MINNESOTA 1900

Art and Life on the Upper Mississippi
1890–1915

The American Arts Series/University of Delaware Press Books

Minnesota 1900

Art and Life on the Upper Mississippi
1890–1915

MICHAEL CONFORTI, EDITOR

With essays by Marcia G. Anderson, Michael Conforti and Jennifer Komar, Mark Hammons, Alan K. Lathrop, Louise Lincoln and Paulette Fairbanks Molin, and Thomas O'Sullivan

DELAWARE

Newark: University of Delaware Press
London and Toronto: Associated University Presses
in association with The Minneapolis Institute of Arts

Associated University Presses
440 Forsgate Drive
Cranbury, NJ 08512

Associated University Presses
25 Sicilian Avenue
London WC1A 2QH, England

Associated University Presses
P.O. Box 338, Port Credit
Mississauga, Ontario
Canada L5G 4L8

Library of Congress Cataloging-in-Publication Data

Art and life on the upper Mississippi, 1890–1915 : Minnesota 1900 / Michael Conforti, editor.
    p.   cm.
    Catalog of an exhibition.
    Includes bibliographical references and index.
    ISBN 0-87413-560-5
    1. Art, American—Minnesota—Exhibitions. 2. Arts and crafts movement—Minnesota—Exhibitions. 3. Art, Modern—20th century—Minnesota—Exhibitions. 4. Minnesota—Social life and customs—Exhibitions. I. Conforti, Michael.
N6530.M6M56   1994
709'.776'074776479—dc20
                               94-4989
                                  CIP

PRINTED IN THE UNITED STATES OF AMERICA

Contents

Preface

THE ART MUSEUM TODAY SERVES MANY CIVIC, AES-thetic, and educational functions in the community. Few responsibilities are as vital, however, as the function of encouraging the region's artistic development and defining the special nature of its collective cultural heritage. Since its opening in 1915, The Minneapolis Institute of Arts has supported the contemporary art of the state. Throughout its early years, annual exhibitions, devoted to the works of local artists, were regularly presented. For nearly two decades the Institute has sponsored the artist-run Minnesota Artists Exhibition Program showcasing the works of artists in the region in the four exhibitions it organizes each year.

The Institute has now become a catalyst for a statewide series of over forty history and art exhibitions devoted to the theme *Minnesota 1900: Art and Life on the Upper Mississippi 1890–1915* and centered around an exhibition of the same name at The Minneapolis Institute of Arts. The Institute's show is intended to focus on the range of artistic activities supported by middle– and upper–middle-class patrons at the turn of the century, that is, artistic commissions ranging from architecture and interior design to paintings and decorative arts created in the state's art schools and guilds to works produced by the region's indigenous peoples whose native craft tradition increasingly reflected the imposition of training and the effects of a non-Indian marketplace.

To foster clarity as well as a fresh scholarly perspective, six subjects have been selected to tell this complex story. Each subject not only focuses on the visual culture of the era but also represents a vital topic in the consideration of the period's artistic production. The success of the exhibition and its accompanying catalogue is due to the authors who have contributed so much time, experience, and intelligence to their essays and accompanying exhibition installations. Al Lathrop's discussion of Minnesota architecture combines his special knowledge of architectural prac-titioners of the time with an awareness of international stylistic trends, particularly in the tradition of the *École des Beaux-Arts*, in the first overview of the state's architecture of the period ever published. Michael Conforti and Jennifer Komar link the development of retailing in the late nineteenth century to the career and wide-ranging interior design practice of John Bradstreet, who joined the aesthetic goals of the Arts and Crafts movement with the reality of the turn-of-the-century Minnesota marketplace. Thomas O'Sullivan's study of one of the region's most respected painters, Robert Koehler, examines not only the artist's work, but his role as catalyst for the artistic community. O'Sullivan considers artists working at their easels and groups of artists joining forces to promote cultural activity at the time by reviewing the careers and work of over two dozen of the period's most respected painters. The special communal nature of Minnesota's artistic life is emphasized in Marcia Anderson's study of the Handicraft Guild of Minneapolis, which presents her years of archival research and clarifies the special nature of the Minneapolis Guild and its place in the international Arts and Crafts movement. Mark Hammons's study of Purcell and Elmslie is the first monograph on this architectural partnership, the most widely commissioned architects of the Prairie School after Frank Lloyd Wright. Hammons not only studies the team-centered working process of the firm and closely analyzes their many commissions, he relates their creative process and formal vocabulary to the contemporary metaphysical discourse which directed Purcell's architectural philosophy. Louise Lincoln joined with Paulette Molin, an enrolled member of the White Earth Chippewa, to examine the nature of relationships between whites and the Anishinabe and Dakota Indians native to Minnesota in a discussion of their material culture. Together they decode a complex, nuanced cultural interchange that results in works embodying both traditional and assimilationist trends by considering both objects made for internal consumption and those intended for sale or as gifts to non-Indians.

The exhibition would not have been possible without the contributions of these scholars, or without the guiding hand of the Institute's chief curator and Bell Memorial Curator of Decorative Arts and Sculpture, Michael Conforti, who conceived this project. Tran Turner of the Decorative Arts and Sculpture Department assisted ably at every juncture. When Tran Turner left the museum in July 1993, his responsibilities were ably assumed by Jennifer Komar, Brian Kraft, and Anna Foxen. Angela Casselton was the masterful coordinator of the exhibition for the Department of African, Oceanic, and New World Cultures and is responsible for the catalog entries in chapter six; Maren Nelson of the same department carried out extensive and meticulous research. Michelle Madson encour-

aged and coordinated the many out-state programs. Each contributed significantly to the final realization of this project.

Minnesota 1900: Art and Life on the Upper Mississippi 1890–1915 has been supported generously by the Blandin Foundation, the National Endowment for the Arts, the Friends of the Institute, and Gabberts Furniture and Design Studio. Major support for the Institute's exhibition program has been provided by the Bush Foundation and Dayton Hudson Foundation on behalf of Dayton's and Target Stores. Promotional sponsorship has been provided by WCCO Television, WCCO News/Talk 8·3·0 and Target Stores. Additional support has been provided by Atherton and Winifred Bean, Lisa and Judson Dayton, and Alfred and Ingrid Lenz Harrison.

Evan M. Maurer
Director

Acknowledgments

MINNESOTA 1900: ART AND LIFE ON THE UPPER MIS-sissippi 1890–1915 has benefitted from the institutions and private collectors around the country who have been generous in supporting this reassessment of Minnesota's cultural heritage. The most significant of the public collections that include works produced in Minnesota are the architectural drawing collection at Northwest Architectural Archives, University of Minnesota Libraries; the Cass Gilbert archive at the New York Historical Society; the Native American collection of the Science Museum of Minnesota; the Minnesota Historical Society's extensive collections of Minnesota paintings and decorative arts, with its special representation of works from the Handicraft Guild of Minneapolis; and the collections of The Minneapolis Institute of Arts.

We would like to thank these and other organizations who have made this exhibition possible and specifically acknowledge our debt to Judith Barter, Field-McCormick Curator of American Art, The Art Institute of Chicago; Horst Rechelbacher, Founder and CEO, AVEDA Corporation; Mark Edevold, Executive Director, Beltrami County Historical Society, Bemidji, Minnesota; Renee Geving, Coordinator, Cass County Museum, Walker, Minnesota; Cathedral of St. Paul; Ray Wade and David Peterson, Church of St. Paul's on the Hill, St. Paul; Beverly Swanson, City of Minneapolis; Milton Sonday, Curator of Textiles, Gillian Moss, Assistant Curator of Textiles, Lucy Commoner, Textile Conservator, and Bradley Nugent, Photographic Services, Cooper-Hewitt National Museum of Design, Smithsonian Institution, New York; Jane Swingle, Management Specialist, Art Collection, First Bank System, Inc., Minneapolis; Polly L. Glynn, First State Bank of LeRoy, Minnesota; First National Bank of Adams, Minnesota; Michael Lane, Director, Glensheen, University of Minnesota, Duluth; Goldstein Gallery, University of Minnesota; Hirschl & Adler Galleries, Inc., New York; Dennis Galleon and Daniel Morris, Historical Design Collection, New York; Susan Meehan and Craig Johnson, James J. Hill House, St. Paul; Minora Pacheco, Assistant Loans Coordinator, and Eileen Sullivan, Photography and Slide Library, Metropolitan Museum of Art, New York; Dorothea Guiney, Director, The Hennepin County History Museum, Minneapolis; Minneapolis College of Art and Design, Minneapolis; Edward Kukla and Bev Anderson at the Minneapolis History Collection, Minneapolis Public Library and Information Center; Pat Harpole, Patty Dean, Linda McShannock, Deborah Swanson, Mark Greene, Patrick Coleman, Kay Spangler, Debbie Miller, Alan Woolworth, Sherri Gebert-Fuller, Tracey Baker, and the archival and reference staffs at the Minnesota Historical Society, St. Paul; Minnesota Museum of Art; Carolyn Kompelien, Minnesota State Capitol, St. Paul; Holly Hotchner, Mary Beth Betts, and Jim Francis, The New-York Historical Society, New York; Patricia Maus, Northeast Minnesota Historical Center, Duluth, Minnesota; Barbara Bezat, Northwest Architectural Archives, University of Minnesota Libraries, St. Paul; Ken Wilcox, Norwest Bank Owatonna, Owatonna, Minnesota; Dave Rambow, Director, and Dawn Hagen, Pipestone County Historical Society, Pipestone, Minnesota; Rosemary Thorson, Plymouth Congregational Church, Minneapolis; Bonnie McDonough, Executive Director, and Martina Bursik, President, Rice County Historical Society, Faribault, Minnesota; Dr. Louis B. Casagrande, Senior Vice President, Melissa Ringheim-Stoddart, Curator of Collections, Sherry Butcher, Curator of Collections, Dan Swan, former curator of Ethnology, Bridget Lips, Registrar, Science Museum of Minnesota, St. Paul; Gregory J. Kieffer, Headmaster, Shattuck–St. Mary's School, Faribault, Minnesota; Judith Payne, Director, and Carrie Krbechek, Sibley Historic Site,

Mendota, Minnesota; Sigma Chi Fraternity, Madison, Wisconsin; Stewart Memorial Church, Minneapolis; Martin DeWitt, Director, Tweed Museum of Art, University of Minnesota-Duluth, Duluth, Minnesota; John Rupp, University Club, St. Paul; Mark Peterson, Director, Winona County Historical Society, Winona, Minnesota; and Lee Townsend, Woodbury County Court House, Sioux City, Iowa.

We would also like to thank the following collectors who have graciously agreed to lend their objects to the exhibition: Peter and Nancy Albrecht, Susan D. Barrows; Lee Baxandall; Mrs. Monica Bessesen Bjornnes; Jennifer Braznell and W. Scott Braznell; James Brewer; Frank and Jean Chesley; James and Darlene Dommel; Arthur Dyson; Father Bill Gamber; Dr. David S. Gebhard; Randy Gegner; Adam Granger; Zev Greenwald and Moira McManus; Rolf Grudem; Mr. and Mrs. Gary Harm; Richard P. Hickenbotham; James E. Johnson; Peter Johnson and Linn Ann Cowles; Gerald B. Johnston; Monroe P. Killy; Ed and Maureen Labenski; Dr. and Mrs. John E. Larkin; Delores Lewis; David Matchan; Nancy M. Rose; Alice Rosekrans; Steve Schoneck; Clara Jean Schumacher; Anthony Scornavacco; Nick Steffen; Colin T. Taylor; Mr. and Mrs. Robert Turnbull; Mark Walbran; Barbara Vodrey Wamelink; Ben Wiles; Robert Winter, and many others who have chosen to be anonymous.

We would like to thank those at the following institutions that have been extremely helpful with research: The Deutsches Historisches Museum, Berlin, Germany; The Huntington Library, San Marino, California; W. Thomas White at the James Jerome Hill Reference Library, St. Paul; members of the Minnesota Art Pottery Association; Walter Gegner at the Art and Music Department, and Carol Van Why at the History Department, Minneapolis Public Library and Information Center; National Archives, Washington, D.C.; Roger G. Kennedy, Director Emeritus of the National Museum of American History; Pewabic Pottery; Betty McSwain, Park Ranger, at Pipestone National Monument, Pipestone, Minnesota; The Pennsylvania Academy of Fine Arts; The Pratt Institute; Maryanne Norton, formerly at the St. Louis County Historical Society, Duluth, Minnesota; St. Paul Public Library, St. Paul; Andrew Kraushaar, Iconographic Collections, at the State Historical Society of Wisconsin; and David J. Klaassen, Social Welfare History Archives, University of Minnesota Libraries.

We would also like to extend our thanks to Nancy Roth, Deborah Karasov, and Richard Kronick for their help in editing the manuscript, to Karen Melvin, architectural photographer, to scholar Susan Larsen-Flemming, and to the various regional photographic services who gladly complied with our deadlines. We appreciate the help of the many individuals who shared their knowledge and information with us throughout the development of this project: Richard Barbeau, Anne Brennan, Tom Burstein, Beth Cathers, Brooks Cavin, Rena N. Coen, Bert Goderstad, Cindy Hall Grey, Arlo Hasse, Candy Hart, Jeffrey Hess and Charlene K. Roise, Leon Kramer and Wesley Kramer, Bruce J. LaBelle, Peter Latner, Laura Linton MacFarlane, Paul Malcolm, Jan Marlese, Jim and Janeen Marrin, Marion Nelson, William Paist, Gladys Pattee, Karen Petersen, Christian Peterson, Cheryl Robertson, Elizabeth Schutt, Marx Swanholm, Tracy Swanholm, Richard Beard Thompson, Hilary Toren, Ken Trapp.

The Minneapolis Institute of Arts staff has worked especially hard in realizing this exhibition. A special thanks and appreciation goes to Bill Skodje, installation designer; Gary Mortensen and Robert Fogt, staff photographers; and Peggy Tolbert, Associate Registrar. We would also like to thank Georgia (Deck) Pavoloni, Jennifer Kurtz, and Mia Johnson, interns in the Department of Decorative Arts and Sculpture; Kate Johnson, Chair, Department of Education; Lorraine McKenzie, Administrative Assistant, Curatorial Division; John Easley, Director of Development, and his staff; Troy Linck and Muriel Morrisette of the Department of Marketing and Communications; Hal Peterson and Michael Boe, Librarians; Elizabeth Sövik, editor.

Introduction:
Art and Life on the Upper Mississippi 1890–1915

Michael Conforti

Our people aimed for Oregon
When they left Newburyport
Great Grandma Ruth, her husband John
But they pulled up in Wobegon
Two thousand miles short
—Garrison Keillor, *Leaving Home:*
A Collection of Lake Wobegon Stories (xx–xxi)

F OR MOST OF THIS CENTURY, THE MIDDLE WEST HAS symbolized the agrarian roots of America, the legacy of a mythic past centered on solid work ethic and conservative lifestyle. To a nation assaulted by decades of industrialization and its even more confusing aftermath, the region represents a comforting antidote, a society built on a value system of honesty and forthrightness, a place where family ties and communal harmony are still afforded special privilege.

The myth has lately assumed special poignancy and popularity through Garrison Keillor's eloquent storytelling. With tales woven around the timeless simplicity of an small imagined Minnesota town, his weekly radio visitations have touched the ever-growing urban population on both coasts and in between. His immigrant Lutheran society of family farmers, imbued with a modesty uncontaminated by contemporary media overstatement, continues to consider hyperbole a sin. It is a neighborly society of hardworking farmers and small-town business people, many of whose ancestors (if we accept his verse), stopped their covered wagons near their current habitat, the Western beacon fad-

ing with the satisfaction found in the quaintly steady, prairie land.

They stayed a week to rest the team
Were welcomed and befriended
The land was good, the grass was green
And slowly they gave up the dream
And there the journey ended
(Keillor, *Leaving Home*, xxi–xxii)

While Keillor's characters convincingly recall the pragmatism of northern Europeans dominant in Minnesota for more than a hundred years, his recollection of the population's origins, and the stable changelessness of their society, not surprisingly bear little relation to reality. The idea of a Midwest with its accompanying populist value system only began to suggest itself in the early years of this century. Eulogized in the political rhetoric of the late 1890s and the progressive politics that strengthened in the decades following, the image solidified as it evoked national sympathy during the farm depression of the 1920s. It is in the economic and social trials of the period between the world wars, a period in which second- and third-generation families came to identify more with each other than with relatives in the East and in Europe, that the society's special nature clarified and an image was created for those outside.

In the second half of the nineteenth century, when this region was first populated by Euro-Americans, the West in name and idea included the upper Mississippi valley, and Minneapolis–St. Paul, at the northernmost navigable point

11

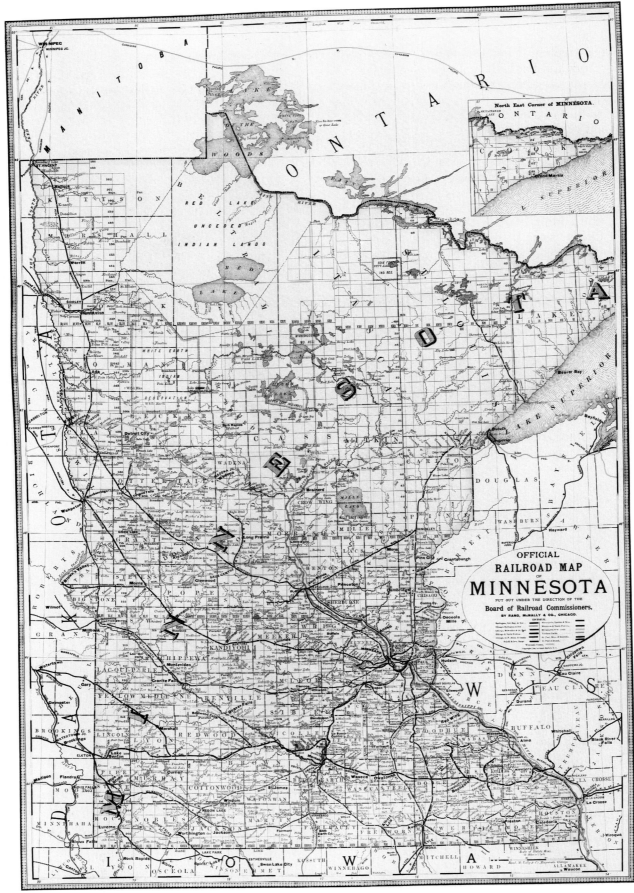

Official railroad map of Minnesota. Rand, McNally & Co.,
1886. Photograph courtesy of the Minnesota Historical Society.

of the great river, represented a special beacon. With the forests of New York and Pennsylvania now gone and those of Michigan almost harvested, the virgin timber of Minnesota took their place, attracting investment and encouraging population growth. As early as the 1850s a Maine legislator rose to complain of the loss of Maine's sons "to the piney woods of the Northwest." The enormous capital generated by the lumber industry in the decade before, and especially in the years after the Civil War, financed the flour mills, the railroad building and the beginnings of iron ore exploration which combined to make Minnesota the fastest growing region in the country in the 1880s. The indigenous population, confined to restricted lands by the middle of the century, initiated its bloodiest act of protest against the system imposed on them in 1862. With hundreds of whites and an equal number of Native Americans killed during the Dakota conflict, the ever-inconvenient issue of American Indian rights became a concern of even fewer of Minnesota's white inhabitants from that point on.

The economic success achieved in the second half of the nineteenth century, especially during the 1880s (the decade of the state's greatest population expansion), was summarized in the rhetoric of civic leaders who convened for "Minnesota Day," 3 October 1893, at Chicago's World Columbian Exposition. A commemorative book published at the time chronicled their words and activities. "Minnesota gained special recognition yesterday by the heartiness with which her celebration was conducted," wrote a Chi-cago newspaper after twenty thousand people from the state converged at Lake Michigan for the event (*Chicago Herald*, 14 October 1983, quoted in *Minnesota Day at the World's Exposition, Friday, October Thirteenth, 1893*, n.p.). With frequent invocation of the New England where most of its leaders were born (e.g., "The beautiful New England-like towns that everywhere adorn [Minnesota's] fair surface"), they touted the achievements of the recent past, convinced of the limitless possibilities for the region's future. The rate of population growth in the previous decade was described as "more than double Chicago's, exceeding that of Boston, Providence, Albany, New Orleans and San Francisco combined." In fact, by 1890 the total population of Minneapolis and St. Paul would have made these neighboring urban communities the ninth largest city in the country. Aspirations for Duluth, "the zenith city of the unsalted seas," had, as yet, no reason to be modified: "The day is not far away when vessels crossing the Atlantic will break bulk in the harbors of our own state."Duluth was envisioned as a transit station for European goods shipped by boat through inland waterways, then carried by rail to the Pacific Coast and Asia. Investors throughout the country were supporting this ambition, making this modest urban center at the western tip of the Great Lakes a center of national real estate speculation.

In 1890, virtually all of Minnesota's leaders had immigrated within the previous forty years, many directly from small northern New England towns. Some families spent

General view showing the state capitol, St. Paul, 1857. Minnesota Historical Society. Photograph by B. F. Upton.

*East side of St. Anthony Falls, Minneapolis, 1865. Minnesota
Historical Society. Photograph by the* Minneapolis Journal.

from a few years to a generation in Ohio or Illinois along
the way. The Pillsburys came directly from New
Hampshire; the Washburns, the Morrisons, and numerous
others, from Maine. The interior designer and retailer John
Bradstreet actually hailed, like Keillor's fictional family,
from the environs of Massachusetts's northern-most coastal
city, Newburyport. Until 1867, when a railroad line connected Minneapolis and St. Paul directly to Chicago, their
journey was made by taking a train to western Illinois.
There they transferred to boats at Mississippi River ports
like Galena for the relatively short trip upstream. Having
arrived in the Northwest, as it was labeled at the time,
they invested varying amounts of capital in the expanding
economy, beginning the work of creating a society based
on the economic and social value system they had known
before.

To meet the economic aspirations of these earliest settlers, to provide the necessary workforce for the growing
number of lumber and flour mills, and to farm the land
now being cleared for the production of grain and other
foodstuffs, they encouraged European immigration. Elaborate systems of trans-Atlantic travel, usually with the promise of land at destination, were organized by the State
Immigration Office and by various church groups, especially Lutheran and Catholic. Immigration agents, the best
known an early Swedish settler named Hans Mattson, who
headed the immigration office in the late 1860s, were sent
abroad by state leaders. Cheap tickets were issued for the
entire journey in an effort to avoid disembarkation earlier
than intended. State-supported shelters were often provided
for the immigrants' first days in the region. Prefabricated

houses were available in 1870, ready for assembling on
land designated for settlement.

In the grasp for land necessary for overnight settlement
and economic growth, from the acquisition of virgin pine
forests whose harvesting drove the state's meteoric rise, to
the division of acreage into family farms to create a food
and grain supply, American–Indian culture was not only
undermined, Indian rights as established by treaty were
regularly subject to manipulation through the legal recon-
sideration of former edicts or land swindling practices. Indian land claims represented little more than an
annoyance, something for the government to "arrange" to
allow the society to expand. The pauperizing effects of the
government's annuity system, and corrupt, politically appointed Indian agents added to the reality of a culture relegated to ever smaller areas of nonproductive land, their
tribal relations shattered, their hunting grounds gone.

In the last half of the nineteenth century, through the
immigration of Europeans and eastern Americans and the
subsequent displacement of the native population, the social fabric of Minnesota had its origins: modest, pragmatic,
and ambitious middle-class Yankees from small New England towns, soon to be outnumbered by poorer, less educated Scandinavian and German immigrants with a similar
work ethic and value system. Afro-American and other
Euro-American ethnic groups joined this society of lumbermen and millers, miners, and farmers. Irish, Czech,
Italians, Jews, and others flavored this homogeneous mix
in urban centers, but they did not substantially redirect the
character of the majority that dominated the region. By
1915, the indigenous population was firmly established on

Peabody and Stearns. James J. Hill residence, 240 Summit Avenue, 1891, photograph about 1905. Photograph courtesy of the Minnesota Historical Society.

tracts of land in the northern part of the state, over time many would settle in the urban center of Minneapolis and St. Paul.

Minnesota did not alter its assumptions of unlimited economic and population growth until after the First World War. In the 1920s, with the lumber industry having depleted its resources and the milling center of Minneapolis challenged by rivals, banks were financially strained, and farms were foreclosed on with regularity. Duluth had also failed to reach its imagined potential because the Panama Canal, which opened in 1914, now provided the easiest route from Asia to Europe. Economic restrictions began to encourage emigration to states farther West. The reorientation of capital to other business ventures initiated at this time would not bear significant fruit until the 1940s and 1950s. Minnesota and the Midwest, imaged by politicians and writers and depicted by the growing regional artist movement of the period between the wars as a place of earnest, honest, and sometimes difficult living, began to solidify in the American consciousness.

For the "progress"-directed Minnesota society at the turn of the century, this sober future was far from the imagination. The state's efforts to capitalize on the potential of its natural resources of timber, fertile land, and iron ore were furthered by a climate that encouraged hard work and by an immigrant population in whom a work ethic was assumed. Life in this prairie civilization combined the comfort of tradition and the promise of innovation. Minnesota resembled both a reconstructed Eastern society and the civilization of the new American West. Freedom from tra-

dition, from the restrictions of Eastern social, familial, and academic boundaries, resulted in special value given to individual opportunity, an individualism that combined with an egalitarian sense of community that would, in turn, have cultural and material expression.

On the one hand, the material aspirations of Minnesota's elite were similar to those of any large American city's upper middle class. In 1890 James J. Hill, increasingly linked in business with J. P. Morgan and other turn-of-the-century Eastern financial barons, was completing the state's largest residence in St. Paul, designed by the Boston firm of Peabody and Stearns. Like his East Coast counterparts, he was collecting French nineteenth-century Barbizon and realist paintings to complement the interior. Harmon Place was a growing residential center for Minneapolis's affluent, but the Washburns and Pillsburys had begun to establish themselves near the Morrison's suburban "Villa Rosa" (1858), now the site of The Minneapolis Institute of Arts (a museum designed by the New York firm of McKim Mead and White, which opened in 1915). In the 1890s Cass Gilbert, who had trained in the McKim Mead and White offices, was planning revival-style houses along eastern Summit Avenue, houses the St. Paul-born F. Scott Fitzgerald would later vehemently disparage. Fitzgerald's critical eye for social nuance was nurtured within St. Paul's stratified turn-of-the-century social hierarchy, an experience that would serve him well chronicling the next generation of defiantly worldly, monied Americans. *The Bellman*, the Minnesota weekly of social and cultural chatter, featured regular reports from correspondents in London and

New York, interspersed with articles ranging from visits to local artists' studios to reflections on recent international cultural trends. One of Puccini's latest operas, *Madame Butterfly*, was described in detail on 16 February 1907, with accompanying illustrations of the costumes created for recent productions in Berlin and Dresden.

Minneapolis and St. Paul's cultural aspirations, however, had to be adapted to certain historical, geographic, and social realities: the newness of a society that was only a few decades old at the turn of the century, its distance from other large cities, a growing urban core, but a modest state population, only 1,300,000 in 1890. To answer the question of how this last metropolis on the railroad west to Seattle, almost two thousand miles away, could establish itself as an important cultural center, the cities' leaders look to the experience of Chicago. The West's largest city, visited by the many Minnesotans who regularly traveled by train to the East, had become a national symbol of western opportunity, a place where it was said society was written with a small "s." Minneapolis and St. Paul, however, would express the liberal social ethos of the western Great Lakes region uniquely, however, by the necessity as well as the opportunity of engaging a communal effort in the formation of a vital cultural life. Groups of businessmen were asked early on to oversee both civic and artistic endeavors. This quickly evolved into support from their companies, establishing a regional tradition that today is now a model for cultural funding throughout the country.

In the 1880s and 1890s, Minnesota's period of greatest economic and population growth, the international movement to establish cultural institutions and associated arts organizations was at its zenith. The goals of these ventures ranged from the avowed civic purpose of public education and moral improvement to the aesthetic-cum-social virtue found in the hand-crafting of useful objects, a virtue that became the philosophical foundation of the Arts and Crafts movement. The liberal tradition of Minnesota's New England and northern European inhabitants embraced the socially driven aesthetic philosophy of the time. To support their goals, however, cultural leaders had to marry their commitment to excellence in the educational and artistic sphere with the pragmatic task of relating to the different backgrounds and experiences of their constituencies. In the process, the implicitly populist assumptions of the new aesthetic ideals had a special reception and articulation. The cosmopolitan aspirations of St. Paul's turn-of-the-century elite may have contributed to F. Scott Fitzgerald's later fiction, but the literary effort of St. Paul–born Dewitt Wallace better symbolizes the character and concerns of the liberal, early twentieth-century Minnesotan. In 1922 Wallace established the *Reader's Digest* which abbreviated contemporary literature for easier public appreciation. Minnesota still distinguishes itself by a greater concern for the collective than for the individual. This is not only reflected in the state's consistent liberal politics, but in its educational and cultural institutions which frequently are arenas for the debate between excellence and accessibility.

The success of Garrison Keillor's myth-making results from his understanding of the subtle regional blending of personal modesty and local pride, often in conflict with other regional attributes: a nagging sense of duty, a belief in the idea of quality, and a commitment to communal participation.

One might assume that identifiable formal qualities in Minnesota's material culture expressed these various regional characteristics. Certainly the cosmopolitanism of Minnesota's turn-of-the-century elite parallels America's appreciation for the historical and the exotic at the time. It is evidenced in the regular commissioning of *Beaux-Arts* inspired architects, the support of the Munich-trained art school director Robert Koehler, and the local success of the fastidious Japan- and London-inspired interior designer and *antiquaire* John Bradstreet. On the other hand, the state's liberal social commitment is manifest in the philosophy and products of the Handicraft Guild of Minneapolis, the assimilation-directed crafts education organized for the

Joseph Ward and Benjamin Waybenais dressed in formal wear and bandolier bags, Red Lake. Reverend Alban Fruth, OSB, A Century of Missionary Work among the Red Lake Chippewa Indians, 1858–1958, page 61.

native American population, and the progressive architecture of Purcell and Elmslie, an architecture directed at providing better housing for the middle class. A more definitive relationship between regional aspiration and material product cannot be established, however. Except for the use of local materials and the evidence of stylistic idiosyncracies of individual artists whose influence can be detected in the region over time, there was little produced that can now be considered as representing a regional vocabulary in the arts. There was certainly no aspiration to create one.

In 1891 the New York critic Montgomery Schuyler spoke of the opportunities afforded by the state's geographical distance from eastern centers: "There are among the emancipated practitioners of architecture in the West, men who have shown that they can use their liberty wisely" ("Glimpses of Western Architecture," *Harper's New Monthly Magazine* 83: 497 [October 1891]). From his late nineteenth-century perspective, however, this freedom did not foreshadow a local western style but rather "the hopeful beginnings of a national architecture." Indeed, if there was a conscious reformulation of established artistic tradition motivating Minnesota's artists, it was their collective contribution to contemporary national concern for the development of a uniquely American style. In John Bradstreet's words this country was "heir to all that was good in every school of design" and out of its choices a style "distinctive of America" would emerge. The progressive movement in architecture had similar goals. Inspired by late nineteenth-century international design movements as well as Japanese precedent, the style's association with its regional, prairie origins came later in its critical life. The desire to associate the regions of America with formal artistic attributes is, like the idea of the Midwest itself, a phenomenon of the early decades of this century.

There are many monuments, many material testaments, to the vitality of Minnesota's artistic life at the turn of the century, from Cass Gilbert's State Capitol, one of the finest "American Renaissance" buildings in the country, to Purcell and Elmslie's house on Lake Place, the paintings of Alexander Fournier and Robert Koehler, and the beadwork of Anishinabe and Dakota women; from Ernest Batchelder's innovative ceramics to the elegant graphic designs of Mary Moulton Cheney, the metal work of the Handicraft Guild, and John Bradstreet's "Lotus" design table. Minnesota's artistic culture, however, is characterized less by its monuments and master artists than by the practice of adapting tradition and directing aesthetic aspirations to practical enterprise. Its most identifiable attribute in the arts, one established at the turn of the century that continues to our own day, is the commitment to process and purpose as much as product, community engagement and public appreciation as much as artistic elegance. Robert Koehler's reputation as an arts advocate was equal to the respect he generated as a painter. He founded the Artist's League in 1893 and later joined forces with other painters to establish an informal artist center in the "Old Bandbox" building, involving himself also in the Minnesota State Arts Society

Elisabeth Augusta Chant in her studio at the Handicraft Guild, ca. 1908. Collection of Sherron R. Biddle, Boiling Springs, PA; courtesy of St. John's Museum of Art, Wilmington, NC.

and the Businessman's Art Club. John Bradstreet's success was based on the commercial viability represented by the range of the offerings in his Craftshouse, though he regularly opened his galleries for public exhibitions and lectured there to encourage the appreciation of his more eccentric wares. The innovative architecture of Frank Lloyd Wright is called "autocratic" in this catalogue and is contrasted to Purcell and Elmslie's team process of design, which resulted in architecture "more expressive of human relationships and needs."

The social and aesthetic ideals of the Handicraft Guild of Minneapolis symbolize the communal aspirations of Minnesota during this period most succinctly. Established from the membership of the "Chalk and Chisel Club," one of the country's first arts and crafts organizations, the Handicraft Guild, like many other American arts and crafts groups, emphasized social change rather than the moral reform espoused by the movement's English founders. Incorporating the international movement's emphasis on hand-process, without adapting it to mechanical production as did other organizations in this country, its avowed

Cass Gilbert. Charles P. Noyes House, 1888–89. Photograph courtesy of the Minnesota Historical Society.

purpose was to educate teachers for Minnesota's schools. The Guild's egalitarian aspirations are is evident in its encouragement of associate members who were not designers. The medieval-inspired principles of early arts and crafts philosophy were also strictly followed, and works were rarely signed. Guild members never defined their careers exclusively in terms of membership in the organization. Their association was as pragmatic as it was ideological, focusing on classes to be taught or attended and on the commercial production of objects to be sold in the Guild's retail shop.

Patronage of the arts also reflected the region's purposefully communal character. Minnesota's population, both small-town Yankee and agrarian northern European, believed in the value of art but lacked the experience of embracing it. Their sense of duty in supporting culture also contrasted with their relative aversion to conspicuous display. Their houses might be large, but the interiors were rarely complemented with significant art works. In the essays that follow we read that William Folwell once encouraged the purchase of Koehler's *The Strike* by suggesting that not supporting its purchase was un-Minnesotan. Folwell knew that an earlier Art School director, Douglas Volk, had returned East because he had lacked patrons. The need to support missionaries like Koehler, whether by purchasing his work or attending his lectures, even those on the new modern art, was taken as the responsibility of the community as a whole.

We are told in this catalogue that John Bradstreet's similar missionary efforts, his promotion of Japanese art as well as his own Japanese-inspired *sugi* furniture, met with mixed

success. Stylistic experimentation in general seems to have had only a tentative acceptance by local patrons. Harvey Ellis's innovative Byzantine modernist design for the Security Bank in Minneapolis was one of the most engaging of his career, but it was never built. In 1893 Cass Gilbert proposed a neo-Federal house for the William Lightners, but it was rejected for a traditional Richardsonian structure even though other local clients had already followed this latest trend. The Charles Noyes residence (1888) is closely modeled on one of the earliest Federal revival houses designed in the country, Stanford White's HAC Taylor house in Newport, Rhode Island (1885–86). The Prairie School is spoken of in this volume as "on the periphery" and, indeed, the patrons of the new progressive architecture were few. Most of Purcell and Elmslie's clients were probably not aware of the metaphysical philosophy which, we are told, drove the formal invention of William Purcell. By commissioning the firm, however, many professionals, bankers, and small-business entrepreneurs supported the reform agenda of this new antirevivalist architecture. Such clients inherently identified progressive design with the values of a new American society developing in the West.

Much can be made of the inspiration Japanese precedent had on Purcell and Elmslie's architecture, but Japanese aesthetics as well as its formal and technical vocabulary had various expressions in Minnesota. No single artistic concern, western or nonwestern, inspired Minnesota's artists as fundamentally as did *japonisme*, both an aesthetic philosophy and formal vocabulary followed internationally in the late nineteenth century. John Bradstreet incorporated Japanese decorative design and woodworking technique in his furniture, furniture whose outlines, however, were often European inspired. Others showed an appreciation of the philosophical foundation as well as the surface quality of Japanese work. Among the Handicrafts Guild members, Japan was honored as a nation that had kept its identity despite the force of industrialization. Ernest Batchelder espoused these views in his writings and lectures, emphasizing the need for craft artists to develop a national design tradition free from European tradition. One of his Guild colleagues, Mary Moulton Cheney, carried many Japanese prints in her retail enterprise "The Artful Shop: Sign of the Bay Tree." She also sold the prints of Bertha Lum, an artist whose woodblock engravings reflected her many Japanese study trips during which she perfected her technique. Lum was one of the first foreigners, and the first woman, to master the many stages of the difficult Japanese print-making process.

Like the other women who formed the teaching staff of the Handicraft Guild, Cheney and Lum represented a generation known at the time as "New Women." The involvement of women in the Guild and other of Minnesota's artistic endeavors paralleled the aspiration to an improved status in the workplace that was a gender concern at the time. This generation of proto-feminist reformers, often college educated and active in the social reform movements of the period, paved the way for the later ad-

Lace makers, Leech Lake, 1906. Photograph courtesy of the Minnesota Historical Society.

vances of women in America. The artists of the Handicraft Guild, along with painters Grace McKinstry, Elizabeth Chant, Elsa Jemme, and Purcell and Elmslie's associate Mary Alice Parker, helped to expand women's educational and vocational opportunities, contributing to the leading position Minnesota has maintained over the years in the recognition of social and economic rights.

The role of women in native American society changed during the period of forced assimilation covered by the years of this exhibition. Their different status, however, reflected cultural disjunction among the American Indian people. In the reconstitution of native life demanded by confinement to reservations and the Federal annuity system, men were robbed of their purpose. Women and children, along with many males, were encouraged to develop or redirect their craft and technical skills to the making of artifacts for different purposes, one driven by the economic realities of a white marketplace.

Traditional techniques, including those of bark-biting and twined fiber, continued in objects created for native use, but products for the new market were also introduced, like nonfunctional miniaturized canoes and cradleboards. Women were also taught to produce European-style lace and to adapt their beadwork tradition, modified from earlier quilling techniques, to ever more diverse functions like pocketbooks and wallets for the white middle class. While the design and technical achievements of the Anishinabe and Dakota are often extraordinary, from intricately fashioned beadwork to delicately knotted lace, these objects are also material evidence of a culture forcibly redirected, a people encouraged to conform. White sympathy at the time could be represented in the ownership and display of Indian-made things. With few exceptions, however, feeling for the Indian cultural loss among whites did not extend beyond such token gestures.

The expansion of Minnesota at the end of the nineteenth century as represented in the rhetoric of the state's leaders at the World Columbian exhibition, as evidenced in the period's architecture, painting, and decorative arts and in the warmly remembered tales of immigrant rural experiences that have descended in so many families, must always be balanced by a consciousness of the devaluation, and the

John S. Bradstreet in Japan, ca. 1905. Photograph courtesy of The Minneapolis Institute of Arts 82.43.45.

near expiration, of an American Indian culture that made this society possible. No recounting of the various inequities of the time is as famous or as sobering as that related by the archaeologist and ethnographer Warren King Moorehead, whose 1909 report on suffering among the Anishinabe on the White Earth reservation in northern Minnesota caused a national scandal. Our own recounting of the achievements of Minnesota's past cannot be appreciated without an awareness of the human cost of building this society on the upper Mississippi, this society, both urban and rural, which is the object of so much regional pride.

With this exhibition we hope to clarify this sometimes heroic and sometimes tragic period, offering various interpretations of Minnesota's turn-of-the-century history along with complimentary considerations of the meaning represented by its artistic heritage.

> They bought a farm just north of town
> A pleasant piece of rolling ground
> A quarter-section, mostly cleared;
> He built a house before the fall;
> They lived there forty years in all
> And by God persevered.
>
> (Keillor, *Leaving Home*, xxii)

MINNESOTA 1900

Art and Life on the Upper Mississippi
1890–1915

1

Architecture in Minnesota at the Turn of the Century

Alan K. Lathrop

THE QUARTER CENTURY BETWEEN 1890 AND 1915 WAS A time of rapid industrialization throughout the United States, and nowhere were the changes more dramatic than in Minnesota. The prominent eastern architectural critic Montgomery Schuyler wrote in 1891 "the marvel even of the marvelous West," referring not only to the extreme speed of the area's recent economic expansion but also the ferocity with which the neighboring cities of Minneapolis and St. Paul competed for cultural supremacy. In the face of an almost sudden prosperity there had arisen an unprecedented demand for new building of all kinds. With its farms and villages as well as its mines and sawmills, its port city at Duluth as well as its full-scale metropolis at Minneapolis–St. Paul, Minnesota presented, within a fairly confined geographical space, the full range of problems and opportunities encountered by early modern architecture in the Western states. Minnesota was not the biggest or the first or the most authoritative architectural center, but its diversity and extremely rapid growth meant that the central issues in contemporary architecture—above all the possibility of finding or developing a single modern natural architectural style—presented themselves with particular intensity. Rivalry between the state's two largest cities further fueled an already somewhat contentious, but also buoyant, dynamic atmosphere. "Evidently," Schuyler continued in his 1891 discussion, "there could be no better places than the twin cities to study the development of Western architecture or rather to ascertain whether there is any such thing."[1]

By 1915 Minnesota could claim a host of professionally designed buildings that reflected the broad spectrum of contemporary architectural practice. Some of the most respected architects in the nation had built here, among them Peabody and Stearns, Daniel Burnham, Bertram Goodhue, Shepley, Rutan and Coolidge, McKim, Mead and White, Louis Sullivan, George Maher, and Frank Lloyd Wright. Perhaps more importantly Minnesota provided a uniquely stimulating environment, especially valuable for younger architects still shaping their own architectural philosophy and technical skill. The Minnesota commissions of Cass Gilbert, Harvey Ellis, and Purcell and Elmslie led to their later national recognition. The firm Franklin Ellerbe founded in 1909 is the largest in the United States today. Many other early Minnesota-based architects deserve greater recognition than they have received to date: Emmanuel Louis Masqueray, the French-born former assistant to Richard Morris Hunt; the firm established by Charles Reed and Allen Stem, the first architects of New York's Grand Central Station; the innovative Harry Wild Jones; the Prairie School architects Bentley and Hausler. They, along with a range of highly competent local talents like Clarence Johnston, Leroy Buffington, and William Channing Whitney, utilized the prosperity and expansionist atmosphere of turn-of-the-century Minnesota to create an architectural fabric that vies successfully with any in the country.

Minnesota was among the fastest growing areas in the nation between 1890 and 1915. Its land was crisscrossed

Downtown Minneapolis at the turn of the century. Photograph courtesy of the Minnesota Historical Society.

Downtown St. Paul at the turn of the century. Photograph courtesy of the Minnesota Historical Society, original in Library of Congress.

by railroads and punctuated by cities and towns. This burgeoning growth incorporated technological changes that were revolutionizing people's lives everywhere. Electricity became almost universally available. Telephones, radios, electric lights, appliances large and small were becoming part of everyday life. With the advent of automobiles, roads had to be paved for the first time. Eager audiences crowded into the first motion picture theaters. In the construction industry, steel and more specialized metal alloys, reinforced concrete—as well as mass-produced central heating and plumbing components, and vastly improved water and sewer systems—opened new design possibilities and raised the technical standards for new building of all kinds.[2]

Technological advances brought standardization, in building as in many other areas of economic development. The enormous demand for housing in the larger cities, in particular, was met with standardized tenements and single-family dwellings, often built by developers from a single master plan. Many such plans came from pattern books produced by architects, lumberyards, or contractors; others were part of the entrepreneurial efforts of manufacturers of portable or prefabricated structures of all types. Just as machinery and the products that it generated could be interchanged with other similar models, so, too, could building components. Heating systems, windows, doors, stairs, woodwork and trim, eaves-troughs, shingles, and a multitude of other products could all be ordered from catalogues and shipped along the vast and efficient rail networks spreading across America. American architecture, like most sectors of industry at the turn of the century, came to depend on the advantages of interchangeable parts.

Building efficiency was further catalyzed by two major developments in American construction technique: the first was the great timesaver, the *balloon frame*, reportedly invented about 1833 by Augustine Taylor of Hartford, Connecticut. Up to that time buildings—large and small—had utilized the New England frame post-and-beam system, which was unnecessarily heavy and cumbersome for houses or smaller structures and difficult to erect with the often crude tools and limited skills existing on the frontier. Balloon frame construction substituted lighter two-by-fours for the frame system's heavy beams. A horizontal sill was laid directly on a base of concrete or masonry, on which vertical studs were nailed at twelve- or sixteen-inch intervals. A plate was fastened to the top of the studs to which the roof rafters were attached. Exterior sheathing was applied to the frame to enclose the building. By this time nails were mass produced, and lumber was available ready-cut to standard lengths. Both developments facilitated construction to an unprecedented degree. The balloon frame could be assembled by virtually anyone capable of handling a saw, hammer, and nails. A group of workers could start a building in the morning and have it enclosed by nightfall.[3]

The second major innovation was the "invention" of the skyscraper in the 1880s. The skyscraper depended on several new technologies: reliable steel manufacturing and fabrication; elevators and telephones to facilitate access and communications within the tall building; electricity to light offices and operate elevators; heating and ventilating systems for very large spaces. Rapidly rising land values in dense city centers intensified interest in this kind of building, for in order to make the most profit from expensive investments in real property, developers were forced to expand in the only direction possible—skyward.

The net result of this standardization and modernization was, among other things, a greater degree of homogeneity in American architecture. By the end of the nineteenth century one could travel coast to coast and encounter similar architectural detail and interior furnishings in houses, banks, churches, schools, offices, and libraries. In Minnesota, as elsewhere in the nation, the excitement of rapid change, as well as an encroaching sameness, produced a

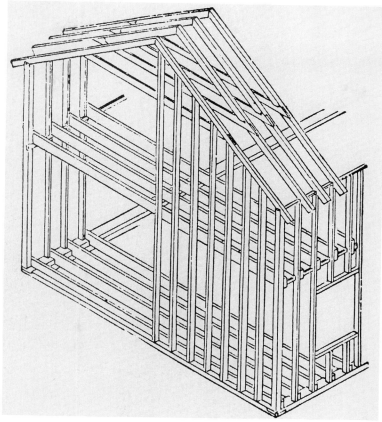

Balloon frame construction, isometric view. George Woodward, Woodward's Country Homes, *1865.*

corresponding fear for the loss of tradition, distinction, and idiosyncracy many felt resulted from the effect of industrialization on everyday life. Differences of belief regarding architectural style could therefore often run deep, engaging political, even religious, as well as aesthetic convictions: conservatives clashed with progressives, individualists with collectivists, democrats with authoritarians. More traditional architects favored the adaptation of forms borrowed from western Europe's past (e.g., classical, medieval, or the Renaissance) to the very different functional requirements of modern life. Their more "progressive" colleagues envisioned an architecture that looked different from anything that had come before, declaring a definitive break with historical traditions.

A key to understanding the bewildering array of architectural styles represented in turn-of-the-century architecture in Minnesota, as elsewhere, is the teaching of the *École Nationale et Spèciale des Beaux-Arts* in Paris, commonly shortened to the "Beaux-Arts" school or style. The preeminent preparation for architectural practice in Europe, it emphasized the value of historical, and especially classical, Greek and Roman forms. By the end of the nineteenth century, schools of architecture had been established at different centers throughout the country.[4] Beaux-Arts thinking, in turn, completely dominated architectural teaching in the United States. The school did not advocate

Leroy S. Buffington. Twenty-story Skyscraper, *Minneapolis, 1894. Northwest Architectural Archives, University of Minnesota Libraries, St. Paul. Photograph by Gary Mortensen and Robert Fogt.*

preservation of older forms for their own sake, as is often mistakenly thought. Instead, its practitioners believed that the forms of the past epitomized eternally valid principles of good architecture. If architects and buildings incorporated the principles that underlay these designs, their new creations, too, would be successful. Architects faithful to Beaux-Arts principles therefore never viewed themselves as *copying* historical styles. The resemblance the resulting buildings might bear to Roman temples or medieval churches was not the goal, they insisted, but the natural effect of their method.

Perhaps even more importantly, the Beaux-Arts school

stood for international standards in architectural education and practice, a force for order and stability in the profession. Rather than any particular architectural style, it actually advocated a standardized way of thinking about design which, it claimed, incorporated essential truths of great architecture of all ages.[5] Through formal lectures and practical assignments in the ateliers—independent studios directed by patrons or master architects—students who attended the *École des Beaux-Arts* learned a method of analysis and the vocabulary of historical styles that would enable them to solve any building problem. Within this logic or "science" of architecture, ornamentation and finish played an important part, both in creating the building's aesthetic power and in establishing its unique identity. These considerations, however, were distinctly secondary to those of order, balance, clarity, and efficient function: Minneapolis architect Cass Gilbert, himself a strong adherent of Beaux-Art principles, put it best when he said, "Aim for beauty [in design]; originality will take care of itself."[6]

Beaux-Arts–trained architects turned out buildings that were orderly, symmetrical, and beautiful—if occasionally, as some argued, unimaginative. Such buildings represented the power and strength of the economic and social establishment, its conservatism and predictability, in an age when these qualities were perceived by many to be essential, particularly in the face of the rapid changes brought about by the technical advances of the modern era. Only a few, such as Louis Sullivan or Frank Lloyd Wright, dared to challenge what had come to seem like the "natural" architectural order. Against the architectural establishment centered in the East, they asserted a belief in a regional architecture that was "democratic"—that is, one serving the distinctive needs of unique individuals, rather than the establishment of institutions of society. In retrospect, the polarization does not seem nearly so extreme: even Sullivan and his disciple Wright were not entirely immune from the

Victor Laloux surrounded by his students, in a courtyard of the Ecole des Beaux-Arts, 1890–91. Photograph courtesy of the Library of the Ecole des Beaux-Arts.

Shepley, Rutan & Coolidge. Study for the Plymouth Congregational Church, *Minneapolis, 1907. Plymouth Congregational Church. Photograph by Gary Mortensen and Robert Fogt.*

persuasive teachings of the Beaux-Arts system. Fundamentally, their approach to design was derived from what Sullivan had learned in Paris and passed on to his astute pupil. Sullivan still admired the "discipline of the Beaux-Arts," which "settled down to a theory of plan" that yielded "results of extraordinary brilliancy."[7]

Architects who were well versed in Beaux-Arts principles knew that the Greek and Roman and, to a lesser extent, medieval, Renaissance, and baroque forms most nearly approximated the ideals and embodied the principles they had been taught. They were also aware that these styles were easily recognizable to their clients and the public at large. Between 1890 and 1915, "revivals" of one kind or another—Romanesque, classical, colonial Renaissance, and Tudor—vied for prominence, each flourishing for brief periods of time within certain categories of building. Besides these European-based styles, several more or less indigenous American architectural vocabularies were adapted to a variety of needs: the shingle and craftsman styles, named for their sources in vernacular materials and practices, and the self-designated progressive or "prairie" style, named for its origins in the midwest, its architectural adaptation of the horizontality of the landscape, and the application of an earth-inspired palette of brown, green, and ochre. Although these styles, too, drew to varying degrees on earlier forms, they also integrated, in a quest for originality, elements of native American, Asian, and other vernacular vocabularies, which were unfamiliar to most of the critical public at the time.

Paradoxically, the architectural eclecticism of the age was the result of an unsuccessful quest for a single style. The American architectural profession as a whole subscribed to the notion that a single style evocative of an age would bring orderliness to society. They understood their own experimentation with one style after another as an ongoing search for the one, appropriate style on which everyone could agree. All that most architects could agree on in fact was that Beaux-Arts methods and techniques

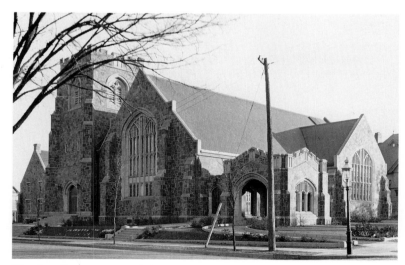

Shepley, Rutan & Coolidge. Plymouth Congregational Church, Minneapolis, 1907. Plymouth Congregational Church.

were necessary if a unifying style was ever to be found. Some architects believed that such a search was pointless, its goal unattainable. Looking around at a cosmopolitan American society, they no longer saw unity or hoped for a single identity. But whether individual architects continued to hope for such a style or not, virtually all of them used a fairly wide vocabulary of historically derived elements in their work, often combining them in a single building.

In practice, of course, the range of all architect's choices depended heavily on the character of the clients they served. True departures from the norm—from recognizable classical and European forms—were not greeted with enthusiasm by most of the American public at the turn of the century. While Americans who wanted to build a unique house, whether in the country or city, might possess high ambitions, their ambitions were frequently circumscribed by conventional taste. Those architects who tried to influence their clients' judgement often failed; many made no effort to experiment beyond testing various combinations of stylistic elements, sometimes piling them one on top of the other like layers of frosting on a cake. Today we may debate whether the architects influenced the tastes of their clients to any appreciable extent. In truth, it worked both ways, with the client often directing the choice offered. Richard Morris Hunt is quoted as telling his protégé, George Post: "The first thing you've got to remember is that it's your client's money you're spending. Your business is to get the best result you can, following their wishes. If they want you to build a house upside down, standing on its chimney, it's up to you to do it and still get the best possible result."[8]

Those architects committed to a more radical originality were rarely successful financially. Even those most admired today, for example, Louis Sullivan, Frank Lloyd Wright, and George Elmslie, made little money directly from architectural practice, and all had long dry spells during which no commissions were forthcoming. Their periodic successes, one could argue, were generated by serendipitous encounters with clients who agreed to support their building experiments. That such encounters occurred at all, however, suggests that as strong as the historical tradition was, it did not completely dominate American architecture of the time. Such encounters also occurred with disproportionate frequency hundreds of miles away from the fonts of Beaux-Arts wisdom at Boston, New York, and Philadelphia. If Minnesota's distance from these centers seemed a grave disadvantage to most traditional architects, more adventurous ones saw that the same distance offered a measure of flexibility, a relaxation from convention, and a range of new opportunities for both architect and client alike.

EARLY ARCHITECTURE IN MINNESOTA

Minnesota had been settled almost entirely by northern Europeans. In the 1850s and 1860s, former New England residents had settled in large numbers along the St. Croix River, particularly in the towns of Taylors Falls and Stillwater. On land much like the wooded hills and valleys of their earlier homes, they built villages that virtually replicated those left behind, with houses, churches, and schools designed in the then-popular Greek Revival style, painted uniformly white and usually trimmed in green.

By the turn of the century Germans accounted for more than half the population, but Scandinavians, including Finns, made up a large percentage as well. The rural areas were primarily populated by the Germans, Scandinavians, and Dutch. The cities, particularly the Twin Cities of Minneapolis and St. Paul, attracted many other groups found

Frank Lloyd Wright. Francis Little house, Minnetonka, Minn., 1914. Henry-Russell Hitchcock, In the Nature of Materials: 1887–1941 The Buildings of Frank Lloyd Wright, *1942, plate 200A.*

only in small numbers elsewhere, especially the immigrants who came from eastern and southeastern Europe—Italy, Poland, the Ukraine, Czechoslovakia, Greece, and a host of other nations—during the great population influx that began in the 1880s. Settling in enclaves within the city, they preserved their language and rich cultural heritage. During the late nineteenth and early twentieth centuries, the style of architecture in each urban quarter tended to reproduce what each group had left behind in Europe. North German Protestants, for example, sought architects of like background to design their churches, clubs, theaters, and even commercial buildings. South German Catholics were similarly employed by those of the same origin. Only infrequently were architects able to cross these strict ethnic, cultural, and religious barriers. Remnants of the resulting architectural particularity are still visible today in the ethnic neighborhoods within Minnesota towns and cities.

Late nineteenth-century architecture in Minnesota clearly reflected the state's economic growth and the affluence it brought to many communities. In smaller towns as well as larger cities, bankers, lawyers, and doctors commissioned homes and offices appropriate to their growing wealth and status. Cities and towns needed banks, office buildings, courthouses, city halls, churches, theaters, and train depots. When professional architects were hired to design these structures, it was less to assure the structural success of a building than to furnish the clients with a suitable symbol for themselves or their activity. Each locality tried to surpass its neighbors in the size and opulence of its civic, commercial, and residential buildings. It was believed hiring an architect with a recognized "name" to design one or more of these structures enhanced the community's prestige, making it more attractive to visitors as well as new residents.

Appearances mattered. Local promoters proudly extolled both their town's natural resources and its man-made improvements in a highly competitive bid for new settlers, often contrasting the deficiencies of neighboring communities for good measure. A good example is the following "advertisement" for Minneapolis, a promotional guide published in 1898 by a Minneapolis newspaper:

Nature is lavish with her favorite haunts. She has endowed the locality with benefits material as well as artistic. The soil is admirably adapted to the erection of buildings. It is only necessary to excavate the soil and lay the foundation in the sub-soil, whereas, in St. Paul it is necessary to blast out rocks, in Kansas City to dig out beds of clay, and in Chicago to drain the soil and drive piles.[9]

In the best tradition of such boosterism, the book claims that "millions and millions of unbroken acres" will "[yield] to [the city] all their riches." It continues:

Minneapolis is drawing upon the surest source of municipal development in the world, and it will start up out of its present dream of future greatness to achieve greatness incomparably beyond its wildest and most expectant dreams, to surprise the world, and to bless mankind, contributing the mighty outpouring of Western agriculture and commerce to the prosperity and peace of humanity and upbuilding the race.[10]

In the 1880s, the neighboring cities of Minneapolis and St. Paul, located approximately fifteen miles from one another on the Mississippi River and both established only at midcentury, could boast the highest growth rate in the nation. Together, they swiftly grew to dominate the political, educational, social, and cultural life of the state, and to form the center of its architectural community.

The first professional architects, that is, individuals who were able to support themselves designing buildings, appeared in Minnesota in the 1850s. Few of them had formal architectural training. They had learned their skills as apprentices with established firms or individual architects in Europe or eastern cities. Such apprentice architects constituted the majority of the architectural practitioners who moved into frontier cities in the mid-nineteenth century. In Minnesota, they settled in Minneapolis, St. Paul, and a few other communities, including the river towns along the Mississippi. Robert Alden was among the first to come to Minneapolis, while Augustus Knight was a pioneer in St. Paul. Charles Maybury set up a business further down the river, in Winona. They were joined by a host of others after the Civil War. Some had earned degrees in engineering, some—after 1880—in architecture, but more often they had begun their careers as carpenters or architectural apprentices. By 1890, more than one hundred architects were practicing throughout Minnesota; twenty-five years later, there were three times as many. Throughout the period, the profession consisted almost exclusively of men, although a rare exception, Marion Alice Parker, worked in the prestigious Minneapolis firm of Purcell, Feick and Elmslie as early as 1910.

MINNESOTA AND THE RICHARDSONIAN ROMANESQUE STYLE

Against the background of stylistic diversity in American architecture in the late nineteenth century one style in particular played a pivotal role. Earlier in the century Henry Hobson Richardson (1838–1886), trained at the *École des Beaux-Arts*, had brought back to America his strong appreciation for the medieval Romanesque architecture he had observed in France and England. Heavily rusticated, his characteristic buildings manifest ashlar-cut stone facing, rounded arches over deeply recessed window and door openings, a tower-like bay often situated near the main entrance, and "eyebrow" windows in the pitched roofs. The buildings of Richardson and his followers had a look of tradition and permanence that particularly appealed to settlers of the new western cities. Furthermore, the style was flexible. Identifiable less by plan than by distinctive details, it celebrated the use of stone which could be adapted to buildings of virtually any size or function, from private residences to commercial buildings. Among

E. Townsend Mix. Northwestern Guaranty Loan Building (Metropolitan Building), 3rd Street and 2nd Avenue, Minneapolis, 1890, photograph ca. 1892. Photograph courtesy of the Minnesota Historical Society.

the best early commercial examples of the latter were the Metropolitan Building (designed by the Milwaukee architect E. Townsend Mix in 1890)—now demolished—and Long and Kees's Lumber Exchange Building (1885) at Hennepin Avenue and South Sixth Street. The era's largest residence, the James J. Hill House in St. Paul (1891), and the Union Depot in Duluth (1892) followed the same style—both designed by the Boston firm of Peabody and Stearns. The Richardsonian Romanesque was ultimately able to accommodate even the unprecedented challenge of the first Chicago skyscrapers.

Although a number of tall offices went up in Minneapolis before the turn of the century, very few of them incorporated the loadbearing steel frame, the key to the "skyscraper" design that evolved in Chicago in the 1890s. Up to the mid-1880s, tall buildings (anything more than two or three stories) were possible only if their outer walls were made incredibly thick at the base and tapered upward in thinness. The walls bore the load of the entire structure;

the structural members inside merely supported the floors and partially braced the walls. In the last decades of the nineteenth century, engineers became increasingly interested in the potential of iron and steel to serve as the skeleton of a building. If a framework of iron or steel beams were erected, these men reasoned, the framework—not the outer walls—could be made to bear the load of the building. The obvious advantage was that walls would be thinner, especially at the base, thus expanding both the interior space and window area, which would be attractive to tenants and owners. The first experiments in this direction were carried out in Chicago in the early 1880s by William Le Baron Jenney and by the architectural office of Daniel Burnham and John Wellborn Root all of whom designed and built the first office buildings featuring load-bearing frames.

Technological developments in tall building construction were understood by Minneapolis's most prominent architect and engineer at the time. Educated in civil engineering in Cincinnati, Leroy Buffington was in an excellent position to appreciate the advancing technology of tall buildings as it was evolving in Chicago. In 1888, he secured a patent for the design of a "cloudscraper" of twenty-eight stories, which used a load-bearing steel frame. His patent was later overturned by a court decision, but he continued to contend that he was the inventor. The notoriety of Buffington's refuted claim has tended to deflect attention from the breadth and distinction of his work. He designed the West Hotel (1884) in Minneapolis and the second Minnesota state capitol in St. Paul (1882), making him one of the few architects of his time to receive prestigious commissions in both of the Twin Cities.

Buffington moved from one stylistic vocabulary to another, selecting one as taste, commission, and client preference dictated. Cantankerous and highly competitive, he was more recklessly adventuresome than most in his profession, and his abrasive personality undoubtedly cost him many large commissions. He tried, and failed, to persuade

Peabody and Stearns. Union Depot, Duluth, 5th Avenue West and Michigan Street, 1892. Northeast Minnesota Historical Center. Photograph by Lyman Nylander.

Harvey Ellis. Charles Pillsbury house, Minneapolis, 1888. Northwest Architectural Archives, University of Minnesota Libraries, St. Paul. Photograph by Gary Mortensen and Robert Fogt.

the city to adopt his "cloudscraper" design in the early 1890s. Several other ambitious and inventive proposals likewise failed to garner adequate support, including a redesign of the Hennepin-Lyndale intersection with a memorial arch, a park, and an auditorium; and the reordering of the Gateway district (between downtown Minneapolis and the Mississippi River) around a City Beautiful axis. His unsuccessful entry in the design competition for the Minnesota Building at the 1893 World's Fair resembled a compacted version of the state capitol, borrowing heavily from all the

Harvey Ellis. S. C. Gale house (interior), Minneapolis, 1888. Northwest Architectural Archives, University of Minnesota Libraries, St. Paul. Photograph by Gary Mortensen and Robert Fogt.

Leroy S. Buffington. Library, Sutton, New Hampshire, 1890. Northwest Architectural Archives, University of Minnesota Libraries, St. Paul. Photograph by Gary Mortensen and Robert Fogt.

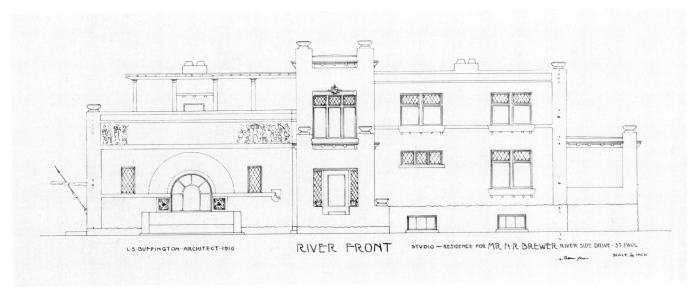

Leroy S. Buffington. N. R. Brewer house, St. Paul, 1910. North-
west Architectural Archives, University of Minnesota Libraries,
St. Paul. Photograph by Gary Mortensen and Robert Fogt.

classical conceits. But Buffington also was capable of sur-
prises: his unbuilt project for a studio-residence for the
painter Nicolas R. Brewer was a curious amalgam of a
Roman villa and an early twentieth-century secessionist
style.

Buffington's architectural failures also tend to obscure
his ability to spot talent in others. He employed several
outstanding draftsmen including the most talented of all,
Harvey Ellis (1854–1904), who worked for Buffington from
1887 to 1890. Widely emulated, Ellis became renowned
in his own time as a master renderer. His reputation continued to grow after his death, in part through the publicity
efforts of fervent disciples such as Claude Bragdon, an architect and critic well known in the 1920s and 1930s. Today

Ellis's name is better known among students of architectural history than that of Buffington. Some historians believe that Ellis learned the Romanesque style while working
briefly for Richardson in Boston, and that he later introduced it to Buffington and to Minnesota. He was, in fact,
employed first in the St. Paul office of Mould and Mc-
Nichol and then in that of J. Walter Stevens (1885–87);
both offices are known for Richardsonian Romanesque designs—probably due to Ellis's influence.

Among Ellis's projects are Pillsbury Hall at the Univer-

Harvey Ellis. Gale's New City Market, Minneapolis, 1891.
Northwest Architectural Archives, University of Minnesota Li-
braries, St. Paul. Photograph by Gary Mortensen and Robert
Fogt.

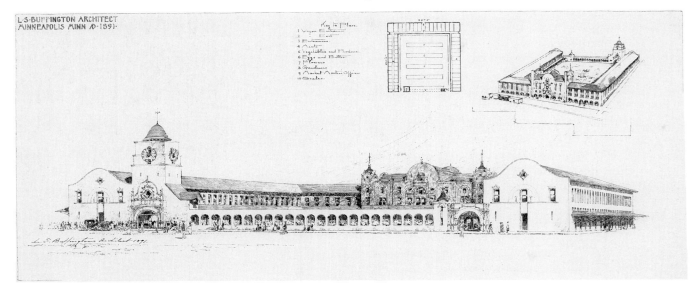

Harvey Ellis. Security Bank, Minneapolis(?), 1891. Northwest Architectural Archives, University of Minnesota Libraries, St. Paul. Photograph by Gary Mortensen and Robert Rogt.

sity of Minnesota (1887); the Mabel Tainter Memorial Library (1890) and Louis Tainter house (1891), both in Menomonie, Wisconsin; and Gale's New City Market and the Security Bank (unbuilt projects), both in Minneapolis. The latter is a particularly harmonious merger of the massively proportioned Richardsonian Romanesque style with a lighter idiom, one that is informed by Sullivan's work and foreshadows the popular Prairie School. In 1890 Ellis moved to Missouri, where he created a number of handsome buildings for the firm of Eckels and Mann. He returned to his home town of Rochester, New York, in 1895, and rejoined a brother in private practice. Late in his life, Ellis designed furniture and interior decor for Gustav Stickley, the well-known designer and manufacturer of arts-and-crafts furniture.

After Ellis, many Minnesota architects adopted the Richardsonian Romanesque, especially for churches and courthouses. Warren H. Hayes (1847–99) used it primarily in church design, executing literally hundreds of commissions, all for Protestant denominations. Some historians credit Hayes with introducing Minneapolis to the "Akron Plan," a spatial system thought to have originated in Akron, Ohio, in the 1880s, in which the auditorium of a church could be closed off from adjacent rooms by means of sliding doors. These doors could be opened to create one large, open space, or closed to form separate rooms for Sunday school, meetings, or other purposes. Working steadily throughout the 1880s and 1890s until his premature death in 1899, Hayes erected some of the Twin Cities's most distinguished buildings in the Richardsonian style, including Wesley Methodist (1889–90), First Congregational (1886), Andrew-Riverside Presbyterian (1890), West-

minster Presbyterian (1896–98) in Minneapolis, and Central Presbyterian (1889) in St. Paul.

Clarence H. Johnston (1859–1936), a prominent St. Paul architect, had attended both Massachusetts Institute of Technology (MIT) and the *École des Beaux-Arts*. Born in Waseca, Minnesota, Johnston worked in New York City for a few years after returning from Paris. He moved to St. Paul in 1883 and set up his first partnership with William Willcox (1832–1929). Although the collaboration lasted only about four years, it resulted in some highly successful

Harvey Ellis. Entry arch, Mabel Tainter Memorial Library, Menomonie, Wisc., 1889. Wayne Andrews, Architecture in Chicago and Mid-America, 1968, p. 31.

buildings, including Summit Terrace (1889) at 587–601 Summit Avenue, famous as a residence of F. Scott Fitzgerald. Both this building and nearby Laurel Terrace (1884), at 286–294 Laurel Avenue, are good examples of middle- or upper-middle-class nineteenth-century row houses carefully executed in, respectively, the Richardsonian Romanesque and Queen Anne styles.

After the breakup of the partnership with Willcox in 1890, Johnston established his own office and began a long and lucrative practice. Much of it consisted of commissions he received while serving as architect to the State Board of Control. These included projects at state-owned educational institutions, such as the University of Minnesota, and various state correctional facilities, notably the state prison at Oak Park Heights near Stillwater. Johnston's most memorable building, however, was a private residence. At Glensheen between 1904 and 1906, he designed and built a house for the wealthy Duluth attorney Chester Congdon. The structure is large and opulent without being overwhelming. Its roomy interior spaces are proportioned to retain a sense of intimacy. Its details—wood paneling, light fixtures, tile and brickwork—all testify to Johnston's extremely high standards of design consistency and craftsmanship.

The adapted Romanesque style, with its characteristic unbroken surfaces and deeply recessed portals, found an unexpected resonance in Duluth. Durable and easily cut and carved, brownstone had already become the favored material for commercial structures. Stone from quarries situated close to Duluth on the Minnesota and Wisconsin sides of Lake Superior could be transported cheaply to the building sites by rail and ship. Oliver Traphagen (1854–1932), one of the earliest architects in the city, specialized in the Richardsonian style. His First Presbyterian Church (1891), Chester Terrace apartments (1890), and Munger Terrace flats (1891–92) are outstanding examples of his skill, as is his own house (1892). Duluth's other prominent brownstone structures include the Lakewood Pumping Station (1897), Central High School (1891–92), and the Torrey Building (1892).

Another firm that successfully adopted the Richardsonian Romanesque was the partnership of Franklin Long (1842–1912) and Frederick Kees (1852–1927). First established in the early 1880s, it quickly became one of the busiest and largest in the Twin Cities. Its Minneapolis projects not only included the Masonic Temple (1888), but the Lumber Exchange (1885), public library (1884), and the First Baptist Church (1887–88), as well as numerous residences. All except the public library survive today. In 1897, Kees left the partnership and formed another successful practice with Serenus Colburn, formerly a draftsman in William Channing Whitney's office. Working in a variety of styles the firm designed such outstanding buildings as the Grain and Flour Exchanges (1900–1902 and 1892–93, 1909, respectively), the Advance Thresher/Emerson-Newton Plow Company warehouse and office building

(1900–1904), and the Northern Implement Company (better known as Pittsburgh Plate Glass) warehouse (1910–11), all in Minneapolis, as well as the Lowry Building in St. Paul (1910–13). Kees and Colburn flourished until Colburn's death in 1925. Kees died two years later.

After the departure of Frederick Kees, Long continued to practice with his son, Louis (1870–1925), until the elder Long's death in 1912 ended the partnership. Louis Lamoreaux (1861–1925) was named a partner in 1909 and was responsible for most of the firm's designs executed after that date, which tended to move away from the Richardsonian Romanesque and toward more classicizing designs. These include, most notably, the Minneapolis City Hospital (1911), at the time one of the most notable of the city's Beaux-Arts classical structures. Obscured by later additions, it was virtually forgotten until the 1980s, when demolition of the complex (by then part of the Hennepin County Medical Center) revealed it once more.

BEAUX-ARTS CLASSICISM

Until the 1890s, many Minnesota architects—even those with first-hand Beaux-Arts training such as Clarence Johnston—tended to find medieval precedents, particularly the Romanesque, more appropriate than classicism for the design problems at hand. At the end of the century, however, the symmetry, clarity, and grandeur of classical architecture began to exert its appeal with a special force. This interest was stimulated by the World's Columbian Exposition, which opened in Chicago in 1893 and presented the nation with a grandiose vision of cities unified and beautified by classical design. The career of Cass Gilbert

Cass Gilbert. Photograph courtesy of the Minnesota Historical Society.

(1859–1934), among those who went on to national and international prominence after establishing himself in Minnesota, reflects especially well the transition from one stylistic mode to the other.

Gilbert arrived in St. Paul in 1882. Born in Ohio, he attended MIT and worked for two years for McKim, Mead and White, an office that was at the forefront of Beaux-Arts style in the country and which employed the architects later chosen to design The Minneapolis Institute of Arts (1911–1915). In 1885 he entered into a partnership with native St. Paulite James Knox Taylor (1857–1929), who had also studied at MIT. Gilbert and Taylor collaborated on a number of prominent commissions; a particularly successful one was the Endicott Building (1888-89) at Fourth and Robert streets in downtown St. Paul. This structure, a fine example of the Italian Renaissance revival style, has an arched entrance and channel-jointed, rusticated stonework on its lower stories. The Endicott and its neighbor, the Pioneer Building (1888–90; Solon Beman, architect), are perhaps the most distinguished pair of commercial buildings to be found anywhere in Minnesota.

Gilbert's shift from predominantly medieval to more distinctly classical sources can be traced in a series of distinguished residences he designed on or near Summit Avenue, which, by the 1890s, was the city's most fashionable street.

He had begun his career in St. Paul by working in the popular shingle style, as seen in the house for J. B. Tarbox at White Bear Lake and another planned for Virginia Street. The architect's own 1890 house at 1 Heather Place incorporates English arts and crafts elements with Tudor half-timbering and stucco. Gilbert soon began to offer clients more modern, classical houses, a shift represented in the 1893 proposal for the William Lightner house, one of the earliest Federal revival residences designed in the country. Lightner himself, however, favored something more traditional, and his house at 318 Summit Avenue successfully integrates a simple Beaux-Arts plan with the massive materials and detailing of the Richardsonian Romanesque. Gilbert's neo-Federal style projects eventually became more accepted, however, as is evident in the Charles Noyes house on Virginia Street and the Emerson Hadley house on Farrington, both begun in the mid-1890s.

Taylor left Gilbert in 1892 to become a senior draftsman in the office of the Supervising Architect of the Treasury in Washington, D.C. In 1897, he took over the post of the supervising architect itself, which he held until 1912 when he was appointed director of the Department of Architecture at MIT. After two years at MIT, he worked in various cities until his retirement in 1928 to Tampa, Florida. After Taylor left the firm, Gilbert came into his own as a leading

- SKETCH OF COTTAGE AT WHITE BEAR FOR MR. J.B.TARBOX -

Gilbert & Taylor Architects.
59 Gilfillan Block.

Cass Gilbert. J. B. Tarbox house, *White Bear Lake, Minn.,* 1889.
Photograph courtesy of the New-York Historical Society.

Cass Gilbert. House on Virginia Avenue, *St. Paul, n.d. Photograph courtesy of the New-York Historical Society.*

Cass Gilbert. Study for the W. H. Lightner house, *St. Paul, 1893. Photograph courtesy of the New-York Historical Society.*

exponent of the Beaux-Arts classical style. His design for the Minnesota state capitol (1895–1905) won him a national reputation. An excellent example of the Classical revival style, the capitol was his greatest accomplishment, not even surpassed by his later designs for the Supreme Court in Washington, D.C. (1932–35) or for the Woolworth Tower (1911–13) in New York City.

Gilbert's traditional Beaux-Arts training shows to best advantage in his designs for the malls at the University of Minnesota (1906) and the state capitol (1904–06). Both also confirm the ideals of the City Beautiful movement of the time. Relying heavily on Beaux-Arts principles of order, characteristic City Beautiful plans called for long, straight boulevards that radiated axially from nodes or plazas. These boulevards, leading from one green space to another, were to provide uncluttered scenic vistas and health-giving open areas. They also would segregate such "clean" activities as government, finance, and shopping from the unsightly, but necessary functions of industry and transportation. Lined with uniform rows of monumental buildings, the avenues or promenades also would recall similar plans in the great capital cities of Europe (e.g., *Unter den Linden* in Berlin or the *Champs-Elysées* in Paris). The well-known European models, however, built on the ruins of older, less orderly urban neighborhoods, often had been the projects of imperial governments at the height of power, governments who directed these changes with the full cooperation of financial and industrial sectors. Except in the instance of Washington, D.C. (laid out by Pierre Charles L'Enfant long before the concept of a "city beautiful" formally existed), such plans usually required too strong and too centralized an authority to be effectively implemented in the United States, where the legitimate scope of federal authority was understood very differently.

Cass Gilbert. Entrance, G. C. Squires house, *St. Paul, n.d. Photograph courtesy of the New-York Historical Society.*

Neither of Gilbert's plans was completely executed. He had intended his capitol building to stand at the end of a long axial drive into downtown St. Paul, but this mall was only partly constructed and now terminates in a contemporary office building. For the University of Minnesota, Gilbert had planned a similar tree-lined vista stretching from Northrop Memorial Auditorium at one end to the Mississippi River at the other. In 1940, the student union building was erected, breaking this line of open space. Under present conditions, it is difficult to envision Gilbert's grand scope, the sweeping ambition that animated the architect's original designs.

One of Gilbert's apprentices was Thomas Holyoke (1866–1925), who was educated in Paris and whose designs regularly achieved the picturesque classicism so prized at the Paris École. Under Gilbert, Holyoke became the chief draftsman for the Minnesota State Capitol. When Gilbert moved to New York early in this century, Holyoke took over his teacher's St. Paul office. In 1916, he formed another partnership with St. Paul architects Magnus Jemne and Holyoke Davis. Holyoke made residential work his specialty. He proficiently designed in a range of styles, from Tudor to the Chateau and Colonial revivals. His lake cot-

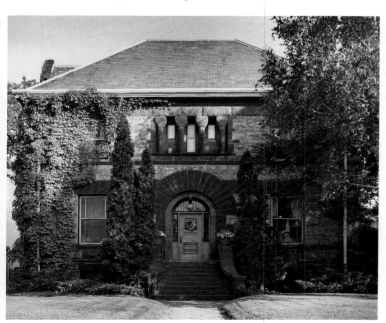

Cass Gilbert. W. H. Lightner house, *318 Summit Avenue, St. Paul, 1893. Photograph by Karen Melvin, Minneapolis.*

tage design for William Mitchell (1907) demonstrates his exceptional skill as an artist and delineator.

The only Minnesota-based architect who was both French-born and École-trained, Emmanuel Louis Masqueray (1861–1917), arrived in St. Paul in 1905. He came at the behest of Archbishop John Ireland to design a new Cathedral of St. Paul and the Procathedral of Minneapolis (later, the Basilica of St. Mary). Masqueray graduated from the *École des Beaux-Arts* in 1884. He probably first came to the United States at the invitation of John Carrère, a partner in the New York-based partnership of Carrère and Hastings and a colleague of Masqueray in Paris. He worked for Carrère and Hastings until 1892, when he joined the firm of New York-based architect Richard Morris Hunt, the first American trained at the École. A year after Hunt's death in 1895, Masqueray entered the New York office of Warren and Wetmore (Whitney Warren was also an alumnus of the École). At about the same time, he set up his own atelier in New York City on East Twenty-third Street. In 1901 Masqueray was hired as chief of design for the Louisiana Purchase Exposition in St. Louis (often called the St. Louis World's Fair), to be held in 1903, marking the centenary of the land acquisition that had nearly doubled the nation's physical size. He worked on the Fair's design until it opened in 1904, a year later than originally planned.

Masqueray was probably approached by Archbishop Ireland at the fair and asked to design a new cathedral for the archdiocese of St. Paul. He agreed to come to St. Paul after making a tour of French churches "for inspiration."[11] The Cathedral of St. Paul (1905–25) on Summit Hill overlooking downtown St. Paul was Masqueray's most important commission. French baroque in style, it utilized the form of a Greek cross to support a large dome above the crossing. His design for the Procathedral of Minneapolis (renamed the Basilica of St. Mary at its dedication in 1926), located on Hennepin Avenue near downtown Minneapolis, borrowed from the French Renaissance revival style with its mansard-inspired dome and highly articulated facade.

Through Archbishop Ireland's influence, Masqueray ob-

Emmanual Louis Masqueray. Cathedral of St. Paul, St. Paul, 1905, photograph ca. 1918. Minnesota Historical Society. Photograph by C. P. Gibson.

Emmanual Louis Masqueray. St. Paul's Church on the Hill, St. Paul, 1913. St. Paul's Church on the Hill. Photograph by David Peterson.

tained many commissions for Catholic parishes in Minnesota, South Dakota, and Iowa. For these, his designs almost always were in an Italian or French-derived Renaissance or baroque style, the St. Louis Church (1909) on Cedar Street in downtown St. Paul being a particularly successful example. Masqueray's name became known to Protestant congregations as well. St. Paul's Church on the Hill, one block east of Snelling Avenue on Summit Avenue in St. Paul (1912), for example, was designed for an Episcopal congregation that had moved out of the downtown area. The quiet stone structure is an exemplary adaptation of an English country Gothic building, utilizing rustic stone and wood which Masqueray preferred for Protestant churches.

In 1891, Charles Reed (1858–1911) of New York and Allen Stem (1856–1931) of Ohio formed a partnership that produced some of the most notable—and least appreciated—buildings in St. Paul. They specialized in large commercial and civic structures, including the St. Paul Auditorium, University Club (1913), and St. Paul Hotel (1910). They also executed several prestigious residential commissions, such as the Thomas B. Scott house at 340 Summit Avenue (1894), successfully exploiting the area's dramatic slopes and vistas. Within the specialization of large public and commercial buildings, Reed and Stem developed a subspecialty of railroad depots, most of them for the Great Northern, Northern Pacific, and New York Central railroads. They produced union stations for Tacoma, Detroit, Schenectady, Albany, and Rochester in New York, crowning their efforts with the magnificent Grand Central Station (1903–13) in the heart of New York City. In carrying out this enormous project, they were joined by the New York firm of Warren and Wetmore, which had once employed Masqueray. Reed and Stem may have received the commission for one of the world's largest

Reed and Stem. University Club, St. Paul, 1913. University Club, St. Paul. Photograph by Gary Mortensen and Robert Fogt.

*D. H. Burnham and Company. St. Louis County Courthouse,
Duluth, Minn., 1908–9. Duluth's Legacy, vol. 1, p. 95.*

*Edward H. Bennett. Bird's Eye view of the Station Plaza, 1917.
Municipal Archives, City of Minneapolis. Photograph by Gary
Mortensen and Robert Fogt.*

Louis Lamoreaux. T. B. Sheldon Memorial Auditorium, Red Wing, Minn., 1904. Sheldon Theater. Photograph from the Photographic Collection of Phil Revoir . . . Red Wing, Minn.

train stations through Reed, whose brother-in-law was the vice president for engineering of New York Central, the builder of Grand Central terminal. Reed moved to New York to oversee the project and work more closely with Whitney Warren, but died there suddenly in 1911, the victim of a heart attack. Stem continued to practice in St. Paul until his retirement in 1920.

The classical vision found perhaps its most complete expression in Duluth. Duluth was considered one of the most promising regional centers in the country around 1900. The city was controlled by eastern monied interests who believed it would be a transit center rivaling Chicago, linking western rail lines to the Great Lakes and Europe. Wheat, timber, and iron ore also brought prosperity to Duluth, resulting in an unexpectedly varied and opulent architecture. Its architectural ambition parallelled its image of both present and future economic success. "Few cities the size of Duluth," writes Minnesota historian Lawrence Sommer, "can boast of so many homes as elegant as those constructed by the magnates of Minnesota's iron mining."[12]

The nationally recognized architect and urban planner Daniel Burnham (1846–1912), head of the huge and prestigious D. H. Burnham and Company of Chicago, was awarded the commission for a downtown Civic Center (1908–30). "Make no little plans," Burnham is reputed to have said; "they have no magic to stir men's blood." In keeping with his convictions, Burnham's concept of a city center, with its huge majestic buildings of overpowering scale, had a kind of magic for those who saw them. Their scale and classical vocabulary gave the impression of per-

manence and confidence. With the completion of the City Hall (1928) and Post Office-Federal Building (1930), Burnham completed his entire civic center project for Duluth, one of the most complete realizations of the City Beautiful movement in Minnesota. Burnham's office also was responsible for the ambitious 1917 *Plan of Minneapolis*, drawn by Edward Bennett. Widely circulated, the *Plan* was published in a richly illustrated, hard-bound book, with water color perspective drawings highly evocative of the "streetscapes" of Paris or Vienna.

The Renaissance revival style of the T. B. Sheldon Memorial Auditorium (1904) in Red Wing, a gift to the city by the grain merchant Theodore Sheldon, presents a somewhat different aspect of turn-of-the-century classicizing trend. Designed by Louis Lamoreaux of Long, Lamoreaux and Long of Minneapolis, it was built for $87,000 and was the first municipal playhouse in the nation. A description published in 1971, in a souvenir brochure by the local art association, ran as follows:

The inside was embellished with gold and ivory. Marble walls glittered with the sparkle of two many-tiered chandeliers, each purchased for $350, and with the light from ceiling beams heavily studded with electric lights. Playgoers were surrounded by plaster busts of Shakespeare, Goethe, Beethoven, and Wagner in ornate niches as well as large oil [portrait] of Sheldon.[13]

Following a disastrous fire, the building has been completely restored to its former elegance.

ECLECTICISM AT THE TURN OF THE CENTURY

Although Edwin H. Hewitt (1874–1939) was the first Beaux-Arts-trained architect to practice in the Twin Cities, he was less committed to classical models than most École alumni. He worked frequently in the gothic style, preferring it for religious, educational, and even residential architecture. A native of Red Wing, Minnesota, he attended MIT, the most acclaimed of the few American schools modeled on the École des Beaux-Arts. He then studied in Paris in the atelier of Jean-Louis Pascal. He finally returned to Minnesota in 1900 to open his own office in Minneapolis. Hewitt executed several highly successful designs while practicing alone and continued to be one of the city's top architects after forming a partnership in 1910 with Edwin H. Brown (ca. 1875–1930). Hewitt was responsible for St. Mark's Episcopal Cathedral (1909), an exemplary adaptation of English Gothic in stone and stained glass. In collaboration with Brown, he later designed the Hennepin Avenue Methodist Church (1914) as well. The latter project incorporated the plan and Norman gothic ornament of Ely Cathedral near Cambridge, England. Hewitt's building reproduces the earlier church's distinctive octagonal tower over the crossing of the nave and transepts. His early twentieth-century refinement was to add a spire atop the octagonal base. Hewitt's two churches still stand within a block of one other, at the junction of Hennepin and Lyndale avenues in Minneapolis.

Blake School (1912) in Hopkins is a fine example of Hewitt's English Collegiate Gothic, recalling the crenelated detailing of Eton College in England. The Charles Pillsbury house (1912) at 106 East Twenty-second Street in Minneapolis retraces the developmental steps of the Elizabethan style in its combination of Gothic and Renaissance elements. One of the firm's most notable classical efforts was the Gateway Pavilion, built in 1916–17, at the intersection of Hennepin and Nicollet avenues in downtown Minneapolis. After the turn of the century, however, Hewitt began to adopt the conventions of craftsman style. His own house, at 126 East Franklin Avenue in Minneapolis (1906), follows a craftsman precedent as it incorporates half-timbering and stucco to stress the flavor of English Tudor revival.[14]

William Channing Whitney. J. R. Kingman house, *Minneapolis, 1903. Northwest Architectural Archives, University of Minnesota Libraries, St. Paul. Photograph by Gary Mortensen and Robert Fogt.*

William Channing Whitney. William Dunwoody house, Minneapolis, 1905. Northwest Architectural Archives, University of Minnesota Libraries, St. Paul. Photograph by Gary Mortensen and Robert Fogt.

William Channing Whitney. Frank Heffelfinger house, "Highcroft," Lake Minnetonka, Minn., 1894. Northwest Architectural Archives, University of Minnesota Libraries, St. Paul. Photograph by Gary Mortensen and Robert Fogt.

Another MIT alumnus was the prolific residential designer William Channing Whitney (1851–1945). Born in Massachusetts, Whitney came to Minneapolis in the late 1870s. During his long career, he demonstrated extraordinary facility with all the fashionable residential styles, often successfully combining them in a single edifice. He seems to have favored the classical tradition, however. His design for the Minnesota Building at the World's Columbian Exposition of 1893 is a typical example of his work.[15] The building mixes Beaux-Arts classicism with Renaissance revival styles, creating an austere Roman temple-like building in fancy dress. Whitney is best remembered today,

William Channing Whitney. J. F. Bell house, "Bellford," Lake Minnetonka, Minn., 1900. Northwest Architectural Archives, University of Minnesota Libraries, St. Paul. Photograph by Gary Mortensen and Robert Fogt.

Harry W. Jones. Lake Minnetonka houses and yacht club, Lake Minnetonka, Minn., 1886. Northwest Architectural Archives, University of Minnesota Libraries, St. Paul. Photograph by Gary Mortensen and Robert Fogt.

however, for his large, lavish residences. No complete list of his work has ever been compiled. Even a small sample of his houses, however, many of them for wealthy community leaders of Minneapolis, reflect an admirable command of diverse architectural styles and a consistent ingenuity in solving difficult design problems.

Harry Wild Jones (1859–1935), a native of Michigan, typifies the apprentice architect who achieved success without the benefit of a college education or classical training. At ease with a variety of architectual vocabularies, Jones is widely ranked among the most accomplished architects of his generation in Minnesota. For residences and park buildings, he preferred the shingle style; for apartment buildings, commercial structures, and churches, Romanesque revival. Several of these were constructed in the Lake Minnetonka area, where dozens of large and opulent summer homes were built by the leading businessmen of the Twin Cities from the 1880s through the 1910s. Jones's crowning achievement was Lakewood Cemetery Chapel (1908) in Minneapolis, a Byzantine Romanesque design inspired by the great sixth-century church of St. Sophia in Istanbul.

Both European-born and educated, interior designer Gustav Weber (1870–1960) established an office in Minneapolis in the early 1900s. The Beaux-Arts influence is especially conspicuous in his designs for two rooms in the Minnesota Club (1900) at Fourth and Cedar streets in St. Paul. In typical Beaux-Art fashion, for example, the elevation drawings portray the ceiling as an isometric extension of the wall with no indication of perspective.

Nationally recognized architects and urban planners often were commissioned by the new millionaires of Duluth. Bertram Grosvenor Goodhue of New York (1869–1924) designed four outstanding structures in the city between 1912 and 1915: the Kitchi Gammi Club (1912), Hartley office building (1914), and Cavour Hartley mansion (1915), all on the lake front. St. Paul's Episcopal Church (1912) is one of the firm's small masterpieces. All were created at a time when Goodhue, in breaking away from his long-time partner Ralph Adams Cram and the latter's strict neo-gothic influence, was finding ways to design buildings that still had a Gothic flavor, but were infused with a vitality drawn from other styles, such as Renaissance and Elizabethan.[16]

William Bray (1868–1959) worked successfully in Duluth in a number of styles including those of Tudor revival, Prairie School, and Colonial revival. His first partner was I. Vernon Hill (1869–1904), whose houses usually featured steep roofs and details derived from the English half-timber tradition. After Hill's untimely death at age thirty-five, Bray produced a number of fine residences in East Duluth with

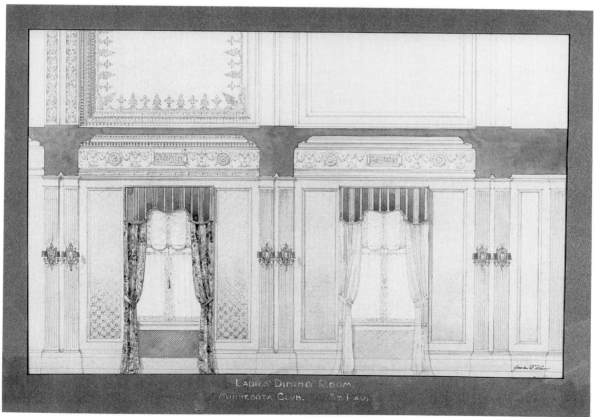

Gustav F. Weber. Minnesota Club, Ladies' Dining Room, *Minneapolis, 1905. Northwest Architectural Archives, University of Minnesota Libraries, St. Paul. Photograph by Gary Mortensen and Robert Fogt.*

Bertram Goodhue. St. Paul's Episcopal Church, Duluth, Minn.,
1912. Duluth's Legacy, vol. 1, p. 129.

his next partner, Carl Nystrom (1868–1944), such as the Prairie style house at 2423 East Second Street designed for the Clark family.

In 1863, Dr. William W. Mayo established a medical practice in Rochester, Minnesota, that would later expand beyond anything he or anyone else could have imagined. His sons, Doctors William and Charles Mayo, joined their father in the 1880s after completing their medical training, and together they built the first group practice medical clinic in the world. It attracted many physicians and scientists whose financial successes were exhibited in the large, attractive homes they built in the southwestern part of the city, today called "Pill Hill." Several architects worked in the city. The most outstanding local designer was Harold Crawford, whose carefully crafted English cottage and Tudor dwellings are among the best to be found anywhere in the state. Franklin Ellerbe (1870–1921) and his son, Thomas (1893–1988), of St. Paul were the principal designers of the buildings for the Mayo Clinic. The first clinic building, erected in 1914 and demolished and replaced by a glass tower in 1985, was a severely functioning building. Few of the turn-of-the century buildings in the city survive.

PROGRESSIVE ARCHITECTS

Although conservative eclecticism, sustained by Beaux-Arts teaching, clearly dominated architectural thinking in Minnesota at the turn of the century, there were a few architects on the periphery who were reconsidering academic training and applying it in unprecedented ways. The hub of this new thinking was Chicago, home of Louis Sullivan and his student, Frank Lloyd Wright, the chief proponents of what they called "progressive" design, termed by others the "Prairie School," acknowledging its regional origins. Both Sullivan and Wright designed important buildings in Minnesota. Sullivan's series of early-twentieth century designs for rural banks, including his masterpiece, the National Farmers' Bank in Owatonna (1906–08), represents a remarkably rich statement of the Prairie School's vision for a distinguished regional architecture, scaled to the particular needs of small communities. When Francis Little moved to Minneapolis from Peoria, Illinois, he asked the architect of his 1903 house in that city, Frank Lloyd Wright, to create a substantial residence for him on Lake Minnetonka. The Little house has received much national publicity since its destruction in 1972 and partial reconstruction in the Metropolitan Museum of Art. The broader impact of the Prairie movement in Minnesota, however, is

I. Vernon Hill. I. Vernon Hill house, Duluth, Minn., 1902.
Duluth's Legacy, *vol. 1, p. 115.*

probably more appropriately attributed to architects based here. The firm that articulated its principles most steadily over an extended period of time, Purcell and Elmslie, is discussed elsewhere in this volume.

The Prairie School was part of a more broadly based desire, shared by American social reformers and intellectuals as well as artists, to return to a greater simplicity in life. Just as rural American society was idealized for its closeness to nature and freedom from the restraints and conventions of urban society, the progressives wanted their buildings to be simple, unpretentious, and on a human scale. Looking to the flat prairie terrain that surrounded them, the architects tried to create buildings with a horizontality and natural palette of colors that would blend unobtrusively with their surroundings. They denounced the artifice, contrivance, and indifference to site that they saw in the Beaux-Arts tradition. Interiors had to be informal, uncluttered and open to free movement. Rather than dominating nature, progressive architecture would harmonize with it.

In keeping with these general principles, Prairie School architects pursued their ideal of beauty through the spareness of their designs. Frank Lloyd Wright believed that because the clean vertical and horizontal lines of his houses were simply rendered, they also represented the best solution to a given design problem. Wright wanted wood cut "in plain, simple ways that resulted in plain, simple rectilinear shapes."[17] Other progressive architects, on the whole, agreed. In contrast to sharp segmentation of more traditional designs, their floor plans reduced the number of dividing walls and other partitions, promoting free movement

*Louis Sullivan. National Farmer's Bank, Owatonna, Minn.,
1906–8. Photograph courtesy of the Minnesota Historical Society.*

*Frank Lloyd Wright. Francis Little house, Minnetonka, Minn.,
1914. Photograph courtesy of The Minneapolis Institute of Arts.*

George Maher. Watkins Company, Winona, Minn., 1911. *Winona County Historical Society, Inc. Photograph by Regan Photography, Winona.*

George Maher. E. L. King house, "Rockledge," Homer, Minn., *1912. Photograph courtesy of the Winona County Historical Society, Inc.*

George Maher. Detail of the fireplace *for the E. L. King house,* "*Rockledge,*" *Homer, Minn., 1912. Winona County Historical Society, Inc. Photograph by Regan Photography, Winona.*

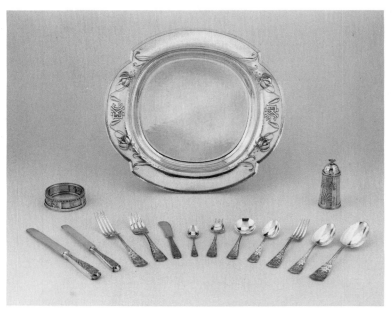

George Maher. Silver service *from "Rockledge," Homer, Minn., 1912. Anonymous lender. Photograph by Gary Mortensen and Robert Fogt.*

and interplay among the activities taking place in the various spaces.

Most Minnesota progressives followed Sullivan and Wright's organic, nature-inspired principles quite closely. Occasionally, however, genuinely eccentric designs appeared, not fully consistent with either Beaux-Arts or progressive ideals. In these buildings, disparate elements often seem at odds with one another. The Winona Savings Bank and Winona National Bank Building (1915), designed by the Chicago-based architect George W. Maher (1864–1926), represents a more harmonious blend of traditional and progressive approaches. On first glance, the bank expresses the heavy, unbroken surfaces of ancient Egyptian architecture, which was regularly adapted to modern functions in the early decades of the nineteenth century, briefly resurfacing in the early 1920s. However, the architect's intentions were more subtle than the mere reissue of a historical revival. Maher had worked for Sullivan in his earlier days and had been imbued with the new progressive ideology. He emphasized, however, that no one "should expect to design on progressive lines who is deficient in architectural training and history. On the other hand, merely familiarizing one's self with the form and style of architecture found in [the] grand ruins of antiquity is not sufficient as a training for our art."[18] Clearly, Maher's objective was a successful composite of historical antecedents with Prairie School theories and practices.

Maher's chief client in Winona was the J. R. Watkins Medical Products Company. He designed the firm's headquarters, an office building (1911) and the adjacent ten-storied factory (1913). The headquarters building is notable as a Beaux-Arts classical structure, consisting of a domed entrance atrium and two wings extending left and right. Although such a plan might seem aberrant to most "progressive" thinking, it is a reminder that the same principles underlay both Beaux-Arts and Prairie School buildings, and that a single architect could, if he chose, combine the principles of the two vocabularies. For the Winona businessman E. L. King, Maher did design a more consistent Prairie School residence, called Rockledge, which better embodied his "progressive" inclinations. Constructed in 1912 outside the town of Homer, Minnesota, it has since been destroyed.

Percy Bentley (1884–1967), born in La Crosse, Wisconsin, was educated at the Armour Institute of Technology in Chicago, where he came to admire Wright and Sullivan's work. After returning to La Crosse to open his own office, Bentley designed a number of Prairie School residences in La Crosse and in Fountain City, Wisconsin. He moved to St. Paul in 1914 and formed a brief partnership with architect Charles Hausler (1884–1971), on whom he had a strong influence. The firm's Strickler residence (1916), with its split-level design, represents something of an oddity among Prairie School houses. The house at 975 Osceola in St. Paul (1917) is a more conventional, two-storied design, so evocative of the strong horizontality found in the work of Purcell and Elmslie or Frank Lloyd

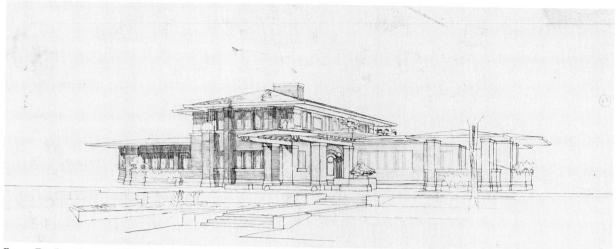

Percy D. Bentley and Charles A. Hausler. Prairie School house, *unknown location, 1918. Northwest Architectural Archives, University of Minnesota Libraries, St. Paul. Photograph by Gary Mortensen and Robert Fogt.*

Wright that it is often mistaken for their work. Bentley's influence on Hausler, who was also employed as St. Paul city architect at the time, is clearly seen in the shelters for Phalen, Mounds, and Como parks and in a police garage on East Third Street, all built between 1914 and 1918.

CONCLUSION

Sharing the ambitions and prospects of the new western regions of the United States at the turn of the century, Minnesotans were most concerned that their architecture reflect, even reproduce the achievements of older American communities in the east and their even earlier antecedents in Europe. They wanted their buildings to be traditional representatives of the prosperity, dignity, and culture they felt their hard work had recreated along the upper Mississippi. Yet far from established centers of architecture in the East, Minnesota architects were comparatively free to represent this achievement in an individualistic way. While the contemporary critic Montgomery Schuyler suggested that this relaxation from restraint often resulted in excesses and incongruities in recent building, it also revealed a promising vigor and inventiveness. "There are among the emancipated practitioners of architecture in the West," he wrote, "men who have shown that they can use their liberty wisely, and whose work can be hailed as among the hopeful beginnings of a national architecture."[19]

Schuyler's concern with the individualistic interpretations of tradition represented in Minnesota's architecture bears little relation to our own current search for a regional identity. Writing only in 1891, this Easterner's underlying motivation was not directed toward defining a peculiarly Minnesota architectural expression but in how Minnesota might have contributed to the articulation of a larger, national architectural style which motivated Schuyler's curiosity. He might have been more encouraged by local achievement if given a preview of the Prairie style that would develop over the next twenty-five years. While critical appreciation of the progressive movement at first emphasizes its regional associations, in our own time the Prairie style has come to express a national separateness and uniqueness, as well as a fundamental proof of the country's architectural sophistication, one that continues to command respect in an international context.

From the perspective of today, with the triumph of the sleek, efficient skyscraper and the proliferation of largely faceless, functional International Style buildings fresh in memory, we should value the architecture of the years around 1900 for reasons other than any national or regionally specific formal associations. Particularly seen against contemporary architecture's enthusiastic, if relatively casual use of materials and "citation" of earlier styles, the material authenticity of the turn-of-the-century revivals appears all the more admirable. That period's consistent regard for craftsmanship, durability, and the functional and aesthetic qualities of materials is readily apparent. Most importantly, the stylistic diversity of the time no longer appears, as it did to many contemporaries—even to Schuyler himself—like evidence of a regrettable confusion, or at best a frustrating search for the "right" way to build. Today it appears more like a point in the long, complex, ongoing effort to identify particular families, towns, professions, and industries within a larger social context. The peculiarities expressed in the juxtaposition of styles within a single block or even a single building now take on a new value exactly for their distinctive adaptation of historical precedent. Whether peculiar to this region or representing a consistent, national trend, it is the record of a singular history, and with it the basis for a particular identity in the present one, worthy of our continued study and respect.

NOTES

1. Montgomery Schuyler, "Glimpses of Western Architecture," *Harper's New Monthly Magazine* 83: 497 (October 1891): 736, 737.

2. See Howard Mumford Jones, *The Age of Energy* (New York: Viking Press, 1971).

3. Carl Condit, *American Building* (Chicago: University of Chicago Press, 1968), 43–44.

4. Quoted in John Burchard and Albert Bush Brown, *The Architecture of America: A Social and Cultural History* (New York: Atlantic-Little, Brown, 1961), 198, 201.

5 See David Van Zanten, "Le Systeme des Beaux-Arts," *L'Architecture d' Aujourd'hui* 182 (November 1975): 97–106.

6. Henry Hope Reed, *Beaux-Arts Architecture in New York* (New York: Dover Publications, Inc., 1988), ix.

7. Quoted in James J. Rossant, untitled remarks, in *Oppositions* 8 (Spring 1977): 163. Sullivan attended but did not graduate from the École.

8. Wayne Andrews, *Architecture, Ambition and Americans* (New York: The Free Press, 1978), 171.

9. *Art Glimpses of Minneapolis, the City of Homes* (Minneapolis: The Times Newspaper Co., 1898), 100.

10. Ibid., 42.

11. See Alan K. Lathrop, "A French Architect in Minnesota," *Minnesota History* (Summer 1980): 43–56.

12. Lawrence Sommer, *Duluth Historical Resources Survey, Final Report* (Duluth: St. Louis County Historical Society, 1984).

13. The T. B. Sheldon Memorial Auditorium," *Souvenir Program* (Red Wing: Red Wing Art Association, 1971), unpaginated.

14. David Gebhard and Tom Martinson, *A Guide to the Architecture of Minnesota* (Minneapolis: University of Minnesota Press, 1977), 65, 124.

15. The Minnesota Building, like most of the fair's structures was a temporary building composed of a wood frame covered in molded plaster mixed with hair or straw, called "staff." Almost all of the art and architecture erected on the fairgrounds was designed to last only a couple years and was demolished when the fair closed.

16. James Scott, *Duluth's Heritage: Architecture* (Duluth: City of Duluth, Department of Research and Planning, 1974), 31.

17. Richard Guy Wilson, "Chicago and the International Arts and Crafts Movements: Progressive and Conservative Tendencies," in *Chicago Architecture 1872–1922: Birth of a Metropolis* (Munich: Prestel-Verlag in association with the Art Institute of Chicago, 1987), 215.

18. Peter B. Wight, "The Winona Savings Bank and Winona National Bank Building Winona, Minnesota," *Architectural Record* 41 (January 1917): 38.

19. Schuyler, "Glimpses of Western Architecture, 755.

BIBLIOGRAPHY

Andrews, Wayne. *Architecture, Ambition and Americans.* New York: The Free Press, 1978.

Art Glimpses of Minneapolis, the City of Homes. Minneapolis: The Times Newspaper Co., 1898.

Barth, Gunther. *City People.* New York: Oxford University Press, 1980.

Borchert, John. *America's Northern Heartland.* Minneapolis: University of Minnesota Press, 1987.

Borchert, John et. al. *Legacy of Minneapolis: Preservation Amid Change.* Bloomington, Minnesota: Voyageur Press, 1983.

Burchard, John and Albert Bush Brown. *The Architecture of America: A Social and Cultural History.* New York: Atlantic-Little, Brown, 1961.

Cable, Mary. *Top Drawer: American Society from the Gilded Age to the Roaring Twenties.* New York: Atheneum, 1984.

Cashman, Sean Dennis. *America in the Gilded Age: From the Death of Lincoln to the Rise of Theodore Roosevelt.* New York: New York University Press, 1988.

Condit, Carl. *American Building.* Chicago: University of Chicago Press, 1968.

Coventry, William D. *Duluth's Age of Brownstone.* Duluth: St. Louis County Historical Society, 1987.

Cram, Ralph Adams. "Influence of the French School on American Architechture." *The Improvement Bulletin,* 16 December 1899.

Crook, J. Mordaunt. *The Dilemma of Style.* Chicago: University of Chicago Press, 1987.

Draper, Joan. "The École des Beaux-Arts and the Architectural Profession in the United States: The Case of John Galen Howard." In *The Architect: Chapters in the History of the Profession,* edited by Spiro Kostoff. New York: Oxford University Press, 1977.

Drexler, Arthur. *The Architecture of the École des Beaux Arts.* New York: Museum of Modern Art, 1977.

Foreman, John and Robbe Pierce Stimson. *The Vanderbilts and the Gilded Age: Architectural Aspirations, 1879–1901.* New York: St. Martin's Press, 1991.

Furnas, J. C. *The Americans: A Social History of the United States, 1587–1914.* New York: Putnam, 1969.

Garner, John S. *The Midwest in American Architecture.* Urbana and Chicago: University of Illinois Press, 1991.

Gebhard, David and Tom Martinson. *A Guide to the Architecture of Minnesota.* Minneapolis: University of Minnesota Press, 1977.

Hansen, Carl O. G. *My Minneapolis.* Published privately by the author, 1956.

Hewitt, Mark Alan. *The Architect and the American Country House, 1890–1940.* New Haven: Yale University Press, 1990.

Hitchcock, Henry-Russell. *Architecture: Nineteenth and Twentieth Centuries.* Baltimore: Penguin Books, 1968.

Jones, Howard Mumford. *The Age of Energy.* New York: Viking Press, 1971.

Jordy, William H. *American Buildings and Their Architects.* Vol. 3. Garden City, N.Y.: Doubleday, 1972.

Kane, Lucile M. *The Waterfall that Built a City.* St. Paul: Minnesota Historical Society, 1966.

Kaplan, Wendy. *"The Art That Is Life": The Arts & Crafts Movement in America, 1875–1920.* Boston: Museum of Fine Arts, 1987.

Kidney, Walter C. *The Architecture of Choice: Eclecticism in America, 1880–1930.* New York: G. Braziller, 1974.

Lane, Michael. *Glensheen: The Construction Years.* Duluth: Glensheen, University of Minnesota, n.d.

Lanegran, David A. and Ernest Sandeen. *The Lake District of Minneapolis: A History of the Calhoun-Isles Community.* St. Paul: Living Historical Museum, 1979.

Larson, Paul Clifford and Susan M. Brown, eds. *The Spirit of H. H. Richardson on the Midland Prairies.* Minneapolis: University Art Museum, of Minnesota, 1988.

Lathrop, Alan K. "A French Architect in Minnesota." *Minnesota History,* Summer 1980.

Monograph of the Work of McKim, Mead and White, 1879–1915. Vol. 4. New York: Architectural Book Publishing Co., 1915.

National Register of Historic Places Nominations. State Historic Preservation Office, Minnesota Historical Society, St. Paul.

Noffsinger, James Philip. *The Influence of the École des Beaux Arts on the Architects of the United States.* Ph.D. Diss., Catholic University of America, 1955.

Platt, Frederick. *America's Gilded Age: Its Architecture and Decoration.* South Brunswick, N.J.: A. S. Barnes, 1976.

Reed, Henry Hope. *Beaux-Arts Architecture in New York.* New York: Dover Publications, Inc., 1988.

Rossant, James J. Untitled remarks. *Oppositions* 8 (Spring 1977).

Roth, Leland M. ed. *America Builds: Source Documents in American Architecture and Planning.* New York: Harper & Row, 1983.

Schuyler, Montgomery. *American Architecture and Other Writings.* Cambridge: Harvard University Press, 1961.

Scott, James. *Duluth's Heritage: Architecture.* Duluth: City of Duluth, Department of Research and Planning, 1974.

Sitte, Camillo. *Der Stadtebau nach seinen Kunstlerischen Grundsatzen.* Vienna, 1899.

Sloane, Florence Adele. *Maverick in Mauve: Diary of a Romantic Age.* Garden City, N.Y.: Doubleday, 1983.

Sommer, Lawrence. *Duluth Historic Resources Survey, Final Report.* Duluth: St. Louis County Historical Society, 1984.

Spreiregen, Paul D. *Urban Design: The Architecture of Towns and Cities.* New York: McGraw-Hill, 1965.

Svendsen, Gustav Rolf. *Hennepin County History.* Minneapolis: Hennepin County Historical Society, 1976.

Szarkowski, John. *The Face of Minnesota.* Minneapolis: University of Minnesota Press, 1958.

"The T. B. Sheldon Memorial Auditorium." Souvenir Program. Red Wing: Red Wing Art Association, 1971.

Torbert, Donald R. "Art and Architecture." In A *History of the Arts in Minnesota,* edited by William Van O'Connor. Minneapolis: University of Minnesota Press, 1958.

———. *Minneapolis Architecture and Architects, 1848–1908.* Ph.D. diss., University of Minnesota, 1951.

Twombley, Robert. *Louis Sullivan: His Life and Work.* New York: Viking, 1986.

Van Zanten, David. "Le systeme des Beaux-Arts." *L'Architecture d'Aujourd'hui* 182 (November 1975).

Wiebe, Robert H. *The Search for Order, 1877–1920.* New York: Hill & Wang, 1967.

Wight, Peter B. "The Winona Savings Bank and Winona National Bank Building, Winona, Minnesota." *Architectural Record* 41 (January 1917).

Wilson, Richard Guy. *The American Renaissance 1876–1917.* New York: Brooklyn Museum, 1979.

———. "Chicago and the Internation Arts and Crafts Movements: Progressive and Conservative Tendencies." In *Chicago: Architecture 1872–1922: Birth of a Metropolis.* Munich: Prestel-Verlag in association with the Art Institute of Chicago, 1987.

CHECKLIST OF THE EXHIBITION

Dimensions = h × w × d

1. Edward H. Bennett
   American, 1874–1954
   City Plan of Minneapolis, 1917
   Book (quarto)
   12¾″ × 9¾″ closed; 12¾″ × 20¼″ open, n.d.
   Northwest Architectural Archives, University of Minnesota, Libraries, St. Paul

2. Edward H. Bennett
   American, 1874–1954
   Minneapolis City Plan: Bird's Eye View of the Station Plaza, 1917
   Watercolor on paper
   Approx. 5′ × 4′
   Municipal Archives, City of Minneapolis

The Minneapolis architect Edward Bennett had worked in the office of D. H. Burnham in Chicago. His city plan of 1917 epitomized all that the City Beautiful movement espoused: wide boulevards and streets that radiated from axes or circular plazas, lined with buildings of uniform height and massing. Despite the emphasis on making cities clean and livable, the scale of buildings in renderings such as this represented anything but human scale. The view is from the site of the now-demolished Great Northern Depot at the foot of Hennepin Avenue near the Mississippi River, looking southeastward toward the present City Hall at the center. This scheme is comparable to one proposed by Leroy Buffington. Each anticipates a Second Empire style hotel for the Nicollet House site at the south end of the plaza (*upper right*). The only portion of this plan actually realized was the Gateway Park and Arcade, the trapezoidal, tree-lined parcel with a pool immediately fronting the hotel.

3. Leroy S. Buffington
   American, 1847–1931
   28-story Skyscraper, about 1887 (study)
   Watercolor on heavy paper stock
   47⅛″ × 25″
   Signed "Harvey Ellis Del 87" lower rt. corner; signed "L.S. Buffington Architect 87" lower left corner (genuine signatures?)
   Northwest Architectural Archives, University of Minnesota Libraries, St. Paul

Reflecting Harvey Ellis's incomparable draftsmanship and his preferred Romanesque revival style, this study illustrates Leroy Buffington's patented "cloudscraper," a pioneering attempt to construct tall buildings with load-bearing metal frames and thin masonry walls. This structure seems to have had a partial load-bearing wall because of the thick massing of stone in its lower floors. This building, designed for Minneapolis, was never executed.

4. Leroy S. Buffington
   American, 1847–1931
   Louis Tainter house, 1889
   Menomonie, Wisc.
   Watercolor on paper
   12⅜″ × 18⅛″
   Signed "E. E. Joralemon" lower left corner, n.d.
   Northwest Architectural Archives, University of Minnesota Libraries, St. Paul

This stone mansion, combining the Gothic and Romanesque revival styles, was designed and built in Menomonie, Wisconsin, for lumber baron Louis Tainter. Tainter commissioned another building designed by Buffington and Harvey Ellis in Menomonie, the Mabel Tainter Memorial Library, named in honor of his daughter.

5. Leroy S. Buffington
   American, 1847–1931
   Library, 1890 (study)
   Sutton, New Hampshire
   Ink on paper
   22½″ × 20¼″
   Signed "E. E. Joralemon Del" lower right corner, n.d.
   Northwest Architectural Archives, University of Minnesota Libraries, St. Paul

This library was designed for a site in Sutton, New Hampshire, and was to be constructed with money provided by John S. Pillsbury, who was born there in 1823. The drawing style closely follows Harvey Ellis's and it proposes a structure in his favorite Romanesque revival style, characterized by thickly massed stonework and an arched doorway.

6. Leroy S. Buffington
   American, 1847–1931
   N. F. Warner house, 1890
   Minneapolis, Minn.
   Pencil, gouache on paper
   25″ × 37″
   Signed "E. E. Joralemon Del" lower left corner, n.d.
   Northwest Architectural Archives, University of Minnesota Libraries, St. Paul

Combining the Romanesque revival style with elements from the shingle and classical vocabulary, the drawing was executed by Edgar E. Joralemon, who succeeded Harvey Ellis as Buffington's chief draftsman. Joralemon came closest to reproducing Ellis's drafting style and may have learned his technique from Ellis himself.

7. Leroy S. Buffington
   American, 1847–1931
   Minnesota Building, 1892

Chicago, Ill. (World's Fair)
Ink on paper
18¾″ × 22⅛″
Signed "Echinus" in block letters upper left corner, n.d.
Northwest Architectural Archives, University of Minnesota Libraries, St. Paul

Buffington's unsuccessful entry in the competition to design Minnesota's building at the Chicago World's Fair was in the Beaux-Arts style, resembling—though on a much smaller scale—Cass Gilbert's later state capitol. The high cost of constructing the building may have been the deciding factor in its rejection.

8. Leroy S. Buffington
   American, 1847–1931
   Burton Hall, University of Minnesota, 1893
   Minneapolis, Minn.
   Watercolor, pencil on paper
   17″ × 28½″
   No marks, n.d.
   Northwest Architectural Archives, University of Minnesota Libraries, St. Paul

This classical building in the form of a Greek temple was built to house the University of Minnesota Library. The exterior was designed by Buffington and the interior by Charles Sedgwick. Tradition has it that the two men hated each other. In a bid to embarrass Buffington, Sedgwick designed the interior so as to make it impossible to get from one side of the structure to the other without having to go outside. Unfortunately, no plans exist to prove—or disprove—this story, as the building has been renovated and is today divided into offices and classrooms.

9. Leroy S. Buffington
   American, 1847–1931
   Opera house, 1893 (study elevation)
   Watercolor, ink on paper
   15¾″ × 21⅞″
   Signed "L. S. B. 93 Arch." lower right corner
   Northwest Architectural Archives, University of Minnesota Libraries, St. Paul

This study follows earler nineteenth-century French prototypes and is the closest Buffington came to designing a contemporary Beaux-Arts building in the European style. This design appears never to have been built.

10. Leroy S. Buffington
    American, 1847–1931
    20-story Skyscraper, 1894 (study)
    Watercolor, ink on paper
    28¼″ × 18½″
    Signed "L. S. Buffington Archt 94" lower right corner
    Northwest Architectural Archives, University of Minnesota Libraries, St. Paul

From about 1887 on, Buffington was constantly trying to market his "cloudscraper" invention. He resurrected this concept more than 35 years later when he entered the competition for the Tribune Tower in Chicago with a similar design.

11. Leroy S. Buffington
American, 1847–1931
Hotel, 1895 (study)
Colored pencil, ink on board
27¼" × 17"
Signed "LSB" lower left corner; signed "L. S. Buffington Archt." right center, n.d.
Northwest Architectural Archives, University of Minnesota Libraries, St. Paul

Buffington had designed Minneapolis's foremost hostelry, the West Hotel, in 1884, in a combination of the Queen Anne and Tuscan gothic style. This later design, which adapts the mansard roof, a characteristic of Second Empire French architecture, to a modern high-rise building is a similar expression of Buffington's ability to combine seemingly disparate stylistic vocabularies into a single work of architecture.

12. Leroy S. Buffington
American, 1847–1931
Fraternal or Office Building, 1903 (study)
Watercolor, ink on paper
17¾" × 20½"
Signed "L. S. Buffington Architect 03" lower right corner
Northwest Architectural Archives, University of Minnesota Libraries, St. Paul

Although the site for the structure does not appear to be in Minnesota, the Dutch gables and tower suggest that the building was designed to house the meeting rooms and offices of a secret society.

13. Leroy S. Buffington
American, 1847–1931
Big Island Pavilion, 1910 (study)
Lake Minnetonka, Minn.
Watercolor, ink on paper
22" × 30½"
No marks, n.d.
Northwest Architectural Archives, University of Minnesota Libraries, St. Paul

This resort building for Lake Minnetonka adopts the Spanish mission revival style, which became a favorite for early twentieth-century resort architecture because of its tropical connotations. As far as is known, it remained an unbuilt project. Buffington had been aware of the mission revival style at least since 1890 when Harvey Ellis designed a market for Samuel Gale in a similar vocabulary.

14. Leroy S. Buffington
American, 1847–1931
N. R. Brewer house, 1910
St. Paul, Minn.
Ink on tracing paper
12¼" × 24¼"
No marks other than architect's title, n.d.
Northwest Architectural Archives, University of Minnesota Libraries, St. Paul

One of the few commissions Buffington received for a building in St. Paul, this house reveals strong sympathy with Prairie School ideals, as well as desire to integrate this regional idiom with the plan of a Mediterranean villa. The result is a studio/residence for River Road in St. Paul that has few precedents in the Minnesota architectural tradition.

15. Leroy S. Buffington
American, 1847–1931
City Beautiful plan (rendering), 1913
Minneapolis, Minn.
Colored pencil on paper mounted on board
15" × 20¼"
Initials "¹²⁄₁₀ LSB 1913" right center
Northwest Architectural Archives, University of Minnesota Libraries, St. Paul

Buffington's proposal for redesigning Bridge Square, where Hennepin and Nicollet avenues met a block from the Mississippi River, reflects the City Beautiful movement models. Buffington introduced its Beaux-Arts classicism in the large civic building on the left in the drawing. The Second-Empire-styled hotel in the right center was intended to replace the old Nicollet House, which was, in fact, torn down in 1922 for a new Nicollet Hotel.

16. Harvey Ellis
American, 1852–1904
Pillsbury Hall, University of Minnesota, 1887
Minneapolis, Minn.
Watercolor and ink on paper
17¾" × 28¾"
Harvey Ellis D.L. 87
Northwest Architectural Archives, University of Minnesota Libraries, St. Paul

Pillsbury Hall is often considered Harvey Ellis's greatest work in the Richardsonian style in Minnesota. Its successful massing of windows and subtle medieval decoration integrate the elements of what could have been an unwieldy structure into a single, elegant architectural whole.

17. Harvey Ellis
American, 1852–1904
Charles Pillsbury house, 1888
Minneapolis, Minn.
Ink on paper

20⅛″ × 36″
Signed "Harvey Ellis Del 88" lower right corner
Northwest Architectural Archives, University of Minnesota Libraries, St. Paul

This Buffington/Ellis design, done in the mainstream of the Romanesque revival, suggests a fortress rather than a private home, much in the manner of Henry H. Richardson's Glessner house in Chicago. As far as is known, this house was never constructed.

18. Harvey Ellis
    American, 1852–1904
    S. C. Gale house (interior), 1888
    Minneapolis, Minn.
    Ink on paper
    14″ × 19″
    Signed "Harvey Ellis Del '88" lower left corner
    Northwest Architectural Archives, University of Minnesota Libraries, St. Paul

A rare interior rendered by Harvey Ellis, this drawing depicts the Gale house, one of a number of mansions which once lined Harmon Place near downtown Minneapolis. All but one of the largely Richardsonian structures are gone today. This entrance hall reflects the period's appreciation for wood panelling in combination with decorative plaster ceilings.

19. Harvey Ellis
    American, 1852–1904
    Gale's New City Market, 1891
    Ink on paper
    17¼″ × 33¾″
    Signed "L. S. Buffington Architect 1891" lower right corner
    Northwest Architectural Archives, University of Minnesota Libraries, St. Paul

Harvey Ellis is thought to have made a trip to the Southwest sometime in 1890 or 1891. This project is one of the earliest Spanish mission style commercial complexes ever designed in this country. The market seems never to have advanced beyond the project stage in this form, however. It was probably intended for the market district between 3rd and 4th avenues north and 6th and 8th streets north, on the southwest side of what became the Minneapolis warehouse district.

20. Harvey Ellis
    American, 1852–1904
    Security Bank, 1891
    Minneapolis, Minn.
    Pencil on paper
    15¼″ × 34½″
    Signed "L. S. Buffington Architect Minneapolis Minn. 1891" in block letters lower left corner

Northwest Architectural Archives, University of Minnesota Libraries, St. Paul

The bank is a sensitive blend of both Moorish and Romanesque revival detailing in an almost proto-modernist structure. Although never constructed, it represented the ambition of Minnesota architecture and the creativity of Harvey Ellis, probably more than any other project conceived at this time.

21. Jakob Fjelde
    American
    Minerva
    Bronze
    88″ × 27″
    Marks: none
    Minneapolis Public Library

This work was commissioned from Jakob Fjelde, a local sculptor responsible for several significant public works. It was originally commissioned in 1883 for the first Minneapolis public library, a Romanesque revival building designed by Long and Kees. The library was torn down in the late 1950s.

22. Daniel Chester French
    American, 1850–1931
    Wisdom, 1898–1900
    State Capitol, St. Paul, Minn.
    Plaster
    58″ high
    Marks: none
    Hirschl & Adler Galleries

In 1898 D. C. French was commissioned by Cass Gilbert to create sculptures for the facade of Gilbert's new Minnesota state capitol building. French's sculptural program included six allegorical figures representing the civic and personal virtues of Truth, Bounty, Wisdom, Prudence, Integrity, and Courage. They were placed above the second-story arcade, beneath his gilded quadriga, or Chariot group, entitled *Progress of the State*.

French prepared working the models for the six allegorical figures and completed them in 1900. The plasters were then sent to Purdy and Hutcheson, St. Paul stone carvers, to be enlarged in marble to approximately twice their size for the capitol building facade.

23. Cass Gilbert
    American, 1859–1934
    J. B. Tarbox house, 1889
    White Bear Lake, Minn.
    Ink, ink wash on board
    22″ × 15½″
    Signed "Sketch of Cottage at White Bear for Mr. J. B. Tarbox Gilbert & Taylor Architects 39 Gilfillan Block." "C Gilbert. 1889."

New-York Historical Society 18.52

This frame house built in the water-side community of White Bear Lake north of St. Paul, represents a combination of the shingle and Richardsonian Romanesque styles. With its central tower, it reflects, though in residential form employing cheaper materials, Harvey Ellis's Pillsbury Hall, designed at about the same time.

24. Cass Gilbert
American, 1859–1934
Minnesota Building, 1892
Chicago, Ill. (World's Fair)
Graphite on trace
14¼″ × 13⅞″
Marks: none
New-York Historical Society 5.4

Cass Gilbert's Minnesota Building, designed at the time he was separating from his partner, James Knox Taylor, follows the classical Beaux-Arts style for which he would become famous.

25. Cass Gilbert
American, 1859–1934
Minnesota State Capitol, 1893
St. Paul, Minn.
Orange chalk, graphite on tracing paper
5½″ × 6¼″
Signed "CG '93"
New-York Historical Society 12.181

This drawing was executed before the actual competition, but plans for a new capitol were already being discussed and a state commission had been formed.

26. Cass Gilbert
American, 1859–1934
W. H. Lightner house, 1893
St. Paul, Minn.
Watercolor, ink, graphite on drawing paper
18¾″ × 24⅞″
Signed "Study for House for Mr. W. H. Lightner. St. Paul. Minn. Cass Gilbert Arch't."
New-York Historical Society 18.81

One of Cass Gilbert's early designs in the neo-Federal style, this frame house for the W. H. Lightners was rejected in favor of a Richardsonian Romanesque work which followed a similar plan.

27. Cass Gilbert
American, 1859–1934
W. H Lightner house, 1893
St. Paul, Minn.
Watercolor, ink, gouache and graphite on paper
15¼″ × 17¾″

Signed "Study for library Mr. Lightner's House"
New-York Historical Society 18.67

William Lightner commissioned two houses from Cass Gilbert: a single house (see catalogue entry 26) and a double house next door, also in a Romanesque style. The former's northwest-facing room on the ground floor was the family library, with decorative motifs relating to reading and other activities of the bibliophile. This is a study for the west wall of that room, which was not constructed precisely to this plan.

28. Cass Gilbert
American, 1859–1934
W. H Lightner house, 1893
St. Paul, Minn.
Watercolor, ink, gouache and graphite on paper
11½″ × 15½″
Signed · C.G ·
Randy Gegner Collection

This is the final study for the house as completed by Gilbert in 1893, and it successfully integrates medievalizing surface treatment and ornament in a standard classicizing house plan of the time. The executed building closely follows this model.

29. Cass Gilbert
American, 1859–1934
Minnesota State Capitol, 1901
St. Paul, Minn.
Watercolor, gouache on drawing paper
45⅜″ × 26¾″
Signed "T. R. Johnson Del/01"
New-York Historical Society 12.180

This is a presentation study for the Minnesota state capitol. Thomas R. Johnson (1872–1915), the renderer, was an architect trained in Toronto. He joined Gilbert's New York office shortly after the 1899 U.S. Customs House competition. One of the primary designers on staff, he is credited with a major role in planning the Essex County Court House and the Woolworth Building.

30. Cass Gilbert
American, 1859–1934
University of Minnesota Plan, 1910
Minneapolis, Minn.
Watercolor, pencil and ink on paper
28″ × 82¾″
No marks other than titles, n.d.
Northwest Architectural Archives, University of Minnesota Libraries, St. Paul

Cass Gilbert's original plan for the University of Minnesota's East Bank campus mall provided for its continuation to the banks of the Mississippi River, with a small park at its terminus. A shortage of funds forced the administration to abbreviate the plan, ending the mall at Coffman Union near Washington Avenue. Gilbert's Beaux-Arts inspiration, emphasizing monumentality, symmetry, and classical detail, adapted City Beautiful ideas to a university plan.

31. Cass Gilbert
    American, 1859–1934
    E. G. Long house, n.d.
    St. Paul, Minn.
    Watercolor, ink and graphite on board
    22½″ × 28½″
    Signed "Gilbert and Taylor Architects 39 Gilfillan Block St. Paul," n.d.
    New-York Historical Society 18.220

This large house is one of the most elegant and lavish residences designed by Cass Gilbert in St. Paul. Although this study proposes a Tudor design, the patron eventually selected a more traditional Romanesque revival style. The house is distinguished by beautiful carved woodwork in oak, mahogany, and maple.

32. Cass Gilbert
    American, 1859–1934
    G. C. Squires house, n.d.
    St. Paul, Minn.
    Watercolor, ink on paper
    17½″ × 25½″
    Signed "Sketch of house for Mr. GC Squires Summit Court St. Paul Minn.," n.d.
    New-York Historical Society 18.104

33. Cass Gilbert
    American, 1859–1934
    G. C. Squires house, entrance, n.d.
    St. Paul, Minn.
    Watercolor, ink, graphite on drawing paper
    17⅞″ × 15¼″
    Signed "Entrance to Residence of G. C. Squires, Esq. Gilbert and Taylor Architects St. Paul," n.d.
    New-York Historical Society 18.99

A Richardsonian Romanesque/Classical revival design. Gilbert submitted a sketch of this classically-inspired brick house to the Architectural League of New York's annual competition, shortly after the house was completed. The drawing was published in their catalog and was labelled "Country house near St. Paul by Cass Gilbert."

34. Cass Gilbert
    American, 1859–1934
    House on Virginia Avenue, about 1892
    St. Paul, Minn.
    Watercolor, ink on paper
    16⅞″ × 21½″
    Signed "House for Virginia Ave: St. Paul Minn: Cass

Gilbert. Architect. 49 Gilfillan Block. St. Paul Minn."
New-York Historical Society 18.08

Situated on a narrow corner lot, this house at Virginia and Laurel in St. Paul is more modest than its rendering would suggest. This vernacular shingle style design was probably produced for a builder rather than a specific patron.

35. Edgar C. Gilivson
    American
    Design for a house in the Mission style
    Duluth, Minn.
    Watercolor, pencil on paper
    10¾″ × 21¾″
    "E. C. Gilivson. 1909." bottom right corner
    Northeast Minnesota Historical Center, University of Minnesota, Duluth

Little is known about E. C. Gilivson except that his work in Duluth reflects a variety of architectural vocabularies. This house in a mission style still survives at 4640 London Road in Duluth.

36. Edgar C. Gilivson
    American
    Prairie/Arts & Crafts house, Duluth, 1910
    Watercolor on paper
    17⅛″ × 25¼″
    E. C. Gilivson 1910, lower right corner
    Northeast Minnesota Historical Center, University of Minnesota, Duluth

This two-story house incorporates walls sloping outward, a feature repeated at the entrance. The stylistic characteristic, popular in arts-and-crafts inspired architecture in the upper midwest, was often a prominent feature of George Maher's work.

37. Percy D. Bentley & Charles A. Hausler
    Americans, 1884–1968 and 1889–1971
    "Ethylglenne," Strickler Estate, St. Anthony, St. Paul, 1913
    Watercolor, pencil on board
    16″ × 28″
    Initials "CAH 1913" lower right corner
    Northwest Architectural Archives, University of Minnesota Libraries, St. Paul

This is an unusual split-level Prairie School design—the entrance is at ground or basement level, and the main living quarters are probably on the floor above.

Although Hausler's initials are on the drawing, it is not known if Percy Bentley also contributed to the design.

38. Percy D. Bentley & Charles A. Hausler
    Americans, 1884–1968 and 1889–1971

Prairie School house, 1918
For an unknown location
Ink, pencil on board
13″ × 32″
Initials "CAH 1918" lower right corner
Northwest Architectural Archives, University of Minnesota Libraries, St. Paul

This house represents the influence that Percy Bentley, a careful practitioner of the Prairie School style, had over his partner, Charles Hausler, during their brief partnership in St. Paul. Excellent examples of Bentley's built designs are also extent in Fountain City and La Crosse, Wisconsin.

39. Thomas Holyoke
American, 1866–1925
William D. Mitchell cottage, 1907
White Bear Lake, Minn.
Watercolor, ink on paper mounted on board
10¼″ × 16″
Signed "T.G.H. del Jan/07" lower right corner
Northwest Architectural Archives, University of Minnesota Libraries, St. Paul

This Tudor revival style house was designed as a summer cottage on White Bear Lake. Holyoke was a student of Cass Gilbert, and like his teacher, he was a strong proponent of Beaux-Arts principles. He later took over Gilbert's practice in St. Paul.

40. Harry W. Jones
American, 1859–1935
Lake Minnetonka houses & yacht club, 1886
Ink on paper mounted on board
19¾″ × 27½″
Each drawing (8 in all) is titled
Northwest Architectural Archives, University of Minnesota Libraries, St. Paul

Along with William Channing Whitney, Harry Jones was one of Minneapolis's most popular residential architects at the turn of the century. The drawing reviews the most important of his early stick, shingle, and Queen Anne designs on Lake Minnetonka.

41. Harry W. Jones
American, 1859–1935
Lakewood Cemetery Chapel, 1908
Minneapolis, Minn.
Colored pencil or pastel, pencil on paper mounted on board
11½″ × 24″
Signed "Harry W. Jones Architect" lower left corner, n.d.
Northwest Architectural Archives, University of Minnesota Libraries, St. Paul

Jones abbreviated the scale and decoration of the vast Hagia Sophia of Istanbul in this beautifully detailed Byzantine revival ecclesiastical structure.

42. George Maher
American, 1864–1926
Watkins Company, 1911, 1913
Winona, Minn.
Watercolor on paper
Approx. 24″ × 36″
Signed "George Maher"
Winona County Historical Society, Inc.

This factory and office building was designed by George Maher, whose work is best understood through his association with the Prairie School. Maher was something of an architectural maverick, adhering closely to Beaux-Arts principles while experimenting with the formal innovations of the Progressive movement. He could handle each style deftly, although his attempts to blend them has often dissatisfied contemporary critics.

ROCKLEDGE
43. George Maher
American, 1864–1926
Exterior, 1912 (sketch)
E. L. King residence, "Rockledge," Homer, Minn.
Ink on tracing paper
Approx. 18″ × 12″
Marks: none
Winona County Historical Society, Inc.

44. George Maher
American, 1864–1926
Pier, 1912 (sketch)
E. L. King residence, "Rockledge," Homer, Minn.
Ink on tracing paper
Approx. 18″ × 12″
Marks: none
Winona County Historical Society, Inc.

45. George Maher
American, 1864–1926
Fireplace, 1912 (sketch)
E. L. King residence, "Rockledge," Homer, Minn.
Ink on tracing paper
Approx. 18″ × 12″
Marks: none
Winona County Historical Society, Inc.

46. George Maher
American, 1864–1926
Armchair, about 1912
E. L. King House, "Rockledge," Homer, Minn.
Oak and Leather
46¼″H × 25⁵⁄₁₆″W × 22″D

Marks: none
The Minneapolis Institute of Arts
Gift of Mr. and Mrs. Sheldon, Mr. and Mrs. Henry
Hyatt and the Anne and Hadlai Hull Fund 88.45

47. George Maher
    American, 1864–1926
    Carpet runner, about 1912
    E. L. King House, "Rockledge," Homer, Minn.
    Wool
    33'¾" × 46½"
    The Minneapolis Institute of Arts
    The William Hood Dunwoody Fund 91.143

48. George Maher
    American, 1864–1926
    Silver service, about 1912
    E. L. King House, "Rockledge," Homer, Minn.
    Sterling silver, fifteen pieces
    Historical Design

Rockledge, one of George Maher's masterpieces, is one of the few substantial houses ever planned for the cliffs along the Mississippi River. Situated a little more than 100 miles downriver from the Twin Cities, the King estate consisted of a main house, a studio-house, and caretaker's cottage. The main house embodies Maher's characteristic monumentality, although the caretaker's cottage is little more than a bungalow with a hipped roof. The studio was the most fascinating of the three buildings, combining Pueblo revival and Vienna secessionist elements within a Prairie idiom. Unlike almost any other house of the time, the interiors of Rockledge, everything from its furniture to its rugs and silver, were designed by the building's architect. Although the house was updated about twenty years after its creation in a similarly "spare no expense" manner, all the earlier decorative arts objects were put into storage at the time. A sale of almost all the house's contents was conducted in the early 1980s, and the building itself was demolished a few years later.

49. Emmanuel L. Masqueray
    French, 1861–1917
    St. Paul's on the Hill, 1913
    St. Paul, Minn.
    Watercolor, ink on paper
    33⅜" × 40⅝"
    E. L. Masqueray–Architect/St. Paul 1913
    St. Paul's Episcopal Church, St. Paul

In the English Gothic style, this church was designed by one of St. Paul's most noted Beaux-Arts architects, Emmanuel Masqueray. He was also responsible for the Cathedral of St. Paul, the Basilica of St. Mary in Minneapolis, and several Catholic and Protestant parish churches in each city.

50. Charles Reed & Allen Stem
    American, 1858–1911, and 1856–1931
    University Club, 1912
    St. Paul, Minn.
    Pencil, colored pencil on heavy board
    31" × 43½"
    Marks: none
    University Club, St. Paul

With the exception of ecclesiastical architecture, the University Club in St. Paul was one of the first nonresidential structures in the Tudor style in Minnesota. It was organized for the quasi-suburban neighborhoods of Ramsey Hill and Crocus Hill in St. Paul and its special position as a social center was underscored by F. Scott Fitzgerald's reference to it in his writings.

51. Shepley, Rutan & Coolidge (George F. Shepley, Charles H. Rutan, Charles A. Coolidge)
    Americans, 1860–1903, 1851–1914, and 1858–1936
    Plymouth Congregational Church, 1907–8
    Minneapolis, Minn.
    Colored pencil on paper
    24" × 36"
    Marks: none
    Plymouth Congregational Church, Minneapolis

This beautiful stone church built in the rustic English Gothic style was designed by successors of H. H. Richardson. The Gothic style was revived around the turn of the century and touted by devotees such as Ralph Adams Cram as the epitome of all that was good in architectural design.

52. John Wangenstein
    Norwegian-American, about 1860
    House for John Gronska, ca. 1890
    Duluth, Minn.
    Pen, ink on paper
    13½" × 16¼"
    " · J · WANGENSTEIN · ARCHT · DULUTH · MINN ·," block letters upper left corner.
    Northeast Minnesota Historical Center, University of Minnesota, Duluth

John Wangenstein's proposal for the Gronska house incorporates the pedimented roof, corner tower, wrap-around porch, and stained glass windows typical of Queen Anne style residences popular in the 1880s.

53. Gustav F. Weber
    American, born in Paris, 1870–1960
    Minnesota Club, Ladies' Dining Room, 1905
    Watercolor, pencil on paper
    15" × 22¾" (21½" × 29" incl. mat)
    Signed "Gustav F. Weber" lower right corner. n.d.
    Northwest Architectural Archives, University of Min-

nesota Libraries, St. Paul

Gustav Weber was trained in Europe and became an interior designer in Minneapolis, where he worked for many years. These two drawings reflect the academic tradition of rendering interiors as flat, impersonal elevations. No attempt has been made to create perspective.

54. Gustav F. Weber
American, born in Paris, 1870–1960
Minnesota Club, Pool Room, 1905
Watercolor, pencil on paper
17½″ × 22″ (25″ × 29″ incl. mat)
Signed "Gustav F. Weber" lower right corner, n.d.
Northwest Architectural Archives, University of Minnesota Libraries, St. Paul

55. William Channing Whitney
American, 1851–1945
H. J. Burton house, 1890
Lake Minnetonka, Minn.
Watercolor on paper
22⅞″ × 10″
Signed "Wm Channing Whitney Architect 1890" lower right corner
Northwest Architectural Archives, University of Minnesota Libraries, St. Paul

Whitney proved himself an early and successful proponent of the then popular "shingle" style with this lakeside house for H. J. Burton. The house site sloped to the back, allowing windows on the basement level to benefit from views of the lake.

56. William Channing Whitney
American, 1851–1945
Minnesota Building, 1893
Chicago, Ill. (World's Fair)
Watercolor on board
14⅝″ × 17⅝″
No marks, n.d.
Northwest Architectural Archives, University of Minnesota Libraries, St. Paul

This exuberant Beaux-Arts design was constructed to house Minnesota's exhibits at the Chicago World's Fair of 1893. Like almost all of the buildings at the Fair, it was built of wood frame and plaster and was expected to survive only as long as the Fair itself.

57. William Channing Whitney
American, 1851–1945
"Highcroft," residence for Frank Heffelfinger, 1894
Lake Minnetonka, Minn.
Ink on paper
13″ × 28″
Signed "S. M. Colburn, del/94" lower right corner

Northwest Architectural Archives, University of Minnesota Libraries, St. Paul

This was the Lake Minnetonka retreat first of Frank H. Peavey and then of milling magnate Frank Heffelfinger, It is strongly Colonial revival in style with a gambrel roof and a large portico reminiscent of those fronting Southern antebellum mansions.

58. William Channing Whitney
American, 1851–1945
"Bellford," J. F. Bell house, 1900
Lake Minnetonka, Minn.
Watercolor, pencil on paper
14½″ × 27½″
Signed "L. B. Clapp" lower right corner, n.d.
Northwest Architectural Archives, University of Minnesota Libraries, St. Paul

Built as a lakeside estate, J. S. Bell's home illustrates how readily the Classical style lent itself to grand, stately residences. Here two-story columns frame the front entrance in a Southern manner.

59. William Channing Whitney
American, 1851–1945
J. R. Kingman house, 1903
Minneapolis, Minn.
Watercolor, pencil on paper
14¼″ × 20½″
Signed "Clifford T. McElroy '03" lower left side
Northwest Architectural archives, University of Minnesota Libraries, St. Paul

This late example of a large shingle-style residence proves how popular the style remained in the early years of this century. The gambrel roof, shingles, lap siding, and field stone foundation all are typical of the idiom, which was at the height of its popularity from 1880–1900.

60. William Channing Whitney
American, 1851–1945
R. B. Langdon house, 1905
Minneapolis, Minn.
Watercolor on paper
11″ × 18¼″
Signed "E. Bartholomew" lower right corner, n.d.
Northwest Architectural Archives, University of Minnesota Libraries, St. Paul

The rigid symmetry on the front facade of this eclectic house, as well as its incorporation of stone sheathing, is characteristic of the Beaux-Arts style. Combining this vocabulary with more decidedly Colonial revival elements, the house is a testament to the flexibility and imagination of Whitney's work. Ethel Bartholomew was one of the pioneer women architects in Minnesota.

61. William Channing Whitney
    American, 1851–1945
    William Dunwoody house, 1905
    Minneapolis, Minn.
    Watercolor, pencil on heavy paper stock
    14¼″ × 22½″
    Signed "C. B. Chapman" left center, n.d.
    Northwest Architectural Archives, University of Minnesota Libraries, St. Paul

Once the largest private residence in the city, the Dunwoody house stood on Mt. Curve Avenue. Despite its suburban Minneapolis setting, its Tudor revival style hearkened back to English country houses of the sixteenth century.

62. William Channing Whitney
    American, 1851–1945
    McMillan house, 1910
    Minneapolis, Minn.
    Watercolor, pencil on paper
    12¾″ × 19″
    No marks, n.d.
    Northwest Architectural Archives, University of Minnesota Libraries, St. Paul

Although Whitney often utilized Eastern and European architectural prototypes in his work, this residence combines Colonial revival detailing with the openness and horizontality popular in regional prairie houses of the time.

63. Frank Lloyd Wright
    American, 1867–1959
    Hallway, 1912–15
    Francis Little house, "Northome," Wayzata, Minn.
    Wood, leaded glass
    18′ × 6′

The Minneapolis Institute of Arts
The David D. Dayton Fund 72.11

"Northome" is considered one of the prime examples of Frank Lloyd Wright's refined Prairie School style. Wright built the house in 1913 as a summer home for Francis Little, a long-time client of Wright's and a Chicago investment banker and utilities owner. In 1908, the Littles decided to sell their Peoria residence and move to the cooler climate of Minnesota, were Mary Little's parents had made their home. In 1908, Wright began drawings for a house to be set into a rugged lakeside landscape, but building was delayed for six years because Wright departed for Europe in 1909. Although impatient with their architect and friend, the Littles remained loyal to him. Living in the small cottage constructed near the proposed site, they waited for the completion of Wright's design.

64. Carved by Ian Kirschmeyer
    American
    Pair of dining room chairs, 1891
    James J. Hill house, St. Paul, Minn.
    Peabody and Stearns, architects
    Mahogany
    Chair: 54¾″ × 24″ × 24½″; Seat: 24″ × 22″
    Marks: none
    James J. Hill House/Minnesota Historical Society Collections

The James J. Hill House was one of the last designed in the Richardsonian Romanesque style in Minnesota. Like its neighbor, Cass Gilbert's Lightner house, also in Romanesque style, it integrates a classical plan with this medieval inspired architecture. The designer of these high-back chairs, made of mahogany from the Virgin Islands, is unknown, although it has been assumed that they emanated from Peabody and Stearns's office.

2
Bradstreet's Craftshouse: Retailing in an Arts and Crafts Style

Michael Conforti and Jennifer Komar

In THE FAST-GROWING METROPOLIS OF TURN-OF-THE-century Minneapolis the name of John Scott Bradstreet, along with that of his company's Craftshouse, was synonymous with the best in interior design and decoration. During his forty-year career, Bradstreet espoused and reinterpreted American avant-garde interior design as it moved from the historicism and exoticism of the last quarter of the nineteenth century to the simplicity and moral imperative of the early twentieth. Attracted first to the Gothic revival in the 1870s, Bradstreet in the 1880s and early 1890s focused on the Moorish and Japanese styles popular in avant-garde design circles of the time. Only after 1900, however, did he finally combine the oriental influences that shaped so much of his aesthetic with the formal design principles of the Arts and Crafts movement, creating a unique style of furniture based on the traditional Japanese technique of carved and treated cypress wood, *jin-di-sugi*. In 1904 he opened a workshop and salesroom known as the Craftshouse to manufacture and market his *sugi* paneling and furniture and to sell the myriad of antique and imported objects that constituted his art and decorating trade. The national publicity surrounding the establishment of the Craftshouse brought Bradstreet commissions from around the country, capping his reputation as the leading interior designer of the Northwest.

Bradstreet cultivated an image of traditional craftsmanship by comparing the Craftshouse to Kelmscott Manor, the workshop of Arts and Crafts movement founder William Morris:

[The Craftshouse] is as distinctive as the Kelmscott Manor made famous by Morris in the output of its workshop, and besides has for sale a vast number of curios and valuable articles brought from many distant lands.[1]

The Craftshouse was more than just a manufacturer of handcrafted furnishings. Unlike Elbert Hubbard's Roycroft Studios, which featured products in one stylistic idiom, and the national popularity of Gustav Stickley's signature line of oak furniture, Bradstreet's success was based on his retailing flexibility. He presented his own art furniture, along with a collection of antique and contemporary goods from around the world, with his services as a supplier of custom-designed interiors. In combining the roles of decorator, antiquarian dealer, and general importer with the product and philosophy of an arts and crafts guild, Bradstreet was able to both address the range of taste represented by the breadth of Minnesota's market and to compete as an alternative to the growing appeal of the department store. The Craftshouse provided clients with specialized attention and a broad range of aesthetically presented objects in the context of a gallery overseen by a recognized artistic visionary. The resulting enterprise was an innovative commercial venture that integrated aesthetic objectives with the reality of consumer taste.

EARLY RETAILING IN THE TWIN CITIES

When Bradstreet arrived in 1873 from New England, Minneapolis was less than twenty years old, a growing,

*John S. Bradstreet in Japan, about 1905. Photograph courtesy of
the Minneapolis Public Library, Special Collections.*

bustling lumber and grain milling center, a city of about
25,000 people. A web of railroad lines connected Duluth,
Winona, Brainerd, and other communities to the Minne-
apolis and St. Paul area, and in turn provided service to
Chicago and Milwaukee. A railroad link to Chicago had
only recently been completed, and railroad magnate James
J. Hill and his partners would soon expand the line to Puget
Sound and the Pacific, connecting the entire northern tier
of the country to the East and South through the Twin
Cities of St. Paul and Minneapolis.

In these early years Twin Cities retail commerce centered on "dry goods," the necessities required by early
Minnesota settlers and others traveling further westward.
Wholesale merchants, who could offer large quantities at
lower prices than retail by selling from warehouses or warerooms, were the most prominent businesses. They provided
not only clothing, textiles, and related materials, but also
groceries, or "wet goods," especially dairy and meat products, liquor, and tobacco.

The Twin Cities had not yet developed retail establishments specializing in interiors. If one can speak of interior
design at all, it was provided by furniture dealers and
"art sellers," none of whom saw quality products in the
latest fashion as their special purview. William L. Pingree's
"Cheap Cash Furniture Warerooms," for instance, proclaimed a large selection of furniture at low prices. Fred-
richs, Winnen and Company advertised "Furniture, of best
quality and latest styles," although their store displays
seemed to emphasize variety rather than quality or style.
While cabinetmakers existed, they were jacks-of-all-trades,
involved in the construction of handcrafted caskets among
other things.[2] Although Beal's Mammoth Art Gallery
claimed to have all the art necessary to equip an up-to-
date home, up-to-date probably meant fitting an interior
with Victorian America's favorite wall decoration: framed
prints of Italian Renaissance and Baroque paintings.[3] Specialized decorative items were available only to those who
could import them from the East Coast or Europe.

By the time Bradstreet arrived in the early 1870s, the
Twin Cities' retail furniture market had become more specialized. Out-of-state businessmen were trying to both supply and shape the growing demand for more stylish
merchandise. The owner of J. B. Hanson Furniture, Bedding, and Upholstery Business, for example, with thirty

years of experience from his businesses in Boston and Chicago, offered the "Latest Styles which may be found East or West."[4] With appetites whetted for high-quality, fashionable furnishings and accessories to fill their new homes, Minnesotans were ripe for an artistic and retail entrpreneur like Bradstreet. Once established, he almost singlehandedly cornered the specialized, artistic end of retailing in interior design.

BRADSTREET'S RETAIL HISTORY 1870–1890

Like most of his fellow Minneapolis businessmen, John Bradstreet was from New England, born in 1845 in northern Essex County, Massachusetts, where his ancestors had settled in 1634. Early in his professional life, he contracted tuberculosis and, in 1873, like a number of others so afflicted at that time, he decided to move to the drier air of Minnesota.[5] Bradstreet's beginnings in Minneapolis were modest. He worked as a salesman in a now-forgotten furni-

ture store. After the store closed, he operated a small shop of his own for a time, specializing in furniture. In 1878, he met Edmund Phelps, a man his own age recently arrived from Aurora, Illinois, where he, too, had owned a furniture company. Phelps had recently sold his interest, however, and the two became partners that same year. The new firm was remarkably successful, eventually occupying six floors of the Syndicate Block on the east side of Nicollet Avenue between Fifth and Sixth streets. It claimed to be "the largest, most elegant and complete furniture store under one roof in America."

Although Phelps and Bradstreet offered a range of furnishings, they specialized in the latest orientalizing trends in interior decoration. Providing imported and look-alike Japanese and Near-Eastern goods, the firm also followed a presentation technique used by the London retailer Arthur Lasenby Liberty in which objects for sale were incorporated into artificial, artistically manipulated "aesthetic" interiors within the retail space, giving customers a sense of how such objects might be placed in their own homes. As at Liberty's, Phelps and Bradstreet, too, regularly created faux

Craftshouse of John S. Bradstreet & Company, 327 South 7th Street, Minneapolis, opened 1904. Photograph courtesy of the Minneapolis Public Library, Special Collections.

room settings for their window displays, prominently showcasing their selection of furniture in appealing interior environments.[6]

The "artistic" furniture alluded to in early Phelps and Bradstreet advertisements was, for the most part, simply constructed alternatives to the carved neo-rococo goods that had been popular up to that time. The market for such alternatives was spreading in the 1870s and 1880s, causing manufacturers to shift the style of their products.[7] The firm did not limit itself to the new aesthetic furniture line, however. During these years, Bradstreet learned that in order to succeed in a growing western community, he would have to cater to the entire range of monied taste. Throughout his career, while encouraging clients to accept his stylish but sometimes esoteric decorative schemes, Bradstreet was always equally ready to provide high-quality objects in a more conventional mode. The juxtaposition of conservative and progressive offerings in his shop never changed, even after his reputation had been fully established. The pragmatic

alliance of trend consciousness with a more consumer-driven eclecticism was a key factor in his enduring local success.

In 1883 Edward Phelps retired from the partnership to enter banking. Bradstreet soon encouraged the Thurber family, owners of the Gorham Manufacturing Company, the Rhode Island firm where he had begun his career, to join him in business. Dexter Thurber moved to Minneapolis to help direct the operation, which remained at the Syndicate Block site until the early 1890s.[8] While Phelps and Bradstreet had specialized in furniture, Bradstreet, Thurber and Company put an almost equal emphasis on decorative accessories. These included stained glass, fabrics, the new Bretby art pottery from England, and novelties of all kinds, such as "Bronzes/Persian and East Indian brass goods/Salviati Venetian glass/Embroideries from Turkey, Algiers and Japan," the materials with which Bradstreet would model his first orientalizing rooms. Bradstreet created some of the most memorable aesthetic interiors ever

Bradstreet, Thurber and Company, Minneapolis, during the Harvest Festival, 1891. Photograph courtesy of the Minneapolis Public Library, Special Collections.

Bradstreet, Thurber and Company pamphlet, 1884. Photograph courtesy of the Minneapolis Public Library, Special Collections.

produced in the Moorish style, which was extraordinarily popular throughout the country in the 1880s.[9]

Bradstreet's Near-Eastern interiors established his reputation as a decorating innovator, but his deeper and more lasting commitment was to the art and design of Japan. The Gorham Company had been early champions of Japanese art, whose design tradition attracted both Europeans and Americans in the decades after Captain Matthew Perry's trade treaty in 1854. While Bradstreet had already included Japanese objects in the 1870s, after entering into partnership with the Thurbers he began visiting Japan every two years, alternating these tours with buying trips to Europe.[10] Bradstreet always returned from the Orient with a large supply of goods to sell. At first, his Minnesota clients did not fully appreciate these oriental imports.[11] Familiarity brought acceptance, however. The "plunder," as Bradstreet

Drawing Room, Edmund G. Walton house, 802 Mount Curve Avenue, Minneapolis, 1893. Decorated by John S. Bradstreet. Photograph courtesy of the Minnesota Historical Society.

called it—Japanese bronzes, screens, and textiles—was slowly absorbed into the homes of local citizens. As the years progressed, a significant number of private collections of Asian objects were formed in Minneapolis, probably inspired in part by Bradstreet's tutelage or example.[12]

Bradstreet was respected in Engish design circles as well. At the innovative firm of Liberty's, whose example Bradstreet followed closely, he was thought to be among the foremost Americans in his field.[13] Having promoted the Moorish and Japanese styles of the late 1880s and 1890s, Liberty's later championed the arts and crafts work of C. F. A. Voysey and C. R. Ashbee. Bradstreet, too, progressed from Near and Far Eastern orientalizing traditions to the products of the Arts and Crafts movement by the turn of the century. Just as furniture companies in the United States were adapting the handcraft style for mass production, Bradstreet, too, interpreted the English arts and crafts tradition with characteristic American pragmatism. Adopting the rhetoric of the movement, he organized a workshop based on arts and crafts principles, combining it all with a commercial furniture and interior design company that would market more mainstream furniture as well. Every object he introduced to the public, however, carried Bradstreet's recognized stamp of approval, which by the 1880s was well recognized in the region.

Bradstreet, Thurber and Company was destroyed by fire in 1893, forcing Bradstreet to establish a temporary shop at 619 Nicollet Avenue.[14] He saw his need for new quarters as an opportunity. Leasing the Morrison-Bigelow family house at 208 South Seventh Street in the late 1890s, Bradstreet directed a team of expert carvers, gilders, painters, and furniture makers in an ambitious remodeling. The result was a communal crafts center inspired by William Morris's Kelmscott Manor. When the new establishment opened in 1899, however, it included both a salesroom for his commercial furniture operation and galleries for the antique and interior decorating trade that formed the backbone of his business. Morris's operation, however, did not deal in imported objects or create interiors in the wide variety of styles that Bradstreet's did.[15]

With the establishment of his retail center, Bradstreet was prepared to make his personal contribution to the Arts

John S. Bradstreet and Company, 208 South 7th Street, Minneapolis, about 1900. Photograph courtesy of the Minneapolis Public Library, Special Collectioons.

and Crafts movement. He introduced a new style of furniture based on the traditional Japanese technique of aging cypress wood, *jin-di-sugi*. Bradstreet's *jin-di-sugi* finish capitalized on the physical properties of cypress wood, which combined extremely hard-grain with soft-grain fibers. The surface was treated to remove the fibers, first by a burning process, then by scrubbing with a wire brush. The hard grain formed a decorative three-dimensional pattern, which was finally washed and waxed for use as paneling or furniture.[16] Bradstreet further elaborated the surface by carving into it, thus combining Japanese technique with the Arts and Crafts movement's appreciation for wood carving. While some of Bradstreet's designs were in a Louis Tiffany-inspired art nouveau style, others were derived from eighteenth-century English or American models, such as the so-called Turtle card table, based on English precedents of about 1740.[17] He even encouraged his friend Tiffany, who since the late 1870s had been the foremost proponent of artistic interiors in America, to speak to the uniqueness of the new products in a letter sent to potential clients in 1903:

> Mr. Louis Tiffany (the well-known art connoisseur of New York), recently in speaking of our latest production, an illustration of which we enclose, remarked "I consider your furniture, as designed and brought out in the Jin-di-Sugi finish, the most

unique and artistic treatment of wood yet produced." By a secret process (patents applied for) developed by Mr. Bradstreet after many years of research and after many voyages to the Orient in making his investigations, we are enabled to slightly eat away the wood-body from the grain, causing the latter to present a raised but most striking and beautifully artistic effect: No other wood, neither rosewood nor mahogany, is more beautiful.[18]

THE MINNEAPOLIS CRAFTSHOUSE

In October 1901, in order to accommodate his growing business and his expanded product line, Bradstreet formed a new company.[19] Within a few years, his quarters also had to expand to accommodate his growing ambitions. He took a ten-year lease on a house at 327 South Seventh Street, remodeling the Italianate structure extensively. In late January 1904 he opened it as the Minneapolis Craftshouse, an expanded version of his earlier 208 South Seventh Street location.[20] All commissioned objects were done on the premises by a staff of workmen. Largely Scandinavian, but including some Japanese, this staff numbered as many as eighty at times during the next decade.

The Craftshouse's distinctive appearance bestowed a memorable identity to Bradstreet's operation. With its re-

Tower Workshop of Bradstreet's Craftshouse, 1905. Photograph courtesy of The Minneapolis Institute of Arts.

John S. Bradstreet and Sam Trubshaw (one of his designers) in the Craftshouse Japanese garden, about 1910. Photograph courtesy of the Minnesota Historical Society.

markable tower workshop, English and Moorish-style windows, and concrete Japanese *torii* gateway at one entrance, the building seemed to emanate from a different and older culture, one unrelated to the ever-expanding and modernizing fifty-year-old city of Minneapolis which surrounded it. The Craftshouse was further distinguished by its Japanese garden, inspired by Bradstreet's tours of gardens in Japan with Josiah Condor, the author of *Landscape Gardening in Japan*, published in 1893. Although physically separate from the merchandise, the garden concept also promoted the specialized landscape work offered by the firm.[21]

The main gallery of the Craftshouse was enormous: fifty-six feet long and two stories high, it featured aged wood floors and a hammer-beam ceiling punctured with skylights. Within the gallery, Bradstreet's antique and contemporary goods were displayed on velvet-covered tables surrounded by walls covered with gold *sackinto* cloth. Almost immediately the Craftshouse became a tourist attraction and a center for cultural activities in Minneapolis. Bradstreet regularly staged exhibitions and concerts there. To some contemporary observers, the objects he assembled represented a museum collection.[22] Indeed, its aesthetic atmosphere suggested Isabella Stewart Gardner's house-as-museum which had opened on Boston's Fenway the year before.

John Bradstreet was among the first in the country to use the vicarious experience of the historic and the exotic to attain retail objectives. Goods were displayed with an

Entrance Hall of Bradstreet's Craftshouse, 1905. Photograph courtesy of The Minneapolis Institute of Arts.

Main Gallery of Bradstreet's Craftshouse, 1905. Photograph courtesy of the Minneapolis Public Library, Special Collections.

aesthetic casualness throughout the Craftshouse to provoke a buyer's curiosity. Shoppers were encouraged to explore all of the shop's nooks and crannies, simulating Bradstreet's own exploration of foreign markets in search of these same items. Besides his own production, Bradstreet promoted pieces brought from lands he visited in his extensive travels—Japan, China, the Near East and Europe—enticing the public with their symbolic reference to another time and place. In one advertisement placed in the local weekly *The Bellman* for 23 January 1909, a hexagonal Japanese temple table was featured, along with the copy: "To those who have travelled in old Japan, cherishing its beauties and its memories, any reminder of it, as this temple table, a lotus bowl, a bronze, or other example of its wonderful art, is appealing."

In promoting exoticism, the Craftshouse followed other retail establishments in Europe and America focusing on the worldly aspirations of their elite clientele.[23] Bradstreet followed, and in some respects exceeded, Liberty's example and his relationship with Tiffany seems to have been one of mutual influence as well as friendship. The Craftshouse's marketing technique and its spirit of individuality parallel that of specialized art dealers of the time such as Siegfried

"A Temple Table from Kyoto," John S. Bradstreet and Co. advertisement, The Bellman, 23 January 1909, page 92.

A Temple Table from Kyoto.

"For the temple bells are callin', and it's there that I would be—"

To those who have travelled in old Japan, cherishing its beauties and its memories, any reminder of it, as this temple table, a lotus bowl, a bronze, or other example of its wonderful art, is appealing.

Many such pieces can be found at the Craftshouse, selected personally with great care, and imported directly by ourselves.

John S. Bradstreet & Co.
327 South Seventh St., Minneapolis
Established 1876

Bing's "L'Art Nouveau" which opened in Paris in 1895, a shop that presented goods in artist-designed interiors, all in the Art Nouveau style. All of these stores, Bradstreet's among them, were reflected in Gump's of San Francisco's eclectic range of imported goods, a merchandiser which dubbed itself "the world's most unusual store" after its opening in 1906. Like Liberty's and Bradstreet's, Gump's created a sympathetic atmosphere for its wares by enclosing them in specially constructed exotic interiors. Their "Jade Room" established their reputation as a center for the sale of Asian objects. The Minneapolis collector T. B. Walker, for example, bought the majority of his jades there.[24]

Like some of his contemporaries, Bradstreet saw European antiques as another form of "exotica." The enthusiasm for antique collecting which had spread throughout Europe in the last decades of the nineteenth century was beginning to become more popular in the United States in the 1890s. The forerunner in this field, the architect and interior designer Stanford White, arranged artificial "collections" for his clients with his stock of old European objects.[25] Although Bradstreet never offered complete collections of furniture for a period interior as Stanford White did, he seems to have been the only Twin Cities purveyor of antique furniture at the turn of the century. Idiosyncratic pieces which he discovered during his travels, items such as "a

fine Dutch chest" or a "beautifully carved Florentine cabinet," could be accommodated into an arts and crafts philosophy interpreted broadly enough to incorporate handcrafted objects from every period. When Bradstreet could not find the style of object he wanted in the antique market, he made the object himself. Liberty and Company, as it happened, featured reproduction antique furniture prominently in its 1905–10 catalogue as well.[26] The variety of Bradstreet's recreations was remarkable, ranging from Venetian eighteenth-century-style commodes to Louis XVI-inspired dressing tables to Hepplewhite-style chairs. His stock represented both actual reproductions and pieces loosely inspired by antique originals.[27] Following Stanford White's example, Bradstreet was more concerned with the flavor of antiquity than with historical precision. Even modern pieces could often incorporate old-style elements. A simple hall table, for instance, integrated "reproductions of fine old carvings found by Mr. Bradstreet in Emden, Germany"; a hall chest included carved lions faithfully reproduced from "originals from Amsterdam."[28]

With the growing popularity of reviving seventeenth- and eighteenth-century furniture styles, Bradstreet's chief Minnesota competitors in interior decorating, William French and Company and William Yungbauer, marketed a standardized range of reproduction antique furniture,

Interior of William A. French and Company, The Western Architect, *June 1910, page 63.*

meeting what was becoming an almost univeral demand. French felt strongly that faithful reproductions of historical styles represented the most appropriate furniture for a home of the time, stating later in life that "I confined my work to American, French, and English furniture. I consider the two latter nations the world's greatest furniture designers. They fit our needs in America better than any other country."[29] Unlike Bradstreet's own creative eclecticism, however, historical precedent seems to have been followed more faithfully by French and Company and by Yungbauer.

With its range of offerings, its new line of *jin-di-sugi*

furniture as well as the variety of oriental, antique, and modern European-style furniture offered, the Craftshouse became the center for the region's specialized decorating trade. Even Bradstreet's most loyal patrons, however, often combined the special styles only offered by the firm with that of the more standard offerings of other decorators. In 1905, the wife of a prominent Duluth businessman, Mina Merrill Prindle, began a search for artists and decorators to create the interiors of her new home. Impressed by the newly opened Craftshouse and its recently developed *jin-di-sugi* line of furniture, she engaged Bradstreet as the principal interior designer of her house, although he was not

William Prindle house, Duluth, Minn., 1905. William ...t, architect (certain windows and other exterior details by ...S. Bradstreet). Photograph courtesy of The Minneapolis In-...te of Arts.

"Lotus" table, 1903, John S. Bradstreet and Co. The Western Architect, April 1903.

its only decorator. After adding exotic window frames to the house's exterior, similar to those he had created for the Craftshouse, Bradstreet concentrated on the living room, which survives as one of his most complete *jin-di-sugi* interiors. Here he outlined the fireplace with Tiffany favrile glass and wrapped the slightly irregular room with brown-toned *jin-di-sugi* paneling, placing beautifully carved *sugi* floral panels above the fireplace and at regular intervals around the perimeter. A bank of bookcases with partially colored leaded glass doors was incorporated opposite the fireplace wall, flanking a bay decorated with Japanese floral and animal carvings and a Japanese bird cage. Bradstreet included his famous "Lotus" table in the setting, as well as a version of his "Turtle" card table, two short and two high-backed chairs, and other furniture in the same *sugi* style. A magnificently carved cypress chandelier with Tiffany favrile shades hung from the *sugi* ceiling. Although other interiors in the house were designed by Bradstreet as well, including the front hall (in an updated Moorish style) and two of the upstairs bedrooms (each following modern Craftsman ideals), William French executed at least two bedrooms in the house and was responsible for other decorating details as well.[30]

Lounging and smoking room, third floor, Glensheen, 1908–9. The Western Architect, April 1910.

Donaldson's Glass Block, 1906. Minnesota Historical Society.
Photograph by C. P. Gibson.

A few years later at "Glensheen," executed for the Chester Congdon family in Duluth, Bradstreet's arts and crafts and French's more conventional styles were combined again to meet a client's need for both the comfortable and the exotically modern. William French and Company was the primary decorator of the house, but Bradstreet was asked to produce the *jin-di-sugi* smoking room and sun room on the ground floor, among the few *sugi* interiors of the time still in situ and the only available for public viewing. Bradstreet also created arts and crafts rooms on the third floor of the Congdon house, incorporating his new line of inlaid mission-style oak furniture in interiors which incorporated Grueby tile fireplace surrounds. The arts-and-crafts elements he supplied—simple oak furniture, decorative tile fireplace surrounds, and stained glass—were fitted into several other Bradstreet commissions during the period. Until the time of Bradstreet's death in 1914, the Bradstreet Company continued to experiment with arts and crafts and other progressive styles. His execution of several pieces of furniture designed by the Prairie School architectural team of William Purcell and George Elmslie are testimony of the local avant-garde's respect for the design and production ability of Bradstreet's firm.[31]

THE CRAFTSHOUSE AND RETAILING AT THE TURN OF THE CENTURY

In offering the customer an intimate, specialized, aesthetic shopping experience, the Craftshouse represented an alternative to the other retailing innovation of the time, the department store.[32] Introduced in the Twin Cities in the late 1890s, department stores arose, as they did throughout the eastern United States, from dry goods merchants and clothiers offering specialized ready-made goods. Minneapolis's Young-Quinlan, for example, began as a purveyor of furs and outerwear; Dayton's was a dry goods merchant.[33] Merchants soon expanded into other areas, however. Bradstreet's competitors, William French and Company, even followed the more publicly oriented department store technique of using display cases that created a largely retail store-like atmosphere. The early twentieth-century department stores of the Twin Cities competed in offering customers not only the best value, but also the anonymity and freedom afforded by large-scale merchandising. Bradstreet's strategy was different. Focusing on a specialized market in search of a uniquely fashionable home, the artistic atmosphere of the Craftshouse made it a shop to be explored, with objects to be discovered. Patrons commanded individual attention in this retail atmosphere, one that was neither aggressively public, very anonymous, nor particularly convenient.

Bradstreet's reputation as an interior design trendsetter, however, was used by department stores in their quest to increase public traffic and boost sales by expanding the experience of shopping. Donaldson's, which expanded into its architecturally striking Glass Block building in 1906, was one of the first merchandisers in the country to combine dining and shopping. Much as tea room commissions had inspired Scottish designer Charles Rennie Mackintosh to originality in design, Donaldson's decision to establish its tea rooms and cafes became an opportunity for John Bradstreet to experiment in interior design.

Each of Bradstreet's six separate dining areas had a different ambience: one was the Gentleman's Cafe, another the Dutch room, others were labeled the Ivory, Gothic, Japanese, and Silver Grey rooms. Although all the dining suites were imaginatively designed, the most modern of the six was the Silver Grey Room. Artificial light was provided by contemporary Craftsman-type wall fixtures, and natural light was filtered through stained glass which depicted geometricized trees, hybrids of Tiffany and Prairie School foliate patterns. The adjacent Japanese Room was partially wainscoted with *sugi* panels. Bradstreet also created Japanese architectural ornaments for the doors and windows, transforming them into *torii*, or formal gates, to look through or walk under. Inexpensive and distinctly different from dining at home, the tea rooms became very popular.[34] In 1912, in an effort to duplicate Donaldson's model, the competing Dayton's Dry Goods Company commissioned the Prairie School architects William Purcell and George Elmslie to draw up designs for their own tea rooms, but the plans were never executed.[35]

As the twentieth century progressed, however, the Dayton Company became one of the leading merchandising innovators in the nation. Famous for its specialized displays and customer service, it also introduced the first enclosed shopping mall in the late 1950s, one of the most influential retailing evolutions of the late twentieth century. Today, the largest of these enclosed shopping centers in the country is located in Minnesota.

Bradstreet's work and example stand as an early, regionally inspired retailing venture of a different kind. His firm

Silver Grey Room, Donaldson's Department Store, Minneapolis, 1906. Interior by John S. Bradstreet and Co., The Bellman, 1906.

understood the effectiveness of name recognition and the personalized artistic experience represented by combining the antique shop and the specialized boutique with an acclaimed firm of interior decorators. Although the success of each of these merchandising services has been proven throughout the twentieth century, Bradstreet integrated all these retailing phenomena in his Craftshouse. Shunning the mass market, his company never advertised in the city directories as did all its competitors; instead, space was regularly leased in the pages of *The Bellman*, a local weekly catering to upper middle-class aspirations. Providing its clients with the experience of the historic and exotic and an appreciation for the handmade, the Craftshouse was an aesthetic shopping alternative which subtly invited visitors to experience its atmosphere in the hope that they would buy.

The artistic shop of the country, unrivaled anywhere, with its quaint buildings and surrounding gardens, its wonderful exhibits of valuable and unique examples of art carefully selected from various parts of the world, gives to Minneapolis a place of interest that no other city of this country can equal. Visitors are always welcome.[36]

NOTES

1. Promotional brochure for John S. Bradstreet and Company, Interior Decorations and Furnishings (Minneapolis: n.p., 1905). Morris's words were inspirational for the "quotations" generated by Bradstreet and Co.:

> The difference between Hand made Furniture and the factory product is very much the same as between a painting of merit and a photograph. One is an artistic production, limited only by the ability of the designer, the other is bound by mechanical limitations. One is original, the other is made in quantities." (*The Bellman*, 14 September 1907, p. 292)

No furniture was actually produced at Morris and Co. Dyeing, printing, and weaving operations were housed in many different locations, including Queen Square in London and later at Merton Abbey in Surrey. See Charles Harvey and Jon Press, *William Morris: Design and Enterprise in Victorian Britain* (Manchester and New York: Manchester University Press, 1991), 107, 132ff.

2. These included H. S. Howe, *Minneapolis Directory*, 1859–60, p. 72; Edsten and Olson, and George F. Warner, *Minneapolis Directory*, 1871–72.

3. It is notable that furniture manufacturers considered the market of framing and gilding significant enough to target. Advertisement for G. F. Warner, manufacturer and dealer in furniture, *Minneapolis Directory*, 1865–66, p. 52.

4. *Minneapolis Directory*, 1871–72, advertisement opposite p. 80.

5. For biographical information on Bradstreet, see George Brainard Blodgette, *Early Settlers of Rowley, Massachusetts* (Rowley, Mass., 1933), 34, 41; William C. Edgar, "John Scott Bradstreet," *The Bellman* 17 (15 August 1914): 215–16; Edwin H. Hewitt, "John S. Bradstreet—Citizen of Minneapolis," *Journal of the American Institute of Architects*, October 1916, pp. 424–27; Horace B. Hudson, *Half Century of Minneapolis* (Minneapolis, 1908), 127–28; *Minneapolis Journal*, 10 August 1914, p. 1; *Minneapolis Tribune*, 11 August 1914, p. 6; Perry Robinson, "John S. Bradstreet and His Work," *The Bellman* 2 (18 May 1907): 597–600. There also is a chapter on John Bradstreet in Rena Neumann Coen, *In the Mainstream: The Art of Alexis Jean Fournier* (St. Cloud, 1985), 36–47, and his work has been discussed recently in Wendy Kaplan, *"The Art That is Life": The Arts & Crafts Movement in America, 1875–1920* (Boston: Museum of Fine Arts, 1987), 151, 225; Julia Meech and Gabriel P. Weisberg, *Japonisme Comes to America: The Japanese Impact on the Graphic Arts 1876–1925* (New York: Harry N. Abrams, 1990), 127–28; and Janet Kardon, editor, *The Ideal Home 1900–1920* (New York: Harry N. Abrams, 1993), 108, 238. For the early history of the Gorham Manufacturing Co., see Charles Carpenter, *Gorham Silver 1831–1981* (New York, 1982) (although no mention is made of Bradstreet's early employment by the firm). A former colleague later stated that Bradstreet had a "small business" in the East before coming to Minnesota (Miriam Lucker Lesley, notes for "John Bradstreet: Minneapolis Interior Designer" [conversation with William Eckert, January 1940, note 5]). Bradstreet's work and career is summarized in Michael Conforti, "Orientalism on the Upper Mississippi: The Work of John S. Bradstreet," *Bulletin of The Minneapolis Institute of Arts* 65 (1981–82): 2–35, from which some of the information in this essay was taken.

6. *St. Paul Pioneer Press*, 8 December 1878, p. 6. For a detailed description from this article, see Conforti, note 7, pp. 32, and 5–6, 8. The successful sale of the latest in progressive European and imported Asian art in mock-home settings induced others to experiment with atmosphere in the promotion of their most special or unusual items. Siegfried Bing used complete room interiors created by young designers as a promotional tactic at the opening of his Paris shop, L'Art Nouveau, in 1895. For a description of the exterior and interiors of L'Art Nouveau, see Gabriel Weisberg, *Art Nouveau Bing: Paris Style 1900* (New York: Harry N. Abrams, 1986), 56–76.

7. Charles Locke Eastlake's manual of design reform, *Hints on Household Taste*, first published in London in 1868, helped popularize "art furniture" as did the presentation of "Japonesque" British furniture at the 1876 Philadelphia Centennial Exposition.

8. Further details of the Bradstreet-Thurber partnership can be found in Fritz Nelson, "First Apostle: John Scott Bradstreet in Minneapolis," unpublished paper, Department of Art History, University of Minnesota, 1980, 4–7.

9. "Announcement of Bradstreet-Thurber and Company second Annual Autumnal Exhibition October 23, 24, 25, 1884," Bradstreet papers. In later years, Bradstreet even made and designed his own brass lamps (*Minneapolis Tribune*, 9 August 1902, part 2, p. 18). For Bradstreet's Moorish style, see Conforti, op.cit., pp. 4-10.

10. Lesley, for "John Bradstreet" (conversation with William Eckert, note 5). Bradstreet's biennial visits to Japan are mentioned in a number of his biographies as well.

11. The cold early reception of Bradstreet's Japanese objects is mentioned in one of his obituaries (*Minneapolis Tribune*, 11 August 1914, p. 6, editorial). Perry Robinson's tribute to Bradstreet also discusses the sharp contrast between Bradstreet's taste and that of the Minneapolis community at this time (Robinson, "Bradstreet and His Work," 587).

12. The many collections formed include T. B. Walker's Chinese jades, Alfred Pillsbury's Chinese Bronzes, Augustus Searle's collection of jades and gold, and Richard Gale's Japanese prints.

13. Bradstreet's friend Perry Robinson related a story:

> Some fifteen years ago [ca. 1892] I was in London on a flying visit and went into Liberty's famous place. On coming away I stopped to ask some questions about the duties on the things which I had bought and intended taking to America. It was the first intimation that the man to whom I spoke had heard that I was from America; and the first question that he asked was if I knew a Mr. Bradstreet.
>
> He could not remember the name of the town where Mr. Bradstreet lived, so I furnished it. "Ah, yes," he said, "of course is it not a remarkable place for such a man to be in? Could he not get a much wider recognition in New York, for instance?" Undoubtedly he could; but, after all, I suggested, the place for a missionary was among the savages. (Robinson, "Bradstreet and His Work," 598)

14. For this period of the Bradstreet firm, see Nelson, "First Apostle," 6, 7. The "business trials" Bradstreet endured, to which Robinson refers, possibly center around this fire and the eventual removal of the Thurbers back to Providence (Robinson, "Bradstreet and His Work," 587).

15. Bradstreet mentions his desire to reflect Kelmscott in the context of describing his larger Craftshouse, where he moved in 1904. "There are various art and crafts movements and enterprises throughout the country, but the Minneapolis Craftshouse is unusual in that it is both a workshop and salesroom. It is as distinctive as the Kelmscott Manor made famous by Morris in the output of its workshop, and besides has for sale a vast number of curios and valuable articles brought from distant lands." The quotation is credited to an employee, William Adams. John S. Bradstreet and Co. promotional brochure, frontispiece.

16. In the traditional *gindai-sugi* (pronounced jin-di-soo-ghee) technique, cypress wood is distressed by burying it underground or under water for many years. This wood often has a sacred function, being used in the building of Shinto temples. The "new treatment of wood called the Sugi finish" was first mentioned in Bradstreet's short brochure in 1901, when the company was at 208 S. Seventh Street.

17. See photos of advertisements in the Bradstreet papers. Also, *Western Architect* 2 (August 1903): 22 and (July 1903): 17.

18. Letter from Frank Waterman, a Bradstreet partner after 1901, to S. O. Barnum, Brooklyn, N.Y., 30 May 1903. Bradstreet papers.

19. The *Minneapolis Journal*, 16 October 1901, p. 7. Bradstreet also became president of the Consolidated Arts Company, 27 East 21st Street, New York, shortly after the establishment of his new Minneapolis company. The firm may have been created to market his and other arts and crafts wares (*Minneapolis Journal*, 30 January 1904, p. 5; the logo for the firm is in the Bradstreet papers).

20. Work had already begun on the building when the lease was announced in the *Minneapolis Journal*, 15 October 1903. We thank Miss Dorothy Burke for this information.

21. For contemporary accounts of Bradstreet's Japanese garden at the Craftshouse, see Frank H. Nutter, "Civic Beauty in the Formal Garden,"

The Western Architect (December 1908): 76–78; Gustav Stickley, "A Garden Fountain," *The Craftsman* (October 1904): 69–75; and Henry H. Saylor, "The Japanese Garden in America: Illustrations from the Japanese Garden of Mr. John S. Bradstreet at Minneapolis, Minnesota," *Country Life in America* (March 1909): 481–84. For his garden for John Burkholz at Minnetonka, Minnesota, see Clay Lancaster, *The Japanese Influence in America*, 2d ed. (New York, 1983), 206, fig. 175. For the vandalization of a Buddha sculpture in Bradstreet's garden, see *Minneapolis Journal*, 1 June 1904, p. 6.

22. "The Craftshouse of John S. Bradstreet and Company," *Minneapolis Journal*, 31 March 1910, p. 7. Bradstreet had begun having exhibitions in his earlier 208 S. Seventh Street establishment, such as the one devoted to Robert Koehler's work in 1900 (*Minneapolis Journal*, 10 November 1900). Invitations to some of the Craftshouse concerts are collected in the Bradstreet papers. For further discussions of the Craftshouse, see *Minneapolis Journal*, 30 January 1904, p. 5; Keith Clark, "The Bradstreet Craftshouse," *House Beautiful* 16 (June 1904): 21ff.; Elliott Randall, "Bradstreet Craftshouse," *Pittsburgh Dispatch*, 23 October 1904; "A Fine Collection in its New Home," *Minneapolis Journal*, 30 January 1904, p. 5; Lesley, notes for "John Bradstreet" (conversation with William Eckert, notes 1, 8, 14, 17, 19).

23. Some British department stores were opening "oriental" departments contemporary with Liberty's, such as Whiteley's & Debenham and Freebody. See Isabelle Anscome, *Arts and Crafts Style* (New York: Rizzoli, 1991), 126.

24. Although the Minneapolis Institute of Arts now owns the best of the original T. B. Walker jade collection, it is not known which pieces were purchased at Gump's; it is only known that Walker shopped there regularly. (From files, Asian Department, Minneapolis Institute of Arts.) Gump's reportedly employed artisans from China and Japan to construct a series of oriental rooms on the premises, but these only lent an atmosphere to the shop and were not reproduced in patrons' homes. See Robert Hendrickson, *The Grand Emporiums: The Illustrated History of the Great Department Store* (New York: Stein & Day, 1979), 158.

25. In the first decade of the twentieth century, various approaches to the creation of antique interiors were promoted by architect/interior designer Ogden Codman, the art dealer Joseph Duveen, and Elsie de Wolfe (see Ogden Codman and Edith Wharton, *The Decoration of Houses* [first published in 1897; reprinted in New York by W. W. Norton, 1978]; Joseph Duveen, *Colour in The Home: with notes on architecture, sculpture, painting and upon decoration and good taste* [London: G. Allen & Co., Ltd., 1912]; and Elsie de Wolfe, *The House in Good Taste*, New York, 1913). See also Michael Conforti, "Decorators and the Antique Room: Collecting European Decorative Arts in The United States from the 1890s to the 1990s," *The Grosvenor House Antiques Fair 1992 Handbook* (London: Published in association with *The Burlington Magazine*, 1992), 20–25.

26. Sarah Nichols, "Arthur Lasenby Liberty: A Mere Adjective?" *Journal of Decorative and Propaganda Arts* 13 (Summer 1989): 84, 86. Bradstreet's adaptations of antique sources also follow the formal precedents of British designers such as George Walton (1867–1932) of Glasgow, who often produced works after early models, as well as designers employed by Liberty's at the turn of the century, like Sir Edwin Luytens (1869–1944).

27. *The Bellman* 9 (10 December 1910); 12 (20 November 1909); 7 (30 October 1909); 6 (17 April 1909); 6 (22 May 1909); 7 (25 December 1909), respectively. Although many of his reproduction pieces undoubtedly survive unrecognized, the Tudor cabinet advertised in 1909 seems identical to one currently in a Minnesota private collection, inscribed with the name Hovey C. Clark and dated 1909.

28. *The Bellman*, 15 February 1908, p. 172, and 22 February 1908, p. 200. Even when a piece was reproduced in its entirety, its particular origin was noted so as to impart a sense of individuality to the furnishing, as with an oak wedding chest, appearing in the 16 May 1908 issue of *The Bellman*, that was "a reproduction of an old chest picked up in London, twenty years ago" (p. 536). By 1 August 1908 Bradstreet's *Bellman* ads were proclaiming the practicality of their reproductions over "genuine" antiques.

"Why pay the cost of freight, duties, and other expenses, to bring from Florence an old and necessarily damaged table, when, here in Minneapolis, as beautiful an Italian Table as the above, exquisitely carved and finished, can be made for you, from original design, at a less price?" (p. 840)

Eventually John S. Bradstreet and Company focused almost entirely on reproductions. Bradstreet's ledgers and design sketches from 1913–32 reveal the extent to which reproduction furniture made up the overall production of the company. In 1913, the year preceding Bradstreet's death, the production of *jin-di-sugi* furniture had ceased to be a moneymaker for the firm; three designs out of approximately 242, or 1.2 percent, were to be executed in Bradstreet's cypress wood treatment. Few designs display any stylistic eccentricities, for example, the incorporation of "old carvings" into new pieces of furniture. From The Studio of John S. Bradstreet and Co., collection of ledger books, 6 vol., indexed, Minneapolis, Minn., 1913–32, Archives of The Minneapolis Institute of Arts.

29. Transcript of article about William French from the *Minneapolis Journal* (1932), n.p., Goldstein Gallery, University of Minnesota, St. Paul, Minn. The article goes on to state that French had used antiques from the Metropolitan Museum of Art as models.

30. The Prindle house living room and its furniture is now in the collection of The Minneapolis Institute of Arts. For a further discussion of the Prindle commission, see Conforti, "The Work of John S. Bradstreet," 24–29.

31. William Purcell Papers, Northwest Architectural Archives, University of Minnesota Libraries, St. Paul.

32. The department store is assumed to have been the creation of the Bouçicaults at Bon Marché in Paris in the 1850s. See Hendrickson, *The Grand Emporiums*, 150. Along with unique policies such as marking goods at a fixed price and offering a return of money to customers if they were not satisfied, the Bouçicaults freed those who entered their shop of the obligation to buy, thus creating a more relaxed atmosphere for customers who had no intention to purchase when entering, but who could be enticed to do so by an attractive display. This phenomenon, later termed "consumer seduction," was an important social and psychological innovation of the nineteenth century. See Alexandra Artley, ed., *The Golden Age of Shop Design: European Shop Interiors 1880–1939* (New York: Whitney Library of Design, 1976), 7. The most prominent early American department store mogul was A. T. Stewart of New York, who expanded his dry goods business as early as 1862, and developed Stewart's as an important early retail center.

33. Many dry goods merchants in the Twin Cities began to expand in the 1870s, and, increasingly, the diversity of their retail offerings and the sophistication of their presentation made these stores resemble department stores of east coast and international fame. Yet the relative newness of the department store phenomenon in the region caused these transitional retail ventures to undergo identity crises. They continued to designate themselves "retail dry goods dealers" for years after they had first called themselves "department stores." For example, William Donaldson and Co., founded by the father of L. S. Donaldson (who developed the family business into a local retail institution), had the honor of being the only department store listed in the Minneapolis city directory of 1895–96, but was listed under "Dry Goods—Retail" throughout the first decade of the twentieth century. Cf. *Minneapolis Directory*, 1895–1910.

34. Donaldson's devoted much advertising space to its new department store feature. For advertisements picturing all the interiors for the tea rooms and cafe executed by Bradstreet and Co., see *The Bellman*, 21 July 1906, p. 3; 4 August 1906, p. 51; 1 September 1906, p. 148; 15 September 1906, p. 196; 22 September 1906, p. 220; 6 October 1906, p. 272; 13 October 1906, p. 300; 20 October 1906, p. 328; 27 October 1906, p. 356; and 10 November 1906, p. 412. An interesting contemporary stylistic parallel to Bradstreet's Japanese Room was designed by Mark Fitzpatrick for Carling's Restaurant in St. Paul (Lancaster, *Japanese Influence*, 226).

35. Their fitting room designs were executed in 1909–11, however. Purcell and Elmslie also worked on the George Draper Dayton home

in 1915. William Purcell Papers. Bradstreet had outfitted the L. S. Donaldson House a few years earlier.

36. John S. Bradstreet and Co. advertisement, *The Bellman*, 21 January 1911, p. 68.

BIBLIOGRAPHY

BOOKS, JOURNALS, AND NEWSPAPERS
The Bellman, Minneapolis, 1907–11.

"The Craftshouse of John S. Bradstreet and Company," *Minneapolis Journal* (31 March 1910): 7.

Conforti, Michael. "Orientalism on the Upper Mississippi: The Work of John S. Bradstreet." *The Minneapolis Institute of Arts Bulletin* 65 (1981–82), 2–35.

Conforti, Michael. "Decorators and the Antique Room: Collecting European Decorative Arts in the United States from the 1890s to the 1990s." *The Grosvenor House Antiques Fair 1992 Handbook*. (Published in association with *The Burlington Magazine*, 20–25, 1992.)

Hendrickson, Robert. *The Grand Emporiums: The Illustrated History of the Great Department Store*. New York: Stein & Day, 1979.

Hess, Jeffrey. *Their Splendid Legacy: A History of the Minneapolis Society of Fine Arts*. Minneapolis: Minneapolis Society of Fine Arts, 1985.

Lancaster, Clay. *The Japanese Influence in America*. 2d ed. New York, 1983.

Minneapolis Journal (16 October 1901): 7; (30 January 1904): 5; (31 March 1910): 7.

Minneapolis Tribune. Obituary (11 August 1914): 6.

Nichols, Sarah. "Arthur Lasenby Liberty: A Mere Adjective?" *Journal of Decorative and Propaganda Arts* 13 (Summer 1989): 84, 86.

Robinson, Perry. "John S. Bradstreet and His Work." *The Bellman* 2 (18 May 1907): 597–600.

St. Paul Pioneer Press (8 December 1878): 6.

UNPUBLISHED AND OTHER SOURCES
Bradstreet, John S. Papers. Minneapolis Collection. Minneapolis Public Library.

Bradstreet, John S. and Co. Promotional brochure. Minneapolis, 1905.

Bradstreet, John S. and Co. Collection of Ledger Books. 6 vol. Archives of The Minneapolis Institute of Arts, Minneapolis, 1913–32.

Lesley, Miriam Lucker. "John Scott Bradstreet: Minneapolis Interior Decorator." Notes from master's thesis, University of Minnesota, 1941.

Minneapolis Directory, 1859–1910.

Nelson, Fritz A. "First Apostle: John Scott Bradstreet in Minneapolis." Paper written for the Department of Art History, University of Minnesota, 1980.

Purcell, William. Papers. Northwest Architectural Archives, University of Minnesota Libraries.

Transcript from an article about William French. *The Minneapolis Journal*. Goldstein Gallery, University of Minnesota (1932) n.p.

CHECKLIST OF THE EXHIBITION

FURNITURE AND DECORATIONS FROM THE WILLIAM PRINDLE HOUSE, DULUTH, MINNESOTA, 1906

dimensions = h × w × d

LIVING ROOM

1. John S. Bradstreet and Co., designer and manufacturer
   American, Minneapolis, Minn.
   Paneling, about 1906
   Cypress
   Various dimensions
   The Minneapolis Institute of Arts
   Gift of Wheaton Wood

2. John S. Bradstreet and Co., designer and manufacturer
   American, Minneapolis, Minnesota
   Armchair, about 1906
   Cypress and velvet
   37″ × 34¾″ × approx. 33¼″
   The Minneapolis Institute of Arts
   Gift of Wheaton Wood 82.43.1

3. John S. Bradstreet and Co., designer and manufacturer
   American, Minneapolis, Minn.
   Sofa, about 1906
   Cypress and velvet
   37½″ × 87½″ × 38½″
   The Minneapolis Institute of Arts
   Gift of Wheaton Wood 82.43.2

4. John S. Bradstreet and Co., designer and manufacturer
   American, Minneapolis, Minn.
   Side chairs, about 1906
   Cypress and embossed leather
   42″ × 17¼″ × 19″
   The Minneapolis Institute of Arts
   Gift of Wheaton Wood 82.43.3.1,2

5. John S. Bradstreet and Co., designer and manufacturer
   American, Minneapolis, Minn.
   Side chairs, about 1906
   Cypress and embossed leather
   42″ × 17¼″ × 19″
   The Minneapolis Institute of Arts
   Gift of Wheaton Wood 82.43.4.1,2

6. John S. Bradstreet and Co., designer and manufacturer
   American, Minneapolis, Minn.
   Lolling chair, about 1906
   Oak, cypress and embossed leather
   46½″ × 20½″ × 19″
   The Minneapolis Institute of Arts
   Gift of Wheaton Wood 82.43.5

7. John S. Bradstreet and Co., designer and manufacturer
of case, and Steinway
American, Minneapolis, Minn.
Piano, about 1906
Cypress and mahogany
54½″ × 63½″ × 27¾″
The Minneapolis Institute of Arts
Gift of Wheaton Wood 82.43.9

8. John S. Bradstreet and Co., designer and manufacturer
American, Minneapolis, Minn.
Piano bench, about 1906
Oak and cypress
The Minneapolis Institute of Arts
Gift of Wheaton Wood 82.43.10
26″ × 48″ × 18″

9. John S. Bradstreet and Co., designer and manufacturer
American, Minneapolis, Minn.
Lotus table, about 1906
Cypress
28⅜″ high, 30″ diameter
The Minneapolis Institute of Arts
Gift of Wheaton Wood 82.43.11

10. John S. Bradstreet and Co., designer and manufacturer
American, Minneapolis, Minn.
Double desk, about 1906
Cypress
30½″ + 72¼″ × 42⅛″
The Minneapolis Institute of Arts
Gift of Wheaton Wood 82.43.12

11. John S. Bradstreet and Co., designer and manufacturer
American, Minneapolis, Minn.
Chest, about 1906
Cypress
The Minneapolis Institute of Arts
19⅜″ × 48¼₆″ × 18¼₆″
Gift of Wheaton Wood 82.43.13

12. John S. Bradstreet and Co., designer and manufacturer
American, Minneapolis, Minn.
Low table or footstool, about 1906
Cypress root
The Minneapolis Institute of Arts
13″ × 29″ × 22½″
Gift of Wheaton Wood 82.43.14

13. John S. Bradstreet and Co., designer and manufacturer
American, Minneapolis, Minn.
Seven wall sconces, about 1906
Cypress, favrile glass, and bronze
24½″ × 8″ each
The Minneapolis Institute of Arts
Gift of Wheaton Wood 82.43.17,1-7

14. John S. Bradstreet and Co., designer and manufacturer
American, Minneapolis, Minn.
Chandelier, about 1906
Cypress, favrile glass and bronze
24″ high, 24″ diameter
The Minneapolis Institute of Arts
Gift of Wheaton Wood 82.43.18

15. John S. Bradstreet and Co., designer and manufacturer
American, Minneapolis, Minn.
Pair of floor lamps, about 1906
Cypress with silk shades
71¾″ high, 27¼″ wide cross piece, approx. 22″ diameter of shade
The Minneapolis Institute of Arts
Gift of Wheaton Wood 82.43.15, 16

16. Manufacturer unknown
American or Japanese
Candlestick, about 1905
Brass
58″ high, 10¾″ diameter of base
The Minneapolis Institute of Arts 82.43.27
Gift of Wheaton Wood 82.43.27

17. Manufacturer unknown
Standing ashtray, about 1905
Bronze and glass
31″ high, 8¾″ diameter of base
The Minneapolis Institute of Arts
Gift of Wheaton Wood 82.43.41

18. John S. Bradstreet and Co., designer and manufacturer
American, Minneapolis, Minn.
Table with pair of tripod supports, about 1906
Maple
30″ × 43¾″ × 30½″
The Minneapolis Institute of Arts
Gift of Wheaton Wood 82.43.6

19. John S. Bradstreet and Co., designer and manufacturer
American, Minneapolis, Minn.
Table with single tripod support, about 1906
Maple
29″ × 23¼″ × 20⅜″
The Minneapolis Institute of Arts
Gift of Wheaton Wood 82.43.8

20. John S. Bradstreet and Co., designer and manufacturer
American, Minneapolis, Minn.
Fu dogs, about 1906
Cypress
12½″ × 2″ × 11½″
The Minneapolis Institute of Arts
Gift of Wheaton Wood 82.43.29, .30

21. Manufacturer unknown

American or Japanese
Lantern in form of owl, about 1905
Bronze
18¾" × 11½"
The Minneapolis Insitute of Arts
Gift of Wheaton Wood 82.43.19

22. Manufacturer unknown
American or Japanese
Hanging lantern in form of rustic birdhouse, about 1905
Wood, metal
17" × 15¼" × 12½"
The Minneapolis Institute of Arts
Gift of Wheaton Wood 82.43.20

23. Manufacturer unknown
American or Japanese
Lantern, about 1905
Polychromed enameled bronze
14½" + 12"
The Minneapolis Institute of Arts
Gift of Wheaton Wood 82.43.22

24. Manufacturer unknown
American or Japanese
Lantern, about 1905
Polychromed enameled bronze
17¼" × 16¼"
The Minneapolis Institute of Arts
Gift of Wheaton Wood 82.43.23

25. Manufacturer unknown
American or Japanese
Pair of candlesticks, about 1905
Iron and brass
.24: 33" high, 9⅜" diameter of base
.25: 35½" high, 9⅜" diameter of base
The Minneapolis Institute of Arts
Gift of Wheaton Wood 82.43.24,.25ab

26. Manufacturer unknown
American or Japanese
Incense burner, about 1900
Brass
23½"
The Minneapolis Institute of Arts
Gift of Wheaton Wood 82.43.38a–c

27. Manufacturer unknown
American or Japanese
Cranes, about 1905
Wrought iron
.31: 58¾" × 8" × 18½"
.32: 51¼" × 8" × 17½"
.33: 34½" × 8" × 28"
The Minneapolis Institute of Arts

Gift of Wheaton Wood 82.43.31,.32,.33a–d

28. Manufacturer unknown
American or Japanese
Butterfly, about 1905
Brass
25" × 21⅝"
The Minneapolis Institute of Arts
Gift of Wheaton Wood 83.43.34

29. Manufacturer unknown
Probably American
Candleholder, about 1905
Bronze with green glass simulating enamel
22⅜" high, 5¼" diameter at base
The Minneapolis Institute of Arts
Gift of Wheaton Wood 82.43.26c

30. Tiffany Studios
American, New York
Planter, about 1905
Bronze and glass
3" high, 9¼" diameter
The Minneapolis Institute of Arts
Gift of Ruth and Bruce Dayton 91.148.3

The finest preserved interiors by John Bradstreet are the sunroom and smoking room of "Glensheen" in Duluth, Minnesota, and various rooms from the Duluth home of William and Mina Merrill Prindle, designed by William Hunt in 1905. William Prindle was prominent in the early real estate and commercial development of Duluth. Mina Prindle chose John Bradstreet as her primary interior designer after visiting Bradstreet's Twin Cities Craftshouse in 1905. Although Bradstreet designed many rooms in the house, the living room was the most distinctive, with a fireplace outlined in Tiffany favrile glass and *jin-di-sugi* paneling and furniture throughout. Mrs. Prindle added Japanese-style accessories (also listed here) from the Craftshouse in 1915, yet the room was otherwise little altered even after her death in 1965. When The Minneapolis Insitute of Arts acquired the interior paneling and its contents in 1981, labels in Mrs. Prindle's hand were attached to most objects listing their origins and date of purchase.

Bradstreet imported many objects from Japan and the Near East, and reproductions or interpretations of such objects were also produced for sale in the Craftshouse. All were intended for use in unique oriental decorating schemes, either indoors (e.g., the *fu* dogs), or outdoors (e.g., the incense burners and lanterns). All were purchased by Mrs. Prindle for her home. The planter (30), which utilized Tiffany Studios' "turtleback" tiles, though not from the Prindle House, is identical to a planter known to have been in the living room.

OTHER ROOMS

31. John S. Bradstreet and Co., designer and manufacturer
    American, Minneapolis, Minn.
    Curtain, about 1904
    Linen with embroidery
    62½″ × 20¾″
    Minnesota Historical Society Collections 1988.255.1

This curtain is from the "yellow bedroom" of the Prindle house, which was decorated in light colors and accentuated with arts and crafts-style furnishings. This horizontal panel was framed by two vertical panels in a window of the room.

32. Manufacturer unknown
    American or Japanese
    Lotus panels, about 1905
    Polychromed wood
    25½″ × 44½″
    The Minneapolis Institute of Arts Collection

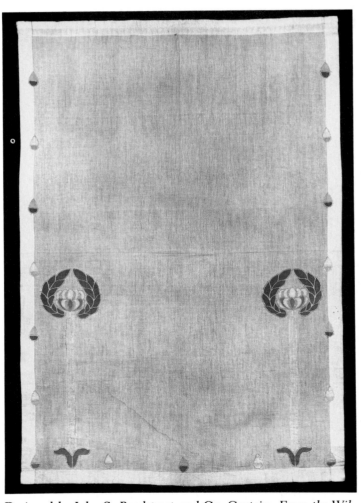

Designed by John S. Bradstreet and Co. Curtain. From the William Prindle house, Duluth, Minn., 1906. Minnesota Historical Society Collections. Photograph by Gary Mortensen and Robert Fogt.

These four panels, when assembled horizontally, create a panoramic view of lotus leaves and flowers. Their thickness and texture, polychroming, and gold wash are similar to those panels installed in the cabinet from Bradstreet's office, now in the collection of the Minnesota Historical Society. They were either imported from Japan or manufactured by Bradstreet in the Japanese taste. It is not known whether they were ever used.

33. From the Studio of John S. Bradstreet and Co.
    American, Minneapolis, Minn.
    Ledger book, 1913–14
    Pencil drawings on paper
    12¼″ × 5⅝″ × ½″
    The Minneapolis Institute of Arts Archive

The first in a series of at least six ledger books from the Craftshouse design studio, this one, dating the year before Bradstreet's death, documents the substitution of the *jin-di-sugi* style popular in the previous decade with reproduction French and English interior styles. It is indexed and each drawing notes the customer for which the piece was made.

34. Paul Fjelde
    American, 1892–?
    John Bradstreet, 1915
    Bronze plaque
    35¼″ × 25¼″ × 1½″
    The Minneapolis Institute of Arts
    Gift of Friends of John Scott Bradstreet 16.3

This plaque was commissioned from local sculptor Paul Fjelde to commemorate Bradstreet's great contributions toward the realization of The Minneapolis Institute of Arts, which opened in 1915, the year after his death. It hung at the entrance to the John S. Bradstreet Memorial Room, which occupied a gallery on the third floor of the newly finished building. The room displayed objects bequeathed by John Scott Bradstreet to the Minneapolis Institute of Arts, including Japanese robes and prints and *jin-di-sugi* furniture.

35. John S. Bradstreet and Co., designer and manufacturer
    American, Minneapolis, Minnesota, 1845–1914
    Two carved light panels, about 1910
    Stained and painted cypress
    From the L. S. Donaldson House, Minneapolis, Minnesota
    23½″ × 37¾″
    23½″ × 33⅜″
    Anonymous loan

These two *jin-di-sugi* panels are two of a series from the sunroom created by Bradstreet for the L. S. Donaldson home on Mount Curve Avenue, Minneapolis. Each of the light panels contains a lotus flower in a different stage of bloom.

J. S. Bradstreet Memorial Room, The Minneapolis Institute of Arts, 1915. Bulletin of the Minneapolis Institute of Arts, Vol. 4, *January–February 1915, p. 15.*

36. John S. Bradstreet and Co., designer and manufacturer
American, Minneapolis, Minn.
Cabinet door, about 1905
Cypress
36½" × 28¾"
Richard Hickenbotham—Geometrie

This door, one of four, is from a now unknown commission.

37. John S. Bradstreet and Co., designer and manufacturer
American, Minneapolis, Minn.
Cabinet, about 1905
Cypress with inset polychromed wood panels
4'7¼" × 6'7" × 18½"
Minnesota Historical Society Collections 1987.160

This cabinet was originally located in Bradstreet's office in the Craftshouse and later belonged to the Minneapolis Institute of Arts, where it was on view in the John S. Bradstreet Memorial Room. Its panels are highlighted with a gold wash, a technique used by Bradstreet to accentuate his *sugi* woodwork, suggesting that they were also manufactured in the Craftshouse.

38. Design attributed to John S. Bradstreet
Manufactured by Grueby Faience Company

American, Boston, Mass.
Fireplace surround, about 1902
Glazed earthenware tile
69½" × 98"
The Minneapolis Institute of Arts
Gift of the Decorative Arts Council 91.47

In this fireplace surround from the home of Captain Joseph Sellwood in Duluth, two trees are depicted with their roots expressively exposed. The individual tiles were produced by the Grueby Faience Company, one of the most prominent manufacturers of art pottery and architectural ceramic work during the first decade of this century. Given the similarity of its design to favorite Bradstreet compositions (such as Glensheen and the Edson S. Woodworth home), the closeness of the Bradstreet firm to Grueby at this time and the Grueby company's use of outside artists during this period, we can tentatively attribute this work to John S. Bradstreet and Co.

39. John S. Bradstreet and Co., designer and manufacturer
American, Minneapolis, Minn.
Double doors, 1908
From the Edson S. Woodworth house, Minneapolis
Leaded and stained glass
Approx. 7–8' × 4'
Mrs. Monica Bessesen Bjornnes Collection

Design and manufacture attributed to John S. Bradstreet and Co. Armchair. From Glensheen, Duluth, Minn., 1908–9. Collection of Glensheen/University of Minnesota-Duluth, about 1908–9. Photograph by Gary Mortensen and Robert Fogt.

These doors belong to one of the only extant *jin-di-sugi* interiors in the Twin Cities. The room also features a magnificent carved cypress fireplace surround inlaid with iridescent glass, incorporating a similar design.

40. John Scott Bradstreet, designer and manufacturer
    American, Minneapolis, Minn.
    Chest of drawers, about 1910
    Oak with inlay
    Approx. 4' × 3'
    Stamped "JOHN S. BRADSTREET AND CO. MAKERS 1910"
    Anthony Scornavacco Collection

41. Design and manufacture attributed to John S. Bradstreet
    American, Minneapolis, Minn.
    Armchair, about 1908–9
    Oak with inlay
    33" × 32½" × 30"
    GLENSHEEN—University of Minnesota

42. Design and manufacture attributed to John S. Bradstreet
    American, Minneapolis, Minn.

Side chair, about 1908–9
Oak with inlay
36" × 16½" × 16½"
GLENSHEEN—University of Minnesota

Numbers 40–42 represent inlaid oak furniture manufactured by John S. Bradstreet and Co. beginning around 1909. The chairs are among the earliest pieces in this style, created for the third floor suite of rooms at Glensheen. These arts-and-crafts interiors were completed with fireplaces of Grueby tile and regularly accented with simple embroidered textiles. The chest of drawers is part of a suite of bedroom furniture for a Twin Cities home.

SELECTED LIST OF JOHN S. BRADSTREET AND COMPANY INTERIOR COMMISSIONS

In 1901, Bradstreet published a list of his most prominent commissions to date, including various Pillsburys, Clinton Morrison, William H. Dunwoody, and Edward C. Gale, all prominent businessmen who were instrumental in the cultural development of the Twin Cities. Many of these commissions have been linked with existing photographs

Design and manufacture attributed to John S. Bradstreet: Side chair, about 1908–9. Photograph by Gary Mortensen and Robert Fogt (Glensheen/University of Minnesota-Duluth).

in the collection of the Minnesota Historical Society (for further discussion of these commissions, see Michael Conforti, "Orientalism on the Upper Mississippi: The Work of John S. Bradstreet," *Minneapolis Institute of Arts Bulletin* 65, 1981–82 [1986], 2–35). There are two other sources for Bradstreet's commissions. One, from the later years of the company, is a set of ledger books from the design department of the firm, documenting the client for each sketch of furniture. The ledger books are in the collection of The Minneapolis Institute of Arts (see no. 33). The other is the *Western Architect*, an architecture journal which illustrated interiors produced by John S. Bradstreet and Company during their most prosperous period, from about 1904–10 (in many cases these represented second homes for many of the Minneapolis patrons he listed in 1901). The following list summarizes these commissions while including others firmly attributable to the company.

1. Charles J. Martin Residence
   Minneapolis, Minnesota, 1904
   William Channing Whitney, architect
   1300 Mount Curve Avenue
   Illustrations: *Western Architect*, November 1908: hall, dining room, porch, living room
   Present Status: Privately owned

Bradstreet outfitted the front hall of the Martin residence with exotic oriental furniture and rugs, accented with plants. His idiosyncratic furnishings extended to the columned "porch," which had potted trees and its own balcony. The living and dining rooms were filled with eighteenth- and nineteenth-century-style furniture.

2. Samuel J. Hewson Residence
   Minneapolis, Minnesota, 1905
   Kees and Colburn, architects
   2008 Pillsbury Ave. S.
   Illustrations: *Western Architect*, March 1908: living room, dining room, den
   Present Status: Privately owned

In the living room of the Hewson residence, Bradstreet introduced a tree design on the fireplace tiles and leaded glass cabinet doors, related to the Grueby tile fireplace from the Joseph Sellwood home, (no. 38). Willow trees are pictured with their branches illusionistically hanging down

Hall, Charles J. Martin residence, Minneapolis, 1904. Interior by John S. Bradstreet and Co. The Western Architect, November 1908.

Living room, Samuel J. Hewson residence, Minneapolis, 1905. Interior by John S. Bradstreet and Co., The Western Architect, *March 1908.*

from the top of the fireplace surround, as if one were looking at trees through a window.

3. Cavour Langdon Residence
   Minneapolis, Minnesota, 1905
   William Channing Whitney, architect
   2200 Pillsbury Ave. S.
   Illustrations: *Western Architect,* April 1907: reception hall, library, music room, dining room
   Present Status: razed

Cavour Langdon commissioned Wiliam Channing Whitney as architect and John S. Bradstreet as decorator for his home. Bradstreet used distinctive Asian furnishings, such as a massive carved settle and armchair, to define the large reception hall and library of the Langdon residence.

4. Edson S. Woodworth Residence
   Minneapolis, Minnesota, 1908
   William Kenyon, architect
   2222 Pillsbury Ave. S.
   Illustrations: *Western Architect,* December 1909: ex-

terior
Present Status: Privately owned

The small smoking room executed for the Woodworth home is one of the most complete Bradstreet interiors known to have survived in the Twin Cities. The fireplace surround is carved *jin-di-sugi* whose design consists of two interlocking stylized trees laid on a background of iridescent glass tile. This motif is very similar to that used in the Hewson fireplace surround executed three years earlier. The surround was featured in a John S. Bradstreet and Co. advertisement in *The Bellman* on 21 December 1907, where they proudly proclaimed their contribution to "the lounge of one of the beautiful homes in Minneapolis." The fireplace surround is complemented by the stained glass doors leading onto the porch, which also feature stylized trees in stained glass (no. 39). Bradstreet may have been responsible for the decoration of the house's other principle rooms, such as the living room, which includes lighting fixtures with Tiffany favrile glass shades identical to those used in the Prindle house living room.

Reception hall, Cavour Langdon residence, Minneapolis, 1905.
Interior by John S. Bradstreet and Co., The Western Architect,
April 1907.

5. John DeLaittre Residence
   Minneapolis, Minnesota, around 1908
   William Channing Whitney, architect
   122 W. Franklin
   Illustrations: *Western Architect*, December 1908: hall,
   living room
   Present Status: razed 1948

The hall of the DeLaittre residence was somewhat sparse
except for a few oriental furnishings and two massive urns.
The living room represents an eclectic mix of the antiques
and modern furnishings Bradstreet kept on hand. The combination of Chippendale, Victorian, arts and crafts, and
Asian furniture reflects the Craftshouse's interior.

6. William H. Dunwoody Residence
   Minneapolis, Minnesota, about 1908
   William Channing Whitney, architect
   104 Groveland Terrace
   Illustrations: *Western Architect*, November 1908: living
   room, billiard room
   Present Status: razed 1967–86

The Dunwoody residence was one of the largest and
most magnificent homes in Minneapolis. Bradstreet created
a living room which contained a fireplace surround with
pictorial tiles creating a foliate pattern similar to that in the
Hewson residence.
   Bradstreet and Co. also executed the interior of the billiard room and possibly other rooms in the house.

7. Chester Congdon Residence, "Glensheen"
   Duluth, Minnesota, 1908–9
   Clarence H. Johnson, architect
   3300 London Road, Duluth, Minnesota
   Illustrations: *Western Architect*, April 1910: hall, living
   room, smoking room, breakfast room, second floor
   bedrooms, third floor rooms
   Present Status: Owned by the University of Minnesota, Duluth

Although William French and Co. was employed by
Chester Congdon to execute the interiors at Glensheen,
Bradstreet was subcontracted to produce the most unique
rooms in the home, the sunroom and the ground floor

smoking room. The sunroom was described in *Western Architect*:

> This room is most unusual. The floor and lower walls are of Rookwood tile in shades of dull green. The panels of the upper walls and the rafters of the ceiling are of cypress, stained green to harmonize with the green of the tile and growing plants. The oak leaf motif has been used in the ornamental glass which is set in bronze, and the same design has been carried out in the green furniture. On the rear wall is a font, the tiles of which are full of color and still carrying out the oak leaf motif. This fountain and the open work grilles of faiance [sic] tile concealing radiators are features of special interest.

Many of the arts-and-crafts style furnishings in the third floor suite of rooms were also provided by Bradstreet. The inlaid oak mission-style furniture (no. 41, 42) are similar to the built-in bookcases in the L. S. Donaldson house and other extant pieces of Bradstreet work in oak (no. 40).

8. Minneapolis Club
    Minneapolis, Minnesota, about 1908
    Gordon, Tracy and Swartwout, New York City, architects, and William Channing Whitney, associate architect
    Illustrations: *Western Architect*, November 1908: exterior and interior
    Present Status: same function

Bradstreet was commissioned to produce furniture for the large dining room of the Minneapolis Club, which still reflects his original scheme. His use of rustic, medieval-style carved chairs for the dining room fits very appropriately with the Club's beamed ceilings and Tudor-style wall paneling.

9. Sarah Smith Langdon Residence
    Minneapolis, Minnesota, 1910
    William Channing Whitney, architect
    2201 Pillsbury Ave. S.
    Present Status: La Storta Jesuit community

Some original elements, such as the fireplaces, chandeliers, and some woodwork, remain in the Sarah Langdon residence. No known photographs exist to record the original interiors produced for the home.

10. L. S. Donaldson Residence
    Minneapolis, Minnesota, 1906, remodeled 1910
    Kees and Colburn, architects
    1712 Mt. Curve Avenue
    Present Status: Privately owned

No doubt as a result of his diverse and successful tearoom interiors for Donaldson's Department Store, Bradstreet was commissioned by L. S. Donaldson in 1910 to create a series of rooms in his home, including a colorful

Fireplace mantel, Edson S. Woodworth residence, Minneapolis, 1907. John S. Bradstreet and Co. advertisement, The Bellman, 21 December 1907.

sunroom in carved cypress wood, stained a light chalky green. A polychromed frieze of animals and foliage surmounted a series of carved light panels, each one containing a lotus flower in bloom (No. 35). The gilt and polychromed overmantel contained two exotic birds which combined with the panels must have produced a wonderful play of light and silhouette. Decorated at the same time as the sunroom, the library's oak woodwork was inlaid identically to Bradstreet's arts-and-crafts furnishings on the third floor at Glensheen.

11. Charles A. Pillsbury Residence
    Minneapolis, Minnesota, 1885–87, remodeled about 1900
    2200 Stevens Ave. S.
    Illustrations: Isaac Atwater, *History of Minneapolis, Minnesota* (Minneapolis, 1893): Exterior
    Present Status: razed, paneling of smoking room in private Minneapolis collection

*Living room, John DeLaittre residence, Minneapolis, about 1908.
Interior by John S. Bradstreet and Co., The Western Architect,
December 1908.*

*Living room, William H. Dunwoody residence, Minneapolis,
about 1908. Interior by John S. Bradstreet and Co., The Western
Architect, November 1908.*

Chester Congdon residence, "Glensheen," Duluth, Minn., 1908–9. Photograph courtesy of Gleensheen/University of Minnesota-Duluth.

Colonial Bedroom, "Glensheen," Duluth, Minn., 1908–9, The Western Architect, April 1910.

Dining room, Minneapolis Club, Minneapolis, 1908. Interior by John S. Bradstreet and Co., The Western Architect, *November 1908.*

Little is known about the original appearance of the smoking room Bradstreet provided for the Pillsbury home, which occupied what is now a corner of Fair Oaks Park, near The Minneapolis Institute of Arts. The cypress wainscoting from the room has carved elements of animals and plants, such as bats and dragons, interspersed throughout.

3
Robert Koehler and Painting in Minnesota, 1890–1915

Thomas O'Sullivan

ROBERT KOEHLER: FROM THE OLD WORLD TO THE NORTHWEST

A CHILD OF THE OLD WORLD YET A PRODUCT OF THE American west, an honored painter in Europe and a respected citizen of Minneapolis, Robert Koehler fused in his life and art those qualities of cosmopolite and good neighbor that Minnesotans sought to reconcile in their young state's art. Koehler came to Minneapolis to teach in its little wooden art-school building in 1893; when he died in 1917, he was honored as a builder of its marble-halled museum. For his personification of the period's art ideals, as well as his regional importance as a painter and a teacher, Koehler serves as a pivotal figure for the art of painting and the cultural history of Minnesota during the years 1890 to 1915.

Born in Hamburg in 1850 and brought to America in 1854, Koehler was the son of a seamstress and a mechanic whom he remembered fondly as a talented and inventive craftsman.[1] Ernst and Louise Koehler settled their family in Milwaukee, a city with a robust German community and a busy printing trade. As a young man Robert Koehler attended Milwaukee's German-English schools and studied art under Henry Vianden and Heinrich Roese. He worked in the lithographic shops of Milwaukee, Pittsburgh, and New York while continuing his art studies in night classes. By 1873 he embarked for Europe. His family heritage, his command of the language, and the attraction of an art center that was drawing other talented Americans, like Koehler's contemporaries and fellow midwesterners William Merritt Chase and Frank Duveneck, made Munich Koehler's destination. "I felt at once at home," he recalled years later, "for I could speak the language (better than the natives, too!) and beheld many things that were already familiar to me from pictures and descriptions, and I was in the home of art, where I had longed to be these many, many years!"[2] He stayed for two years, studying with Alexander Straehuber, Ludwig von Loefftz, and Franz von Defregger, respected painters of anecdotal realist works.

Koehler returned in 1875 to New York City. He studied at the National Academy of Design and the Art Students League, two institutions at the heart of American art training. By 1879 he was on his way to Germany again, to resume his residency in Munich where he would stay for more than a decade. There he taught private classes, established an art school of his own, and refined his art and his reputation for a passionate involvement in the artist life of the city. Koehler maintained a close connection with America throughout the period; his wife Marie, whom Koehler had met at an Uberlingen resort in 1886, reported eleven ocean crossings.[3] His Munich studio was a convivial gathering place for students and fellow painters among the substantial cadre of Americans there. Koehler was president of Munich's American Artists Club and arranged the representation of American painters in international exhibitions, just the kind of organizational roles that he would bring to the nurturing of art and artists in Minnesota.

Robert Koehler, about 1900. Minnesota Historical Society. Photograph by Sweet Studio, Minneapolis.

In this long Munich period Koehler, like many American and European contemporaries, painted portraits and genre scenes of peasant life. His firm grounding in the painterly realism synonymous with Munich is evident in Koehler's 1881 study of an old woman. The closely allied narrative strain in academic Munich circles is clearer still in *Holy-day Occupation*, Koehler's painting of an old man reading the Bible.

But while in Munich Koehler also turned his hand to less common and comforting subjects than the dignities of peasant life. In paintings with strong, even shocking overtones of radical action and labor strife, Koehler brought contemporary social issues into the exhibition hall. His works of the 1880s include paintings of laborers at work and at rest, exhibited with titles like *Her Only Support* and *Twenty Minutes for Refreshments.*[4] *The Socialist* is an 1885 portrayal of a man afire with the zeal of his cause. With

the smoldering eyes and wild hair of a biblical prophet, the portrait approaches melodrama, yet freezes its fist-pounding action successfully at a moment of high tension.

Koehler elaborated this knack for characterization and incipient drama into a history painting for his times in *The Strike*. Painted in 1886, this nine-foot-wide canvas was a rare depiction of labor strife. The scene is based on Koehler's recollections of a Pittsburgh incident a decade earlier, memories quickened by the artist's trip to London to observe the struggles of workers there.[5] *The Strike* telescopes elements of class and gender, age, costume, and architecture into one densely packed image of society at the boiling point. A crowd of some fifty figures, rough-clad workmen and their families, confront a top-hatted capitalist on the steps of his home. Incidents and actions abound, such as the factory owner's impassive reception of his workers, the

Robert Koehler. Studio Still Life, 1879. Gerald B. Johnson Collection. Photograph by Gary Mortensen and Robert Fogt.

bert Koehler. The Socialist, *etching after his 1885 painting.
otograph courtesy of the Minnesota Historical Society.*

A COMMUNITY OF ART INTERESTS

At the time of Koehler's arrival in 1893, Minnesota had a population of more than 1,300,000 people.[8] It was a promising time for local artists and their supporters, as individual efforts began to coalesce into fruitful associations of art interests statewide. Minnesotans considered orchestras,

pleadings of a young mother, and the variety of expressions with which the people in the crowd reveal fear, doubt, and resolve. One man reaches for a stone, signaling the violence soon to erupt.

Despite its provocative theme, *The Strike* was a success. Its timeliness was no doubt a factor in its popularity. The painting was reproduced in *Harper's Weekly* in the very week of May 1886 when a railroad workers' strike in Chicago led to a bloody encounter that left strikers and policemen dead in Haymarket Square.[6] *The Strike* received honorable mention at Paris's Exposition Universelle in 1889, praise from the New York *Times*, and an enthusiastic reception in Milwaukee, where a drive to purchase it for the city nevertheless failed to raise sufficient funds.[7] On his return to America in 1892, Koehler again took up residence in New York City. But just a few months later he accepted an invitation to teach in Minneapolis's art school. He headed west, to the city that would become his home for the rest of his life.

Etching by Robert Koehler, 1885. Invitation to the "Anglo-American Fancy Dress Ball" of the American Artists' Club, Munich. Photograph courtesy of the Minnesota Historical Society.

Robert Koehler. Holy-Day Occupation (A Holiday Occupation),
about 1885. The Pennsylvania Academy of the Fine Arts, Phila-
delphia. Gift of Joseph E. Temple.

Robert Koehler. Head of an Old Woman, 1881. *The Minneapolis*
Institute of Arts; Gift of Art School Students.

Robert Koehler. The Strike, 1886. *Photograph courtesy of the*
Deutsches Historisches Museum.

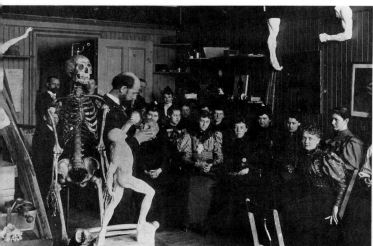

...nneapolis School of Art class, about 1895. Koehler is in the ...rway at left. Photograph courtesy of the Minnesota Histori-Society.

A school tour at The Minneapolis Institute of Arts, about 1915. Photograph courtesy of The Minneapolis Institute of Arts archives.

museums, and schools worthwhile in themselves, and also saw them as proof, to fellow citizens and to the world at large, that civilization flourished here. Koehler took a leading role in Minnesota's community of resident and visiting artists, collectors, students and exhibit-goers.[9]

Minneapolis had established its preeminence as the region's art capital with the founding of the Minneapolis Society of Fine Arts in 1883.[10] A private association of art-minded citizens, the Society raised public interest in art by exhibiting works borrowed from local collections. In 1886 the Society founded the Minneapolis School of Art, with New England painter Douglas Volk as its first director. The society also held exhibitions in the Minneapolis Public Library. When the society opened the doors of its museum, the Minneapolis Institute of Arts, in 1915, Koehler's *Head of an Old Woman* was the only painting by a local artist in the inaugural exhibition.[11]

Other Minnesota cities boasted artists and art institutions

of their own. St. Paul, Minneapolis's neighbor and the state's capital city, had resident painters who also gave art lessons as early as the 1850s.[12] Years later, their efforts showed little sign of making St. Paul the cultural mecca its boosters had predicted. But late in the century, the prospect was brighter. New York painter Charles Noel Flagg held art classes in the city in the mid-1880s. An art school opened under Burt Harwood's direction was incorporated in 1894 as the St. Paul School of Fine Arts. By 1908, it became part of the new St. Paul Institute of Arts and Sciences, an ambitious organization that offered art classes, exhibitions, and lectures among its diverse programs. New Ulm, a city in the Minnesota River valley emphatically German in character, had its own short-lived art school in 1892.[13] The citizens of Duluth, Minnesota's northern port city on Lake Superior, founded its Art Institute in 1907. Many smaller communities, including Faribault, Red Wing, Winona, and Moorhead, had groups that fostered interests in the arts through regular meetings in clubrooms, libraries, and members' homes.

Artists banded together in associations that combined business, pleasure, and common interests. Koehler is credited with founding the Artists League (sometimes known as the Art League) on his arrival in Minneapolis in 1893. This group held exhibitions that "would do credit to the art talent of any large city" in the estimation of one reporter.[14] The Chalk and Chisel Club was formed in 1895 and continued after 1899 under the name Arts and Crafts Society. The closely allied Handicraft Guild later offered classes in metalwork, design, jewelry, pottery, and art education, as well as a sales room, beginning in 1904. Other clubs and associations had more specialized characters or purpose: the Attic Club of commercial artists met in the evening to hone their fine-art skills, for example, while the Businessmen's Art Club afforded its members firsthand involvement in the arts.[15]

Students at the St. Paul Institute School of Art, about 1912. Photograph courtesy of the Minnesota Historical Society.

At the turn of the new century, a movement to establish a public, statewide art organization took shape. The movement began in discussions at a St. Paul study club. Art and History Club member Mrs. W. E. Thompson presented a plan for a state arts commission to the Federated Woman's Clubs of Minnesota in 1898. After five years of "persistency and effort," in the words of one clubwoman, the Minnesota legislature passed a bill to create the Minnesota State Art Society.[16] Its first president was Robert Koehler; its mission, "to advance the interests of the fine arts, to develop the influence of art in education, and to foster the introduction of art in manufactures."[17] The statement summarized Minnesotans' thinking about art as a worthy end in itself, an uplifting element in society, and an important factor in the state's productive sectors. In the dozen years after its founding as the second state-supported art organization in the nation, the Minnesota State Art Society sought to bring its program to citizens across the state through lectures, publications, and especially through exhibitions.

Exhibitions had long been the focal point of arts activities in Minnesota. As a social event, a showcase for an artist's most recent work, and an opportunity for sales, an exhibition offered artists and viewers alike the chance to involve themselves in their community's artistic expression. The work of local artists, craftspeople, and photographers had been featured prominently in regional fairs as early as the 1850s.[18] By the 1880s, exhibitions were becoming more

regular events. Loan exhibitions had helped citizens of Minneapolis and St. Paul launch their efforts to rouse public interest in the arts. Galleries like Stevens and Robertson in St. Paul and John Scott Bradstreet's Craftshouse in Minneapolis held occasional special showings of an artist's recent work, and artists opened their studios for formal showings that gained attention as social as well as artistic events.[19]

Years before collections of art were easily and regularly accessible to the average Minnesotan, touring exhibitions offered opportunities to view specialized collections. Exhibits of the works of local and nationally renowned artists were a notable feature of the Minneapolis Industrial Exposition, a commercial fair held in a commanding building at the side of St. Anthony Falls in the late 1880s and 90s. The 1886 exhibit, for example, presented a selection of works by artists of the Munich school, as well as forty-two paintings by the American landscapist Albert Bierstadt. The Exposition Building boasted a Hall of Antique Statuary with plaster casts of the Venus de Milo and the Elgin Marbles, displayed under the latest in electrical lighting.[20] A few years later the featured artist was native son Alexis Fournier, who showed more than two hundred oils and watercolors.[21] Other local artists were included among the exhibitors at the Industrial Expositions, and in 1900 the Minneapolis Society of Fine Arts began holding its own annual exhibitions of American artists' works.[22]

Alexis Jean Fournier. View of St. Anthony Falls, 1890. *The Minneapolis Industrial Exposition building is the many windowed building at right. First Bank Systems, Inc. Photograph by Gary Mortensen and Robert Fogt.*

The State Art Society extended the concept of an annual exhibition of local and national artists to a touring show that brought fine art to Minnesotans outside of the metropolitan center. State law charged the society with mounting its annual exhibitions in different Minnesota cities year by year. In 1904 a correspondent in St. Cloud noted the importance of such decentralization of artistic opportunity: "This pretty little city will hereafter be remembered as the scene of the first annual exhibition of the Minnesota State Art Society, an exhibition which inaugurated a novel and promising plan for educating the people of this state in art appreciation. There is no doubt in the minds of the board and of those interested in making the local arrangements that the plan of exhibitions in different parts of the state is destined to exert a splendid educational influence."[23] Held in St. Cloud's new Carnegie library building, the exhibition of more than three hundred items included work not only by Minnesotans like Alexis Fournier, Grace McKinstry, and Koehler himself, but nationally known American painters like J. Alden Weir and Edward Potthast, architectural exhibits, metalwork, pottery, jewelry, and textiles from across the state and the country.

The State Art Society's annual exhibition appeared in subsequent years in Northfield, Fergus Falls, Duluth, Rochester, and other cities, in addition to its annual Twin Cities showings. A headline in the *New Ulm Review* proclaimed "New Ulm the Mecca of Art Lovers During the Ten Days' Exhibit" in April 1910.[24] Brought to town by the women of the Current News Club, the exhibition featured more than six hundred items. More than seven thousand saw the customary variety of paintings, prints, handicrafts, architectural drawings, and students' artwork. A selection of Bohemian lace, made by New Ulm women, was on display in the Brown County Courthouse,[25] as a particularly well-publicized example of the State Art Society's effort to promote local crafts. Rev. J. A. Heinz of New Ulm delivered an address at the exhibition in which he "admonished the Bohemian mothers to cherish this art, as they do their mother tongue, and to teach their daughters this handicraft, not alone on account of artistic merits, but because it is highly profitable as well. . . . The state art society has promised to endeavor to obtain the best prices possible for the local product in the future."[26] The newspaper illustrated several works from the show, including Koehler's portrait of his son, paintings by Frank W. Benson of Boston and E. Irving Couse of New York, and (on the front page) an "artistic photograph" by Sweet Studio of Minneapolis, *Hunter and Dog.*[27]

By means ranging from individual artists' initiatives to an act of the legislature, a sense of artistic community thus developed in Minnesota. The story was hardly one of steady progress toward enlightenment, however. In her social history of the Minnesota State Fair, Karal Ann Marling points out that "No firsthand testimony survives to suggest whether the estimated 150,000 visitors who wandered through the galleries of the Minneapolis Exposition paid their dimes

Hall of Antique Statuary at the Minneapolis Industrial Exposition, about 1890. Minnesota Historical Society. Photograph by Jacoby.

Prospectus for the State Art Society's annual exhibit, 1915. Photograph courtesy of the Minnesota Historical Society.

out of real enthusiasm or bought tickets out of a nagging sense of duty—a vague feeling that cultural interests were expected out of respectable citizens, the notion that art was somehow good for a person."[28] The art exhibits at the fair were in fact discontinued in 1890, though they returned under the vigorous sponsorship of the State Art Society

The MINNESOTAN
The Individual   The Home
The Community

Volume 1   DECEMBER 1915   Number 5

Published Monthly by
Minnesota State Art Commission
Old Capitol, St. Paul.

The Minnesotan, *the monthly magazine of the Minnesota State Art Society. Photograph courtesy of the Minnesota Historical Society.*

after 1900. Similarly, artists rarely prospered by their work, even after the opportunities for Minnesotans to see and buy art increased dramatically. Volk had been lured to Minneapolis in 1886 with the promise of sales and portrait commissions to augment his modest teaching salary, but the lack of local patrons was a factor in his decision to return to the East.[29] William Watts Folwell, first president of the University of Minnesota and indefatigable supporter of the arts, often scolded his fellow citizens for their lukewarm support of working artists. In 1901, for example, Folwell expressed his vexation at the lack of purchases from Koehler's retrospective exhibition in a letter to the Minneapolis *Journal:* "This is not the Minneapolis way of doing things. A number of the minor works should have been purchased on the spot."[30]

But the general trend was an optimistic awareness of the presence and potential of Minnesota's art interests. City directories listed artists by the dozens; exhibitions and awards helped establish the acknowledged leaders on the local scene. Art was a newsworthy topic, with exhibit reviews, profiles of artists, and even a column called "Art Aids for Busy People" to put knowledge about such topics as Impressionism or Rubens's masterpieces at the fingertips of Minneapolis readers.[31] The State Art Society's magazine published a series called "Who's Who in Minnesota Art Annals." Illustrated profiles of painter Alexis Fournier, sculptor Paul Manship, etcher George Plowman, and others introduced readers to fellow citizens who had earned a measure of fame in the world of art beyond Minnesota's borders.[32] But with a network of artists, insitutions, and events in place at home, the desire to study and paint no longer necessarily drove artists out of the state. Men and women born and trained in Minnesota joined the ranks of professional artists. Contemporaries from other states and countries settled here as well, leavening local art circles with their presence and helping to tie Minnesota into a loose-knit network of artists. While individual origins, experiences, and allegiances varied, the examples of a handful of painters may serve to introduce the artists of turn-of-the-century Minnesota.

MINNESOTA'S PAINTERS

Robert Koehler took a respected place in Minnesota's art community on his arrival in 1893. He taught in the Minneapolis School of Art for a year before being named Volk's successor as director; in this capacity he would base his broad range of activities, from the studio to the lecture hall to the committee meeting. Koehler taught drawing from life and from the antique, as well as painting in the studio and out of doors. He also broadened the curriculum during his directorate to include decorative design and handicrafts, under the direction of Mary Moulton Cheney.[33] This philosophy of making art a useful and pervasive part of life also was a key aspect of the State Art Society under Koehler's founding presidency. Koehler carried out this program for democratization as a popular lecturer as well. He spoke around the state on such topics as "Art in Photography," "Modern Tendencies in Art," and "how to look at a picture from an artistic standpoint."[34]

Koehler was the founder and leading light of an important local group, the Artists League.[35] This association of some of the leading painters of the area exhibited at Bradstreet's gallery and at other venues. Newspaper coverage and the league's own catalogues, with illustrations and artist biographies, attest to how seriously its work was received. Over the years it became something of a social club, as "Mr. Koehler brought to this western American business city the finest ideals of artistic social intercourse."[36] A member recalled how artists gathered weekly to discuss and debate art, music, and world affairs under the aegis of Koehler's cosmopolitan acceptance of art forms and fashions: "it was perfectly delightful to hear and see him pointing out the possible hidden beauties and meanings of the modern extreme schools."

Robert Koehler's studio in Minneapolis. Minnesota Historical Society. Photograph by Sweet Studio, Minneapolis.

Koehler did make time to paint, among his varied teaching and civic duties. The painter of the notorious *Strike*—which was finally bought for the Minneapolis Society of Fine Arts in 1901—mellowed in subject and style in his Minneapolis years.[37] His later work production included portraits of scholars and family members; landscapes in a quiet, Inness-like mode; genre subjects and city scenes that mirrored Minnesota's comfortable bourgeoisie. *Rainy Evening on Hennepin Avenue* evokes twilight on Minneapolis's main thoroughfare, with passers-by (including the artist's wife, son, and dog) strolling rain-slick streets that reflect gas lights and streetcars. His portraits are often somber studies of bookish types, like librarian Etta Ross (Etta Ross Memorial Library, Faribault County Historical Society, Blue Earth, Minnesota) and Koehler's friend Frederick Wulling of the University of Minnesota (Weisman Art Museum, University of Minnesota, Minneapolis). Koehler's portrait of Alvina Roosen (Minneapolis Institute of Arts), livelier in its finery, lush bouquet, and sly smile, offers a hint of the painter's enjoyment of Minnesota society.

Koehler held two substantial exhibitions of his work, aside from his regular participation in Art League and other group undertakings. His first retrospective in 1900 featured *The Strike*, as well as a generous sampling of his European and American work.[38] Koehler's 1916 exhibition was some-

Robert Koehler. Landscape, *undated (about 1900). Private collection. Photograph by Gary Mortensen and Robert Fogt.*

Robert Koehler. Portrait of Etta C. Ross, *undated. Faribault County Historical Society, Blue Earth, Minn. Photograph by Photos by GT, Blue Earth, Minnesota.*

carries on through the gropings of my youth in an untoward environment that offered no advantages for the realization of the ideals and aspirations that germinated within me as a barefoot boy."[41] Born in rural Olmsted County, Brewer (1857–1949) availed himself of the scant training he could then find in Minnesota. An early lesson in drawing charcoal portraits from photographs afforded a source of income and a reinforcement of his wish to become a professional artist. He set up his own studio in St. Paul, and eventually studied with the tonalist landscape painter Dwight W. Tryon in New York. A long and peripatetic career took Brewer to Washington, D.C., Texas, Arkansas, and twenty other states to paint local dignitaries and socialites. He retained his ties to Minnesota, and built a substantial home for his large family in St. Paul.

Brewer's professed admiration for Tryon and George Inness suggests the vision that informed his own landscape work. He painted modest vistas of streams, hills and meadows, suffused with morning or evening light or washed in sunshine. "Who can overestimate the value of mood in landscape? The most thrilling and delightful effects we see are usually evanescent, fleeting," he wrote.[42] He was also

Robert Koehler. Portrait of a Woman (Alvina Roosen), *undated. The Minneapolis Institute of Arts; Gift of Coord F. Roosen.*

thing of a final summation, with thirty paintings ranging from a view of New York in 1879 to landscapes from a recent painting trip to Gloucester, Massachusetts.[39] Koehler had by that time been relieved of his directorial duties at the art school, and had been appointed docent, or lecturer, at the newly opened Minneapolis Institute of Arts. Still painting and still active in art circles, he had attained many of his goals for the cause of art. Koehler's official title was "director emeritus" of the school, but he was widely recognized—by students and by artists now established in their own careers—as "Papa Koehler."[40]

Other artists were prospering in the region as well. "My story begins with the hardships and hazards of pioneer life," recalled Nicholas R. Brewer in his autobiography, "and

Nicholas R. Brewer. The Story Book, *1914. Mr. and Mrs. James F. Brewer Collection. Photograph by Gary Mortensen and Robert Fogt.*

a diligent portraitist, whose best work in the genre parallels his philosophy of landscape. Brewer refrained from lavish settings and grand gestures in favor of portrayals which captured his sitters in a reflective mood; he employed mellow coloring and subtle brushstrokes, in preference to the dazzling displays of a Chase or a Sargent. A critic of 1918 summed up Brewer's achievement: "he is an honest, straightforward painter who convinces us of the veracity of his point of view and of his faithfulness to his subject."[43]

Grace McKinstry (1859–1936) traveled widely in America and Europe throughout her life, but maintained her home and studios in Faribault and Minneapolis. She studied in the Art Institute of Chicago, New York's Art Students League, and the Academie Julian in Paris and then refined her painting with further studies of the great painters of

Nicholas R. Brewer. Portrait of Clara Gerdtzen Blair (Mrs. Burr D. Blair), *1915. Winona County Historical Society, Inc. Photograph by Regan Photograph, Winona.*

Grace E. McKinstry. Portrait of Alexander Ramsey, 1903. Minnesota Historical Society Collections.

Spain and Holland.[44] "As a portrait painter Miss McKinstry will be known, in all probability, to succeeding generations, but her activities do not cease here. Unsparing of herself and untiring in her efforts to arouse interest in the history and achievement of painting, she has organized clubs with committees in each large town in the State for the purpose of awakening and maintaining a general interest in the study of art. She is sanguine herself and so carries an enthusiasm for it wherever she goes."[45] McKinstry was a founding officer of the State Art Society, and appeared on the boards and juries of art groups around Minnesota. She popularized art history for audiences statewide in talks such as "The Land of Rembrandt and Israels," "Famous Studios and Their Owners," and "Art Fads," earning the praise of the Red Wing *Republican* for "an unusual fund of anecdote and experience which she is not slow to make use of in her happy lecture."[46]

Many of Minnesota's notables—governors, educators, and religious leaders—sat for McKinstry. She painted them in a searching, often somber fashion that attests to her admiration of Dutch and Spanish masters, as clearly as her popular lectures bespoke her fascination with their lives and works. Her painting of Alexander Ramsey, for instance, portrays Minnesota's first territorial governor as a bewhis-

Alexis Jean Fournier in his Paris studio, about 1900. Photograph courtesy of the Minnesota Historical Society.

Homer Dodge Martin. View on the Seine *(also known as* Harp of the Winds)*, 1895. Metropolitan Museum of Art; Gift of Several Gentlemen.*

kered patriarch, at rest in the twilight of a public life.

Alexis Jean Fournier (1865–1948) was born in St. Paul and made his "western" origins a part of his professional persona as a worldly artist from humble frontier roots.[47] He began his career in a sign painter's shop, but soon took up stage-scene painting as well. Beginning around 1885, he painted a series of landscape studies of the environs of Minneapolis and St. Paul, as well as murals in Minneapolis houses. Fournier was among Douglas Volk's first pupils when Volk arrived to open Minneapolis's art school in 1886. Exhibiting his works regularly, Fournier gained the support of Minnesota patrons who collected a fund for his study in Paris at the Academie Julian. He returned to Europe several times, but remained a Minnesotan in spirit and in the press: "Minneapolis is my home," he told a reviewer in that city years after he had taken up residence in upstate New York.[48] Before his death in 1948, Fournier also lived in southern Indiana, where his work took on a more vibrant cast in the afterglow of Impressionism. Whatever his address, Fournier was a visible presence in the Minnesota art scene. His paintings were regularly included

in Minnesota exhibitions, where they often hung with the invited selection of work by leading Americans, enhancing his reputation as local painter made good in the world of art.

In his rambles about the French countryside, Fournier worked on his homage to the painters he held in highest esteem: a series of twenty canvases collectively known as *The Homes and Haunts of the Barbizon Masters.*[49] These views of the houses and studios of Millet, Daubigny, Jacque and others—the shrines of Fournier's aristic pilgrimage— carried the open-air, Barbizon feel of Fournier's early Minnesota landscapes to a conceptual and artistic culmination of his generation's love for the "Men of 1830." Fournier exhibited the "Homes and Haunts" in Minneapolis, St. Paul, and Duluth in 1911, as well as in New York, Chicago, and other cities.[50]

Knute Heldner (1877–1952) left his boyhood home in Sweden for adventures which typify the vagaries and the romance of the immigrant artist's story, though contradictory versions of the story are recorded in different sources.[51] He may have served in his native country's navy, probably

Elsa Laubach Jemne. The Red-Haired Girl, 1916. *Adam Granger Collection. Photograph by Gary Mortensen and Robert Fogt.*

washed dishes in Chicago and herded sheep in Wyoming, and apparently worked in Minnesota's mines and logging camps before settling in Duluth as a cobbler, as well as a determined painter. "Every morning at sunrise would find him on the Lake Shore or in the hills about Duluth, where he would paint at least one sketch before going to his cobbler's bench," reads the brochure for a one-man exhibition. "Every evening found him in the open where he painted, until darkness changed the colors on his pallette [sic], eating, if his last money had not been spent for a tube of paint."[52]

Heldner took classes in the Minneapolis School of Art, the Art Students League, and the Art Institute of Chicago, and gained public recognition and awards for his paintings by 1915. His early landscapes have the soft-edged forms and gentle colors of the Impressionist-influenced landscape style popular among American painters and their audiences. Later work showed a harsher, even expressionistic side of Heldner, and subjects that reflected a concern for labor like his erstwhile teacher Koehler.

Elsa Laubach Jemne (1888–1974) belongs to a younger generation, for while she was an important Midwestern muralist during the Depression, she earned wide acclaim for her easel paintings. Born in St. Paul, Jemne attended the St. Paul School of Art and the Pennsylvania Academy of Fine Art.[53] Two scholarships for travel in Europe allowed Jemne to study mural techniques, which she later utilized for commissions in the Stearns County Courthouse, St.

Cloud; the Ely, Minnesota, post office; the Minneapolis Armory; and in other states.[54] Jemne's paintings reflect the strong sense of structure and design that suited her for larger public works. Her early exhibitions featured figure compositions which a fellow artist recognized as "successful portraits, lovely in color and having an artistic raison d'etre quite apart from their value as portraits."[55] *The Red-Haired Girl,* for instance, plays the likeness of a stylish young woman against a framed Holbein portrait and an Oriental jar, to tease the viewer with objects and influences.

Whether Minnesota-born or immigrants to the state, these painters and many others called the state home for substantial parts of their careers. But Minnesota was also the last resting place for one of America's greatest nineteenth-century landscapists, Homer Dodge Martin, and an early stop on the road to fame for the American modernist Max Weber. Martin (1836–1897) lived in Minnesota for the final years of his life, arriving in 1893 to join his wife in St. Paul.[56] Battling poor health and failing eyesight, Martin completed his last paintings here, works that went unnoticed by Minnesota. Critic Frank Jewett Mather found some advantage in this anonymity: "Isolated by their pride and poverty amid a prosperous and hospitable community, it was the first time in more than thirty years that the Martins had not been sought by the best people. And yet the lack of congenial associations meant concentration, which with heroic abstinence from his beloved beer, made the St. Paul years extraordinarily productive."[57] Martin's widow recounted that he worked at a farm outside St. Paul to complete canvases on which he had earlier sketched landscape compositions. Their titles, such as *Normandy Farm, The Adirondacks,* and his best-known work, a view on the Seine known as *Harp of the Winds,* suggest how Martin found a natural setting without undue interruptions

Knute Heldner. Third Avenue Bridge #1, 1914. *First Bank Systems, Inc. Photograph by Albert Asch-AJA Photo, West Bend, Wisc.*

more conducive to his painting than being in the presence of his motif.[58] These last works have a breadth of composition, softness of color, and richness of surface that mark the culmination of Martin's work from its Luminist origins.

Max Weber (1881–1961), on the other hand, was just beginning his career when he came to Duluth in 1903. He taught in the Art and Manual Training Department of the State Normal School, the predecessor of today's University of Minnesota, Duluth.[59] Weber entered his work in the Minnesota State Fair's annual exhibition in 1904. "I shall never forget how thrilled I was with the announcement that my two pictures were accepted for exhibition," he recalled forty years later. "After the opening of this exhibition I received a most complimentary and encouraging letter from Mr. Kohler [sic] who was, I believe, the director of the Art Society of Minneapolis. His enthusiasm and advice gave me the courage to plan and embark on the long and arduous road of art."[60] Weber's Duluth earnings enabled him to follow that road to Paris. There he engaged academic tradition at the Academie Julian, and more importantly for his own and American art, pursued his more progressive bent with Matisse and other makers of modern art.

FINDING A PLACE IN THE ART WORLD

Whatever their ties to Minnesota, these painters and their colleagues in the state were also citizens of the wider world of art. Some were as active in developing schools and organizations as they were in making paintings. Many participated in exhibitions across the nation. The local press reported their successes in New York and elsewhere outside the region. But Minnesota's artists faced an ambivalent reception at home. Grace McKinstry, for example, was described in 1907 as "an artist whose growing fame is placing her in the front rank of American painters." She nonetheless risked pursuing her career in her home town: "With her eyes open to its isolation from even our national art centers, knowing full well how suicidal it might prove to inspiration, loyalty to home and family brought her west to Minnesota and into Faribault, there to establish her workshop."[61] Robert Koehler's friends recalled his "sacrifice": "If he had stayed in New York, he undoubtedly would have made money, but he kept the school here alive, established it on a sound basis, and seemed happy to do missionary work in art."[62]

Although the state's artists were often the pride of their communities, their work was overshadowed by the paintings of contemporaries from other parts of the country, as measured by showings in Minnesota museums, purchases for Minnesota collections, and commissions for Minnesota buildings. The case of the state capitol in St. Paul, "the showplace of the state, where every citizen may go without let or hinder,"[63] illustrates the dilemma for local artists. The building was the work of St. Paul architect Cass Gilbert. The capitol's sumptuous interior featured murals of

Grace McKinstry's studio in Faribault, Minn., 1907. Photograph from the Bellman, *16 February 1907.*

"subjects that would appropriately represent the growth and progress of the Northwest in the direction of manufacturers, commerce and agriculture from pioneer days to the present time."[64] Gilbert and the citizen commissioners of the capitol project chose for this task some of the nation's most prestigious muralists: Edward E. Simmons, Kenyon Cox, Edwin H. Blashfield, and others. These painters conceived and executed their grand allegories in New York or Paris studios and shipped their canvases to St. Paul for installation. Although experienced muralists were present

Gallery of the Minneapolis Society of Fine Arts at the Minneapolis Public Library, 1908. The largest painting behind the women is Koehler's The Strike. *Photograph courtesy of the Minnesota Historical Society.*

Rotunda of the Minnesota State Capitol, St. Paul, with two panels of Edward E. Simmons's four-panel mural, The Civilization of the Northwest. *Minnesota Historical Society. Photograph by C. P. Gibson, about 1920.*

in Minnesota early in the century, their work was typically commissioned for homes and businesses. None received commissions for the capitol project. Fournier, as noted above, painted decorative murals in Minneapolis homes; Lauros Phoenix, who taught a class in mural decoration at the St. Paul Institute School of Art, received commissions from the city's hotels and restaurants. David Tice Workman painted murals in the schools of Minnesota's iron range communities.[65] Lee Woodward Ziegler, director of the St. Paul Institute School, found mural work only on his return to the East.[66]

One notable aspect of the rise of art interests in Minnesota was the involvement and prominence of women artists and organizers. Their roles ranged from behind-the-scenes maneuvering to the appointment to visible public positions. One participant in the movement to secure an art museum for Minneapolis recalled how women set the stage for a public campaign and then stepped aside in favor of their male counterparts: "It was still a men's world in 1909, so all the ladies resigned [from the Board of Directors] gracefully and left the new board quite unencumbered."[67] The State Art Society, too, was the brainchild of Minnesota's women's clubs, and a number of women including Mary Moulton Cheney, McKinstry, Carleton College Dean Margaret Evans, and suffrage leader Clara Ueland served as officers.

As individual practitioners, or "art workers" in the parlance of the day, women frequently constituted a majority of the art students and exhibitors listed in catalogues and articles. They were also well represented among the teachers and organizers of art institutions around the state. Reporting on *Vocations Open to College Women* in 1913, the director of the State Art Society and Handicrafts Guild stated, "There is hardly a field at the present time more full of opportunities for women than that of art, nor one in which women can find more satisfactory renumeration

Gertrude Barnes. Still Life with Purple Bowl, *1915. Minnesota Historical Society Collections.*

Ada Wolfe. Sails on Lake Minnetonka, *1914. Minnesota Historical Society Collections.*

Magnus Norstad. City on a Hill, 1917. *Minnesota Historical Society Collections.*

for the efforts expended." The choices included teaching, commercial art, design for manufacturing, and "plying the crafts of jewelry, pottery, weaving, lacemaking, etc., as specialized industries."[68]

The Minnesota art community—its collectors and art-going public—balanced an appreciation for its own potential and accomplishments against a self-consciousness of its distance from established cultural centers. The surest index of the Minnesotans' successes, it seemed, was the approval of out-of-town commentators, and especially Eastern critics. When local talent took up local subject matter, a more confident demeanor emerged. Besides portraits and still lifes, Minnesota's artists painted farms, towns, city streets, and industrial sites, as well as the people who lived and worked in them. Ada Wolfe insisted that "One does not have to go to Provincetown or Marblehead or any of those artists' colonies on the Atlantic coast to get sketching material; everything one needs is near by."[69] Her landscapes, painted along the Mississippi, on the shores of Lake Superior, and around the Twin Cities, provided ample support for her point of view. Winter scenery was another natural resource that Minnesota offered its artists. Magnus Norstad's much-praised view of St. Paul, *City on a Hill,* was considered a painting that "should appeal to the hearts of all natives of this rugged Northwest, since it portrays the severity of its icy winter climate, only in a mysteriously soft and benignant aspect."[70] Nathaniel Pousette-Dart of

Elizabeth Chant. River Scene, 1899. *Sibley House Association of the Minnesota Society, Daughters of the American Revolution; Gift of Mrs. Glenn Wyer, Monument Chapter, D. A. R. Photograph by Gary Mortensen and Robert Fogt.*

St. Paul also was lionized as a painter of snow scenes.[71] This kind of affection for "paintable places," as Wolfe called them, established the local scene as a primary theme years before the term "regionalism" took on the air of a movement.[72]

"THE SEED HAS BEEN SOWN"

The years 1890 to 1914 were not only a key formative time for art in Minnesota, but across the country as well. Among the cities that expressed their support for the arts by founding museums, schools, and associations were Cleveland, Detroit, Pittsburgh, St. Louis, and San Francisco.[73] These and many smaller communities became nodes in an art network that can be traced in the travels of artists and exhibits around the country. For example, Minneapolis painter Elizabeth Chant founded an art colony in North Carolina, while her teacher Burt Harwood settled in New Mexico. Iowa-born Edwin Dawes left Minneapolis, where he established his career, for Nevada and California. Heldner divided his time between Duluth and New Orleans. Alexander Grinager, a popular exhibitor with Minneapolis's Artists League, moved to New York, as did Twin Cities' painter-teachers Volk and Pousette-Dart. An influx of painters also came to Minnesota, as young artists starting out (like Weber) or as veterans seeking commissions or positions (like Gustav Goetsch, etcher, painter, and teacher at the Minneapolis School of Art). Brewer, Fournier, and Frances Greenman were on the move frequently, while maintaining a presence in Minnesota through exhibits and news articles.

A parallel commerce in ideas, manifest in paintings, exhibitions, and writings, also circulated through this nationwide network. Minnesotans could see the works of major European and American painters in annual exhibitions and in museum shows. In reviews and studio reports, commentators remarked on how local painters interpreted styles and motifs. They recognized similarity between the *plein-air* painting of the Barbizon school and the early work of Fournier and Larpenteur, for instance. Whistler's influence was observed in the paintings of artists like David Ericson and Ada Wolfe. Impressionism, which had an impact on the palette and brushwork of many Minnesota painters, found a curiously ambivalent reception. Although the works of the French Impressionists and their legions of followers were seen at first hand in the state—most notably in a 1908 exhibit of 98 paintings, circulated by the New York branch of the Durand-Ruel gallery— the style seemed acceptable only if linked with more traditional values.[74] An anonymous reviewer of Nathaniel Pousette-Dart's 1911 exhibit spelled this out: "Wholly and progressively modern it is, and impressionistic to a degree, yet at bottom it is sane and conservative. For its modernity rests on the safe foundation of a thorough academic training, and is of a kind that comes through study and appreciation of the old masters, rather than through blind worship of the new ones."[75]

Alexander Grinager. Venice (Venetian Idyll), *undated (about 1905). Colin Taylor, New York. Photograph by Color Group, Hawthorne, New York.*

"Modernity" soon became a topic of discussion in Minnesota, with cubism serving as its bugbear in the press. New York's International Exhibition of Modern Art, the immense 1913 assembly of European and American art better known as the Armory Show, pushed new modes of painting and sculpture into the news nationwide. The Winona, Minnesota *Independent* addressed modern art on its editorial page: "Some painters calling themselves 'Cubists' or 'Futurists', or whatever, have precipitated a crazy art."[76] When a portion of the Armory Show was hung at the Art Institute of Chicago, a Minneapolis journalist printed a vitriolic review of "that silly sensation of the hour." "Since early childhood I had reverenced pictorial art," he wrote, "and in a shocking instant this life-long reverence turned to disgust—not so much disgust for the obsessed and misguided creators of this wild riot of foolishness as for the sheep-like quality in humanity which causes it so invariably to be led astray by the crazy theories of decadent or perverted zealots."[77]

David Ericson. Morning of Life, 1907. *Tweed Museum of Art, University of Minnesota, Duluth; Gift of Mrs. George P. Tweed.*

Such diatribes as this led Robert Koehler to view the Chicago exhibition and share his response in illustrated lectures. "It was not an enjoyable task from the beginning," he wrote of the trip, "indeed at the end of the first two hours I felt dizzy and fled to one of the galleries of old masters where the rich deep harmonies of color soothed my over-wrought nerves, which had been set on edge by the wild tumult of loud and discordant notes and unintelligible forms among which I had been moving." He extended the musical analogy in urging his audiences to ponder the moderns' exploration of subjectivity through new forms. Koehler praised Cezanne, Van Gogh, and Gauguin, "the masters, who have not exhausted the possibilities of their theories by any means." He found the work of Matisse "most fascinating by its very audacity, and I must confess to being attracted to it again and again, while I could pass by more pleasing canvases. It was not the charm of the serpent that exerted this influence, but the desire to get at the root of things, to solve the strange riddle. In this I did not succeed and Matisse still remains an enigma to me."[78] Koehler urged tolerance and fairness upon his listeners in viewing the new artists, and predicted: "At all events, we shall hear more of them soon." A year later, Koehler brought a selection of modern works to the Minneapolis

Society of Fine Arts' galleries in the public library with the assistance of Armory Show organizers Arthur B. Davies and Walter Pach. He reported afterward to Pach, "I feel the seed has been sown and it will depend on proper nourishment to make this wider appreciation of art a living thing."[79]

Robert Koehler held his final exhibition in 1916; six months later he died of a heart attack on a Minneapolis streetcar. One report had him en route to an art lecture. By another account, he was on his way downtown to oversee the lighting of an Artists League exhibition.[80] In either case, it is typical and significant that his final errand was in service to art in his adopted community. Tributes in Minnesota newspapers stressed this devotion. "It is safe to say there is not a man to whom Minneapolis is more indebted for the cultivation of its arts," said Minneapolis Institute of Arts director Joseph Breck.[81] The Minneapolis *Journal* published an account of Koehler's life and noted, "He loved the art school, and his ambitions for it were greater than any he held for himself."[82]

Koehler's memory was still honored a decade later, when a memorial plaque was unveiled in the halls of the Minneapolis School of Art.[83] But with the passing of the years and of generations of students and collectors, his reputation

Edwin M. Dawes. Channel to the Mills, 1913. *The Minneapolis Institute of Arts; given anonymously.*

faded. His *Rainy Evening on Hennepin Avenue* remained a popular and much reproduced work, favored for its graceful evocation of Minneapolis's gaslight era. But a reporter examining the painting in 1954 received this dismissive response to her query about the artist: "[Koehler] has other works, but he was primarily a teacher. He studied in Munich, and this picture suggests the Munich school."[84] His masterwork fared even worse. *The Strike* was relegated to storage and later deaccessioned by the Minneapolis Institute of Arts. In 1971, author and labor historian Lee Baxandall's purchase of the picture galvanized local interest in the artist and his work, but a local museum official dismissed it as "an interesting curiosity."[85]

Baxandall hung *The Strike* in the headquarters of a New York City labor union and in 1975 lent it to the Whitney Museum of American Art's *The Painter's America* exhibit.[86] There it once more drew attention for its subject and treatment: "A harsh, brutal painting bullied its way into the Whitney Museum's 19th Century 'Painter's America' exhibition recently. Amid the genteel genre works depicting 'Afternoon Tea' and 'Country Wedding', it shoves for attention and gets it," reported New York's *Village Voice*.[87] A century after its first exhibition successes, *The Strike* has today returned to a museum collection—and to Germany—with some fanfare. The Deutsches Historisches Museum in Berlin made Koehler's painting the focal point of its 1992 exhibition, *Streik: Realitat und Mythos*, with a catalogue tracing the labor theme in the history, art, and material culture of Koehler's day.[88]

Koehler was not the only long-overlooked American artist to be "rediscovered" in the 1970s. Spurred in part by a broad-based interest in American history and culture during the 1976 Bicentennial, museums in many states and cities reappraised their artists in exhibitions and publications. That interest has continued, with scholarly studies of individual artists and locales, as well as landmark works like William H. Gerdts's *Art Across America: Two Centuries of Regional Painting, 1710–1920*.[89] A century after Koehler's arrival in Minneapolis, his works and those of his contemporaries find the market and audience that often eluded them in their lifetime. Today Robert Koehler appears as a kind of Janus-figure for the arts of his adopted state. He faced back to Europe in his own art, and personified the solid traditions of the art of painting. At the same time, he looked ahead to the styles and theories of younger artists and movements. The ideals and even some of the associations to which he subscribed are still alive today, while the "local artist" classification remains a complex issue for many critics and collectors. Koehler's advocacy of an open-minded, all-embracing approach to art as a vital part of a lively community, however, offers a lesson and an example of his continuing relevance in our time.

Nathaniel Pousette-Dart. Downtown, *about 1915. Minnesota Historical Society Collections; Gift of John E. Larkin Jr., M.D.*

NOTES

1. Robert Koehler's life is treated in depth in Robert and Marie Koehler, "History of the Koehler Family" ed. and trans. Lee Baxandall, 1898/1927, Minnesota Historical Society; Harriet S. Flagg, "Robert Koehler," *Minneapolis Journal*, 29 April 1917 (copy in Robert Koehler file, Minneapolis History Collection, Minneapolis Public Library and Information Center); Roy A. Boe, "The Development of Art Consciousness in Minneapolis and the Problem of the Indigenous Artist," Master's thesis (University of Minnesota, 1947); and Peter C. Merrill, "Robert Koehler: German-American Artist in Minneapolis," *Hennepin County History* 47, no. 3 (Summer 1988): 20–27.

2. Koehler, "Chapters from a Student's Life," *Minneapolis Society of Fine Arts Bulletin* 1, no. 11 (September 1906): 4.

3. "History of the Koehler Family," 22.

4. "Twenty Minutes for Refreshments" is illustrated in Charlotte

Whitcomb, "Robert Koehler: Painter, and Director of the Minneapolis School of Fine Arts" (unidentified newspaper clipping, Robert Koehler file, Minneapolis History Collection, Minneapolis Public Library and Information Center).

5. Charlotte Whitcomb, "Buy Koehler's Masterpiece," *Minneapolis Journal*, 23 March 1901, p. 10.

6. *Harper's Weekly* 30, no. 1532 (1 May 1886): 280–81.

7. Merrill, "Robert Koehler: German-American Artist in Minneapolis," 23; "History of the Koehler Family," 24; Robert Koehler papers, Minnesota Historical Society, includes correspondence pertaining to the Milwaukee purchase efforts.

8. Theodore C. Blegen, *Minnesota: A History of the State*, 2d ed. (Minneapolis: University of Minnesota Press, 1975), 340.

9. Donald R. Torbert, "A Century of Art and Architecture in Minnesota," in A *History of the Arts in Minnesota*, William Van O'Connor, ed. (Minneapolis: University of Minnesota Press, 1958), 28–29.

10. Jeffrey A. Hess, *Their Splendid Legacy: The First 100 Years of the Minneapolis Society of Fine Arts* (Minneapolis: Minneapolis Society of Fine Arts, 1985), 5.

11. *Catalogue of the Inaugural Exhibition* (Minneapolis: Minneapolis Institute of Arts, 1915), 42.

12. Torbert, "Century of Art and Architecture," 13; Isaac O. Peterson, "Art in St. Paul as Recorded in the Contemporary Newspapers," Master's thesis (University of Minnesota, 1942), 12, 34.

13. Coen, *Painting and Sculpture*, 74.

14. "Have Done Good Work," *Minneapolis Journal*, 12 May 1897.

15. "Attic Club's Exhibition of Sketches and Caricatures Shows Talent of Members," *Minneapolis Journal*, 21 May 1911; "Business Men Get Hammerlock on Old Man Art," *Minneapolis Journal*, 4 March 1923.

16. Mrs. J. H. Palmer, "The Women's Clubs of Minnesota and the State Art Society," *Minnesota State Art Society* 1, no. 1 (February 1923): 3.

17. *Constitution and Bylaws of the Minnesota State Art Society* (St. Paul: Minnesota State Art Society [?], 1903) 2, 3; "History of the Minnesota State Art Society," undated typescript, manuscript collection P210, Minnesota Historical Society; "State Art Society," *Minneapolis Journal*, 25 April 1903.

18. Torbert, "Century of Art," 12.

19. See, for example, "In the Studio," *Minneapolis Journal*, 16 December 1899, p. 10; Martha Scott Anderson, "Minneapolis Artists Lose a Landmark," *Minneapolis Journal*, 12 December 1903, p. 4.

20. *Complete Catalogue of the Art Department of the First Minneapolis Industrial Exposition* (Minneapolis: Minneapolis Industrial Exposition, 1886), 7–31, 32–34.

21. *Art Catalogue '92* (Minneapolis: Minneapolis Industrial Exposition, 1892), 5–11.

22. Boe, "Development of Art Consciousness," 33–38.

23. "Art Exhibition Opens at St. Cloud," *Minneapolis Journal*, 5 April 1904, p. 5.

24. *New Ulm Review*, 13 April 1910, p. 1.

25. Ibid., 27 April 1910, p. 1.

26. *Brown County Journal*, 23 April 1910, p. 1.

27. *New Ulm Review*, 13 April 1910, pp. 1, 4; *Brown County Journal*, 16 April 1910, p. 2.

28. Karal Ann Marling, *Blue Ribbon: A Social and Pictorial History of the Minnesota State Fair* (St. Paul: Minnesota Historical Society Press, 1990), 230.

29. Hess, *Their Splendid Legacy*, 13; Coen, *Painting and Sculpture*, 108.

30. Quoted in Boe, "Development of Art Consciousness", 41.

31. Martha C. Wells, "Art Aids for Busy People," *Minneapolis Journal*, 18 February 1900; Wells, "On Impressionist Art," *Minneapolis Journal*, 22 April 1908, p. 12.

32. For Fournier, see "Who is Who in Minnesota Art Annals," *The Minnesotan* 1, no. 6 (January 1916): 15–18; Manship, "Who is Who in Minnesota Art Annals," *The Minnesotan* 1, no. 1 (July 1915): 14–17; Plowman, "Who is Who in Minnesota Art Annals," *The Minnesotan* 1, no. 2 (August 1915): 15–17.

33. Hess, *Their Splendid Legacy*, 14.

34. *Minneapolis Society of Fine Arts Bulletin* 1, no. 7 (March 1906); *Minneapolis Institute of Arts Bulletin* 3, no. 3 (March 1914); *Brown County Journal*, 16 April 1910, p. 8.

35. Boe, "Development of Art Consciousness", 30–31.

36. H. G., "Robert Koehler and the Art League," n.d., unpaged pamphlet. Inscriptions in a copy in the Minnesota Historical Society identify the author as Harlow Gale.

37. Torbert, "A Century of Art and Architecture," 29.

38. "A Retrospective Exhibition of Robert Koehler's Art," *Minneapolis Journal*, 10 November 1900, sec. 2, p. 1; exhibition catalogue, "Exhibition and Sale of Paintings, Drawings and Etchings: The Works of Robert Koehler," J. S. Bradstreet and Co. [Minneapolis], 12 to 18 November 1900.

39. Gladys M. Hamblin, "Oil Paintings by Robert Koehler on View at Handicraft [sic]," *Minneapolis Journal*, 22 October 1916; exhibition catalogue, "Exhibition of Recent Paintings by Robert Koehler," Edmund D. Brooks (Minneapolis), 16 to 31 October 1916.

40. "Koehler Did Most for Art in City, Former Pupil Says," *Minneapolia Journal*, 29 April 1917, p. 5.

41. Nicholas R. Brewer, *Trails of a Paintbrush* (Boston: Christopher Publishing House, 1938), 13–14.

42. Ibid., 297.

43. Harvey B. Fuller, "Local Artist Wins Success: N. R. Brewer is a Minnesota Product," *St. Paul Pioneer Press*, 10 March 1918.

44. "Rites for Miss Grace McKinstry to be Saturday," *Faribault Journal*, 3 December 1936, p. 1; Minnesota Biographies Project files, Minnesota Historical Society.

45. Evangeline Newhall, "A Western Studio," *The Bellman*, 16 February 1907, p. 185.

46. Quoted in "Art Talks by Miss McKinstry," n.d., unpaged pamphlet, Minnesota Historical Society.

47. Florence Lehmann, "Minnesota Artist to Return with World Famed Painting," *Minneapolis Journal*, 30 March 1930, sec. 2, p. 2; "Alexis Jean Fournier, Noted Artist, Dies", *St. Paul Pioneer Press*, 21 January 1948, p. 5; Rena Neumann Coen, *In the Mainstream: The Art of Alexis Jean Fournier* (St. Cloud, Minn.: North Star Press, 1985), 5–6.

48. "The Tribune Girl," "'Minneapolis is My Home', Said Alexis Jean Fournier," undated newspaper clipping, Alexis J. Fournier Papers, Minnesota Historical Society.

49. Coen, *In the Mainstream*, 63–76.

50. "Fournier Series for Art Museum," *Minneapolis Journal*, 14 November 1911; Coen, *In the Mainstream*, 71.

51. Daniel N. Wiener, "Heldner Painted for Art, Not Money," *Duluth News-Tribune*, 11 January 1981, 1E–4E; Mary T. Swanson, *The Divided Heart: Scandinavian Immigrant Artists, 1850–1950* (Minneapolis: University Gallery, University of Minnesota, 1982), 22.

52. "The Art of Knute Heldner," undated pamphlet, 12.

53. Minnesota Biographies Project files, Minnesota Historical Society; *Private Collectors and Art by Women* (Minneapolis: Women's Art Registry of Minnesota, 1984), 21–22.

54. Nancy A. Johnson, *Accomplishments: Minnesota Art Projects in the Depression Years* (Duluth: Tweed Museum of Art, 1976), 23.

55. Alice E. Hugy, "Elsa Laubach Jemne—An Appreciation," *Minnesota State Art Society* 2, no. 1 (August 1922): 2.

56. Elizabeth Gilbert Martin, *Homer Martin: A Reminiscence* (New York: William Macbeth, 1904), 50; "Genius in St. Paul was Unrecognized," *St. Paul Pioneer Press*, 8 May 1909, p. 3.

57. Frank Jewett Mather, Jr., *Homer Martin: A Poet in Landscape* (New York: Privately printed, 1912), 57–58.

58. Martin, *Homer Martin*, 50.

59. Lloyd Goodrich, "Max Weber Retrospective Exhibition" (New York: Whitney Museum of American Art, 1949), 8.

60. Max Weber, "A Letter from Weber," *Walker Art Center Activities* 2, no. 2 (November 1946): 2.

61. Newhall, "A Western Studio," 184.

62. "Friends Here Honor Robert Koehler by Art School Tablet," *Minneapolis Tribune*, 2 January 1927.

63. "Eminent Artists to Work on Minnesota's New Capitol," *Minneapolis Journal*, 19 December 1903, p. 9.

64. Julie C. Gauthier, *The Minnesota State Capitol: Official Guide and History* (St. Paul, 1907), 16; Neil B. Thompson, *Minnesota's State Capitol: The Art and Politics of a Public Building* (St. Paul: Minnesota Historical Society Press, 1974), 65–72.

65. "Rip Van Winkle Resumes Sleep, Prohibition Makes Him 'Retired,'" *St. Paul Daily News*, 15 November 1925, p. 9; "Epic of Iron Age is Made into Mural Painting for Inspiration of School Children of Hibbing," *St. Paul Pioneer Press*, 3 August 1913 (copy in Minnesota artists files, St. Paul Public Library).

66. Unidentified newspaper article, St. Paul artists file, St. Paul Public Library.

67. Florence Welles Carpenter, "How the Art Institute Was Built 1883–1915," undated typescript, 4, manuscript collection FN583/C295 (Minnesota Historical Society).

68. Maurice Irwin Flagg, "Vocational Art," in *Vocations Open to Women, Bulletin of the University of Minnesota*, extra ser. 1 (1913): 34–35.

69. Elizabeth McLeod Jones, "A Minneapolis Artist and Her Art," *Minneapolis Tribune*, 9 December 1917.

70. "A Friendly Critic" [Alice E. Hugy?], "Home Artists Discouraged," unidentified newspaper clipping, Alice E. Hugy Papers, Minnesota Historical Society.

71. Henry A. Castle, *History of St. Paul and Vicinity* (Chicago: Lewis Publishing Co., 1912), 2: 509.

72. Jones, "A Minneapolis Artist."

73. Nathaniel Burt, *Palaces for the People: A Social History of the American Art Museum* (Boston: Little, Brown & Co., 1977), 173–74.

74. Martha G. Wells, "On Impressionist Art," *Minneapolis Journal*, 22 April 1908, p. 12.

75. "Paintings by Local Artist Exhibited: Nathaniel J. Pousette, Born and Brought Up Here, Is Producing Minnesota Art," *St. Paul Pioneer Press*, 19 November 1911 (unpaged copy in Minnesota Artists file, St. Paul Public Library).

76. "Impressionism," *Winona Independent*, 8 April 1913, p. 2.

77. Caryl B. Storrs, "Gazing at Weird Work of the Cubists is Rude Shock to One's Nervous System," *Minneapolis Sunday Tribune*, 6 April 1913, p. 2.

78. Robert Koehler, "Lecture about 'post-impressionists' and 'cubists'" (Robert Koehler files, Minneapolis History Collection, Minneapolis Public Library and Information Center).

79. Robert Koehler to Walter Pach, 7 March 1914 (Minneapolis Institute of Arts Archives).

80. "Koehler Funeral Set for Tomorrow," *Minneapolis Journal*, 24 April 1917, p. 8; Wanda Gág, *Growing Pains* (New York: Coward, McCann Co., 1940; reprint ed., St. Paul, Minnesota Historical Society Press, 1984), 459.

81. "Koehler Funeral Set for Tomorrow," 8.

82. Harriet S. Flagg, "Robert Koehler," *Minneapolis Journal*, 29 April 1917 (copy in Robert Koehler file, Minneapolis History Collection, Minneapolis Public Library and Information Center).

83. "Friends Here Honor Robert Koehler by Art School Tablet," *Minneapolis Tribune*, 2 January 1927.

84. Betty Bridgman, "Mrs. Bridgman Reports from the Minneapolis Institute of Arts," *Christian Science Monitor*, 2 November 1954 (unpaged clipping in Minnesota Artists Files, St. Paul Public Library).

85. Peter Ackerberg, "Library Painting Gains Recognition," *Minneapolis Star*, 5 February 1975, pp. 1A–4A.

86. Patricia Hills, *The Painters' America: Rural and Urban Life, 1810–1910* (New York: Praeger Publishers, 1974), 123.

87. Jean B. Grillo, "Socialism Comes to the Whitney," *New York Village Voice*, 2 December 1974 (copy in Robert Koehler file, Minneapolis History Collection, Minneapolis Public Library and Information Center).

88. Agnete von Sprecht, *Streik: Realitat und Mythos* (Berlin: Deutsches Historisches Museum, 1992).

89. William H. Gerdts, *Art Across America: Two Centuries of Regional Painting 1710–1920*, 3 vols. (New York: Abbeville Press, 1990).

SELECT BIBLIOGRAPHY

American Renaissance 1876–1917. Brooklyn: The Brooklyn Museum, 1979.

Barter, Judith A., and Lynn E. Springer. *Currents of Expansion: Painting in the Midwest 1820–1940*. St. Louis, Mo.: St. Louis Art Museum, 1977.

Blegen, Theodore C. *Minnesota: A History of the State*. 2d ed. St. Paul: Minnesota Historical Society Press, 1975.

Boe, Roy A. "The Development of Art Consciousness in Minneapolis and the Problem of the Indigenous Artist." Master's thesis, University of Minnesota, 1947.

Brewer, Nicholas R. *Trails of a Paintbrush*. Boston: Christopher Publishing House, 1938.

Burke, Doreen Bolger, et al. *In Pursuit of Beauty: Americans and the Aesthetic Movement*. New York: Metropolitan Museum of Art, 1986.

Burt, Nathaniel. *Palaces for the People: A Social History of the American Art Museum*. Boston: Little, Brown & Co., 1977.

Coen, Rena N. *Painting and Sculpture in Minnesota 1820–1915*. Minneapolis: University of Minnesota Press, 1976.

————. *In the Mainstream: The Art of Alexis Jean Fournier*. St. Cloud, Minn.: North Star Press, 1985.

Davidson, Abraham A. *Early American Modernist Painting 1910–1935*. New York: Harper & Row, 1981.

Gág, Wanda. *Growing Pains*. Reprint. St. Paul: Minnesota Historical Society Press, 1984.

Gauthier, Julie C. *The Minnesota Capitol: Official Guide and History*. St. Paul: Pioneer Press Manufacturing Departments, 1907.

Gerdts, William H. *American Impressionism*. New York: Abbeville Press, 1984.

————. *Art Across America: Two Centuries of Regional Painting*. 3 vol. New York: Abbeville Press, 1990.

Hess, Jeffrey A. *Their Splendid Legacy: The First 100 Years of the Minneapolis Society of Fine Arts*. Minneapolis: Minneapolis Society of Fine Arts, 1985.

Hills, Patricia. *The Painter's America: Rural and Urban Life, 1810–1910*. New York: Praeger Publishers, 1974.

Kaplan, Wendy. *"The Art That Is Life": The Arts & Crafts Movement in America, 1875–1920*. Boston: Museum of Fine Arts, 1987.

Mendelowitz, Daniel M. *A History of American Art*. New York: Holt, Rinehart & Winston Inc., 1970.

Morgan, H. Wayne. *The New Muses: Art in American Culture, 1865–1920*. Norman: University of Oklahoma Press, 1978.

Nelson, Marion. *Norway in America*. Decorah, Iowa: Vesterheim, 1989.

O'Connor, William Van, ed. *A History of the Arts in Minnesota*. Minneapolis: University of Minnesota Press, 1958.

Peterson, Isaac O. "Art in St. Paul as Recorded in the Contemporary Newspaper." Master's thesis, University of Minnesota, 1942.

Post-Impressionism: Cross-Currents in European and American Painting 1880–1906. Washington, D.C.: National Gallery of Art, 1980.

Swanson, Mary T. *The Divided Heart: Scandinavian American Immigrant Painting 1850–1950.* Minneapolis: University Gallery, University of Minnesota, 1982.

Thompson, Neil B. *Minnesota's State Capitol: The Art and Politics of a Public Building.* St. Paul: Minnesota Historical Society Press, 1974.

von Sprecht, Agnete. *Streik: Realitat und Mythos.* Berlin: Deutsches Historisches Museum, 1992.

Weisberg, Gabriel P. *Beyond Impressionism: The Naturalist Impulse.* New York: Harry N. Abrams Inc. 1992.

CHECKLIST OF THE EXHIBITION

Dimensions = h × w

1. Gertrude Barnes
   American, b. 1865
   Still Life with Purple Bowl, about 1915
   Oil on canvas
   20″ × 30″
   Signed at lower left, "Gertrude J. Barnes"
   Minnesota Historical Society Collections AV1991.204

A Massachusetts native, Gertrude Barnes studied with the Boston painter Dennis Miler Bunker and later with Douglas Volk in Minneapolis. Her sizeable exhibition record in Minnesota lists miniature portraits; landscapes of Minnesota, Mexico, and New England; and flower still lifes. When one of the latter earned an award in a seven-state exhibit of 1916, a commentator pronounced that "Still life of the kind that Mrs. Barnes exhibits is in the class by itself and embodies all the requisites of drawing, good color and decorative quality that make up a good painting of any sort."

2. Nicholas R. Brewer
   American, 1857–1949
   Wabasha Streetscape (View of St. Paul), undated (about 1910)
   Oil on canvas
   16″ × 20″
   Signed at lower left, "N. R. Brewer"
   Minnesota Historical Society Collections
   Bush Foundation Purchase AV1983.263

Cityscape was an uncharacteristic theme for Brewer, who professed, in words and in paint, a fondness for the quiet pastorals of his teacher Dwight Tryon and his hero George Inness. This view from his studio window, however, describes the vitality of turn-of-the-century St. Paul with a sure and fluid touch. The growth of the city is evident in the newly completed Minnesota State Capitol on the horizon, the work of hometown architect Cass Gilbert.

3. Nicholas R. Brewer
   American, 1857–1949
   The Story Book, 1914
   Oil on canvas
   36″ × 46″
   Signed at lower left "N R Brewer 1914" and at lower right "N R Brewer"
   James Brewer Collection

Some of Nicholas Brewer's most engaging portrayals capture families at their ease together. Here Brewer's niece and son enjoy a story in the artist's substantial St. Paul home. Typical Brewer landscapes hang in the background, while a buffalo hide at the lady's feet serves not only as a rug, but as a symbol of the triumph of culture over the frontier days of Brewer's own childhood.

4. Nicholas R. Brewer
   American, 1857–1949
   Portrait of Clara Gerdtzen Blair (Mrs. Burr D. Blair), 1915
   Oil on canvas
   41⅜″ × 51″
   Signed at lower right, "N R Brewer"
   Winona County Historical Society, Inc.

A pallid muse of Minnesota culture, Mrs. Blair occupies her sturdy Mission rocker like a throne. Brewer's portrayal of the Winona clubwoman eschews lavish display in favor of dress, book, and armchair which suggest the sitter subscribed to the progressive social ideas and aesthetic of her day.

5. Nicholas R. Brewer
   American, 1857–1949
   Winter Scene, Minnesota: Train in a Snowy Landscape, undated (about 1920)
   Oil on canvas
   25¼″ × 30″
   Signed at lower left, "N R Brewer"
   Minnesota Museum of American Art
   Collections Fund Purchase 88.5.1

Winter Scene distills the brittle beauties of the season that epitomizes Minnesota to many people. Fleeting effects of sunlight and air, here heavy with locomotive breath, are the kind of motifs Brewer explored in small outdoor studies. He later worked these into larger studio paintings, as he noted in his autobiography, allowing memory and imagination to help shape the final image. Such paintings are often not identifiable as specific locations: viewers may find a corresponding place in their own memory.

6. Elisabeth Chant
   American, born in England, 1865–1947
   River Scene, 1899

Oil on canvas
14″ × 22″
Signed at lower left, "E A Chant '99"
Sibley Historical Site, Mendota, Minnesota 31.81

Elisabeth Chant was trained as a nurse before studying art in the young Minneapolis School of Art and taking an active part in two of the city's important groups, the Handicraft Guild and the Artists League. She also exhibited regularly in Minnesota before moving to Wilmington, North Carolina, to establish an art colony. *River Scene* is one of some forty paintings completed during her summer of study with Burt Harwood's art classes at the Sibley House in Mendota, just south of Minneapolis.

7. Edwin M. Dawes
   American, 1872–1945
   Channel to the Mills, 1913
   Oil on canvas
   51″ × 39½″
   Signed at lower left, "Edwin M Dawes"
   The Minneapolis Institute of Arts
   Given Anonymously 15.296

Beginning his career as a self-taught sign painter, Iowa-born Edwin Dawes gained fame as a Minnesota landscapist and later painted in Nevada and California. *Channel to the Mills* treats Minnesota's most frequently painted cityscape, the flour mills that line the banks of the Mississippi River in Minneapolis and which produced the city's wealth for decades. Dawes's major work in Minnesota, the painting plays the curves of water and smoke against the geometric battlements of the massive stone mills.

8. David Ericson
   American, born in Sweden, 1869–1946
   Morning of Life, 1907
   Oil on canvas
   27″ × 22¼″
   Signed at lower left, "David Ericson/ 1907"
   Tweed Museum of Art, University of Minnesota, Duluth D59x.32

Of Minnesota's many disciples of the art of James McNeill Whistler, David Ericson was one painter whose tonalities and composition reflected the master's work most directly. Ericson studied art in Duluth before moving on to New York's Art Students League and to Europe. He spent his later life in Duluth, where the cachet of his travels and his teaching skills made him a leader among local artists. This painting is a portrait of his son, and at the same time, a gentle allegory of youth at the start of life's journey.

9. Alexis Jean Fournier
   American, 1865–1948
   Coming Around the Bend (The Minnesota River, Pike Island and the Mississippi), 1889

Oil on canvas
27⅞″ × 50″
Signed at lower right, "Alex. Fournier 89."
Dr. and Mrs. John E. Larkin, Jr. Collection

The bluff-lined river valleys near Fournier's birthplace in St. Paul afforded him bucolic motifs for dozens of paintings around 1890. No wilderness for this son of the midwest: here, grazing cattle, a well-trod path, and an approaching steamboat bespeak the comfortably settled state of his environs. Ambitious early works like this attracted patrons who helped Fournier travel abroad to study at firsthand the French origins of his landscape style.

10. Alexis Jean Fournier
    American, 1865–1948
    View of St. Anthony Falls, 1890
    Oil on canvas
    38″ × 64½″
    Signed at lower left, "Alex. Fournier"
    First Bank Systems, Inc.

The force of the Mississippi tumbling over St. Anthony Falls captured artists' and travelers' imaginations even before businessmen harnessed the waterpower for sawmills and flour mills. Fournier's river-edge vantage point carefully cropped out the view of mills and bridges to dramatize the waterfall in a Niagaralike rendition. In the background is the Minneapolis Exposition Building, a gaudy showplace of commerce and art where Fournier showed over two hundred works in 1892.

11. Alexis Jean Fournier
    American, 1865–1948
    In Daubigny's Country, 1912
    Oil on canvas
    30″ × 40″
    Inscribed at lower right, "Alex. Fournier. 12"
    Private Collection

On a 1907 trip to France, Fournier began a series of paintings that paid homage to the artists who had shaped his own vision. His *Homes and Haunts of the Barbizon Masters* formed a travelogue in paint of the fields, forests, and skies which had been the inspiration of the *Men of 1830. In Daubigny's Country* also recalls the open compositions and calm vistas of Fournier's own early works like *Coming Around the Bend.*

12. Anton Gág
    American, born in Bohemia, 1859–1908
    Raspberries, 1904
    Oil on canvas
    15⅜″ × 20⅜″
    Signed at lower right, "Anton Gág/ 1904"
    Mr. and Mrs. Gary Harm Collection

Raised among the German-speaking immigrants of New Ulm, Minnesota, Anton Gág painted portraits, landscapes, church interiors, and a 110-foot-long panorama of the Dakota Conflict, an Indian war of 1862. This rustic still life attests to Gág's keen interest in straightforward renderings of his world, a feature that marks his best easel paintings. Gág's eldest child was the important twentieth-century printmaker and children's book author/illustrator, Wanda Gág (1893–1946).

13. Frances Cranmer Greenman
    American, 1890–1981
    Agona-Coma-Goqui (Woman Who Rides the Wind), 1912
    Oil on canvas, mounted on board
    50″ × 36″
    Signed at upper left, "Frances Cranmer 1912"
    Minnesota Historical Society Collections
    Gift of the Artist AV1988.45.360

"I was planning to be the world's greatest painter of Indians," recalled Frances Cranmer Greenman of a short-lived youthful ambition. Back in the Midwest after studies with William Merritt Chase and Robert Henri in New York, she painted this Anishinabe elder "alone with her memories" on the White Earth Reservation in northern Minnesota. Greenman traveled the country for another six decades, painting portraits of statesmen and socialites from Washington to Hollywood.

14. Alexander Grinager
    American, 1865–1949
    Boys Bathing, 1894
    Oil on canvas
    59″ × 34″
    Signed at lower left, "Alex Grinager"
    The Minneapolis Institute of Arts
    Gift of Mr. and Mrs. Alexander Grinager 47.23

Alexander Grinager began his art training in Minneapolis with the Danish-born painter Peter Gui Clausen before touring Europe in the 1890s. Active in the Artists League at the turn of the century, Grinager gained much local acclaim before moving to New York state. His scene of boys on the banks of the Mississippi was a widely exhibited and lavishly praised exercise in sun-drenched naturalism.

15. Alexander Grinager
    American, 1865–1949
    Venice (Venetian Idyll), undated (about 1905)
    Oil on canvas
    40″ × 28″
    Signed at lower right, "Alexander Grinager"
    Colin T. Taylor Collection

Venice is a portrait of Grinager's wife and fellow artist Margaret, posed in a noble Old World setting and rich brocade which led a Minneapolis journalist to liken her to Queen Guinevere. Like Fournier, Volk, and a few other painters with Minnesota ties, Grinager continued to exhibit and draw praise in the state years after relocating in the East.

16. Knute Heldner
    American, born in Sweden, 1877–1952
    Third Avenue Bridge #1, 1914
    Oil on canvas
    29″ × 33″
    First Bank Systems, Inc.

Settling in Duluth after wanderings as a worker in fields, mines, and factories, Knute Heldner mastered his art to win a gold medal in a 1914 statewide exhibit. Many of his early landscapes were Impressionist-influenced reveries. In a series of paintings of Minneapolis and Duluth buildings, Heldner introduced more structured compositions and rugged paint textures to his work. He spent much of his life in New Orleans after 1925.

17. Elsa Laubach Jemne
    American, 1888–1974
    The Red-Haired Girl, 1916
    Oil on canvas
    27½″ × 33½″
    Signed at lower left, "Elsa Laubach"
    Adam Granger Collection

Honored in an important 1916 exhibition of upper Midwest paintings, this work crystallized the standard of its time and place. Jemne's art balanced traditional and contemporary tastes as deftly as *The Red-Haired Girl* juxtaposed a Holbein drawing with a stylish young woman. Within a few years of her successful showings of portraits "permeated by the artist's ever-present sense of decorative arrangement," as one critic noted, Jemne began painting murals for municipal and federal buildings around Minnesota.

18. Robert Koehler
    American, born in Germany, 1850–1917
    Studio Still Life, 1879
    Oil on canvas
    50″ × 34″
    Signed at upper right, "Robt Koehler/ 1879"
    Gerald B. Johnston Collection

This sumptuous array of Old World artifacts suggests Robert Koehler's possession of not just the furnishings of an artist's studio but the skills needed to proceed from the lithographer's shop to the painter's atelier. Painted on the foundation of his art studies in Milwaukee, New York, and Munich, the still life served perhaps as the tour de force of an artist ready to engage his European heritage in depth. Koehler embarked for Germany by the end of 1879 for a sojourn which lasted three years.

19. Robert Koehler
American, born in Germany, 1850–1917
Head of an Old Woman, 1881
Oil on canvas
18″ × 14½″
The Minneapolis Institute of Arts
Gift of Art School Students 01.1

This small study, which, in the words of Minnesota's art historian Rena Neumann Coen, "captures with a few sure strokes and in a thick impasto the image of old age," bears witness to the technical and thematic approach to art that Koehler perfected in Munich. It was exhibited in The Minneapolis Institute of Arts' 1915 inaugural exhibition, the only work by a Minnesota painter to be so honored.

20. Robert Koehler
American, born Germany, 1850–1917
Portrait of the Artist, 1898
Oil on canvas
38½″ × 23″
Signed at upper right, "Robt Koehler 1898"
Private Collection

Five years after his arrival in Minneapolis, Robert Koehler appraised his own image in a somber portrayal. A touch of bourgeois formality in his well-tailored garb also suggests Koehler's respected place in the city's professional class.

21. Robert Koehler
American, born in Germany, 1850–1917
Landscape, undated (about 1900)
Oil on canvas
19½″ × 15½″
Signed at lower left, "R. Koehler"
Private Collection

Once settled in Minnesota and busy with his teaching, Koehler tended to find his subjects close to home. A family tradition of the first owner of this landscape held that Koehler painted it near the house he built in south Minneapolis, improvising the two bare trees to enliven the foreground. Like the small liberties he took with nature, the gently back-lit grove and soft-edged treatment are typical of Koehler's later work.

22. Robert Koehler
American, born in Germany, 1850–1917
Edwin, My Son, 1908
Oil on canvas
40″ × 23½″
Signed at lower right, "Robt Koehler/ 1908"
Private Collection

Perched on a rough-hewn chair amid the props of his father's studio, young Edwin Koehler conveys the amiable union of family and art that his father found in Minneapolis. As he did for the figures in *Rainy Evening on Hennepin Avenue*, Koehler used a photograph of Edwin for this painting.

23. Robert Koehler
American, born in Germany, 1850–1917
Rainy Evening on Hennepin Avenue, undated (about 1910)
Oil on canvas
25¾″ × 24″
Signed at lower left, "Robert Koehler"
The Minneapolis Institute of Arts
Gift by subscription 25.403

An urban masterpiece for Minnesota, *Rainy Evening* sums up Koehler's life in his adopted city. The busy main thoroughfare was the site of his first Minneapolis studio and exhibits. His wife, son, and dog take center stage in a painting that also displayed Koehler's often-stated admiration for the subtle atmospheric effects of Whistler's work.

24. James D. Larpenteur
American, 1847–1915
St. Paul from Pig's Eye Lake, 1888
Oil on canvas
36½″ × 58″
Signed at lower right, "J. D. Larpenteur./ 88."
Minnesota Historical Society Collections
Gift of the Family of Dr. Harry B. Zimmermann and Dr. Bernard Zimmermann AV1986.279

The son of an early St. Paul settler, James Larpenteur studied in France as a young man. He later served as superintendent of the State Fair's art program, and also assisted railroad magnate James J. Hill in tending and hanging his celebrated art collection. This autumn scene encompasses the view up the Mississippi valley to the St. Paul skyline—a thoroughly domesticated landscape, with well-fed cattle, neatly stacked hay, and a couple at right taking the view from a conveniently placed seat.

25. James D. Larpenteur
American, 1847–1915
George W. Langevin in His Cutter, 1888
Oil on canvas
96″ × 120″
Signed at lower left, "J. D. Larpenteur"
Raymond Seliski Collection

Larpenteur was acclaimed as an animal painter by his fellow Minnesotans. In its bold size, loving attention to equine finery, and vignette of a race on the snow, this portrayal of a St. Paul businessman with his team epitomized the sportsman's pride of ownership and skill.

26. Homer Dodge Martin
    American, 1836–1897
    View on the Seine (also known as *Harp of the Winds*), 1895
    Oil on canvas
    28¾″ × 40¾″
    Signed at lower right, "H D Martin 1895"
    Metropolitan Museum of Art
    Gift of Several Gentlemen 97.32

Homer Dodge Martin spanned the styles and themes of nineteenth-century American landscape art, from Hudson River School clarity to Barbizon reverie to the lyricism of his final canvases. His last works, painted in a farmhouse near St. Paul, gave form and color to the recollected vistas of his past. Martin's presence in the city went uncelebrated, however. St. Paul painter Nicholas Brewer noted that a prominent local collector "passed by Homer Martin's *Harp of the Winds* (now a valued possession of the Metropolitan Museum) when it stood unframed on the floor in a St. Paul art shop while its author lived in a cheap flat on Rice Street unable to buy enough coal to keep his family warm, or to obtain shoes for their feet."

27. Grace E. McKinstry
    American, 1859–1936
    Portrait of Alexander Ramsey, 1903
    Oil on canvas
    44″ × 36″
    Signed at upper right, "G. E. McKinstry 1903"
    Minnesota Historical Society Collections AV1983. 149.18

Daughter of a Minnesota newspaperman, Grace McKinstry traveled widely before settling in Faribault as a portraitist and art lecturer. She painted many of the state's notables, such as territorial governor Alexander Ramsey and educator Maria Sanford (Weisman Art Museum Collection, University of Minnesota, Minneapolis). From her studio, "'a bit of Paris' set down in the little town of Faribault," McKinstry proselytized successfully for culture in general and a state-supported art society in particular.

28. Magnus Norstad
    American, born in Norway, 1884
    City on a Hill, 1917
    Oil on canvas
    36″ × 30″
    Signed at lower right, "Norstad/ '17"
    Minnesota Historical Society Collections AV1983. 149.16

Noted for "canvases that sparkle with the spirit of winter," Magnus Norstad frosted St. Paul's skyline, rail yards, and river front with cold hues in a painting that won acclaim in several Midwestern shows. The richly textured surfaces and pearly tones of sky and shadows characterized the Impressionism of the early twentieth century, which was popular from Norstad's homeland to the exhibit halls of his adopted state.

29. Nathaniel Pousette-Dart
    American, 1886–1965
    Downtown, undated (about 1915)
    Oil on board
    13¾″ × 9⅝″
    Signed at lower left, "Nathaniel Pousette Dart"
    Minnesota Historical Society Collections
    Gift of John E. Larkin Jr., M.D. AV1980.368.9

Nathaniel Pousette-Dart studied art in his home town of St. Paul, New York's Art Students League, and the Pennsylvania Academy of Fine Arts. Back in Minnesota, he taught at the College of St. Catherine and the St. Paul Institute School of Art. Pousette-Dart, who hyphenated his name at the time of his marriage to poet Flora Dart, also wrote extensively on art, and he championed the work of modern and abstact artists (including his son, the New York School painter Richard Pousette-Dart). The elder Pousette-Dart was known in Minnesota for snowy landscapes in an Impressionist mode; later in his career he, too, became an abstract painter.

30. Douglas Volk
    American, 1856–1935
    After the Reception, 1887
    Oil on canvas
    34¾″ × 25½″
    Signed at lower left, "Douglas Volk"
    The Minneapolis Institute of Arts
    Gift of Mr. and Mrs. E. J. Phelps 23.42

Son of a sculptor, raised on the Continent and trained in Paris, Douglas Volk was the founding director of the Minneapolis School of Art from 1886 to 1893 (today the Minneapolis College of Art and Design). This portrayal of a family friend suggests the storytelling nature of much of Volk's work and anticipates his costume pieces set in colonial America. Volk also painted two mural-sized history paintings for the Minnesota State Capitol—the only artist with Minnesota connections to be so honored.

31. Douglas Volk
    American, 1856–1935
    John Scott Bradstreet in His Judd House Rooms, undated (about 1890)
    Oil on canvas
    17¼″ × 22¼″
    Signed at lower right, "Douglas Volk"
    The Minneapolis Institute of Arts
    Gift of John Scott Bradstreet 06.2

Volk's portraits conveyed the sensibilities of a sitter through setting and pose as much as likeness. His painting of interior designer John Scott Bradstreet at his ease, amid what a Minneapolis editorial termed "the fellowship of good things," captures Bradstreet's eclectic aesthetic. A Massachusetts native like Volk, Bradstreet was an influential tastemaker for the Midwest through his Craftshouse firm.

32. Ada Wolfe
    American, 1878–1945
    Sails on Lake Minnetonka, 1914
    Oil on canvas
    30″ × 40″
    Inscribed at lower left, "Ada A Wolfe/ 1914"
    Minnesota Historical Society Collections AV1988.
    45.317

"Like most young artists, Miss Wolfe went through a 'Whistler period'" noted a Minneapolis critic in 1917. "It is represented by a group [of pictures] possessing delicate beauty of coloring, and distinctive composition." Wolfe's first-prize award for this painting in 1914 offers proof that

Magnus Norstad's caricature of himself painting outdoors, from a letter to Louis W. Hill, 4 November 1917. James J. Hill and Louis W. Hill Papers, James J. Hill Reference Library, St. Paul. Photograph by Gary Mortensen and Robert Fogt.

Whistler was a respected influence in Minnesota art circles. A student of Koehler and Gustav von Schlegel in Minneapolis and of William Merritt Chase in New York, Wolfe turned in her later paintings from the misty veils of "Whistler" hues to deeper colors, heavier brushwork, and forms given greater solidity through dense, dark contours.

4

Art for Life's Sake: The Handicraft Guild of Minneapolis

Marcia G. Anderson

MINNESOTA OWES MUCH OF ITS REPUTATION AS AN active center of the international Arts and Crafts movement to one small but energetic organization: The Handicraft Guild of Minneapolis. Active between 1904 and 1918, the guild shared many of the social and aesthetic goals of arts and crafts organizations worldwide. It championed the distinctive properties of materials, the skill of individual craftsmen, and the satisfaction to be found in making and using unique, handmade objects. The guild understood its work to be an alternative to mass-produced and often indifferently crafted factory products and the repetitive labor required to produce them. In Minnesota, however, these broad arts and crafts ideals assumed a distinctive local inflection.

The Handicraft Guild was founded, led, and to a large extent was staffed by diversely talented and highly motivated women. For some of them—notably those who had been trained as painters, sculptors, or art educators before joining—arts and crafts work offered a way around the traditional gendering of "fine art" as male, "craft" as female. Perhaps even more importantly, the guild offered a means of publicly asserting and disseminating certain social values. The Arts and Crafts movement had cultivated personal attributes such as patience, self-knowledge, and cooperation among its adherents. In Minneapolis such values assumed primary importance, however, colored further by the region's populist commitment. As arts and crafts workers, and specifically as guild members, Minnesota women quietly offered an alternative to a cost-centered, success-oriented, male-dominated society by spreading a different value system. The singular lasting accomplishment of the Handicraft Guild was to permanently institutionalize these ideals into the region. Through the design and construction of useful objects, one would learn not only technical skills, but aesthetic discrimination, personal self-discipline, and ultimately a sense of one's own value within a harmonious social community.

The Arts and Crafts movement began in England in the mid-nineteenth century. In analyzing the process and product of the Industrial Revolution in England, John Ruskin, William Morris, Thomas Carlyle, Augustus W. N. Pugin, and others concluded that inferior quality machine-made goods had diminished the beauty in everyday life. They decried inappropriate use of materials, ineffective design, and poor construction of industrial products, as well as the tedium of factory labor. As a model for an alternative, more humane system of production, these writers looked to the crafts guilds that had built the Gothic cathedrals of medieval Europe. Each guild, a professional organization representing a particular craft, not only trained apprentices but set and maintained standards for work and wages, provided a vehicle for social interaction, and sometimes supported members unable to work.

Among the first to put arts and crafts principles into practice was C. R. Ashbee, who founded his London School and Guild of Handicraft in 1887 and 1888. His guild, a communal society made up primarily of male artists directed by a single, recognized leader, served as a

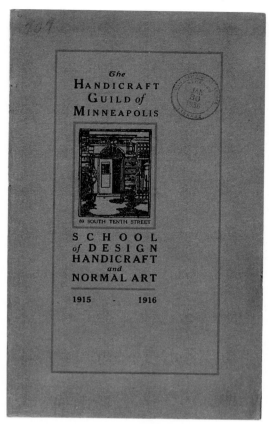

1915–16 Handicraft Guild of Minneapolis session booklet cover. Minnesota Historical Society Collections. Photograph by Gary Mortensen and Robert Fogt.

model for many later arts and crafts organizations. In East London in 1888 he identified the guild's two chief goals: "[to] establish a standard in craftsmanship . . . [and an] education in the crafts."[1] A local economic depression coupled with disputes among the artists—difficulties which were to plague subsequent arts and crafts groups as well—led to the guild's failure in 1908, although some members continued to work and teach after that time.

In contrast to most English arts and crafts organizations, which emphasized social concerns, the group active at the Glasgow School of Art in Scotland, under the leadership of the architect Charles Rennie Mackintosh, concentrated on design reform. Combining the formal language of the art nouveau style with arts and crafts ideals, the Glasgow style proved more influential on the continent and in America than in England. In Austria it was admired by the founders of the *Wiener Werkstätte* (loosely, "Viennese Workshops"), Josef Hoffman and Koloman Moser, who had, in turn, also profited from their visits to Ashbee's Guild.

In 1897, a year after the death of the Arts and Crafts movement's chief proponent, William Morris, Boston's Society of Arts and Crafts was founded. That same year it staged its first arts and crafts exhibition, an event considered the first institutionalized presentation of arts and crafts objects in this country. Other U.S. cities with crafts organiza-

tions developed quickly from that point on. American arts and crafts associations varied greatly from city to city, however; some were affiliated with fine arts or academic institutions, such as the school of the Art Institute of Chicago, The Chicago Arts and Crafts Society, and The Detroit Society Arts and Crafts.[2] Others had no institutional affiliation but were inspired by a local hand craft tradition, such as the Society of Blue and White Needlework of Deerfield, Massachusetts and the Hull-House settlement in Chicago. In some cases, individuals provided the focus for an arts and crafts association, a workshop, or studio serving as a community center for fellow artists and a marketplace for arts and crafts objects.[3] Certain programs centered on one craft medium, art pottery being the most common. Others, the Handicraft Guild of Minneapolis among them, represented a variety of aesthetic and social concerns that stretched well beyond any particular product or skill.[4]

The American public was introduced to principles of the Arts and Crafts movement through these societies and associations, whose mission was spread by local newspapers, existing arts organizations, and specialized periodicals (e.g., *House Beautiful, The Ladies Home Journal, The International Studio, Arts and Decoration, Keramic Studio,* and *The Craftsman*). These publications printed exhibition reviews, statements of new design philosophy, and suggestions for home decoration. They advertised lecture tours and announced curricula offered by guilds and schools. It was through these pages that the ideals of the American Arts and Crafts movement became familiar to Americans.

With no medieval craft tradition, no examples of Romanesque or Gothic building, and only a fledgling group of civic museums to visit, proponents of the Arts and Crafts movement in America created a unique identity for themselves and developed a style drawing on their respective regional building traditions as well as the technical and functional requirements of objects. The movement in the East came closest to following the medieval models and romantic ideals of William Morris, while in the Far West interest focused on the Spanish, Mexican, and Indian heritage of the region. In the wide expanse between the coasts, craftsmen and art educators did not turn to indigenous cultures of the region for inspiration. In articulating the design ideals of a new society, they turned to function as a *raison d'être*, often utilizing Japanese precedent as a stylistic foundation.

Perhaps because Americans did not embrace a common past, American theorists were also less concerned with historical precedent than their European counterparts. With a pragmatism characteristic of the New World population, discussions focused on the appropriate social function of craft training and product and object use. Leaving religious principles of European medievalism aside, the American movement's ideal of social responsibility and improvement was seen to be integrated in craft technique itself, the goals of discipline, patience, and cooperation into technical skill. In the June 1902 issue of *House Beautiful*, Gardner C.

*Handicraft Guild building, 89 South 10th Street, Minneapolis,
about 1909. Minnesota Historical Society. Photograph by Elgin
R. Shepard, Minneapolis.*

Teall summed up contemporary attitudes. He proposed a list of "essential" books for the library of every craftsperson, because "technical literature is what we have to take the place of the medieval system of apprenticeship" in America.[5]

The ideals of the Arts and Crafts movement clashed with modern economic theory most dramatically over the appropriate use of machines. English arts and crafts followers were categorically opposed to the employment of machines for any craft production. The more practical, modernist Americans were not as averse. The range of views over machine use, however, reflected a full spectrum of opinions regarding identity and labor. A 1902 debate between Oscar Lovell Triggs, a writer and member of Chicago's Industrial Art League, and the Minnesota-born Thorstein Veblen, a prominent economist and author of *The Theory of the Leisure Class*, presented the polar attitudes of the time[6].

While Triggs believed in the use of machinery in crafts production, he was most concerned with camaraderie among craftsworkers and the spirit of self-determination in the workplace. Veblen, on the other hand, disdainfully referred to these attitudes, as represented in Britain's Arts and Crafts movement, as "sentimental," an archaic off-shoot of nineteenth-century romanticism. Medieval guilds and past societies, he said, offered no solutions to the problems of a twentieth-century democracy. The movement had no hope of success because it denied the machine process which he believed was integral to the development of a modern culture. To abandon the machine process, he insisted, was to abandon all hope of commercial viability; hand-crafted objects were simply too costly for general consumption. Incorporating the professed arts and crafts goals of beauty in "honest" work and products for "everyman," Veblen proposed an association of art and labor aimed at a larger output of low-cost, standardized goods. Functional goods with a beauty of line and color, he wrote, could be achieved "in fuller measure through the technological expedients of which the machine process disposes."[7]

The attitude of American arts and crafts associations regarding the use of machines in craft production varied widely. At nearly opposite poles were two of the country's best-known organizations, Elbert Hubbard's Roycrofters and Byrdcliffe, led by Ralph Whitehead. Both were located in New York state. The Roycrofters, in East Aurora, was a group founded on Hubbard's dream of creating an American counterpart to William Morris's Kelmscott Press, but it quickly expanded to include cabinetry, metalwork, and other crafts. As early as 1909, the Roycrofters's small metal pieces (items such as letter openers, vases, stamp boxes, and trays) were available around the country in shops and by mail. Hubbard's community of cottages served as both school and factory and he maintained economic and social control until his death in 1915. The Roycroft shops were a commercial success, making arts and crafts objects widely available.

Sustained mainly through Whitehead's independent wealth and commitment to the Arts and Crafts movement, Byrdcliffe, located in Woodstock, New York, flourished between 1902 and 1915. Byrdcliffe's furniture did not sell well, however. It was both bulky in design and the labor required to produce its characteristic decorative detail made it expensive. As a center for the exchange of ideas, however, Byrdcliffe was extraordinarily successful. With his connections to artists and arts organizations in both the United States and Great Britain, Whitehead was able to attract a steady stream of visitors, lecturers, and aspiring artists, generating an atmosphere of informal interaction that still exists among the many artist communities in the Woodstock area.

THE TWIN CITIES' ART COMMUNITY AND THE ORIGINS OF THE HANDICRAFT GUILD

In contrast to the Roycrofters or Byrdcliffe, the Arts and Crafts movement in Minnesota had neither a single dynamic personality nor a personal fortune at its center. Instead, its arts and crafts organizations, those preceding and including the Handicraft Guild of Minneapolis, were well integrated into an active metropolitan arts community from which each drew support and membership. When the Handicraft Guild was formed in 1904, it adopted a pragmatism and a populism characteristic of the region as it simultaneously addressed three broad areas of concern in the arts community. First was the need for art education and formal craft training, which had been expressed in Minnesota as early as the 1860s, but by 1904 had been only partially addressed in the local schools. At the same time, artists and craftspeople, as well as students, were in need of studio and workshop space and opportunities for the exhibition and sale of work. Finally, there was a less tangible need, seen most clearly by the guild's female leaders, to publicly assert a set of values that challenged modern industrial society's goals of economy, efficiency, and speed. The guild's history is largely a record of how these multiple needs were interrelated within the framework of a single institution.[8]

If the Twin Cities arts community had a geographical center at the turn of the century, it was the studio spaces in the "Old Bandbox" building at 719 Hennepin Avenue.

Bandbox studio rooms. Minneapolis Journal; *Womenkind, 27 April 1901.*

Because many of the artists who maintained studios there also were teachers or members or leaders of various local arts organizations, the building facilitated a spirited exchange of ideas within these groups. Among its prominent tenants, for example, was Robert Koehler, who had moved to Minneapolis as the new director of the Minneapolis School of Fine Arts in 1892 and who had founded the Art League in 1897.[9] Following Koehler's arrival, Burt Harwood, an instructor at the same school and studio tenant in the "bandbox," served tea from a Russian samovar on a regular basis, providing an occasion for local artists to gather informally at the end of each week. The Russian tea tradition survived into the early 1900s under the auspices of two other studio occupants, Elisabeth A. Chant and Margarethe E. Heisser, both of whom were early and active members of the city's local Arts and Crafts Society. At an October 1899 opening reception for an exhibition of their own work, tea was served in rooms adjoining Chant and Heisser's studio, namely those of the Art League. In November of that year, still within the same building, the Arts and Crafts Society of Minneapolis met to plan the coming year's work.[10] The building, therefore, functioned as an informal "clearing house" for arts information, where those concerned with the community's need for craft instruction as well as professional studio and exhibition space could gather, providing a forum for the discussion of contemporary social and aesthetic issues at the same time.

When Koehler took over his post as director of the Minneapolis School of Fine Arts in 1893, the school offered classes in "industrial art," which included instruction in the theory of handicraft, but with little accompanying workshop experience. St. Paul, too, felt the pressure to provide more applied arts training for public school teachers and members of the community. In 1895, St. Paul's school board had expanded course offerings in manual training and separated those courses from the core curriculum. The board also created the new, co-educational Mechanic Arts High School, which offered four-year courses emphasizing art, craft, shop, drawing, and domestic science.[11] By the turn of the century, however, it was attracting more students than could be comfortably accommodated in existing studio and workshop facilities.

It is evident that the pressure for more applied arts training was not solely a Twin Cities phenomenon. State-wide support for the movement led to the formation of the Minnesota State Art Society in 1903. The society sought "to advance the interest of fine arts, to develop the influence of art in education, and to foster the introduction of art in manufacture." Minnesota was recognized around the country for its innovation in promoting a state-wide art program.[12] The demolition of the "Bandbox" studios in 1903 left the downtown Minneapolis art community in need not only of individual studio space, but of a center, a place for both formal and informal meetings. At the same time, the demand for applied art courses was growing. A popular course in decorative design was begun in 1899 at the Minneapolis School for Fine Arts. By the early twentieth century, the more specific studio needs of the school had become acute as well.[13]

In the 1890s, as local schools were struggling to meet a growing demand for art and craft training, a series of small associations were addressing the different, if related aesthetic and social interests of local women. The Chalk and Chisel Club—the name reflects its formation as a merger of woodcarvers and designers—began humbly with a handwritten note dated 5 January 1895. In the note, Gertrude J. Leonard invited Nellie Trufant to a meeting at Leonard's home "to consider the formation of a club of ladies for study in wood-carving and design."[14] Membership grew to between twelve and fifteen women. The articles of the club's constitution reflected arts and crafts ideals of mutual support, education, and the exhibition of hand-crafted objects. There were monthly meetings and an annual November exhibition, in which all members were expected to participate. Some of their programs were quite ambitious. An early handwritten agenda for one year of monthly meetings, for example, lists the art, architecture, and design of France, Italy and England as topics. The 1895–96 agenda featured programs on historic furniture—Gothic; Moresque; the Renaissance in Italy, Germany, France, and the Netherlands; and Louis XVI, Empire, Tudor, Stuart, Sheraton and Colonial styles. Meetings in 1897–98 focused on flower varieties as themes, with the lecturer discussing the use of particular flowers in ornament and decorative design.[15]

In November 1898, the Chalk and Chisel Club sponsored Minnesota's first exhibition of arts and crafts. The results were unexpectedly gratifying. Of the eighty-two exhibitors, thirty were Minnesotans. Two members exhibited in the cabinet work and wood carving section: Gertrude Leonard (writing desk, stand, tabouret) and Mary Helmick (colonial mirror, jewel casket). Elizabeth (Mrs. F. G.) Hol-

brook, Adeline T. Gates, Mary Moulton Cheney, and Hope McDonald had entries in designs and book decoration, metal, glass and casts. The quality and geographic distribution of work in the exhibition attests to the standards Chalk and Chisel Club members set for themselves from the beginning. Exhibitors included Otto Zahn of Memphis (bookbinding and leather work), Arthur G. Grinell of Bedford, Massachusetts (cabinet work and wood carving), Samuel Bridge Dean of Boston (ceramics), the Rookwood Pottery Co., Charles Volkmar (ceramics), Grueby Faience Co. and Dedham Pottery, Eleanor Klapp of Chicago (jewelry), and The Deerfield Society of Blue and White Needlework (embroideries and textiles).[16]

The growing community interest in the applied arts led Chalk and Chisel Club members to revise their by-laws and reorganize under the name of Arts and Crafts Society of Minneapolis in 1899.[17] The principal objective of this new organization was "to encourage the production of artistic handicraft, to establish mutual and helpful relations between designer and craftsman, and to stimulate the appreciation of harmony and fitness in design."[18] At this point the society began to admit associate members who were not designers or craftspeople. This is the first evidence of the pragmatic, populist principles that would shape the Arts and Crafts movement's development in Minnesota, distinguishing it from others in the United States. The newly named society, which continued to be comprised solely of women, chose to study manuscripts, printing, and bookbinding at its first meetings, with special focus on recent developments in bookmaking in America.[19]

In the fall of 1904, eleven local women, many of whom were members of the Arts and Crafts Society of Minneapolis, founded the Handicraft Guild of Minneapolis. Beginning with the Chalk and Chisel Club, formal arts and crafts organizations had been active in the city for about nine years, which is the basis for Minnesota's claim of having

Chest by Mary A. Helmick. The International Studio, *vol. 28, 1906.*

1900 Minneapolis Arts & Crafts Show. Brush and Pencil, *vol. 6, June 1900.*

the oldest arts and crafts society in the nation. Grace Margaret Kiess served as president until the newest organization was formally incorporated in March 1905. An announcement in *The Craftsman* for May 1905 described the motivating factors:

> The [Handicraft] Guild came into existence last fall to meet a pressing need for craft classes especially suited to requirements for training teachers of the public schools in handicrafts. There was also a recognized want of such training by others and there was no salesroom for artistic craft projects nor any means of bringing the work of the local craftsmen to the notice of the buying public. The project of a salesroom in which a stock of articles could be kept and orders taken was heartily approved and furthered by the local Arts and Crafts Society, which is one of the oldest and most successful in the United States.[20]

Put simply, the guild integrated the resources of the Arts and Crafts Society of Minneapolis with the needs of the arts education community.

The subject of the position of women in craft production was not addressed explicitly in statements issued by the Chalk and Chisel Club, nor by any of the various Minnesota arts and crafts groups. It is clear, however, that the movement's focus on the individual worker's needs for social interaction, recognition, and a sense of personal accomplishment, in addition to wages and security, spoke to women in an unusually forceful way. The history of the Handicraft Guild suggests that it functioned differently from most business or educational institutions run by men at the time in ways that might justifiably be designated as feminist. Rather than a clear-cut administrative hierarchy which pursued fixed institutional goals, for example, the guild more closely resembled a network of individuals whose interests—in crafts, education, and personal development—stretched out into the community in many different directions, merging to produce thoughtfully designed and constructed objects and programs. The organization itself was dynamic, constantly adapting to the changing interests and needs of a larger community, even to the point of surrendering its independent identity altogether, in 1918, to become part of the University of Minnesota.

The founders and most active guild members were professional women—artists, educators, entrepreneurs. The majority of those with the longest and most distinguished records apparently resolved the conflict between marriage and career by not marrying at all; some who did marry discontinued their active participation in the guild at that point. No member, however, defined her career primarily in terms of the guild. The staff consisted of trained and experienced artists and teachers who simultaneously held positions in other, usually educational institutions, or operated their own small businesses. The guild, in short, provided established professionals with an opportunity to expand and extend their work in new directions, to experience economic independence, to find camaraderie and mutual support, to exchange ideas with other artisans, and to experience personal and artistic growth. As such it attracted participants at various stages of different careers and served their needs in a wide range of ways.[21]

Emma Roberts, for example, the guild's founder and its president between 1906 and 1917, was a teacher in the Minneapolis public school system where she supervised drawing and art appreciation for twenty-four years. She was primarily concerned with the introduction of an aesthetic dimension into everyday life and saw the products of the arts and crafts movement as a way to achieve this goal. She both taught and wrote textbooks. In her guild work she pursued the same goals, although largely among older, more advanced students, many of whom planned to become or already were teachers.

Mary Moulton Cheney, whose educational philosophy closely paralleled that of Roberts, was prominent in the Arts and Crafts movement in Minnesota well before the guild was founded. She was a graphic designer of national reputation, a teacher—and later director—at the Minneapolis School of Fine Arts, and the proprietor/partner in a business specializing in craft work. The volume and diversity of Cheney's activity in design, sales, exhibition, teaching, and administration made her a key figure in the formation of the arts community in the Twin Cities metropolitan area.

The guild offered transitional artistic and occupational opportunities to its members. To its president from 1905 to 1906, the interior designer Mary Linton Bookwalter, the guild provided an early glimpse into the entrepreneurial possibilities of design work. Bookwalter later moved to New York City, where she was instrumental in the design, financing, and construction of important early apartment cooperatives. Already well known as an artist and china painter before coming to the guild as a student, Henrietta Barclay Paist moved from a fairly conservative, realist style of painting to a flattened, patterned, "modern" one in the course of her studies and work. Gladys Pattee adapted her guild training not only to innovative teaching methods at the public school level, but eventually—in the wake of World War I—to the development of a new occupational therapy program.

THE GUILD HOUSE

The guild was housed initially on the fourth floor of the Dayton Building at 710 Nicollet Avenue and functioned primarily as a permanent exhibition and showroom for handmade items by craftspeople from around the United States. Limited courses were offered in clay modeling, leather work, and Irish embroidery. By December 1904 there was already a growing demand for more courses, and it became clear that additional space had to be sought elsewhere. A lease was acquired for a large residence at 926 2nd Avenue. By March 1905 the guild had moved in and

Handicraft Guild fireplace. Construction Details, *August 1914, p. 59. Photograph courtesy of the Minnesota Historical Society.*

Handicraft Guild auditorium, 10th Street and Marquette Avenue, about 1910. Photograph courtesy of the Minnesota Historical Society.

a pottery class was in session as remodeling was still underway. Exhibition and lecture rooms were at the front of the building; rear rooms were used for clay and metal work. Studios for artists and craftsworkers were located on the second and third floors.[22]

In July 1905 the guild was less than a year old, but its directors announced that they would begin work to acquire yet another new facility. In February 1906, the officers announced the selection of a site and plans to build a permanent home for the guild. Minneapolis philanthropist Joseph R. Kingman provided the capital for the construction of the building. A local architect of national reputation, William Channing Whitney, agreed to design the multifunction facility. By November 1907 a jubilant group of officers and staff moved into the guild's new home at 89 S. 10th Street, which was equipped to meet the needs not only of the guild, but those of others in the art community, local craftsworkers, educators, shopkeepers, and charitable groups as well.[23]

The three-story brick and stone Georgian revival structure at 89 S. 10th Street offered precisely what the Minneapolis art community had sought for more than a decade. The large auditorium could accommodate lectures, general assemblies, exhibitions, and concerts. The long sales/display room featured a fireplace decorated with guild tiles. There was a luncheon and tea room, a book shop, work shops, classrooms, stock rooms for supplies, and studios for craftsworkers, designers, and painters, as well as shops and offices for interior designers. Writing in 1908, Elisabeth Chant expressed her surprise and admiration at what the guild had accomplished in a short time. It had demonstrated how "art applied to everyday uses can really be made to pay; that even here, in a Western city, a corporation built on lines that demand the cultivated tastes of the public for its support has flourished and grown important; and that without large capital or financial backing it has proved successful in a business as well as an artistic way." At long last guild founders were able to implement their founding goals in this new facility which included an attractive sales area "for the advancement of industrial art interests [and] to furnish complete training for students desirous of becoming Craftsmen, Designers, and Teachers."[24]

Among the special facilities in the new building was a pottery studio. Judson T. Webb, a pottery instructor at the Chicago Art Institute School, was first engaged to come to Minneapolis in April 1905 and supervise the installation of

ndicraft Guild sales area. Construction Details, *Ausust 1914,* *59. Photograph courtesy of the Minnesota Historical Society.*

Elizabeth Augusta Chant (1865–1947) in her studio at the Handicraft Guild, about 1908. Collection of Sherron R. Biddle, Boiling Springs, Penn. Photograph courtesy of St. John's Museum of Art, Wilmington, N.C.

potters' wheels similar to those used in Chicago. Due to the expense of professional power wheels, both the Minneapolis and Chicago schools initially used wheels powered by sewing machine treadles. Two kilns were installed, a small one for biscuit ware (the initial firing prior to glazing) and a larger one for firing glazed pieces. The guild's decision to use local Red Wing clay for its pottery production was likely reached in consultation with Webb who was a proponent of the use of American clays.[25]

The guild house itself may have articulated arts and crafts principles as eloquently as any of the organization's members. Beamed ceilings, dark rafters, and wainscoting details combined with warm brown wall and yellow ceiling tones to produce a subtle, welcoming atmosphere that promoted the exchange of ideas. The floor plan relegated noisy shop areas to the back of the building. The building quickly became a center for artists, craftspeople, and students across the metropolitan area. The Woman's Club of Minneapolis held its weekly meetings there; visiting artists spoke and exhibited their work in the guild auditorium and galleries; specialists were invited to lecture on topics related to the guild's coursework. In January 1910 May Morris, daughter of William Morris (British founder of the Arts and Crafts movement), was a featured speaker at the guild during her exhibition tour of the United States.[26]

The guild facility also offered studio space to artists, designers, and craftspeople working in various media, further strengthening its relationship to the art community. Over the years those spaces were occupied by Elizabeth Norris, Susan Christian, bookbinders Winifred Cole and Edith Griffith, leatherworkers Nelbert Murphy and Margaret Sheardown, photographers Margaret Sheridan and Gertrude E. Mann, rare book dealer Edmund D. Brooks, the decorating studio of Gustav F. Weber, portraitist Hildur Peterson-Frey, jeweler Ida Pell Conklin, and painter Elisabeth Chant. The last Saturday of the month served as a day to informally visit studios and join a gathering in the guild tea room. More than fifty years later, the guild building remained a center of activity for local craftsworkers. Commercial artists, a violin maker, fashion designers, and cabinetmakers had successful showrooms and workshops in the guild building as late as 1973. They were drawn there, as fashion designer Agnes Reed said, because it felt like home.[27]

Ernest Batchelder. Photograph courtesy of Robert Winter and Allan Bachelder.

THE PROGRAM

In keeping with the broad ideals of the arts and crafts movement, the guild fostered an appreciation for fine materials, a respect for skilled work, and for cooperative effort of its members. In translating these ideals, first articulated in Europe, to the practical, socially liberal young American city of Minneapolis, emphasis shifted from the training of individual artists to the training of teachers who could disseminate the ideas as broadly as possible.

Because the guild initially functioned as an extension or supplement to existing educational programs, a summer school represented its first programmatic focus. To direct its first *Summer School of Design Applied to Crafts*, held in the summer of 1905, the guild hired Ernest A. Batchelder of Throop Polytechnic Institute, Pasadena, California (now Caltech). Batchelder believed in a universality of

good design that could be fostered by craftsworkers, not theorists, who would then teach the applied arts. He recommended the analysis of exemplary objects as a way of understanding the need for order, for clear and coherent expression, and for the effective functioning of a work. Batchelder felt that the true strength of design could be found in the structural relationship of its various elements. One of his simplest statements spoke most eloquently of his perspective on the goals of a true craftsman. "We try for order and hope for beauty."[28]

Batchelder presented four aims for the summer school program: "1. To stimulate the imagination. 2. To impart sufficient technical skill to develop the limitations and possibilities of leather, metal and clay as means of expression. 3. To induce pupils to think in terms of lines, areas and tones. 4. To lead the individual expression of an idea in accordance with sound principles."[29] The first summer school session drew eighty students and much favorable comment. Batchelder agreed to return for the summer of 1906 before leaving to study at industrial art and technical schools in England and Europe.[30] After the first successful summer program, the guild added two faculty members to its staff in the fall of 1906. Harry S. Michie, a 1902 design graduate of Pratt Institute in Brooklyn, who also spent a year at the Camberwell School of Arts and Crafts in London, joined the faculty as a metalwork specialist. Ida Pell Conklin, a 1906 Pratt graduate in jewelry and metal-chasing, began a long affiliation with the guild as jewelry instructor.[31] In December of the same year, the guild participated in the "Fifth Annual Exhibition of Original Designs for Decorations and Examples of Art Crafts Having Distinct Artistic Merit" at the Art Institute of Chicago. Guild students and faculty went on in the years ahead to show their work regularly in Chicago, Boston, Detroit, New York, Los Angeles, Kansas City, Philadelphia, and Fargo, North Dakota, as well as throughout Minnesota. Handicraft Guild work was shown in 1907 exhibitions organized by the Brooklyn Handicrafters, the New York Keramic Arts group, and the Eastern & Western Drawing & Manual Training Teachers' Associations meeting in Cleveland.

Despite poor health in the previous year, Batchelder returned to direct the summer school program in 1907. There were ninety-eight students registered for the course, half of whom came from outside the Twin Cities, including some from as far away as Oregon, Ohio, and Missouri. Determined efforts were made to encourage a broad-based student body. The guild advertised its program regularly in such publications as *The Craftsman, International Studio,* and *School Education,* and the summer school brochure offered addresses of boarding facilities in Minneapolis. Many of the students were established professionals, already engaged in teaching, designing, or crafts production, who sought to improve their skills and knowledge under the stimulating curriculum designed by Batchelder and the other well-known instructors.[32] Classes at the guild in 1907 included metalwork, jewelry, leather, pottery, book-bind-

Metalwork executed by the Handicraft Guild. The International
Studio, vol. 28, 1906.

ing, woodworking, wood carving, wood-block printing, and a special course in watercolor painting. The guild also advertised facilities for the firing and glazing of pottery and sold modeling tools, clay and leather tools, and "whole skins."[33]

Batchelder returned to direct the summer school of 1908, and in December of that year it was announced that he would also return in February 1909 for his first tenure as director of design for the winter term. He remained in Minneapolis for the 1909 summer school session as well. Batchelder's fame as an authority on design and composition had grown considerably by this point. He had served as director of the art department at Throop, as president of the Pacific Manual Training Association, and as a design instructor at the Harvard summer school. His regular contributions in *The Craftsman* and his book, *Principles of Design*, were read and debated across America. When, at the conclusion of the 1909 courses, he ended his formal association, the guild lost an important asset as well as the inspiration of a fine theorist, artist, and designer.[34]

With the summer school course of 1910, the guild entered a new phase under the directorship of Maurice Irwin Flagg of Boston, the second of the three most influential personalities to direct the Guild's educational efforts. At this time the guild building and its various programs continued to be managed by its corporate officers: Emma Roberts, Florence D. Willets, and Florence Wales. In September 1910, the normal art department was added to the curriculum to "train students to fill positions as teachers in public

or private schools, and give them a knowledge of handicraft which may lead to professions." By 1912 the guild was advertising its expanded programs as the "School of Design, Handicraft, and Normal Art," with diplomas awarded at the completion of the two-year course. New courses also were offered in other subjects, including stained glass, interior decoration, art in advertising, costume design, and illustration.[35] In 1912 Maurice Irwin Flagg also accepted the part-time position of director of the Minnesota State Art Society. Flagg's work at the State Art Society consumed more and more of his time, until he finally found it necessary to leave his position at the guild in 1914. He was replaced briefly by Mary C. Scovel.[36]

The arts and crafts movement in Minnesota reached its peak of recognition and acceptance around 1914–15. At the same time, however, the impact of World War I and the expanded roles of the Minnesota State Art Society and the Minneapolis School of Art contributed to its gradual decline. Ruth Raymond, who was hired in 1914 as a design and composition instructor and who took over as principal the following year, became the guild's last administrator. In 1916 Emma Roberts and Florence Willets, who had been serving respectively as guild president and secretary-treasurer almost since the organization's formation, felt they could no longer manage the administration of both the building and the program. At their suggestion, discussions began with the University of Minnesota for the possible transfer of the guild program. From information gathered in public schools and normal schools state-wide, there was

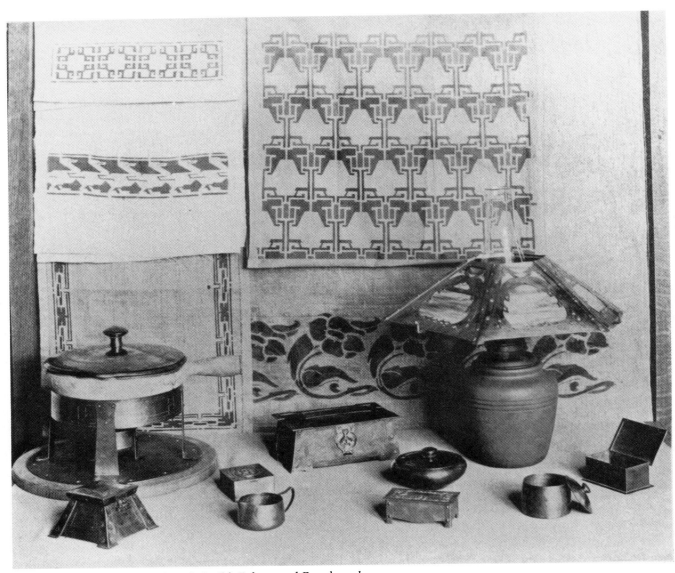

Varied works from the Handicraft Guild. Palette and Bench, *vol.*
1, October 1908, *p. 24.*

1914 junior class, Handicraft Guild. Photograph courtesy of the
Minnesota Historical Society.

a clear need for a degree program to train special teachers of art and music. In 1917 a two-year negotiation began to have the guild absorbed as the University of Minnesota's art education department. After this was accomplished, Raymond stayed on as head of the new department at the university until her retirement in 1947.[47]

THE WORK

The work produced by the guild incorporated many of the formal and technical traditions now identified with the Arts and Crafts movement. Identifiably handworked pots, exposed furniture joints, hammer marks, and visible, over-sized rivets on metalwork asserted the superiority of hand-made objects. In conscious contrast to mechanized production that masked all evidence of construction, the aim of all arts and crafts artists was to make process a component of design. Despite the accessibility of the so-phisticated work of Douglas Donaldson, James H. Winn, or Batchelder, many guild products retained a quality of stark simplicity and an absence of studied decorative elements. Emphasis was as much on process as on product. A successful student could acquire some level of technical skill, and would experience the satisfaction of working with his or her hands, recreating the experience with and for others.

To the extent that a prevailing aesthetic or design philosophy is discernible in guild work, it seems most closely linked to Japanese precedent. From the perspective of nineteenth-century romanticism, of which the philosophy of the Arts and Crafts movement was an extension, Japan was honored as a nation which had kept its identity against the force of Western industrialization. Japanese culture was seen as conservative, against innovation, a quality championed by romantics seeking to escape the machine production of the industrial age. Compared to the American style of life, obsessed with consumerism and wasteful spending, the Japanese appeared to live simply and well. They also did not separate and elevate "art" to a special place over "craft," as was the case in Western culture.[38]

Art periodicals were the most pervasive tool for spreading Japanese images and ideas. *Japonisme*, the term broadly designating this late nineteenth-century Western enthusiasm for things Japanese, contributed to the popularity of certain birds, flowers, insects, trees, and fish, especially carp, as design motifs in America and Europe at the turn of the century. The Japanese sensitivity to the look of specific seasonal and weather conditions also was emulated. The "cracked-ice" or "crackled-glaze" motif had a significant impact on ceramic and graphic work. Many of these qualities (e.g., the juxtaposition of movement against static natural backgrounds, bird's-eye viewpoints, irregular division of space, and flatter images with absent or altered perspectives) inspired Western artists of the time. Ernest Batchelder, the guild's most influential teacher, was among them.

Batchelder's writings emphasized the need for American craft artists to develop a national design vocabulary that was not based on Western historical tradition. His writings and his instruction emphasized that good design required a unity of all elements. The successful solution to any design problem amalgamated decisions about line, composition, and color and the strength of any work lay in the structural relationship of these various elements. Batchelder was greatly influenced by Japanese design, viewing it as a unification of nature and abstract form. He admired the Japanese artist who did not replicate nature, but rather expressed an idea of it. Consequently, although he encouraged his own students to study nature, he gave greater emphasis to the use of natural materials, naturally fashioned; iron should look like iron and copper like copper, and neither should look like draped silk or a dragonfly's wing.

Other influential guild members had a strong commitment to Japanese art as well. At her shop, The Artcraft Shop: Sign of the Bay Tree, Mary Moulton Cheney intro-

Peacock lamp designed and executed by Douglas Donaldson. Palette and Bench, vol. 2, February 1910, p. 111.

duced prints imported from Japan as early as 1901, and she regularly carried the prints of contemporary artist, Sogo Matsumoto. She also copyrighted illuminated designs of her own that featured sparrows in flight and human figures reminiscent of those in Japanese block prints. The peacock and the phoenix—two popular icons of American *japonisme*—were hallmarks of her graphic design. These motifs were used not only by Cheney, but by Batchelder, Twin Cities china painter Henrietta Barclay Paist, and other students and instructors at the guild and other Twin Cities arts and craft schools.

Bertha Lum, who trained at the School of the Art Institute of Chicago before marrying and moving to Minneapolis in 1893, taught wood-block printing at the guild in 1905,

1906, and 1915. Her early fascination with Japanese woodblock prints lasted a lifetime and led to several visits to and apprenticeships in Japan between 1893 and 1912. In Japan, the production of a color woodcut print was divided among several artists, each specializing in one particular component of creation and execution. Lum, in contrast, mastered the entire process. Her prints, often based on the work of other Japanese artists or the heroines of Japanese folklore and legends, so impressed her Japanese teachers and fellow artists that she was the only Westerner (and the only woman) whose work was shown at a Tokyo exhibition in 1912.[39] Lum's regular incorporation of the Tori Gate image, her distorted landscape perspectives, use of silhouette, and the interior light of her color woodcuts is echoed in the work of other guild instructors and students.[40]

The Minneapolis community's exposure and sensitivity to *japonisme* were further advanced by the local interior designer John Scott Bradstreet. The galleries of his Craftshouse extended the walls of the guild's classroom, where students were exposed to Oriental art, furnishings, and Bradstreet's own *jin-di-sugi* design contribution to the arts

Handicraft Guild of Minneapolis. Copper hood detail of the downstairs fireplace in the Hewitt residence, Minneapolis, Minn. Photograph by Gary Mortensen and Robert Fogt.

Wall light fixture with same piercework motifs as Wycroft fixtures and Burtha Lum print. Palette and Bench, vol. 2, February 1910, p. 109.

and crafts movement. A column in a local publication, *Keith's Magazine*, describes Bradstreet's exaggerated Japanese-inspired furniture designs with an appreciation for both his innovative use of Eastern design motifs and the creation of a unique decorative style.[41]

In the crafted products of the guild, elaborate detail was the exception rather than the rule. The graphic, flat nature of guild designs, even of most of its repoussé metalwork, encouraged more abstract, less representational imagery, particularly evident in pierced metalwork. The guild's design vocabulary was reminiscent of the work of Charles Rennie Mackintosh and the women embroiderers of the Glasgow School, and at least two popular regional publications discussed and illustrated Glasgow School work. Batchelder's travels to Europe no doubt exposed guild members to the Glasgow School's innovative design principles.[42]

The best-known products of guild students and faculty are either in metal or ceramic. The ceramic forms are predominantly functional and include vases, pots, candlesticks, bookends, trivets, flower frogs, tiles, lamp bases, ink wells, wall sconces, and covered vessels.

Each of the three primary processes of potting—building, throwing, and molding—were utilized at the guild. Although there are examples of thin-walled, wheel-turned pots, the majority of surviving examples are thick walled, sometimes with rough applied designs or stamp work and usually coated with heavy, blended glazes.[43] These slab or coiled vessels appear to have been created primarily as instructional pieces and apparently were not earmarked for retail sale. The molded versus hand-built pieces are more appealing, their success relying on the glazing skill of the student or instructor and the quality of the original mold.

Red Wing clay was brought directly from the beds fifty miles from the Twin Cities, then kneaded and formed into soft bricks of a workable size for the potters' use. Full-scale working drawings were prepared before work on a vessel was begun. Decorating and finishing were done entirely by hand. All guild pots were biscuit-fired, glazed and fired again.[44] The rustic quality of most guild pottery, which did not always lend itself well to vessel forms, was better suited to decorator tiles and household ornaments. Residential work by guild craftsworkers seems to have focused on metal light fixtures and fireplace faces. Guild fireplaces in particular have a scale, texture, and color that expressed the American arts and crafts ideal of incorporating craft production into the heart of the newly simplified and cozy home.[45]

In a 1905 feature article of the *Minneapolis Journal*, society editor Martha Scott Anderson described the guild's pottery-making process and suggested that a new art industry might emerge from the pottery work of guild students. But the small number of extant guild ceramics and the few interiors executed by the organization indicate that their commissions were limited to a small group of committed patrons.[46]

Of the surviving handicrafts produced by the guild,

Handicraft Guild of Minneapolis. Ceramics. Steve Schoneck,
Rolf Grudem, Nancy M. Rose, and the Rev. William Gamber
Collections. Photograph by Gary Mortensen and Robert Fogt.

Women in a pottery class at the Handicraft Guild. 1916–1917
Handicraft Guild of Minneapolis Session Booklet, *p. 21.*

Fireplace from the M. E. J. Couper residence, Minneapolis. Construction Details, *vol. 6, August 1914, p. 61.*

metalwork is the most prevalent and often the most successful from a design and functional perspective. These objects represent nearly every metalwork technique and function, everything from hammered light fixtures, to cut spoons, to enameled desk sets. Early metalwork courses at the guild included only hammering and etching. Chasing and braising were soon added. By 1912–13 courses offered both beginners and advanced workers instruction in the finer points of constructing and decorating trays, bowls, spoons, desk

1916–17 pottery display. 1916–1917 Handicraft Guild of Minneapolis Session Booklet, *p. 6.*

sets, lamp shades, and other items. Among the techniques taught were hammering, riveting, soldering, etching, saw piercing, raising, repoussé, and enameling.[47] Surviving guild metalwork suggests that instructors and students were heavily influenced by work done at Pratt Institute and Bradley Polytechnic and by artisans and educators such as Ernest Batchelder, Ida Pell Conklin, Harry S. Michie, Augustus F. Rose, Arthur Frank Payne, his student Harold L. Boyle, James Winn, and Douglas Donaldson. The form and finish of many surviving examples of metalwork suggest that spinning also was taught. Metal blanks seem to have been purchased elsewhere and used by the guild for pierced work and other decorative techniques.

In 1910, *Palette and Bench* featured an article by guild metalwork instructor, Douglas Donaldson, "The Making of Metal Lampshades." The oriental decorative elements of these pierced and repoussé metal shades suggest that while a clean, rectilinear style prevailed in American arts and crafts design, metalwork at the guild featured decoration that flared and curved, often resembling Japanesque pagoda-like forms.[48] The balance of positive and negative space and the frequent incorporation of peacocks and other exotic birds in metalwork bear further witness to guild members' admiration for Japanese precedent.

An undated brochure succinctly describes the guild's view of the educational and aesthetic value of metalwork. The basic but elegant forms developed as raised bowls, nut sets, and pierced spoons are among the guild's most representative and finest work.

> A metal bowl should be made from the flat material. The metal is annealed again, fashioned over stakes and gradually coaxed into shape until the ideal of the maker is expressed in the finished piece.
> Such an article demands our respect and admiration, and possesses a commercial, as well as an artistic value, far exceeding a machine made piece."[49]

Group of metalwork from the Handicraft Guild. Arts and Decoration, *vol. 2, September 1912, p. 399.*

Handicraft Guild of Minneapolis. Brass etched tray and picture frame, brass and copper match holder. *Steve Schoneck and David Matchan Collections. Photograph by Gary Mortensen and Robert Fogt.*

...mp fixtures executed by the Handicraft Guild of Minneapolis. ...lette and Bench, *vol. 2, February 1910, p. 111.*

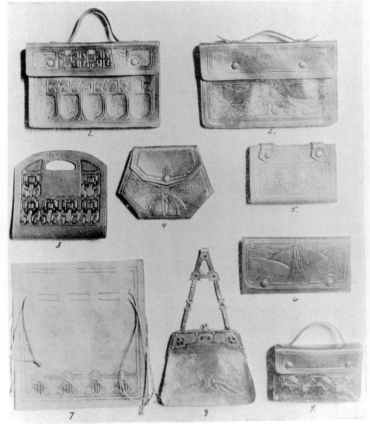

Handicraft Guild tooled leather works. Palette and Bench, *February 1909, p. 119.*

Handicraft Guild metal shop. 1916–1917 Handicraft Guild of Minneapolis Session Booklet, *p. 8.*

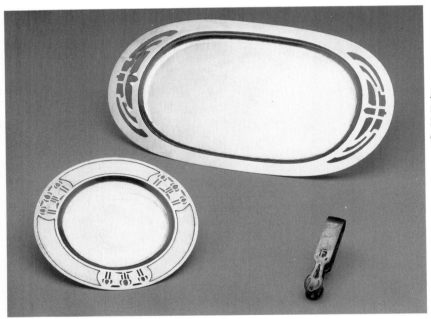

Handicraft Guild of Minneapolis. Silver plated tray, calling card tray, and sugar tongs. Minnesota Historical Society and Steve Schoneck Collections. Photograph by Gary Mortensen and Robert Fogt.

Handicraft Guild jewelry. 1916–1917 Handicraft Guild of Minneapolis Session Booklet, *p. 19.*

Few examples remain of guild jewelry, leather work, stenciling, woodblock printing, weaving, basket making, and graphic design. However, a 1909 issue of *Palette and Bench* featured a photograph of nine pieces of guild leather work and identified their makers, each of them a woman.[50]

nent place in the international Arts and Crafts movement, but also as a model of resilience, responsiveness, and institutional modesty that demanded no monument and no tribute beyond the assurance that its ideals would be conveyed to students of the crafts for generations to come.

CONCLUSION

Although varied in size, goals, and membership, American arts and crafts organizations at the turn of the century shared a deep-seated antipathy to the social impact of industrialization, finding expression for a sense of personal and cultural loss, a fragmentation of experience occasioned by industrial progress, and the hope that life could be restored to a more fulfilling, more natural state. In Europe, this hope was conveyed effectively through reference to a medieval past, the time before machine production played so decisive a part in everyday life. In America, however, with scant memory of a pre-industrial past, the hope was more appropriately formulated in terms of the present and future. Embedded in the experience of craft technique and process (although, with characteristic pragmatism, often willing to incorporate machine work), the ideal of a full, humane life was to be preached as widely as possible, enough to augment and even, at times, displace efficiency and economy, the prevailing values of modern industrial society.

Although both Europeans and Americans rejected the loss of individuality implicit in industrial production, American arts and crafts organizations more often sought broad social change as opposed to moral reform. The successful craft product required hard-won skills and the personal engagement of a particular craftsman, and it invariably demanded a great deal of time. Arts and crafts guilds, schools, and individual artists were certainly not averse to selling hand-made products at a profit, however. On the contrary, each sale, particularly of objects for everyday use, became a small victory of the hand-made over the industrially produced.[51] More broadly, this represented a symbolic victory of a utopian ideal over the unpalatable realities of life in a modern industrial society.

In its determined pragmatism, in its populist sentiments, and in its strong educational emphasis, the Handicraft Guild of Minneapolis was an exemplary American arts and crafts organization. In acute awareness of the larger arts community in which it functioned, however, it may well be unique. Although the guild focused its utopian efforts on change in individuals, the goal would be achieved through education. This small and relatively short-lived organization effectively matched its members' interests with a series of recognized community needs. The guild fulfilled these needs, went on to continuously redefine its own programs for more than a decade, and finally accommodated itself within the structure of a large state university. Then, it quietly and permanently stepped aside. As we approach the turn of the next century, it becomes possible to see the guild not only as the basis for Minnesota's claim to a promi-

NOTES

1. Lionel Lambourne, *Utopian Craftsmen: The Arts and Crafts Movement from the Cotswolds to Chicago* (Salt Lake City: Peregrine Smith, Inc., 1980), 125–40.
2. Other institutionally affiliated arts and crafts associations include the Chicago Arts and Crafts Society, Throop Polytechnic Institute in Pasadena, Pratt Institute in Brooklyn, Newcomb Pottery at Sophie Newcomb Memorial College in New Orleans, the Mechanic Arts High School in St. Paul, the Minneapolis School of Fine Arts, and the California College of Arts and Crafts in Oakland.
3. These include the Furniture Shop of Arthur and Lucia Mathews in San Francisco, Charles Rohlf's Workshop in Buffalo, New York, Old Mission Kopper Kraft shops in San Jose and San Francisco, the Kalo Shop in Chicago, and the Shop of the Crafters in Cincinnati.
4. These include the Hartford Arts & Crafts Club, the Arts & Crafts League of Evansville (Illinois), The Arts & Handicrafts Guild of Greensboro (North Carolina), The Chicago Arts and Crafts Society, and the Handicraft Workers of Peterborough (New Hampshire).
5. Gardner C. Teall, "The Craftsman's Library," *House Beautiful* 12, no. 1 (June 1902): 18.
6. Thorstein Veblen, *The Theory of the Leisure Class: An Economic Study in the Evolution of Institutions* (New York: Macmillan Co., 1899).
7. Eileen Boris, *Art and Labor: Ruskin, Morris and the Craftsman Ideal in America* (Philadelphia: Temple University Press, 1986): 48, 49; Thorstein Veblen, "Arts and Crafts," *The Journal of Political Economy* (December 1902–September 1903): 108–11.
8. "All Hand Work: The Chalk and Chisel Club Exhibition Opens To-Night," *Minneapolis Journal*, 16 November 1898, p. 6; "Arts and Crafts Exhibition: Formerly Opened by a Private View Last Night," 17 November 1898, p. 7; "At the 'Arts and Crafts': Book Lovers Go There to Rave," 18 November 1898. The exhibitions first sponsored in 1898 by the Chalk and Chisel Club of Minneapolis exposed Minnesota artists to a variety of handicrafts and inspired designers, architects, and artists to experiment with new materials and technologies. Local merchants began to stock Rookwood, Grueby fireplace tiles, Craftsman furniture, Kalo silver, Van Briggle pottery, Deerfield Society blue and white embroidery, and other fine crafts for this newly enlightened populace. Minnesotans were anxious to have local commercial access to such goods.
9. "Minneapolis Artists Lose a Landmark: The Old Studio on Hennepin was Most Intimately Identified with the Beginnings of Art in this City," *Minneapolis Journal*, 12 December 1903, p. 4; "Artists Planning a Studio Center," 24 September 1906, p. 5. Other tenants in the 1890s included Alexis Fournier, Mary Helmick, Rhoda Casterlin, and E. H. Center.
10. Martha Scott Anderson, "Two Young Women Artists and their Charming Studios: Miss Heisser and Miss Chant Work for the Encouragement of Art Interests—Some of their Recent Experiments," *Minneapolis Journal*, 10 March 1900.
11. St. Paul Department of Education, *A Course Book for the High Schools of St. Paul, Minnesota* (St. Paul, 1912–13): 64–68. Minnesota's public school applied arts programs were as sophisticated as some of the nationally established arts and crafts societies. Mechanic Arts High School students, for example, developed the color scheme and furniture design for the Minnesota Building at the St. Louis Universal Exposition of 1904. Half of the furniture was produced by Mechanic Arts students, the other half by students in Minneapolis high schools. The exhibition hall was critically reviewed in the *New York Staatzeitung*. Dr. M. Baumfield's review discussed the setting as "furniture in an independent variation of the Mission style, [which] harmonizes well in color [greens] with

the wood-work and a carpet of perfect design. The colored glass windows . . . are of great decorative value . . . well worth seeing." The exhibition won the gold medal. Support for the school sometimes came directly from the St. Paul community, as suggested in a report of The Woman's Civic League of St. Paul in that city's *Directory of Charitable and Benevolent Organizations* (1913). Organized in 1899, this league sponsored "Arts & Crafts" and industrial education exhibitions in 1901–2. The proceeds were used to purchase a year's supply of manual training supplies for St. Paul schools and a china kiln for Mechanic Arts High School.

12. On the origins of the Minnesota State Art Society, see State of Minnesota, *The Constitution and By-Laws of the Minnesota State Art Society*, (1903): 3–15; M. K. Bailey, "An Annual Art Exhibition," *The Bellman*, 26 March 1910, pp. 386–88; "The Beginning of the Minnesota State Art Commission," *The Minnesotan*, 1, no. 1 (July 1915): 24, 26; "Minnesota State Art Society," reprint from the *Magazine of Art*, Walker Art Center edition (ca. 1948): n.p. (from the pamphlet collections of the Minnesota Historical Society); Minnesota State Archives, Minnesota State Arts Board Administrative Files, State Art Society Scrapbook 1905–14, Minnesota Historical Society Collections (box 70 G4 7B); O. R. Geyer, "Putting Art to Work for the Masses," *Scribner's Magazine*, 62 (1917): 769–72; William Gray Purcell, "Made in Minnesota: The Story of Native Resources, Their Use and Possibilities," *The Minnesotan*, 1, no. 9 (April 1916): 7–13. With annual appropriations as small as $2,000, the Minnesota State Art Society was able not only to purchase Minnesota art and handicrafts which were lent for study and exhibition statewide, but to sponsor exhibitions and offer cash prizes, provide training around the state, offer lantern slide illustrated programs, and publish *The Minnesotan*, a short-lived state arts magazine. The State Art Society had a difficult time maintaining its momentum over the years. But it was successful in disseminating ideas, encouraging the use of natural resources, and in taking programs and exhibitions to rural Minnesota, charitable institutions such as orphan asylums, and into ethnic communities in efforts to revive native and foreign crafts.

13. The Minneapolis Society of Fine Arts had its first official gathering in January 1883. Its first program was the Art Loan Exhibition, which provided art exhibitions from private collections in the area. Although some early supporters already felt a museum would be the appropriate next step, the limited funds available and the perception that arts education was a pressing need argued that a school would be a more practical first effort. The three-year course in decorative design was initiated in 1899 under the direction of Mary Moulton Cheney, an active member of the Minneapolis arts and crafts community. Cheney served as head of the department until 1917 when she became the director of the Minneapolis School of Fine Arts. She was the first woman to hold the position.

14. Nellie Trufant Papers, Minneapolis History Collection, Minneapolis Public Library. Gertrude J. Leonard, handwritten note, dated 5 January 1895.

15. *The Chalk and Chisel Club Outline of Study for 1895–1896, 1897–98*, and for an undated year, Minneapolis, n.p. The member names listed follow: Mrs. George Backus, Miss Gene G. Banker, Mrs. Edward Center, Mary Moulton Cheney, Miss Elena Jay Darling, Miss Emily Fairfield Darling, Miss Clara Derickson, Miss Adeline Gates, Miss Agnes Harrison, Mrs. Mary Helmick, Mrs. F. G. Holbrook, Mrs. T. J. Janney, Miss Gertrude J. Leonard, Miss Charlotte B. Long, Miss Hope McDonald, Mrs. E. H. Monroe, Mrs. Milton O. Nelson, Miss Marion Parker, Mrs. William Reno, Miss Mary Ella Simpson, Mrs. Ruth Wilson Tice, Miss Nellie Stinson Trufant, and Miss Hattie Eliza Welles.

16. The Chalk and Chisel Club, *An Exhibition of the Arts & Crafts Under the Auspices of the Chalk & Chisel Club* (Minneapolis, 16–19 November 1898): 1–30. The influence of the Arts and Crafts Society's exhibitions on Minnesota artists and educators was evident in an article which described a show of work by women with studios at the "Old Bandbox." ("In the Studio: The Busiest and Most Attractive Spots in Town this Week," *Minneapolis Journal*, 16 December 1899, p. 10.) The columnist described it as "the most beautiful [work] they have ever

shown." Elizabeth Chang's illuminations incorporated heraldic motifs, and Mrs. A. M. Wang showed work in burnt and stained woods. An eastern woodworker who had exhibited in the previous year (undoubtedly Arthur G. Grinnel of New Bedford, Massachusetts) had directly influenced the work of Mrs. Wang.

17. Chalk and Chisel Club co-founder Mary Helmick hosted the last meeting of the year in her home in Washburn Park. That meeting was both a formal farewell to Minnesota's first arts and crafts organization and a symbol of the larger community network now supporting the arts and crafts movement in Minnesota.

18. *Constitution and By-Laws of the Minneapolis Society of Arts and Crafts* (Minneapolis, n.d.), 5.

19. "Clubs and Charities," *Minneapolis Journal*, 18 November 1899, p. 12. In the late nineteenth and early twentieth centuries, advanced education for many women was not a viable option. A national proliferation of women's clubs and study groups at the turn of the twentieth century permitted women to expand their knowledge and exchange ideas. Minnesotans were no exception, and many of these clubs evolved into the formal organizations and programs that still exist today. Chalk and Chisel Club and Handicraft Guild members belonged to many such clubs and appeared frequently on the programs as participating members or guest speakers.

20. "Summer School Handicraft Guild," *The Craftsman* 8 (May 1905): 267.

21. "Art," *Minneapolis Journal*, 1 July 1905, p. 12.

22. *The Fourth Exhibition of the Arts & Crafts Society of Minneapolis, Minnesota* (15–21 November 1904): 29; *Minneapolis Journal*, 1 March 1905, p. 7.

23. "May Build a School," *Minneapolis Journal*, 20 July 1905, p. 4; "Handicraft to Build," 22 February 1907, p. 7; *The Dual City Blue Book* (Householder's Directory), 1907–9, p. 302. A guild advertisement notes that after October 1907, the guild would be in its new facility at 89 South 10th Street.

24. Elisabeth A. Chant, "The Handicraft Guild," *The Bellman*, 21 March 1908, p. 317–19. *The Handicraft Guild of Minneapolis School of Design Handicraft and Normal Art, Eighth Annual Session* (17 September 1912–31 May 1913): 3.

25. "Able Craftsmen for Summer Work: Art Institute will Send Jewelry and Pottery Teachers," *Minneapolis Journal*, 27 March 1905, p. 7; "Guild Workers Take up Pottery: First Effort of the Kind in Minneapolis," 19 April 1905, p. 12. Partly due to Webb's efforts, native clay deposits in Hot Springs, Arkansas, and Menominie, Wisconsin, were being mined to expand the American clay industry.

26. "The Village Gossip," *The Bellman*, 22 January 1910, p. 122; "The Village Gossip," 29 January 1910, p. 158.

27. Barbara Flanagan labeled the guild building a "little Greenwich Village" in 1973, reviving an appellation first used in 1916. "Handicrafts Flourish in City's 'Greenwich Village,'" *The Minneapolis Star*, 11 May 1973, p. 1B.

28. Ernest A. Batchelder, *Design in Theory and Practice* (New York: The MacMillan Company, 1912), 7.

29. "Summer School Handicraft Guild," *The Craftsman* 8, no. 2 (May 1905): 267.

30. Handicraft Guild, *Summer School of Design Applied to Crafts* (19 June–19 July 1905): 1–4. Principal instructors working with Batchelder, some of whom continued at the guild throughout that first full year, included Florence D. Willets of The Art Institute of Chicago (pottery), Nelbert Murphy of Pratt Institute in Brooklyn (leatherwork adapted for public schools), James H. Winn of The Art Institute of Chicago (jewelry and metalwork), and John Ellsworth Painter of Minneapolis public schools (woodwork). Local craftsworkers serving as assistant instructors included Edith Griffith and Winifred Cole in book binding, Grace Kiess in pottery, Bertha Lum in wood-block printing, Mary Moulton Cheney in design, and Corice Woodruff in sculpture and painting.

31. "Art Metal Course: Pratt Institute Recently Opened a Class for Women," *Minneapolis Journal*, 26 July 1901, p. 11. This article discussed the innovations at Pratt Institute in Brooklyn, which was offering a new program to teach the art of metalwork in silver and gold. It

noted the high percentage of women enrolled and the opportunities such training offered them. So much interest was evident that an art metal class was opened expressly for women. Such a program, available for the first time in America, supplanted the previously limited options of apprenticeship in a factory or of study abroad. Shared goals between Pratt Institute and arts and crafts organizations in Minnesota resulted in an enriching exchange of students and instructors to teach handicrafts and train educators in the years to come.

32. *Minneapolis Society of Fine Arts Bulletin*, 2, no. 6 (Midsummer 1907): 10; *School Education* (September 1910): 53.

33. Handicraft Guild, *Summer School of Design and Handicraft: Third Annual Session*, (19 June–20 July 1907): 1–6.

34. *Minneapolis Journal*, 27 March 1905, p. 7; Handicraft Guild, *Summer School of Design Applied to Crafts* (19 June–19 July 1905): 1–4; *The Craftsman* 8, no. 2 (May 1905): 267; *Minneapolis Journal*, 20 July 1905, p. 4; *The Craftsman* 10, no. 1 (April 1906): 137; "Local Art Notes," *Minneapolis Society of Fine Arts Bulletin* 1, no. 10 (July 1906): 5; 2, no. 3 (March 1907): 11, 12; "Art Notes," *Minneapolis Society of Fine Arts Bulletin* 2, no. 5 (May 1907): 3; 2, no. 6 (Midsummer 1907): 10; Elisabeth A. Chant, "The Handicraft Guild," *The Bellman* 21 March 1908, p. 317–19; "Summer Schools," *The International Studio* 35, no. 7–10 (1908): xxiii; "Batchelder will Teach: Authority on Designs Opens Class at Handicraft Guild Feb. 1," *Minneapolis Journal* 9 December 1908, p. 13. Due to the varied material published on the career of Ernest Allen Batchelder, an extensive citation is provided to substantiate the discussion in the text related to the dates of his association with the guild. He also is listed in the 1909 Minneapolis city directory. There is no evidence that Batchelder played any direct role in the founding of the Handicraft Guild. He was brought in to direct the first summer course offered by the guild, and his retention in that role confirms that his talents and reputation were recognized and sought by guild officers and faculty to establish a program that promoted quality in design and coursework.

35. *The International Studio* 44 (September 1911): n.p.

36. In his position at the Minnesota State Art Society, Flagg became an active advocate for the revival of foreign crafts as commercial endeavors in rural locations, for the promotion and use of natural materials in craft work, for courses and lectures on arts and crafts, for traveling exhibition programs, and for the promotion of low-cost model house plans for use in rural and suburban areas.

37. University of Minnesota president's office, 1911–45, box 34, University of Minnesota College of Education folder 1916–40, University of Minnesota Archives, Minneapolis, Minn. Correspondence and memos between University of Minnesota administrators and faculty, Emma Roberts, Florence Willets, Ruth Raymond, Harington Beard, Minneapolis Civic and Commerce Association, and others related to the dissolution of the guild and its adoption by the University of Minnesota as its new art education department.

38. The exposure to Japanese material culture in goods as diverse as fans, embroidery patterns, and art pottery greatly influenced middle-class Americans, women in particular, and promoted among them a desire to own Japanese-inspired goods.

39. Julie Meech and Gabriel P. Weisberg, *Japonisme Comes to America: The Japanese Impact on the Graphic Arts, 1876–1925* (1990): 126–56; Mary Evans O'Keefe Gravlos and Carol Pulin, *Bertha Lum, American Printmakers, A Smithsonian Series* (Washington, D.C.: Smithsonian Institution Press, 1991).

40. The Minneapolis Institute of Arts acquired a major collection of Bertha Lum's color woodcuts for its holdings in 1916.

41. Henrietta P. Keith, "Decoration and Furnishing," *Keith's Magazine*, 10, no. 4 (October 1903): 185.

The Japanese artists are probably unsurpassed by any in the world in producing decorative effects with wood. Western woodworkers have indeed studied these Eastern models to much purpose, as was evidenced in some extremely beautiful pieces of furniture seen recently in the artistic rooms of a leading decorator [Bradstreet]. Notable among these was a table of cypress wood, treated with the new process of eating out the soft parts of the wood by acids, bringing out the natural markings and veinings of the wood strongly, yet leaving an indescribably soft and beautiful finish to the surface. This wood lends itself admirably to such treatment, on account of its large, decided grain. This table was for a library, with slightly hexagonal outline, and around the natural veinings and markings of the center which looked like a piece of watered silk moire, was carved a broad border of large plantain leaves and interlacing stems. The price of this rich and beautiful table was but $85.00 . . . Those who know furniture only as the product of the department stores, have no conception of its refinements, when submitted to the hands of such artists.

42. Henrietta P. Keith and Eleanor A. Cummins, *Practical Studies in Interior Decoration and Furnishing*, 2d ed. (Minneapolis, M. L. Keith, 1909–10): 34, 110, 146, 153; M. L. Keith, *Interiors Beautiful and Their Decoration* (illus.), 3d ed. (Minneapolis, 1911–12), 62, 88. These publications appear to be compilations of published work and article research done for *Keith's Magazine*. The discussions and images of interior treatments identified as the "New Idea" Glasgow School style suggest the local constituency was well versed in this design school.

43. Pottery instruction was given by Florence Wales, secretary-treasurer of the guild. She, along with Margaret Hubbard, Jeannette Gunkel, Katherine Whitney, and Annette Wales were the first to produce guild pottery marked with its "characteristic monogram." A script variation of the HG cipher was used in published form from 1904 until early 1905. These marks illustrate the many methods used to mark Handicraft Guild pieces from 1905–18.

44. In the 1905 and 1907 summer school brochures the pottery course was described as including building, molding, throwing, and glazing. On page 13 of *The Handicraft Guild of Minneapolis School of Design Handicraft and Normal Art, Eleventh Annual Session* (21 September 1915–3 June 1916) the course was described as offering students several choices in pottery techniques, including "the making of low bowls, tall vases, jars with handles, tiles with incised designs, the modeling of low reliefs and the glazing and firing of these pieces."

45. "Society Biographies: The Handicraft Guild, Minneapolis," *Handicraft* 3 (December 1910): 341–42. "The Handicraft Guild pottery has become well known for its beauty of form and quiet, rich color. Architects are interested in the tiles produced and orders for specially designed mantles are frequently received." "Society Biographies: Handicraft Guild of Minneapolis," *Handicraft* 4, no. 5 (August 1911): 170–71. "In all departments a large part of the work executed is to fill special orders. The growing demand for tiles and copper hoods for fire places [sic], lamps, lanterns and other articles for specific places indicates more thought for decorative interiors." A small number of documented guild interiors have come to light but without any surviving records of the guild itself it is very difficult to demonstrate what part custom interior work might have actually played in guild production.

46. Martha Scott Anderson, "A New Art Industry May Grow from the Pottery Work of the Handicraft Guild," *Minneapolis Journal*, 2 September 1905, p. 12. The photographs which accompany this article are by Arus S. Williams and also appear in some of the guild's promotional material.

47. *The Handicraft Guild of Minneapolis School of Design Handicraft and Normal Art, Twelfth Annual Session* (19 September 1916–3 June 1917): 7.

48. Douglas Donaldson, "The Making of Metal Lampshades," *Palette and Bench* 2 (February 1910): 109–11. According to this article, guild workers used metal and pottery lamp bases created in their shops as well as examples produced by other American craftsworkers. Donaldson noted in the article that the goal was for the base and shade to harmonize with each other, resulting in a beautiful and functional piece.

49. Handicraft Guild of Minneapolis, "Made in Minneapolis," (n.d.): 1–4. An undated promotional brochure for the Handicraft Guild.

50. *Palette and Bench* (February 1909): 119. A large photograph features nine pieces of tooled leather done by students of the Handicraft Guild ranging from purses to folders. The pieces were made by Mrs. Taylor, Miss Ekers, Miss Everett, Miss Carter, Miss Lodwig, Mrs. Seamar, Mrs. Stevens, and Mrs. Ingold.

51. *Minneapolis Society of Fine Arts Bulletin* 2, no. 2 (February 1907): 7. "The spread of the arts and crafts influence cannot take exactly the same lines of advance as in the old days of the guilds, for commerce

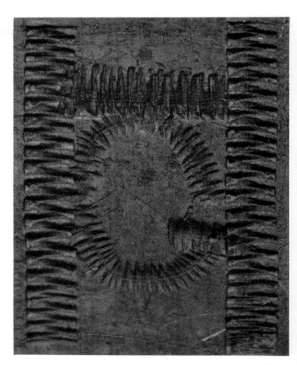

Details of Handicraft Guild markings. Photographs courtesy of the Minnesota Historical Society, Peter Latner, Gary Mortensen, and Robert Fogt.

now demands wide markets for its products and seeks to reach the every-day life. If art is to become a livelihood, it must follow the signs of the times, and appeal to the average purse."

BIBLIOGRAPHY

BOOKS

American Federation of Artists. *American Art Annual XIV.* 1917.

Anderson, Timothy J., Eudorah M. Moore, and Robert W. Winter, eds. *California Design 1910.* Salt Lake City: Gibbs Smith, 1989.

Anscombe, Isabelle and Charlotte Gere. *Arts and Crafts in Britain and America.* New York and London, 1978.

Bank, Mirra. *Anonymous Was a Woman.* New York: St. Martin's Press, Inc., 1979.

Boris, Eileen. *Art and Labor: Ruskin, Morris, and the Craftsman Ideal in America.* Philadelphia: Temple University Press, 1986.

Bowman, Leslie Green. *American Arts & Crafts: Virtue in Design.* Los Angeles: Los Angeles County Museum of Art in conjunction with Bullfinch Press, 1990.

Callen, Anthea. *Women Artists of the Arts and Crafts Movement, 1870–1914.* New York: Pantheon Books, 1979.

Carruth, William Hubert, *Each in His Own Tongue.* 3d ed. Minneapolis, n.d.

Carruthers, Annette. *Ashbee to Wilson: Aesthetic Movement, Arts and Crafts, and Twentieth Century.* Cheltenham, England, 1986.

Carruthers, Annette and Frank Johnson. *The Guild of Handicraft 1888–1988.* England, 1988.

Castle, Henry A. *History of St. Paul and Vicinity.* Vol. 2. Chicago and New York: The Lewis Publishing Company, 1912.

Cathers, David M. *Furniture of the American Arts and Crafts Movement: Stickley and Roycroft Mission Oak.* New York: New American Library, 1981.

Chapter XIII of the First Epistle to the Corinthians. Written by Paul the Apostle. Minneapolis: Mary Moulton Cheney, 1903.

Clark, Robert Judson, ed. *The Arts and Crafts Movement in America 1876–1916.* Princeton: Princeton University Press, 1972.

Colby, Joy Hakanson. *The Detroit Society of Arts and Crafts 1906–1976: An Introduction.* N.p., n.d.

Darling, Sharon S. *Chicago Ceramics and Glass: An Illustrated History from 1871 to 1933.* Chicago: Chicago Historical Society, 1979.

———.*Chicago Metalsmiths: An Illustrated History.* Chicago: Chicago Historical Society, 1977.

Evans, Karen, ed. and comp. *The Society of Arts and Crafts, Boston Exhibition Record. 1897–1927.* Boston: Boston Public Library, 1981.

Foster, Mary Dillon. *Who's Who Among Minnesota Women.* St. Paul: Mary Dillon Foster, 1924.

Frackelton, S. S. *Tried by Fire: A Work on China Painting.* New York, 1886.

Garwood, Darrell. *Artist in Iowa: A Life of Grant Wood.* New York: W. W. Norton & Co., 1944.

Glasgow Girls: Women in the Art School 1880–1920. Glasgow, Scotland: The Mackintosh Museum, Glasgow School of Art, 1988.

Gravlos, Mary Evans O'Keefe and Carol Pulin. *Bertha Lum, American Printmakers, A Smithsonian Series.* Washington, D.C.: Smithsonian Institution Press, 1991.

Gray, Stephen, ed. *Arts and Crafts Furniture: Shop of the Crafters at Cincinnati.* New York: Turn of the Century Editions, 1983.

Guptill, Arthur L. *Freehand Drawing Self-Taught: With Emphasis on the Techniques of Different Media.* New York, 1933.

Hamilton, Charles F. *Roycroft Collectibles: Including Collector Items Related to Elbert Hubbard. Founder of the Roycroft Shops.* San Diego, 1980.

Hess, Jeffrey A. *Their Splendid Legacy: The First 100 Years of the Minneapolis Society of Fine Arts.* Minneapolis: The Minneapolis Society of Fine Arts, 1985.

History of Minneapolis: Gateway to the Northwest. Vol. 3. Minneapolis: S. J. Clarke Publishing Co., 1923.

History of the City of Minneapolis, Minnesota. Part 1. Munsell & Co., 1893.

Hosley, William. *The Japan Idea: Art and Life in Victorian America.* Hartford, Conn.: Wadsworth Atheneum & William Hosley, 1990.

Hudson, Horace B., ed. *A Half Century of Minneapolis.* Minneapolis: Hudson Publishing Co., 1908.

Hudson, Horace B. *Hudson's Dictionary of Minneapolis & Vicinity: A Guide & Handbook.* Minneapolis: Hudson Publishing Co., 1909–17, annually.

Jeffries, Richard. *Saint Guido.* Minneapolis: The Chemith Press, 1902.

Kaplan, Wendy. *"The Art that is Life": The Arts & Crafts Movement in America. 1875–1920.* Boston: Little, Brown & Co., 1987.

Keith, Henrietta P., and Eleanor A. Cummins. *Practical Studies in Interior Decoration and Furnishing.* 2d ed. Minneapolis: M. L. Keith, 1909–10.

Keith, M. L., comp. *Interiors Beautiful and Their Decoration.* 3d ed. Minneapolis, 1911–12.

Lambourne, Lionel. *Utopian Craftsmen: The Arts and Crafts Movement from the Cotswolds to Chicago.* Salt Lake City: Peregrine Smith, Inc., 1980.

Lancaster, Clay. *Japanese Influence in America.* New York, n.d.

Lawrence, Maude and Caroline Sheldon, *The Use of the Plant in Decorative Design for the Grades.* Scott, Foreman & Co., 1912.

Leland, Charles G. Revised by John J. Holzapffel. *A Manual of Wood Carving.* New York, 1891.

Ludwig, Coy L. *The Arts & Crafts Movement in New York State 1890s–1920s.* Hamilton, N.Y.: Gallery Association of New York State, Inc., 1983.

Marling, Karal Ann. *Blue Ribbon: A Social and Pictorial History of the Minnesota State Fair.* St. Paul: Minnesota Historical Society Press, 1990.

Meech, Julia and Gabriel P. Weisberg. *Japonisme Comes to America: The Japanese Impact on the Graphic Arts 1876–1925.* New York, 1990.

Minneapolis School of Art. *The 1922 Sketch Pad.* Vol. 1. Minneapolis, 1922.

Mourne, Nancy Dustin Wall. *Publications in Southern California Art 1, 2 & 3.* Los Angeles, 1984.

Nelson, Marion John. *Art Pottery of the Midwest.* Minneapolis: University Art Museum, University of Minnesota, 1988.

Paist, Henrietta Barclay. *Design and the Decoration of Porcelain.* Syracuse, New York: Keramic Studio Publishing Co., 1916.

Payne, Arthur Frank. *Art Metalwork with Inexpensive Equipment for the Public Schools and the Craftsman.* Peoria, Ill.: The Manual Arts Press, 1914.

Polk's Minneapolis City Directory. St. Paul: R. L. Polk & Co., 1873–present.

Polk's St. Paul City Directory. St. Paul: R. L. Polk & Co., 1879–present.

Priestman, Mabel Tuke. *Handicrafts in the Home.* St. Paul: Methuen & Co., Ltd., 1910.

Realf, Richard. *A Fragment of the Poem Symbolism, by Richard Realf.* Minneapolis: The Chemith Press, 1906.

Reed, Cleota. *Henry Chapman Mercer and the Moravian Pottery and Tile Works.* Philadelphia: University of Pennsylvania Press, 1987.

Roach, Inez. *A History of the Science Museum of Minnesota 1907–1975.* St. Paul: The Science Museum of Minnesota, 1981.

Robinson, Stuart. *A Fertile Field: An Outline History of The Guild of Gloucestershire Craftsmen and the Crafts in Gloucestershire.* Cheltenham, England, 1983.

Rose, Augustus F. *Copper Work: An Illustrated Text Book for Teachers and Students in the Manual Arts.* 3d ed. Worcester, Mass.: The Davis Press, 1909.

Saint Paul Department of Education. *A Course Book for the High Schools of St. Paul, Minnesota.* St. Paul, 1912–13.

Slack, Hiram Worcester, comp. *Directory of Charitable and Benevolent Organizations: A Classified and Descriptive Reference Book of the Charitable, Civic, Educational, and Religious Resources of St. Paul, Minnesota. Together with Legal Suggestions.* St. Paul, 1913.

Spear, Ray P. and Harry J. Frost. *Minnesota State Fair: The History and Heritage of 100 Years.* Minneapolis: Argus Publishing Company, 1964.

Tames, Richard. *William Morris: An Illustrated Life of William Morris 1834–1896.* Aylesbury, England, 1972.

Todd, Mattie Phipps and Alice W. Cooley. *Hand-Loom Weaving. A Manual for School & Home.* Rand, McNally & Co., 1902.

University of Minnesota. *Glensheen.* Duluth, n.d.

Veblen, Thorstein. *The Theory of the Leisure Class: An Economic Study in the Evolution of Institutions.* New York: Macmillan Co., 1899.

Volpe, Tod M. and Beth Cathers. *Treasures of the American Arts and Crafts Movement 1890–1920.* London: Thames & Hudson Ltd., 1988.

White, Mary. *How to Make Baskets.* New York, 1901.

Withey, Henry F. and Elsie Rathburn. *Biographical Dictionary of American Architects (Deceased).* Los Angeles: New Age Publishing Co., 1956.

Woodmere Art Gallery. *Arthur Meltzer Retrospective.* Philadelphia, 1983.

PUBLISHED ARTICLES

"Able Craftsmen for Summer Work: Art Institute will send Jewelry and Pottery Teachers." *Minneapolis Journal* (27 March 1905): 7.

"All Hand Work: The Chalk and Chisel Club Exhibition Opens To-Night." *Minneapolis Journal* (16 November 1898): 6.

Anderson, Martha Scott. "A New Art Industry May Grow from the Pottery work of the Handicraft Guild." *Minneapolis Journal* (5 September 1905): 12.

———. "Two Young Women Artists and their Charming Studios: Miss Heisser and Miss Chant Work for the Encouragement of Art Interests—Some of their Recent Experiments." *Minneapolis Journal* (10 March 1900).

Armstrong, Della M. "Art Progress in the Northwest: The Handicraft Guild." *Fine Arts Journal* (September 1910): 158, 160, 163.

"Art." *Minneapolis Journal* (1 July 1905): 12.

"Art Metal Courses: Pratt Institute Recently Opened a Class for Women." *Minneapolis Journal* (26 July 1901): 11.

"Artists Planning a Studio Center." *Minneapolis Journal* (24 September 1906): 5.

"Arts and Crafts Exhibition: Formerly Opened by a Private View Last Night." *Minneapolis Journal* (17 November 1898): 7.

"The Arts and Crafts Movement at Home and Abroad." *Brush and Pencil* 6 (June 1900): 110–21.

"At the 'Arts and Crafts': Book Lovers go there to Rave." *Minneapolis Journal* (18 November 1898).

Ayres, William S. "Rose Valley Furniture." *Art & Antiques* (January/February 1983): 92–99.

Bailey, M. K. "An Annual Art Exhibition." *The Bellman* (26 March 1910): 386–88.

"Batchelder will Teach: Authority on Designs Opens Class at Handicraft Guild Feb. 1." *Minneapolis Journal* (9 December 1908), p. 13.

Beard, Emma E. "The Recent Exhibition of the Minnesota State Art Society." *The International Studio: An Illustrated Magazine of Fine and Applied Art* 28 (March–June 1906): cxiii–cxviii.

"The Beginning of the Minnesota State Art Commission." *The Minnesotan* 1, no. 1 (July 1915): 24, 26.

"The Bradstreet Craftshouse: An Art Institution of which Minneapolis is Justly Proud." *The Commercial West* (3 December 1904): 22–23.

"Bradstreet Island." *The Bellman* (20 January 1912): 73–76.

Brandimarte, Cynthia A. "Somebody's Aunt and Nobody's Mother: The American China Painter and Her Work. 1870–1920." *Winterthur Portfolio* (1988): 203–24.

Chant, Elisabeth A. "The Handicraft Guild." *The Bellman* (21 March 1908): 317–19.

Clark, Keith. "The Bradstreet Craftshouse." *House Beautiful* (June 1904): 21–23.

"Clubs and Charities." *Minneapolis Journal* (18 November 1899): 12.

Construction Details 6, no. 2 (August 1914): 40, 56–61.

Dennett, Mrs. Hartley. "Aesthetics and Ethics." *Handicraft* (May 1902): 29–47.

Donaldson, Douglas. "The Making of Metal Lampshades." *Palette and Bench* 2 (February 1910): 109–11.

Flagg, Maurice Irwin. "The Dollar and Cents Value of Art: Making Art A Democratic Possession By Relating Art to the Natural Resources of Minnesota." An address given before The Minnesota Federation of Women's Clubs Convention. Rochester, Minn., 7 October 1914. Reprint by the Minnesota State Art Commission.

Geyer, O. R. "Putting Art to Work for the Masses." *Scribner's Magazine* 62 (1917): 769–72.

"The Guild House." *Minneapolis Journal* (1 March 1905): 7.

"Guild Workers Take up Pottery: First Effort of the Kind in Minneapolis." *Minneapolis Journal* (19 April 1905): 12.

"Handicraft to Build." *Minneapolis Journal* (22 February 1907): 7.

"Handicrafts Flourish in City's 'Greenwich Village'." *The Minneapolis Star* (11 May 1973): 1B.

Hewitt, Edwin H. "John S. Bradstreet—Citizen of Minneapolis: An Appreciation of His Life and Work." *Journal of the American Institute of Architects* (October 1916): 424–27.

"In the Studio: The Busiest and Most Attractive Spots in Town this Week." *Minneapolis Journal* (16 December 1899): 10.

Keith, Henrietta P. "Decoration and Furnishing conducted by Mrs. Henrietta P. Keith." *Keith's Magazine on Home Building* 10, no. 4 (October 1903): 185.

Lovett, Eva. "The Exhibition of the Society of Arts and Crafts. Boston." *The International Studio: An Illustrated Magazine of Fine and Applied Art* 31 (March –June 1907): xxvii–xxxii.

Macomber, H. Percy. "The Future of the Handicrafts." *American Magazine of Art* (March 1918): 192–95.

"May Build a School." *Minneapolis Journal* (20 July 1905): 4.

McDonald, Hope. "Halsey C. Ives." *The Bellman* (18 January 1908): 71.

"Minneapolis Artists Lose a Landmark: The Old Studio on Hennepin was Most Intimately Identified with the Beginnings of Art in this City." *Minneapolis Journal* (12 December 1903): 4.

"Minnesota State Art Society." Reprint from *The Magazine of Art*, Walker Art Center edition (ca. 1948): n.p.

Palette and Bench (February 1909): 119.

Payne, Arthur F. "The Influence of the Arts and Crafts Movement Upon Manual Training." *Handicraft* 4, no. 7 (October 1911): 243–48.

Pearson, Jane. "What to Give for Wedding Presents." *House Beautiful* (June 1904): 8–9.

Poesch, Jessie. "The Newcomb Women." *Design History* (January/February 1987): 58–61.

Pond, Theodore Hanford. "The Arts and Crafts Exhibition at the Providence Art Club." *House Beautiful* (June 1901): 98–101.

Purcell, William Gray. "Made in Minnesota: The Story of Native Resources. Their Use and Possibilities." *The Minnesotan* 1, no. 9 (April 1916): 7–13.

Sampson, C. S. J. Sister Ann Thomasine. "St. Agatha's Conservatory and the Pursuit of Excellence." *Ramsey County History* 24, no. 1 (1989): 3–14.

Smith, Katherine Louise. "An Arts and Crafts Exhibition at Minneapolis." *The Craftsman* (March 1903): 373–77.

"Society Biographies: The Handicraft Guild. Minneapolis." *Handicraft* 3 (December 1910): 341–2.

"Society Biographies: Handicraft Guild of Minneapolis." *Handicraft* 4, no. 5 (August 1911): 170–71.

Sterrett, Frances R. "The Arts and Crafts Exhibition in Minneapolis." *House Beautiful* (April 1901): 225–30.

"Summer School Handicraft Guild." *The Craftsman* 8, no. 2 (May 1905): 266–67.

"Summer Schools." *The International Studio* 35 (July–September 1908): xxiii; *The International Studio* (September 1911): n.p.

Teall, Gardner C. "The Craftsman's Library." *House Beautiful* 12, no. 1 (June 1902): 18–20.

Veblen, Thorstein. "Arts and Crafts." *The Journal of Political Economy* 11 (December 1902): 108–11.

"The Village Gossip." *The Bellman* (22 and 29 January 1910): 122, 158.

"What the Art Schools are Doing." *Arts and Decoration* (September 1912): 398–99.

Whitcomb, Charlotte. "Arts and Crafts in Minneapolis." *Brush & Pencil* (March 1901): 344–52.

MAGAZINES, BULLETINS, NEWSLETTERS, DIRECTORIES, ETC.

The Bellman. 1906–19. Published by The Bellman Co., Minneapolis, William C. Edgar, ed. Weekly, which professed truthful commentary but also provided regional social news as well as local and national art and economic news, book reviews, poetry, fashion, theater, music, and architecture. Advertisements by many local businesses were also featured (particularly John Scott Bradstreet).

Construction Bulletin. (other early titles absorbed: *Improvement Bulletin, Architect, Builder and Decorator, Street Railway and Electrical News,*) 1893————. Chapin Publishing Company, Minneapolis. In the early twentieth century this weekly included regular data on new construction locally and regionally, architectural drawings and photographic plates, and advertisements to the trade.

Construction Details. Began in Chicago in 1911 by G. L. Lockhart, manager. Three numbers were issued. Publication discontinued until July 1912, when vol. 2, no. 1 was published in St. Paul. Frank A. Greenlaw, president and manager. Publication ceased with vol. 7, no. 3, March 1915.

The Craftsman. 1901–16.

The Dual City Blue Book (Householders' Directory). 1885–1924. A social directory of the Twin Cities of Minneapolis and St. Paul, Minnesota which indexed private addresses for over twenty-four thousand householders and included a ladies' calling and shopping guide.

Handicraft. 1902–12.

House Beautiful. 1898–1908.

International Studio. 1906–13.

Keith's Magazine on Home Building (aka *Home Builder, Keith's Home Builder, Keith's Beautiful Homes Magazine, Beautiful Homes Magazine*) 1899–1931. Published by the Keith Publishing Co. and edited by Walter J. Keith, Minneapolis. Included a variety of articles/columns on topics ranging from architectural studies to construction, remodeling, interior decoration, gardening, physical plants, and so on. Mrs. Harriet P. Keith was a regular contributor (decoration department editor) and authored a series on"Special Studies in House Decorating."

Keramic Studio. 1897–1924.

The Merriam Park Woman's Club Yearbooks. St. Paul, 1896–1918.

The Minneapolis Institute of Arts. Bulletin. 1905–present.

The Minnesotan. Organ of the Minnesota State Art Commission (MSAC) published monthly from 1 July 1915–September 1916. Maurice Irwin Flagg served as editor and publisher. In October 1916 the magazine incorporated with no mention of the MSAC. The last issue was dated September 1917.

The Woman's Club of Minneapolis (Incorporated). Bulletin. 1913–present.

SCHOOL AND EXHIBITION CATALOGUES, PAMPHLETS, ETC.

The Art Institute of Chicago. *Catalogue of the First Annual Exhibition of Original Designs for Decorations and Examples of Art Crafts Having Distinct Artistic Merit. December 16, 1902, to January 10, 1903.* Chicago.

———. *Catalogue of the Third Annual Exhibition of Original Designs for Decorations and Examples of Art Crafts Having Distinct Artistic Merit. December 6 to 21, 1904.* Chicago.

———. *Catalogue of the Fourth Annual Exhibition of Original Designs for Decorations and Examples of Art Crafts Having Distinct Artistic Merit. December 5 to 21, 1905.* Chicago.

———. *Catalogue of the Fifth Annual Exhibition of Original Designs for Decorations and Examples of Arts Crafts Having Distinct Artistic Merit. December 2 to 20, 1906.* Chicago.

———. *Catalogue of the Sixth Annual Exhibition of Original Designs for Decorations and Examples of Arts Crafts Having Distinct Artistic Merit. December 10 to 22, 1907.* Chicago.

———. *Catalogue of the Seventh Annual Exhibition of Original Designs for Decorations and Examples of Arts Crafts Having Distinct Artistic Merit. December 8 to 22, 1908.* Chicago.

———. *Catalogue of the Eighth Annual Exhibition of Original Designs for Decorations and Examples of Arts Crafts Having Distinct Artistic Merit. December 7 to 23, 1909.* Chicago.

———. *Catalogue of the Ninth Annual Exhibition of Original Designs for Decorations and Examples of Arts Crafts Having Distinct Artistic Merit. December 6 to 23, 1910.* Chicago.

———. *Tenth Annual Art Crafts Exhibition, 1911. October 3 to 25, 1911.* Chicago.

———. *Eleventh Annual Art Crafts Exhibition, 1912. October 1 to 23, 1912.* Chicago.

———. *Catalogue of the Fourteenth Annual Exhibition of Examples of Applied Art and Original Designs for Decorations, October 7–November 3, 1915.* Chicago.

———. *Catalogue of the Fifteenth Annual Exhibition of Applied Art and Original Designs for Decorations. October 12–November 15, 1916.* Chicago.

———. *Applied Arts Exhibition, 1917.* Chicago.

———. *Catalogue of the Seventeenth Annual Exhibition of Applied Art and Original Designs for Decorations, October 8 to 27, 1918.* Chicago.

———. *Circular of Instruction of the School of Drawing. Painting. Modelling. Decorative Designing. Normal Instruction and Architecture 1906–1907, with a Catalogue of Students for 1905–1906.* Chicago.

Art League. *Minneapolis Art League Illustrated Catalogue of the Third Exhibition, May 1897.* Minneapolis.

Arts Guild. *The Arts Guild of St. Paul Summer School of Design and Handicrafts, June 15 to July 15, 1908.* St. Paul.

Art Workers' Guild. *Art Workers' Guild Exhibition of Watercolors and Pastels, April 4 to 15, 1905.* St. Paul.

Art Workers' Guild. *Art Workers' Guild of St. Paul Annual Report for the year ending May 1, 1906.* St. Paul.

Attic Club. *The Minneapolis Institute of Fine Arts Presents the Attic Club in Exhibition. November–December 1913.* Minneapolis.

Bradstreet, John S. & Co. *Interior Furnishings and Decorations.* Minneapolis, 1905.

Chalk and Chisel Club. *An Exhibition of the Arts & Crafts Under the Auspices of the Chalk & Chisel Club.* Minneapolis, 16–19 November 1898.

———. *Names of Members and Outline of Study.* n.d.

———. *Constitution, Names of Members, and Outline of Study for 1895–'96.* Minneapolis, Minn.

———. *Names of Members and Outline of Study for 1897–'98.*

Handicraft Guild. *Summer School of Design Applied to Crafts.* Minneapolis, 19 June–19 July 1905.

———. *Summer School of Design and Handicraft: Third Annual Session.* Minneapolis, 19 June–20 July 1907.

———. *The Handicraft Guild of Minneapolis School of Design Handicraft and Normal Art. Eighth Annual Session.* Minneapolis, 1912–13.

———. *The Handicraft Guild of Minneapolis School of Design Handicraft and Normal Art. Tenth Annual Session.* Minneapolis, 1914–15.

———. *The Handicraft Guild of Minneapolis School of Design Handicraft and Normal Art. Eleventh Annual Session.* Minneapolis, 1915–16.

———. *The Handicraft Guild of Minneapolis School of Design Handicraft and Normal Art. Twelfth Annual Session.* Minneapolis, 1916–17.

Handicraft Guild of Minneapolis. *Made in Minneapolis.* Minneapolis, n.d.

Manual Arts Bulletin. Volume 2, Number 1. Minneapolis, September 1917.

Minneapolis Society of Arts and Crafts. *Constitution and By-Laws of the Minneapolis Society of Arts and Crafts.* Minneapolis, n.d.

———. *Constitution of the [Minneapolis] Society of Arts and Crafts.* Minneapolis, Minn., 1900.

———. *The Second Exhibition of the Arts & Crafts Society, February 5 to 9, 1901.* Minneapolis.

———. *The Third Exhibition of the Society of Arts & Crafts. January 20 to 24, 1903.* Minneapolis.

———. *The Fourth Exhibition of the Society of Arts & Crafts. November 15 to 24, 1904.* Minneapolis.

———. *The Fifth Exhibition of the Minneapolis Society of Arts and Crafts. November 21 to 27, 1906.* Minneapolis.

The Minneapolis Society of Fine Arts. *First Public Loan Exhibition, 1883.* Minneapolis.

———. *Minneapolis School of Fine Arts Exhibition of Studies and Sketches by the Late Royal A. Rheem, December 1909.* Minneapolis.

———. *Minneapolis Society of Fine Arts First Exhibition of Work of the Alumni Association of the Minneapolis School of Art, January 1913.* Minneapolis.

———. *Minneapolis Institute of Arts Third Annual Exhibition by the Alumni Association of the Minneapolis School of Art, March 1915.* Minneapolis.

———. *The Minneapolis Institute of Arts First Annual Exhibition of the Work of Minneapolis Artists, 1915.* Minneapolis.

———. *Minneapolis Institute of Arts Second Annual Exhibition. Work of Minneapolis Artists, 1916.* Minneapolis.

———. *Minneapolis Institute of Arts Third Annual Exhibition. Work of Minneapolis Artists, 1917.* Minneapolis.

———. *Minneapolis Institute of Arts Work of Minneapolis Artists. Sixth Annual Exhibition, 1920.* Minneapolis.

———. *Third Annual Catalogue of the Minneapolis School of Fine Arts, 1888.* Minneapolis.

———. *Fourth Annual Catalogue of the Minneapolis School of Fine Art, 1889–90.* Minneapolis.

———. *Minneapolis School of Fine Art Catalogue, 1890–91.* Minneapolis.

———. *Minneapolis School of Fine Art Catalogue, 1905–06.* Minneapolis.

———. *Minneapolis School of Fine Arts. Twenty-Fifth Year, 1909–10.* Minneapolis.

———. *Minneapolis Society of Fine Arts & School of Art Circular of Information Regarding Instruction. Twenty-Sixth School Year. 1910–11.* Minneapolis.

———. *Minneapolis Society of Fine Arts & School of Art Circular of Information Regarding Instruction. Twenty-Seventh School Year, 1911–12.* Minneapolis.

———. *Minneapolis Society of Fine Arts & School of Art Circular of Information Regarding Instruction. Twenty-Eighth School Year, 1912–13.* Minneapolis.

———. *Minneapolis School of Art Special Short Course in Design & Handicraft, 1912–13.* Minneapolis.

———. *Minneapolis Society of Fine Arts & School of Art Circular of Information Regarding Instruction. Twenty-Ninth Year, 1913–14.* Minneapolis.

———. *Catalogue of the Minneapolis School of Art. Thirtieth School Year, 1914–15.* Minneapolis.

———. *The Minneapolis Society of Fine Arts Annual School Catalogue. The Minneapolis School of Art Thirty-Third School Year, 1917–18.* Minneapolis.

———. *The Minneapolis Society of Fine Arts Annual School Catalogue. The Minneapolis School of Art Thirty-Fourth School Year, 1918–19.* Minneapolis.

———. *The Minneapolis School of Art Catalogue, 1925–26.* Minneapolis.

———. *The Minneapolis School of Art List of Students, 1905–06.* Minneapolis.

Minnesota State Art Commission. *Catalogue of the Art Collections in Galleries, 1914.* St. Paul.

———. *The Thirteenth Annual Exhibition of the Minnesota State Art Commission given in conjunction with Minnesota State Fair and Exposition, September 4 to 9, 1916.* Hamline, Minnesota.

———. *14th Annual Exhibition. Minnesota State Art Commission & The Minnesota State Fair Catalogue of the Fine Arts, September 3 to 11, 1917.* Hamline, Minnesota.

Minnesota State Art Society. *The Constitution and By-Laws of the Minnesota State Art Society. 1903.*

———. *The Annual Report for the Year 1912. 1913.*

———. *Report of the Governing Board of the Minnesota State Art Society for the Years 1903 and 1904.* St. Paul.

———. *Report of the Governing Board of the Minnesota State Art Society for the Years 1905 to 1911.* St. Paul.

———. *Report of the Minnesota State Art Society for the Year 1948.*

———. *First Annual Exhibition, April 4 to 16, 1904.* St. Cloud, Minn.

———. *Second Annual Exhibition, April 13 to 22, 1905.* Minneapolis.

———. *Third Annual Exhibition, 1906.* Mankato, Minn.

———. *Fourth Annual Exhibition, March 2 to 11, 1907.* Fergus Falls, Minn.

———. *Fifth Annual Exhibition.* Minnesota, 1908.

———. *Sixth Annual Exhibition, April 13 to 24, 1909.* Faribault, Minn.

———. *Seventh Annual Exhibition, April 14 to 25, 1910.* New Ulm, Minn.

———. *Eighth Annual Exhibition, April 27 through June 16, 1912.* St. Paul, Stillwater, Anoka, and Duluth, Minn.

———. *Ninth Annual Exhibition, March 1 through April 21, 1913.* St. Paul, Minneapolis, and Owatonna, Minn.

———. *Tenth Annual Art Exhibit, March 14 through May 20, 1914.* St. Paul, Minneapolis, Crookston, and Austin, Minn.

Minnesota State Art Society. *Catalogue of Eleventh Annual State Art Exhibit Given in Connection with The Minnesota State Fair and Exposition, September 6 to 12, 1914.* Hamline, Minn.

———. *Catalogue of Twelfth Annual State Art Exhibit Given in Connection with The Minnesota State Fair and Exposition, September 6 to 12, 1915.* Hamline, Minn.

Pratt Institute. *Pratt Institute Catalogs* for 1891–1892, 1899–1900, 1901–1902, 1905–1906, 1907–1908. Brooklyn, N.Y.

Pratt Institute. *Student Diploma Lists* for 1893, 1900, 1902, 1906, and 1909. Brooklyn, N.Y.

Rochester Art Center. *Rochester Art Center First Exhibition, January 1947.* Rochester, Minn.

St. Paul Institute. *Exhibition of Fine and Industrial Arts, December 14 to 20, 1908.* St. Paul.

———. *First Year-Book of the St. Paul Institute of Arts and Sciences: A Record of Its Activities from Its Incorporation April 28, 1908 to June 1, 1909.* St. Paul.

———. *Professional Art Section of St. Paul Institute. Third Annual Exhibition. March 11 to 16, 1912.* St. Paul.

———. *Prospectus for the Summer School of Arts and Crafts, June 14 to July 14, 1909.* St. Paul.

———. *St. Paul Institute School of Art First Year Calendar, 1908–09.* St. Paul.

———. *St. Paul Institute School of Art Second Year Calendar, 1909–10.* St. Paul.

———. *St. Paul Institute School of Art Fifth Year Calendar, 1912–13.* St. Paul.

———. *St. Paul Institute School of Art Seventh Year Calendar, 1914–15.* St. Paul.

———. *St. Paul Institute School of Art Ninth Year Calendar, 1916–17.* St. Paul.

———. *St. Paul School of Fine Arts, 1904–05.* St. Paul.

———. *St. Paul School of Fine Arts, 1905–06.* St. Paul.

Society of Arts and Crafts. *Annual Report, 1907, 1908, 1909, 1918.* Detroit, Mich.

The Woman's Civic League of St. Paul. *Civic League Program Calendar for Nineteen Hundred and Two: Devoted to a Study of The Arts and Crafts with casual attention to the methods of The Artful and Crafty.* St. Paul, 1901.

The Woman's Club of Minneapolis. *Woman's Club 1913–1914 Report.* Minneapolis.

———. *Woman's Club 1916–17 Report.* Minneapolis.

NEWSPAPERS

The Duluth News Tribune. 2 June 1912.

Minneapolis Journal. 1890–1925.

The New Ulm Newspaper. 16 April 1910. New Ulm, Minn.

The St. Paul Pioneer Press. 1890–1925.

MANUSCRIPT COLLECTIONS

Ames, Charles W. and Mary Lesley Ames and Family Papers. Minnesota Historical Society, St. Paul. Several boxes contain correspondence, reports, speeches, and so on, with particular association to the St. Paul Institute, 1907–81. Ames was a founder and first president of the Institute.

Arts Board Collection. Minnesota State Archives. Minnesota Historical Society, St. Paul. Administrative files 1903–86, five boxes. Annual and biennial reports, 1904–77, one box. Contains a variety of materials documenting the Minnesota State Art Society (Commission) including histories, reports, correspondence, published materials, photographs, scrapbook, and so on.

Berglund, Hilma, Collection. American Swedish Institute Collections, Minneapolis. Archival material, family history, and objects acquired by the institute in 1979. Includes journals/diaries by Hilma and her mother. Art work, textile work, and signed ceramic pieces by Hilma are likely from her period of association with the St. Paul Institute.

Bookwalter, Mary Linton. Laura Linton MacFarlane, Pasadena, California. Personal collection of family papers, printed ephemera, and so on, which documents the career of Mary Linton Bookwalter. Minimal personal correspondence.

Cheney (Mary Moulton and family) Papers, one box. Minnesota Historical Society, St. Paul. Contains minimal correspondence between Cheney and other artists, monogram sketchbooks, bookplate materials, two order books from her shop, and some summary biographical material with corrections provided by her.

Cheney, Mary Moulton. Papers. Uncataloged, one box. Minnesota Historical Society, St. Paul. Contains primarily original artwork by Cheney, sketches for everything from monograms to bookplates, greeting cards, stationery, stained glass windows, andirons, oils, and conventionalization of floral specimens. Also includes brochures from her business, The Artcraft Shop, loose product samples, and an order book from her shop. Work by her partners and others who did design work for her is also included.

Paist, William and Herbert. Papers. Minnesota Historical Society, St. Paul. Political, military, and business career documentation, and family genealogy information. Herbert was the husband of artist Henrietta Barclay Paist.

University of Minnesota President's (papers) Office, 1911–45. Box 34. University of Minnesota College of Education folder 1916–40. University of Minnesota Archives, Minneapolis. Includes correspondence and memos relating to the absorption of the Handicraft Guild by the university as the new art education department.

Wheeler, Cleora. Papers. Uncataloged, nine boxes. University of Minnesota Archives, Minneapolis.

Winters, Robert. The author generously allowed me to read sections of his unpublished biography of Ernest A. Batchelder.

PERSONAL ACCOUNTS AND MISCELLANEOUS

Anderson, Marcia. Paper on the Handicraft Guild of Minneapolis, 1990 Winterthur Conference, "The Substance of Style."

Bergslund, Theodora. Letters of inquiry and response between her and the Handicraft Guild. Guild student card.

The Camlet Needlecraft Shop, dated invoice. Minneapolis, 1918.

Letter from Marjorie M. Haish to her sister, 28 January 1915.

Paist, William B. St. Anthony Park, Minnesota. Several meetings and conversations between Bill and Marcia Anderson from 1990–present. Bill is the grandson of artist Henrietta Barclay Paist.

Pattee, Gladys. Minneapolis. Several meetings and conversations between Gladys and Marcia Anderson from 1985 until her death in December 1991.

Letter from Louise Pickney to Mr. A. C. Gooding, 15 July 1909.

Schutt, Elizabeth. Minneapolis. Several meetings and conversations between Elizabeth and Marcia Anderson from 1992–present. Elizabeth is the niece of Harriett Carmichael, partner with Mary Moulton Cheney in the Artcraft Shop from 1908–12.

CHECKLIST OF THE EXHIBITION

Dimensions = h × w × d

1. Handicraft Guild of Minneapolis
American, Minnesota, 1908–18
Jardiniere, about 1912
Copper
9⅘" × 12⅘"
Marks: base, struck incuse HANDICRAFT GUILD/
MINNEAPOLIS
Minnesota Historical Society Collections
Purchase 1984.162.1

This hammered copper jardiniere is embellished with an applied band of pierced copper and copper handles attached with copper rivets. The form appears to be the same as that of a vessel in the 1912 Barnum Trunk Company window display of Guild products.

2. Handicraft Guild of Minneapolis
American, Minnesota, 1904–18
Vase, 1905–18
Ceramic
11⅕" × 6½"
Marks: Base, stick applied HG (cipher with G enclosed in the bottom half of the H)
Minnesota Historical Society Collections
Purchase 1985.78.1

Six landscape panel scenes are impressed on the circumference of the lower section of this vase, a particularly successful example of guild ceramics. Although matte glaze is found most frequently on guild ceramics, high glaze finishes also appear on both the interior and exterior surfaces. This vase exterior combines the two.

3. Handicraft Guild of Minneapolis
American, Minnesota, 1904–18
Spoon, 1905–18
Copper
8¾"
Marks: handle, struck incuse HG (cipher with G enclosed in the bottom half of the H)
Minnesota Historical Society Collections
Purchase 1986.115.1

Typical of the nut spoon form produced in arts and crafts organizations nationwide, this example in hammered copper features a pierced terminal.

4. Handicraft Guild of Minneapolis
American, Minnesota, 1904–18
Bowl, 1905–18
Copper
3⅕" × 9½"
Marks: base, struck incuse HANDICRAFT GUILD .
MINNEAPOLIS
Minnesota Historical Society Collections
Purchase 1986.305.1

This shaped bowl, raised from a single sheet of copper, is one of the simplest expressions of American arts and crafts metalwork. Twenty-five similar bowls outlined the Handicraft Guild window display at the Barnum Trunk Company in Minneapolis, November 1912.

5. Handicraft Guild of Minneapolis
American, Minnesota, 1904–18
Spoon, 1905–18
Copper
9⅘" × 3 7/10"
Marks: handle, struck incuse HG (cipher with G enclosed in the bottom half of the H)
Minnesota Historical Society Collections
Purchase 1986.305.2

Hammered copper spoon has stylized repoussé panel on handle and pierced design in bowl. This spoon and bowl (1986.305.1) were probably originally acquired to furnish the home of a newly married Massachusetts couple.

6. Handicraft Guild of Minneapolis
American, Minnesota, 1904–18
Bookends, 1905–18
Copper
5½" × 5 3/10" × 6⅘"
Marks: top side of base, struck incuse HANDICRAFT GUILD/MINNEAPOLIS
Minnesota Historical Society Collections
Purchase 1989.153.1–2

7. Handicraft Guild of Minneapolis
American, Minnesota, 1904–18
Coffee service, about 1911
Copper, sterling silver, and wood
Tray: 8½" × 11⅘"
Covered coffee pot: 6 9/10" × 4"(base) × 7 7/10"(handles)
covered sugar bowl: 3" × 2⅕(base) × 4 3/10"(handles)
Creamer: 2⅗" × 3⅗"(handles) × 2⅕"(base)
Marks: base of tray, sugar, creamer and coffee pot all struck incuse HANDICRAFT GUILD/MINNEAPOLIS. Covers unmarked.
Minnesota Historical Society Collections
Purchase 1990.478.1–4

The interior surface of the creamer and coffee covers are silver washed, as is the coffee pot interior. A nearly identical coffee service was illustrated in an article on the guild in the May 1911 issue of *Arts and Decoration*. Two other examples of the same coffee pot form by the guild also survive in private collections.

Handicraft Guild of Minneapolis. Coffee set *including copper chocolate style pot with wood handle and cover; sugar and cover; creamer and rectangular tray. Minnesota Historical Society Collections. Photograph courtesy of* ARK Antiques.

8. Arthur Frank Payne
    American
    Piano lamp, 1914 or earlier
    Copper and glass
    12″ × 14″ on 8″ × 8″ base
    Marks: none
    Minnesota Historical Society Collections
    Gift of the artist's daughter, Mrs. Walter Jones 71.67.1

This hammered copper cantilever piano lamp with frosted green glass and copper shade is illustrated in plate 56 on p. 104 of Payne's 1914 book, *Art Metalwork with Inexpensive Equipment for the Public Schools and for the Craftsman.* Payne's student Harold Boyle supervised the guild's metalwork program from 1909 to 1913, and the Oriental lantern style incorporated in this piano lamp suggests shared stylistic influences between Bradley Polytechnic Institute in Peoria, Illinois, and the Handicraft Guild.

9. Arthur Frank Payne
    American
    Art Metalwork with Inexpensive Equipment for the Public Schools and for the Craftsman (Peoria, Ill.: The Manual Arts Press, 1914).
    Paper and cloth
    9³⁄₁₀″ × 6⅞″
    Minnesota Historical Society Collections
    Gift of the artist's daughter, Mrs. Walter Jones NK6404.P3

Some of the objects donated to the MHS collections are illustrated in this annotated copy of Payne's book.

10. Handicraft Guild of Minneapolis
    American, Minnesota, 1904–18
    Calling card tray, 1905–18
    Sterling silver
    ⅓″ × 6¹⁄₁₀″

Marks: base, struck incuse HANDICRAFT GUILD/ MINNEAPOLIS/STERLING
Minnesota Historical Society Collections
North Star Fund Purchase 1992.473.1

Such examples of guild silver work are rare. The calling card tray rim features three pierced conventionalized floral sections separated by hammered panels. The quality of work and restrained use of piercing and hammering on this small piece suggests it was produced by an instructor or skilled guild member.

11. Harriet Carmichael
American, Colorado Springs, Colorado, 1865–1940
Card folder, 1912 or earlier
Leather
6 2/5" × 3 9/10"
Marks: none
Minnesota Historical Society Collections
Gift of Elizabeth Schutt 1993.16.25

The blue leather card folder with black lacing and all other pieces attributed to Harriet Carmichael were given to relatives in Minneapolis before she moved to Colorado in 1912. The folder was either made by her or others at the Artcraft Shop, Minneapolis. The folder is typical of the leatherwork taught in Minnesota schools between 1900 and 1920.

12. Harriet Carmichael
American, Colorado Springs, Colorado, 1865–1940
Photo album, 1912 or earlier
Leather and paper
5 3/10" × 8 7/10" × 1/10"
Marks: none
Minnesota Historical Society Collections
Gift of Elizabeth Schutt 1993.16.1

The tooled pine motif on the cover of the green leather album is also found on copyrighted printed pieces made and sold by the Artcraft Shop in Minneapolis where Carmichael was a partner from 1908 to 1912.

13. Harriet Carmichael
American, Colorado Springs, Colorado, 1865–1940
Necklace/dress clip, 1912 or earlier
Sterling silver and turquoise
10" × 1 3/5"
Marks: none
Minnesota Historical Society Collections
Gift of Elizabeth Schutt 1993.16.4

The rough casting, piercework, and floral motif is typical of jewelry made by guild members as well as those at the St. Paul Institute and the Minneapolis Institute School of Art in the same years.

14. Harriet Carmichael
American, Colorado Springs, Colorado, 1865–1940
Watch fob, 1912 or earlier
Leather, copper, and set stone
7 9/10" × 1 2/5"
Marks: none
Minnesota Historical Society Collections
Gift of Elizabeth Schutt 1993.16.5

A photograph of Carmichael taken after her move to Colorado in 1912 shows her wearing a similar fob on the waistband of her skirt. Apparently it was not customary practice to sign such objects because no marked pieces of jewelry by guild members have been identified.

15. Corice Woodruff
American, Minneapolis, Minnesota, b. 1878
Plaque entitled *Baby*, early twentieth century.
Painted and cast plaster
1/2" × 7 7/10"
Marks: none
Minnesota Historical Society Collections
Gift of Elizabeth Schutt 1993.16.3

Baby is illustrated as no. 5 in an undated sales catalog with color illustrations, *Relief Plaques*, by Corice Woodruff. Elizabeth Schutt, Harriet Carmichael's niece, helped Woodruff to paint plaques as her first high school job.

16. Corice Woodruff
American, Minneapolis, Minnesota, b.1878
Sales catalog, *Relief Plaques*. First quarter twentieth century
Paper
6 1/10" square
Marks: none
Minneapolis History Collection, Minneapolis Public Library

There is considerable discussion of Woodruff's work in local periodicals, exhibition catalogs, and in the personal reminiscences of Elizabeth Schutt in the MHS accession files regarding Woodruff's plaster cast and sculptural work. Woodruff also placed frequent advertisements in local arts and crafts exhibition catalogs.

17. Mary Moulton Cheney
American, St. Anthony Park, Minnesota, about 1871–1957
Chapter XIII of the First Epistle to the Corinthians Written by Paul the Apostle. Designed, illustrated, and published by Cheney. Printed by Hahn and Harmon. Bound by A. J. Dahl. #407/500. 1903.
9 3/5" × 5 1/5"
Marks: none.
Minnesota Historical Society Collections
Gift of Mary Moulton Cheney Z276.C52b

All of Cheney's camera-ready illustrations for this book are in the manuscript collections of the Minnesota Historical Society. The influence of *japonisme* is evident in the cover image of *Corinthians XIII*.

18. Florence D. Willets
    American, Minnesota, active 1905–56
    Covered pot, about 1915
    Ceramic
    Cover: 1½" × 4³⁄₁₀"
    Pot: 5¹⁄₁₀" × 6³⁄₁₀"
    Marks: base, stick applied HG (cipher with G enclosed in the bottom half of the H)
    The Minneapolis Institute of Arts
    Gift of Florence D. Willets 16.720

This dark blue vessel has scenic images stamped into the sides of the pot body. Several examples of Willets's work were illustrated in a 1906 issue of *The Bellman*. Although this piece is unsigned, its attribution can be established on the basis of its similarity to her documented work shown in *The Bellman*.

Florence D. Willets. Covered jar. Photograph courtesy of The Minneapolis Institute of Arts.

19. Handicraft Guild of Minneapolis
    American, Minnesota, 1904–18
    Tile, about 1912
    Ceramic
    5½" square
    Marks: back, remains of Handicraft Guild paper label.
    Goldstein Gallery
    Gift of Jean Stange, 87.8.1

The tile has incised landscape forms and glazes in blue, ochre, and dark green. This is one of two landscape tiles of the same subject in the collections of the Goldstein Gallery. The glaze coloration and tile sizes vary slightly. Both were collected locally by Harriet and Vetta Goldstein about 1912.

20. Handicraft Guild of Minneapolis
    American, Minnesota, 1904–18
    Covered box, 1905–18
    Copper, amethysts, and silk lining
    2¼" × 5"
    Marks: base, struck incuse HANDICRAFT GUILD/ MINNEAPOLIS
    Jennifer Braznell Collection

Many such covered boxes, displaying similar floral motifs, were produced within the arts and crafts movement during the period from 1902 to 1915. Examples closely resembling this one by the guild include an inkwell made by Gilbert Marks of London, 1902, and a box cover illustrated in *Art Metalwork with Inexpensive Equipment for the Public Schools and for the Craftsman*, 1914, by Arthur Payne.

21. Handicraft Guild of Minneapolis
    American, Minnesota, 1904–18
    Teaspoon, 1905–18
    Sterling silver
    4⅘"
    Marks: back, struck incuse HG(cipher with G enclosed in the bottom half of the H).
    Barbara Vodrey Wamelink Collection

This teaspoon has descended from Margaret Kelly Cable to the present owner. Cable may have made it herself or acquired it from the guild shops where she was a student and gave instruction in pottery from 1907 to 1910.

22. Margaret Kelly Cable
    American, Minnesota, active 1906–10
    North Dakota, active 1910–49
    Vase, 1917
    Ceramic
    10"
    Marks: Signed MKC/1917 below the blue ink stamp for the University of North Dakota School of Mines
    Barbara Vodrey Wamelink Collection

23. Handicraft Guild of Minneapolis
    American, Minnesota, 1904–18
    Jar with cover, 1905–18
    Ceramic and copper
    Jar: 5⁷⁄₁₀" × 5³⁄₁₀"
    Cover: 4⁷⁄₁₀" × 1⅗"
    Marks: Jar base: struck incuse HG (cipher with G enclosed in the bottom half of the H).

Margaret Kelly Cable. Vase with pine tree design. *Object and photograph courtesy of Barbara Vodrey Wamelink.*

Peter Johnson and Linn Ann Cowles Collection

24. Handicraft Guild of Minneapolis
American, Minnesota, 1904–18
Bowl, 1905–18
Copper
2½″ × 12″
Marks: base, struck incuse HANDICRAFT GUILD/
MINNEAPOLIS
Ben Wiles, Jr. Collection

This bowl features the stylized leaf and vine motif, a saw-pierced design set in panels below the lip. It is one of several related motifs characteristic of guild metalwork.

25. Handicraft Guild of Minneapolis
American, Minnesota, 1904–18
Vase, 1905–18
Ceramic
11½″ × 7½″
Marks: Base, struck incuse HANDICRAFT GUILD/
MINNEAPOLIS
The Rev. William Gamber Collection

26. Handicraft Guild of Minneapolis
American, Minnesota, 1904–18
Picture frame, 1905–18
Brass
5″ × 3½″
Marks: back, struck incuse HANDICRAFT GUILD/

MINNEAPOLIS
David Matchan Collection

This frame is reminiscent of the etching technique and motifs utilized by the Frost Arts and Crafts Workshop, Dayton, Ohio. Frost goods were sold in the guild shop quite early and appear to have had some influence on the work of students and instructors.

27. James Winn
American, Chicago, Illinois, 1866–1943
Pendant
Sterling silver and amethyst
2½″ × 1½″
Marks: engraved WINN
ARK Antiques, New Haven, Connecticut

Although exhibition catalogs and award records indicate that Winn was a recognized and prolific craftsman, few examples of his work are known today.

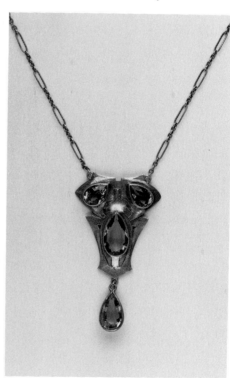

James Winn. Pendant with chain. *ARK Antiques. Photograph by Gary Mortensen and Robert Fogt.*

28. Handicraft Guild of Minneapolis
American, Minnesota, 1904–18
Letter rack, 1905–18
Copper
3³⁄₁₀″ × 4½″ × 1⅕″
Marks: struck incuse HANDICRAFT GUILD/MIN-
NEAPOLIS
Dolores P. Lewis Collection

Desk sets were a popular product of arts and crafts metal-work students across the nation. The repetition of a bird or animal form as a mirror image, seen clearly in this letter rack, is typical of guild work.

29. Handicraft Guild of Minneapolis
    American, Minnesota, 1904–18
    Vase, 1905–18
    Ceramic
    $9\frac{1}{2}'' \times 4\frac{7}{10}''$
    Marks: base, scratched HG (cipher with G enclosed in the bottom half of the H).
    Dolores P. Lewis Collection

The matte glaze on this vase is typical of Guild work. Guild glazes are traditionally opaque and often incorporate a second color in a heavy overglaze.

30. Handicraft Guild of Minneapolis
    American, Minnesota, 1904–18
    Match holder, 1905–18
    Brass and copper
    $2\frac{3}{5}'' \times 4\frac{1}{2}''$
    Marks: base, Dremel tool-engraved HG (cipher with G enclosed in the bottom half of the H).
    Steve Schoneck Collection

The successful integration of materials, design, and piercework decoration distinguish this small example of guild metalwork.

31. Handicraft Guild of Minneapolis
    American, Minnesota, 1904–18
    Oval tray, about 1912
    Silver plated copper
    $7\frac{3}{10}'' \times 12\frac{3}{10}'' \times \frac{2}{5}''$
    Marks: back, incuse struck HANDICRAFT GUILD/MINNEAPOLIS
    A small, unidentified manufacturer's mark suggests that guild students purchased metal blanks from commercial sources and then decorated them.
    Steve Schoneck Collection

A photograph of guild work in a September 1912 issue of *Arts and Decoration* illustrates this tray or one just like it.

32. Handicraft Guild of Minneapolis
    American, Minnesota, 1904–18
    Vase, 1905–18
    Copper
    $6\frac{3}{5}'' \times 3\frac{1}{2}''$
    Marks: base, struck incuse HANDICRAFT GUILD/MINNEAPOLIS
    Steve Schoneck Collection

There are several documented examples of square vases

executed in metal or clay by guild members. Metal ones, such as this, were normally lined with glass.

33. Handicraft Guild of Minneapolis
    American, Minnesota, 1904–18
    Sugar tongs, 1905–18
    Sterling silver
    $3\frac{2}{5}'' \times \frac{3}{4}''$
    Marks: inside surface, struck incuse HANDICRAFT GUILD/MINNEAPOLIS/STERLING
    Steve Schoneck Collection

This pair of sugar tongs is one of the very few extant examples of guild work done in silver.

34. Handicraft Guild of Minneapolis
    American, Minnesota, 1904–18
    Pair of bookends, 1905–18
    Copper
    $5\frac{7}{10}'' \times 7'' \times 5\frac{3}{5}''$
    Marks: base, struck incuse HANDICRAFT GUILD/MINNEAPOLIS
    Steve Schoneck Collection

The piercework panels on these bookends demonstrate design principles taught at the guild. Students were encouraged to create spatial balance within a confining shape. In this example, the perimeters are clearly visible: the vertical bars separate these panels like the leading in stained glass. In other guild metalwork, the perimeters are not integrated into the design.

35. Handicraft Guild of Minneapolis
    American, Minnesota, 1904–18
    Inkwell, 1905–18
    Copper
    $3\frac{1}{2}'' \times 3\frac{3}{10}''$
    Marks: base, struck incuse HANDICRAFT GUILD/MINNEAPOLIS
    Steve Schoneck Collection

36. Handicraft Guild of Minneapolis
    American, Minnesota, 1904–18
    Pair of bookends, 1905–18
    Copper
    $5\frac{3}{10}'' \times 7\frac{3}{5}'' \times 5\frac{3}{10}''$
    Marks: base, struck incuse HANDICRAFT GUILD/MINNEAPOLIS
    Steve Schoneck Collection

The piercework grape and leaf motif was one of the guild's most common design motifs and recurs in various object forms and design variations.

37. Handicraft Guild of Minneapolis
    American, Minnesota, 1904–18
    Tray, 1905–18

Brass
11″ × 3⁄10″
Marks: reverse, metal rectangular label HANDICRAFT/.GUILD./MINNEAPOLIS soldered to tray.
Steve Schoneck Collection

All guild students were required to produce an etched tray in their first metalwork class.

38. Handicraft Guild of Minneapolis
American, Minnesota, 1904–18
Tray, 1905–18
Copper
1⁄2″ × 11 1⁄2″
Marks: base, struck incuse HANDICRAFT GUILD/MINNEAPOLIS
Steve Schoneck Collection

39. Handicraft Guild of Minneapolis
American, Minnesota, 1904–18
Flower bowl with frog in the form of a turtle, 1905–18
Ceramic
Bowl: 2″ × 7 4⁄5″
Frog: 2 1⁄10″ × 5 1⁄2″ × 4 1⁄5″
Marks: Bowl unmarked; frog base, struck incuse HANDICRAFT GUILD/MINNEAPOLIS
Steve Schoneck Collection

Many glazed ceramic turtle flower frogs with guild marks survive.

40. Handicraft Guild of Minneapolis
American, Minnesota, 1904–18
Inkwell, about 1912
Ceramic and glass
Covered: 3 1⁄10″ × 5 3⁄10″
Marks: base, stick applied HG (cipher with G enclosed in the bottom half of the H), rectangular paper label HANDICRAFT GVILD/HG (cipher with G enclosed in the bottom half of the H)
Steve Schoneck Collection

An inkwell of the same form is illustrated in the guild's eighth annual session pamphlet, 1912–13.

41. Handicraft Guild of Minneapolis
American, Minnesota, 1904–18
Vase, 1905–18
Ceramic
13 4⁄5″ × 5 2⁄5″
Marks: base, stick applied HG (cipher with G enclosed in the bottom half of the H)
Steve Schoneck Collection

This is a lightweight, well-proportioned vase which exemplifies the guild's preference for layering glazes on pottery pieces.

42. Handicraft Guild of Minneapolis
American, Minnesota, 1904–18
Pair of bookends, 1905–18
Ceramic
3 9⁄10″ × 5 7⁄10″ × 3 1⁄5″
Marks: reverse of each bookend, struck incuse HANDICRAFT GUILD/MINNEAPOLIS, and below this mark a rectangular paper label HANDICRAFT GVILD/HG (Cipher with G enclosed in the bottom half of the H)/MINNEAPOLIS
Steve Schoneck Collection

Molded ceramic pieces such as this were among the most popular of guild products in the first community recognition of its work documented in a 1905 issue of the *Minneapolis Journal*.

43. Handicraft Guild of Minneapolis
American, Minnesota, 1904–18
Pot, 1905–18
Ceramic
1 7⁄10″ × 6 1⁄10″
Marks: base, struck incuse HANDICRAFT GUILD/MINNEAPOLIS. Evidence of original paper sticker.
Steve Schoneck Collection

The thin walls and graceful lines of this small pot are exceptional in guild ceramic work.

44. Handicraft Guild of Minneapolis
American, Minnesota, 1904–18
Pot, 1905–18
Ceramic
1 7⁄10″ × 4 3⁄5″
Marks: base, struck incuse HAND[ICRAFT] GUILD/MINNEAPOLIS, signed in pencil M. Brown.
Steve Schoneck Collection

The vivid, bright glaze color and delicacy of this object distinguish it from most guild pottery.

45. Handicraft Guild of Minneapolis
American, Minnesota, 1904–18
Pot, 1905–18
Ceramic
2 1⁄2″ × 7⁄10
Marks: base, struck incuse HANDICRAFT GUILD/MINNEAPOLIS
Steve Schoneck Collection

46. Handicraft Guild on Minneapolis
American, Minnesota, 1904–18
Pot, 1905–18
Ceramic
2 2⁄5″ × 7 7⁄10″
Marks: base, struck incuse HG (cipher with G enclosed in the bottom half of the H)

Steve Schoneck Collection

47. Handicraft Guild of Minneapolis
American, Minnesota, 1904–18
Sconce, 1905–18
Copper and other metal
$13\frac{1}{2}'' \times 7\frac{4}{5}'' \times 1\frac{1}{2}''$
Marks: reverse, rectangular metal label HANDICRAFT/.GUILD./MINNEAPOLIS. is soldered to surface.
Steve Schoneck Collection

This particularly well-crafted example of repoussé metalwork features a symmetrical bird motif which occurs frequently in guild work of varied media. A similar guild sconce is illustrated in an article entitled "Art Progress in the Northwest," in the September 1910 issue of *Fine Arts Journal*.

48. Handicraft Guild of Minneapolis
American, Minnesota, 1904–18
Sconce, 1905–18
Ceramic
$10\frac{1}{2}'' \times 4\frac{3}{10}'' \times 3\frac{3}{10}''$
Marks: back, stick applied HG (cipher with G enclosed in the bottom half of the H), and paper label with the HG cipher and HANDICRAFT GVILD/MINNEAPOLIS.
Steve Schoneck Collection

The rondel at the top of this wall sconce features a common arts and crafts landscape motif.

49. Handicraft Guild of Minneapolis
American, Minnesota, 1904–18
Letter rack, 1904–18
Copper
$4\frac{4}{5}'' \times 7\frac{1}{2}'' \times 4\frac{3}{10}''$
Marks: struck incuse HANDICRAFT/GUILD/MINNEAPOLIS
Steve Schoneck Collection

50. Handicraft Guild of Minneapolis
American, Minnesota, 1904–18
Bowl, 1905–18
Copper
$2\frac{3}{10}'' \times 7\frac{1}{10}''$
Marks: base, struck incuse HANDICRAFT GUILD/MINNEAPOLIS
Steve Schoneck Collection

51. Handicraft Guild of Minneapolis
American, Minnesota, 1904–18
Bowl, 1905–18
Copper and glass
$2\frac{2}{5}'' \times 8\frac{9}{10}''$
Marks: copper bowl base, struck incuse HANDICRAFT GUILD/MINNEAPOLIS
Steve Schoneck Collection

Many of the guild copper bowls, such as this one, were originally fitted with glass liners so they might function as containers for flowers, food, and so on. Others were produced with a silver washed or enameled interior. Hammer marks were usually left on the interiors of piercework bowls; the exterior surface was usually burnished.

52. Handicraft Guild of Minneapolis
American, Minnesota, 1904–18
Vase, 1905–18
Ceramic and tin
$15\frac{2}{5}'' \times 6\frac{1}{10}''$
Marks: base, struck incuse HANDICRAFT GUILD/MINNEAPOLIS, HG stick applied (cipher with G enclosed in the bottom half of the H)
Nancy M. Rose Collection

The tin insert of this tall, slender vase indicates that it was intended to be functional.

53. Handicraft Guild of Minneapolis
American, Minnesota, 1904–18
Vase, 1905–18
Ceramic
$7\frac{1}{2}'' \times 3\frac{9}{10}''$
Marks: base, struck incuse HANDICRAFT GUILD/MINNEAPOLIS
Nancy M. Rose Collection

54. Handicraft Guild of Minneapolis
American, Minnesota, 1904–18
Nut bowl set, 1905–18
Copper
Serving bowl: $2\frac{3}{10}'' \times 7\frac{1}{10}''$; individual bowls: $1\frac{2}{5}'' \times 4''$
Marks: all but one individual bowl struck incuse HANDICRAFT GUILD/MINNEAPOLIS on base
Richard P. Hickenbotham—Geometrie

The serving bowl is embellished with four rectangular pierced panels set below the lip, and each of the six individual bowls features three such rectangular pierced panels. All have the stylized iris motif common to much guild work.

55. Attributed to Handicraft Guild of Minneapolis
American, Minnesota, 1904–18
Table lamp, 1905–18
Ceramic, copper, and glass
Base: $9\frac{1}{2}''$; shade: $5'' \times 13\frac{1}{10}'' \times 13\frac{1}{10}''$
Marks: none
Richard P. Hickenbotham—Geometrie

This peacock table lamp, decorated with the guild's signature opposed peacock figures, has a molded ceramic base

Handicraft Guild of Minneapolis. Copper bowl with pierced design. *Steve Schoneck Collection. Photograph by Gary Mortensen and Robert Fogt.*

Handicraft Guild of Minneapolis. Nut bowl set, *seven pieces. Richard Hickenbotham—Geometrie. Photograph by Gary Mortensen and Robert Fogt.*

in green and brown glazes with a copper pierced shade backed with green glass. The peacock motif used in the lamp base in very similar to one illustrated in Ernest Batchelder's *Design in Theory and Practice*, 1912, figures 141–144, demonstrating the direct connection between Batchelder's theory and guild practice.

56. Handicraft Guild of Minneapolis
American, Minnesota, 1904–18
Convertible candleholder or sconce, 1905–18
Copper
$1\frac{5}{8}'' \times 3\frac{5}{8}'' \times 8\frac{1}{2}''$
Marks: base, struck incuse HANDICRAFT GUILD/MINNEAPOLIS
Richard P. Hickenbotham—Geometrie

57. Handicraft Guild of Minneapolis
American, Minnesota, 1904–18
Bowl, 1905–18
Copper
Dr. Robert Winter, Pasadena, California

The particular hammering technique used in making this bowl is known as fluting. It is well illustrated in *Art Metalwork with Inexpensive Equipment for the Public Schools and for the Craftsman*, a popular metalwork text of the period by Arthur Frank Payne.

58. Ernest Batchelder
American, California, 1875–1957
Planter, ca. 1912
Ceramic
$12'' \times 16''$
Dr. Robert Winter, Pasadena, California

The use of the opposed birds motif and engobe glaze on this piece by Batchelder confirms his personal interests in these motifs and techniques which are so evident in examples of guild work during and after his tenure as instructor.

59. Ernest Batchelder
American, California, 1875–1957
Tile assemblage, after 1909
Ceramic, unidentified casting medium
Marks: none
Dr. Robert Winter, Pasadena, California

This tile grouping, assembled at some point after the tiles were created, embodies the color palette and texture of Batchelder's work. The historical sailing ship image is another motif associated closely with Batchelder and the guild.

60. Ernest Batchelder
American, California, 1875–1957
Tile
Ceramic
4″ square
Marks: back stamped BATCHELDER/LOS ANGELES
Zev Greenwald and Moira McManus Collection

Such circular interpretations of plant forms occurred frequently in ceramic trivets and tiles produced by the Handicraft Guild. The greens, pale blues, and muted browns, typical of tiles from Batchelder's California factory, also were the glazes seen most frequently in guild tiles.

61. Gustav F. Weber
American, Minnesota (b. Paris) 1870–1960
Rendering of a period interior by G. F. Weber Studio, 1911–13
920 Nicollet Avenue, Minneapolis, Minn.
Colored pencil on paper
$16\frac{1}{2}'' \times 36''$
Marks: G. F. Weber Studio/920 Nicollet
Northwest Architectural Archives, University of Minnesota Libraries, St. Paul
Gustav F. Weber Papers

This colorful rendering by Weber's interior decorating studio at 920 Nicollet (Myers Arcade), Minneapolis, very likely depicts the type of work he used to illustrate his lectures to guild students.

62. Gustav F. Weber
American, Minnesota, (b. Paris) 1870–1960
Design for a floor lamp, n.d.
Colored pencil on paper
$11\frac{1}{2}'' \times 5\frac{4}{5}''$
Marks: signature, lower right corner, G. F. Weber Studio/Mpls
Northwest Architectural Archives, University of Minnesota Libraries, St. Paul
Gustav F. Weber Papers

Weber's use of the peacock motif reconfirms the design influence of *japonisme*, Batchelder, and his instructors on the larger Minnesota artistic community.

63. Handicraft Guild of Minneapolis
American, Minnesota, 1904–18
Pair of bookends, 1905–18
Copper
$6\frac{1}{10}'' \times 7\frac{1}{5}'' \times 5\frac{7}{10}''$
Marks: base, struck incuse HANDICRAFT GUILD/MINNEAPOLIS
James and Darlene Dommell Collection

64. Handicraft Guild of Minneapolis
American, Minnesota, 1904–18
Bowl, 1905–18
Ceramic

3½" × 7⁷⁄₁₀"
Marks: base, struck incuse HANDICRAFT GUILD/
MINNEAPOLIS.
James and Darlene Dommel Collection

65. Handicraft Guild of Minneapolis
American, Minnesota, 1904–18
Pot, 1911
Ceramic
3" × 4½"
Marks: base, struck incuse HANDICRAFT GUILD/
MINNEAPOLIS, stick applied 1911, black ink Q3,
green pencil 654, and detached paper label HANDI-
CRAFT GVILD/621/HG (cipher with G enclosed in
the bottom half of the H)/MINNEAPOLIS
Rolf Grudem Collection

Dated examples of guild work are extremely rare.

66. Handicraft Guild of Minneapolis
American, Minnesota, 1904–18
Vase, 1905–18
Ceramic
6¼" × 3¹⁄₁₀"
Marks: base, stick applied HG (cipher with G enclosed
in the bottom half of the H)
Rolf Grudem Collection

Many period illustrations of guild work depict such
pieces as this, which show slab construction vases displaying similar impressed/incised panel decoration.

67. Handicraft Guild of Minneapolis
American, Minnesota, 1904–18
Convertible candleholder or sconce, 1905–18
Brass
1⅖" × 8³⁄₁₀" × 3⅖"
Marks: base, struck incuse HANDICRAFT GUILD
MINNEAPOLIS
Rolf Grudem Collection

The candle bracket swivels to permit its use either as a
candleholder or as a wall sconce.

68. Handicraft Guild of Minneapolis
American, Minnesota, 1904–18
Nut bowl, 1905–18
Copper
1½" × 4¹⁄₁₀"
Marks: base, struck incuse HANDICRAFT GUILD/
MINNEAPOLIS
Rolf Grudem Collection

69. Handicraft Guild of Minneapolis
American, Minnesota, 1904–18
Shelf or desk clock, 1905–18
Copper with enameled face, clock works by Waterbury

Clock Co., USA
4¹⁄₁₀" × 8⁷⁄₁₀" × 3⅖"
Marks: back, struck incuse HANDICRAFT GUILD/
MINNEAPOLIS
Rolf Grudem Collection

The scale of this clock and the use of a popular guild
decorative motif often seen in desk sets suggests it might
have been part of such a set.

70. Bertha Lum
American, Minneapolis, Minn., 1869/79–1954
The Homecoming, 1905
Color wood-block print
9⁵⁄₁₆" × 3⁷⁄₁₆"
Marks: Copyright 05 by Bertha Lum, lower edge
The Minneapolis Institute of Arts
Gift of Ethel Morrison Van Derlip, 1916   P.63

There are many shared *japonisme* influences in Lum's
early work and the design work featured in Mary Moulton
Cheney's Artcraft Shop in the first decade of the twentieth century.

71. Bertha Lum
American, Minneapolis, Minn., 1869/79-1954
O Yuki, 1904
Color wood-block print
13¾" × 2³⁄₁₆"
Marks: Bertha Lum/Copyright 1904/no. 97
The Minneapolis Institute of Arts
Gift of Ethel Morrison Van Derlip, 1916   P.82

The narrow, vertical format of this print is evidence of
the *japonisme* influence adopted in Minnesota and nationwide during the American arts and crafts era.

72. Handicraft Guild of Minneapolis
American, Minnesota, 1904–18
Light fixture, 1908
From the dining room at Wycroft, Osceola, 1908
Copper and glass
Horst Rechelbacher, Aveda Spa, Osceola, Wis.

Several Light fixtures and three ceramic tile fireplaces
remain in the former residence of Oliver C. Wyman, a
Minneapolis mercantile owner and president of Wyman,
Partridge & Co., Inc. Wycroft was designed and built by
Edwin H. Hewitt for Wyman in 1908.

73. Handicraft Guild of Minneapolis
American, Minnesota, 1904–18
Wall light, 1908
From the dining room at Wycroft, Osceola, 1908
Copper, glass and wood
Horst Rechelbacher, Aveda Spa, Osceola, Wis.

Waterbury Clock Company. Clock. *Rolf Grudem Collection.*
Photograph courtesy of the Minnesota Historical Society.

A nearly identical wall light with conventionalized peacock designs rendered in piercework is illustrated in the guild's 1912–13 annual session pamphlet which confirms this as guild work.

74. Handicraft Guild of Minneapolis
    American, Minnesota, 1904–18
    Candlestick, 1905–18
    Ceramic
    6½″ × 5⁷⁄₁₀″
    Marks: base, struck incuse HANDICRAFT GUILD/
    MINNEAPOLIS
    Steve Schoneck Collection

Candlesticks of many forms and construction methods were popular among guild pottery workers. Similar examples are illustrated in the guild's course schedule.

75. Handicraft Guild of Minneapolis
    American, Minnesota, 1904–18
    Vase, 1905–18
    Ceramic
    8⅓″ × 8″
    Marks: base, struck incuse HANDICRAFT GUILD/
    MINNEAPOLIS.
    Steve Schoneck Collection

The bottom edge of this thrown pot has been drilled for use as a lamp base.

76. Handicraft Guild of Minneapolis
    American, Minnesota, 1904–18
    Bowl, 1905–18
    Copper and glass
    Copper bowl: 2⅗″ × 7⁹⁄₁₀″
    Glass liner: 2⅖″ × 7⁹⁄₁₀″
    Marks: bowl, base, struck incuse HANDICRAFT
    GUILD/MINNEAPOLIS
    Steve Schoneck Collection

77. Handicraft Guild of Minneapolis
    American, Minnesota, 1904–18
    Inkwell, 1905–18
    Copper and enamel
    3″ × 3⅓″
    Marks: base, Dremel-tooled HG (cipher with G enclosed in the bottom half of the H)
    Steve Schoneck Collection

This inkwell is part of an enameled copper desk set including writing pad ends, pen tray, stamp box, letter holder, and picture frame.

Mary Linton Bookwalter Ackerman. Laura Linton MacFarlane collection. Photograph courtesy of the Minnesota Historical Society.

ing. In later years she focused on issues that had long been a priority in her personal life, assisting women to achieve recognition and rewards for their accomplishments in business and professional life. Bookwalter Ackerman died in New York in 1953 and would no doubt be gratified to know

that Harperly Hall and its interiors have continued to serve their function and that the building has received special recognition as a national historic landmark.

HENRIETTA BARCLAY PAIST

Henrietta Barclay Paist is an example of an established artist who profited greatly from her experiences at the guild. She was born in Red Wing, Minnesota, in 1870 and went on to become a nationally known artist and china painter. As an artist, Paist's training began early at the knee of another artist, her mother. Studies followed with Franz A. Bischoff, a ceramic artist; in factories in Dresden and Berlin; with Gertrude Barnes, a watercolorist in Minneapolis; with Ernest A. Batchelder in design; and with Mrs. Greenleaf, a miniaturist, in Chicago. Paist also was a founding member of the Twin City Keramic Club.

In the late nineteenth century she was a recognized painter of portraits on porcelain, winning an award for one of her pieces at the 1900 Paris Exposition. She was well known in America as an instructor of china and watercolor painting, and she advertised instruction and design studies for sale and rent in the China Teacher's Directory of *Keramic Studio* magazine. Paist's nineteenth-century work was in the popular natural realism style. In 1896 she won the gold medal at the National Exhibition of Ceramic Workers in Chicago for the best of "One Hundred and Eight Collections of Decorated Porcelain" exhibited. She continued to copy nature into the twentieth century, but as her work grew more abstract and stylized, it became increasingly apparent that it was heavily influenced by *japonisme* and her training under Ernest Batchelder. Batchelder even used some of her designs as illustrations in his 1910 book, *Design in Theory and Practice*.[8]

Paist's watercolor studies and designs for specific forms such as vases, pitchers, and plate borders appeared regularly in such periodicals as *Keramic Studio* from the 1890s until shortly before her death in 1930. She exhibited her work in the Twin Cities, Chicago, New York, and Detroit, and published frequently in American pottery publications. For four years in the late 1910s Paist's name appeared frequently in individual issues of *Keramic Studio* as page and/ or assistant editor. Some of her designs were included in Keramic Studio's 1906 book entitled *The Fruit Book: Studies for the Painter of China and Student of Water Colors*. The dog-eared copy of this book, still in use at the Minneapolis Public Library, was checked out repeatedly in the 1910s and 1920s. Paist's own book, *Design and the Decoration of Porcelain*, was published by Keramic Studio in 1916.

At the same time that she was busy with the roles of wife, mother, businesswoman, dressmaker, milliner, musician, poet, author, and practicing artist she was also the principal instructor in ceramics at the St. Paul Institute from 1908–10. For more than twenty years, Paist served as porcelain judge at the Minnesota State Fair.

HILMA BERGLUND

Berglund was born in Stillwater in 1886 to immigrant

parents from Småland, Sweden. Her father built a business as a carpenter, building contractor, and designer, and the family eventually moved to St. Paul. Due to illness, Berglund was prevented from finishing a formal education and spent many of her early years pursuing art while convalescing at home. In the first decade of this century she began to focus her studies through the normal art course offered at the St. Paul Institute School of Art, housed in the St. Paul Auditorium.

In the winter of 1909 Berglund kept a journal which included entries describing her coursework at the St. Paul Institute School. At her first lesson on 6 October in tooled leather work with Miss Nabersberg, Berglund was the only student in attendance. "I had to make an original design for the cardcase which I am going to make. There is lots of measuring to be done as every line must be accurate. I took my lesson from 9 to 12." On 13 October she finished the cardcase. She also completed a purse, notebook cover, and bill folder during the course, employing drawing, stamping, tooling, skiving, coloring, and stitching in their creation.[9]

Berglund was developing and printing her own photographs and decorating painted china at home while she was enrolled in the leather work course at the Institute. From late November through early December she made several visits to the auditorium with family, friends, and fellow students to view the industrial arts exhibit there.

In December she began a course in metalwork. In her first class on 2 December she began with a letter opener and then started a copper bowl on 12 December, which occupied her for much of the month. Her description of her Christmas gifts that year is evidence of the local availability and popularity of crafts work at the time. Berglund received a burnt wood (pyrography) glove box, a thermome-

ter in a burnt wood frame, and an embroidered silk pillow cover kit.

From 1910 to 1916, Berglund taught at the St. Paul Institute of Art and continued to pursue art studies at the Handicraft Guild and the Minneapolis School of Art. She assembled photographic albums as journals of her early art school years and later as records of her extensive travels and study abroad. The photographs she included serve as one of the few known documents of work by St. Paul Institute students and female instructors.

While she worked in embroidery, china painting, and pottery, Berglund is best remembered for her commitment and contribution to the art of weaving. She spent considerable time studying abroad, particularly in Sweden, Japan, and China, in a lifelong pursuit of ideas and skills. She incorporated this broad knowledge into her experiments with new weaving forms and into a teaching approach which offered students the widest possible exposure to design and technical innovation.

She went on to receive art education and masters degrees from the University of Minnesota and joined the faculty to teach weaving, design, and other crafts in the art department from 1930 until her retirement in 1954. In 1955 she patented "The Minnesota Loom," a four-harness tabletop loom that was easily converted to a foot power loom. The loom's "removable innards" made it possible for several students to work on projects with the same loom frame, and its small size suited it well to crowded classroom spaces.

Berglund was a modest woman whose unassuming manner and appearance was somewhat at odds with her energy and drive. "One lifetime isn't long enough for all the things I'd like to do," she once said.[10] In 1940 she joined with Mrs. Lynwood Downs and Mrs. George Glockler to found the Weavers Guild of Minnesota, which is still in existence. Berglund died in 1972.

RUTH RAYMOND

The guild's last director, Illinois native Ruth Raymond, graduated in design from the School of the Chicago Art Institute. Raymond enjoyed early success as a commercial artist and was an originator of the Kalo Shop in Chicago. She taught design at the University of Chicago with Lillian Cushman (Brown) and left there to study at the Church School of Art.

In 1914, she came to Minnesota as an instructor and went on to serve as principal of the Handicraft Guild. She served that role until 1917, when she began a project that would become her life's work. Working closely with Dean Coffman, she convinced trustees at the University of Minnesota to take over the guild as a degree program for teachers in art education. Her curriculum plan and the support of the arts community and guild officers won the university over. By 1919 the Handicraft Guild, fifty students, and its

Hilma Berglund, at Lake Elmo, early 1900s. Photograph courtesy of the Minnesota Historical Society.

Metal and leather work examples from the St. Paul Institute School of Art, 29 May 1910. Photograph courtesy of the Minnesota Historical Society.

KEY FIGURES:
Charles W. Ames, L. P. Ordway, Arthur Sweeney, William R. French, George B. Zug.

ACTIVITIES:
Major programs included the evening schools (1907–52), lecture programs and concerts (1910 to the 1920s), Museum of Natural and Applied Sciences (1910–present), School of Art and the Art Gallery (1908–31). Lectures, free art exhibitions, concerts, art school, school of commerce, classes for teachers, home economics classes, grade and high school evening schools; departments/committees— art, music, municipal art, language and literature, natural and physical sciences.

COMMENTS:
The following St. Paul cultural organizations grew out of the St. Paul Institute: The International Institute, Minnesota Museum of Art, University of Minnesota extension classes, Metropolitan College, The Woman's Institute, the vocational schools, and the Science Museum of Minnesota.

ST. PAUL INSTITUTE OF SCIENCE & LETTERS
Begun September 1906 at the Minnesota Club.
Incorporated: 11 January 1907.
Reincorporated: 28 April 1908 as *St. Paul Institute of Arts & Sciences.*

FOUNDING PRINCIPLES:
"To promote among all classes of people the knowledge and enlightenment which are essential to right living and good citizenship; seek to accomplish this purpose through lectures, instruction classes, publications and other means designed to stimulate interest in the practical arts, hygiene, literature, history, the fine arts, economics, government and all departments of arts and sciences, but without sectarian bias or political partisanship."

KEY FIGURES:
Charles W. Ames, Thomas Irvine, C. P. Noyes, Arthur Sweeney, L. P. Ordway.

ACTIVITIES:
Free lecture series, elementary and high school night schools (in conjunction with the St. Paul school board and aimed at the immigrant population).

ST. PAUL INSTITUTE SCHOOL OF FINE ART
Department of the *St. Paul Institute*—same facilities.

FOUNDING PRINCIPLES:
The institute modeled itself after the Brooklyn Institute of Arts and Sciences and sought "to provide a foundation of drawing, color and composition. The time has come when all arts can be elevated to the plane of fine arts; when a design for a poster, a lamp, a flower pot or a fabric has a need of the same lofty principles as a painting or a piece of sculpture."

KEY FIGURES:
Elizabeth Bonta, Hilma Berglund, Henrietta Barclay Paist, Berta Nabersberg, Lauros M. Phoenix, Lee Woodward Ziegler, Tyler McWhorter, Jessie H. Neal, George W. Rehse, Edith Griffith, D. E. Randall, Drusilla Paist, Hazel Tusler, Ida Kueffner.

ACTIVITIES:
Academy of fine arts and a school of applied arts. Courses offered in metalwork, pottery, keramics, block printing, stenciling, leather work, bookbinding, portrait painting, general design, mural decoration, illustration, cartoon and caricature, commercial design, jewelry, and a special course for teachers. Offered a special summer school of arts and crafts in 1909.

ST. PAUL SCHOOL OF FINE ARTS
Incorporated: 1896.
1896–1912?

LOCATION:
48 E. 4th Street, St. Paul, Minn.

FOUNDING PRINCIPLES:
"The mutual improvement of its members by advancement in the study, knowledge and love of art; the acquisition of books and papers for the formation of an art library; the establishment of a studio of information, and such other means of art culture as come within the province of similar associations."

KEY FIGURES:
Mrs. C. W. Ames, Mrs. D. A. Monfort, Mrs. Herbert Davis, Ellen Wheelock, Mrs. E. P. Sanborn, Annie Carpenter, Clara Sommers, Elizabeth B. Bonta, Eleanor Jilson, Mrs. S. C. Olmstead.

ACTIVITIES:
Classes in life, draped model, still life, composition and illustration, antique, sketching, design (two years), out-of-door sketching. Offered classes mornings, evenings, Saturdays, October through May.

Martha Larson working metal, 27 March 1913. St. Paul Institute School of Art. Photograph courtesy of the Minnesota Historical Society.

TWIN CITY KERAMIC CLUB
Organized 1912 by fourteen china painters living in Minneapolis and St. Paul.

LOCATION:
Meyers Arcade, Minneapolis (1916).

MEMBERS:
Miss Elizabeth Hood (president, 1913), Miss M. Etta Beede (vice president, 1913; secretary, 1916), Henrietta Barclay Paist, Mrs. R. K. Alcott, Miss Ora V. White (vice president, 1916), Miss Florence Huntington, Mrs. M. F. Carlyle. Mrs. Arch Coleman (president, 1916), Frances E. Newman (treasurer, 1916).

ACTIVITIES:
Annual exhibitions (in 1913 it was held in Minneapolis at the Handicraft Guild and in St. Paul at the St. Paul Hotel). Annual meeting held in May. Under the suggestion of Mary Moulton Cheney, the club members conducted an

amateur class in china painting and design for the students of the Minneapolis Institute School of Art. Held luncheons with presentations on art by invited speakers. Membership in 1916 was forty-three.

APPENDIX III: MINNESOTA ARTS AND CRAFTS INDEX

The following index lists many of the people and organizations which had connections to the arts and crafts movement in Minnesota. It includes a record of any individual identified with association to the Chalk and Chisel Club, Arts and Crafts Society of Minneapolis, and the Handicraft Guild of Minneapolis. Individuals who were identified as exhibiting/working in a medium which is or could possibly be classified as arts and crafts/design related were included. All individuals with controlling positions (i.e., director) or who served as faculty at programs/schools that included arts and crafts/design introduction courses in their curricula were included. Business people who supported arts and crafts activity in Minnesota and businesses with processes, products, or merchandise with connection to the arts and crafts were included here as well.

This index was compiled from city directories, articles in school bulletins, annual reports, exhibit catalogs, newspaper articles, periodical articles, general art references, biographical references, published histories, and so on. The general sources or specific citations are noted in the bibliography. A more complete and annotated index exists in database form in the museum collections reference holdings of the Minnesota Historical Society, St. Paul. The information appears in this order:

- Name of individual/organization

- Birth-death/years in existence

- Address and date at that location

- Role(s) within the movement, such as artist, board member, officer, teacher, student, member, executive committee member

- Art Medium (i.e., crochet, wood-block printing, sculpture, metalwork, and so on)

- Organizational affiliations (i.e., Handicraft Guild, Art Workers' League of St. Paul, and so on)

- Expanded text comments

Aanstad, Sarah Margrethe
Dates unknown
Location: Eau Claire, Wisconsin (1913–14); Minneapolis (1915)
Role(s): Student
Medium: Illustration
Affiliations: Minneapolis Society of Fine Arts, Minneapolis School of Art

Adelaide, Sister
Dates unknown
Location: Winona (1905–6)
Role(s): Student
Medium: Design
Affiliations: Minneapolis School of Fine Arts
Comments: MSA List of Students—Winona Seminary

Agnew, Chalmer
Dates unknown
Location: Duluth
Roles(s): Artist
Medium: Art Handicraft
Comments: 1908—MSAS Prize; MSAC 1917 Catalog lists Wm. Chalmers Agnew Jr., 518 Hawthorne Rd., Duluth, Painting.

Akerberg, Knut(e)
Dates unknown
Location: 430 Moore Bldg., St. Paul (1904); Naples, Italy (1905)
Role(s): Artist, Student
Medium: Sculpture
Affiliations: St. Paul Institute of Arts & Sciences
Comments: 1904—MSAS Prize; 1894–98—SPIAS Student

Akerberg, Knute, Mrs.
Dates unknown
Role(s): Student
Affiliations: St. Paul Institute of Arts & Sciences
Comments: 1894–98—SPIAS Student; Maiden Name—Miss Verne Ayer.

Albert, Allen D.
Dates unknown
Location: Minneapolis
Role(s): Artist, Member
Medium: Painting, Sculpture
Affiliations: Minnesota State Art Society, Handicraft Guild
Comments: 1912—MSAS Exhibit Committee, MSAS Juror; 1912–13—HG Session Lecturer; 1914—MSAS Treasurer; 1917—MSAC Vice President

Alcott, R. R., Mrs.
Dates unknown
Location: 508 Oak St. S.E., Minneapolis (1908)
Role(s): Artist
Medium: Ceramics

Knut(e) Akerberg. Minnesota State Art Society Exhibit Catalog, *1903 and 1904, p. 49.*

Alcott, Robert K., Mrs.
Dates unknown
Location: 1424 W. 26th St., Minneapolis (1913–14)
Role(s): Artist, Student
Medium: Ceramics, China painting
Affiliations: Twin City Porcelain and Keramic Club
Comments: 1914—MSAS First Place Ceramic Art

Allen, Katherine (Kate)
Dates unknown
Role(s): Student
Medium: Pottery
Affiliations: Handicraft Guild

Alsdurf, Pearl E.
Dates unknown
Role(s): Student
Medium: Textile design
Affiliations: St. Paul Institute of Art

Altman, Harry I.
Dates unknown
Location: 609 Delaware St. S.E., Minneapolis
(1912)
Role(s): Artist
Medium: Pottery, Textiles

Alwin, W. G., Mrs.
Dates unknown
Location: 13 N. Broadway St., New Ulm (1912)
Role(s): Artist
Medium: Lace

Ames, Charles W., Mrs.
Dates unknown
Location: St. Paul (1914)
Role(s): Officer, Member
Affiliations: Art Workers' Guild of St. Paul, St. Paul
Institute of Arts & Sciences, Minnesota State
Art Society
Comments: 1908–9—SPIAS Vice Chair; 1912,
1914—SPIAS President of Art Dept.; 1914—
MSAS Exhibit Committee; 1916—SPIAS Com-
mittee Member

Ames, Charles W.
Dates unknown
Location: St. Paul (1914)
Role(s): Board Member, Member
Affiliations: Art Workers' Guild of St. Paul, St. Paul
Institute of Arts & Sciences, Minnesota State
Art Society
Comments: 1907–21—President of The St. Paul In-
stitute Board of Trustees; 1908, 1909, 1912,
1914—SPIAS President; 1914—MSAS Exhibit
Committee; 1916—SPIAS Chairman and
President

Ames, Charlotte Phoebe
Dates unknown
Role(s): Student
Medium: Textile Design
Affiliations: . Paul Institute of Art

Anderson, Adah E.
Dates unknown
Role(s): Artist, Student
Medium: Leaded glass (Applied Art), Textiles, Sten-
ciling
Affiliations: Minneapolis School of Fine Arts, Min-
neapolis Institute of Arts, Minneapolis School
of Art
Comments: 1917–18—MSFA Student in Applied
Arts; Awarded 2nd Prize by Art Alliance of
America Competition in NYC.

Anderson, Eleanor
Dates unknown
Role(s): Student
Medium: Textile design
Affiliations: St. Paul Institute of Art

Andrews, Cecile
Dates unknown
Role(s): Artist
Medium: Ceramics
Affiliations: St. Paul Institute School of Art

Atkinson, Flossie
Dates unknown
Location: Litchfield
Role(s): Artist
Medium: Basketry
Affiliations: Litchfield Handicraft Guild

Austin, Alice
Dates unknown
Location: Boston & St. Paul (1912)
Role(s): Artist
Medium: Photography
Comments: Not listed in St. Paul City Directories
1911–13

Avery, Bertha, Mrs.
Dates unknown
Location: Anoka (1913); 1013 University Av. S.E.,
Minneapolis (1914)
Role(s): Artist
Medium: Illumination, Photography

Avis, James L.
Dates unknown
Role(s): Artist
Medium: Chafing Dish
Affiliations: Handicraft Guild

Axtell, Mary E., Miss
Dates unknown
Location: 645 Central Park Pl., St. Paul (1914); 563
Laurel Av., St. Paul (1908)
Role(s): Member, Teacher
Medium: Pottery, Jewelry
Affiliations: Art Workers' Guild of St. Paul, Arts
Guild of St. Paul
Comments: 1908—AGSP Summer School; Instruc-
tor of Drawing and Crafts at Cleveland High
School, St. Paul.

Babbidge, Eleanor Winship
Dates unknown
Location: St. Paul
Role(s): Artist
Medium: Art Handicraft, Textile Design
Affiliations: St. Paul School of Fine Arts
Comments: 1908—MSAS Prize

Babcock, Rose Estella
Dates unknown
Role(s): Student
Medium: Textile Design
Affiliations: St. Paul Institute

Backus, Catherine F., Mrs.
Dates unknown
Location: 615 9th Av. S.E., Minneapolis (1904–5);
610 13th Av. S.E., Minneapolis (1906)
Role(s): Artist, Member
Medium: Sculpture
Affiliations: Minneapolis Arts & Crafts Society,
Chalk & Chisel Club
Comments: 1905—MSAS Prize; Married Name—
Mrs. George J. Backus

Backus, Clara Marie
Dates unknown
Role(s): Artist
Medium: Book Plates
Affiliations: Minneapolis School of Fine Arts
Comments: See Marie Backus and Marie Backus
Chapman

Backus, Marie
Dates unknown
Location: Independence, Iowa (1905–6)
Role(s): Student

Medium: Design
Affiliations: Minneapolis School of Fine Arts, Min-
neapolis School of Art
Comments: 1905, 1906—Student at 12 N. 13th; see
Marie Backus Chapman

Bahr, Pauline
Dates unknown
Location: 2429 Colfax Av. S., Minneapolis (1912)
Role(s): Artist
Medium: Ceramics

Baird, Allen G.
Dates unknown
Location: 500 S. 3rd St., Minneapolis (1906)
Role(s): Artist
Medium: Stained Glass

Baker, E. D., Mrs.
Dates unknown
Location: Finlayson, Minnesota (1915)
Role(s): Artist
Medium: Textiles

Baker, Jane, Mrs.
Dates unknown
Location: 1932 Aldrich Av. S., Minneapolis (1912)
Role(s): Artist
Medium: Lace

Baldwin, Inez, Miss
Dates unknown
Location: Curtis Court, Minneapolis (1906)
Role(s): Artist
Medium: Ceramics
Comments: 1905—Listed as Decorator; 1906—
Listed as Artist; 1908—Listed as China Decorator

Barber, Bell, Miss
Dates unknown
Role(s): Artist
Medium: Textile Design
Affiliations: St. Paul Institute

Barber, Bessie
Dates unknown
Location: St. Paul
Role(s): Student
Affiliations: Handicraft Guild

Barnes, Gertrude J., Mrs.
Dates unknown
Location: 719 Hennepin, Minneapolis; 1812 Emer-
son Av. S., Minneapolis (1904–5, 1908,
1912–15, 1917)
Role(s): Artist, Teacher, Member, Student
Medium: Painting
Affiliations: Handicraft Guild, Minnesota State Art
Society, Minneapolis School of Fine Arts, The
Woman's Club of Minneapolis, Minneapolis
School of Art
Comments: 1904—MSAS Prize; 1908—MSAS Ex-
hibit Committee; 1910—MSAS Honorable
Mention; 1916—State Art Exhibit Prize; Married
Name—Mrs. Henry A. Barnes

Barrett, Alice M., Miss
Dates unknown
Location: 2735 Humboldt Av. S., Minneapolis
(1912)
Role(s): Artist
Medium: Lace, Textiles

Barrett, Helen H., Mrs.
Dates unknown
Location: Minneapolis (1903)
Role(s): Artist
Medium: Woodcarving

Barsness, Edward
Dates unknown
Role(s): Student
Medium: Design

Gertrude J. Barnes. Minnesota State Art Society Exhibit Catalog, *1903 and 1904, p. 51.*

Affiliations: St. Paul Art Gallery, St. Paul Institute of Art
Comments: 1915—SPIAS Student

Bartholomew, Ethel, Miss
Dates unknown
Location: Sheraton, Iowa (1906); Minneapolis (1912); Curtis Court, Minneapolis (1914)
Role(s): Artist, Member
Medium: Architecture
Affiliations: Minnesota State Art Society, Minneapolis Arts & Crafts Society
Comments: 1912—MSAS Extension Committee

Bartlett, Madge
Dates unknown
Role(s): Artist
Medium: Leather
Affiliations: Minneapolis School of Fine Arts

Barton, J. C.
Dates unknown
Location: 814 Nicollet Av., Minneapolis (1903)
Medium: Pottery

Batchelder, Ernest A.
1875-1857
Location: Pasadenda, California; Los Angeles, California
Role(s): Artist, Teacher
Medium: Metal Work, Design, Pottery/tiles
Affiliations: Handicraft Guild
Comments: 1901–9(?)—Instructor at Throop Ploytechnic Institute; 1905–9—Director of HG

Summer School; 1909—Director of HG Winter Course, HG Instructor; 1908—Author of *Principles of Design*; 1909—MSAS Juror; 1910—Author of *Design in Theory and Practice*; 1910–20—Developed Tile Manufacturing Business in Pasadena; 1920–32—Expanded Tile Business in Los Angeles; 1936–49—Developed Ceramic Art Pottery Line, "Kinneloa," in Los Angeles

Bealz, George, Mrs.
Dates unknown
Role(s): Artist
Medium: Ceramics
Affiliations: St. Paul Institute School of Art

Beans, Jesse E.
Dates unknown
Location: 1001 Hennepin Av., Minneapolis (1907); 1617 Stevens Av., Flt. 3, Minneapolis (1908)
Role(s): Teacher
Medium: Drawing, Jewelry
Affiliations: Minneapolis School of Fine Arts
Comments: 1907—-MSFA Asst.; 1908—Listed as a Designer for the Artcraft Shop, made pieces designed by Mary Moulton Cheney for MSAS Exhibit

Beard, Harington
Dates unknown
Role(s): Officer
Affiliations: Minneapolis Society of Fine Arts
Comments: 1914—MSFA Trustee, Director of The Beard Art Galleries, Minneapolis; 1917—MIA Committee Chair; his gallery served as the loca-

tion for many early art exhibits—MACS, etc.

Beaver, Alice Chant
Dates unknown
Location: 616 E. Franklin Av. (1906)
Medium: Textiles

Beede, Caroline
Dates unknown
Role(s): Artist
Medium: Design

Beede, M. Etta
Dates unknown
Location: 310 Medical Blk., Minneapolis (1904, 1906, 1908, 1913–14); 333 Meyers Arcade, Minneapolis (1915)
Role(s): Artist
Medium: Ceramics, China Painting
Affiliations: Twin City Keramic Club
Comments: 1903, 1906—A&CS Exhibit Ad; 1916—Won AIC Atlan Ceramic Art Club Prize; 1916—Secretary of TCKC

Bell, Barbara
Dates unknown
Location: 229 5th Av. S.E., Minneapolis (1914, 1915)
Role(s): Artist, Student
Medium: Sketching
Affiliations: Minneapolis School of Art
Comments: 1914—MIA 3rd Year Student in Design, ½ Year Scholarship

Benedict, Ida
Dates unknown
Location: Moorhead
Role(s): Student, Artist
Affiliations: Handicraft Guild

Benson, Agnes B., Miss
Dates unknown
Location: 2013 18th Av. S., Minneapolis (1908); 2405 Elliot Av. S., Minneapolis (1912)
Role(s): Artist
Medium: Textiles, Embroidery
Affiliations: Handicraft Guild
Comments: 1906—Winner of Handicraft Guild Scholarship, South High School; 1908—MSAS Prize

Berg, Agnes
Dates unknown
Location: St. Paul
Role(s): Artist
Medium: Basketry

Berger, Maria
Dates unknown
Location: 1978 Como Av. W., St. Paul (1915)
Role(s): Artist
Medium: Textile Design, Painting
Affiliations: St. Paul Institute

Berglund, Hilma
1886-1972
Location: 1860 Feronia Av., St. Paul (1915)
Role(s): Teacher, Student, Member
Medium: Weaving, Painting, Metal Working, Pottery, Stenciling, Leather, Block Printing, Photography, Basketry
Affiliations: St. Paul Art Gallery, St. Paul Institute of Arts & Sciences, Handicraft Guild, Minnesota State Art Society
Comments: 1909—Student at St. Paul Institute Art School, took courses in Leather Work, China, Painting, and Metal Work; 1910–16—Affiliated with HG, Taught Crafts (Metal Work, Pottery, Leather Work, Stencil-block Printing) at SPI; 1914—MSAS Exhibit Committee; 1914–15—St. Paul Art School Sketch Class; 1930–54—Taught

Weaving in U of M Art Department; 1940—One of Three Founders of The Weavers Guild of Minnesota; 1955—Invented and Patented "The Minnesota Loom"; Student at HG (no date)

Bergmeier (Kranstover), Etta
Dates unknown
Location: 614 Fountain St., St. Paul (1915)
Role(s): Student
Medium: Illustration, Painting, Water Color Design, Wall Paper Design
Affiliations: St. Paul Institute of Arts & Sciences, St. Paul Art Gallery

Berry, Louise Du Bois
Dates unknown
Location: Curtis Court, Minneapolis (1906)
Role(s): Artist
Medium: Cabinetry, Leather
Affiliations: Handicraft Guild
Comments: 1908—Designed and made articles with Nelbert Murphy for MSAS Exhibit; Teacher at Central High School, Minneapolis

Betlach, J. W.
Dates unknown
Location: 638 Huron St. S.E., Minneapolis
Role(s): Artist, Student
Medium: Book Plates
Affiliations: Minneapolis School of Art

Bierstettel, Henry J. (J. Henry)
Dates unknown
Role(s): Student
Medium: Illustration
Affiliations: St. Paul Institute of Arts & Sciences

Billau, Helen Frances
Dates unknown
Location: 1919 Iglehart Av., St. Paul
Role(s): Artist
Medium: Crochet, Copper, Illustration

Bishop, Caroline Robert
Dates unknown
Location: 2017 St. Anthony Av., St. Paul
Role(s): Artist
Medium: Ceramics

Blackburn, Oscar T.
Dates unknown
Location: 3525 Park Av., Minneapolis (1912, 1914)
Role(s): Artist
Medium: (Commercial Art) Book Plates

Blaisdell, Helen
Dates unknown
Role(s): Student
Medium: Ceramics
Affiliations: Handicraft Guild

Blanch, Arnold A.
Dates unknown
Location: Minneapolis; St. Louis Park (1915)
Role(s): Student
Medium: Illustration
Affiliations: Minneapolis Society of Fine Arts, Minneapolis School of Art

Blase, Annette
Dates unknown
Location: North St. Paul (1905–6)
Role(s): Student
Medium: Design
Affiliations: Minneapolis School of Fine Arts, Minneapolis School of Art

Blashfield, Edwin H.
Dates unknown
Location: New York (1913)
Role(s): Artist
Medium: Drawing
Affiliations: Handicraft Guild

Blymyer, Elizabeth, Mrs.
Dates unknown
Location: 1776 Humboldt Av. S., Minneapolis (1906)
Medium: Weaving

Bodlak, Zdenek
Dates unknown
Role(s): Student
Medium: Poster Design
Affiliations: St. Paul Institute of Arts & Sciences
Comments: 1912—SPIAS Student

Bond, Marie Palmer, Mrs.
Dates unknown
Location: 1120 Chestnut Av., Minneapolis (1908)
Role(s): Artist
Medium: Photography
Comments: Married Name—Mrs. Charles E. Bond

Bonta, Elizabeth Brainard, Miss
Dates unknown
Location: 486 Marshall Av., St. Paul (1905); 275 Kent St. (1908); 48 E. 4th St., St. Paul (1908)
Role(s): Student, Artist, Teacher, Member
Medium: Jewelry, Painting, Design
Affiliations: St. Paul Art Gallery, Art Workers' Guild of St. Paul, St. Paul Institute of Arts & Sciences, Minnesota State Art Society, St. Paul School of Fine Arts, Handicraft Guild
Comments: 1903–4—Came from New York to Direct Life and Design Classes at SPIAS; 1904—MSAS Juror; 1905–18—in charge of Design and Decorative Art classes at SPIAS; 1908—Teacher and Curator at SPSFA, MSAS Secretary; 1912—MSAS Extension Committee; 1914—MSAS Exhibit Committee; 1916—SPIAS Exhibitor. Taught Courses at SPIAS in Design, Watercolor, Metalwork and Jewelry.

Bookwalter Ackerman, Mary Linton, Mrs.
Dates unknown
Location: 1031 6th St. S., Minneapolis (1903–6), New York, New York (1906)
Role(s): Officer, Member
Medium: Screens, Oils, Woodcarving, Interior Decorating
Affiliations: Handicraft Guild, Minneapolis Arts & Crafts Society
Comments: 1905—HG Director and Treasurer; 1906—A Decorator located at the HG building; Married names—Mrs. Joseph Bookwalter, Mrs. Frederick Lee Ackerman. Designed interior of Edwin H. Hewitt residence built in 1906 at 126 E. Franklin Ave., Minneapolis. Wrote a series of articles on Interior Design for *The Craftsman.* Interior Decorator in NYC where she served as chairman of the building committees and designed the apartments for the cooperatives Harperly Hall (1910) and the Gainsborough.

Bosworth, Miss
Dates unknown
Location: Rochester
Comments: 1912—MSAS Gave Talk on Handicraft

Boutell Brothers

Elizabeth Brainard Bonta, 29 March 1916. Photograph courtesy of the Minnesota Historical Society.

Dates unknown
Location: Minneapolis
Role(s): Artist
Medium: Furniture
Comments: 1884–1971—Furniture and Home Furnishings

Bovey, Charles A., Mrs.
Dates unknown
Location: Minneapolis
Role(s): Officer
Affiliations: Handicraft Guild
Comments: HG President

Bowers, Ray
Dates unknown
Role(s): Student
Affiliations: St. Paul Art Gallery
Comments: MSAS 1914 Exhibit Lists James Raymon Bowers, Student at St. Paul Institute of Art, Illustration

Boyle, Harold L.
Dates unknown
Role(s): Teacher, Artist
Medium: Metalworking
Affiliations: Handicraft Guild
Comments: 1909–13—HG Faculty; 1909, 1910—AIC Award of Distinct Artistic Merit; 1911—Foreman in Metal Shop at HG; Student of Arthur F. Payne of Bradley Polytechnic, Peoria, Il; and of Silversmith R. Wallace of Walling, Ct.

Boyle, W. G., Mrs.
Dates unknown
Location: Mora, Minnesota
Role(s): Artist
Medium: Textiles
Affiliations: M. E. Parsonage

Brace, Ruth
Dates unknown
Location: 89 S. 10th St., Minneapolis (1914)
Role(s): Student, Artist
Medium: Jewelry
Affiliations: Handicraft Guild
Comments: 1914—MSAS Prize; 1923—Jeweler at

Kirchner & Renich, Minneapolis.

Bradstreet, John Scott
1845–1914
Location: Minneapolis
Role(s): Officer, Member
Medium: Interior Decorator/Designer
Affiliations: Minneapolis Society of Fine Arts, Minneapolis Art Commission, Handicraft Guild
Comments: 1903, 1904, 1906—Ads in A&C Exhibit Catalogs; MSFA Trustee; Opened the Craftshouse in 1904—Gallery There Served as Adjunct Instruction for MSFA and HG Students

Brandtjen, Minnie
Dates unknown
Role(s): Artist
Medium: Ceramics
Affiliations: St. Paul Institute School of Art

Breck, Joseph
Dates unknown
Location: Minneapolis
Role(s): Artist
Medium: Painting
Affiliations: Minneapolis Institute School of Art, Minneapolis School of Art
Comments: 1914–16—Director of Minneapolis School of Fine Arts; Director of Minneapolis Institute School of Art; Director of Minneapolis Society of Fine Arts.

Brewer, Edward
Dates unknown
Location: Minneapolis (1917)
Role(s): Artist
Medium: Commercial Art
Comments: Ad for Cream of Wheat Co.

Bright, Agnes
Dates unknown
Role(s): Artist
Medium: Dish
Affiliations: Handicraft Guild

Brill, Ethel Claire, Miss
1877–1962
Location: St. Anthony Park (1905–6); 2365 Carter

Av., St. Paul (1908, 1910, 1912, 1913)
Role(s): Artist, Student
Medium: Writer, Artist, Jewelry, Metal Working
Affiliations: Handicraft Guild, St. Paul Institute of Arts, Minneapolis School of Art
Comments: 1902—Student at U of M; 1903—Instructor U of M; 1906—Metal Worker, MSCFA Student; 1907—HG Student; 1908—HG Asst., Douglas Donaldson and Ruth Starr Made Pieces She Designed for MSAS Exhibit; Taught High School for Two Years. MHS Collections hold three portfolios of her pencil and watercolor drawings from the early 1900s, some of which were used to illustrate her many children's books.

Brink, Floyd Curtis
Dates unknown
Location: St. Paul
Role(s): Student
Medium: Illustration
Affiliations: St. Paul Institute of Arts & Sciences
Comments: 1914—MSAS Prize, Student

Brioschi, Charles
Dates unknown
Location: 246 W. 3rd St., St. Paul (1914, 1915); St. Paul (1912)
Role(s): Artist
Medium: Sculpture
Comments: 1914—MSAS Prize

Brock, Emma Lillian, Miss
1886–
Location: 1983 St. Anthony Av., St. Paul (1907, 1912–13); 89 S. 10th St., Minneapolis (1910); Ft. Snelling (1915).
Role(s): Artist, Student, Teacher
Medium: Stenciling, Book Plates, Pottery, Writer, Artist, Painting, Illustration
Affiliations: Minneapolis School of Art, Handicraft Guild
Comments: 1905—Student at U of M; 1907—Student; 1910—HG Clerk; 1912—MSAS 1st Place Stencil; 1914—MSAS Prize, Teacher; 1914–21 & 1928–32—Librarian Minneapolis Public Library; 1918–19—On The Faculty of The Minneapolis School of Art; Graduate, University of Minnesota. Graduate and post-graduate, MSA. Pupil of George Bridgman, The Art Students' League, New York. Designer for the Art Craft Shop, Minneapolis. Writer/artist of children's books.

Brock, Vinnia
Dates unknown
Location: 89 10th St. S., Minneapolis (1908)
Role(s): Artist
Medium: Pottery
Affiliations: Handicraft Guild
Comments: 1908—AIC of Distinct Artistic Merit Award

Brockway, Helen, Miss
Dates unknown
Location: 500 10th St. S., Minneapolis (1906)
Role(s): Student, Member
Affiliations: Handicraft Guild, Minneapolis Arts & Crafts Society
Comments: 1906—Student at HG and Teacher, North High School

Brooks, Edith M., Mrs.
Dates unknown
Location: 1779 Emerson Av. S., Minneapolis (1906); 1779 James Av. S., Minneapolis (1913)
Role(s): Artist, Member
Affiliations: Minneapolis Arts & Crafts Society, The Woman's Club of Minneapolis

Ethel Claire Brill. Photograph courtesy of the Minnesota Historical Society.

Comments: Married Name—Mrs. Edmund D. Brooks.

Brooks, Edmund D.
1866–1919
Role(s): Officer
Affiliations: Minneapolis Society of Fine Arts
Comments: 1902–19—Bookman and Rare Book Importer with a Shop in the HG Building from 1907 until His Death; 1914—MSFA Trustee

Brown, Alice L., Mrs.
Dates unknown
Location: 920 Nicollet Av., Minneapolis (1914); 216 Meyers Arcade, Minneapolis (1915)
Role(s): Artist, Student
Medium: Ceramics
Affiliations: Twin City Keramic Club
Comments: 1914—MSAS Honorable Mention, Listed as Artist in City Directory

Brown, Helen
Dates unknown
Location: 2811 2nd Av. S., Minneapolis
Role(s): Artist, Student
Medium: Textiles
Comments: 1913—MSAS 1st Place Student Painting

Brown, Robert A.
Dates unknown
Role(s): Student
Medium: Illustration, Painting
Affiliations: St. Paul Institute of Arts & Sciences, St. Paul Art Gallery
Comments: 1914—SPIAS Student; 1915—Listed as Artist; 1917—MSAC 1st Place Student Painting

Brownell, Grace Borden
Dates unknown
Role(s): Student
Medium: Textile Design
Affiliations: St. Paul Institute of Art

Bryant, Nettie, Miss
Dates unknown
Location: Elk River, Minnesota (1905–6); Minneapolis (1907)
Role(s): Artist, Student
Medium: Leather, Copper
Affiliations: Minneapolis School of Fine Arts, Minneapolis School of Art
Comments: 1907—Student; 1908—MSAS Prize, Made Pieces Designed by Mary Moulton Cheney for MSAS Exhibit

Buechner, Erna
Dates unknown
Role(s): Student
Medium: Textile Design
Affiliations: St. Paul Institute
Comments: 1913—Student, St. Paul Institute

Buell, May Whitney
Dates unknown
Location: 2219 Knapp St., St. Paul (1905)
Role(s): Artist, Student
Medium: Design, Bookplate, Metal Working, Leather
Affiliations: School of Fine Arts

Burbank, Elizabeth, Miss
Dates unknown
Role(s): Teacher
Affiliations: Handicraft Guild
Comments: 1916–17—Instructor at HG; Art Instructor at Vocational School.

Burke, Elizabeth, Mrs.
Dates unknown
Location: Minneapolis
Role(s): Artist, Teacher, Student
Medium: Art Handicraft, Painting

Affiliations: Minneapolis School of Fine Arts, Minneapolis School of Art
Comments: 1905, 1906—MSAS Prize

Burnett, Edah F.
Dates unknown
Location: 666 Holly Av., St. Paul
Role(s): Artist
Medium: Design, Painting
Affiliations: St. Paul School of Fine Arts
Comments: 1908—Student

Burnside, Ada M.
Dates unknown
Location: Duluth (1905–6)
Role(s): Artist, Student
Medium: Leather
Affiliations: Minneapolis School of Fine Arts, Minneapolis School of Art
Comments: 1906—Student MSFA

Burr, Alice, Mrs.
Dates unknown
Role(s): Artist, Student
Affiliations: Handicraft Guild
Comments: 1912—Received HG Scholarship, Central High School; 1912–14—Student HG; 1915—Teacher HG Summer School; Married Name—Mrs. M. C. Burr

Bushnell, H. J., Mrs.
Dates unknown
Location: 1776 Humboldt Av. S., Minneapolis (1906)
Medium: Weaving

Buttrud, John Herbert O.
Dates unknown
Location: 516 Oak St. S.E., Minneapolis (1905); 209 Washington Av. N., Minneapolis (1912)
Role(s): Artist
Medium: Glass, Painting
Comments: 1907, 1912—Listed as Artist at Ford Bros. Glass Co., Minneapolis.

Buzza, George E.
Dates unknown
Location: 426 S. 6th St., Minneapolis (1916–19)
Role(s): Artist
Medium: Designer
Comments: 1914—Founded the art publishing co. which became The Buzza Co. in 1917–26, Factory on Lake St. Was Known as "Craftsacres"; 1916–19—SA&C, Boston Exhibitor

Byholt, Clara
Dates unknown
Medium: Leather
Affiliations: Handicraft Guild

Byron, Elizabeth
Dates unknown
Role(s): Student
Medium: Stencil
Affiliations: Minneapolis School of Art
Comments: 1918—Minnesota State Fair Prize

Cable, Margaret Kelly
Dates unknown
Location: 89 10th St. S., Minneapolis
Role(s): Student, Artist
Medium: Pottery, Photography
Affiliations: Handicraft Guild
Comments: 1910—MSAS Photography Prize; 1907–10—HG Student and Instructor; 1910—Hired as First Director of New Ceramic Department at University of North Dakota; 1910–1949—University of North Dakota Ceramics Dept.; 1910–13—Summer Employee at The White-ware Potteries, East Liverpool, Ohio; 1911—Student of Frederick H. Rhead; 1918—Student of Charles F. Binns; aka Marguerite B. Cable

Calderwood, Ruth
Dates unknown
Location: Newport, Minnesota (1910)
Role(s): Artist
Medium: Jewelry, Metal Working, Water Colors
Affiliations: St. Paul Institute School of Art
Comments: 1910—MSAS Prize, Student

Calhoun, Frederic D.
Dates unknown
Location: 1900 Dupont Av S., Minneapolis (1903); 1611 Dupont Av. S., Minneapolis (1914); 89 S. 10th St., Minneapolis (1917)
Role(s): Artist
Medium: Design, Painting
Comments: 1907—Teacher at U of M; 1911—Artist, MacMartin Adv. Co.; 1917—Rep. for Artists' League of Minneapolis

Cameron, Mary B., Mrs.
Dates unknown
Location: 1605 Hennepin Av., Minneapolis (1913, 1914)
Role(s): Artist
Medium: Ceramics

Camlet Art Needlecraft Shop, The
Dates unknown
Location: 210–211 Meyers Arcade (1918)

Campbell, Donald
Dates unknown
Location: Minneapolis (1910–14, 1916, 1919)
Role(s): Student, Artist
Medium: Copper
Affiliations: Handicraft Guild
Comments: 1910–14, 1916, 1919—Draughtsman

Campbell, George A.
Dates unknown
Location: 2934 Oakland Av., Minneapolis (1917)
Role(s): Member
Affiliations: Manual Arts Club of Minneapolis
Comments: 1917—MACM President; Teacher at Central High School

Campbell, Jess(ie) G.
Dates unknown
Location: 386 Cleveland Av., Merriam Park, St. Paul (1912); 55 E. 4th St., St. Paul (1914, 1915); North St. Paul (1917)
Role(s): Artist
Medium: Painting, Etching
Comments: 1917—MSAC 1st Place Etching; MSFA 1913 Exhibit lists Jessie Campbell of Turner, Oregon

Campbell, Mae Louise
Dates unknown
Location: 63 The Buckingham, St. Paul (1904)
Role(s): Artist
Medium: Weaving

Cantieny, Delphine
Dates unknown
Role(s): Student
Medium: Poster
Affiliations: Minneapolis School of Art
Comments: 1917—MSAC 1st Place Student Poster

Cantieny, Josephine
Dates unknown
Location: Detroit, Mi (1915)
Role(s): Student
Affiliations: Minneapolis School of Art
Comments: 1917—Graduated from MSA Applied Arts Dept. and first place student poster.

Carey, Clarence
Dates unknown
Role(s): Teacher
Medium: Mechanical Drawing
Affiliations: St. Paul Institute of Arts & Sciences

*zza Company "Crafters"] George E. Buzza. Minnesota His-
cal Society. Photograph by Norton and Peel, 1923.*

Margaret Kelly Cable, 1926. Barbara Vodrey Wamelink.

Carey, Gertrude L., Miss
Dates unknown
Location: Duluth
Role(s): Artist, Member
Affiliations: Duluth Art Association
Comments: 1908—MSAR Juror, 1912—Duluth
Art Association Member

Carlborg, Andrew J.
Dates unknown
Location: 1416 Hennepin Av., Minneapolis (1906);
1414 Hennepin Av., Minneapolis (1907)
Role(s): Artist
Medium: Cabinetry
Comments: 1907—Cabinetmaker

Carlson, Thorgny
Dates unknown
Comments: 1906—Won Handicraft Guild High
School Scholarship, Attended East High
School, Minneapolis

Carlyle, Margaret
Dates unknown
Location: 509 Wabasha Av., St. Paul (1914)
Role(s): Student
Medium: Ceramic Art
Comments: 1914—MSAS Prize

Carlyle Studio
Dates unknown
Role(s): Artist
Medium: China Painting
Affiliations: St. Paul Institute

Carmichael, Harriet E., Miss
1865–1940
Location: 2100 James Av. S., Minneapolis
(1906–12)
Role(s): Artist, Student
Medium: Leather, Design, Printingmaking, Jewelry
Affiliations: Minneapolis Arts & Crafts Society,
Minneapolis School of Fine Arts, Minneapolis
School of Art
Comments: 1906—A&CS Ad; 1907 SA&C, Boston
Exhibitor; 1907–12—Partner with Mary Moulton

Cheney in Artcraft Shop: Sign of the Bay Tree;
1910—MSFA Ad; 1912–Moved to Colorado
Springs where she had a craft shop with her
niece, Mary Ruth Maxwell; 12/18/40—Died in
Colorado Springs

Carter, Albertine, Mrs.
Dates unknown
Location: 4147 Vincent Av. S., Minneapolis (1915)
Role(s): Artist
Medium: Basketry

*Harriet E. Carmichael. Photograph courtesy of the Minnesota
Historical Society.*

Carter, Deborah, Miss
Dates Unknown
Location: 270 Mackubin St., St. Paul (1908)
Role(s): Artist, Member
Medium: Jewelry, Metal Working, Leather
Affiliations: Minnesota State Art Society, Handi-
craft Guild
Comments: 1908—Mechanic Arts High School
Teacher; 1912—MSAS Exhibit Committee,
MSAS Juror

Carter, Lillie M.
Dates unknown
Location: 4147 Vincent Av. S., Minneapolis (1915)
Role(s): Artist
Medium: Basketry

Case, Elizabeth
Dates unknown
Role(s): Student, Artist
Medium: Jewelry
Affiliations: Handicraft Guild

Cavanaugh, Josephine
Dates unknown
Location: St. Paul (1908)
Role(s): Artist
Medium: Pottery
Comments: 1908—Teacher, Ericsson School, St.
Paul

Cederberg, Ruth
Dates unknown
Location: 689 Bedford St., St. Paul (1907)
Role(s): Artist
Medium: Textile Design, Painting
Affiliations: St. Paul Institute of Art, St. Paul
School of Fine Arts
Comments: 1907—MSAS Honorable Mention;
1907–13—St. Paul Resident Intermittantly Listed
as Artist, Painter, Student

Center, Amelia H., Mrs.
Dates unknown
Location: 124 W. 14th, Minneapolis (1897); Oak Park, Il. (1906)
Role(s): Artist, Member
Medium: Leather Work
Affiliations: Chalk & Chisel Club, Minneapolis Arts & Crafts Society
Comments: 1904—MSAS Juror, Entry Made in Care of Chicago Industrial Art League; Married Name—Mrs. Edward H. Center.

Chace, May
Dates unknown
Location: Minneapolis (1908)
Role(s): Artist
Medium: Ceramics

Chant, Elisabeth A., Miss
1862?–1947
Location: 616 E. Franklin Av., Minneapolis (1905–6); 926 2nd Av. S., Minneapolis (1906); 89 S. 10th St., Minneapolis (1908)
Role(s): Member, Artist
Medium: Painting, Embroidery, Murals, Design, Pottery
Affiliations: Minneapolis Arts & Crafts Society
Comments: 1901—MSAC Member; 1907—SA&C, Boston Exhibitor, A&CS Member; Active Member of A&CS with studio at 719 Hennepin & in the HG after 1907. Also spelled name as Elizabeth. Resided in Minneapolis 1895–1911, moved to Springfield, MA, died in Wilmington, NC.

Chant, Sarah, Miss
Dates unknown
Location: 616 E. Franklin Av., Minneapolis (1906)
Role(s): Artist, Member
Affiliations: Minneapolis Arts & Crafts Society

Chapman, Marie Backus, Mrs.
Dates unknown
Location: Minneapolis (1915)
Role(s): Artist, Student
Medium: Embroidered Panel, Illuminated Cards, Design
Affiliations: Minneapolis School of Fine Arts
Comments: See Marie Backus

Chatfield, E. C.
Dates unknown
Role(s): Member
Affiliations: Minneapolis Art Commission

Cheney, Mary Moulton, Miss
1871–1957
Location: 401 Evanston Bldg., Minneapolis (1904–5); St. Anthony Park (r. 1904–5); 926 2nd Av. S., Minneapolis (1906), 425 Auditorium Bldg., Minneapolis (1906–8); 2239 Gordon Av., St. Paul (r. 1912–13, 1917)
Role(s): Teacher, Member, Officer
Medium: Calligraphy, Illumination, Jewelry, Design, Leather, Stenciling, Book Plates, Printmaking, Stained Glass, Furniture, Interior Decoration
Affiliations: Handicraft Guild, Minnesota State Art Society, Minneapolis Society of Fine Arts, Chalk & Chisel Club, Minneapolis Arts & Crafts Society, Minneapolis School of Fine Arts, The Woman's Club of Minneapolis, Arts Guild of St. Paul
Comments: (Her art school teaching work and her own studio and art shop work co-existed from 1897 to 1917.) 1897, 1907—SA&C, Boston Exhibitor; 1898—Chalk & Chisel Club Treasurer; 1902—Designed a candlestick purchased for production by Tiffany Studios; 1902—Co-owner Chemith Press; 1903, 1904, 1906—A&CS Ex-

hibits Ad; 1904, 1905—MSAS Board, Designer; 1906–15/16—Owned Artcraft Shop: Sign of the Bay Tree; 1907—MSAS Juror, MSAS Extension Committee; 1908—MSAS Prize, J. E. Beans and Nettie Bryant made pieces she designed for MSAS Exhibit, Harvard Summer School; 1908, 1914—MSAS Exhibit Committee; 1912—MSAS Extension Committee; 1914—MIA Dean of Women, Instructor, Dept. of Applied Arts; 1917–26—Director of MIA School; 1928–42—Served on faculty of Vocational High School; Served as Principal of Department of Design & Handicrafts, Minneapolis School of Fine Arts. Education and training—School of Boston Museum of Fine Arts, pupil of Dr. Denman Ross of Cambridge, Miss Jessie M. Preston of Chicago, and George Elmer Browne of Provincetown. Printed, designed, and illustrated many books, printed and organization logos/ciphers. Owned and operated summer art school at Camp Danworth near Walker, MN (1930s). Retired to Bend, OR. Large collections of her work held at MHS, St. Paul.

Christian, George S., Mrs.
Dates unknown
Role(s): Officer
Affiliations: Handicraft Guild
Comments: HG President.

Christian, John
Dates unknown
Location: 1826 Fond Du Lac Ave., Milwaukee, Wisconsin (1905)
Role(s): Artist
Medium: Metal Working

Christian, Susan
Dates unknown
Role(s): Student
Medium: Ceramics
Affiliations: Handicraft Guild

Clark, Martha C., Mrs.
Dates unknown
Location: 467 Holly Av., St. Paul (1908)
Role(s): Artist
Medium: Photography
Comments: Married Name—Mrs. C. H. Clark

Clarke, Wallace R.
Dates unknown
Location: 518 8th St. S., Minneapolis (1903)
Role(s): Artist
Medium: Cabinetry, Stained Glass

Claypool, Jennie L.
Dates unknown
Location: 627 12th Av. S.E., Minneapolis (1903)
Role(s): Artist
Medium: Design

Clements, Loraine
Dates unknown
Location: Faribault, Minnesota (1915, 1917)
Role(s): Artist
Medium: Jewelry
Comments: 1917—MSAC 1st Place Jewelry

Clopath, Henriett(e)(a)
Dates unknown
Location: 1426 6th St. S.E., Minneapolis (1904); 1425 6th St. S.E., Minneapolis (1905); 813 Fulton St. SE, Minneapolis (1912).
Role(s): Artist
Medium: Painting, Woodcarving
Comments: 1903—U of M

Cockburn, Janette
Dates unknown
Location: Glenwood, Minnesota (1915)
Role(s): Artist

Medium: Tatting

Coffin, Gertrude
Dates Unknown
Location: 2816 Fremont Av. S., Minneapolis
Role(s): Artist, Student
Medium: Basketry, Pottery
Affiliations: Minneapolis School of Art
Comments: 1920—MIA 1st Place Student Pottery

Cograve, Nellie
Dates unknown
Location: St. Paul
Role(s): Artist
Medium: Basketry

Cole, Stella Frances
Dates unknown
Location: Faribault, Minnesota
Role(s): Artist
Medium: Illumination, Leather
Comments: 1914—MSAS Prize

Cole, Winifred, Miss
Dates unknown
Location: 545 Syndicate Arcade, Minneapolis (1904); 926 2nd Av. S., Minneapolis (1906, 1907)
Role(s): Artist, Teacher, Officer, Member
Medium: bookbinding
Affiliations: Handicraft Guild, Minneapolis Arts & Crafts Society, The Woman's Club of Minneapolis
Comments: 1905–7—Assistant or Instructor at HG; 1905–12—Bookbinder with Shop in HG Building, 1906—A&CS Exhibit Ad

Coleman, Arch, Mrs.
Dates unknown
Location: Minneapolis (1916)
Role(s): Member, Artist
Medium: (Applied Art) China Painting
Affiliations: Twin City Keramic Club
Comments: 1917—Pres. TCKC

Colson's Incorporated
Dates unknown
Location: Minneapolis
Comments: 1908–18—Decorative Art; 1908–10—Interior Decorators Located in HG; Officers—W. H. Colson, President; Harold Johnson, Vice President; R. E. Boutell, Secretary-Treasurer

Colter, Mary E. J., Miss
Dates unknown
Location: 269 Selby Av. St. Paul (1903)
Role(s): Artist
Medium: Metalworking, Design
Affiliations: Art Workers' Guild of St. Paul
Comments: 1905—MSAS Juror; 1906—Gave Talk to AWGSP on Metalworking; Teacher at Mechanic Arts High School, St. Paul.

Conaughy, Clarence W.
Dates unknown
Location: Minneapolis (1905–6, 1913)
Role(s): Teacher, Student
Medium: Illustration, Drawing
Affiliations: Minneapolis Society of Fine Arts, Minneapolis School of Art
Comments: 1905—Student at School of Arts, Minneapolis., MSAS Honorable Mention for Sketch; 1913—MSFA Exhibit "by Permission of Mac Martin Advertising Co."; 1914–15—MSA Drawing and Sketch Instructor; Pupil at Minneapolis School of Art and New York School of Art.

Conaughy, Madge B.
Dates unknown
Role(s): Artist
Medium: Applied Art

Conklin, Ida Pell, Mrs.

Ida Pell Conklin (advertisement with cipher). Dual City Blue Book, 1915–16, p. 73.

Dates unknown
Location: 926 2nd Av., Minneapolis (1906, 1907); 89 S. 10th St., Minneapolis (1910, 1912, 1914, 1916–18)
Role(s): Teacher, Student, Member, Artist
Medium: Jewelry, Metal Working
Affiliations: Handicraft Guild, Minneapolis School of Fine Arts, Minneapolis
Comments: Ca. 1906—Came to Minnesota; 1906—A&CS Exhibit Ad; 1906–18—Associated with HG as Jewelry Maker and Instructor, Had Studio There; 1907—Student at Pratt Institute; 1907, 1911, 1914

Cooley, Alice W.
Dates unknown
Medium: Weaving
Comments: Supervisor in Minneapolis Primary Schools

Copelin, M. J., Mrs.
Dates unknown
Location: 2929 Clinton Av., Minneapolis (1912)
Role(s): Artist
Medium: Embroidery

Corbett, Bertha Louise, Miss
Dates unknown
Location: Minneapolis
Role(s): Student
Medium: Water Color, Charcoal, Silhouettes
Affiliations: Minneapolis School of Fine Arts

Corcoran, Elizabeth, Miss
Dates unknown
Location: 781 Cedar St., St. Paul (1905–7)
Role(s): Artist
Medium: Ceramics, Pottery
Comments: 1905—MSAS Prize, Piece Glazed by Prof. Geo. Weit

Corning, Emily A., Miss
Dates unknown
Location: 481 Dayton Av., St. Paul (1908)
Role(s): Executive Committee Member, Member
Medium: Photography
Affiliations: Art Workers' Guild of St. Paul
Comments: 1906—AWGSP Secretary

Coterie, The
1892–1936
Location: Minneapolis
Comments: Twin Cities Literary and Cultural Discussion Group

Cox, Marie
Dates unknown
Location: 3228 Blaisdell Av., Minneapolis (1910)
Role(s): Artist
Medium: Stenciling, Leather, Book Plates

Craig, William
Dates unknown
Role(s): Member
Affiliations: Duluth Art Association
Comments: Founding Member of Duluth Art Asso-

ciation.

Crawford, Isabel, Miss
Dates unknown
Location: Minneapolis (1905–6, 1910); New York (1913)
Role(s): Artist, Teacher, Member, Student
Medium: Art Handicraft, Painting (Commercial Art) Ad Poster
Affiliations: Minneapolis School of Fine Arts, Attic Club, Minneapolis School of Art
Comments: 1910—MSAS Prize; 1915—Attic Club; 1917—Studio at HG; 1918–19—Lectured at The Minneapolis School of Art on The Processes of Commercial Art

Crowley, J. H., Mrs.
Dates unknown
Role(s): Member
Affiliations: Duluth Art Association
Comments: Founding Member of Duluth Art Association

Crowley, Ruth
Dates unknown
Role(s): Artist
Medium: Book Plates
Affiliations: St. Paul Institute

Curry, E. H., Mrs.
Dates unknown
Role(s): Artist
Medium: Ceramics
Affiliations: St. Paul Institute School of Art

Dale, Frederic Cowderoi
Dates unknown
Role(s): Artist, Member
Medium: Water Color
Affiliations: Attic Club
Comments: 1915—Attic Club Exhibitor; 1917—Studio at HG

Daniels, John K.
Dates unknown
Location: 1524 St. Anthony Av., St. Paul (1905); 959 Lombard, St. Paul (1912)
Role(s): Artist, Student
Medium: Sculpture, Painting, Wood Carving
Affiliations: St. Paul Institute of Arts & Sciences
Comments: 1894–98—SPIAS Student; 1909, 1913—MSAS Prize; 1916—State Art Exhibitor

Darling, Elena J., Miss
Dates unknown
Location: 2647 Lake of The Isles Blvd., Minneapolis (1897)
Affiliations: Chalk & Chisel Club
Comments: Charter Member Chalk & Chisel Club

Darling, Emily F., Miss
Dates unknown
Location: 2647 Lake of The Isles Blvd., Minneapolis (1897)
Affiliations: Chalk & Chisel Club
Comments: Charter Member Chalk & Chisel Club

Davis, Alice D.
Dates unknown
Role(s): Artist
Medium: Textiles

Davis, Daisy W.
Dates unknown
Location: 2205 Chicago Av., Minneapolis (1908)
Role(s): Artist
Medium: Ceramics

Dawes, Edwin M.
Dates unknown
Location: 318 Meyers Arcade, Minneapolis (1912); 20 Western Av., Minneapolis (1914); 415 Essex Bldg., Minneapolis (1915).
Role(s): Artist
Medium: Painting
Comments: 1917—at Sweet Studios, MSAC 2nd Place Painting

Dawson, Anna
Dates unknown
Role(s): Artist
Medium: Pottery
Affiliations: St. Paul Institute School of Art

Day, Ellen A.
Dates unknown
Location: Farmington
Role(s): Artist
Medium: Lace

De Haven, E. P., Mrs.
Dates unknown
Location: 2435 Pillsbury Av., Minneapolis (1906)
Role(s): Artist, Member
Affiliations: Minneapolis Arts & Crafts Society

Delano, Lila Marie
Dates unknown
Location: 419 S. 9th St., Minneapolis (1906–7)
Role(s): Artist
Medium: Weaving

Densmore, Mabel
Dates unknown
Location: 629 4th St., Red Wing (1912)
Role(s): Artist
Medium: Jewelry

Denton, C. C., Mr.
Dates unknown
Location: 62 Syndicate Block, Minneapolis (1905)
Role(s): Artist
Medium: Art Handicraft, Photography
Comments: 1905—MSAS Prize

Derickson, Clara M., Miss
Dates unknown
Location: 59 Highland Av., Minneapolis (1906)
Role(s): Artist, Member
Medium: Water Color, Pastel
Affiliations: Minneapolis Arts & Crafts Society, Chalk & Chisel Club

Derickson, George P. Mrs.
Dates unknown
Location: 59 Highland Av., Minneapolis (1906); 238 Franklin Av. W., Minneapolis (1913)
Role(s): Artist, Member
Affiliations: Minneapolis Arts & Crafts Society, The Woman's Club of Minneapolis

Deshon, Marguerite, Miss
Dates unknown
Comments: 1906—Won Handicaft Guild High School Scholarship, Attended Central High School, Minneapolis

Devoist, P. L., Mrs.
Dates unknown
Role(s): Member
Affiliations: Duluth Art Association

Comments: Founding Member of Duluth Art Association

Dewanz, Helena
Dates unknown
Role(s): Artist
Medium: Designer, Pottery
Affiliations: Handicraft Guild

Dickman, Hortense Starkey
Dates unknown
Role(s): Student
Medium: Textile Design
Affiliations: St. Paul Institute of Art

Dietz, Otto O., Mrs.
Dates unknown
Location: 4042 Pillsbury Av., Minneapolis (1915)
Role(s): Artist
Medium: Basketry, Photography

Dike, Abbie Griffin, Mrs.
Dates unknown
Location: 3030 Colfax Av. S., Minneapolis (1906)
Medium: Textiles

Dillingham, E. B.
Dates unknown
Location: 2448 Portland Av., Minneapolis (1906)
Role(s): Student, Artist
Medium: Copper
Affiliations: Handicraft Guild
Comments: Dentist

Dion, Adele
Dates unknown
Location: St. Paul
Role(s): Artist
Medium: Basketry

Dion, Anna
Dates unknown
Location: St. Paul
Role(s): Artist
Medium: Basketry

Dobie, Harry
Dates unknown
Role(s): Student

Douglas Donaldson. Photograph courtesy of the Northwest Architectural Archives, University of Minnesota Libraries, St. Paul.

Medium: Painting, Illustration
Affiliations: St. Paul Institute of Arts & Sciences
Comments: 1912, 1914—SPIAS Student

Dodge, Fred B., Mrs.
Dates unknown
Location: 917 New York Life Bldg., Minneapolis (1903), Minnetonka Beach, Lake Minnetonka (1904, 1906, 1913)
Role(s): Artist, Member
Medium: Bookbinding
Affiliations: Minneapolis Arts & Crafts Society, The Woman's Club of Minneapolis

Donaldson, Douglas
Dates unknown
Location: Minneapolis (1909); 4128 Walton Av., Los Angeles, Ca (1912); 4156 Walton Av., Los Angeles (1915–16); 1100 W. 71st St., Los Angeles (1917); 2316 La Salle Av., Los Angeles (1918–19); 4968 Melrose Hill, Los Angeles 1920–27)
Role(s): Artist, Teacher, Member
Medium: Copper, Jewelry, Lamps
Affiliations: Handicraft Guild, Minneapolis Arts & Crafts Society
Comments: 1907—Nonresident Craftsman Member of Detroit Society of A&C; 1908—M. Hagen Executed Two Pieces He Designed for MSAS Exhibit; 1909—MSAS Prize, Instructor at Handicraft Guild; 1915–27—SA&C,Boston Exhibitor;

1916—AIC Prize; Married E. Louise Towle C. 1909

Donaldson, Ethel
Dates unknown
Role(s): Artist
Medium: Jewelry
Affiliations: Handicraft Guild
Comments: 1917—Taught Manual Arts at North High School, Minneapolis

Donaldson, Louise, Mrs.
Dates unknown
Location: 129 W. 33rd St., Minneapolis (1910); 4128 Walton Av., Los Angeles, California (1912); 4960 Melrose Hill, Hollywood, California (1926–27)
Role(s): Artist, Teacher, Member
Medium: Jewelry, Copper
Affiliations: Handicraft Guild, Minneapolis Arts & Crafts Society
Comments: 1908–9—Asst. at HG; 1926–27—SA&C,Boston Exhibitor; Maiden Name—E. Louise Towle

Donlin, Flossie
Dates unknown
Location: 49 Como Av., St. Paul
Role(s): Artist
Medium: Lace

Dorsey, Jean Muir, Mrs.
Dates unknown
Location: 2132 Carter Av., St. Anthony Park, St. Paul
Role(s): Artist
Medium: Basketry

Drake Marble & Tile Co.
Dates unknown
Location: Minneapolis & St. Paul
Comments: 1912–14—Importers and Dealers in Grueby, Rookwood, Foreign and Domestic Tiles for Mantles, Fireplace Goods in Period or Mission Styles in Black, Brass, Copper Plated, Flemish

Drummond, Mildred
Dates unknown
Location: Eau Claire, Wisconsin
Role(s): Student
Affiliations: Handicraft Guild
Comments: 1912—Won Edmund D. Brooks Book Plate Award; HG Graduate

Drummond, Willis
Dates unknown
Role(s): Artist
Medium: Photography

Duncan, Charles H., Mrs.
Dates unknown

Location: 482 Laurel Ave., St. Paul
Role(s): Member, Artist
Medium: Jewelry
Affiliations: Art Workers' Guild of St. Paul

Duncan, Charles H.
Dates unknown
Location: 482 Laurel Av., St. Paul (1908, 1913)
Role(s): Member, Officer, Artist
Medium: Jewelry
Affiliations: Art Workers' Guild of St. Paul, St. Paul Institute of Arts & Sciences
Comments: 1906—AWGSP Treasurer

Dunn, J. W. G.
Dates unknown
Location: 1033 Lincoln Av., St. Paul (1908)
Role(s): Artist
Medium: Photography

Dunwoody, Kate L. Patten, Mrs.
1845–1915
Location: 104 Groveland Ter. (1913)
Role(s): Officer, Member
Affiliations: Handicraft Guild, The Woman's Club of Minneapolis
Comments: Married Name—Mrs. William Hood Dunwoody.

Dunwoody, William Hood
1841–1914
Role(s): Officer
Affiliations: Minneapolis Society of Fine Arts
Comments: William Hood Dunwoody Bequest in 1914 Led to the Establishment of The Dunwoody Industrial Institute

Dvorak, Mary, Mrs.
Dates unknown
Location: Hopkins
Role(s): Artist
Medium: Textiles

Dyson, Arthur
Dates unknown
Role(s): Student
Medium: Cabinet Maker, Stained Glass
Affiliations: Minneapolis School of Art
Comments: 1920—Won Part-time Scholarship to Minneapolis School of Art; Worked at Forman, Ford and Company and Was a Lead Glazier (Stained and Leaded Glass Work)

Eastman, Miss
Dates unknown
Location: 563 Ashland Av., St. Paul (1908)
Role(s): Artist
Medium: Photography

Eaton, Marion
Dates unknown
Role(s): Artist
Medium: Metal Working
Affiliations: Handicraft Guild

Eck, Seth
Dates unknown
Role(s): Artist
Medium: Metalworking

Edwards, Austin S., Dr.
Dates unknown
Role(s): Teacher
Affiliations: Handicraft Guild
Comments: 1916–17—HG Faculty; Instructor of Psychology at U of M

Edwards, J. H.
Dates unknown
Role(s): Member
Affiliations: Duluth Art Association
Comments: Founding Member of Duluth Art Association

Ellingson, Dina
Dates unknown
Location: Minneapolis
Role(s): Student
Affiliations: Handicraft Guild

Ellis, Florence E.
Dates unknown
Role(s): Student, Artist
Medium: Wood Blocking
Affiliations: Handicraft Guild
Comments: President of Western Drawing Teacher's Association

Ellis, Kathryn H.
Dates unknown
Location: 67 The Buckingham, St. Paul (1904)
Role(s): Artist
Medium: Leather, Wood

Ellsworth, J.
Dates Unknown
Role(s): Artist
Medium: Metal Painting
Affiliations: Handicraft Guild

Erickson, C. A.
Dates unknown
Role(s): Artist
Medium: Wood Carving
Affiliations: St. Paul Institute

Erickson, David
Dates unknown
Location: St. Paul
Location: 89 S. 10th St., Minneapolis (1912); St. Paul (1912)
Role(s): Artist, Member
Medium: Painting
Affiliations: Art Workers' Guild of St. Paul, Handicraft Guild, Minnesota State Art Society
Comments: 1911, 1912—MSAS Extension Committee; 1912—HG Artist

Erickson, George P. (R.)
dated unknown
Role(s): Student
Affiliations: St. Paul Institute of Arts & Sciences
Comments: 1912, 1913, 1915—SPIAS Student; 1914–15—Artist at Brown & Bigelow

Eustis, C. B.
Dates unknown
Location: 5 S. 7th St., Minneapolis (1912)
Role(s): Artist
Medium: Jewelry

Eustis, C. B., Mrs.
Dates unknown
Location: 1368 Spruce Pl., Minneapolis (1908); 2117 Colfax Av. S., Minneapolis (1913)
Role(s): Artist
Medium: Jewelry

Evans, Doris Rebecca
Dates unknown
Role(s): Student
Medium: Textile Design
Affiliations: St. Paul Institute of Art

Farnsworth, Ethel Newcomb, Miss
Dates unknown
Location: 1414 Mt. Curve Av., Minneapolis (1903); 1418 Mt. Curve Av., Minneapolis (1915)
Role(s): Artist, Student
Medium: Watercolors, Bookplates, Painting, Poster
Affiliations: Handicraft Guild, Minneapolis School of Fine Arts, Minneapolis School of Art, Minneapolis Arts & Crafts Society
Comments: 1918–19—Instructor of Illustration and Composition at Minneapolis School of Art; Studied at University of Minnesota.

Faulkner, Raymond Lloyd
Dates unknown
Role(s): Student
Medium: Illustration
Affiliations: St. Paul Institute of Arts & Sciences, St. Paul School of Art
Comments: 1912–14—SPIAS Student; 1914—Student, MSAS Honorable Mention

Feely, Elizabeth
Dates unknown
Location: St. Paul
Role(s): Artist
Medium: Needlework

Fergus Falls State Hospital
Dates unknown
Location: Fergus Falls, Minnesota
Medium: Basketry, Iron Work, Textiles

Fitch, Mrs.
Dates unknown
Role(s): Artist
Medium: Textiles

Fjelde, Pauline, Miss
Dates unknown
Location: Minneapolis (1916)
Role(s): Student, Artist
Medium: Tapestry
Affiliations: Minneapolis School of Fine Arts
Comments: 1915—Won AIC Mrs. Julius Rosenwald Prize

Fjelde Sisters Decorative Art Needlework
Dates unknown
Location: Syndicate Arcade (1898–1907)
Comments: Pauline Fjelde and Tomane Hansen

Flagg, Harriet S., Mrs.
Dates unknown
Location: Hampshire Arms, Minneapolis (1912); 89 S. 10th St., Minneapolis (1912–14); 2101 Blaisdell Ave., Minneapolis (1913, 1915–16).
Role(s): Artist, Member
Medium: Jewelry
Affiliations: The Woman's Club of Minneapolis, Minneapolis Arts & Crafts Society
Comments: 1912–16—SA&C,Boston Exhibitor; Married Name—Mrs. Maurice I. Flagg.

Flagg, Maurice Irwin
Dates unknown
Role(s): Teacher, Board Member
Affiliations: Handicraft Guild, Minnesota State Art Society
Comments: 1910?–13—HG Director; 1912, 1914, 1917—MSAS Director; After 1919—Managed Publicity Services for The Architects' Small House Service Bureau, Inc.; Former Director of Swain School of Design in New Bedford, Massachusetts

Flinn, Georgia Johnstone
Dates unknown
Location: 2434 Pleasant Av., Minneapolis (1914)
Role(s): Artist, Student
Medium: Stenciling, Book Plates, Design
Affiliations: Minneapolis Society of Fine Arts, Minneapolis School of Art
Comments: 1913–14—MIA 2nd Year Student in Design; 1914—MSAS Honorable Mention

Folsom, Mary Louise
Dates unknown
Location: 1632 W. 26th St., Minneapolis (1914–15)
Role(s): Artist, Student
Medium: Book Plates, Stenciling, Block Printing
Affiliations: Minneapolis Society of Fine Arts, Minneapolis School of Art
Comments: 1914—MIA Post Graduate, MSAS 1st Place Block Printing

Folwell, Sarah Heywood, Mrs.
1838–1931
Location: Minneapolis
Role(s): Student
Affiliations: Minneapolis School of Fine Arts
Comments: Married Name—Mrs. William Watts
Folwell.

Folwell, William Watts, Prof.
1833–1929
Role(s): Officer
Affiliations: Minneapolis Society of Fine Arts
Comments: 1883—MSFA President; President of U
of M

Forsberg, Brunhild
Dates unknown
Location: 602 Mendota Av., St. Paul (1908)
Medium: Jewelry, Metal Working

Fournier, Marietta, Mrs.
Dates unknown
Location: 3505 Sheridan Av. N., Minneapolis
(1914–15)
Role(s): Artist, Student
Medium: Stenciling, Book Plates, Wood Block
Printing
Affiliations: Minneapolis School of Fine Arts, Min-
neapolis School of Art
Comments: 1914—MIA 2nd Year Student, MSAS
2nd Place Block Printing

Frank, Arthur
Dates unknown
Role(s): Student
Medium: Cabinetmaker
Affiliations: Minneapolis School of Art
Comments: 1920—Won a Scholarship to MSA;
Employed by John S. Bradstreet and Co. (Cabi-
netmakers)

Franke, Kurt
Dates unknown
Location: 114 Iglehart St., St. Paul
Role(s): Artist
Medium: Woodworking

Freeman, H. G., Mrs.
Dates unknown
Location: St. Louis Park (1914)
Role(s): Artist
Medium: Stenciling, Leather
Comments: 1914—MSAS Prize

French, William A.
Dates unknown
Location: 44 E. 6th St., St. Paul (1903); 6th &
Cedar Sts., St. Paul (1904)
Role(s): Artist
Medium: Furniture Design
Comments: 1910?–1941—President of William A.
French & Co., Fine Furniture and Decorators,
Minneapolis. Interiors at Glensheen Mansion,
Duluth, by Wm. A. French and Co.

Fuller, Harvey B.
Dates unknown
Location: 186 W. 3rd St., St. Paul (1914)
Role(s): Artist
Medium: Photography
Affiliations: St. Paul Institute of Arts & Sciences

Fuller, Helen
Dates unknown
Location: 738 Lincoln Av., St. Paul (1912)
Role(s): Student, married name—Mrs. Harry
Lawton
Medium: Drawing
Affiliations: St. Paul Institute of Arts & Sciences
Comments: 1894–98—SPIAS Student, married
name—Mrs. Harry Lawton

Fuller, Mark K.
Dates unknown
Role(s): Student
Medium: Wood Blocking
Affiliations: Handicraft Guild

Fuller, W. H., Mrs.
Dates unknown
Role(s): Artist
Medium: Applied Art, China Painting

Fuller, Jr., Harvey B.
Dates unknown
Location: 186 W. 3rd St., St. Paul (1914)
Role(s): Officer
Medium: Sculpture
Affiliations: St. Paul Institute of Arts & Sciences

Fulton, Edith, Miss
Dates unknown
Location: 120 S. 8th St., St. Paul (1915–16)
Comments: Needlecraft Specialty Shop

Gag, Hazel Wanda
1893–1946
Role(s): Student
Medium: Illustration, Block Printing, Author
Affiliations: St. Paul Institute of Arts & Sciences,
Minneapolis School of Art
Comments: 1912–14—SPIAS Student; 1914—Stu-
dent, MSAS Honorable Mention; 1917–18—
Awarded Tuition Scholarship by The Art Stu-
dents' League of New York

Gage, Carl A.
Dates unknown
Location: 716 4th Av. S., Minneapolis (1908)
Role(s): Teacher
Medium: Architecture, Mechanical Drawing
Affiliations: Minneapolis School of Fine Arts

Gale, Edward C.
Dates unknown
Location: Minneapolis
Role(s): Board Member, Member, Officer
Affiliations: Minnesota State Art Society, Handi-
craft Guild, Minneapolis Art Commission, Min-
neapolis Society of Fine Arts & School of Art
Comments: 1912, 1914—MSAS Treasurer; 1917—
MSAC Treasurer, MIA 2nd Vice President,
Member of Art Commission of Minneapolis;
1914—MSFA Trustee

Gale, Jane
Dates unknown
Role(s): Artist
Medium: Stenciling

Galloway, George W.
Dates unknown
Role(s): Teacher
Medium: Woodcarving
Affiliations: Minneapolis School of Fine Arts

Gardner, Sadie E.
Dates unknown
Location: Minneapolis (1905–6)
Role(s): Student
Medium: Design
Affiliations: Minneapolis School of Fine Arts, Min-
neapolis School of Art

Gardner, Sarah E.
Dates unknown
Location: Fergus Falls, Minnesota
Role(s): Student
Affiliations: Handicraft Guild

Garvey, James J.
Dates unknown
Location: 1216 Harmon Pl., Minneapolis (1903)
Role(s): Artist
Medium: Cabinetry

Comments: Affiliated with Central High School,
Minneapolis

Gates, Adeline T., Miss
Deceased by 1898
Role(s): Artist
Medium: Sculpture
Affiliations: Chalk & Chisel Club

Gaus, Janette Ricker, Mrs.
Dates unknown
Location: South End House, 20 Union Park, Bos-
ton, Ma (1918–20); Poland Springs, South Po-
land, Me (1919–20); Amherst, Ma (1921–26);
1101 E. River Rd., Minneapolis (1927)
Role(s): Artist, Member
Medium: Metal Working
Affiliations: Minneapolis Arts & Crafts Society
Comments: 1918–27—SA&C, Boston Exhibitor;
Married Name—Mrs. John M. Gaus.

Gauthier, Julie Celina, Miss
1857–22 June 1924
Location: 901 Fairmount Av., St. Paul (1905,
1906); The Willard, St. Paul (1906, 1908); 163
Kent St., St. Paul (1912)
Role(s): Artist, Member
Medium: Weaving, Decorative Modeling
Affiliations: Art Workers' Guild of St. Paul, Minne-
sota State Art Society
Comments: 1904, 1905, 1907—MSAS Exhibit
Committee; 1912—MSAS Juror, MSAS Exhibit
Committee; Studied Art in Boston, New York,
France, and Italy. Pupil of Charles Noah Flagg,
Carl Guthrez, Henry Bacon, Benjamin Constant
and Jules LeFebvre. Instructor and later supervi-
sor of Drawing in St. Paul high schools for over
30 years.

Geist, Emil
Dates unknown
Role(s): Artist
Medium: Jewelry
Affiliations: St. Paul Institute
Comments: 1912—SPI Professional Art Section

Gerlach, Sophia
Dates unknown
Role(s): Artist
Medium: Textiles, Embroidery
Comments: 1904—Made Pieces Designed by Mrs.
Sumner Le Duc for MSAS Exhibit

Gerow, Grace D.
Dates unknown
Role(s): Artist
Medium: Leather Work

Giddings, Thaddeus P.
1869–1954
Role(s): Teacher
Medium: Music
Affiliations: Handicraft Guild
Comments: 1910–42—Supervisor of Music in Min-
neapolis Public School System; HG Supervisor
of Music

Giehler, H., Mr.
Dates unknown
Location: Room 301 Dispatch Building, St. Paul
(1905)
Medium: Drawing
Affiliations: St. Paul Institute of Arts & Sciences

Gift Shop, The
Dates unknown
Location: Minneapolis
Comments: 1920–21—Mrs. Emily Singer,
Manager.

Gilbert, Caroline
Dates unknown
Location: 582 Dayton Av., St. Paul (1908); 563

Julie Celina Gauthier. Who's Who among Minnesota Women, 1924, p. 116.

Gustav Goetsch. Minnesota State Art Society Exhibit Catalog, 1903 and 1904, p. 52.

Laurel St., St. Paul (1913)
Role(s): Artist, Student
Medium: Pottery, Leather
Affiliations: St. Paul Institute of Arts & Sciences

Gilbertson, Albert N.
Dates unknown
Location: Minneapolis
Role(s): Teacher
Affiliations: Handicraft Guild
Comments: 1912—Teacher at Minneapolis Kindergarten Normal School; 1916—Moved

Giles, Robert Tait
Dates unknown
Location: 221–225 2nd Av. S., Minneapolis (1904); 111 S. 6th St., Minneapolis (1906–7); 500 S. 3rd St., Minneapolis (1910, 1912); 720 Ridgeland Av., Oak Park, Il (1915); Chicago (1917)
Role(s): Artist, Teacher
Medium: Stained Glass (Windows and Lamp Shades), Sculpture
Affiliations: Minneapolis School of Fine Arts
Comments: 1904, 1906—A&CS Ads; 1910—MSAS Prize; 1913–14—MSFA Lecturer; 1914–15—HG Lecturer; Owned Stained Glass Firm R. T. Giles & Co.

Gillit(t), Anna
Dates unknown
Role(s): Artist
Medium: Textiles, Photograph Case
Comments: 1904—Made Pieces Entered in MSAS by Alice Sumner Le Duc

Glessner, Agnes
Dates unknown
Location: 701 7th Sv. Se (1903)
Role(s): Artist
Medium: Design

Goetsch, Gustav F.
Dates unknown
Location: St. Louis Mo (1913); Minneapolis (1915, 1917)
Role(s): Artist, Teacher
Medium: Painting, Etching
Affiliations: Minneapolis School of Art, Minnesota State Art Society, Minneapolis School of Fine Arts
Comments: 1904—MSAS Prize; 1909—MSAS Exhibit Committee; 1914–15—MSA Principal; Instructor in Painting and Drawing. Pupil at MSA, the New York School of Art, and The Atelier Julien, Paris. Asst. Instructor at MSA. Instructor at St. Louis School of Art. Affiliated with J.S. Bradstreet firm.

Goldstein, Samuel, Mrs.
Dates unknown
Comments: 1917—Organized Nine Women as The Arts & Crafts Organization of Foreign Women. Once a year they exhibited handicraft work of their native lands.

Goodell, T. N., Mrs.
Dates unknown
Location: Madelia
Role(s): Artist
Medium: Centerpiece

Goodrich, Harriet M., Miss
Dates unknown
Location: 204 W. Wabasha St., Winona, Minnesota (1905)
Role(s): Artist
Medium: Art Handicraft, Wood Carving

Mrs. Samuel Goldstein. Who's Who among Minnesota Women, *1924, p. 279.*

Comments: 1905—MSAS Prize

Gottlieb, Harry
Dates unknown
Location: 1300 8th St. S., Minneapolis (1917)
Role(s): Student
Medium: Stenciling

Gove, Margaret Thorpe, Miss
Dates unknown
Role(s): Artist
Medium: Art Handicraft
Comments: 1907—MSAS Prize; MIA 1915 Exhibit by Alumni Association of MSA Refers to Margaret Gove Camfferman

Gowdy Jean
Dates unknown
Location: 1813 Elliott Av., Minneapolis (1903)
Role(s): Artist
Medium: Basketry

Graah, Wilhelmine, Miss
Dates unknown
Location: 3327 Longfellow Av., St. Paul (1912–14)
Role(s): Artist
Medium: Textiles, Lace, Embroidery (Hedebo)
Affiliations: Handicaft Guild
Comments: 1914—MSAS Honorable Mention

Gramps, Beatrice Winifred
Dates unknown
Location: 3624 Park Av., Minneapolis (1914, 1915)
Role(s): Artist, Student
Medium: Illumination, Illustration
Comments: 1914—MIA Illustration Class Honorable Mention, Column by Winifred Gramps on Science Applied to Art in MIA *Bulletin*

Gray, Helen
Dates unknown
Role(s): Artist
Medium: Pottery
Affiliations: St. Paul Institute School of Art

Gray, Horace, Mrs.
Dates unknown
Location: 2015 Stevens Av., Minneapolis (1913)
Role(s): Teacher, Officer
Medium: Handicraft
Affiliations: The Woman's Club of Minneapolis
Comments: 1912—Organized Handicraft Class in Mound, Minnesota

Gray, Mabel
Dates unknown
Location: Minneapolis (1905–6)
Role(s): Artist, Student
Affiliations: Handicraft Guild, Minneapolis School of Art
Comments: 1902—Teacher, Calhoun School; 1905—Artist; 1906—MSFA Student, 1907—Craftsworker HG

Gray, Nellie J.
Dates unknown
Location: Minneapolis
Role(s): Artist
Medium: Pottery

Gray, R. A., Mrs.
Dates unknown
Role(s): Artist
Medium: Ceramics

Greeley, May Dudley
Dates unknown
Location: 804 Nicollet Av., Minneapolis (1906)
Role(s): Artist
Medium: Ceramics

Greene, S. R., Mrs.
Dates unknown
Location: 1504½ E. 3rd St., Duluth (1912)
Role(s): Artist
Medium: Basketry

Greenman, Frances Willard Cranmer
1890–1981
Location: 2742 S. Girard Av., Minneapolis (1917)
Role(s): Artist, Teacher
Medium: Oil Painting
Affiliations: Handicraft Guild, Minneapolis School of Art
Comments: Author and Artist Originally from Aberdeen, South Dakota

Gregory, Mary W.
Dates unknown
Role(s): Artist
Medium: Leather
Affiliations: St. Paul Institute School of Art

Griffith, Edith, Miss
Dates unknown
Location: 1307 4th Av. S., Minneapolis (1903–5), 926 2nd Av. S., Minneapolis (1906–7); Studio 12, HG building (1908).
Role(s): Artist, Teacher
Medium: Art Handicraft, Bookbinding, Weaving
Affiliations: Handicraft Guild, Minnesota State Art Society, Minneapolis Arts & Crafts Society, Minneapolis Society of Fine Arts, St. Paul Institute of Arts & Sciences
Comments: 1904—MSAS Exhibitor, A&CS Ad; 1905—MSAS Prize; 1905–7—Assistant or In-

structor at HG; 1906—A&CS President and Ad, Studio at HG; 1919—Weaving instructor at Minneapolis School of Art; 1925–26—Instructor in Weaving at The Minneapolis School of Art. Student of Ellen Gates Starr of Chicago, Frank P. Lane of Florice, MA, Carleton College and U of M in Design.

Gun(c)kel, Jea(n)nette T.
Dates unknown
Location: 1614 2nd Av. S. Minneapolis (1908, 1910, 1913)
Role(s): Student, Artist
Medium: Leather, Design
Affiliations: Handicraft Guild
Comments: 1905—Student; 1906—Leatherworker, HG

Haavold, Andrew Anderson, Mrs.
Dates unknown
Location: 3944 36th Av. S., Minneapolis (1915)
Role(s): Artist
Medium: Wall Cover

Hagen, Martin P.
Dates unknown
Location: Minneapolis
Role(s): Student, Artist
Medium: Metal Working
Affiliations: Handicraft Guild
Comments: 1909—MSAS Prize; 1900–1905—Tinner at Minneapolis Treshing Machine Co.; 1909–11—HG Metalwork Asst.; MSAS 1908 Exhibit Lists M. Hagen Who Made Pieces Designed by Douglas Donaldson and Florence Willets

Haish, Marjorie M.
Dates unknown
Location: Cloquet, Minnesota
Role(s): Artist
Medium: Jewelry
Comments: Designer and Maker of Handwrought Jewelry

Haldemann, Florence Ann, Miss
Dates unknown
Location: 3200 Columbus Av., Minneapolis
Role(s): Student
Affiliations: Minneapolis Society of Fine Arts
Comments: Affiliated with The Art Craft Shop.

Hall, Elizabeth, Miss
Dates unknown
Affiliations: Handicraft Guild
Comments: 1916–17—Lecturer at HG; Assistant Superintendent of Minneapolis Public Schools

Hall, J. C., Mrs.
Dates unknown
Location: 1818 Portland Av., Minneapolis
Role(s): Officer
Affiliations: Handicraft Guild

Hall, James L.
Dates unknown
Role(s): Teacher, Student
Medium: Design
Affiliations: Minneapolis Society of Fine Arts, Minneapolis School of Art
Comments: 1912–13—Taught Class in Window Decorating at MSA

Hamlin, Lenora, Mrs.
Dates unknown
Location: 615 St. Albans, St. Paul
Role(s): Member
Medium: Civic Art
Affiliations: Minnesota State Art Society

Comments: 1912—MSAS Exhibit Committee, MSAS Juror

Hannah, Nellie
Dates unknown
Role(s): Artist
Medium: Photograph Case
Comments: 1904—Made Pieces Entered in MSAS Exhibit by Alice Sumner Le Duc

Hansen, Anne
Dates unknown
Location: Hopkins (1914)
Role(s): Artist
Medium: Stenciling, Ceramics
Comments: 1914—MSAS Prize

Hansen, Grethe
Dates unknown
Location: 1596 Marshall Av., St. Paul
Role(s): Artist
Medium: Weaving

Hanson, Arthur C.
Dates unknown
Location: 1912 Columbus Av., Minneapolis (1915)
Role(s): Artist
Medium: Sculpture, Painting

Hara, Emma T.
Dates unknown
Role(s): Student
Medium: Ceramic Art
Comments: 1914—MSAS Prize

Hare, Margaret Tyler (Emma)
Dates unknown
Role(s): Student
Medium: Design
Affiliations: St. Paul Institute of Arts & Sciences
Comments: 1914—SPIAS Student, MIA Student, MSAS Prize

Harrington, Frances
Dates Unknown
Location: 3239 Lake Av. S., Duluth
Role(s): Artist
Medium: Jewelry

Harrington, Helen, Miss
Dates unknown
Location: 1823 Park Av., Minneapolis (1903–4, 1906)
Role(s): Artist, Student, Member
Medium: Design, Bookplates
Affiliations: Minneapolis School of Fine Arts, Minneapolis Arts & Crafts Society
Comments: 1902—Graduated From U of M; 1904—Attended Minneapolis School of Art; Designed Furniture, Rugs, etc., for John S. Bradstreet & Co.

Harrison, Agnes, Mrs.
Dates unknown
Role(s): Officer, Member
Medium: Watercolor
Affiliations: Handicraft Guild, Chalk & Chisel Club, Minneapolis Art & Crafts Society
Comments: Married Name—Mrs. Perry Harrison

Hart, Lucy
Dates unknown
Location: 2204 Grand Av., Minneapolis (1906)
Role(s): Student
Medium: Pottery
Affiliations: Handicraft Guild

Hartmann, Violet
Dates unknown
Role(s): Artist, Student, Teacher
Medium: Textile Design, Design, Jewelry, Metal Working
Affiliations: St. Paul Institute of Arts & Sciences

Frances Willard Crammer Greenman, 1935. Minnesota Historical Society. Photograph by Kenneth Wright.

Hartwood, Evelyn
Dates unknown
Role(s): Student
Affiliations: Handicraft Guild
Comments: 1906—Student

Harwood, Evelyn
Dates unknown
Role(s): Student
Medium: Leather, Pottery
Affiliations: Handicraft Guild

Harwood, Stanley
Dates unknown
Location: 2638 Aldrich Av. S., Minneapolis (1906)
Role(s): Artist
Medium: Copper
Affiliations: Handicraft Guild

Hauser, George
Dates unknown
Role(s): Artist
Medium: Woodcraving
Comments: Affiliated with Central High School, Minneapolis

Haven, Frank
Dates unknown
Role(s): Artist
Medium: Woodcarving
Comments: Affiliated with Central High School, Minneapolis

Hawkins, Lydia
Dates unknown
Location: Minneapolis (1903); 1923 Crystal Lake Av. (1904)

Role(s): Student
Medium: Design
Affiliations: Minneapolis School of Fine Arts

Hayes, Mrs.
Dates unknown
Role(s): Artist
Medium: Textiles

Heisser, Helen
Dates unknown
Location: Minneapolis (1903)
Role(s): Artist
Medium: Woodcarving

Heisser, Margarethe E.
1871 or 1872–1908
Location: 719 Hennepin Av., Minneapolis (1898); 3012 Humboldt Av. S., Minneapolis (1903, 1907–8); Moorhead, Minnesota (1903)
Role(s): Student, Artist
Medium: Design, Illumination, Metalwork, Calligraphy, Painting, Woodwork, Glass, Pyrography
Affiliations: Minneapolis School of Fine Arts, Handicraft Guild, Minneapolis Arts & Crafts Society, Samovar Club
Comments: 1899—Studied in Paris; 1901—in Arts/Crafts Show; 1902–3—AIC Distinctive Artistic Merit Award in Illumination; 1897–1901—Shared Studio at 719 Hennepin with Elizabeth Chant; Art Teacher at Moorhead Normal School. Manual Art teacher at the School for the Feeble Minded, Faribault, MN (ca. 1899–1901). Died Grand Forks, ND.

Helmick, Dan S.
Dates unknown
Location: Washburn Park (1906); 5227 Nicollet Av., Minneapolis (1910)
Role(s): Artist
Medium: Woodworking, Bookbinding

Helmick, Mary A., Mrs.

Mary A. Helmick. Minnesota State Art Society Exhibit Catalog, *1903 and 1904, p. 54.*

Dates unknown
Location: 7227 Nicolett Av., Minneapolis (1906); Washburn Park, Minneapolis (1903, 1905–6, 1908, 1912); 1607 4th St. S.E., Minneapolis (1913); 1014 13th Av. S.E., Minneapolis (1913, 1917); 1014 16th Av. S.E., Minneapolis (1914); 1604 4th St. S.E., Minneapolis (1914)
Role(s): Artist, Officer, Member
Medium: Art Handicraft, Wood Carving, Design
Affiliations: Chalk & Chisel Club, Minneapolis Arts & Crafts Society, The Woman's Club of Minneapolis, Minneapolis Society of Fine Arts, Minneapolis Art School
Comments: 1904, 1906, 1914—MSAS Prize; 1905—Made Object Designed by William Fry of Cincinnati for MSAS Exhibit; 1912—MSAS 1st Place Wood Carving; 1917—MSAC 1st Place Wood Carving Group; Co-founder & Charter Member of Chalk & Chisel Club

Hendrickson, H. M., Mrs.
Dates unknown
Location: Anoka, Minnesota (1904)
Role(s): Artist
Medium: China
Comments: 1904—Made China Jar Designed by Miss Beede

Hewitt, C. N., Mrs.
Dates unknown
Role(s): Student
Medium: Ceramics
Affiliations: Handicraft Guild

Higbee, Paul A., Mrs.
Dates unknown
Location: 307 Masonic Temple
Role(s): Student
Medium: Ceramics
Affiliations: Handicraft Guild

Hill, Georgia B.
Dates unknown
Location: St. Paul (1905–06)

Role(s): Artist, Student
Medium: Stenciling, Jewelry
Affiliations: Minneapolis School of Fine Arts, Minneapolis School of Art
Comments: 1910—Partner with Ethel C. Williams in The Art Craft Shop (Arts and Crafts) in The Edison Building, Duluth

Hirt, Archie E., Mrs.
Dates unknown
Location: Hector
Role(s): Artist
Medium: Textiles

Hodgeman, Dallas V.
Dates unknown
Location: 2009 Lyndale Av. S., Minneapolis (1914); 915 W. 44th St., Minneapolis (1915)
Role(s): Artist
Medium: Stenciling, Embroidery
Affiliations: Minneapolis School of Fine Arts

Hofflin, Elizabeth G., Miss
Dates uknown
Location: Minneapolis (1915)
Role(s): Artist
Medium: Jewelry, Book Plates
Affiliations: Minneapolis School of Fine Arts

Hoffman, Minnie
Dates unknown
Location: New Ulm (1912)
Role(s): Artist
Medium: Textiles

Holbrook, Elizabeth, Mrs.
Dates unknown
Location: Harvard Chambers, Minneapolis (1904, 1906, 2320 Fremont Av. S., Minneapolis (1906); 11 S. 12th St., Minneapolis (1910); 554 Chambers of Commerce Annex, Minneapolis (1912); 1374 Spruce Pl., Minneapolis (1913–15)
Role(s): Artist, Student, Member
Medium: Lace, Embroidery, Jewelry, Design, Glass, Stenciling
Affiliations: Minneapolis Arts & Crafts Society, The Woman's Club of Minneapolis, Minneapolis School of Art, Chalk & Chisel Club, Minneapolis Society of Fine Arts
Comments: 1914—MSAS Prize; Married Name—Mrs. Franklin G. Holbrook.

Holbrook, Emily, Miss
Dates unknown
Location: 1374 Spruce Place, Minneapolis
Role(s): Student
Medium: Jewelry
Affiliations: Minneapolis School of Fine Arts

Holbrook, William R.
Dates unknown
Location: 5300 Penn Av. S., Minneapolis (1917)
Role(s): Artist
Medium: Textiles

Holmes, Edythe Josephine
Dates unknown
Location: 3108 Humboldt Av., Minneapolis (1915)
Role(s): Artist
Medium: Leather, China Painting

Holter, (K)(C)lara Alice
Dates unknown
Location: 1601 Elliot Av., Minneapolis
Role(s): Artist
Medium: Jewelry

Holth, Julia
Dates unknown
Location: St. Paul
Role(s): Artist
Medium: Basketry

Hood, Elizabeth, Miss
Dates unknown
Location: 342 Market St., St. Paul (1914)
Role(s): Member
Medium: Ceramics
Affiliations: Art Workers' Guild of St. Paul

Hough, Laura M.
Dates unknown
Location: 699 Laurel Av., St. Paul (1908)
Role(s): Artist
Medium: Jewelry, Metal Working

Howe, Mary S.
Dates unknown
Location: Minneapolis (1906)
Role(s): Student
Medium: Pottery
Affiliations: Handicraft Guild
Comments: 1906—Student; 1908—Principal, Irving School

Howland, Ida
Dates unknown
Location: Perley
Role(s): Artist
Medium: Textiles

Hubbard, Margaret T.
Dates unknown
Role(s): Artist, Student
Medium: Ceramics, Jewelry
Affiliations: Handicraft Guild
Comments: 1900—Student

Hubbell, Lucille, Miss
Dates unknown
Role(s): Student
Medium: Weaving
Affiliations: Minneapolis School of Art

Hughes, Elizabeth
Dates unknown
Role(s): Artist
Medium: Pottery
Affiliations: St. Paul Institute School of Art

Hugy, Alice Elizabeth
Dates unknown
Location: 612 Cherokee Av., St. Paul (1908, 1914–15, 1917)
Role(s): Artist, Student
Medium: Drawing, Painting
Affiliations: St. Paul Institute of Arts & Sciences
Comments: 1894–98—SPIAS Student; 1906—Artist at Bureau of Engraving, Minneapolis

Hunt, Wm. M.
Dates unknown
Location: Duluth
Role(s): Artist
Comments: 1908—MSAS Juror

Huntington, Florence A.
Dates unknown
Location: 2245 Knapp St., St. Paul (1913, 1914)
Role(s): Artist, Teacher
Medium: Ceramics, Design, Handicraft, China Painting
Affiliations: Twin City Porcelain and Keramic Club, Minneapolis School of Art
Comments: 1914–15—MSA Assistant Instructor in Design and Handicraft (decoration of China); 1914—Listed as Artist; 1916—TCKC Vice President; Pupil of Miss Anna Riis, Cincinnati Art Academy; of Mrs. Henrietta Barclay Paist; and of Miss Mary Moulton Cheney, Minneapolis School of Art.

Ickler, E. E.
Dates unknown
Location: 648 Delaware Av., St. Paul

Role(s): Artist
Medium: Pottery

Industrial Shops
Dates unknown
Location: 97 S. 10th, Minneapolis
Comments: 1912–13—Rug Manufacturers, Henrietta C. Olberg, Sophia H. Stearns

J. B. Hudson & Son, Inc.
Dates unknown
Location: 37–39 S. 7th St., Minneapolis (1887–Present)
Comments: Jewelers, Silversmiths, Stationers.

Jager, Selma E., Mrs.
Dates unknown
Location: 801 E. 15th St., Minneapolis (1904); 5241 Upton Av. S., Minneapolis (1906, 1912–13, 1917); 5241 Royal Rd. (1906).
Role(s): Artist, Teacher
Medium: Needlework, Textiles, Embroidery, Lace
Affiliations: Minneapolis School of Fine Arts
Comments: 1904, 1906, 1912—MSAS Prize; 1917—MSAC 1st Place Lace; Attended Imperial and Royal School of Lace-making, Vienna. Instructor in lace making and embroidery at MSA. Married name—Mrs. John Jager.

James, Henry C., Mrs.
Dates unknown
Location: 1043 Laurel Av., St. Paul (1904, 1905)
Role(s): Artist
Medium: Illumination, Pen Drawing

Janney, T. J., Mrs.
Dates unknown
Affiliations: Chalk & Chisel Club
Comments: Charter Member Chalk & Chisel Club

Jarvie, Robert
Dates unknown
Role(s): Artist
Medium: Designer, Metal Worker
Comments: 1913—Affiliated with The Fine Arts Shop, Chicago

Jehle, Clara Antonia
Dates unknown
Role(s): Student
Medium: Textile Design
Affiliations: St. Paul Institute, St. Paul (1913)

Jilson, Eleanor Burrill
Dates unknown
Location: Flat 6, The Seville, St. Paul (1905, 1907)
Role(s): Artist
Medium: Illumination, Jewelry, Design, Painting
Affiliations: St. Paul Institute of Arts & Sciences, St. Paul School of Fine Arts
Comments: 1905—MSAS Honorable Mention

Johnson, Ella Caroly
Dates unknown
Role(s): Student
Medium: Textile Design
Affiliations: St. Paul Institute of Art

Johnson, Josephine
Dates unknown
Location: 2523 Johnson St. N.E., Minneapolis (1915)
Role(s): Artist
Medium: Textiles

Johnson, Nellie
Dates unknown
Role(s): Artist
Medium: Pottery
Affiliations: St. Paul Institute School of Art

Johnston, Elizabeth
Dates unknown
Location: 3140 2nd Av. S., Minneapolis (1917)
Role(s): Artist
Medium: Stenciling

Jones, Edward
Dates unknown
Role(s): Artist
Medium: Woodcarving
Comments: Affiliated with Central High School, Minneapolis

Selma E. Jager. Minnesota State Art Society Exhibit Catalog, *1903 and 1904, p. 57.*

Kaercher, Mabel G., Miss
Dates unknown
Location: St. Paul (1909); Ortonville (1915, 1917)
Role(s): Artist, Student
Medium: Art Handicraft, Leather, Illustration, Ceramics, Jewelry
Affiliations: St. Paul Institute of Arts & Sciences
Comments: 1910—MSAS Prize

Kaiser, August
Dates unknown
Location: 505 Essex Bldg., Minneapolis
Role(s): Artist
Medium: Commercial Art, Poster, Painting

Kane, Kathleen Constance
Dates unknown
Location: 2927 Oakland Av., Minneapolis (1914, 1915)
Role(s): Artist, Teacher, Student
Medium: Book Plates, Illustration
Affiliations: Minneapolis School of Fine Arts, Minneapolis School of Art
Comments: 1913–14—MIA 2nd Year Student; 1914—MSAS Prize; 1915—Student

Kast, E. C., Mrs.
Dates unknown
Role(s): Artist
Medium: Ceramics

Keister, Florinda
Dates unknown
Role(s): Student, Artist
Affiliations: Handicraft Guild
Comments: 1912—Received HG Scholarship, South High School

Keith, Henrietta, Mrs.
Dates unknown
Location: Minneapolis (1897–1901)
Comments: Advertised as Interior Decorator in Keith's Magazine. Married name—Mrs. George H. Keith

Keith's Magazine
1899–1931
Comments: Magazine Published in Minneapolis and Chicago by Keith Corporation under Several Titles ("Home Builder," "Keith's Home Builder," "Keith's Magazine on Home Building," and "Keith's Beautiful Homes Magazine") Its articles and illustrations are a rich source of commentary on local arts and crafts-style designers, architects, and residential interiors.

Kellogg, Ella
Dates unknown
Role(s): Student
Medium: Pottery
Affiliations: Handicraft Guild
Comments: 1908—M. Hagen and Louise Towle Made Pieces She Designed for MSAS Exhibit

Kelly, Alice M.
Dates unknown
Location: 658 Lincoln Av., St. Paul (1910)
Role(s): Artist
Medium: Design
Affiliations: St. Paul Institute School of Art
Comments: 1910—MSAS Prize

Kerbug, K. A.
Dates unknown
Location: St. Paul
Role(s): Artist
Medium: Decorative Molding

Kiess, Grace Margaret
Dates unknown
Location: 1610 Harmon Pl., Minneapolis (1906)
Role(s): Teacher

Medium: Leather
Affiliations: Handicraft Guild
Comments: HG First Director

Killorin, John, Mrs.
Dates unknown
Role(s): Member
Affiliations: Duluth Art Association
Comments: Founding Member of Duluth Art Association

King, Mrs.
Dates unknown
Location: Litchfield
Role(s): Artist
Medium: Basketry
Affiliations: Litchfield Handicraft Guild

King, Katherine, Miss
Dates unknown
Role(s): Member
Affiliations: Duluth Art Association
Comments: Founding Member of Duluth Art Association

King, Katherine M., Miss
Dates unknown
Location: 212 Concord St., St. Paul (1905, 1906); 2400 Stevens Av., Minneapolis (1913)
Role(s): Artist, Member
Medium: Textile Design
Affiliations: The Woman's Club of Minneapolis

Kingsland, Fred
Dates unknown
Role(s): Student, Artist
Medium: Copper
Affiliations: Handicraft Guild

Klees, Emil
Dates unknown
Location: 2523 28th Av. S., Minneapolis (1914); 28 College Av., St. Paul (1912)
Role(s): Artist
Medium: Wood Carving, Painting

Klinkerfues, Fulton
Dates unknown
Location: 858 E. 5th St., St. Paul (1914, 1915)
Role(s): Student
Medium: Sculpture
Affiliations: St. Paul Institute of Arts & Sciences

Knight, Mary C.
Dates unknown
Role(s): Artist
Medium: Design

Knowles, Katherine Howland
Dates unknown
Location: 752 Lincoln Av., St. Paul (1915, 1917)
Role(s): Artist
Medium: Basketry

Knuppe, Belle
Dates unknown
Location: 1381 Summit Av., St. Paul (1908)
Role(s): Artist
Medium: Ceramics, Leather, Painting
Affiliations: Arts Guild of St. Paul

Koehl, Howard
Dates unknown
Location: Minneapolis
Role(s): Artist
Medium: Art Handicraft, Painting
Comments: 1907—MSAS Prize

Koehler, Robert
28 November 1850–1917
Location: Minneapolis (1913); 4816 Portland Av., Minneapolis (1904–5, 1908, 1915)
Role(s): Artist, Officer, Member, Teacher
Medium: Painting

Affiliations: Minneapolis Society of Fine Arts, Minnesota State Art Society, Minneapolis Art Commission, Minneapolis School of Fine Arts, Minneapolis Art League
Comments: 1894–1914—Director of Minneapolis School of Fine Arts, Director Emeritus from 1914 until Death in 1917; 1903–5, 1908, 1913—MSAS President; 1904–7, 1910—MSAS Exhibit Committee; 1908—President of Minneapolis Art League; 1912—MSAS Extension Committee, MSAS Exhibit Committee; 1914—MSAS Exhibit Committee; 1915–16—HG Lecturer; Born in Hamburg. Student of National Academy of Design and Art Students' League, New York, with Lifftz and Defregger at the Royal Academy, Munich. President of Minnesota Art League.

Koenig, Nellie (Nell)
Dates unknown
Role(s): Artist
Medium: China

Kraft, Emma
Dates unknown
Location: Minneapolis (1905–6)
Role(s): Student
Affiliations: Minneapolis School of Art

Krayenbuhl, Harold
Dates unknown
Role(s): Artist
Medium: Woodcarving
Comments: Affiliated with East Side High School, Minneapolis

Krebs, Nell
Dates unknown
Location: St. Paul
Role(s): Artist
Medium: Basketry

Kronberg, Herbert
Dates unknown
Location: 3446 11th Av. S., Minneapolis (1917)
Role(s): Artist
Medium: Metal Work
Comments: 1917—MSAC 1st Place Metal Work

Kruger, Pauline
Dates unknown
Location: 67 Syndicate Block, Minneapolis (1903)
Role(s): Artist
Medium: Woodcarving

La Berge, Myrtle, Mrs.
Dates unknown
Location: St. Paul (1912)
Role(s): Student
Affiliations: Handicraft Guild
Comments: HG Graduate

La Combe, Bertha, Mrs.
Dates unknown
Location: 719 Portland Av., St. Paul (1905, 1906)
Role(s): Artist
Medium: Needlework, Lace
Comments: 1905—MSAS Prize; Married Name—Mrs. Grunow La Combe

La Du, Roy W.
Dates unknown
Role(s): Member
Affiliations: Manual Arts Club of Minneapolis
Comments: 1917—MACM Secretary/Treasurer

La Fond, Irene
Dates unknown
Location: 1379 Breda St., St. Paul
Role(s): Artist
Medium: Crochet
Comments: 1914—MSAS First Place Crochet

Lacina, Katie, Mrs.

Dates unknown
Location: Canby (1915, 1917)
Role(s): Artist
Medium: Lace

Lambert, Elisabeth Van Wedel Staedt
Dates unknown
Location: 1400 Willow St., Minneapolis (1910)
Role(s): Artist
Medium: Ceramics

Larsen, Lina B.
Dates unknown
Location: 822 Charles St., St. Paul (1905)
Role(s): Artist
Medium: Design

Larson, Martha
Dates unknown
Role(s): Student
Medium: Poster Design
Affiliations: St. Paul Institute of Art

Lavell, Lulu Verharen, Mrs.
Dates unknown
Role(s): Artist
Medium: Ceramics, China Painting

Layman, Edna E., Miss
Dates unknown
Location: 2823 Cedar Av., Minneapolis (1904, 1906)
Role(s): Artist, Student, Member
Medium: Embroidery, Design, Book Plate
Affiliations: Minneapolis School of Fine Arts, Minneapolis Arts & Crafts Society

Le Duc, Alice Sumner
Dates unknown
Location: 702 Marshall Field Bldg., Chicago, Il (1902–3); Hastings, Minnesota (1904, 1906, 1908, 1912); 2512 Humbolt Av. S., Minneapolis (1927)
Role(s): Artist, Member
Medium: Textile Design, Designer, Craftsworker
Affiliations: Minneapolis Arts & Crafts Society
Comments: 1902–3—AIC Distinct Artistic Merit Award; 1904—Pieces Entered in MSAS Were Withdrawn, Designed by Mrs. Sumner Le Duc, Made by Sophia Gerlach, Anna Gillit, Nellie Hannah; 1906—Designed Table Cover Executed by Anna Gillitt for MSAS Exhibit; 1912, 1927–SA&C,Boston Exhibitor; Did Embroidery Design Work for John S. Bradstreet and Co. and William A. French & Co. (See MHS Museum Collections for patterns, etc.)

Le Duc, Sumner, Mrs.
Dates unknown
Role(s): Artist
Medium: Design
Comments: 1904—Designed Pieces Entered and Then Withdrawn by Alice Sumner Le Duc

Le Mieux, Delvina
Dates unknown
Location: 620 6th St. W., Faribault
Role(s): Artist
Medium: Knitting, Crochet
Comments: 1914—MSAS 2nd Place Crochet

Leavenworth, Louise
Dates unknown
Role(s): Artist
Medium: Woodcarving
Comments: Affiliated with East Side High School, Minneapolis

Lederer, Katherine
Dates unknown
Role(s): Artist
Medium: Jewelry

Affiliations: Handicraft Guild

Lengby, Hilda C.
Dates unknown
Location: 708 E. Lawson St., St. Paul
Role(s): Artist
Medium: Pottery

Lenionen, K. F.
Dates unknown
Role(s): Artist
Medium: Metalworking

Lenz, Louise M.
Dates unknown
Location: 2217 Bryant Av. N., Minneapolis (1915)
Role(s): Artist
Medium: Tatting, Crochet

Leonard, Gertrude J., Miss
Dates unknown
Location: 2121 Blaisdell Av., Minneapolis (1904, 1906)
Role(s): Officer, Artist, Member
Medium: Wood Carving
Affiliations: Chalk & Chisel Club, Minneapolis Arts & Crafts Society
Comments: 1898—Chalk & Chisel Club President; Co-founder and Charter Member Chalk & Chisel Club

Lere, Gudrun Oalbu, Mrs.
Dates unknown
Location: 1418 E. Lake St., Minneapolis (1915)
Role(s): Artist
Medium: Crochet

Lillie, Ella May, Mrs.
Dates unknown
Location: Chicago
Role(s): Artist
Medium: Poster

Lindback, H. P., Mrs.
Dates unknown
Location: 1219 Monroe St. N.E., Minneapolis (1915)
Role(s): Artist
Medium: Hand Carving

Lindberg, Beatrice E., Miss
Dates unknown
Location: Faribault, Minnesota (1908); 504 W. 7th St., Faribault (1914–15, 1917); 315 W. 3rd St., Faribault (1917)
Role(s): Artist
Medium: Design, Weaving, Embroidery, Rugs
Affiliations: Minnesota State Art Society, Handicraft Guild
Comments: 1908—MSAS Prize, MSAS Extension Committee; 1912—MSAS Extension Committee, MSAS 1st place Weaving; 1914—MSAS 1st place Embroidery

Lindberg, Isaac, Mrs.
Dates unknown
Location: Fairbault, Minnesota
Role(s): Artist
Medium: Weaving

Linsley, Laura S., Miss
Dates unknown
Location: 19 Royalston Av.
Role(s): Artist
Medium: Basketry

Litchfield Handicraft Guild
Dates unknown
Location: Litchfield, Minn.

Lockwood, Mary C., Miss
Dates unknown
Location: Minneapolis (1905–6, 1910); 501 5th St.

S.E., Minneapolis (1908, 1910)
Role(s): Artist, Teacher, Student
Medium: Jewelry, Design
Affiliations: Minneapolis School of Fine Arts, Minneapolis School of Art
Comments: 1907, 1910—MSAS Prize

Lodwick, Agnes I.
Dates unknown
Location: Studio 18; 2665 Irving Av. S., Minneapolis (1909); 2012 James Av. S., Minneapolis (1910); 2647 Irving Av. S., Minneapolis (1911–12)
Role(s): Artist
Medium: Leather, Stenciling, Painting, Photography
Affiliations: Handicraft Guild
Comments: 1908–11—Teacher, West High School, Minneapolis; 1910—MSAS Prize

Long, Olive M., Miss
Dates unknown
Location: 443 Carroll St., St. Paul (1905)
Role(s): Member
Medium: Art Handicraft, Illustration
Affiliations: Art Workers' Guild of St. Paul
Comments: 1905—MSAS Prize

Longer, Clara
Dates unknown
Location: 360 Auditorium Bldg., Minneapolis (1916)
Role(s): Artist, Member
Medium: Modeler
Affiliations: Minneapolis Arts & Crafts Society
Comments: 1916—SA&C,Boston Exhibitor

Lougee, Clara
Dates unknown
Location: 1103 5th St. S.E., Minneapolis (1917)
Role(s): Artist, Member
Medium: Modeler
Affiliations: Minneapolis Arts & Crafts Society
Comments: 1917—SA&C,Boston Exhibitor

Lounsberry, Esther
Dates unknown
Role(s): Student
Medium: Design
Affiliations: Minneapolis Institute of Arts
Comments: 1918—MIA 1st Year Design Illustration

Lovell, Ruth Stilwell
Dates unknown
Location: 2620 Dupont Av. S., Minneapolis (1914)
Role(s): Artist, Student
Medium: Stenciling, Embroidery, Design
Affiliations: Minneapolis School of Fine Arts, Minneapolis School of Art
Comments: 1913–14—MIA 1st Year Student, received Scholarship

Lowry, Ethelwyn
Dates unknown
Location: 519 Oakland Av., St. Paul (1914, 1917)
Role(s): Artist
Medium: Pottery, Sculpture, Painting
Affiliations: St. Paul Institute School of Art

Luisoni, Marie Louise
Dates unknown
Location: 943 Summit Av., St. Paul (1912)
Role(s): Artist
Medium: Textiles

Lum, Bertha Boynton Bull, Mrs.
1869 or 1879–1954
Location: Hamshire Arms, Minneapolis (1904); 1804 Park Av., Minneapolis (1904–5); 1812 S. Humboldt, Minneapolis (1906, 1908, 1913); 89 S. 10th St., Minneapolis (1912)

Role(s): Artist, Teacher, Member, Student
Medium: Japanese Woodcut, Wood Blocking, Design, Painting, Photography
Affiliations: Handicraft Guild, Minneapolis Arts & Crafts Society, The Woman's Club of Minneapolis, Minneapolis School of Art, Artists' League of Minneapolis
Comments: 1905, 1906, 1915–16—Instructor or Lecturer in Wood Block Printing at HG; 1908—MSAS Membership Committee; 1915–16—HG Lecturer; Student at Chicago Art Institute Art School, under Frank Holme of Chicago, with Anna Weston, Igami Bonkotsu, and Nishimura Kumakichi. Married names—Mrs. Bert Francis Lum (1903).

Lunachek, Mary, Mrs.
Dates unknown
Location: 1524 Logan Av. N., Minneapolis (1912)
Role(s): Artist
Medium: Lace

Lundquist, Olga, Mrs.
Dates unknown
Location: 852 Selby Av., St. Paul (1917)
Role(s): Artist
Medium: Lace
Comments: 1917—MSAC 2nd place Lace

Luther, Jessie Willcox
Dates unknown
Role(s): Artist
Medium: Metal Working

Luther, Mabel Wilcox
Dates unknown
Location: 15 Westminster St., Providence, Ri (1905)
Role(s): Artist
Medium: Metal Working, Jewelry

Mack, Catherine, Mrs.
Dates unknown
Location: 233 Nelson Av., St. Paul
Role(s): Artist
Medium: Basketry

Maetzold, Bertha
Dates unknown
Location: Litchfield
Role(s): Artist
Medium: Leather
Affiliations: Litchfield Handicraft Guild

Maine, Maurice
Dates unknown
Location: 716 4th Av. S., Minneapolis (1908)
Role(s): Artist
Medium: Photography

Mairs, Clara G.
Dates unknown
Location: 414 Holly Av., St. Paul (1908)
Role(s): Student, Artist
Medium: Painting, Ceramics, Textiles
Affiliations: St. Paul Institute of Arts & Sciences
Comments: MHS has a ceramic pot made by her.

Man, Gertrude E., Miss
Dates unknown
Location: Minneapolis (1888–89); 89 S. Tenth St., Minneapolis (1908); Mound, Minnesota (1908); 2015 Stevens Av., Minneapolis (1913)
Role(s): Artist, Member, Student
Medium: Photography
Affiliations: The Woman's Club of Minneapolis, Minneapolis School of Fine Arts
Comments: 1908—Studio in HG building. Her work was included in exhibitions in London, Liverpool, Dresden, and Turin.

Mann, Leonora C.
Dates unknown

Location: 2804 Garfield Av. S., Minneapolis
Role(s): Artist, Student
Medium: Silver
Affiliations: Handicraft Guild, Minneapolis School of Fine Arts, Minneapolis School of Art
Comments: Assistant at Minneapolis Public Library

Manship, Paul
1885–1966
Role(s): Student, Artist
Medium: Drawing, Sculpture
Affiliations: St. Paul Institute of Arts & Sciences
Comments: 1894–98—SPIAS Student; 1908—at Pennsylvania Academy of Fine Arts, Philadelphia, Pa; 1914—MSAS Prize; 1916—Designed SPIAS Award Medal

Marie Teresa, Sister
Dates unknown
Location: St. Margaret's Academy (1912, 1914)
Role(s): Artist
Medium: Painting, Lace
Comments: 1914—MSAS 1st Place Lace

Marshall, H. C., Mrs.
Dates unknown
Role(s): Member
Affiliations: Duluth Art Association
Comments: Founding Member of Duluth Art Association

Martin, Mrs.
Dates unknown
Role(s): Artist
Medium: Textiles

Martin, Ida
Dates unknown
Role(s): Student
Medium: Design
Affiliations: Minneapolis School of Fine Arts

Martin, M. M., Mrs.
Dates unknown
Role(s): Artist
Medium: Ceramics
Affiliations: St. Paul Institute School of Art

Mastrangelo, Luigi T.
Dates unknown
Role(s): Artist
Medium: Commercial Art

Maunsell, Lee
Dates unknown
Location: 424 N. 3rd St., Stillwater, Minnesota
Role(s): Artist, Student
Medium: Weaving
Affiliations: St. Paul Institute School of Art
Comments: 1913—SPI Student; 1913—MSAS Prize

Maxwell, Helen
Dates unknown
Location: Hampshire Arms, Minneapolis (1903)
Role(s): Artist
Medium: Basketry

May, Sarah
Dates unknown
Role(s): Artist
Medium: Leaded Glass

McBride, Marian
Dates unknown
Role(s): Artist
Medium: Stenciling

McCall, Helen Frances, Miss
Dates unknown
Location: 220 E. 27th St., Minneapolis (1910, 1912); 3040 Harriet Av., Minneapolis (1914–15, 1917)
Role(s): Artist, Student

Medium: Stenciling, Leather, Textiles, Book Covers, Photography, Book Plates
Affiliations: Minneapolis Society of Fine Arts
Comments: 1912—MSAS 1st place Book Decoration: 1914—MSAS 1st place Stencil; MIA 1st Annual Exhibit of Minneapolis Artists lists Helen Frasier McCall

McCarthy, Nathaniel
Dates unknown
Location: 622 Nicollet Av., Minneapolis (1903)
Role(s): Artist
Medium: Bookbinding

McClelland, Alice
Dates unknown
Role(s): Student
Medium: Design
Affiliations: Minneapolis School of Fine Arts

McClumpha, C. F.
Dates unknown
Location: 323 6th Av. S.E., Minneapolis (1903)
Medium: Bookbinding

McCormick, Ella Sudduth
Dates unknown
Role(s): Teacher
Medium: Design, Handicraft
Affiliations: Minneapolis School of Art
Comments: 1918–19—Instructor in Design and Handicraft at MSA; Graduate of Vassar College and Church School of Art, Chicago

McDermott, Gertrude
Dates unknown
Location: Hudson, Wisconsin
Role(s): Artist
Medium: Design
Affiliations: Minneapolis School of Fine Arts

McDonald, Harriet, Miss
Dates unknown
Location: 301 Oak Grove St., Minneapolis (1906)
Role(s): Artist
Medium: Silver, Jewelry, Woodcarving
Comments: 1906—MSAS Prize

McDonald, Hope, Miss
Dates unknown
Location: 301 Oak Grove St., Minneapolis (1906); 201 Ridgewood Av., Minneapolis (1913)
Role(s): Artist, Member
Medium: Woodcarving
Affiliations: Minneapolis Arts & Crafts Society, The Woman's Club of Minneapolis, Chalk & Chisel Club
Comments: 1913–14—WC Lecturer

McDonald, Williamina
Dates unknown
Role(s): Artist
Medium: Jewelry
Affiliations: Handicraft Guild

McEwen, Nora
Dates unknown
Role(s): Artist
Medium Leather

McGill, Drusilla Paist, Mrs.
1888–1968
Location: 2293 Commonwealth Av., St. Paul (1908)
Role(s): Artist
Medium: Ceramics
Comments: 1910–11 SPI Keramics Instructor Daughter of Henrietta Barclay Paist. Married name—Mrs. Thomas Martin McGill.

McGirk, I. B., Mrs.
Dates unknown
Location: Minneapolis (1903)
Role(s): Artist

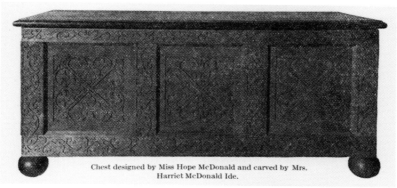

Chest designed by Miss Hope McDonald and carved by Mrs. Harriet McDonald Ide.

Harriet McDonald Ide and Hope McDonald (chest designed by Hope, carved by Harriet). The Bellman, 24 November 1906, p. 471.

Grace E. McKinstry. Who's Who among Minnesota Women, 1924, p. 194.

Medium: Design
Affiliations: Minneapolis School of Fine Arts
Comments: MSFA 1913 Exhibit Lists A Mrs. Mary McGirk

McGolrick, James, Bishop
Dates unknown
Location: Duluth
Role(s): Member

Affiliations: Minnesota State Art Society, Duluth Art Association
Comments: 1908—MSAS Membership Committee; 1911, 1912—MSAS Extension Committee; 1912—MSAS Juror

McGrory, Mabel M.
Dates unknown
Location: Yale Flats, Minneapolis (1904); 500 S. 3rd St., Minneapolis (1906)
Role(s): Artist
Medium: Stained Glass
Comments: 1903—Artist, Pittsburgh Plate Glass Co.

McKechnie, Ruth Starr, Mrs.
Dates unknown
Location: 647 Holly Av., St. Paul (1910); 647 Holly Av., St. Paul (1914)
Role(s): Artist
Medium: Jewelry, Metal Working
Comments: Married name—Mrs. Alexander A. McKechnie

McKinstry, Grace E., Miss
Dates unknown
Location: Faribault, Minnesota (1904, 1905, 1908); 315 W. 3rd, Faribault (1912, 1917)
Role(s): Member, Artist, Student
Medium: Painting
Affiliations: Minnesota State Art Society, St. Paul Art Workers' Guild, Minneapolis School of Fine Arts, Arts Guild of St. Paul, Minnesota State Art Commission, Minneapolis Artists League
Comments: 1904, 1905—MSAS Prize; 1906, 1908, 1909—MSAS Exhibit Committee; 1908—Member of Society of Washington Artists, League of American Pen Women; 1912—MSAS Board Member, MSAS Juror; 1914-15—HG Lecturer; 1914, 1917—MSAS Recording Secretary; Studied at Art Students' League, New York, Academie Julian, Academie Colarossi, Paris, student of Raphael Collin, Paris

McKinstry, June
Dates unknown
Location: 618 E. 15th St., Minneapolis (1908)
Role(s): Artist
Medium: Leather, Design
Affiliations: Minneapolis School Fine Arts

McLeod, Elizabeth
Dates unknown
Role(s): Student
Medium: Design
Affiliations: Minneapolis School of Fine Arts

McMillan, Bertha, Miss

Dates unknown
Location: 802 4th St. S.E., Minneapolis (1904, 1906)
Role(s): Artist, Officer
Medium: Cabinetry, Metalwork
Affiliations: Minneapolis Arts & Crafts Society

McMillan, Emily Dana, Miss
Dates unknown
Location: 505 10th Av. S.E., Minneapolis (1904, 1913–14); Minneapolis (1916)
Role(s): Member
Medium: Painting, Sculpture
Affiliations: Minnesota State Art Society, The Woman's Club of Minneapolis
Comments: 1912—MSAS Exhibit Committee, MSAS Juror; 1914—MSAS Prize; 1916—SPIAS Exhibitor

McMillan, Margaret
Dates unknown
Role(s): Student
Medium: Design, Jewelry
Affiliations: Minneapolis School of Fine Arts, Handicraft Guild

McWhorter, Tyler, Mrs.
Dates unknown
Location: 369 Winslow St., St. Paul (1908); 52 W. Delos St., St. Paul (1908)
Role(s): Artist
Medium: Stenciling, Embroidery, Rugs

McWhorter, Tyler
Dates unknown
Role(s): Teacher, Officer
Medium: Cartooning
Affiliations: St. Paul Institute of Arts & Sciences
Comments: 1916—SPIAS Committee Member

Meeker, H. L., Mrs.
Dates unknown
Role(s): Artist
Medium: Ceramics
Affiliations: St. Paul Institute School of Art

Meltzer, Arthur
1893–
Location: 919 N. Emerson Av., Minneapolis (1914)
Role(s): Artist, Student
Medium: Stained Glass, Painter
Affiliations: Minneapolis School of Fine Arts
Comments: 1911–17—Student of Robert Koehler at MSFA; 1909–15?—Worked at Ford-McNutt Stained Glass Co.

Mendenhall, Luther
Dates unknown
Role(s): Member
Affiliations: Duluth Art Association
Comments: Founding Member of Duluth Art Association

Mero, Lee V.
Dates unknown
Location: Studio 15, 89 10th St. S., Minneapolis (1917)
Role(s): Artist, Student, Member
Medium: Illustration, Tempora, Painting
Affiliations: Minneapolis School of Art, Attic Club
Comments: 1913—With The Buzza Co.; 1915—Attic Club Exhibitor; 1917—MSAC Prize

Methven, Don
Dates unknown
Role(s): Artist
Medium: Stenciling

Meyer, A. C.
Dates unknown
Location: 958 Reaney St., St. Paul (1908)
Role(s): Artist
Medium: Photography

Michie, Harry S.
Dates unknown
Role(s): Artist, Teacher
Medium: Metalworking, Textiles
Affiliations: Handicraft Guild
Comments: 1906—Handicraft Guild Instructor in Metalwork; Graduate of Pratt Institute; studied at Camperwell School of lArts & Crafts, London.

Miller, Elizabeth
Dates unknown
Role(s): Artist
Medium: Leather
Affiliations: St. Paul Institute School of Art

Miller, Hattie S. F.
Dates unknown
Role(s): Artist
Medium: Basketry
Affiliations: St. Paul Institute School of Art

Miller, Margaret
Dates unknown
Role(s): Artist
Medium: Textiles

Milligan, William, Mrs.
Dates unknown
Location: St. Paul (1916)
Role(s): Artist
Medium: Needlework

Milnor, Mary F.
Dates unknown
Role(s): Artist
Medium: Jewelry
Affiliations: Handicraft Guild

Milton, Florence Ruth, Miss
Dates unknown
Location: 217 Dayton Av., St. Paul (1914)
Role(s): Artist, Teacher, Student
Medium: Wood Blocking
Affiliations: Minneapolis School of Art
Comments: 1914—MIA Student

Moak, Mildred A. K.
Dates unknown
Location: St. Paul (1904)
Role(s): Student
Medium: Design

Moen, Ragna I.
Dates unknown
Role(s): Student
Medium: Textile Design
Affiliations: St. Paul Institute of Art

Monson, Richard
Dates unknown
Role(s): Student
Medium: Cabinetmaker
Affiliations: Minneapolis School of Art
Comments: 1920—MSA Student, Won a part-time Scholarship; Cabinet maker at William A. French and Co.

Moore, H. W., Mrs.
Dates unknown
Location: 521 S. 9th St., Minneapolis (1907)
Role(s): Artist
Medium: Lace

Moran, Nellie
Dates unknown
Location: 2735 Emerson Av. S., Minneapolis (1906)
Medium: Textiles

Morison, Evelyn
Dates unknown
Role(s): Artist
Medium: Leather
Affiliations: Handicraft Guild

Morrison, Miss
Dates unknown
Location: Minneapolis (1911)
Role(s): Artist
Medium: Art Handicraft
Comments: 1909—MSAS Joint Prize with Miss Edith Griffith

Morrison, Rose B.
Dates unknown
Role(s): Student
Medium: Pottery
Affiliations: Handicraft Guild

Morton, Louise H.
Dates unknown
Location: 827 Nicollet, Minneapolis
Comments: 1909—Manager of Priscilla's Tea Shop in The New England Furniture & Carpet Co.; Proprietor, Morton's Quality Shop; 1901–12—Maintained a Gift Shop and Tea Room at various addresses. She regularly advertised in The Bellman, and the ads frequently featured nationally recognized Arts & Crafts merchandise.

Morton, Mary W.
Dates unknown
Role(s): Artist, Student
Medium: Design
Affiliations: Minneapolis School of Fine Arts

Mowbray, L. Althea
Dates unknown
Location: 1012 Nicollet Av., Minneapolis
Role(s): Artist
Medium: Ceramics

Mowry, Jason L.
Dates unknown
Role(s): Artist
Medium: Copper
Affiliations: Handicraft Guild

Mueller, Maude
Dates unknown
Location: Minneapolis (1905–6)
Role(s): Student
Medium: Design
Affiliations: Minneapolis School of Fine Arts, Minneapolis School of Art

Mull, Adelaide
Dates unknown
Location: 277 Pleasant Ave., St. Paul, Minnesota (1913)
Role(s): Student
Medium: Textile Design
Affiliations: St. Paul Institute
Comments: 1913—SPI Student

Munns, Ernest
Dates unknown
Location: 329 Central Av., Minneapolis (1903)
Role(s): Artist
Medium: Cabinetry

Murdock, Alice, Miss
Dates unknown
Location: Stillwater, Minnesota (1888, 1908)
Role(s): Student, Member
Affiliations: Minneapolis School of Fine Arts, Minnesota State Art Society
Comments: 1908—MSAS Membership Committee

Murphy, Helbert, Mr.
Dates unknown
Role(s): Student, Artist
Affiliations: Handicraft Guild

Murphy, Nelbert, Miss
Dates unknown
Location: Montevideo, Minnesota (1903), East Orange, New Jersey (1907)

Role(s): Teacher
Medium: Leather, Metalwork
Affiliations: Handicraft Guild
Comments: 1906–7—Assistant Supervisor of Drawing at Minneapolis Public Schools; 1908—Designed and made articles with Louise Berry for MSAS Exhiibit

Nabersberg, Bert(h)a, Miss
Dates unknown
Location: 131 S. St. Albans St., St. Paul (1906); 1834 Summit Av., St. Paul (1907, 1908, 1910)
Role(s): Student, Artist, Teacher, Member
Medium: Wood Block Printing, Embroidery, Metalwork, Leather, Pottery
Affiliations: Handicraft Guild, Art Workers' Guild of St. Paul, Minnesota State Art Society, St. Paul Institute of Arts & Sciences
Comments: 1906—Student; 1907—Handicraft Guild instructor/assistant. 1907–8—Supervisor of industrial work for St. Paul public schools; 1909–11—instructor at SPIAS; 1911—teacher, Central High School, St. Paul.

Nash, Franklin
Dates unknown
Role(s): Teacher
Medium: Cabinetmaking, Wood Block Carving
Affiliations: Arts Guild of St. Paul
Comments: 1908—AGSP Summer Session Teacher of Joinery, Wood Block Carving, and Cabinetmaking; Instructor of Manual Training in St. Paul Public Schools

Nash, Lucy
Dates unknown
Location: Minneapolis (1905–6)
Role(s): Student
Medium: Design
Affiliations: Minneapolis School of Fine Arts, Minneapolis School of Art

Naughton, Mary, Miss
Dates unknown
Location: Duluth
Role(s): Artist
Medium: Sculpture
Comments: 1908—MSAS Honorable Mention

Neal, Grace Anita, Mrs.
Dates unknown
Location: 416 Stryker Av., St. Paul (1905); 633 Holly Av., St. Paul (1912)
Role(s): Artist, Student, Member
Medium: Sculpture
Affiliations: Art Workers' Guild of St. Paul, St. Paul Institute of Arts & Sciences, Minnesota State Art Society
Comments: 1894–98—SPIAS Student; 1906, 1907—MSAS Prize; 1909—MSAS Exhibit Committee; Maiden name—Grace Pruden. Married name—Mrs. Jesse H. Neal

Neff, E. B.
Dates unknown
Role(s): Member
Affiliations: Duluth Art Association
Comments: Founding Member of Duluth Art Association

Neilson, Caroline
Dates unknown
Location: Red Lake Falls, Minnesota
Role(s): Artist
Medium: Lace

Nelson, Agnes
Dates unknown
Location: Litchfield, Minnesota
Role(s): Artist
Medium: Leather

Affiliations: Litchfield Handicraft Guild

Nelson, Daisy
Dates unknown
Location: Litchfield, Minnesota
Role(s): Artist
Medium: Rugs
Affiliations: Litchfield Handicraft Guild

Nelson, Florence
Dates unknown
Location: St. Paul
Role(s): Artist
Medium: Basketry

Nelson, Mabel
Dates unknown
Location: Litchfield, Minnesota (1914)
Role(s): Artist
Medium: Rugs, Basketry, Weaving
Affiliations: Litchfield Handicraft Guild
Comments: 1914—MSAS Prize

Nelson, Milton O., Mrs.
Dates unknown
Role(s): Officer
Affiliations: Chalk & Chisel Club
Comments: Charter member Chalk & Chisel Club

Nelson, N. C., Mrs.
Dates unknown
Location: 3155 14th Av. S., Minneapolis (1910)
Role(s): Artist
Medium: Embroidery (Hedebo)

Nelson, O. M., Mrs.
Dates unknown
Location: Wanamingo
Role(s): Artist
Medium: Textiles

Nelson, Ora L.
Dates unknown
Location: 3528 5th Av. S., Minneapolis (1915)
Role(s): Artist, Student
Medium: Furniture Drawing (Commercial Art), Design

Nelson (Nelsen), Lillian (Lilian)
Dates unknown
Role(s): Student
Medium: Design
Affiliations: St. Paul Art Gallery, St. Paul Institute of Art

Nelson Needlecraft Shop
Dates unknown
Location: 382 St. Peter, St. Paul (1910–11)
Comments: Proprietor, Almina C. Nelson

New England Furniture & Carpet Co.
Dates unknown
Location: Minneapolis
Comments: 1887–1950s.
Purveyors of contemporary furniture styles ranging from 'Mission' to 'Period' (Revival), 'Chinese Chippendale' and Berkley and Gay Furniture Co. lines

New Ulm Lace Makers (Workers)
Dates unknown
Location: New Ulm
Role(s): Artist
Medium: Lace
Comments: 1908—New Ulm Lace Industry Showed Collection by Bohemian Women of New Ulm; 1914—Four Lace Makers in Group, MSAS Prize

Newcomb, Olive, Miss
Dates unknown
Location: Minneapolis
Role(s): Artist, Teacher, Student

Medium: Ceramics, Metalwork
Affiliations: Handicraft Guild, Minneapolis School of Art
Comments: 1900–1903—Teacher at Prescott and Hawthorn School; 1906—MSAS Prize; 1906–8—HG Instructor/Assistant

Newman, Cornelia A.
Dates unknown
Role(s): Artist
Medium: Ceramics, Embroidery

Newman, Frances Ellen (Allen)
Dates unknown
Location: 615 Medical Block, Minneapolis (1904); 616 Medical Block, Minneapolis (1906, 1908); 323 Meyers Arcade, Minneapolis (1914); 308 Meyers Arcade, Minneapolis (1915)
Role(s): Artist
Medium: Ceramics, China Painting
Affiliations: Twin City Keramic Club
Comments: 1917—TCKC Treasurer; 1914—MSAS Prize

Newport, Mary Morgan, Miss
Dates unknown
Location: St. Paul
Role(s): Executive Committee Member, Member
Affiliations: Art Workers' Guild of St. Paul, Minnesota State Art Society
Comments: 1910—MSAS Exhibit Committee; 1912—MSAS Board; 1912, 1914—MSAS Treasurer

Newton, Bessie E.
Dates unknown
Role(s): Artist
Medium: Stencils

Nolan, William F.
Dates unknown
Location: 679 Cornwell Av., St. Paul
Role(s): Artist
Medium: Wrought Iron

Nordberg, Oscar N.
Dates unknown
Role(s): Student
Medium: Textile Design
Affiliations: St. Paul Institute of Art

Norris, Elizabeth, Miss
Dates unknown
Location: 3200 Garfield Av., Minneapolis (1903–4); 926 2nd Av. S., Minneapolis (1906)
Role(s): Artist, Student, Officer, Member
Medium: Ceramics, Copper, Bookplates, Stenciling, Illustration
Affiliations: Handicraft Guild, Minneapolis Arts & Crafts Society
Comments: 1900–1901—Teacher; 1902–3—Instructor at U of M; 1904—Illustrator; 1905–7—Teacher at South High School; 1908—Designed pieces made by Olive Newcomb for MSAS Exhibit; 1908–9—Studio in HG building

Norstad, Lillian R.
Dates unknown
Location: 383 Wheeler Av., St. Paul (1914)
Role(s): Artist
Medium: Jewelry

Northfield, Susan, Mrs.
Dates unknown
Location: 2133 Emerson Av. N. (1906)
Role(s): Artist, Officer
Medium: Basketry
Affiliations: Minneapolis Arts & Crafts Society
Comments: 1907—SA&C, Boston Exhibitor

Northrop, Cyrus, Dr.
Dates unknown

Location: Minneapolis
Role(s): Board Member
Affiliations: Minnesota State Art Society
Comments: 1903/04—MSAS Ex officio member; 1911, 1912—MSAS President

Nye, Elmer
Dates unknown
Role(s): Student
Medium: Poster Design
Affiliations: St. Paul Institute
Comments: 1913—SPI Student

Ober, Elsie
Dates unknown
Role(s): Student
Medium: Textile Design, Applied Arts
Affiliations: Minneapolis School of Art
Comments: 1918—Minnesota State Fair Prize

Ober, Florence
Dates unknown
Location: 707 Marshall Av., St. Paul (1908)
Role(s): Artist
Medium: Leather

Olds, R. E., Mrs.
Dates unknown
Location: 131 S. St. Albans St., St. Paul (1908)
Role(s): Artist
Medium: Photography, Leather

Olmstead, Clara Halm, Miss
Dates unknown
Location: 646 Laurel Av., St. Paul (1905); St. Paul (1911)
Role(s): Artist

Medium: Art Handicraft, Design, Book Cover
Comments: 1905—MSAS Prize

Olstad, Betsy, Miss
Dates unknown
Location: Wanamingo, Minnesota
Role(s): Artist
Medium: Textiles

Oredalen, Turina
Dates unknown
Location: Kenyon, Minnesota
Medium: Needlework, Hardanger, Crochet
Comments: 1914—MSAS 3rd place Prize

Osborne, E. W., Mrs.
Dates unknown
Location: 794 Laurel Av., St. Paul (1912)
Role(s): Artist
Medium: Embroidery
Comments: 1912—MSAS 1st place Embroidery

Osborne, S. E., Mrs.
Dates unknown
Location: Hampshire Arms, Minneapolis
Role(s): Artist
Medium: Basketry

Ostrem, Sophie
Dates unknown
Location: Perley
Role(s): Artist
Medium: Lace
Affiliations: Handicraft Guild

Page, Madeline
Dates unknown

Location: California (1912)
Role(s): Student
Affiliations: Handicraft Guild

Painter, John Ellsworth
Dates unknown
Location: 613 Franklin Av. E., Minneapolis (1906)
Role(s): Student, Artist
Medium: Metalwork
Affiliations: Handicraft Guild
Comments: 1900–1926—Supervisor of Manual Training, Minneapolis Public Schools; 1905–7 Handicraft Guild Assistant/Instructor

Paist, Henrietta Barclay, Mrs.
Dates unknown
Location: 2298 Commonwealth Av., St. Paul (1904, 1908, 1913, 1914); 804 Nicollet Av. (1890s)
Role(s): Artist, Teacher
Medium: Ceramics, Painting (oil & watercolor)
Affiliations: Twin City Keramic Society, St. Paul Institute of Arts & Sciences
Comments: 1904—Detroit SA&C Exhibitor; 1906—A&CS Ad; 1910—Contributor and Assistant Editor of "Keramic Studio"; 1916—President of Twin City Keramic Club. Author of Design and Decoration of Porcelain, 1914. Examples of her watercolor and ceramic work in Minnesota Historical Society Collection.

Palmer, Pauline, Mrs.
Dates unknown
Location: Chicago
Role(s): Artist
Comments: 1908—MSAS Juror

Parker, George W.
Dates unknown
Location: 731 E. 14th (1912?–14?)
Comments: Artist and President of George W. Parker Art Co., publisher of greeting cards.

Parker, Marion Alice, Miss
Dates unknown
Location: 516 4th St. S.E., Minneapolis (1904, 1906, 1914)
Role(s): Artist, Officer, Member
Medium: Rugs, Textiles, Architecture
Affiliations: Chalk & Chisel Club, Minneapolis Arts & Crafts Society
Comments: 1914—MSAS Prize; Charter Member Chalk & Chisel

Parker, R. Barton
Dates unknown
Role(s): Teacher
Affiliations: Handicraft Guild
Comments: 1914–15—HG Lecturer; 1914—Secretary at Gustav Weber Studio; Studied at the school of the Museum of Fine Arts, Boston

Parlin, Florence "Polly", Miss
Dates unknown
Role(s): Teacher, Member
Medium: Painting
Affiliations: Handicraft Guild, Rochester Art Center
Comments: 1947—Chair of RAC Exhibit Committee; Taught at HG and at North High School, Minneapolis. Founding member of Rochester Art Center, Rochester, Minn. Examples of her work in Minnesota Historical Society Collection.

Patrick, F. A.
Dates unknown
Role(s): Member
Affiliations: Duluth Art Association
Comments: Founding Member of Duluth Art Association

Henrietta Barclay Paist. Who's Who among Minnesota Women, 1924, p. 246.

Patrick, Isabel, Miss
Dates unknown
Location: Duluth
Role(s): Artist
Medium: Art Handicraft
Comments: 1908—MSAS Prize

Pattee, Gladys, Miss
1892–1991
Location: 2029 Queen Av. S., Minneapolis
Role(s): Student
Medium: Metal Working, Ceramics, Jewelry
Affiliations: Handicraft Guild
Comments: HG Graduate

Patten, Jennie
Dates unknown
Location: 385 Ashland Av., St. Paul
Role(s): Artist
Medium: Ceramics

Patten, Sarah E., Miss
Dates unknown
Location: 178 14th St., St. Paul (1904–6, 1908)
Role(s): Artist, Member
Medium: Painting, Textiles, Stencil Design
Affiliations: Art Workers' Guild of St. Paul

Patterson, Helen
Dates unknown
Role(s): Artist
Medium: Ceramics

Payne, Arthur Frank, Dr.
Dates unknown
Comments: 1905–7—Director of Arts & Crafts
School, Columbus, Oh; 1909–16—Asst. Professor of Manual Arts, Bradley Polytechnic Institute;
1920–23—Asst. Professor in U of M Education
Dept.; Author of *Art Metalwork with Inexpensive
Equipment for The Public Schools and for the
Craftsman*, 1914 and 1926; *Administration of
Vocational Education*, 1924; *Organization of Vocational Guidance*, 1924; *What Do You Know?*
1927

Pease, Alleyne W., Mrs.
Dates unknown
Location: 3204 Elliot Av., Minneapolis (1915)
Role(s): Artist
Medium: Textiles

Peck, A. E., Mrs.
Dates unknown
Location: 926 2nd Av. S., Minneapolis (1906)
Role(s): Member
Affiliations: Minneapolis Arts & Crafts Society

Peck, Grace
Dates unknown
Role(s): Artist
Medium: Candlestick
Affiliations: Handicraft Guild

Peck, Helene D.
Dates unknown
Location: 576 Lexington Av., St. Paul (1908)
Role(s): Artist
Medium: Leather

Pelton, Ruth
Dates unknown
Location: Minneapolis (1913)
Role(s): Artist
Medium: Metal, Leather

Perkins, Eunicia Lutine
Dates unknown
Location: 3754 2nd Av. S., Minneapolis (1904–5)
Role(s): Artist
Medium: Ceramics

Perkins, Evelyn Hope
Dates unknown

Location: Minneapolis
Role(s): Student, Artist
Medium: Leather, Pottery
Affiliations: Handicraft Guild, Minneapolis School
of Fine Arts
Comments: 1906—Student; 1908—Assistant at HG

Peter, Minnie
Dates unknown
Location: St. Paul, Minnesota (1916)
Role(s): Artist
Medium: Textiles

Petersen, S. N., Mrs.
Dates unknown
Location: Perley, Minnesota
Role(s): Artist
Medium: Textiles

Peterson, Alma W.
Dates unknown
Location: Grand Meadow, Minnesota (1915)
Role(s): Artist
Medium: Lace

Peterson, Carl
Dates unknown
Comments: 1906—Won HG High School Scholarship, Attended North High School, Minneapolis

Peterson, Clara A.
Dates unknown
Location: Grand Meadow
Role(s): Artist
Medium: Lace

Peterson, Helen Christine
Dates unknown
Location: 2724 Oakland Av., Minneapolis (1915)
Role(s): Artist
Medium: Ceramics

Peterson, Vivian
Dates unknown
Location: 1519 Jefferson St. N.E., Minneapolis
(1912)
Role(s): Student
Medium: Illustration
Affiliations: Minneapolis Society of Fine Arts

Peterson Art Furniture Company
1865–1960
Location: 708 NW 5th St., Faribault, Minnesota;
28 NE 4th St., Faribault, Minnesota
Comments: Created through the amalgamation of
other local furniture factories including Flint
Furniture Factory, Daisy Woodcraft, North Star
Furniture Co.

Petrin, Emilie, Mrs.
Dates unknown
Location: Wayzata, Minnesota
Role(s): Artist
Medium: Cloth, Hardanger

Pfendler, May
Dates unknown
Location: 2407 Bloomington Av., Minneapolis
(1907)
Role(s): Artist
Medium: Lace

Phelan, Margaret, Miss
Dates unknown
Location: 853 Lincoln Av., St. Paul (1904)
Role(s): Artist
Medium: Glass Etching

Phelps, Ruth Shepard, Miss
18 June 1876– ?
Location: Minneapolis
Comments: Graduate of Smith College and M.A.
from Columbia.

Phoenix, Lauros Monroe

Dates unknown
Location: Minneapolis (1914)
Role(s): Teacher, Member
Medium: Mural Decoration
Affiliations: St. Paul Institute of Arts & Sciences,
Minneapolis Society of Fine Arts, Minneapolis
School of Art, Minnesota State Art Society, Federal School of Commercial Designing
Comments: 1914—MSAS Exhibit Committee;
1914–16—HG Lecturer on Mural Painting;
1914–15—MSA Instructor in Antique, Mural
Painting, Theory of Color, Illustration, and
Sketch Classes; 1917—Exhibited Commercial
Art, Director of The Federal School of Commercial Designing, Minneapolis; Graduate of Chicago Art Institute. Student of Alphonse Mucha
and Howard Pyle.

Pilcher (Lott), Hazel Edith
Dates unknown
Role(s): Student
Medium: Textile Design
Affiliations: St. Paul Art Gallery, St. Paul Institute
of Art

Pinckney, Louise
Dates unknown
Location: Minneapolis (1905–6); Minnetonka
Beach, Minnesota (1909); Los Angeles, Ca (1915)
Role(s): Student, Teacher
Medium: Painting, Drawing
Affiliations: Minneapolis School of Fine Arts,
Handicraft Guild, Minneapolis School of Art
Comments: 1900—Started at MSFA; 1908–9—Acting Director of School of Art at Dakota Wesleyan
University in Mitchell, SD; 1909—MSFA
Teacher; Student of Batchelder at HG and at Columbia University, N.Y.

Pine, Fidelia Auten
Dates unknown
Role(s): Student, Officer
Medium: Textiles, Painting
Affiliations: St. Paul Art Gallery, St. Paul Institute
of Arts & Sciences
Comments: 1909–11—Student at SPIAS; 1912—
SPIAS Teacher, MSAS Prize in Student Textile
Design Competition; 1913—SPIAS Registrar;
1914–15—St. Paul Art School Sketch Class

Pittsburgh Plate Glass Co.
1898–1960s
Location: Minneapolis
Comments: One of several local companies doing
artistic stained glass work.

Plowman, George Taylor
Dates unknown
Location: 169 Main St., Winthrop, Massachusetts
(1915)
Role(s): Artist
Medium: Etching

Porter, Winifred
Deceased by 1911
Location: 504 Medical Block, Minneapolis (1905)
Role(s): Artist
Medium: Art Handicraft, Photography
Comments: 1905—MSAS Prize

Potter, C. Fredrick
Dates unknown
Location: 620½ Nicollet Av., Minneapolis (1908)
Role(s): Artist
Medium: Photography

Pousette-Dart, Nathaniel J.
Dates unknown
Location: 746 Jessie St., St. Paul (1908); 1550 Selby
Av., St. Paul (1914); 1649 Marshall Av., St. Paul
(1915, 1917)

Role(s): Artist, Student, Teacher, Member
Medium: Drawing, Painting, Etching
Affiliations: St. Paul Institute of Arts & Sciences, Minnesota State Art Society
Comments: 1894–98—SPIAS Student; 1912—SPIAS Teacher; 1914—MSAS Exhibit Committee; 1916—SPIAS Exhibitor, SPIAS Committee Member, MSAS Prize

Preston, Jessie M., Miss
Dates unknown
Location: Fine Arts Bldg., 203 Michigan, Chicago (1904–5, 1908)
Role(s): Artist, Teacher
Medium: Jewelry, Metal Work
Affiliations: Minneapolis School of Fine Arts, Arts Guild of St. Paul
Comments: 1896—Graduate of Chicago Art Institute School; 1906—MSAS Juror; 1907—Special Instructor in Jewelry and Metal Work at Minneapolis School of Art; 1908—Instructor at AGSP Summer School

Purcell, Wm. Gray
Dates unknown
Location: 2409 Lake of The Isles Blvd., Minneapolis (1908); 2311 Humboldt Av. S., Minneapolis (1910); 2328 Lake Place, Minneapolis (1913–14)
Role(s): Artist
Medium: Design, Architecture, Painting
Comments: Prairie School architect who promoted the use of natural materials and the goals of the MSAS in his article in The Minnesotan I, no. 9 (April 1916) entitled "Made in Minnesota: The Story of Native Resources, Their Use and Possibilities," pp. 7–13.

Race, Josephine

Dates unknown
Role(s): Student
Medium: Design
Affiliations: Minneapolis School of Art
Comments: 1913–14—MIA Midyear Student

Raetz, Fred W.
Dates unknown
Location: 2916 Park Av., Minneapolis (1915)
Role(s): Artist
Comments: 1915—He had Studio 19 at Handicraft Guild, and boarded at Park Avenue address.

Ralston, Elsie
Dates unknown
Location: Litchfield, Minnesota
Role(s): Artist
Medium: Basketry
Affiliations: Litchfield Handicraft Guild

Ramsey, C. F.
Dates unknown
Role(s): Officer
Affiliations: Minneapolis School of Fine Arts
Comments: 1916–17—Director of MSFA; Student of The Pennsylvania Industrial School of Philadelphia and Pennsylvania Academy, and The Academie Julian, Paris

Randall, D. Ernest, Mr.
Dates unknown
Location: 409 Pittsburgh Bldg., St. Paul (1908); 702 Pittsburgh Bldg., St. Paul (1908)
Role(s): Member, Executive Committee Member, Artist, Teacher
Medium: Painting
Affiliations: Art Workers' Guild of St. Paul, St. Paul Institute of Arts and Sciences, Minnesota State Art Society

Comments: 1906—MSAS Exhibit Committee; 1908—MSAS Prize

Raymond, Ruth, Miss
6 October 1867–1964
Location: 408 Greenwood Av., Evanston, Il (1907–8)
Role(s): Teacher, Artist
Medium: Monograms, Stenciling, Book Plates
Affiliations: Handicraft Guild
Comments: 1900—Graduate of Chicago Art Institute Department of Design and Chicago School of Applied and Normal Art; 1907—AIC Silver Medal Winner; Former Instructor at Chicago Art Institute; U of Chicago Art Department; Classical School, Evanston, Il; and Summer School, Chatauqua, New York. One of the Kalo Shop originators. 1914–17—Principal (Director) of Handicraft Guild. When Handicraft Guild became the nucleus of the U of Minnesota Art Education Department she served as the Department Head.

Rees, Georgia May
Dates unknown
Location: Minneapolis (1913)
Role(s): Teacher
Medium: Painter, Metalworking
Affiliations: Minneapolis School of Fine Arts

Renning, Eva
Dates unknown
Location: Kasson, Minnesota
Role(s): Student
Affiliations: Handicraft Guild

Resler, George E.
Dates unknown
Location: 431 Bidwell St., St. Paul (1905); 395 Winslow Av., St. Paul (1912, 1914)
Role(s): Member, Teacher, Student
Medium: Painting, Etching
Affiliations: Art Workers' Guild of St. Paul, St. Paul Institute of Arts & Sciences
Comments: 1905—MSAS Prize, Student

Rheem, Royal
–7/5/1909
Location: Minneapolis
Role(s): Artist, Student
Medium: Art Handicraft, Commercial Art
Affiliations: Minneapolis School of Fine Arts
Comments: 1904, 1905—Student at MSFA; 1905—MSAS Prize; MSFA 1909 Exhibit was a One-Man Show

Rice, Lorilla M., Miss
Dates unknown
Location: 1778 S. Lyndale Av., Minneapolis (1910)
Role(s): Artist, Student
Medium: Stenciling, Embroidery
Affiliations: Minneapolis Society of Fine Arts

Richards, J. B., Mrs.
Dates unknown
Role(s): Member
Affiliations: Duluth Art Association
Comments: Founding Member of Duluth Art Association

Rideout, Mrs.
Dates unknown
Role(s): Artist
Medium: Pottery
Affiliations: St. Paul Institute School of Art

Rishatch, Katherine
Dates unknown
Role(s): Artist
Medium: Pottery
Affiliations: St. Paul Institute School of Art

Robbins, Adelaide, Miss

Jessie M. Preston (jewelry executed by her). Minneapolis Society of Fine Arts Bulletin, vol. 2, no. 2 (February 1907): 3.

Dates unknown
Role(s): Student, Artist
Affiliations: Handicraft Guild
Comments: Married Name—Mrs. Ralph P. Gilette

Roberts, Catherine
Dates unknown
Medium: Leather
Affiliations: Handicraft Guild

Roberts, Mary Emma, Miss
Dates unknown
Location: 409 E. 16th St., Minneapolis (1906); 14 E. 51st St. (1914–32)
Role(s): Artist, Officer, Member
Medium: Basketry, Watercolor
Affiliations: Handicraft Guild, Minnesota State Art Society, Minneapolis Arts & Crafts Society
Comments: 1890s—Artist; 1898—Teacher; 1906—MSAS Juror; 1908—HG Instructor in Watercolor; 1915–17—HG Lecturer; 1905–17—Handicraft Guild president. Founder of the Handicraft Guild. Supervisor of the Drawing at the Minneapolis Public Schools (24 years); and author of several textbooks.

Robertson, Victor, Mrs.
Dates unknown
Location: 554 Portland Av., St. Paul (1907)
Role(s): Artist, Officer, Member
Medium: Bookbinding
Affiliations: Art Workers' Guild of St. Paul
Comments: 1906—Gave Talk on Bookbinding to AWGSP; 1908—SPIAS Sec.

Robinson, Bessie
Dates unknown
Role(s): Artist
Medium: Pottery
Affiliations: St. Paul Institute School of Art

Rochester State Hospital
Dates unknown
Location: Rochester, Minnesota
Medium: Handicraft

Roepke, Otto
Dates unknown
Role(s): Artist
Medium: Woodcarving
Comments: Affiliated with Central High School, Minneapolis

Rogers, Edna Caro
Dates unknown
Location: 2729 Bryant Av. S., Minneapolis (1913)
Role(s): Artist, Student
Medium: Wood Blocking, Decorative Landscape, Design for Tapestry
Affiliations: Minneapolis School of Art

Rogers, George Jacob
Dates unknown
Location: Nicollet & Ninth, Minneapolis (1917)
Role(s): Artist
Medium: Photography

Roiger, Frances
Dates unknown
Location: 808 Willow St., Mankato (1914)
Role(s): Artist
Medium: Lace
Comments: 1914—MSAS 2nd place Lace

Rollins, Alice
Dates unknown
Location: 520 E. 14th St., Minneapolis (1903)
Role(s): Artist
Medium: Basketry

Romieux, Magdeleine, Miss
Dates unknown
Location: Minneapolis; 1222 E. 4th St., Duluth,

Minnesota (1908); 813½ East 4th St., Duluth (1909)
Role(s): Artist
Medium: Art Handicraft, Embroidery, Lace
Affiliations: Handicraft Workers
Comments: 1909—MSAS Prize

Rosenkranz, C. S. (C. C.)
Dates unknown
Location: 7 W. Superior St., Duluth (1912, 1915, 1917); Duluth (1916)
Role(s): Artist
Medium: Painting
Affiliations: Duluth Art Association
Comments: 1916—SPIAS Exhibitor

Rosland, Lillian S.
Dates unknown
Location: 216 13th St., St. Paul (1905, 1906)
Role(s): Artist
Medium: Textile Design

Rost, Antoinette A.
Dates unknown
Location: 5250 Penn Av., Minneapolis (1917)
Role(s): Artist
Medium: Weaving
Comments: 1917—MSAC 1st place Weaving

Rounce, Esther, Miss
Dates unknown
Location: 536 Boston Block, Minneapolis (1904–5)
Role(s): Artist, Teacher, Student
Medium: Art Handicraft, Embroidery, Design, Book Plates
Affiliations: Minneapolis Society of Fine Arts, Minneapolis School of Fine Arts, Minneapolis Arts & Crafts Society
Comments: 1905—MSAS Prize

Rubins, Winfield
Dates unknown
Location: 1812 3rd Av. S., Minneapolis, (1904, 1905)
Role(s): Artist
Medium: Painting, Metal Working/Woodworking?
Comments: 1905, 1906—MSAS Prize; MSFA 1913 lists W. H. Rubins

Rye, Archie
Dates unknown
Role(s): Artist
Medium: Woodcarving
Comments: Affiliated with Central High School, Minneapolis

Sandy, Winifred Davis
Dates unknown
Location: 3032 James Av. S., Minneapolis (1913); 3137 James Av. S., Minneapolis (1914)
Role(s): Artist
Medium: Ceramics, China Painting
Affiliations: Twin City Porcelain and Keramic Club

Sasse, Fred
Dates unknown
Role(s): Student
Medium: Design
Affiliations: St. Paul Art Gallery, St. Paul Institute of Art, St. Paul Institute of Arts & Sciences
Comments: 1915—SPIAS Student

Schibsby, Fanny Marie
Dates unknown
Location: 2008 3rd Av. S., Minneapolis (1914); 2107 Pleasant Av., Minneapolis (1917)
Role(s): Artist, Student
Medium: Stenciling
Affiliations: Minneapolis School of Art
Comments: 1914—MSAS Prize; 1917—Graduated from MSA, MSAC 1st place Stencil

Schlimme, John F.

Dates unknown
Location: 3418 Park Av., Minneapolis (1917)
Role(s): Artist
Medium: Photography

Schlimme, Lucille (Lucile)
Dates unknown
Location: 3418 Park Av., Minneapolis (1915)
Role(s): Artist, Student
Medium: Embroidery
Affiliations: Minneapolis School of Art
Comments: 1917—Graduated from MSA Applied Arts Dept.

Schmidt, Margaret, Miss
Dates unknown
Role(s): Artist
Medium: Textile Design
Affiliations: St. Paul Institute

Schnee, Cora, Mrs.
Dates unknown
Location: 340 E. 22nd, Minneapolis (1912)
Role(s): Artist
Medium: Textiles

School for Feeble Minded and Colony for Epileptics
Dates unknown
Location: Faribault, Minnesota (1913)
Role(s): Artist
Medium: Basketry, Textiles, Ceramics, Metal Working

School for The Blind
Dates unknown
Location: Faribault
Role(s): Artist
Medium: Textiles

Scovel, Mary C.
Dates unknown
Location: Minneapolis
Role(s): Teacher
Affiliations: Handicraft Guild
Comments: 1906–7—Taught at AIC Normal Art School; 1912–13—Instructor HG; 1914–15—HG Principal (Director); Graduate of Pratt Institute Normal Dept.

Scrugham, Elizabeth
Dates unknown
Location: 2107 Aldrich Av. S., Minneapolis (1915)
Role(s): Student
Affiliations: Minneapolis School of Art
Comments: 1917—Graduated from MSA Applied Arts Dept.

Sedgwick, Jr., Charles S.
Dates unknown
Location: Minneapolis
Role(s): Student, Artist
Medium: Poster
Affiliations: Minneapolis Society of Fine Arts

Seeley, Arthur
Dates unknown
Role(s): Artist
Medium: Woodcarving
Comments: Affiliated with Central High School, Minneapolis

Seidel, Emory P.
Dates unknown
Location: St. Paul (1910); McClurg Bldg., Chicago, Il (1912, 1914)
Role(s): Artist
Medium: Sculpture
Comments: 1910—MSAS Honorable Mention

Sewall, Samuel, Mrs.
Dates unknown
Location: 224 Ridgeway Av., Minneapolis (1913)

Role(s): Member, Officer
Medium: Handicraft, Industrial Art
Affiliations: Minnesota State Art Society, The Woman's Club of Minneapolis
Comments: 1912—MSAS Exhibit Committee, MSAS Juror

Sewell, Samuel
Dates unknown
Role(s): Artist
Medium: Vase
Affiliations: Handicraft Guild

Seymour, Robert M., Mrs.
Dates unknown
Location: 326 E. Superior St., Duluth (1912)
Role(s): Member
Affiliations: Minnesota State Art Society, St. Paul Institute of Arts & Science, Duluth Art Association
Comments: 1905—MSAS Board; 1908, 1909—MSAS Exhibit Committee; 1911, 1912—MSAS Extension Committee; 1916—SPIAS Committee Member

Sheardown, Margaret, Miss
Dates unknown
Location: 926 2nd Av. S., Minneapolis
Role(s): Student, Artist, Member
Medium: Copper, Leather
Affiliations: Handicraft Guild, Minneapolis Arts & Crafts Society
Comments: 1903–26—Teacher at South High School; 1907—SA&C, Boston Exhibitor; 1908—Studio in HG Building; 1914—Leatherworker at HG; 1917—Taught Manual Arts at South High School, Minneapolis

Shedorsky, Sarah
Dates unknown
Role(s): Artist
Medium: Pottery
Affiliations: St. Paul Institute School of Art

Sherman, Martha
Dates unknown
Location: Winona, Minnesota (1905–06)
Role(s): Student
Affiliations: Art Institute of Chicago
Comments: 1905–6—Student at AIC "Normal Art School"

Siewert, A. B., Mr.
Dates unknown
Role(s): Member
Affiliations: Duluth Art Association
Comments: Founding Member of Duluth Art Association

Siewert, A. B., Mrs.
Dates unknown
Role(s): Member
Affiliations: Duluth Art Association
Comments: Founding Member of Duluth Art Association

Silberstein, E. A., Mr.
Dates unknown
Role(s): Member
Affiliations: Duluth Art Association
Comments: Founding Member of Duluth Art Association

Simonds, Edith
Dates unknown
Location: Minneapolis (1914)
Role(s): Student
Affiliations: Handicraft Guild
Comments: 1914—Scholarship from Women's Club during her junior year at HG

Simpson, Mary E., Miss
Dates unknown

Mary E. Simpson. Minnesota State Art Society Exhibit Catalog, 1903 and 1904, p. 55.

Location: 1512 Laurel Av., Minneapolis (1904–5); 26 N. 16th St., Minneapolis (1906, 1914)
Role(s): Artist, Teacher, Member, Student
Medium: Art Handicraft, Metal Working, Painting
Affiliations: Minneapolis Society of Arts and Crafts, Minneapolis School of Fine Arts, Minneapolis Art School, Chalk & Chisel Club, Minneapolis School of Art
Comments: MSAS 1903/04—Bio; 1904, 1905—MSAS Prize; Charter Member of Chalk & Chisel

Sjodahl, Nels, Mrs.
Dates unknown
Location: Wayzata, Minnesota (1915)
Role(s): Artist
Medium: Textiles

Skinner, L. J.
Dates unknown
Location: 1915 Hennepin Av., Minneapolis (1908)
Role(s): Artist
Medium: Photography

Sloan, Marion W.
Dates unknown
Location: Winona (1905)
Role(s): Artist
Medium: Basketry

Smith, Clarence D.
Dates unknown
Role(s): Artist
Medium: Textiles

Smith, Gertrude
Dates unknown
Role(s): Artist
Medium: Jewelry
Affiliations: Handicraft Guild

Smith, H. F., Mrs.
Dates unknown
Location: 1410 Willow St. (1913)
Role(s): Artist
Medium: Macrame

Smith, Helen, Miss

Dates unknown
Location: Hotel Summers (1906)
Role(s): Artist, Member
Medium: Metalwork
Affiliations: Minneapolis Arts & Crafts Society, Handicraft Guild
Comments: MSA List of Students 1905–6 lists Helen H. Smith, Minneapolis, as Saturday Night Student

Smith, Mamie A. M., Miss
Dates unknown
Location: 201 W. 7th St., St. Paul (1905)
Role(s): Artist, Student
Medium: Design, Tile
Affiliations: Minneapolis School of Fine Arts

Smith, May Marsh, Miss
Dates unknown
Location: 2239 Gordon Av., St. Anthony Park (1906)
Role(s): Artist, Officer, Member
Medium: Printing, Bookbinding
Affiliations: Minneapolis Arts & Crafts Society, Minneapolis School of Fine Arts
Comments: 1912–15—Partner with Mary Moulton Cheney in Artcraft shop. Studied at MSFA and privately with Robert Koehler, Elisabeth Chant and Margarethe Heisser.

Smith, Xamieve, Miss
Dates unknown
Location: 1110 Plymouth Av. N., Minneapolis (1906)
Role(s): Artist, Member
Affiliations: Minneapolis Arts & Crafts Society

Snook, Florence Elizabeth, Miss
Dates unknown
Location: 3110 Fremont Av. S. Minneapolis (1904); 3013 Aldrich Av. S., Minneapolis (1904, 1906); 425 Auditorium Bldg. Minneapolis (1906)
Role(s): Artist, Student, Teacher, Member
Medium: Drawing, Metal Working, Design, Illumination
Affiliations: Minneapolis School of Fine Arts, Minneapolis Arts & Crafts Society, Minneapolis School of Art
Comments: 1904, 1906—MSAS Prize; 1905–6—MSFA Asst. Instructor of Decorative Design; 1906—A&CS Ad, Designer for Artcraft Shop, Minneapolis

Snyder, Corydon G.
Dates unknown
Role(s): Teacher
Medium: Fashion Design
Affiliations: St. Paul Institute of Arts & Sciences

Sole, Caspara P.
Dates unknown
Location: Marshall, Minnesota (1905–06); St. Paul (1915)
Role(s): Student
Medium: Design, Monograms
Affiliations: Minneapolis School of Fine Arts, Minneapolis School of Art
Comments: 1914—Clerk at Haynes Photo Studio

Somes, Dora
Dates unknown
Location: Minneapolis (1905–6)
Role(s): Student
Medium: Design
Affiliations: Minneapolis School of Fine Arts, Minneapolis School of Art

Sorter, A. L., Mrs.
Dates unknown
Location: Minneapolis (1905–6, 1913)
Role(s): Artist, Student
Medium: Painting
Affiliations: Minneapolis School of Art

Soulen, Harvey H.
Dates unknown
Role(s): Artist
Medium: Wood Working

South, Helen
Dates unknown
Location: Black Duck, Minnesota (1914)
Role(s): Student
Affiliations: Handicraft Guild
Comments: 1914—Scholarship from Women's
   Club her junior year at HG

Sparrow, Kate, Miss
Dates unknown
Location: Mankato, Minnesota (1911)
Role(s): Artist, Student
Medium: Art Handicraft
Affiliations: Handicraft Guild
Comments: 1895—Student at Normal School;
   1897–1925—Instructor at State (Normal School)
   Teachers College; 1906—MSAS Prize; 1927–
   28—Moved to Rochester, Minnesota

Sperry, Ernest D. L., Mrs.
Dates unknown
Location: 2163 Iglehart Av., St. Paul (1913)
Role(s): Artist
Medium: Ceramics
Affiliations: Twin City Porcelain and Keramic
   Club, St. Paul Institute School of Art

Spettel, Gertrude
Dates unknown
Role(s): Student, Artist
Affiliations: Handicraft Guild
Comments: 1896–1946—St. Paul Seamstress and
   Dressmaker, who worked with her sisters; a hand-
   wrought copper candle holder donated by her is
   in MHS Collections

Spilkman, Bertha
Dates unknown
Location: Winona, Minnesota
Role(s): Student, Artist, Teacher
Affiliations: Handicraft Guild

Spink, James L.
Dates unknown
Location: 303 S. 9th, Minnesota (1901–2); Big
   Lake, Minnesota (1904)
Role(s): Artist
Medium: Illumination
Comments: 1904—Detroit Soc. of A&C Exhibitor

Spink, Louise, Miss
Dates unknown
Location: Minneapolis (1903/04); Big Lake, Minne-
   sota (1905)
Role(s): Artist
Medium: Metal

Spink, Marie Louise
Dates unknown
Location: 500 S. 8th St., Minneapolis (1904)
Role(s): Artist, Student
Medium: Design, Illumination, Book Cover
Affiliations: Minneapolis School of Fine Arts

St. Joseph's Academy
Dates unknown
Location: 314 Houston Av., Crookston, Minne-
   sota (1914)
Medium: Embroidery

St. Margaret's Academy Day School for Girls

Dates unknown
Location: Minneapolis
Comments: Art and Music Courses

Stair, Ruth
Dates unknown
Role(s): Student, Artist
Medium: Copper
Affiliations: Handicraft Guild

Stark, Laura G.
Dates unknown
Location: Two Harbors, Minnesota (1905–06)
Role(s): Artist, Student
Medium: Woodworking
Affiliations: Minneapolis School of Art

Starr, Mary G.
Dates unknown
Location: Excelsior, Minnesota
Role(s): Artist
Medium: Kodak Book

Starr, Ruth M.
Dates unknown
Location: 2317 Aldrich Av. S., Minneapolis (1908)
Role(s): Student, Artist
Medium: Metal Working
Affiliations: Handicraft Guild
Comments: 1905–7—Student; 1908—Made piece
   designed by Ethel Brill for MSAS Exhibit

Stebbins, George W.
Dates unknown
Role(s): Artist
Medium: Design

Stebbins, Mary S.
Dates unknown
Medium: Jewelry
Affiliations: Handicraft Guild

Stebbins, Vera
Dates unknown
Role(s): Student
Medium: Design
Affiliations: Minneapolis School of Fine Arts

Stedman, Nada
Dates unknown
Role(s): Artist
Medium: Glass

Steele, Jessie Grant, Miss
Dates unknown
Location: 335½ E. Winifred, St. Paul (1904)
Role(s): Member, Student
Affiliations: Art Workers' Guild of St. Paul, Minne-
   sota State Art Society, St. Paul Institute of Arts
   & Sciences
Comments: 1894–98—SPIAS Student; 1904—
   Artist

Steele, Rowena
Dates unknown
Role(s): Student
Medium: Textile Design
Affiliations: St. Paul Institute
Comments: 1913—SPI Student

Sterrett, Lavinia, Miss
Dates unknown
Location: 2309 Girard Av. S., Minneapolis (1906)
Role(s): Member
Affiliations: Minneapolis Arts & Crafts Society
Comments: Newspaper Reporter and Art Commen-
   tator at *Minneapolis Journal*

Stevens, James V.
Dates unknown
Role(s): Member
Affiliations: Art Workers' Guild of St. Paul
Comments: Stevens & Robertson Art Store at 62 E.
   6th, St. Paul

Stevens, Janet
Dates unknown
Location: 1929 Humboldt Av., Minneapolis (1906)
Role(s): Artist
Medium: Leather

Stevens, Jeanette
Dates unknown
Location: Faribault
Role(s): Student, Artist
Affiliations: Handicraft Guild

Steward, Maud(e) H.
Dates unknown
Location: 812 Delaware St. S.E., Minneapolis
   (1903); 38 Oak St. S.E., Minneapolis (1904); 328
   Oak St. SE, Minneapolis (1905).
Role(s): Artist
Medium: Design, Metal
Comments: 1903—Student at U of M

Stewart, Clarence B.
Dates unknown
Location: Munger Terrace, Duluth, Minnesota
   (1904)
Role(s): Artist
Medium: Cabinet

Stickney, A. B.
Dates unknown
Location: Metropolitan Bldg., St. Paul (1914)
Role(s): Board Member, Artist
Medium: Landscape Architect
Affiliations: St. Paul Institute of Arts & Sciences

Stoner, C. V., Mrs.
Dates unknown
Location: 123 Summit Av., St. Paul (1908)
Role(s): Artist
Medium: Ceramics

Storrs, Caryl B., Dr.
Dates unknown
Location: Minneapolis (1912–13)
Affiliations: Handicraft Guild
Comments: 1912–13—HG Lecturer; Music and
   Drama Critic, *Minneapolis Tribune.*

Streed, Hilda M.
Dates unknown
Location: 2547 25th Av. S., Minneapolis (1908)
Role(s): Artist
Medium: Stenciling, Embroidery

Stringham, Josephine Ann
Dates unknown
Role(s): Teacher
Medium: Music
Affiliations: Handicraft Guild
Comments: Assistant Supervisor of Music in Min-
   neapolis Public Schools

Strong, A. W., Mrs.
Dates unknown
Role(s): Student
Medium: Ceramics
Affiliations: Handicraft Guild

Strong, Frances
Dates unknown
Role(s): Teacher
Medium: Handwork
Affiliations: Arts Guild of St. Paul
Comments: 1908—AGSP Summer Session Teacher
   of Handwork; Instructor of Handwork in Teach-
   ers' Training School, St. Paul

Strunk, Herbert J.
Dates unknown
Location: Shakopee (1912, 1915)
Role(s): Student
Medium: Sculpture, Illustration
Affiliations: St. Paul Institute of Arts & Sciences

Sweet Brothers photographic studio, waiting room, 1903. Photograph courtesy of the Minnesota Historical Society.

Advertisement for the Teco Inn, The Radisson Hotel, Minneapolis. The Minnesotan 1, *no. 10 (May 1916).*

Comments: 1913—MSAS Prize

Suffel, F. H., Mrs.
Dates unknown
Role(s): Student
Medium: Ceramics
Affiliations: Handicraft Guild

Sullwold, H. A.
Dates unknown
Role(s): Artist
Medium: Reading Lamp
Affiliations: St. Paul Institute

Sutton, Jennie, Mrs.
Dates unknown
Location: 312 W. University St., St. Paul
Role(s): Artist
Medium: Textiles

Swanson, E. D., Mrs.
Dates unknown
Location: 901 Chicago Av., Minneapolis (1915)
Role(s): Artist
Medium: Textiles

Swanwick, Aline J.
Dates unknown
Role(s): Student
Medium: Design
Affiliations: St. Paul Institute of Art

Sweet Bros. Photographic Studio
1897–1930
Location: Syndicate Arcade, Minneapolis (1897, 1905); 515 Nicollet Av., Minneapolis (1908)
Medium: Photography
Comments: 1906—MSAS 1st Place Photography; Art Photo Studio and Photographic Images for the Minneapolis periodical *The Bellman.* Operated by Louis and Frank Sweet. Louis designed the Arts and Crafts–style studio gallery and waiting rooms, "one of the cities' show places."

Swenson, Agnes
Dates unknown
Location: Minneapolis
Role(s): Student
Affiliations: Handicraft Guild

Swenson, David F.
Dates unknown

Location: Minneapolis (1912–13)
Role(s): Teacher
Affiliations: Handicraft Guild
Comments: 1894–98—Student at U of M; 1899–1939—Professor of Philosophy at U of M

Swinburne, Bessie
Dates unknown
Location: 4910 39th Av. S., Minnehaha Park, Minneapolis (1904)
Role(s): Student
Medium: Design
Affiliations: Minneapolis School of Fine Arts

Switzer, Myrtle M.
Dates unknown
Location: 1110 5th St. S.E., Minneapolis (1915)
Role(s): Artist
Medium: Jewelry

Sykes, Edith
Dates unknown
Role(s): Student
Medium: Painting, Weaving, Printing
Affiliations: St. Paul Institute of Arts & Sciences
Comments: SPIAS 1912–14 Student

Taflinger, Elmer E.
Dates unknown
Role(s): Teacher
Medium: Mural Painting, Illustration, Life Drawing
Affiliations: Minneapolis School of Art
Comments: 1914–22—Art Director and European Representative for David Belasco; 1925–26—Instructor in Mural Painting, Illustration, and Life Drawing at the Minneapolis School of Art; Pupil of George B. Bridgman, The Art Students League of New York, Frank Vincent Du Mond, Dean Cornwell, Otto Stark, and Ernest M. Gros

Tanner, Ruth M.
Dates unknown
Location: Minneapolis (1915)
Role(s): Teacher, Student
Affiliations: Minneapolis Society of Fine Arts, Minneapolis School of Art
Comments: 1913–14—MIA 1st Year Student in Design

Tateibaumey, M., Mrs.
Dates unknown

Role(s): Artist
Medium: Textiles
Comments: 1912—MSAS piece entered by Harry L. Altman, U of M

Tautges, Louise, Miss
Dates unknown
Location: 2631 Grand Av. S., Minneapolis (1906)
Role(s): Student, Artist
Medium: Copper, Leather
Affiliations: Handicraft Guild, Minneapolis Arts & Crafts Society
Comments: 1906—MSAS Prize, HG Designer; 1909—Teacher; 1911—Artist at G. E. Buzza; 1917–26—Teacher at Sheridan School

Teco Inn
Dates unknown
Comments: One of three cafés in Radisson Hotel, Minneapolis

Thoften, Ole
Dates unknown
Location: 1512 19th St. E., Minneapolis (1913)
Role(s): Student
Medium: Wallpaper Design

Thomas, Alice
Dates unknown
Role(s): Artist
Medium: Metal Working, Jewelry
Affiliations: Handicraft Guild

Thomas, Jr., Frederick F.
Dates unknown
Role(s): Artist
Medium: Illumination
Comments: 1910—Executed design by Wm. Gray Purcell for MSAS Exhibit

Thompson, C. R., Mrs.
Dates unknown
Location: Worthington
Role(s): Artist
Medium: Macrame

Thompson, William E., Mrs.
Dates unknown
Location: Hamline (1904–5); 879 Pascal Av., St. Paul (1912)
Role(s): Member
Affiliations: Minnesota State Art Society, Art Work-

ers' Guild of St. Paul
Comments: 1904, 1905—MSAS Secretary/Treasurer; 1911, 1912—MSAS Extension Committee

Thulin, Otto Edward
Dates unknown
Location: 257 W. 3rd St., St. Paul (1904)
Role(s): Artist
Medium: Design

Tice, Ruth Wilson, Mrs.
Dates unknown
Location: 2435 Pillsbury Av., Minneapolis (1903–4, 1906)
Role(s): Teacher, Member
Medium: Ceramics, China Painting
Affiliations: Minneapolis Arts & Crafts Society, Minneapolis School of Fine Arts, Chalk & Chisel Club

Tinsley, Laura Rollins, Mrs.
Dates unknown
Location: Minneapolis
Comments: Came to Minneapolis in 1860 and taught in public schools. Founder of Industrial Education in grade schools of Minneapolis. Published *Practical and Artistic Basketry* (1904). Married name—Mrs. G. W. Tinsley.

Todd, C. E., Mrs.
Dates unknown
Location: 3805 10th Av. S., Minneapolis (1910)
Role(s): Artist
Medium: Textiles

Todd, Ethel
Dates unknown
Role(s): Student, Artist, Teacher
Affiliations: Handicraft Guild

Todd, Louise
Dates unknown
Role(s): Student, Artist
Affiliations: Handicraft Guild

Todd, Mattie Phipps
Dates unknown
Medium: Weaving
Comments: Author of "Hand-loom Weaving"

Todd, Nell Margaret, Miss
Dates unknown
Location: Minneapolis (1905–6, 1913)
Role(s): Teacher, Student
Medium: Design, Watercolors
Affiliations: Minneapolis Society of Fine Arts, Minneapolis School of Art
Comments: Studied Art at MSFA; Received Chase Scholarship to New York School of Art. Studied under Arthur W. Dow. Taught clases in pratical design and various crafts at MSA.

Tollefson, Tillie, Mrs.
Dates unknown
Location: 105 E. 15th St., Minneapolis (1914)
Role(s): Artist
Medium: Textiles, Embroidery
Comments: 1914—MSAS 2nd place Embroidery

Tomlinson, J. H., Mrs.
Dates unknown
Location: St. Peter, Minnesota (1908, 1912)
Role(s): Member
Affiliations: Minnesota State Art Society
Comments: 1908—MSAS Membership Committee; 1912—Gave talk on Handicraft to MSAS

Towle, Louise
Dates unknown
Role(s): Artist
Medium: Candle shades
Affiliations: Handicraft Guild
Comments: 1908—Made shades designed by Flor-

ence D. Willets for MSAS Exhibit

Traxler, Hazel A.
Dates unknown
Location: 225 W. 24th St., Minneapolis (1914–15)
Role(s): Artist, Student
Medium: Book Plates, Stenciling, Design
Affiliations: Minneapolis Society of Fine Arts, Minneapolis School of Art
Comments: 1913–14—MIA 3rd Year Student, ½ Yr. Scholarship; 1914—MSAS Prize

Treadwell, S. Lydia
Dates unknown
Location: 45 S. Milton St., St. Paul (1915); 201 Goodrich Av., St. Paul (1917)
Role(s): Artist, Student
Medium: Etching, Design, Painting
Affiliations: St. Paul Institute of Arts & Sciences
Comments: 1914—SPIAS Student, MSAS Honorable Mention

Truesdell, Ellen B.
Dates unknown
Role(s): Artist
Medium: Metal Working
Affiliations: Handicraft Guild

Trufant, Nellie Stinson, Miss
Dates unknown
Location: 2614 Clinton Av., Minneapolis (1903–4, 1906)
Role(s): Teacher, Member
Medium: Publishing, Metalworking, Design
Affiliations: Handicraft Guild, Chalk & Chisel Club, Minneapolis Arts & Crafts Society
Comments: 1892–96—Student at U of M; 1895—Founding member of Chalk & Chisel Club; 1898–1903—Instructor at U of M; 1905–7—Teacher at North High School; 1910–13—Designer; 1912–17—Instructor at HG; 1914–40—Teacher at Central High School (Drafting); 1917—Instructor in Manual Training at Central High School, Minneapolis; Pupil of Arthur W. Dow, Ernest A. Batchelder, and James Parton Haney; her personal paper at Minneapolis Public library is a primary source for origins of Chalk and Chisel Club.

Tubesing, Walter
Dates unknown
Location: 714 Ashland Av., St. Paul (1917)
Role(s): Artist, Member
Medium: Tempora
Affiliations: Attic Club
Comments: 1915—Attic Club Exhibitor

Tuohy, E. L., Mrs.
Dates unknown
Role(s): Member
Affiliations: Duluth Art Association
Comments: Founding Member of Duluth Art Association

Tupper, Emily
Dates unknown
Location: Minneapolis
Role(s): Teacher
Affiliations: Handicraft Guild
Comments: 1909–10—Student at HG (Classmate of Gladys Pattee); 1914–17—HG Instructor; 1922–28 (31)—Teacher at Northrop Collegiate School for Girls; Graduate of Handicraft Guild Normal Art Department

Tusler, Hazel
Dates unknown
Location: 900 Laurel Av., St. Paul (1907, 1908)
Role(s): Artist
Medium: Jewelry
Affiliations: Handicraft Guild

Tuthill, Geo. P.
Dates unknown
Location: 713 Lincoln Av., St. Paul (1908)
Role(s): Artist
Medium: Photography

Udell, Elizabeth
Dates unknown
Role(s): Student
Medium: Textiles
Affiliations: St. Paul Institute
Comments: 1912—Honorable Mention MSAS Student Competition

Ueland, Andreas, Mrs.
Dates unknown
Location: Calhoun Blvd., Minneapolis (1913)
Role(s): Board Member, Member
Affiliations: Minnesota State Art Society, The Woman's Club of Minneapolis
Comments: 1910—MSAS Exhibit Committee; 1912—MSAS Board, MSAS Juror, MSAS Exhibit Committee; 1914—MSAS Treasurer; 1917—MSAC Representative

Ueland, Clara
Dates unknown
Role(s): Member
Affiliations: Minnesota State Art Society
Comments: 1912—Chair of MSAS Handicraft Committee

Ueland, Elsa
Dates unknown
Role(s): Artist, Student
Medium: Ceramics
Affiliations: Handicraft Guild
Comments: 1906–07—Student

Upson, Arthur Wheelock
1877–1908
Comments: 1898–90, 1900–1902—Studied at U of M; 1902—Became an Associate of Edmund D. Brooks, Bookseller; 1906—Taught English at U of M; Poet whose published works included "The Sign of the Harp"; "The City" (1904 Printing decorated and illuminated by Mary Moulton Cheney); "Poems"; "The Collected Poems of Arthur Upson" (Published by Edmund D. Brooks); "Norton Northrup" (Published by Edmund D. Brooks); "Westwind Songs" (Published by Edmund D. Brooks); and "Octaves in an English Garden" (Lettered and illuminated by Margarethe Heisser)

Van Leshout, Alexander J.
Dates unknown
Role(s): Teacher
Medium: Illustration
Affiliations: St. Paul Institute of Arts & Sciences

Van Soelen, Theodore
Dates unknown
Location: 1019 Western Av. N., St. Paul (1915)
Role(s): Student
Medium: Painting
Affiliations: St. Paul Institute of Arts & Sciences

Vittum, Percy, Mrs.
Dates unknown
Location: 241 Prescott St., St. Paul (1908)
Role(s): Artist
Medium: Ceramics

Volk, Douglas
Dates unknown
Location: Center Lovell, Me (1893); New York City (1922)
Role(s): Officer, Teacher
Affiliations: Minneapolis Society of Fine Arts
Comments: 1886–93—Director of The Minneapo-

lis School of Fine Arts; Trained in The Ecole Des Beaux Arts of France and for Four Years under Gerome

Von Schlegell, Arthur, Mrs.
Dates unknown
Location: 2002 2nd Av. S., Minneapolis (1903)
Role(s): Artist
Medium: Basketry

Von Tresckow, E. C. M., Miss
Dates unknown
Location: 719 Portland Av., St. Paul
Role(s): Artist
Medium: Needlework

Vrooman, A. L., Mrs.
Dates unknown
Location: 7 6th St. S., Minneapolis (1903)
Medium: Leatherwork

Vysekal, I. G.
Dates unknown
Role(s): Artist
Medium: Screen
Affiliations: St. Paul Institute

Wade, Fern
Dates unknown
Location: Fairmount
Role(s): Student
Affiliations: Handicraft Guild

Wadsworth, Katharine

Dates unknown
Role(s): Artist
Medium: Glass, Stenciling

Wagner, Else
Dates unknown
Location: St. Paul
Role(s): Artist
Medium: Pottery

Wales, Annette, Miss
Dates unknown
Location: Minneapolis
Role(s): Artist, Student
Medium: Ceramics
Affiliations: Handicraft Guild
Comments: 1905—Teacher at Central High School; 1906—Student, MSAS Prize; 1911—Designer for Winifred Cole in HG

Wales, Florence, Miss
Dates unknown
Location: 926 2nd Av. S., Minneapolis (1906); 89 S. 10th St., Minneapolis (1913); 48 E. 13th Street, Minneapolis (1917)
Role(s): Officer, Member
Medium: Watercolors
Affiliations: Handicraft Guild, Minneapolis Arts & Crafts Society, The Woman's Club of Minneapolis
Comments: 1894–96—Artist; 1898–1904—Art teacher at Central High School; 1905—MSAS

Juror, HG Vice President; 1906–18—HG Secretary/Treasurer, HG President; Assistant Art Supervisor in the Minneapolis public schools.

Walker, May Sarah
Dates unknown
Location: 3154 15th Av. S., Minneapolis (1914–15)
Role(s): Artist, Student
Medium: Stenciling Embroidery, Design
Affiliations: Minneapolis School of Fine Arts, Minneapolis School of Art
Comments: 1913–14—MIA 1st Year Student in Design

Walsh, Marie P.
Dates unknown
Role(s): Artist
Medium: Jewelry
Affiliations: Handicraft Guild

Walsh, S. B., Mrs.
Dates unknown
Location: 521 Ashland Av., St. Paul
Role(s): Artist
Medium: Jewelry

Walters, C. A.
Dates unknown
Location: Ft. Madison, Ia (1905–6); 26 S. 13th St., Minneapolis (1912)
Role(s): Artist, Student
Medium: Painting
Affiliations: Minneapolis School of Art

Arthur Wheellock Upson. The Collected Poems of Arthur Upson, *vol. 1, 1909.*

Amy Robbins Ware. Who's Who among Minnesota Women, *1924, p. 272.*

Walton, Nellie
Dates unknown
Role(s): Artist
Medium: Candlestick, Plate
Affiliations: Handicraft Guild

Wang, A. M., Mrs.
Dates unknown
Location: 1517 Stevens Av., Minneapolis (1908)
Role(s): Artist
Medium: Photography

Ware, Amy Robbins, Mrs.
1877 – 1929
Location: 3900 Crystal Lake Av., Robbinsdale, Minnesota (1917)
Role(s): Student
Medium: Crochet
Affiliations: Handicraft Guild
Comments: 1905–6—Attended HG Summer School; 1907—MA from U of M; 1908—Founded The Orchardcrafts Guild at Her Home in Robbinsdale; 1913–14—Studied Handicrafts in Europe; 1917—MSAC 1st Place Crochet; Taught in Army Schools after 1914. Maiden name—Amy Robbins. Married name—Mrs. John Roland Ware.

Ware, Ella
Dates unknown
Role(s): Artist
Medium: Pottery
Affiliations: St. Paul Institute School of Art

Warner, A. L., Mr.
Dates unknown

Gustav F. Weber. Photograph courtesy of G. F. Weber Studios, Inc.

Role(s): Member
Affiliations: Duluth Art Association
Comments: Founding Member of Duluth Art Association

Warner, Lenore
Dates unknown
Role(s): Student
Medium: Pottery
Affiliations: Handicraft Guild

Watson, Blanche Lockhart, Mrs.
Dates unknown
Role(s): Teacher
Medium: Drawing
Affiliations: Handicraft Guild
Comments: 1915–17—HG Faculty; Trained at The Art Institute, Chicago; former Supervisor of Drawing, Kalamazoo, MI.

Way, Elizabeth S., Mrs.
Dates unknown
Location: 3712 Harriet Av., Minneapolis (1912)
Role(s): Artist
Medium: Crochet

Webb, Judson T.
Dates unknown
Location: Chicago, Il
Role(s): Teacher
Medium: Pottery
Affiliations: Handicraft Guild
Comments: Instructor at Chicago Art Institute

Webber, Margaret
Dates unknown
Location: 236 W. 5th St., St. Paul

Role(s): Artist
Medium: Ceramics
Affiliations: Twin City Porcelain and Keramic Club

Weber, Gustav F.
Dates unknown
Location: Minneapolis
Role(s): Teacher
Medium: Publishing, Interior Design
Affiliations: Handicraft Guild
Comments: 1913–19(21), 1933–38—G. F. Weber Studios; 1914–17—HG Lecturer; 1922–32—Weber-Werness Studios, Inc.; 1939–80s—G. F. Weber Studios, Inc. Affiliated with Wm. French and Co. Student of Industrial Art School, Karlsruhe, and Polytechnical School, Stuttgart, Germany.

Weedell, Hazel Elizabeth, Miss
Dates unknown
Location: 2436 Elliot Ave., Minneapolis (1913); 201 N. Kenwood Av., Austin, Minnesota (1917)
Role(s): Student
Medium: Poster Design, Book Plates, Etching
Affiliations: Handicraft Guild
Comments: 1913—Won Edmund D. Brooks Book Plate Award; 1917—MSAC 2nd Place Etching; HG Graduate

Weingartner, Frank S.
Dates unknown
Location: 2900 29th Av. S., Minneapolis (1912); 2424 Garfield Av. S., Minneapolis (1913)
Role(s): Artist
Medium: Bronze, Wrought Iron
Comments: 1913—Draughtsman at Flour City Ornamental Iron Works, Minneapolis

Wellan, Gladys
Dates unknown
Role(s): Student
Medium: Painted Screen
Affiliations: Minneapolis School of Art
Comments: 1918—Minnesota State Fair Prize

Welles, Harriet, Miss
Dates unknown
Affiliations: Chalk & Chisel Club
Comments: Charter Member Chalk & Chisel Club

Wells, Charles S.
Dates unknown
Location: 203 Reid Corner Bldg., Minneapolis (1915); 3004 Hennepin Av. S., Minneapolis (1917)
Role(s): Teacher, Member
Medium: Sculpture
Affiliations: Minneapolis Society of Fine Arts, Minnesota State Art Society
Comments: 1916–17—HG Lecturer; 1914—MSAS Exhibit Committee; 1917—MSAC 2nd Place Sculpture; Graduate of Pratt Institute

Wells, Martha C. Howard, Mrs.
Dates unknown
Location: 3120 James Av. S., Minneapolis (1917)
Affiliations: Minnesota Federation of Women's Clubs, Minnesota State Art Commission
Comments: 1881—Came to Minneapolis; 1917—Chair of Art Committee, Graduated from Rockford College. Maiden name—Martha C. Howard. Married name—Mrs. Cyrus W. Wells

Welter, P.
Dates unknown
Location: 244 W. Third St., St. Paul
Role(s): Artist
Medium: Wood Working

Wertman, Geo. L., Mrs.
Dates unknown

Martha C. Howard Wells. Who's Who among Minnesota Women, 1924, p. 340.

Cleora Clark Wheeler. University of Minnesota Archives, Walter Library. Photograph courtesy of the University of Minnesota.

Location: 3752 11th Av. S., Minneapolis
Role(s): Artist
Medium: Centerpiece, Embroidery

Weston, J. B., Mrs.
Dates unknown
Role(s): Member
Affiliations: Duluth Art Association
Comments: Founding Member of Duluth Art Association

Weston, J. B., Dr.
Dates unknown
Role(s): Member
Affiliations: Duluth Art Association
Comments: Founding Member of Duluth Art Association

Wheeler, Belle H.
Dates unknown
Location: 510 Tenth Street So., Minneapolis (1902–3)
Role(s): Artist
Medium: Design for Church Window
Affiliations: Art Institute of Chicago
Comments: 1902–3—AIC Distinct Artistic Merit Award

Wheeler, Cleora Clark, Miss
1882–1980

Location: 1376 Summit Av., St. Paul (1912–14)
Role(s): Artist
Medium: Book Plates, Photography, Printing, Poetry
Affiliations: Minnesota State Art Association
Comments: 1903—Graduate of The University of Minnesota With B.A. in English; 1912—Student at The School of Fine and Applied Art, New York City; 1918—Director of The Vocational Bureau for Trained Women, St. Paul. Listed as Artist or Designer intermittently (1914–77); substitute teacher in St. Paul high schools; Designer and Illuminator whose work was published in *The Book of Artists' Own Bookplates*, 1933.

Wheeler, Ethel C., Miss
Dates unknown
Location: Minneapolis (1905–6); 425 Forest Av., Minneapolis (1908); Duluth, Minnesota
Role(s): Artist, Student
Medium: Stenciling, Illumination, Leather, Book Plates, Design
Affiliations: Minneapolis School of Fine Arts, Minneapolis School of Art
Comments: 1907—MSAS Prize; 1909–10—Affiliated with The Craft Shop (Arts and Craft) in The Edison Building, Duluth

Wheelock, Hazel Eleanor
Dates unknown
Location: 1924 Colfax Av. S., Minneapolis
Role(s): Artist
Medium: Textiles, Lamp Shade, Illumination, Tapestry

White, A. M., Mrs.
Dates unknown
Location: 1215 Harmon Pl., Minneapolis (1903)
Role(s): Artist
Medium: Woodcarving

White, Jessie Aline
Dates unknown
Location: Hope, ND (1913); Minneapolis (1913–15)
Role(s): Artist, Student, Teacher
Medium: Design, Painting, Illustration
Affiliations: Minneapolis Society of Fine Arts, Minneapolis School of Art
Comments: 1913–14—MIA 1st Year Student in Design; 1914—Listed as Artist; MSAS 1915 Exhibit Lists Essie A. White, 2411 1st Av. S., Minneapolis, Student, Stenciling

White, Margaret
Dates unknown
Role(s): Student
Medium: design

William Channing Whitney. Minnesota State Art Society Exhibit
Catalog, *1903 and 1904, p. 53.*

Affiliations: Minneapolis School of Art
Comments: 1913–14—MIA Midyear Student

White, Margaret Devoe (M. De V.), Miss
Dates unknown
Location: 4314 Nicollet Av., Minneapolis (1914, 1915)
Role(s): Artist
Medium: Sculpture
Affiliations: Attic Club, Handicraft Guild
Comments: 1917—Officer/Representative of Attic Club, MSAC 1st Place Sculpture

White, Ora Valetta
Dates unknown
Location: 1215 Harmon Pl., Minneapolis (1904), 255 Auditorium Bldg., Minneapolis (1915)
Role(s): Artist, Member
Medium: Ceramics
Affiliations: Twin City Keramic Club
Comments: 1915—Won AIC Atlan Club Prize; 1917—TCKC Vice President

Whitely, J. H.
Dates unknown
Role(s): Member
Affiliations: Duluth Art Association
Comments: Founding Member of Duluth Art Association

Whitford, Adeline, Mrs.
1 November 1865–2 May 1922
Medium: Interior Decoration
Comments: Born in St. Paul studied with Douglas Volk, Ernest Batchelder, and at Chicago and Columbia Universities; prepared lecture for MSAS on "Interior Decoration in the Small Home"; Maiden name—Adeline Boynton; Married name—Mrs. Edmund A. Whitford.

Whitney, Katherine
Dates unknown
Location: Minneapolis
Role(s): Student, Artist
Medium: Ceramics, Leather
Affiliations: Handicraft Guild
Comments: 1906–16—Listed intermittently as Student or Artist at U of M

Whitney, Ray

Dates unknown
Location: 1159 Raymond Av., St. Paul (1917)
Role(s): Artist
Medium: Wood Carving

Whitney, William Channing
Dates unknown
Location: 313 Nicollet Av., Minneapolis (1904); 2514 4th Av. S., Minneapolis (1913–14)
Role(s): Artist, Officer, Member
Medium: Architecture
Affiliations: Minneapolis Society of Fine Arts, Minneapolis Art Committee
Comments: 1904—MSAS Prize; 1914—MSFA Trustee; 1917—President of Art Commission of Minneapolis; Architect for HG Building, 89 S. 10th St., Minneapolis

Whitten, Grace J., Miss
Dates unknown
Location: 1219 E. Lake St., Minneapolis (1903); 1529 E. Lake St., Minneapolis (1906)
Role(s): Artist, Teacher, Member
Medium: Design, Commercial Art, Lettering, Woodcarving
Affiliations: Minneapolis School of Fine Arts, Minneapolis Arts & Crafts Society
Comments: 1903—Teacher at Greeley School, Minneapolis; 1925–26—MSA Instructor of Commercial Art, Design, and Lettering; Studied Design and Normal Art at Pratt Institute. Student of Mary Moulton Cheney, Ralph Helm Johnnot, and Charles W. Hawthorne of Provincetown.

Wiard, Charles L.
Dates unknown
Role(s): Artist
Medium: Applied Arts, China Painting

Wickstrom, Clara L.
Dates unknown
Location: 1499 Gibbs Av., St. Anthony Park, Minnesota (1907)
Role(s): Artist
Medium: Ceramics

Wilcox, Hazel, Miss
Dates unknown
Location: Minneapolis
Role(s): Student
Medium: Jewelry
Affiliations: Minneapolis Society of Fine Arts

Wilde, Frances S., Mrs.
Dates unknown
Location: 500 S. 3rd St., Minneapolis (1906)
Role(s): Artist
Medium: Stained Glass
Comments: 1903—Artist at Pittsburgh Plate Glass Co.; Married Name—Mrs. Thomas V. Wilde

Wilde, S. F.
Dates unknown
Location: Minneapolis (1904)
Role(s): Artist
Medium: Glass Painting

Wiley, G. E.
Dates unknown
Location: 716 4th Av. S., Minneapolis (1908)
Role(s): Artist
Medium: Photography

Wilkerson, Carrie
Dates unknown
Role(s): Artist
Medium: Tile, Bowl

Affiliations: Handicraft Guild

Wilkinson, Ora, Miss
Dates unknown
Location: 1205 26th Av. N., Minneapolis (1906)
Role(s): Artist, Member
Affiliations: Minneapolis Arts & Crafts Society

Willard, Miss
Dates unknown
Location: Minneapolis (1912)
Role(s): Artist
Medium: Leather
Affiliations: Handicraft Guild
Comments: 1912—MSAS Prize; Probably Mary L. Willard, Teacher at West High School, Minneapolis, 1914

Willard, George H.
Dates unknown
Role(s): Artist
Medium: Jewelry
Affiliations: Handicraft Guild

Willets, Florence D., Miss
Dates unknown
Location: 89 10th St. S., Minneapolis; 98 10th St. S., Minneapolis (1914)
Role(s): Teacher, Officer, Artist
Medium: Metal Working, Ceramics, Photography, Jewelry, Pottery
Affiliations: Handicraft Guild
Comments: 1895—Graduate of Chicago Art Institute School; 1905–17—HG Instructor; 1906, 1910, 1914—MSAS Prize; 1907–17—HG Vice President; 1912–17—HG Faculty; 1914–56—Resided with Mary Emma Roberts, listed occasionally during those years as a teacher; 1914–15—HG Registrar; Student of Leon Volkmar.

Williams, Catherine
Dates unknown
Location: 235 Arundel St., St. Paul (1908)
Role(s): Artist
Medium: Jewelry, Metal Working
Comments: Sister to Laura Anne Williams (also in index)

Williams, Elijah H.
Dates unknown
Role(s): Member
Affiliations: Manual Arts Club of Minneapolis
Comments: 1917—MACM Vice President

Williams, Ethel O.
Dates unknown
Location: 727 Carroll St., St. Paul (1908)
Role(s): Artist
Medium: Leather

Williams, Laura A., Miss
?–1944
Location: 235 Arundel St., St. Paul (1907, 1908)
Role(s): Student, Artist, Officer, Teacher, Member
Medium: Copper, Pottery, Metalwork, Design
Affiliations: Art Workers' Guild of St. Paul, Handicraft Guild, Arts Guild of St. Paul
Comments: 1895–99—Taught Art and Music at Austin, Minn. Schools; 1899–1915—Supervisor of Art in St. Paul Public and Normal Schools; 1906—Student, Gave Talk on Craft Work in Schools to AWGSP; 1908—AGSP Summer School Chair of Crafts Committee; 1915?–35—in Charge of Modeling and Pottery Department at Central High School; Born in Watertown, Wisconsin; Attended art schools in Chicago and New York and studied with Arthur Dow; Instructor of Art at U of M summer school sessions.

Williams, Lillian May
Dates unknown

Role(s): Artist
Medium: Design
Affiliations: Minneapolis School of Fine Arts

Willink, Theresa Amelia
Dates unknown
Role(s): Student
Medium: Design
Affiliations: St. Paul Art Gallery, St. Paul Institute of Art

Willis, Sadie, Miss
Dates unknown
Location: Janesville, Minnesota (1912)
Role(s): Student
Affiliations: Minneapolis Society of Fine Arts, Handicraft Guild
Comments: HG Graduate

Wilson, Mary
Dates unknown
Role(s): Artist
Medium: Metalworking
Affiliations: Handicraft Guild

Winn, James H.
1866–?
Location: 40 Howland Block, Chicago, Il (1904); 184 Dearborn St., Chicago (1904–5); Fine Arts Building, Chicago (1907–12); 410 S. Michigan Av., Chicago (1914–17)
Role(s): Artist, Teacher, Member
Medium: Jewelry, Metal Work
Affiliations: Handicraft Guild, Society of Arts & Crafts
Comments: 1904—Exhibitor at Detroit Society of A&C; 1907–12, 1914–17—SA&C,Boston Exhibitor; 1909—Won AIC Arthur Heun Prize; 1910—MSAS Juror; Taught at HG

Winnor, Florence French
Dates unknown
Location: Minneapolis
Role(s): Artist
Medium: Pottery

Wise, Floy E., Miss
Dates unknown
Location: Mankato
Role(s): Artist
Medium: Art Handicraft
Comments: 1906—MSAS Prize

Witter, Nellie
Dates unknown
Role(s): Student, Artist
Affiliations: Handicraft Guild

Wood, Grant
Dates unknown
Role(s): Artist
Medium: Box, Copper, Pine Cone Design
Affiliations: Handicraft Guild
Comments: 1910—HG Student at Ernest Batchelder Summer School; In later years Wood commented that his studies with Batchelder were the most important influence on his life as an artist.

Wood, Stella Louise, Miss
1865–1949
Location: Minneapolis
Role(s): Teacher
Affiliations: Handicraft Guild
Comments: 1896—Came to Minneapolis; 1896–1905—Superintendant of Kindergarten Association Normal School; 1905—Kindergarten Association disbanded and turned school over to Miss Wood who ran it through 1948.; 1912–17—HG Faculty

Woodard (Woodword, Woodward), E., Mr.
Dates unknown
Location: New Orleans
Role(s): Member
Affiliations: Minnesota State Art Society, Newcomb Art School (n.o.)
Comments: 1911, 1912—MSAS Extension Committee

Woodruff, Corice, Mrs.
Dates unknown
Location: 50 Highland Av., Minneapolis (1904, 1906); 2012 James Av. S., Minneapolis (1910–14); 2521 Pillsbury Av., Minneapolis (1913, 1915)
Role(s): Artist, Member, Board Member, Student
Medium: Book Decoration, Sculpture, Modeler, Painting, Design
Affiliations: Handicraft Guild, Minnesota State Art Society, Minneapolis Arts & Crafts Society, Minneapolis School of Art, The Woman's Club of Minneapolis
Comments: 1903, 1904—A&CS Ad; 1910—MSAS

Sculpture Prize; 1910–15—SA&C,Boston Exhibitor; 1911, 1912—MSAS Extension Committee; 1912—MSAS Exhibit Committee; 1916—SPIAS Exhibitor; Home Business Creating Bas Relief, Hand-tinted Plaster of Paris Wall Plaques; Married mane—Mrs. Henry Seymour (Hal) Woodruff

Woods, Lillie M. Sorrenson
Dates unknown
Location: 1754 W. Minnehaha St., St. Paul (1908)
Role(s): Artist
Medium: Book Plate

Workman, David Tice
Dates unknown
Location: 1210 1st Av. N., Minneapolis (1914)
Role(s): Artist
Medium: Etching, Painting
Comments: 1914—MSAS Prize

Wright, Florence E.
1894–September 29, 1983
Role(s): Teacher
Medium: Interior Decoration, Design
Affiliations: Minneapolis School of Art
Comments: 1925–26—at Minneapolis School of Art; Instructor in Interior Decoration, Design, and Color Organization; Graduate of Church School of Art, Chicago; Supervisor of Art at Ames, IA; Instructor at State Teachers College, St. Cloud, MN.

Wyllie, Jos.
Dates unknown
Location: Cathedral Apts. (Apt. 207), Minneapolis (1914)
Role(s): Artist
Medium: Ad Design

Wyman, Oliver C.
Dates unknown
Location: Minneapolis
Comments: President of Minneapolis Wholesale Drygoods Business, Wyman, Partridge & Co.; Client of Edwin H. Hewitt for 1908 residence in

James A. Winn. Jewelry class, instructor Winn standing on left. Catalogue of The Art School of The Art Institute of Chicago, 1921–22. Copyright 1993, The Art Institute of Chicago, all rights reserved.

Corice Woodruff (right). Photograph courtesy of the Minnesota Historical Society.

Osceola, WI known as "Wycroft"; fireplaces and copper fixtures at "Wycroft" by HG.

Young, E. B.
Dates unknown
Role(s): Member, Board Member
Affiliations: Art Workers' Guild of St. Paul, St. Paul Institute of Arts & Sciences
Comments: 1914, 1916—SPIAS Art Committee; 1916—SPIAS Vice Chairman, Chairman of Trustee Art Committee

Young, Rowena
Dates unknown
Role(s): Artist
Medium: Fashion Drawing

Yungbauer, William
Dates unknown
Location: 242 W. 3rd St., St. Paul (1898); 181 W. 4th St., St. Paul (1903–8, 1912)
Role(s): Artist, Board Member, Member
Medium: Furniture, Cabinet Maker
Affiliations: Art Workers' Guild of St. Paul, Minnesota State Art Society, St. Paul Institute of Arts & Sciences
Comments: 1903/04, 1904, 1905—MSAS Board;

1906—MSAS Prize, MSAS Extension Committee, A&CS Ad, Gave Talk to AWGSP on Cabinet Making; 1912—MSAS Extension Committee; 1909, 1912, 1914, 1916—SPIAS Art Committee.

Zeigler (Ziegler), Lee Woodward
Dates unknown
Location: St. Paul (1914, 1916)
Role(s): Teacher, Member, Student, Officer
Medium: Drawing, Painting
Affiliations: St. Paul Institute of Arts & Sciences, Minnesota State Art Society, St. Paul Art Gallery, St. Paul Institute School
Comments: 1911—MSAS Extension Committee; 1912–15—St. Paul Institute School Director; 1912, 1914–16—SPIAS Director; 1914 MSAS Exhibit Committee; 1916—SPIAS Exhibitor

Zlatkowsky, I.
Dates unknown
Role(s): Artist
Medium: Pottery
Comments: 1912—Made Piece Entered by Harry L. Altman, U of M, at MSAS Exhibit

5

Purcell and Elmslie, Architects

Mark Hammons

Gᴇᴏʀɢᴇ Gʀᴀɴᴛ Eʟᴍsʟɪᴇ (1869–1952) ᴀɴᴅ Wɪʟʟɪᴀᴍ Gray Purcell (1880–1965) were two men born to meet the challenge of establishing an indigenous American architecture. One came to America an immigrant from the heaths of Scotland, the other was a son from the third generation of a pioneering American family in the midwestern prairie.[1] Brought together in partnership in the first decade of this century, the application of spiritual truth in the making of buildings and all the attendant objects of life was their common goal. To Purcell and Elmslie, this was the noblest of causes, for the most beautiful of results.

The undertaking was inspired by their pride, common ability, and insight into the time and place in which they lived. Unprecedented achievements had arisen from a political democracy nourished by the ideal of individual freedom. The economic wealth and technological power produced in this new world surpassed all historical antecedents. The social authorities controlling these forces, however, preferred to render architectural form in images of the past. Regardless of modern purpose, buildings were draped with revisions or outright copies of ancient Greek and Roman, medieval Romanesque and Gothic, English Tudor, Italian and French Renaissance, Oriental, and even Egyptian designs. To architects like Purcell and Elmslie, such revivalism was a dishonorable betrayal of the American spirit.

Architects who wanted their designs to express the strength of American life charged that there was a basic perceptual error in the revivalist perspective. They asserted that people were romantically attracted to the image of historical architecture because these buildings represented a lasting presence that spoke of the persistence of human values. The survival of antique architecture was emblematic of human identity and, hence, endurance. The reproduction of the historical form in modern buildings was an attempt to claim those qualities in the present. In actuality, however, only an external shape was exhumed from the past. The connection between the appearance of an ancient building and the construction techniques informing the structure was disregarded. For those who despised revivalism, this break in functional continuity was literally the difference between a living culture and a dead one. The definition of beauty hung on their argument.

To revivalists, beauty was a discretely identifiable presence in architecture that could be calculated and applied ready-made. The justification of this view was rooted in the tenets of scientific reductionism, the dominant philosophical orientation then as now. Adherents believed that architectural beauty had already been invented and brought to perfection in ages past. They projected their own nineteenth-century rationalism onto the minds of earlier architects whose designs were then dismembered to form a palette of isolated decorative elements which could be attached piecemeal to new buildings. All the modern practitioner had to do was apply a scale ruler and total the various segments, like an arithmetical sum, then size the historical appearance accordingly. Indeed, the thought of doing more could be considered presumptuous in the face of the architectural attainments of history. This method claimed kinship with that of the flourishing physical sciences, which assumed the eventual elimination of any impediment to the will of man over nature. Beautiful

Exterior of 2328 Lake Place, Edna S. Purcell residence. Photograph courtesy of The Minneapolis Institute of Arts.

architecture, revivalist architects declared, depended on how well the given recipe was followed.

Other architects, distinctly a minority in the profession, held an antithetical view. They believed that beauty perceptible in the form and decoration of historical architecture was not a cause but an effect. To them the true beauty of a structure was the result of a clear understanding and direct expression of contemporary ability and aspiration. The man who focused the argument was a Chicago architect named Louis Henri Sullivan (1856–1924). Fervent in his message, Sullivan asserted, in both work and words, that architectural form was a pure reflection of the building culture. The truth of architecture was not in the image, but in the event. Spiritual honesty, he emphasized, required architectural honesty. The ghostly recreations of historical revivalism were blasphemy.

The creed advanced by Louis Sullivan conceived of ar-

Front hall and bookcases in the living room at Lake Place. Photograph courtesy of The Minneapolis Institute of Arts.

Plant stand at Lake Place. Photograph courtesy of The Minneapolis Institute of Arts.

chitectural design through the biological metaphor of the natural world. In that sphere, of which humans were inextricably part, all experiences evolved from active functions transmitted by the structural form of material objects. All physical things conducted the momentum of the event, like copper wire carrying electricity. One act arose from another in a cascade of interrelationships. This holistic model of experience was the fundamental order of existence, the way everything worked. Sullivan epitomized his view in the phrase "form follows function."

The organic architectural philosophy initiated by Louis Sullivan descended from his own practice principally through two lines. One of these paths encompassed the much-examined work of Frank Lloyd Wright (1867–1959), whose lengthy and metamorphic career has continued to attract a large public following. The other direct lineage was formed by the partnership of George Grant Elmslie and William Gray Purcell. Because their work is scarcer and less well known, the efforts of Purcell and Elmslie for the cause of organic architecture have been less celebrated than those of Wright. Nonetheless, their understanding and articulation of organic design was fully developed on a most profound level:

> These organic procedures exemplified the living relation which was practiced in exposition of democracy within our living world. Architecture as we saw it was called upon to express, in peace and mutual respect, that cooperation between the inanimate—the material world, which we now know is never inanimate or "material"—and the world of Man, together with his companions, the animals and the plants. . . . If these relations within a living democracy cannot be shown as the home and fountain of our mutual life in common with all living creations, then any further attempt to study and explain them becomes futile.[2]

Wright, who appeared and departed from the movement early on, was widely recognized for innovative architectural forms that were often as autocratic as they were creative. Purcell and Elmslie, on the other hand, inspired a team process of design that resulted in architecture that should be taken as more expressive of human relationships and needs.

For Purcell and Elmslie, organic architecture was a matter of faith. Any assessment of their designs must take into account the metaphysical motivations implicit in their work. Their spirituality, however, needs to be separated from the dogmatic connotations of religion. The key to the spiritual concept realized by the organic architects was a kind of gnostic perception, through which the continuities of past and future human life could only be understood in the context of the present. Inner recognition of need came first, and the external formulation of pattern derived from those informing ideas. If done with spiritual conscience, the organization of even the mundane elements of a structure would be endowed with values that represented the initial origins of the design. By the organic standard, this task was the vocation of the architect. Those devoted to this cause envisioned the result to be an important means of social progress, and thus came to be known in general parlance as progressive architects (a usage of the term distinct from, though obviously in character with, the contemporary political drive of the same name). Because this movement was born in the prairie of the American midwestern states, these men and women have also come to be called Prairie architects.[3]

One of the prime influences shaping the American architectural environment at the turn of the century, especially visible in the designs of Purcell and Elmslie, was the increased integration of machinery into ordinary life. The unprecedented liberty of personal movement provided earlier by trains and steamships was being augmented by automobiles and airplanes in the early twentieth century. Audio recordings, motion pictures, telephones, and other innovations quickened individual intellect and desire. Fascination with the rising tide of machinery was a powerful, even an overwhelming social force that is now very difficult to appreciate completely. In architectural terms, for example, mechanical household conveniences eliminated the need for servants' quarters. Therefore, architects could contract domestic architectural forms, omitting entire floors of live-in staff quarters, while at the same time labor-saving devices were absorbed into the fabric of the house. There was an optimism, a nearly unshakable shared belief in the liberating ability of machines to improve the human condition.

Pressure existed for an aesthetic as well as structural response that organized and clarified this change. A variety of approaches emerged in response. Revivalist architects did incorporate modern improvements such as fire-proofing and bathrooms into their designs, though these functions were by and large still hidden within historicist wrappings. Others wanted a more visible mechanical expression, but disagreed over the aesthetic rendition. Designs by Purcell and Elmslie, for example, are often mistakenly grouped with those of the American Arts and Crafts movement. Although the American cousin of the original English Arts and Crafts movement accepted a greater working relationship with machines, the fundamental orientation of the arts and crafts followers was toward the handicraft production of the past. Mechanical expediency was secondary to the aesthetic value of hand process. While some of the craftsman products were used successfully by Purcell and Elmslie in their work, often at the behest of clients, the fundamental philosophy of the firm was outside the objectives declared by the founders of the Arts and Crafts movement.[4]

Some insight into how deeply this consciousness of the machine penetrated the work of Purcell and Elmslie, and its strong correlation with Sullivan's thesis of natural poetic expression, can be seen in a short volume by Gerald Stanley Lee titled *The Voice of the Machines*.[5] George Elmslie recommended the book enthusiastically to Purcell, who called his experience of the writing "an epiphany." The author argued that the modern relationship between man and machines, and by extension machines to architecture, *was* poetry in threefold. First, there was the human motivation to honest labor, like the organic architects to their profession. "Every man who loves his work, who gets his work and his ideal connected, who makes his work speak out of the heart of him, is a poet."[6] Second, machines themselves were the poetry of the age, an expression of modern needs and wants that could not have been understood by people living a half century earlier. Third and

most significantly, the absorption of machinery into life was not fragmentary. Instead, life had been cast organically in the mold of iron, coal, and electricity. Just as surely as each human lived within a body of flesh and blood, so did the race now exist through an entelechy of machines.[7]

The underlying conditions of early twentieth-century life laid the foundations for a dramatic philosophical response from Purcell and Elmslie. They understood design to be the defining act of personal and communal self-identification, a metaphysical creation first made tangible on the surface of the drafting board. Purcell recorded how this was clear when watching Sullivan in his office:

> Sullivan in action built a sort of fourth dimensional motion trace, for Sullivan's architectural concept was never a 'plan and elevation' sequence. His organizing and articulating development moved from origin to fulfillment in three dimensions. The germinal thought expanded concurrently in all dimensions, acknowledging relativity as it moved to its density. . . . Life itself was flowing through his mind . . . as if his hands . . . were recording a general philosophical structure in space, of which the plane of the paper cut through a completely realized geometric concept.[8]

This profound conception of design, of course, did not take place in an intellectual vacuum. What Purcell witnessed in Sullivan was part of a broad and still ongoing change in Western consciousness: the practical understanding of time as a fourth dimension of being inherent in all things. In the early 1900s, mathematicians Albert Einstein (1878–1955) and Hermann Minkowski (1864–1909) rejected the absolute and individual existences of space and time. Instead, they replaced those two separate abstractions with one scheme for a four-dimensional continuum. The basic premise of this new theory bonded all objects that humans perceived as three-dimensional—including themselves—within a higher reality whose essential characteristic was defined by relative movement. As Sullivan suggested in his own prose, objects become what they are only in relationship to each other, all realized through a universal field of change.

Learning to perceive the world in terms of four dimensions was the most challenging mental puzzle of the time. Magazines like *Scientific American* sponsored contests to find explanations that could be easily understood by the popular audience. The problem was that fourth-dimensional consciousness could not be experienced through the physical senses. Only the mind was capable of opening a frame of reference into this new realm of comprehension. Among those bringing logic and projective geometry to bear on the task was a New York architect named Claude Bragdon (1866–1946). In an essay titled "Space and Hyperspace," he taught readers how to draw their own mental portals into the fourth dimension called tesseracts.[9] The resulting graphic device was the analog of a fourth dimensional cube. Seen in the two-dimensional rendering of a line drawing, there were four squares set equidistantly to one another. This implied a fifth yet invisible square,

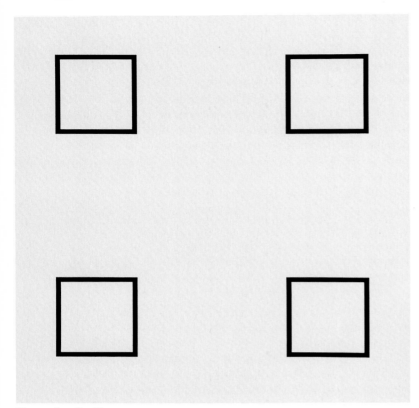

Example of a Tesseract.

whose interior was a cross of open space between the original four visible squares. The image represented a shift from external to internal perceptions of reality. Bragdon called this a "higher level," explaining that the relationship of a higher space to a lower one is always an inner state of recognition.[10]

To Purcell and Elmslie, the conceptual mechanics involved in this symbol perfectly described the process of unfolding organic design. Whether drawn outright or indicated typographically by a pair of joined colons, the device appeared on their presentation drawings, correspondence, advertising brochures, and in the issues of an architectural journal, *The Western Architect*, which they designed to illustrate their work. The tesseract was the summa for all the geometric forms that played within their decorative designs, signifying the creative process from which material objects crystallized. The tesseract declared that the physical, emotional, mental, and spiritual elements of human consciousness interpenetrated in manifest unity at the moment of creation.

To clarify these interrelationships, Bragdon worked to develop a theory of projective geometry to serve as the basis for architectural design. He realized, however, that his treatises on the subject were almost as inaccessible to the vast majority of people as were the elaborate formal proofs of Einstein. For a wider public understanding, ordinary language would have to be the vehicle. His task took an unexpected but well-suited turn when he joined in the translation of books and essays by the Russian author P.

D. Ouspensky, whose principal oeuvre was titled *Tertium Organum*. The text of *Tertium Organum* studied the rationalization of empirical experience from the deductive observations of the early Greeks through the experiment-directed scientific methods of the industrial age. Ouspensky then asserted that fourth-dimensional awareness was the third organon, the next step in the evolution of human understanding. He concluded his book with both logical and philosophical arguments to prove that all natural events occurred within a single vast universal organism. The mystery of this "cosmic consciousness" became comprehensible only when the perspective of isolated objects was abandoned.[11] In the writings of Bragdon and Ouspensky, Purcell and Elmslie recognized a description of the same metaphysical unity posited by Louis Sullivan.[12]

Although this metaphysical order was only newly recognized in the West, these concepts were the essence of ancient religious and philosophical systems of the Far East.

Presentation rendering, *Aviation Cup Trophy for Robert Jarvie, 1912. Northwest Architectural Archives, University of Minnesota Libraries, St. Paul. Photograph by Gary Mortensen and Robert Fogt.*

Progressive architects like Purcell and Elmslie read widely, followed developments in theoretical science, and were open to a variety of spiritual perspectives. They were aware of the studies of Emerson and Thoreau, for example, in Vedic scripture and the mythology of the Indian subcontinent.[13] Their affinity for the transcendentalists has long been a matter of record. Elmslie and Purcell, for example, often cited Walt Whitman and Edward Carpenter as philosopher poets of the organic movement. The theosophical enterprise started by H. P. Blavatsky (1831–91) and the descendant anthroposophy of Rudolph Steiner (1861–1925) attracted some of them, notably Walter Burley Griffin (1876–1936) and his wife Marion Mahoney (1871–1962). A few of the progressives also found a kinship with some of the "mind control" philosophies of the time, as Purcell and Walter Burley Griffin did through Christian Science.

The degree to which this new Western metaphysics was expressed varied with the individual. If there is today a single way of accessing the gnostic understanding in organic design, however, that can be found in the presence of Asian, especially Japanese, art forms. The popularity of Japanese prints in Europe and the United States during the period, for instance, is a widely documented fact. Credit for the importance of their aesthetic values to progressive architecture was given by no less a figure than Frank Lloyd Wright, who said he was uncertain what would have become of his designs had he not encountered the graphic forms called *ukiyo-e*, especially those by Hiroshige (1797–1858). Indeed, Wright was not above noting himself in virtual collaboration with his favorite nineteenth-century artist.[14]

Although the Prairie architects did have a strong appreciation for Asian art, they did not want to copy it any more than they did European examples. What attracted them so strongly was something deeper, a psychological pressure for self-examination. Their own culture was being forced by geographical boundaries, industrialization, and aesthetic quandary to become more introspective. In the fluid dynamic between contemplation and event at the heart of Japanese *ukiyo-e* and other forms of Oriental artwork, many organic architects, artists, designers, writers, and others intuitively perceived the true nature of their adversary at home.[15] Western reductionism believed that human perception and experience could be separated from the framework of the natural world. Louis Sullivan, for one, preached with utmost conviction the message that all true art and architecture was a poetic record of human passage through an enfolding spiritual continuum. Whether or not this realization rose to full consciousness in the work of any given progressive architect—clearly some made the intellectual connection—only a few of the Prairie architects grasped the fullness of his teachings. William Gray Purcell and George Grant Elmslie were among those who deciphered the puzzle and rendered the answer in terms of their architectural design.

The architectural firm that is most widely known as Purcell & Elmslie (P&E) represents three different partnerships that evolved from 1907 to 1921. Purcell joined with a college classmate named George Feick, Jr. (1880–1947) to open an office known as Purcell & Feick from 1907 to 1909. The arrival of George Grant Elmslie in 1910 changed the name to Purcell, Feick, & Elmslie, an arrangement that lasted approximately two and a half years. In 1913, Feick left the practice and the title of the partnership became simply Purcell & Elmslie, by which name the practice was known until dissolution of the firm in 1921. The partnership started with a series of offices in Minneapolis and eventually developed service locations in Chicago (1912), Philadelphia (1916), and Portland, Oregon (1919). In addition to the principals, this continuity of working relationships included contributions by a large number of support staff and job contractors. The character of the firm, however, was very much determined by the long-term friendship, background, and goals shared between Purcell and Elmslie.[16]

Born on a farm called Foot O' Hill in northeast Scotland, George Grant Elmslie passed his childhood in the countryside of the Aberdeenshire Highlands. Deeply impressed by the effects of seasonal change upon the landscape, the youthful Elmslie was instilled with a sense of natural rhythm in the living world of light, color, and texture. Hand in hand with a strict Presbyterian upbringing went an awareness of the ancient Celtic mysticism that permeated the Scottish national consciousness. His formal education began in the Riggins School in Gartly and continued in the famous Duke of Gordon School in Huntly. At the Gordon School he studied in a highly disciplined scholastic environment in which the demand for obedience was balanced by the encouragement to participate in outdoor activities that were structured to emphasize a democratic spirit of teamwork. Elmslie remained in the school until 1884 when, at the age of sixteen, he immigrated to America with his mother and sisters. There they joined his father, John Elmslie, who had left a year earlier and settled in Chicago. After a brief period in a business school, George Elmslie followed the suggestion of his parents and began the study of architecture.[17]

By 1887 Elmslie was working in the office of Joseph L. Silsbee, a prominent Chicago architect, where he joined a staff that included Cecil Corwin, George H. Maher, and Frank Lloyd Wright. When Wright left for employment in the office of Adler & Sullivan in 1889, he asked Elmslie to come with him. The move to the Sullivan office atop the newly completed Auditorium Building tower was propitious. Elmsley found in Sullivan an exacting taskmaster, sometimes caustic but essentially fair in his criticisms and liberal in spending time with an earnest pupil. Although Elmslie did not consider himself a facile student, he persevered in his efforts to understand and express the Sullivan concept of organic design. He learned to follow the practice of thinking a problem through mentally and then turning to the drafting table only after a solution had taken root in his mind. His repeated demonstrations of exceptional renowned National Farmers Bank in Owatonna, Minnesota (1905).[18] Although Elmslie later remarked that to his detriment he perhaps stayed too long with Sullivan, he did so by direct request from his master and friend with the indication that Elmslie was to be the heir of the Auditorium Tower practice. The decline of fortune that afflicted Sullivan after the turn of the century, however, resulted in deteriorated financial circumstances which prevented Elmslie from remaining any longer. Because Elmslie had no capital

Louis H. Sullivan (1856–1924). Photograph, copyright 1993, The Art Institute of Chicago, all rights reserved.

George Grant Elmslie. Photograph courtesy of the Northwest Architectural Archives, University of Minnesota Libraries, St. Paul.

aptitude for the work did not go unrewarded. In the mid-1890s, when Wright was dismissed from the office and after the Adler and Sullivan partnership had been dissolved, Elmslie became Sullivan's chief draftsman and kept that position for more than fifteen years.

In time, the professional and personal relationship between Elmslie and Sullivan became intensely important to both men. Elmslie was increasingly responsible for the development and articulation of architectural compositions only generally outlined by Sullivan. Moreover, he mastered thoroughly the principles and techniques of architectural ornamentation that were the most visible hallmark of Sullivan-inspired design. Elmslie, for example, detailed nearly all of the exterior ornament for the Wainwright Building in St. Louis (1890), designed the ironwork entrance and interior finish for the Schlesinger & Mayer [now Carson, Pirie, Scott] department store in Chicago (1900/1903), and has been shown to be almost entirely the author of the

of his own, he was faced with finding a position where his income would be secure.

Since August 1903, Elmslie had been on friendly terms with William Gray Purcell, a young architect whom he met at a dinner party of mutual friends in Oak Park, Illinois. Subsequently, Elmslie arranged for Purcell to work in the Sullivan office. Among the designs being completed by Elmslie when Purcell arrived for work were the delicate modular screen panels for the Schlesinger & Mayer store. Purcell recorded his thrill in watching these dazzling forms come from Elmslie's hand:

All the Schlesinger and Mayer ornament of the second unit of their building built in 1902–1903, at the corner of State and Madison, was from the hand of George Grant Elmslie. There was no one in the office at that time [except Elmslie] capable of doing such work. I sat beside him as he did much of the interior sawed detail. I recall the excitement when he produced so easily that five-ply miracle sonatina in wood—

Sawed wood screen panel, 1903. From the Schlesinger & Mayer Store, Chicago, Ill. Photograph, copyright 1993, The Art Institute of Chicago, all rights reserved.

the unit panel of the great screens for the dining room, rest rooms, and so on.[19]

The experience formed the beginning of a solid and fruitful friendship, both professional and personal, that was anchored in their shared commitment toward progressive architecture. Ten years older than Purcell, Elmslie had not only his extraordinary gift for architectural composition, but also had a Presbyterian-Scottish heritage in common with his younger friend. The two men were even distantly related. Purcell, for his part, was well situated financially and possessed a talent and enthusiasm for design that had already enabled him to win a significant architectural competition.[20] George Elmslie was greatly charmed by the warmhearted eagerness of his newfound friend toward the cause of progressive architecture.

If Louis Sullivan regarded Elmslie as the inheritor of his architectural mantle, he surely must have found in William Gray Purcell the kind of young architect for whom he had written the treatise on organic design called *Kindergarten Chats*. In background and lineage, Purcell came from a hardy stock of pioneering Scots-Irish families who settled

in Pennsylvania prior to the Revolutionary War. In 1806, the family moved across the Allegheny mountains to homestead a farm called Pleasant Run in the Ohio wilderness. Purcell was named after his maternal grandfather, William Cunningham Gray (1830–1901), who had been among the first generation of the family born on the newly settled frontier. Educated as a lawyer, Gray became an editor and publisher whose naturalist musings were read worldwide in *The Interior*, the Presbyterian weekly newsmagazine he owned in partnership with Cyrus Hall McCormick. Establishing his household in the Chicago suburb of Oak Park in the early 1870s, W. C. Gray became an influential voice both for social reform and preservation of the environment. In 1879, his daughter Anna married Charles A. Purcell, a prosperous grain trader who had years earlier come to Oak Park from West Bend, Nebraska, to be educated in the renowned village schools and stayed on to join with his brother in a malt dealership. Their son William was born a year later.

William Cunningham Gray. Photograph courtesy of the Northwest Architectural Archives, University of Minnesota Libraries, St. Paul.

William Gray Purcell was raised largely by his grandparents. His grandmother, Catherine Garns Gray, was responsible for his early exposure to the arts, especially poetry and drawing. In the succession of homes built by the Grays in Oak Park, they hosted many prominent authors, clergymen, and social reformers in a vibrant literary atmosphere. From the time he was allowed to be present in this distinguished company, Purcell began to acquire progressive cultural attitudes and a spirit of social activism. His formal education came through the nationally respected Oak Park schools, as well as a liberal private academy. More significant to his philosophical evolution were the experiences he enjoyed during annual summer living at a retreat established by his grandfather in northern Wisconsin. There, amid the clear waters of a glacial lake, stood an island crowned with towering pine trees on which the family lived in a camp they called, naturally enough, Island Lake.

At this isolated settlement, W. C. Gray evoked the life he had experienced in his youth at the Pleasant Run homestead in Ohio. A series of log cabins was built on the same pattern he had known as a child, and life was lived by harvesting as much as possible from the surrounding forest. Members of this community ranged from the Cyrus Hall McCormick family to Ojibway Indians, all sharing conversation and song around a common campfire. Their communion would later by symbolized in every fireplace designed by Purcell. The Island Lake experience was the frame within which he found his place as a human being. The vibrant rhythmic interplay of wind, water, light, and human life in the forest served as a well of inspiration for the rest of his long life. Purcell was delivered to his architectural vocation with a rich appreciation for the continuity of this heritage, a keenness for meeting practical necessities, and a strong faith in the fundamental wholesomeness of life.

The vision of organic architecture was familiar to Purcell when he left Chicago in 1899 to attend the College of Architecture at Cornell University, then considered to be the most modern architectural education available in the United States. He already knew the designs of Sullivan from his frequent attendance at the Columbian Exposition, where the Golden Door of the Transportation Building had opened for him a world of great and marvelous machines. Throughout his youth he had attended operas and musicals in the vastness of the Chicago Auditorium, which he sometimes viewed from the stage as a supernumerary. In later years he declared that the spirit of architecture first spoke to him in 1890, at age ten, beneath the sweeping electric arcs of that great theater. The voice he heard calling was that of Louis Sullivan. Also, Purcell was fifteen when Frank Lloyd Wright built his Oak Park studio on the same block of Forest Avenue where his father lived. Purcell had been introduced to Wright's designs when he was shown a pen and ink perspective for the new building by family friends, the Loziers. During his high school years he spent many after-school hours wandering throughout the vicinity to see all the Wright-designed houses as they were built. He eventually made personal acquaintance with the architect.[21]

Four years of revivalist architectural college education proved to be a largely unpleasant task for Purcell. Fired with enthusiasm for organic design, he found his inevitable clash with the classically oriented curriculum at Cornell to be a foretaste of the greater contest yet to come. He spent many hours mastering the rote drafting techniques required of him, turning out rendering after rendering of

William Purcell, Willie Purcell, Dorothy Gray, and another unidentified child at a small log cabin in northern Minnesota. Photograph courtesy of the Northwest Architectural Archives, University of Minnesota Libraries, St. Paul.

imitated Greek and Roman facades. At every opportunity, Purcell challenged his teachers to discussions that contrasted the eclectic mix of class assignments to designs by Sullivan and Wright. His efforts were of little avail. Meeting Elmslie two months after graduation and thereafter getting five months of employment in the Sullivan office seemed the best possible redemption. Yet, all too soon, he had to leave for the balance of his apprenticeship years on the West Coast in Berkeley, California, and Seattle, Washington. Then, at the behest of his father in 1906, Purcell departed for a year-long tour of Europe. Accompanied by Cornell classmate George Feick, Jr., he studied the classical sites of Greece and Italy, Byzantine remains in Constantinople, and medieval cathedral cities in France and England. Stretching their money, the two men made an extra effort to meet progressive European architects, among them Henrik P. Berlage, Ferdinand Boberg, and Martin Nyrop, who welcomed the young Americans with showings of their latest work. These contacts excited Purcell and spurred the desire to get started with his own architectural practice. Although Purcell had intended on his return to go to California and wanted to try for work with Myron

Hunt in Los Angeles, George Feick convinced him through the course of their journey together that there might be a better opportunity in establishing a partnership firm in Minnesota. [22]

In February 1907, Purcell and Feick rented an office in Minneapolis and sent out engraved cards announcing that they were open for business. For the next two years they worked to establish their credentials as earnest practitioners of the Sullivan-derived "form and function" architecture. The dedication of Purcell and Feick to a new and largely unknown architectural philosophy made securing work even more difficult than the usual obstacles facing any fledgling practice in an environment filled with long-established competitors. The principles underlying proposed designs often had to be explained to potential clients. With his gift for friendly conversation, Purcell undertook those relations. His presentations involved a time-consuming educational process that depended on an open-mindedness not always present in his listeners. The lack of completed buildings as examples to demonstrate the effectiveness of the Purcell & Feick approach was another handicap to getting work. During their first year, the architects recorded

William Gray Purcell and George Grant Elmslie in their office.
Photograph courtesy of the Northwest Architectural Archives, University of Minnesota Libraries, St. Paul.

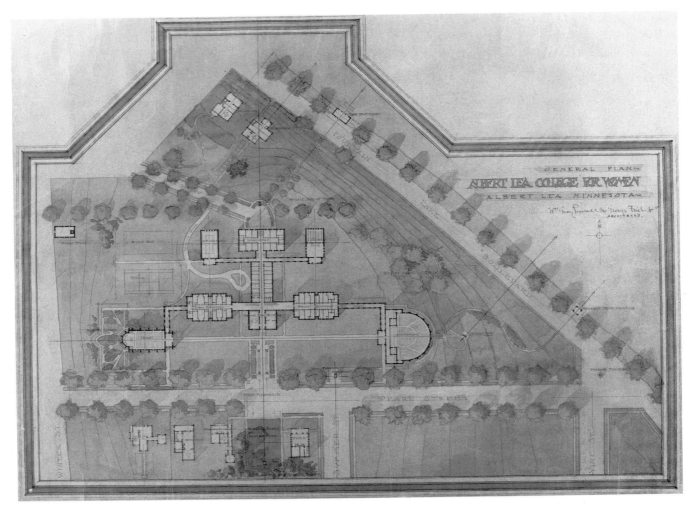

Presentation rendering, *showing grounds and floor plan, 1908.*
Alberta Lee College for Women. Northwest Architectural Archives, University of Minnesota Libraries, St. Paul. Photograph by Gary Mortensen and Robert Fogt.

only twelve entries on their accounting system, of which seven were for unrealized projects, minor alterations to existing structures, or insignificant consultations. When they did get a commission the circumstances were not always in tune with their preferred methods, but they could not afford to turn down work that might bring in money and lead to future opportunities.

One of their early projects was the Cargill Science Hall, designed in 1907 for the Albert Lea College for Women in Albert Lea, Minnesota. The severe economic constraints of the job required that the classroom building be as inexpensive as possible. The result was a strictly rectangular, standardized box form with trimly set fenestration. For their first large (and to them important) building, the plan was presented in a lush watercolor rendering that showed both existing and optimistically planned future structures on the grounds of the institution. Purcell and Feick also worked out a novel series of time and motion studies to prove the efficiency of the design. Their effort was successful, but Purcell was not prepared for the unyielding difficulties with

the building committee that prevented the architects from approving materials and supervising construction. To their disappointment, all they were allowed to do was provide a set of working drawings. Purcell later remarked that the insistent fiscal conservatism of the client, rather than any agreement with organic architectural views, may ultimately have been the only reason they could sell such a plain and unornamented building.[23]

An opposite circumstance in another early job seemed to work against their progressive intentions as well. The vestry building committee in 1908 for the Anglican Christ Church of Eau Claire, Wisconsin, was made up of prosperous lumbermen. From the first, Purcell recognized that these people would not be led toward any modern form. For organic architects in the first eighteen months of business, this situation presented a thorny dilemma. They could walk away on principle and do nothing, or compromise in order to serve what were otherwise friendly and responsive clients. In a result that could be superficially called the firm's only fallback into revivalism, Purcell and

Feick resigned themselves to a building plan for what was basically an ancient and unchanged religious liturgy:

We decided to search among historical ecclesiastical forms for the very simplest, most primitive way of putting masonry around Christian worship, and of forming its simplest need for window openings and doors. An important consideration was the saving in cost which this promised, and at the very least, [we intended] to have nothing but genuine materials and methods, none of the tin and lumber gothic of the time.[24]

Having made the decision to work within the tradition, the firm resolved that all construction should be done with as honest a structural approach as possible. Lancet windows pierced thick stone walls in the familiar pattern because the form was correctly suited to the masonry techniques used in the construction. The architects made sure that set buttresses actively carried the structural load. George Feick provided roller slideways hidden behind the interior coping of the meeting hall to accommodate internal roof truss movement. He integrated modern sealing techniques within the building sheathe to counter weather stresses. Purcell and Feick detailed moldings, column elements, brackets, and similar features as plainly as possible. Interior wooden roof supports in the sanctuary hall were left unconcealed. Purcell noted decades later that the effect was "too

much influenced by the Gustav Stickley 'craftsman-fumed-oak' period" and seemed heavy. If the architects undertook the project in hopes of later opportunities to do genuinely progressive work in the same area of Wisconsin, however, they were rewarded over the next five years with a series of projects for residences, furniture, and another church building. A decorative memorial window design also was commissioned for the Christ Church building in 1915.[25]

A reputation for the sincerity and quality of their work spread mostly by word of mouth, although Purcell sent letters as far away as the southwestern United States to inquire of Presbyterian church building committees about building programs under consideration. Many early business relations sprang from contacts with old friends of W. C. Gray or Charles A. Purcell, such as H. C. Garvin of Winona, Minnesota. Like several other supporters of Purcell & Feick in small towns of the agricultural countryside, Garvin believed in the same philosophy that motivated the firm. He provided his own commissions and worked to deliver other customers. This growing network of rural businessmen, especially bankers, broadened chances for commissions in Minnesota, Wisconsin, Iowa, and the Dakotas. From contacts in his home town of Sandusky, Ohio, Feick brought staple if mundane business to the firm, including a series of speculative houses and a somewhat inno-

Advertising card, *Goosman's Motor Inn*, 1908. *Northwest Architectural Archives, University of Minnesota Libraries, St. Paul. Photograph by Gary Mortensen and Robert Fogt.*

vative multi-story office building for his father, a construction contractor. He also handled sundry small buildings for local friends and acquaintances.

One of the earliest commissions in a progressive idiom was the "Motor Inn," an automobile garage erected for Henry Goosman in 1908. Goosman, a jovial Dutchman who maintained a prominent livery service in Minneapolis for many years, understood the importance of the new "automatics." His commission represented the first time a building had been erected in the city specifically to service these machines. The project was under discussion for more than a year before construction went ahead, providing ample time to develop the design. With the site located on a busy downtown street corner, Purcell & Feick could have asked for no better project to illustrate the accommodation for modern life that was at the core of their work.

The round shape of the main service entrance was a humorous recognition of the wheels that brought the automotive machine inside. A bright green garage door panel lifted hydraulically—a pioneering application that received trade publicity—and contained an arrowhead window set within equilateral triangular framing to sign the accessway. Foot traffic entered at an office doorway on the right. A rank of three windows separated by thin brick piers balanced the left side of the front elevation, giving a view of arriving customers and bringing natural illumination into the garage space. Doors and windows were framed by red and tan coursework accents against a background of cream-colored brick. Specially designed gilded lettering completed the polychrome exterior treatment. The geometric symbol of the inset door triangle was further developed into electric light fixtures and used as an advertising mark on business stationery. Inside the office, horizontal board-and-batten paneling emphasized a sense of linear motion. Within the garage proper, a thirty-inch deep, six-inch high curb along

the perimeter wall formed a sidewalk that served as a handy ledge for tools while providing a stop for the bumper-less cars of the day. For a young architectural office still in the throes of establishing a clientele, the "Motor Inn" design presented a complex and creditable response to practical work functions, business presentation needs, and possibilities for aesthetic enhancement.

Purcell and Feick believed that their architectural philosophy was applicable to every kind of structure, but they were particularly keen to get a bank commission. This type of building epitomized modern midwestern independence and democratic community. Bankers like Sullivan's Owatonna client Carl K. Bennett, however, were scarce exceptions to the conservative breed of men (rarely, if ever, women) who kept the financial lockboxes of small countryside towns. They were serious about the obligations of their positions and wanted no hint of irresponsibility in their buildings. New, better, and beautiful were fine qualities, so long as no imprudence, frivolity, or extravagance clouded the picture. This situation placed the burden of proof squarely at the feet of the organic architects.

Of all unbuilt Purcell & Feick commercial designs, the one to fail because they did their work too convincingly was the First National Bank project of 1907 for Winona, Minnesota. H. C. Garvin, who had been an associate in the grain business with Charles A. Purcell, arranged for a presentation by the firm to the building committee. The design was a cubic form based on a pier and girder construction that lifted dramatically above a brick and stone envelope. The dynamic interleaving of the wall planes drew the attention of the arriving customer inward, focusing on entrances beneath deep eaves extending from the flat roof. The overhanging roof panels defined a cruciform, filled out at each corner by separately rising curtain walls. Large terra-cotta cartouches punctuated the interplay of the wall

First National Bank, Winona, 1907. Photograph courtesy of David S. Gebhard.

planes. The interior would have been largely open to sunlight from a wide skylight and street-side walls glazed over half their surface.

Ironically, efforts to make clear one of the most creative aspects of the proposed bank building contributed greatly to rejection of the design. As they had done with the Goosman garage, Purcell and Feick wanted the structure to be very colorful. In addition to carefully detailed renderings to show the use of polychrome features, the architects asked the committee members to visit the Farmers National Bank finished recently about a hundred miles away in Owatonna, Minnesota, by Louis Sullivan and George Grant Elmslie. Rather than taking the brilliant finish of that building as a recommendation, the richness and variety of color disturbed the bankers. Adding more injury to the prospects of the firm, Purcell recorded, was another special effort undertaken to make their case:

> We made a plaster model which showed a carefully worked out color scheme. The gorgeous color of the Owatonna project, so welcome after returning to bleak America from my Italian journey [of 1906] . . . made me enthusiastic to get the joy of color into our buildings. This model didn't seem to help our cause at all, and we first realized what few architects realize today, how much imagination it takes to visualize a model into a full size building. . . . Standing around the model, the bank committee was visibly embarrassed. They felt taken in, like men who had paid admission to a boxing match and then were asked to enjoy aesthetic dancing.[26]

Generally, other projects of this period were attempts by Purcell & Feick to bring their message to a wider public audience. Most of these designs did not proceed beyond sketches and were undertaken without the kind of inside assistance supplied by men like Garvin. The form and function argument had to appeal not only to propriety and pocketbook, but also do so in a form that the entire community found distinctly attractive. The bank model failed as a medium of communication, leaving presentation renderings as the principal means of convincing people to step inside the living idea of architecture. A typical example is the project for an Elk's club in Mankato, Minnesota (1908). The drawings show a conservative form, the solidly dignified brick body of the structure set on a stone plinth with regularly placed entrances and windows. An inviting arbor envisioned for a third floor terrace was protected on one side by a high pitched roof rising over an interior meeting hall. Benevolent fraternal respectability set the overall tone of the composition, but the design was not built. Closer to home and on a much smaller scale, the firm did execute a meeting house on Lake Minnetonka for the Reel and Rudder Club that same year. The plain pencil rendering that was circulated among the membership for approval showed a two-story wooden structure with straight clean lines for a sturdy yet pleasant appearance. Purcell found the little-altered building still in use when he inquired fifty years later.

With the successful completion of utilitarian work like a warehouse and ordinary residential alterations, the firm became known to prosperous and influential Minneapolitans such as A. W. Armitage, George Draper Dayton, and Seares E. Brace. Through these social contacts the architects were presented with opportunities to compete for more substantial work. In 1908 they prepared sketches for a large memorial arch to have been sited in a Minneapolis park by C. M. Loring, who was then busy establishing the extensive city park system. For wealthy E. C. Warner, oversized monochrome presentation sketches were drawn for a large house to be placed on a hill overlooking suburban Lake Calhoun. To research the requirements in designing a dwelling of that size, Purcell wrote to Louis Sullivan asking for plans of the Henry B. Babson house, whose forty thousand dollar cost was the same amount Warner said he wanted to spend. Despite these efforts to provide what the client asked for, the plain horizontal Purcell & Feick composition was unsuccessful. The commission went instead to competitors Tyrie and Chapman, who correctly assessed Warner's desire for a grand image and built a much more expensive baronial Tudor house for him.[27]

The largest commission completed by Purcell & Feick was the Steward Memorial Church, designed for a Presbyterian congregation in south Minneapolis during 1909. The general form descended from the unsuccessful First National Bank project at Winona, particularly in the area given over to large window openings. In the church, however, the pier treatment prominent in the bank design disappeared and the enclosing corner walls assumed definite support functions. Roof slabs reached beyond the basic cubic form of the auditorium on all sides, while an auditorium wing facing the pulpit contained a balcony and secondary seating areas. Entrances passed into both flanks of this extension in symmetrically organized stairwells. Exterior and interior detailing for doors, coping, and window lights, as well as ornamental ceiling and wall moldings, took on a variety of cruciform motifs to echo the basic symbol of the worship practice. One sanctuary wall was filled by a large sliding wood and glass door meant to open into the court of a Sunday school wing added at a later date.[28]

Purcell believed that the design addressed for the first time some basic needs of the Presbyterian service, the religion in which he had been raised. Despite high ceilings, the interior possessed a friendly intimacy. The square plan brought the members of the congregation closer toward the altar, choir, and each other, strengthening their sense of participation. Rows of seating divided into three groups by surrounding aisles faced the pulpit platform directly, with a section of benches at a tangent on the side. The placement of trafficways and seating logically determined the disposition of windows and entryways throughout the building. Because no bell was required for this neighborhood mission, no tower or similar features appeared on the exterior. Instead, the flat roof was mounted with four small chimneys (forming a tesseract symbol, as did some of the cruciform detailing) to service ventilation. Wall sconces

DWELLING for MR. E. C. WARNER
overlooking LAKE CALHOUN
WM CRAY PURCELL AND GEORGE FEICK JR - ARCHITECTS.

E. C. Warner house. *Northwest Architectural Archives, University of Minnesota Libraries, St. Paul. Photograph by Gary Mortensen and Robert Fogt.*

Interior of the Stewart Memorial Church. Photograph courtesy of the Northwest Architectural Archives, University of Minnesota Libraries, St. Paul.

and rectangular plateaus of electric bulbs suspended from the high ceiling provided artificial light for the interior. Shortly after completion, revision of the choir to contain a large pipe organ thrust the lectern further forward into the auditorium, further increasing the effectiveness of the design. Purcell reported the benefits of the church in an article for the successor of his grandfather's old newsmagazine that explained the practical aesthetic of the building as a matter of honest expression in church design.[29]

In these early years, the type of project that would make the most substantial contribution to the later achievements of the firm was residential design. One of the first tasks that faced Purcell and Feick when their office first opened in February 1907 was to complete some visible architectural scheme that could demonstrate their abilities and intentions. Like many architects seeking to create a professional reputation, Purcell decided to build a dwelling for himself. Fortunately, millionaire Charles A. Purcell had provided a

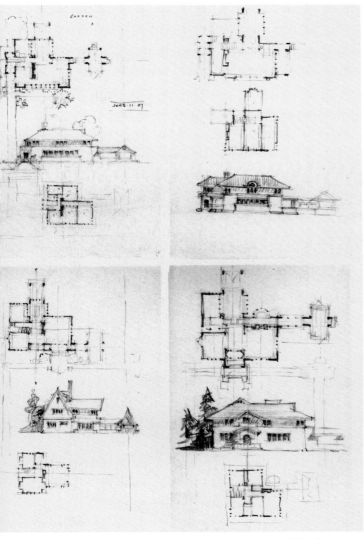

up of four sketches, 1907. *Catherine Gray residence. North-Architectural Archives, University of Minnesota Libraries, 'aul. Photograph by Gary Mortensen and Robert Fogt.*

large sum of money to get his son started in life. With these resources, Purcell bought a prominent lot on Lake of the Isles in what was then a suburb of Minneapolis. Originally titled the W. G. Purcell residence, the dwelling was later referred to as the Catherine Gray house, honoring his grandmother who came to live there. This starting venture for his architectural career was undertaken very soberly by Purcell, and the work turned out to be more demanding than he anticipated.

For the first time, Purcell was faced with initiating and sustaining responsibility for a building from beginning idea through construction, something that until then had been only theory for him. A group of four sketches that are the earliest known drawings for this project provide insight into his difficulties. He approached the problem from a variety of fronts, experimenting with the possible compositional effects of a high-pitched or low-hipped roof treatment. The floor plans of the house evolved more stubbornly. In the first effort Purcell revealed his lifelong attraction to the aspirational sense of a high-pitched roof. The plan, however, would have none of it. The pitch of the roof subsides quickly across the sequence of sketches, with two intermediate ideas for dormers finally disappearing entirely in the fourth version.[30]

More significantly, Purcell found himself grappling with a fundamental conflict in his approach to the composition. Several considerations were obvious. The length of the lot faced the shore of the lake, commanding a lovely view, but also establishing the most logical unfolding of the plan across the width of the land. Purcell understood that setting the structure deeper into the site was a natural response to balance the relationship of the house to the lake. In turn, this influenced the placement of door openings and fenestration. Purcell was intent on adding a pergola and summer pavilion, an element that in the first sketch had a duncecap roof, flirted with being an attached porch in the second and third, then in the fourth sketch finally settled at a comfortable distance from the house. A telling change in the layout occurs between the first two drawings and the last half of the series. In the earlier pair, Purcell situated the principal entrance in the middle of the front elevation, creating awkward internal divisions that he attempted to resolve by introducing walkways. In the later set of drawings, he has harkened to Frank Lloyd Wright's recently published *Ladies Home Journal* plan for a "Fireproof House for $5,000" and aligned the front and service entrances at the side of the house.[31] Each variation contained a mixture of experimental theory and bits of practicality. None of these approaches seemed workable. Purcell admitted to himself that he was caught in a welter of disconnected relationships.

When examining his trial by fire with the Catherine Gray house some thirty-five years later, Purcell saw more clearly the beginning of his insight into organic design. There were problems and influences at work in a house that would take time to understand. This journey required him to practice the same kind of internal meditation that

Sullivan had taught Elmslie. "Plainly," he wrote, "there was much pure analytical thinking to be done before any broad concept for a true building could be crystallized." He also admitted freely that "to gradually integrate this factual material until it was related to a particular building and at the same time create a living architecture, rather than a thesis on building construction, took more than Purcell and Feick had in them at that time."[32] Frustrated, Purcell set his sketches aside entirely and realized there was a better way to learn.

Throughout the years since his apprenticeship employment in the Sullivan office, Purcell had continued to develop his relationship with George Grant Elmslie. When in Chicago, he would always visit in the Auditorium Building tower to see his friend and look over the work on the drafting tables. Over the years Elmslie consulted gladly with Purcell on some competitive projects and encouraged him to read books by authors such as Edward Carpenter and P. D. Ouspensky. After spending more than a month of uneasy struggle with his ideas for the Catherine Gray house, Purcell decided he knew the best thing to do:

> After a series of studies for this project which were wholly unsatisfactory, and with the confusion and dead end [of the first try] in mind, we turned to George G. Elmslie, with data on lot, lake view, winter flowers room, and wish for a detached pavilion porch, out of sight in winter, similar to a Fair Oaks, Oak Park house of F. L. Wright's. G. G. E. replied with a pencil plan that seemed just right. W. G. P. articulated the mechanics of the plan and developed the elevations for this house.[33]

Elmslie had the necessary understanding to lay out an integrated pattern for the elements of the program Purcell wanted to realize. His suggestions showed Purcell that he had been closer to a good outcome than he thought. The final design was made to work by deleting a number of trafficways to leave a crisp open floor plan. The rest of the design work was up to Purcell, who found himself carefully questioning every aspect of the material fabric. The relationship of wooden frame construction to brick walls came to be understood as the natural distinction between skeleton and skin:

> Having satisfied my conscience I began with confidence . . . to create both of the enveloping areas and the solid masses of the various parts and utilities in such a way that they would counteract in movement, bulk, and shape, against the other elements of the building and thus establish a sequence, subordination and movement of part with part, and part with the whole.[34]

Interior elements were subject to the same exacting scrutiny. Many design components to make their first appearances in this structure became regularly used features in the repertoire of the firm. These included a raised hearth, tented ceilings, and corner-set casement windows. Most importantly, Purcell and Feick began to articulate their own version of a wood trim system for interior finish that placed definition of the surface plane of the wall over the traditionally emphasized presence of door and windows. One of the flaws in this design represented a problem that often would be encountered in the future. The need to incorporate pre-

Catherine Gray residence. Photograph courtesy of the Northwest Architectural Archives, University of Minnesota Libraries, St. Paul.

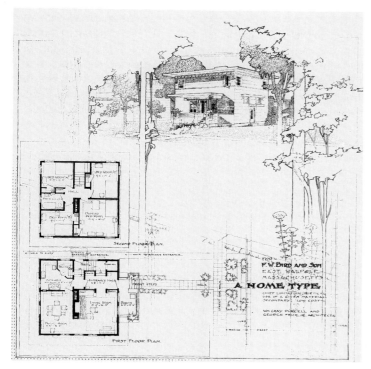

Presentation rendering, *Home Type for F. W. Bird and Son.* *Northwest Architectural Archives, University of Minnesota Libraries, St. Paul. Photograph by Gary Mortensen and Robert Fogt.*

existing furniture in the new building negatively affected the values of the architecture. In an effort to accommodate some large bookcases owned by Catherine Gray, the house reached the stage of working drawings with a windowless south living room wall. Elmslie criticized these plans, as did Frank Lloyd Wright when Purcell stopped by the Oak Park studio to show him the design. Long afterwards, when writing the history of his firm, Purcell lamented, "I wish now he [Elmslie] had insisted upon opening up the south wall—a defect sufficiently glaring that I can hardly imagine myself so blind as not have seen it."[35]

The experiment with the open floor plan at the heart of the Catherine Gray house set Purcell and Feick, later Purcell & Elmslie, on a road to a series of successful variations on the theme. The plan had to yield a sense of inner movement, as Purcell noted. Most often, the living room and dining space were set at a tangent to each other, and the turning of the plan pivoted around a chimney stack. Entrance, staircase, and kitchen filled the remaining area on the first floor to complete a square or rectangular enclosure. Most of these houses were two-storied, and upstairs there were usually two or three bedrooms and a bath. The first public presentation by the firm of this form was in a house scheme entered into a competition for designs using the product line of the F. W. Bird Company, a manufacturer of building and roofing materials. The resourceful design was ignored in favor of a Colonial cottage plan. Still hopeful of getting some favorable publicity, Purcell & Feick

made a subsequent study for a similar house that they wanted to appear in the *Ladies Home Journal.* Their approach accomplished the feat of including five well-proportioned bedrooms in a two-story plus attic house measuring only twenty-two by thirty feet. Whether the design was actually submitted is unknown, but such experiments came to produce practical results. Although the plan for the *Journal* was never executed, a cottage based in part on the design was erected for J. D. R. Stevens in Eau Claire, Wisconsin, during the spring of 1909. The harmonious arrangement of the Stevens cottage so pleased the owner that when a second, much bigger and more formal house was required, Purcell & Feick got the commission.

One house designed by Purcell in 1909 stands apart from the others of the Purcell & Feick era as an interesting benchmark. He was beginning to realize his growing working relationship with Elmslie might deprive him of some basic educational experiences. However easily he might be able to rely on the skills of someone else, Purcell wanted to make sure that he remained competent on his own. Deliberately, he sequestered from Elmslie the development of a commission for his father, Charles A. Purcell. In this residential design the demons he had battled two years before in the Catherine Gray house were fully vanquished. The first floor plan sweeps neatly through the necessary areas of entry, staircase, living room, dining room, and kitchen. Using his familiarity with the living patterns of the client, Purcell customized the plan with a glass-enclosed room labeled "the Smoker" just off the side of the living room so his father could enjoy a cigar without having to disturb others.

The massing of the house rests trimly within a large square suburban lot. In the backyard Purcell specified land-

Charles A. Purcell residence. Photograph courtesy of the Northwest Architectural Archives, University of Minnesota Libraries, St. Paul.

scape plantings and installed a round fountain with a sculpture by Richard Bock. On the back of the house a small balcony opens off the master bedroom on the second floor. This was the prototypical beginning of the sleeping porches that would later appear in many Purcell and Elmslie dwellings. The deep extension of the eaves to more than three feet was exactly the kind of technical challenge that Purcell wanted to resolve himself:

> . . . making a plastic transition with exterior stucco from gable soffit to a flat undereave. A part of the problem was to insure solid support for the widely projecting corners without resorting to brackets. It was also necessary to give support to projecting gable rafter ends, which in this instance had a 3'–6" projection—too much for a 2 × 4 cantilever, and 2 [foot by] 6 [foot boards] would make to thick a facia edge. The resultants effected many factors in the total design of the building: a lower area for the plaster wall end; an easier 120 degree bend between the vertical wall and upward sloping soffit; an angle brace system under the entire length of gable. Thus we were able to get a better plastic feeling in the marginal frame of wood bands.[36]

One of the most sensitive features of this dwelling has long since vanished. For the exterior, Purcell devised a color scheme of red-brown brick, sandy green plaster, blue slate roof, neutral olive plaster framing strips, and a small accent line of patinated brass. He later attempted to recall this effect by handpainting a photograph of the house. The result, though somewhat garish as rendered in the different medium, delivers a feeling of liveliness. This characteristic of bright, almost effervescent coloration was an essential part of Purcell and Elmslie designs. Sadly, most of this color has since disappeared under numerous coats of paint.[37] For his father's house Purcell also executed one of his rare ventures into designing art glass, providing decorative panels for the front entrance, the built-in dining room buffet, and especially a triangular-shaped tympanum above the central windows of the smoking room.

Purcell experienced trouble finding a solution for the house within the imposed economic limits and came to regard his unaided completion of the design as a point of honor. Relying solely on his own ideas, he finished the residence and a slightly self-conscious garage for a total of fifteen thousand five hundred dollars, with one thousand dollars of that amount going for the driveway and the car shelter. The garage still stands almost completely intact, with glass-paneled doors, deep soffits, and detailed moldings to match those on the main house. Purcell was satisfied with the result of this diligent effort toward self-development, but in 1915 the house would be further decorated with Elmslie-designed leaded glass, sawed wood, and a fireplace mural by Albert Fleury.[38]

From 1907 to 1909, the work of Purcell & Feick was characterized by a straightforward accommodation to basic functional needs, but, beyond the openly utilitarian, there was evidence of a growing sensitivity to deeper organic consciousness. Designs such as the First National Bank project

at Winona and the Stewart Church in Minneapolis reflected the potential of the firm. There also were some indications of trouble. George Feick, for example, had difficulty handling the structural requirements of the roof trusses for the Goosman "Motor Inn." Luckily, he was rescued by another friend of progressive architecture, E. Fitch Pabody of the American Bridge Company in St. Paul. The uneasiness of Feick in handling the innovative engineering required for the new, often experimental forms was a weakness that became a continuing source of friction as the partnership progressed.

The early years saw the beginning of important personal relationships that would effect the story of the firm. Catherine Gray moved to be near her grandson. Just before Christmas 1908, Purcell married Edna Summy, a graduate of Wellesley and the daughter of a music company owner in Chicago. From the beginning, the two women had a discordant relationship. As a result of the disharmony, Purcell and his wife left the house on Lake of the Isles to rent an apartment several blocks away. More happily, Purcell became involved with a circle of people who shared his interests in art and architecture. He participated in activities at the Handicraft Guild of Minneapolis and joined several social organizations. He also lectured from time to time on the goals of organic architecture. At one of these talks in 1908 he met John Jager (1871–1959), a Slovenian-born architect who studied with Otto Wagner in Vienna. Since Jager had been involved with the Secessionist movement in Austria and was well informed about progressive European and American architecture in general, these common interests formed the basis for an intense intellec-

Purcell, Feick & Elmslie Office. George Grant Elmslie standing. Photograph courtesy of the Northwest Architectural Archives, University of Minnesota Libraries, St. Paul.

tual friendship between him and Purcell that lasted the rest of their lives.

John Jager had left Europe in 1901 when he was appointed architect to the Austrian mission to Peking. In China he designed and rebuilt the Austro-Hungarian legation building, which had been destroyed a year earlier during the Boxer Rebellion. Jager was greatly impressed with Chinese culture and began a lifelong study of the Chinese language and arts. Shortly afterward he also visited Japan where he collected examples of vanishing handicrafts, particularly metalwork, textiles, and wood-block printing. By 1902 Jager relocated to the American midwest where he was reunited with his brothers who had earlier immigrated to Minnesota. Soon he had opened his own architectural office in Minneapolis. His commissions during the first year included several Catholic churches for ethnic parishes, notably St. Bernard's, located in a German neighborhood in the north end of St. Paul, and St. Stephen's in Brockway Township, Minnesota. In 1903, Jager published a booklet titled *Fundamental Ideas in Church Architecture* that argued against the rote use of historic forms in modern buildings. He also discovered that he was among the few architects in the state who advocated the use of reinforced concrete construction, which many contractors at the time considered merely a passing trend that was ill-suited to the extreme variations of the northern climate.

Jager continued to develop a presence in public affairs that gained him a strong local reputation. He eventually became actively involved with the Minneapolis City Planning Commission and was an author of the city plan of 1905.[39] After becoming a friend of Purcell, he contributed an essay to one of the *Western Architect* issues illustrating the work of P&E. Titled "What the Engineer Thinks," the text asserted the organic view that there was a beautiful and naturally perfect relationship of technological function and engineering form.[40] Given his careful and reserved character, Jager published the piece under the pseudonym E. Van Regay, a reversed spelling that played on the pronunciation of his name. Purcell and Jager often spent evenings walking alongside Minnehaha Creek, near Jager's country home, discussing Sullivan, the organic thesis, and the history of languages, a subject in which Jager was doing extensive research. These conversations energized Purcell and supported his education in organic design. Although Jager did not ever actually work in the P&E office, his constant moral support earned him the sobriquet of "silent partner" in the Purcell firm.[41]

As the office became more established and business warranted a supporting staff, Purcell & Feick began to hire associates to do drafting and other work. Over the next ten years, a changing community of drafters, artists, designers, contractors, and others came to be part of the enterprise that Purcell referred to as "the Team." Many members of the Team regarded their office as the most challenging and interesting place in town to be employed. In contrast to common practice in most architectural offices at the time, active participation in the design process by all employees

was both recognized and encouraged. Drafters were to sign their work and could suggest changes. The idea of the Team meant each individual who was part of the production process shared in the credit for each project. Gertrude Phillips, for example, the office secretary who made the first alphabetic index of the office commissions, was as fully appreciated in her work as Purcell and Elmslie were in performing their own functions as principals. Most of these men and women came to share a special commitment to the progressive ideals. The camaraderie of the Team as a fellowship was rooted not in time cards, salaries, or commission fees, but in a common belief in the organic procedures through which they joined together in the building art. Purcell described the situation:

> There were no important differentials of class or station, no priorities of talent. The good idea—the resolution of a tough problem could come from anyone in the office or on the job, and usually without controversy. One who hit the right answer, no matter whom, had the good word from all and everyone was happy about it. Such an approach automatically expanded our team to everyone who had *anything* whatever to do with the project. We all continually developed our contacts with the shovel men, bench craftsman, trowelers, carriers, plumbers, painters, weavers, wood carvers, glass makers, modelers, bankers, realtors in such a way as to make them feel that their experience and their wise know-how was going to make the building the best. Without Necessity, and the old barn-raising spirit of the pioneers, we knew a building would have no life. One could not invent a building; one could only *grow* it [emphasis original].[42]

In 1908, the firm hired the first full-time permanent drafter, a woman named Mario Alice Parker (1875?–1935). She had moved to Minneapolis from New Hampshire, where she went to drafting school and gained her first practical experience at a planing mill owned by her uncle. Having worked in a series of other Minneapolis offices before coming to Purcell & Feick, Parker proved herself to be competent and dependable. Over the decade she spent with the firm her previous eclectic attitude toward architectural design gave way to a full commitment to organic principles. She was the only member of the Team who came close to mastering the poetic forms of ornamental treatment produced by George Elmslie. Eventually Parker became a successful independent architect in Minneapolis, though some of her earliest commissions were carried through the Purcell & Elmslie accounting system.[43]

A succession of other drafters came and went in the office. The same year that Parker arrived she was joined at the drafting tables by Lawrence B. Clapp, who remained through the change of the partnership to Purcell, Feick, & Elmslie until 1912.[44] In March 1912 a drafter named Paul Haugen, then leaving the Purcell, Feick & Elmslie office, was asked to find someone to fill his place before departing. Haugen knew that a friend, Lawrence A. Fournier (1878–1944), was unhappy with his position at the Minneapolis Ornamental Iron Works. Haugen arranged for Fournier to interview with Purcell, who offered him a job. Although

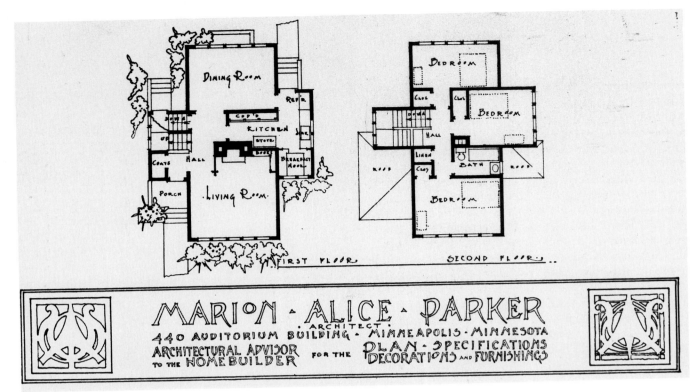

Business card, *Marion Alice Parker. Purcell & Elmslie, designers.*
Photograph courtesy of the Northwest Architectural Archives, University of Minnesota Libraries, St. Paul.

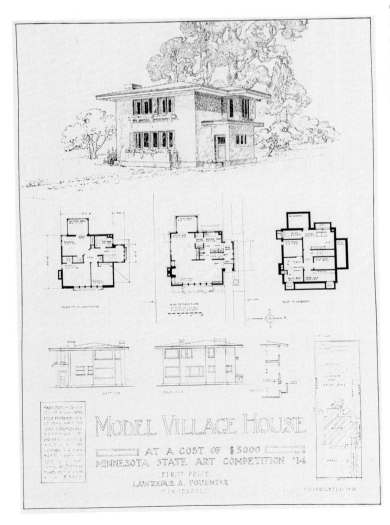

Fournier had previous experience in the offices of Kees & Colburn and William Kenyon in Minneapolis, he was at first self-conscious about his carpenter-drafting background and intimidated by the idea of working for a highly creative firm without the benefit of a formal education. Only a brief time back at his drafting board in the ironworks persuaded him to make the change, however, and the next day he telephoned Purcell to accept. Over the following decade Fournier worked intensively on most of the major commissions built by the firm. In addition, he regularly entered competitions for small houses sponsored by the Minnesota State Arts Commission. He took first place in a 1914 Model Village House contest, and the plan was published in folio along with the second prize entry of Marion Alice Parker. His two-story design for a brick house with an estimated cost of $2,500 won third mention in 1916 and appeared a year later in *The Minnesotan*, a publication of the art commission. When the P&E operation in Minneapolis was reduced to a smaller staff in 1917, Fournier transferred to the Chicago office and remained with George Elmslie after the firm was disbanded in 1921.[45]

The most longstanding figure in the history of the Team came to the firm in 1912. A native-born Minnesotan, Frederick A. Strauel (1887–1974) first worked on the Thomas Snelling residence built in Waukegan, Illinois (1913), and ultimately came to be regarded as the chief drafter of Purcell & Elmslie. The meticulous reliability of Strauel was an article of faith in the office, and Purcell recorded that

Competition for a Model Village House, *for Lawrence A. Fournier, Minnesota State Arts Competition. Northwest Architectural Archives, University of Minnesota Libraries, St. Paul. Photograph by Gary Mortensen and Robert Fogt.*

over the years he had not known Strauel to have ever let a mistake slip by in his work.[46]

Other drafters passed through the firm at different periods, some on the way to establishing their own successful architectural practices. The most prominent of these was John A. Walquist, who became a highly successful architect in New York City. Leroy A. Gaarder exemplified the colorful, sometimes eccentric character of the office personnel. He came to Purcell, Feick & Elmslie in 1912 from earlier experience with a church architect, stayed for five years, and later opened his own office in Albert Lea, Minnesota. While working for P&E, Gaarder attended night classes in architecture at the University of Minnesota, leading Purcell to remember him by his notable habit of carrying a derringer pistol for protection. Other drafters who worked for the firm at various times and about whom little is known beyond their signature on drawings include Oscar H. Banville, L. F. Collins, Kenneth Harrison, Clyde W. Smith, and A. H. Wider.

The Team extended to the many service professionals who contributed design details, mechanical systems, construction, landscaping, ornamentation, and the myriad other aspects of bringing a building into existence. General contractor Fred M. Hegg handled masonry, carpentry, roofing, plastering, and painting for many Purcell & Elmslie buildings. His first job for the firm was the Harold Hineline residence in Minneapolis (1910). Hegg was nearly always the lowest bidder on projects to be built, and his highly regarded crews and subcontractors undertook construction for P&E throughout Minnesota, Iowa, Wisconsin, Illinois, Montana, and the Dakotas. The Hegg foreman was Fritz Carlson, who supervised banks built by the firm in Madison and Hector, Minnesota, as well as the Clayton F. Summy residence (the parents of Edna S. Purcell) designed in 1924 by George Elmslie in Hinsdale, Illinois. Both Carlson and Edward Goetzenberger, a tinsmith, were so pleased to be working with P&E that they had their own homes designed by the firm, an unusual indication of respect for the practice.

Numerous Purcell & Elmslie residences and other structures often required specially built furniture or interior decoration. These craft jobs were sometimes taken by the office staff. Drawings for some of the more finely finished furniture done by the firm were detailed by Emil Frank, a draftsman whose father was the foreman of the woodworking shop of John S. Bradstreet and Company. Frank also collaborated with Harry Rubins, the president of the Bradstreet company after Bradstreet's death, to produce the furniture, paneling, and interior trim of the house for Louis Heitman in Helena, Montana (1916). Ralph B. Pelton, a craftsman, cabinetmaker, and superintendent of construction for the Gallaher residence built in 1909, produced a structurally complex floor lamp designed by Elmslie for the Edna S. Purcell residence in Minneapolis (1913), as well as other handcrafted objects. His demeanor was characteristic of those working for the firm, whose involvement often

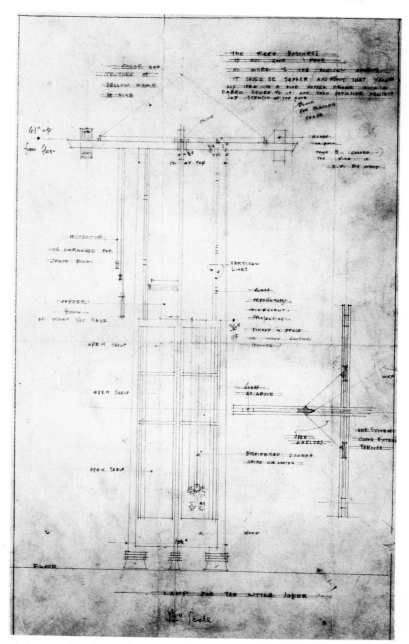

Plan, standing lamp fixture at the Lake Place residence, Minneapolis. Photograph courtesy of the Northwest Architectural Archives, University of Minnesota Libraries, St. Paul.

went far beyond making a living. Purcell was impressed by the man for many years afterwards:

> He was a well educated man of most charming manner; seemed a gentleman born, without pretense; and since he was a very capable craftsman in wood, a jeweler in fact, he perhaps represented a good example of William Morris' builder of the Democratic Future of Man. . . . His work was carried out with precision and a perfection far beyond the call of any contract. His charges bore no relation to the time spent—as I recall $60 for the lamp and $6 for the cases. Hand dovetailed, they were the last of this art I have met with. I should say he

could not have made fifty cents an hour on these jobs—just worked for the love of it.[47]

Two individuals deserve special note in the successful ornamentation achieved by Purcell & Elmslie. The first was a modeler, Kristian Schneider, who worked for many years either at or as a consultant with the American Terracotta and Ceramic Company in Illinois. The Norwegian-born Schneider had been personally tutored by Louis Sullivan over the years and had worked in many cases with Elmslie in the production of various models for clay, cast-iron, and plaster designs. Purcell paid due respect to what the modeler could and could not do:

> Schneider had first come under Sullivan's spell in the Schiller Theater building, 1893, and from then on developed his art in close cooperation with Sullivan and Elmslie. He learned to work from the very simplest of small scale drawings with no need for details. Every pencil trace of Mr. Elmslie's delicate draftsmanship carried full meaning and instruction—mutually understood. Schneider with all his virtuosity of hand and experienced taste in manipulating the plastic clay, could not originate designs and his attempts to produce ornament for others are stale and uninteresting. What George Elmslie did was really poetry and it took Elmslie to conceive and Schneider to call it out of the clay.[48]

Another important craftsman belonging to the role call of the Team was Edward L. Sharretts, who first happened to work with the firm through an order placed with the Minneapolis office of his then employer, the Pittsburgh Plate Glass Company. P&E had some difficulty finding people who could work with the fine lines and color requirements of their leaded glass designs. Sharretts was the man they found to execute some particularly delicate window panels for alterations to the house of George W. Stricker in Minneapolis during 1910. Recognizing an opportunity, he left the glass company where he worked to open his own studio called the Mosaic Art Shops. Sharretts maintained a large stock of the best available glass and reserved the finest pieces for his work with Purcell & Elmslie. Purcell considered the color sense and imagination possessed by Sharretts to be a major contribution in the beauty of the final rendering of the designs. Between 1910 and 1920, the Mosaic Art Shops provided leaded glass panels, mosaics, and lamp fixtures out of a small Minneapolis workshop for nearly every commission built by P&E.

Lastly, there were occasions when a commission could afford the very highest quality of available craftsmanship. Metalwork designs were often executed for Purcell & Elmslie by the studio of Chicago silversmith Robert Jarvie. In addition to the living room light fixtures in the Edna S. Purcell house of 1913, for example, Jarvie completed specially detailed furniture (since missing), a silver flatware service, and personal items for the dwelling. He also executed a silver memorial loving cup commemorating the retirement of James B. Angell from the University of Michigan in 1909. In addition, Jarvie turned to P&E for designs when he was asked to create trophy cups for an aviation meet in 1911. When a large amount of fine furniture was needed quickly, Purcell & Elmslie sent their business to George Niedecken & Company in Milwaukee. The Niedecken company produced a cascade of chairs, sofas, rugs, and other commercial and household furnishings for the firm over a ten-year period.

In November 1909, longstanding events of critical importance to the future of the practice came to a head. George Elmslie had for several years grown increasingly distressed by the deteriorating situation he witnessed in the office of Louis Sullivan. A major financial crisis forced him to take reluctant but unavoidable action. When Sullivan could no longer pay him even a small salary, Elmslie was compelled to find a more reliable situation. Purcell and Elmslie had long talked of working together. In 1910 Elmslie left the Sullivan office and moved to Minneapolis as a full partner in Purcell, Feick, & Elmslie. With his arrival, the firm reached a new creative balance that resulted in advanced organic designs rarely equalled by any other progressive firm.

The degree to which the potential of Purcell & Elmslie was recognized by other organic architects is suggested by an incident involving Frank Lloyd Wright. In November 1909, Purcell received a telephone call from Wright, who was at the Union Depot station in Minneapolis. Saying that he had business to discuss, Wright requested cryptically that Purcell come to the train station and declined an offer to meet at the Purcell & Feick office only a five-minute walk away. When Purcell arrived, Wright said he was leaving for an extended stay in Europe and indicated that he wanted the Purcell firm to take over his own architectural practice.[49] Purcell listened to Wright, then re-

George Feick, Jr., Edna S. Purcell, Catherine Gray, William Gray Purcell, George Grant Elmslie, and Bonnie Elmslie dining in Catherine Gray Residence, 1910. Photograph courtesy of the Northwest Architectural Archives, University of Minnesota Libraries, St. Paul.

*Electric Carriage and Battery Company. Edna S. Purcell in car,
M. L. Hughes, William Gray Purcell, and George Grant Elmslie
standing in front. Photograph courtesy of the Northwest Architectural Archives, University of Minnesota Libraries, St. Paul.*

turned to his office to relate the business proposition to
Elmslie. Although the offer appeared attractive and could
have meant considerable business prospects and prestige,
Elmslie expressed his view of the deal by saying, "Well,
you know Wright." Shortly afterward, Purcell and Elmslie
telegraphed their regrets and declined the opportunity.
Only four years later, Walter Burley Griffin also would ask
Purcell & Elmslie to represent his American commissions
when he left the United States for Australia. [50]

With the arrival of Elmslie in 1910, Purcell was exposed
to a creative talent that had been seasoned for more than
fifteen years by close association with the founding master
of organic architecture, Louis Sullivan. The slow, careful
pace at which Purcell had been developing his understanding of architecture was suddenly interrupted by the presence of Elmslie, a man capable of a voluminous flow of
sophisticated expression. At times, Purcell was unable
wholly to digest the new forms. The two men spent many
hours in deep discussion of the means and ends of organic
design. This frank and intimate communication resulted
in a synergistic working relationship that balanced their
respective strengths and weaknesses, and the division of
labor in the office was restructured along those lines. With
his natural, poetic facility for composition, Elmslie assumed much of the creative work of formulating designs.

Given his bent for structural details, George Feick was in
charge of writing specifications and, when he could meet
the need, engineering. Between these two specializations
Purcell was responsible for managing the flow of the work
between client, office, and contractors, as well as remaining
abreast of the work done by his partners. Part of his management role meant guiding Elmslie toward solutions that
were in line with client needs. As George Feick grew more
uncomfortable with the experimental forms produced by
the firm, Purcell often had to articulate the technical elements of the structures himself. When Elmslie was otherwise occupied, Purcell also handled basic design.

Against the background of democratic give-and-take that
was the office rule, designs went from one production phase
to another with each person bringing forward some contribution to the project. Generally speaking, Purcell would
supply Elmslie with notes and drawings to convey the essential elements of the situation. Elmslie would then render
a delicate pencil study to transform the ideas into graphic
form. In many instances, drawings show that the preliminary ideas Purcell sketched during client interviews appeared unchanged in the final design. On other jobs,
Elmslie provided a wholly different direction for the composition. In subsequent conferences the partners synthe-
sized their understanding into one commonly held view of

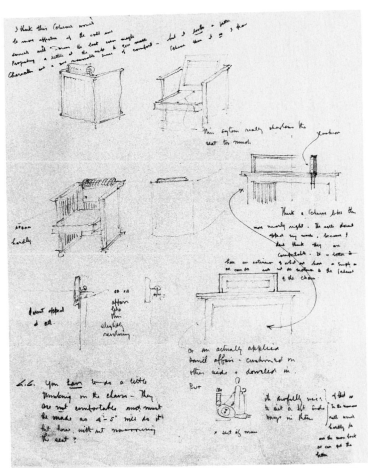

Sketch, with annotations, 1912. A letter by George Grant Elmslie concerning chairs for the Merchant's Bank of Winona. Northwest Architectural Archives, University of Minnesota Libraries, St. Paul. Photograph by Gary Mortensen and Robert Fogt.

values of a single job also can be followed in relationship to other commissions that represent a sequence of type, as with the small open floor plan houses or the commercial interiors of the Edison Shops. Third, the strong interaction between Team members provoked an interweaving of thought in the designs themselves. The varying involvement of office personnel, contractors, and others effected the result, for example, when work was handled separately by the staff of P&E offices that opened in different cities over the years. These three qualifying circumstances vary in impact, and there are some designs that stand out more distinctively than other work. Generally speaking, however, the organic creative process of the firm evolved along these lines.

Relations with clients were naturally one of the most important aspects of the design process. Beyond the obvious fact that without the client there would be no work, Purcell & Elmslie regarded themselves as facilitators, rather than dictators, of the architecture. This attitude encouraged clients to participate in the process and assured that the final design would be a clearer expression of their personalities, living habits, special requirements, and aesthetic inclinations. The P&E approach stood in contrast to the common practice by many competitors of selling historical images from architectural magazines and then squeezing the clients in, with as little reshuffling of the floor plans as possi-

William Purcell and George Elmslie. Chair, 1912. Merchant's Bank of Winona. The Minneapolis Institute of Arts; The Driscoll Arts Accession Fund 93.1.

the design. Often, Purcell prepared a presentation rendering to more easily introduce the concept to the client. If the work was approved, office drafters undertook working drawings, while Feick prepared specifications for construction bids. Once the decision to build was made, full-scale diagrams for built-in furniture or other significant details were drawn by the office staff from a scaled study supplied by Elmslie. Finally, Elmslie or Marion Parker produced drawings for terra-cotta, leaded glass panels, stencils, and other decorative elements that were passed along to craftspeople and technicians.

To gain a better insight into the continuity of the P&E creative process, the designs of the firm can be examined in three interrelated contexts. First, by organic definition, any specific project required unique analysis in terms of site and other conditions. Second, the conception of one project inevitably occurred when other designs also were taking shape. In the P&E office there might be several banks, larger and smaller houses, churches, graphic schemes, or diverse other works-in-progress at the same time. The challenges of one project could and usually did bring some immediate inspiration to another. The design

Interior of the Edison Shop, Kansas City. Photograph courtesy of the Northwest Architectural Archives, University of Minnesota Libraries, St. Paul.

ble. The process of self-discovery suggested by Purcell & Elmslie worked best with residences, where clients controlled directly the decision to build and were often already aware of the kind of house they could expect from the firm. Satisfied P&E clients returned periodically to the firm for further development of their properties such as enlarging alterations, further interior decoration, furniture, garages, landscape fencing, and so on. [51]

Other situations were less predictable. Much of the commercial and institutional design work had to be presented to building committees. The nature of a group decision forced P&E to educate their clients about the progressive ideals in the simplest of terms. This was a balancing act without a net. When the situation was receptive, there might be the danger of succeeding too well. The firm lost an important commission for the St. Paul Methodist Church in Cedar Rapids, Iowa (1912), because Purcell was overly enthusiastic about Louis Sullivan who, still practicing, was a competitor to whom the builder subsequently

turned. [52] On other occasions not even the best of preparations could prevent dissension in conferences with people whose astonishment turned to outrage when confronted with the unconventional new architectural forms, as was one stockholder of the First National Bank at Rhinelander, Wisconsin (1910). [53] Internal company politics might also interfere with getting a job. Henry B. Babson needed no convincing about organic designs, but his brother Fred Babson did not believe them sufficiently mainstream to appeal to the Eastern sense of taste in the commercial marketplace. When Henry Babson was traveling in Europe, his brother made the decision to build a new Edison Shop in New York City without Purcell & Elmslie. This deprived the firm of building on a prominent Fifth Avenue site. They were greatly disappointed to lose such an opportunity.

Ultimately, P&E could only do so much. The decision to build, of course, was finally up to the client. Although Purcell and Elmslie could understand the failure of their own efforts to meet the needs of a situation, sometimes the

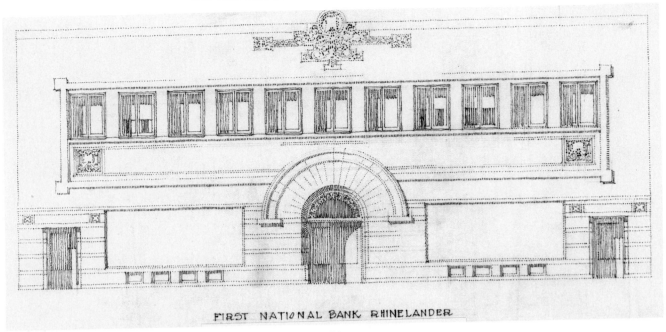

FIRST NATIONAL BANK RHINELANDER

Elevation drawing, *First National Bank, Rhinelander, Wisc.* *Northwest Architectural Archives, University of Minnesota Libraries, St. Paul. Photograph by Gary Mortensen and Robert Fogt.*

Construction of the First National Bank, Rhinelander, Wisc. Photograph courtesy of the First National Bank, Rhinelander.

design was not the source of rejection. They learned that all their hard work was useless against the inhibitions of some people. To feel safer in their decision making, building committees might simply want to buy from the same places as their peers. A prime example of this occurred with events surrounding the proposed First National Bank at Mankato, Minnesota (1911). Magnificent presentation drawings were left for further study with the bank building committee, which was apparently enthusiastic about the organic cause. Only a few weeks later, however, a competi-

tor not known for progressive work landed the job by underbidding with a design that Purcell regarded as an outright transcription of his firm's presentation.[54] The flattery of the imitation was no consolation.

The sting of such disappointments came with the territory. Other events also seemed to have mixed results. Before coming to Minneapolis to live, Elmslie had met and fallen in love with a young Scots woman named Bonnie Hunter. The deep passion that he felt for his work now had a personal focus. She agreed to marry him and came to Minnesota, where the Elmslies took a flat in the same apartment building where the Purcells lived. For two years, George Elmslie was extremely happy in both of his new partnerships. The brooding moodiness to which he was sometimes victim vanished and the character of his work brightened into lighter, more playful expressions. In 1912, however, just two years after they were married, Bonnie died from a failed surgical operation. In spite of efforts by Purcell to get him to stay, Elmslie left Minneapolis and returned to Illinois to live with his sisters. He opened a P&E office in Chicago, arguing that the business of the firm would improve and the location would be more convenient for important clients like Henry Babson. Although he threw himself more deeply than ever into his work, the tragic shock of losing his wife never left him. Periodically over the course of the next decade, Elmslie experienced periods of manic productivity followed by repeated hospitalizations for what was termed nervous exhaustion but was likely depression.

Meanwhile, George Feick continued to become more and more peripheral to the work of the firm. Often, the

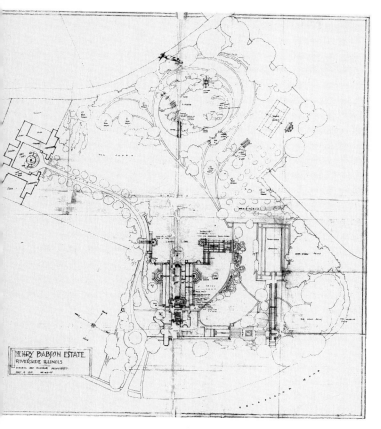

Presentation drawing, 1915. *Landscaping for the Henry B. Babson estate, Riverside, Ill. Photograph courtesy of David S. Gebhard.*

engineering that he should have handled was subcontracted. During his two years in the partnership after Elmslie joined the firm, Feick participated less and less in the flow of projects outside of those he brought to the office himself. Relations with colleagues in the firm were also strained by his gruff personality. After a fractious dispute over personnel, Feick left in the spring of 1912 for a site supervision assignment at the Crane estate in Woods Hole and he never returned to the office. Although in later years Purcell wanted to credit his former partner with some participation as a matter of friendly historical record, he also admitted that at heart Feick was not greatly motivated by the progressive cause. The significant designs through which the firm would find acclaim were therefore largely unaffected by the presence or departure of George Feick, Jr.

Some time would pass before the new working arrangements in the office with Elmslie were optimally realized, but from the beginning there were signs of a powerful achievement in the making for the firm. After 1910 the amount of work in the office more than doubled. George Elmslie brought important business contacts that resulted

Henry B. Babson Service Buildings. Photograph courtesy of the Northwest Architectural Archives, University of Minnesota Libraries, St. Paul.

Babson sleeping porch. Photograph courtesy of the Northwest Architectural Archives, University of Minnesota Libraries, St. Paul.

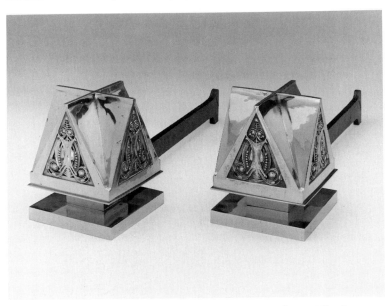

George Grant Elmslie. Andirons, *for Henry B. Babson. The Art Institute of Chicago; Gift of Mrs. George A. Harvey 1971.788a-b.*

in a growing number of commissions from former Sullivan clients, such as Henry B. Babson, Charles R. Crane, and Crane's daughter and son-in-law, the Harold C. Bradleys. Though few in number, these wealthy people were solid patrons of the firm who readily accepted the design forms presented to them. From Babson, for example, P&E inherited the development of his country estate in Riverside, Illinois, that had begun with the original house designed by Sullivan and Elmslie in 1908. Over the next decade Elmslie produced for this dwelling a stream of furniture and embellishments, including a tall clock, leaded glass windows and doors, a variety of fireplace andirons, and numerous electric light fixtures. Sometimes the architects regretted the continual desire of the client to make changes to the house but did their best to accommodate his wishes, as with the enclosure of the sleeping porch in 1912. These unhappy alterations were few, however, and in the context of the larger estate P&E had magnificent opportunities of their own in the development of a master landscaping plan (1914) and service buildings (1915).

Although a man of greater sensitivity than personal wealth, Carl K. Bennett, for whom Sullivan and Elmslie had produced the great National Farmers Bank in Owatonna, Minnesota, also came to Purcell & Elmslie with a variety of commissions. Any changes or additions to the bank building were naturally referred to the firm. Bennett wanted a speculative project developed for small houses (1912), and had graphic materials designed for his various businesses in 1910 and 1914. Over the ten-year period after Elmslie joined the firm, Bennett commissioned two formidable schemes for personal residences (1914 and 1918), both of which met his vision of architecture but were beyond his purse. Aside from a separate landscaping plan executed in 1913, he was unable ever again to realize his creative ambition for building that first blossomed in the Owatonna bank. Nonetheless, Bennett stood ready to lend his prestige and support as needed. Through this connection Purcell and Elmslie continued to develop a wider circle of productive friendships with men who lived in small towns throughout the Midwest, enlarging the network of sympathizers in the agricultural countryside who kept the firm advised of potential jobs.

In order to advertise the message of the new architecture on a larger scale, Purcell regularly delivered addresses to a variety of groups, including architectural clubs, social meetings, and conventions of contractors and suppliers. He gave newspaper interviews and published essays in progressive magazines. In these articles he meant to sensitive readers to the immediate need for Americans to abandon historically derived building forms and express directly the glories of their own unique cultural achievements. One of the best examples of this purpose was the campaign conducted by Purcell against the classical design proposed for the Lincoln Memorial in Washington, D.C. Starting in a nationally syndicated full-page newspaper piece in which he pointed out the illogic of honoring a great American president with a Greek temple, Purcell pressed his arguments later in correspondence with prominent architects such as William Channing Whitney.[55] On a more positive note, Purcell introduced the public to various progressive architects, notably H. P. Berlage and Walter Burley Griffin in *The Craftsman* and *The Western Architect*, respectively. George Elmslie sometimes co-authored these writings.[56]

The principal statement of design philosophy published by P&E appeared in the first of three issues of *The Western Architect* (1913, and two in 1915) that showcased the work of Purcell, Feick, & Elmslie, and later Purcell & Elmslie.[57] Titled "The Static and Dynamics of Architecture," the text described how all great civilizations transmitted the energies of their own singular presences within the creative form of their artifacts. Individual distinctions, however, were possible only because they were simultaneously part of an all-encompassing unity. The essence of any object resulted from an aggregate of dualistic creative expression. In an inescapable, everlasting way there was an archetypal commonality, which they called "the Static," out of which all forms of the same kind arose. This unifying substrate constituted a field of operational function shared by all instances of the class. For example, no matter where or when in the course of history a column was to be found, there was always a relationship of thrust conducted through the form. Each column, however, had a unique existence in any time and place. This was the result of "the Dynamic," an omnipresent interplay of creative energy whose essence was change. Both the unchanging static and the ever-changing dynamic were mutually interpenetrating in all aspects of physical existence.

By nature, the static had the basic quality of utter stillness. This was not conceived of as a vacancy or void, but as an infinite state of potential being. Purcell and Elmslie referred to this virtual state of consciousness as "mind," which could be conceived as the pure source of all functional prototypes. By contrast, the dynamic was a ceaselessly unfolding movement revealed in the specific conditions of any single moment, to be understood in terms of architectonic qualities as the actions of human will, heart, and spirit. Mind and event crystallized together into the building experience. All people since the beginning of humankind shared an inalienable continuity of being, yet within that community the diversity of human response varied with their specific conditions of life. The static quality of mind was the common denominator. Cultural profusion was the dynamic product. In the abstract, this dualistic vision provided a framework to understand design. The actual practice was a sublimely intimate participation with the creative process. To Purcell and Elmslie, an architect had to comprehend the substance of these distinctions.

This spiritual aspect of architectural practice placed the architect in the role of prophet. In this sense the way in which Purcell and Elmslie designed anything was the opposite of professional colleagues who relied on the approach of scientific reductionism. For an organic designer, logic was the child of insight, insight the servant of intuition, and intuition the essence of perceived truth, not the other

way around. A design must reveal, as in an ode of revelation, not only the passage hither but equally the journey hence. The true moment in the birth of a building occurred long before materials were gathered into a physical structure. The result of the past equally informed the cast of the future. In a colloquy with Purcell, Elmslie said:

> We know, of course, that a true architect is under no compulsion to design his building in order to satisfy the inverted logic of the critic. The professors who have catalogued and rationalized a vast body of structural and architectural misstatements, not only believe the nonsense which they have so carefully systematized, but demand that everyone else accept their theology as the spirit and substance of Truth.

Purcell replied in context:

> True enough and as corollary truth to what you say, it is the function of the architect to lead the people as prophet, because when the architect is properly nurtured in true values, he sees things, potential in the seed, which they will come to see only by growth toward flower and fruit, but have not yet seen. In this process of experienced prevision the architect can gently and gradually educate the particular genius and character of any people.[58]

The practical method by which a design translated from inner recognition to a form of external communication was primarily through the graphic arts. Drawings created in the Purcell & Elmslie office were not regarded as an end in themselves, but as vessels, momentary resting places for living ideas. Elmslie emphasized this attitude by often discarding sketches or other drawings once the work of a project had gone past that stage in the conception of a building. The drafting board was viewed as a conduit, a pipeline through which the creative current carried a design forward to the outflow of construction. In the same way, the use of machinery in the building process, such as millworking or other carpentry, was intended only as a similar kind of assistance, not as a statement in itself. This standpoint went hand in hand with the democratic concept motivating the work:

> The drafting board *served*; it was a *tool* for transmitting *free* ideas to craftsmen and machines. The machines were in a sense circumscribed because they were of necessity mechanical tools, but we did not do violence to them and they in turn were not allowed to dictate to us. In this naturally maintained relation, easily maintained because it was seen by us as inevitable, lay our contribution to the first practical demonstration of the democratic relation in the age of manufactured power between man and his machines; between the machine and man; between creative idea and the craftsman; between creative artist and the "consumer" [emphasis original].[59]

The transmission of the living idea was carried beyond the limitations of the graphic method by the actions of the men and women who executed the construction. In moving forward, a design became interactive with the skills and understandings of people other than the architects. Given the dedicated character of people who worked for P&E,

this could result in useful, even essential improvements that had been unforeseen during the creation of the drawing. Purcell, for example, had a humbling experience when he insisted to an experienced work crew that ceramic floor tiles be laid in perfect accord with his straight-lined drawing. After Purcell rejected two earnest attempts by tile layers to meet this demand and ordered the floor redone yet again, the frustrated foreman told the architect to try the work himself. Purcell took up the challenge, and realized very quickly to his embarrassment there was a world of difference between an abstract structural idea on paper and the necessary workings of the building materials to bring that idea into actual use.[60]

Long accustomed to virtually unlimited resources for realization of his architectural visions, George Elmslie had a similar lesson in store shortly after his arrival in Minneapolis. New designs from the firm departed immediately from the plainer, less ornamented constructions of Purcell & Feick, as Elmslie elaborated compositional depth and added powerful decorative expression. One of the first projects that showed what Elmslie could contribute, though, also revealed a potentially fatal inexperience with practicality. Purcell found himself having to chide his new partner, whose flights of unrestrained creativity were "willingly paid for by very wealthy clients. George Elmslie was at first naturally out of key with the modest business of Purcell and Feick which had no such cloth to cut." The incident soon after Elmslie arrived brought things to a head:

> In the [Charles W.] Sexton house that Purcell and Elmslie did at Lake Minnetonka, George detailed a paneled ceiling cornice of enameled cabinet work for the living room of this country house. He called for twenty-two mouldings in that 24″ wide cornice requiring *704!* [emphasis original] mitred and glued joints all made on the job. That was just too much for our able carpenter-foreman, August Lennartz, who greatly admired George and loved to show his own skill in executing his details. Well then and there with the boys in the office to second me, I began to put my foot down. . . . The situation left us open to justifiable criticism that would have [ruined] both our business and our reputation for well balanced architecture at once.[61]

Fortunately for George Elmslie there were to be clients who could and did afford a larger palette. The first major residence to be designed in the Purcell, Feick, & Elmslie period was the E. L. Powers house (1910) near Lake of the Isles in Minneapolis. This house shows clearly the transition by Elmslie from familiar forms used when in the Sullivan office to architectonic treatments that presage the more refined lines of later P&E residential designs. The well-to-do client was a vice president of the Butler Brothers mail merchandising company, who had hired Purcell & Feick to build a temporary warehouse in 1907. He was sympathetic to the progressive architecture and gave them a free hand in the design of his new dwelling. Even so, first estimates placed the costs much higher than what he and his wife were willing to spend. The firm redrew the plans,

making studies of the relationship of cubic footage to construction expenses. Purcell and Elmslie were surprised to find that a thirty percent reduction in size yielded only a four percent cost savings. Reflecting on this experience as they redrafted an alternate scheme at their own expense, the firm learned an important practical lesson in the economies of form:

> Practically the same amount of piping, plumbing, wiring, doors and windows, would serve two houses, one which was as much as 50 percent larger than the other in mere size, if the number of living or utility units were not increased. It was, therefore, plain to us that our efforts to solve the terrific cost pressure placed on us by clients could not be solved by compressing the size of rooms to a point where they were just barely satisfactory to the owners, but that we could be freer to give our clients more living space without endangering the cost factor, providing we could keep to a definite structural simplicity.[62]

The site for the Powers house presented a potentially awkward problem. The property had a view of the lake at the rear of a narrow lot, but there was also the necessity of

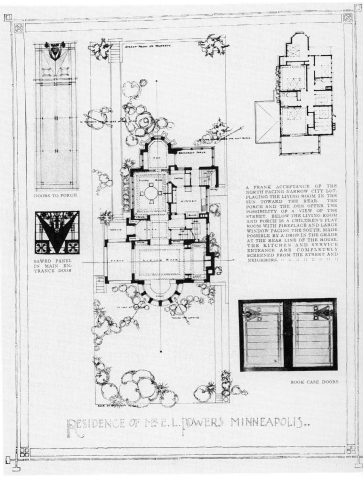

Plan, *1910. E. L. Powers residence, Minneapolis.* The Western Architect, *January 1913.*

Dining room, 1910. E. L. Powers residence, Minneapolis. The
Western Architect, *January 1913.*

Terracotta detail, front entry. E. L. Powers residence, Minneapolis. Photograph by Karen Melvin, Minneapolis.

keeping a suitable presence on the street. Social convention
would have placed the primary rooms forward in the plan
to receive visitors, but in the Powers design the living room
was aligned toward the lake and best seasonal sunlight. The
main entrance was moved deep within the site to open into
the side of the structure. While the mass of the house
largely filled the width of the lot, the entry hall, living
room, and dining room intersected in a wide cruciform
to belie any sense of tightness. Upstairs, there were four
bedrooms, two baths, and a sewing room. To keep a sense
of active use on the street, the presence of a screened porch
and small sitting room on the first floor was emphasized by
a four-sided, piered tower. The balcony above the front
porch was marked with a triple strip of molding, a feature
also seen on a large sleeping porch at the rear. This banding
became a signature that appeared regularly on subsequent
houses by the firm. At the time Elmslie took some office
criticism for his unusual approach but, as he pointed out
some years afterward to his partner, his instincts were good:
"*Well*, I remember the basic layout. It disturbed you greatly
at first in that you were a bit averse to showing it because
it was too unusual and not likely to suit. However, *you sold*
it and all were happy."[63]

Bifold doors, 1910. E. L. Powers residence, Minneapolis. Photograph by Karen Melvin, Minneapolis.

The Powers house offered Elmslie his first substantial opportunity for ornamental treatment since joining the firm. Almost all of the forms of enrichment that appeared in later Purcell & Elmslie designs had a presence in this dwelling. The variety of decorative elements seen in the residence reveal the depths to which the inner rhythms of a design could be detailed. P&E believed that these kinds of beauties derived spiritually, arising out of the interplay of forces being resolved within the plan. Rather than some fanciful glamour, this was meant to be a sheen of gracefulness throughout the structure of joyous pleasure in self-expression.

In the Powers residence, Elmslie began to reign in his passion to find more carefully restrained, but at least equally poetic, decorative forms. To strengthen the presence of the entrance at the side of the house, terra-cotta panels frame the upper half of the front entrance. A rich dark green glazing covers three-dimensional geometric forms that develop into sprays of stylized leaves and berries. Elmslie had done similar panels earlier for the Henry B. Babson house in Riverside, Illinois, but here the effect was richer while more articulate. The cool earthen mood of terra-cotta joined with the dark brown brick of the first floor walls to set a calm, protective atmosphere for the approach to the house. Against the tan floated-plaster surface of the second floor a long dark stained wooden flower box with sawed wood end brackets stretched beneath the length of a

casement window range above the front door, emphasizing the horizontality of the composition. Other sawed wood panels were used visually to expand the narrow front elevation with a patterned frieze at the top of the screened porch facing the street. The result was a mixture of formal propriety and reserved exuberance that undoubtedly expressed the personality of the client.

Inside the residence, Elmslie placed heavy frames of straight-lined oak cornicework in the main rooms. To lessen its visual weight, light-colored plaster frieze panels set below the dark wood were frosted with courses of polychrome stencils. The stencilwork followed the line of the integrated interior trim system, which had elements of both Purcell & Feick and earlier work by Elmslie. In the dining room a built-in buffet with sawed wood panels filled one wall while doors throughout the house (oak downstairs and mahogany upstairs) were inlaid with delicate patterns of wood. Gilded wall sconces with Stueben art glass shades hung symmetrically on first floor walls and cupped bronze electroliers dropped from the principal ceilings to provide sources of artificial light. Built-in book cabinets held leaded glass panels related to those of larger lights in the doors of an adjacent sun porch. At the opposite side of the living room, Elmslie mounted a shield of polychrome terra-cotta above the raised hearth of the fireplace and enclosed the space with a nook of flanking wall seats. The happy burst of green and yellow glazing on the fireplace decoration fulfills the sense of expectation set by the monochrome terra-cotta panels at the front entry. This instance of terra-cotta for hearth enrichment would be one of only two uses of the material in the interior of a house, the other being for an alteration, both dated the first year Elmslie came to the partnership.[64]

Completion of the Powers interior was placed in the hands of a talented designer, Gustav Weber. Born in France of German parents repatriated during the Franco-Prussian war of 1870, Weber learned fine cabinetmaking in Stuttgart and traveled to America in 1893 to see the Columbian Exposition. He remained to study interior design in New York and became head of a large firm. He moved to Minneapolis in 1903 and worked for William A. French & Company before setting up his own business in 1911. Weber was asked to consult with Purcell & Elmslie on the new house after making a furnishings presentation for the Interlachen Country Club where E. L. Powers was a committee chairman. He took enthusiastically to the organic ideals and prepared a large rendering for the dining room furnishings. The watercolor drawing shows an integrated interior scheme fully in harmony with the architectural finish, centered around a table, chairs, and carpet designed by Elmslie. The professional association was a success that continued, and Weber appreciated the opportunity when remembering the outcome of his Powers work:

"That was the beginning. Wakefield, Dr. Owre, I believe [P&E residential commissions (1911 and 1914, respectively)] followed and many others. Wonderful how it all worked out! . . . It was Purcell and Elmslie and you in particular [Purcell] who introduced me to Form and Function, which as far as I was permitted to make use of it has been the dominating thought and principle of my work."[65]

The majority of works by Purcell & Elmslie to proceed through construction were residences, and many of these structures have survived relatively intact. Three categories of P&E houses are apparent. The series of small open-plan houses that had begun with Purcell & Feick in the Catherine Gray house continued to develop after Elmslie joined the firm. Each expression of this idiom found different

emphasis according to variations of site, economy, and client that resulted in an exploration of the possibilities of progressive form. At one end of the spectrum, some of these dwellings were built inexpensively for clients who could afford few if any architectural effects beyond those available from the austere execution of the plan itself. Others, more in the mid-range of cost, mixed the results of smaller size with an allowance for more ornamental enrichment, or traded the potential of creative embellishments for larger square footage. Only rarely was both the expansion of the space and the development of a full decorative treatment possible in open plan projects.

For Purcell and Elmslie, this unfoldment of variations soon led to the development of plans and buildings which they felt were far removed from the original suggestion of the form by Frank Lloyd Wright. Among the designs forming part of this unfolding sequence were residences for H. J. Myers (Minneapolis, 1908), Terrence McCosker (Minneapolis, 1909), Edward Goetzenberger (Minneapolis, 1910), T. R. Atkinson (Bismark, North Dakota, 1910), A. B. C. Dodd (Charles City, Iowa, 1910), Harold E. Hineline (Minneapolis, 1910), John Leuthod (or Beebe house, St. Paul, 1912), Maurice I. Wolf (Minneapolis, 1912 [built in 1919]), and E. S. Hoyt (Red Wing, Minnesota, 1913/1915). The variations seen in the plans for these houses illustrate how flexible the simple idea at their common root could be, reflecting the modern cultural life shared by the clients while at the same time developing personal plan specializations and decorative elements.

The residence designed for C. T. Backus, a piano tuner, in Minneapolis, Minnesota (1915) was one of the simplest and least costly of the open plan houses done by P&E, but the results clearly demonstrated the ability of the firm to transcend monetary limitations and create vibrant architectural forms. The design was a simple cube whose massing was enlivened by broad, deep eaves around the entire two-story house. The front entry was sheltered by a pergola bearing a dark-brown trellis roof supported on plaster piers. The piers and all exterior wall surfaces were finished in a light pink version of the salmon color often found on P&E dwellings. Casement windows, including a slide-panel Whitney window in the living room, punctuated the sides of the house in balanced groups.

The plan of the house incorporated a variety of architectural effects to create a sense of spaciousness that belies the 1,200 feet square of the plan. A strip of small square windows ran nearly the full length of the first floor above a bookcase and built-in buffet that extended along an entire wall, joining living and dining areas with one line of cabinetry. The sunken front entrance was separated from the interior by a low wooden grille bannister. A large wooden grille that grew naturally from the definition of the interior

Exterior perspective, Bachus residence, Minneapolis. Photograph courtesy of the Northwest Architectural Archives, University of Minnesota Libraries, St. Paul.

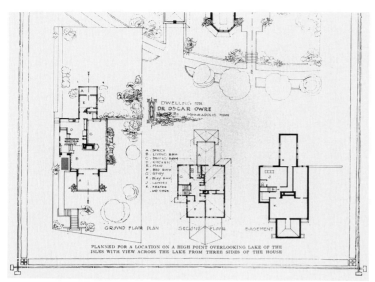

Plan. Oscar Owre residence, Minneapolis. The Western Architect, *January 1913.*

trim moldings took the place usually occupied by a fireplace and chimney stack. This cost-saving solution (Backus could not afford masonry for a fireplace) effectively divided the living and dining rooms into two focal areas. The small rectangular plan of the kitchen included a special P&E innovation, a built-in breakfast nook which lent its own special aura of place. Upstairs the plan contained three bedrooms, two of which opened into each other through a folding panel door wall, and a bathroom with a full wall of built-in storage cabinets. The integration and extension of functional space in the Backus residence established the dwelling as a high watermark in the design of small houses for Purcell & Elmslie.

Intermediate-size open plan dwellings accounted for most of the residences built by P&E. Some, such as the Oscar Owre house in Minneapolis (1911, with later furniture in 1914, garage and landscaping in 1918) were designed for more affluent clients whose budgets could allow for a wider creative latitude. The site was a suburban lot with a waterfront view. The first floor plan was organized around a fireplace with raised hearth, accommodating the usual flow of living room, dining room, kitchen, entrance and stairwell. A large porch placed at the front took advantage of the view and another porch at the rear supported a second floor sleeping porch whose wall carried the typical P&E triple-band moldings. The massing of the design set along the deep axis of the lot created an impression of privacy by extending the roofs with pointed hoods over the front and back. The sides of the house opened to the sunlight through lengths of casement windows.

Owre, a dentist, was intent on having nothing but the best materials and workmanship used in the building of his new home, despite his unwillingness at first to consider extra costs. Under the watchful eye of the client, P&E was able to include inside the house sawed wood, leaded glass panels, and lighting fixtures, and an elaborate exterior fin-

ish treatment including deep flowerboxes with column trim details. The interest Owre had in using sturdy building materials, however, became a problem in another aspect. He demanded that bronze nails be used in shingling the roof. The mouths of the workmen, who traditionally held nails between their teeth as they worked, were badly irritated by the metal. Many of he nails fell into the copper roof flashing, where underfoot they punched tiny holes that went unnoticed at the time. The expensive repairs that later became necessary were a less than amusing result of Owre's attempt to manage house construction with the precision to which he was accustomed in dental work.

The second type of P&E house was larger, generally cruciform in plan, and usually highly detailed with decorative treatment. Few commissions offered the kind of opportunity found in the request of Josephine Crane Bradley for the firm to build a summer residence on the Cape Cod estate of her father, Charles R. Crane. Crane had been a longtime client of Louis Sullivan, but the two men were estranged by Sullivan's demand for payment on services not yet rendered during construction of the first house built by Crane for his daughter in Madison, Wisconsin, in 1909. Because Elmslie was reluctant to abandon the work when he joined in partnership with Purcell, the decoration of this dwelling was subsequently carried as a P&E account. In September 1910, Crane contacted Elmslie to handle some mechanical revisions at his summer house in Woods Hole, Massachusetts. Elmslie was to be married the same evening that Crane called, and Purcell responded in his place. This was the beginning of a lucrative and highly satisfying series of projects for the vacation estate that included a half dozen small houses from 1910 to 1913: an icehouse, toolhouse, and Japanese-style bridge (1912); and a greenhouse, a pier, and a boathouse with second-floor cypress paneled library (1913). All of these designs fitted deliberately into the character of the traditional Cape Cod

Josephine Crane Bradley residence #1, Madison, Wisc. Wayne Andrews, Architecture in Chicago and Mid-America: A Pictographic History, *1968, p. 59.*

Presentation rendering, 1912. *Josephine Crane Bradley summer residence (aka "Bradley Bungalow"), Woods Hole, Massachusetts. Charles R. Crane Estate. Northwest Architectural Archives, University of Minnesota Libraries, St. Paul. Photograph by Gary Mortensen and Robert Fogt.*

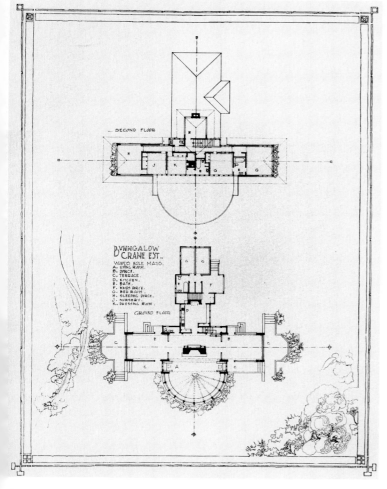

cottage and blended indiscernibly with the existing architectural environment in which they were situated. The commission for the Bradley summer residence, however, was an unparalleled opportunity for the creativity of P&E to express itself.

Originally, the client intended to purchase a three-room portable cabin from a magazine advertisement and have Purcell & Elmslie make some alterations. As Purcell conducted his interview with the Bradleys to determine what they wanted, the pre-fabricated house plan was rapidly left behind. Mrs. Crane said that beyond the basic accommodation for herself, her husband, and children, there must be provisions for guests, a household staff, and entertainment amenities. After Elmslie reviewed Purcell's notes he produced three schemes, two for intermediate-sized houses and one much larger. When Purcell presented these schemes to the Bradleys in May 1912, the two smaller houses were glanced at briefly and set aside. The elaborate third plan represented a complete departure from the more austere arrangements of the first two sketches and was approved for construction nearly unchanged. Only one request was placed on P&E by Crane and the Bradleys: the house had to be ready for a family wedding during the coming October. The architects were given an unlimited budget and told to bring the house into being in five months. Charles R. Crane went to Europe while his daugh-

Plan, 1912. Josephine Crane Bradley summer residence, Woods Hole, Mass., The Western Architect, January 1913.

View to the Josephine Crane Bradley summer residence. The Western Architect, *July 1915.*

ter and son-in-law departed for the summer to California.

Excavation work was ordered by telegram to the Crane estate foreman while working drawings were developed under high pressure in the office. The site was extraordinary. Located on the spur of a rocky peninsula called Juniper Point, the structure was to be placed at the raised tip of the land, full face to the sea with Martha's Vineyard on the horizon. Elmslie perched the body of the house on the small rise, with two flanking wings spread outward above open air porches. The design was nicknamed the "airplane" house by the firm. Household service areas were arranged in an extension toward the Cape and the rest of the Crane estate. Open terraces surrounded the seaside elevations wrapping around a large half-cylinder bow window that followed the curve of water on the beachfront. The central core of the structure rested on a massive arched fireplace whose line moved in response to the window bay. Oak beams revealed in the ceiling were anchored underneath the line of the second floor wall, tethered together visually by finely sawed decorative wood panels. Upstairs, four bedrooms were set in a line across the width of the second floor, terminated at each end by small porches.

The exterior surfaces were finished in cypress shingles, while the house within was warmed by golden-hued oak paneling and woodwork. Matching bookcases and built-in writing desks were positioned symmetrically on the east and west walls of the living room, and the numerous leaded glass windows and doors had open patterns for an unobstructed view. Landscaping included specially prepared local sod and shrubbery, though the rocky core of the site presented some difficulties in placement. Completely furnished with rugs, furniture, monogrammed linen and bedding, and all other equipment, the house stood ready to receive the Bradleys on September 30, 1912. Only once during construction had Charles R. Crane inspected the work, at the prodding of local residents who were disturbed by the modern form of the house. Crane approved wholeheartedly of the results of his commission and paid the $30,000 costs without concern.

A second house descended from the Bradley bungalow

Living room, 1912. Josephine Crane Bradley summer residence. The Western Architect, *July 1915.*

project was built roughly at the same time in 1912 near Lake Minnetonka, Minnesota, for banker Edward W. Decker. Like the Bradley design, the Decker house was intended to be a summer residence. Designed for a wooded lot, the house was similar to the preceding example but somewhat larger. The raised hearth of the fireplace was set back further into the structure and reduced in mass. This arrangement opened the length of the ground floor to open movement from east to west porches across a tiled surface. Unlike the Bradleys, the Deckers required a formal dining room. Paneled in rose pine with dual built-in buffets, the space was furnished with custom-made dining room table and chairs. Seven bedrooms and three baths made up a second floor. A service building that was connected to the main house by a breezeway contained a garage, servant quarters, and other service areas. Leaded glass, electroliers, and sawed wood beam ends decorated the interior throughout the dwelling.[66]

The third group of houses that was designed over the years of the Purcell & Elmslie practice represents those dwellings whose solutions were unique or only distantly

Exterior perspective, E. W. Decker residence, Lake Minnetonka, Minn. The Western Architect, *July 1915.*

Garage, E. W. Decker residence. Photograph courtesy of the Northwest Architectural Archives, University of Minnesota Libraries, St. Paul.

reflective of other residential work. Most of these projects were not built, some in part because the clients were taken aback by the radical nature of the form. Another common reason for unbuilt residential designs was cost. Because the firm prided itself on an ability to deliver work within a budget, expense per se was usually not the barrier. This practice, however, was not always successful. In an instance of one of the small open plan houses, the Palmer-Cantini residence of 1914, P&E got carried away with an exquisite solution that bore no relation to the economic reach of the client. Even though the composition was an eloquent example of the form, construction costs would have been far in excess of most small houses. Purcell considered this unhappy circumstance to have been an occasion when mechanical and architectural considerations on the drafting board had overcome their living purpose and become "a paper project that could not have any reality in that world which the client had to face . . . It deserved not to be built."[67] The third sequence of P&E house designs suffered from these two difficulties in a variety of ways, and this frequently accounts for the rarity of their construction.

One house to be completed, however, suffered from being overwrought because the client demanded it. Purcell & Elmslie were always concerned with the newest developments in domestic engineering and experimented with air conditioning systems, central vacuum cleaning systems, and other work saving devices. Such specialization was carried to extremes at the request of long-time client Josephine Crane Bradley. For the third of her houses to be built or furnished by P&E, she required the services of Team draftsman Lawrence A. Fournier for one full month on site to make detail drawings:

> In this second Bradley house, the emphasis was on "push the button" living, with the house made into a perfect machine for accomplishing all the household life as automatically as possible. The closets and storerooms were a maze of specialized subdivisions for every possible article. The kitchen was a pioneer study in scientific arrangement.

A similar preoccupation with mechanical conveniences had occurred at her behest in earlier work, but the client later admitted, "Well, it's a lovely house and we like it, but perhaps we did overdo the machinery a little bit. Sometimes it feels a bit like living in some kind of glorified office building."[68]

At times P&E failed to accommodate client needs by paying attention to arrangements that already worked well in an existing house. In the residence for Mr. and Mrs. Henry L. Simons of Glencoe, Minnesota (1915), the plan and decorative articulation of this house represented an unusual combination of public and private life. Simons, who was a banker in this small town, was a prominent citizen and enjoyed having his many friends and customers over for visits. The clients were greatly pleased by the proposed design and money was not a problem. One critical element, however, had been overlooked. An atmosphere of relaxed familiarity was a chief characteristic of the existing Simons home. Although the dwelling P&E proposed to build correctly assayed the sophisticated character and intellectual interests of the clients, the expression of those factors in a new and enriched form would not support the easygoing social interaction that the Simons enjoyed. Humility was the element that had been overlooked in the design, and the plans for the new house were set aside.

In one magical instance, a completely novel and unparalleled design formed the exquisite solution to a complex and intensively specific building program. In 1913, Purcell wanted to provide a house for his wife and growing family. Built on a site near Lake of the Isles in Minneapolis, the Edna S. Purcell residence represented a unique moment

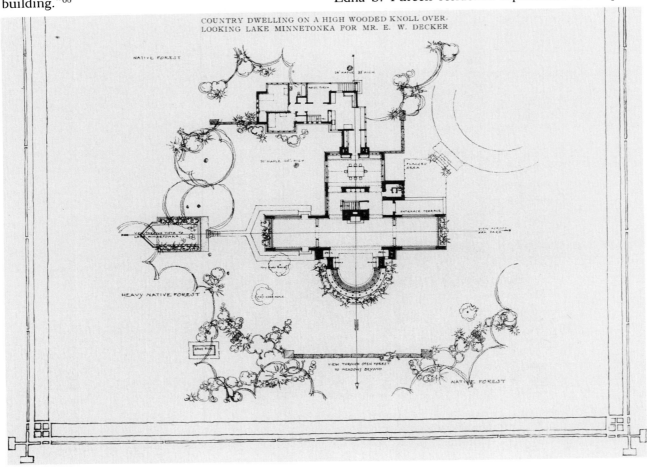

Plan, 1912. E. W. Decker residence. The Western Architect, January 1913.

Presentation rendering, 1914. Palmer-Cantini residence, Minneapolis. Photograph courtesy of David S. Gebhard.

Construction of the Josephine Crane Bradley residence #2, 1914.
Photograph courtesy of the Northwest Architectural Archives, University of Minnesota Libraries, St. Paul.

Exterior, Lake Place during winter. Photograph courtesy of the Northwest Architectural Archives, University of Minnesota Libraries, St. Paul.

The Purcell family portrait near the writing nook at Lake Place. Photograph courtesy of the Northwest Architectural Archives, University of Minnesota Libraries, St.Paul.

in the creative expression of the firm and became the most complete fulfillment in residential design of their architectural ideals. The standard shaped lot was fifty feet wide and one hundred-fifty feet long. In order to avoid the visual crush of surrounding houses and create a sense of privacy, P&E set the body of the dwelling back thirty feet from the street. The ground floor plan consisted of a long rectangle aligned on the linear axis of the lot. A square-shaped footprint for the second floor containing three bedrooms and a bath crossed the lower floor at a tangent, with the whole effect of room arrangements completing a three-dimensional cruciform. From the entryway, steps descended easily to the sunken living room and rose upward to the open dining area set directly in line with a tented ceiling that ran the full length of the house. Outside, a reflecting pool on the eastern front of the house passed morning sunlight through a seven by twenty-eight foot opening of leaded glass windows to shimmer as an aurora within the interior.

The scale of the house accentuated the flowing environment established by the floor plan. The raised hearth in the living room balanced the presence of the tall range of east-facing windows. An intimate writing nook cuddled by bookcases developed from the dining room balcony prow on the other side of the room, with the built-in cabinetry and furniture integrated with a system of oak wall moldings throughout the interior. Brightly colored stencil patterns, embroidered cheviot draperies, and specially designed pendant light fixtures executed by metalsmith Robert Jarvie dressed the geometric plan with a curvilinear playfulness. Artworks incorporated into or acquired for the residence by

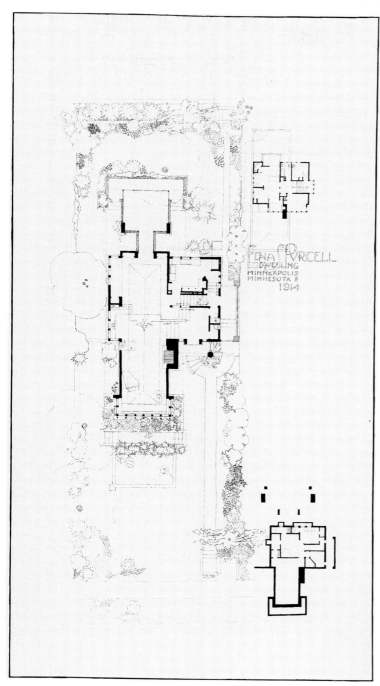

Plan, Lake Place, Minneapolis. Photograph courtesy of the Northwest Architectural Archives, University of Minnesota Libraries, St. Paul.

adopted a second boy, James, and the morning room adjacent to the master bedroom was converted to a bedroom. A pullman-style bed installation incorporated a fold-out study desk, storage drawers for clothes, and a bin for toys.

The house included more than seventy panels of leaded glass, and the windows were arranged so that most had landscape views rather than a look into neighboring houses. In a characteristically humorous touch, a special pair of side lights bearing the legend "Peek A Boo" that flanked the front door were set one facing inside and the other outside. The dramatic effects of light, both natural and artificial, were carefully planned to deliver alternate senses of bright welcome or warm enclosure. Decorative effects accented by the interior color scheme were arranged to deliver a sense of bright welcome or warm enclosure in subtle tones of chamois and pale lavender. A sinuous sawed wood panel set in a trabeated beam by the front entrance contained a poetic summary of the psychological and historical heritage behind the house with the phrase "Gray Days and Gold." To further make the point, a portrait of W. C. Gray that had originally been painted for the Chicago Hall of Fame exhibit at the World's Columbian Exposition was installed on the wall just inside the door. Named after the street on which it was located, the Lake Place house was the most intense effort of the firm to express in architectural terms the supremely important values of family and community at the heart of their work.

Because the last part of a project to be developed—at the point in the process when available money was usually scarcest—was interior furnishings, there the firm met with the most frustration in their desire to achieve a fully integrated environment. In his own Lake Place house, Purcell spent freely to have furniture specially built (though he was forced by circumstance to use an unsuitably colored preexisting dining room suite). Most clients, however, could

the Purcells included paintings by Lawton S. Parker, Albert Fleury, and Charles Livingston Bull, and there was also a sculpture group by Richard Bock. As originally built, the second floor plan featured two bedrooms, a sitting room, a bath, and sleeping porch. The master bedroom opened on the east side through a folding wall panel into a morning room with small raised hearth. Dual cedar storage bins set flush in the floor took advantage of space created by the tented ceiling of the room below. In 1915 the Purcells

Entry, Lake Place, Minneapolis. Photograph courtesy of The Minneapolis Institute of Arts.

not do as much. P&E was often faced with making provisions for existing furniture, and the commercially available or family heirloom pieces clients brought with them were jarring in their new homes. Traditional furniture designs that were often revivalist in form sat uneasily within the clean lines that defined the interiors of P&E houses, while dark finishes and ornate fabrics clashed with the delicate color schemes of the stencils, leaded glass, and terra-cotta. Opportunities to remedy this situation were rare, but on occasion Purcell & Elmslie could later provide new furniture and decoration for houses built years earlier. In general, however, the firm supplied most of the furnishings that they were able to include in the form of built-in cabinets, such as dining room buffets and bookcases, or other permanently installed features like window seats.

One of the great strengths of Purcell & Elmslie was the ability to introduce personal comforts and conveniences into their architecture. Because the writing of letters and personal journals was a frequent occupation of the time, the firm often included built-in desks or writing nooks in their houses. In a remodeling at the Oscar Owre house in 1914, one of the occasions when P&E were able to return to a job at a later time, an upstairs room was equipped for use as a study with a desk and bookcases manufactured by the John S. Bradstreet Company. One of the amenities designed for this installation was a special large drawer that could be pulled out at elbow height to hold a full-sized reference dictionary.

Dining room suites were the most common form of freestanding furniture done by the firm. The earliest table and chairs designed by Purcell were built in 1908 as a wedding gift for his new wife, but after the arrival of Elmslie nearly all the furniture drawings came from his hand. Over the course of a decade two types of dining room furnishing made an appearance. Beginning in 1910, Elmslie created a series of suites that had round or square oak tables grouped with tallback chairs. The most important examples of this type were built for the Harold C. Bradley house, the E. L. Powers house, and as a wedding gift for Bonnie Hunter Elmslie, all in 1910. The table bases had pedestals made of tangent wooden grilles that crossed beneath the center of the tabletop. These grilles could be made of plain shaft rows or frame more complex sawed wood panels. Height in the chairbacks was deliberate, with the intent being to frame the human head for more pleasant visibility under the lighting conditions of the time. The splat of each chair was treated as a decorative field, also in sawed wood, and a monogram usually pierced the headband in a final decorative accent.

Another type of design emerged beginning in 1913. Smaller triangular-backed chairs were grouped with delicate four-footed tables. One of this kind represents the most elegant of the furniture to be designed by P&E. Built in 1915 by the John S. Bradstreet Company under the supervision of Team draftsman Emil Frank, the Hanna table was made of "Cuban white mahogany, inlaid with English holly, strips of copper, and gold leaf backed on irridescent porcelain." Leg supports were ornamented with square tubes of brushed silver fillets, with the legs joined together by a square shelf panel just above the floor. The chair tops had insets of small leaded glass medallions at the top of the back and were covered in a bright silk damask. Square in shape when contracted to the smallest size, the tabletop was left free of a center break by providing end bolsters, complete with matching inlay, that extended to rest on apron shafts operated by finger pulls. A matching serving buffet also was built, complete with a hidden drawer opened by concealed trigger latch. The effect was so pleasing and beautiful to the client that she believed the set should finally rest in a museum.[69] Additional furniture along these lines also was built by the Bradstreet firm for the Louis Heitman house in Helena, Montana (1916).

Other domestic furniture design occurred on a more irregular basis and most often took the form of incidental pieces like chairs, fern stands, and writing desks. Much of this work was done in conjunction with remodeling alterations rather than as part of a complete residential commission. Unfortunately, the surviving records of the firm do not contain a complete account of these projects, and much of the production has disappeared. Various publications show a delicately inlaid writing table and chest of drawers for W. G. A. Millar, a relative of Elmslie (1910); a desk for Josephine Crane Bradley (1910); and a cubic-shaped chair for the sleeping porch remodeling of the Henry B. Babson house in Riverside, Illinois (1912). At the same time as the Babson chair, Elmslie also designed an extraordinary tall clock for the entrance hallway in the house that Purcell christened "the Grandchildren's Clock." Made of mahogany, the front of the case was pierced by a sawed wood panel that revealed the swing of the pendulum in a four part rhythm intended to signify "tick, tock, tick, tock." The cast bronze face of the timepiece was modeled by Kristian Schneider, the metalwork was executed by silversmith Robert Jarvie, and the original clock hands were made of solid gold.[70]

Light sources were an important part in the success of the color scheme for most interiors, and P&E had some lamps custom-made for clients. In commercial designs, these most often took the form of wall sconces, suspended plateaus of upward directed electric lights, and thin long pendant electroliers that could drop more than eight feet in length from a high ceiling. Residential lights were usually a combination of plain dark metal catalog fixtures for room walls and specially-made inverted bronze hemispheres to hang in the center of the room. Wealthier clients could be provided with more elaborate designs, such as the four electroliers placed in the vacation estate library of Charles R. Crane in Woods Hole, Massachusetts (1912). Some of the most successfully integrated fixtures were three matching ceiling lights executed for the John H. Adair house in Owatonna, Minnesota (1913). Each hanging light consists of a metal frame from which dropped the opaque cup of an inverted glass bowl. A fine band of tiny stencils girdles the top of the light saucer with designs that originally

Dining room, Josephine Crane Bradley residence #1. Photograph courtesy of the Northwest Architectural Archives, University of Minnesota Libraries, St. Paul.

Chair, E. W. Decker residence. The Minneapolis Institute of Arts. Photograph by Gary Mortensen and Robert Fogt.

Sideboard and pair of chairs, 1915. Dining room suite for Mrs. Hanna. Private collection. Photograph by Gary Mortensen and Bob Fogt.

Amy Hamilton Hunter Lamp, 1916. Photograph courtesy of the Northwest Architectural Archives, University of Minnesota Libraries, St. Paul.

echoed a similar pattern on the walls. Smaller wall sconces and hall lights completed the treatment.

As their public exposure increased, P&E became recognized as a professional competitor for important commissions across the midwest. Their success, however, was acknowledged less as architecture than as artistic achievement, as if there was some exclusionary rule between the two. An example of the disinterest shown by their professional colleagues in the new architecture can be seen in an incident when Purcell and Elmslie hosted H. P. Berlage, the renowned Dutch architect, during his visit to Minneapolis in 1911. Purcell sent invitations to every architect in Minneapolis and St. Paul to attend a lecture and reception with Berlage, but he later reported that only two respondents came to the event.[71]

The air of practiced aloofness toward the organic architects—the real ones, anyway, as opposed to those who dabbled—coming from their professional peers was palpable. There was a sense of suspicion between the average establishment architect and the progressives. Ironically, the same architectural fraternity that made a living through the rote application of historical ornament viewed the organic decorative forms as whimsical, mere novelties for their own sake. By thinking in those terms they had already missed

Dining room, 1916. Amy Hamilton Hunter residence. Photograph courtesy of the Northwest Architectural Archives, University of Minnesota Libraries, St. Paul.

...ndelier. *John H. Adair residence, Owatonna, Minn. Photo-...n by Gary Mortensen and Robert Fogt.*

the point, as Purcell and others tried to say time and again in print. As a result, those who rested comfortably on their memberships in the American Institute of Architects tended to dismiss not only the ornament, but the entire design and, of course by extension, the organic architects themselves.

The depth of the antipathy from the historical revivalists toward the progressives is difficult to credit, especially at the distance of the intervening seventy-five years. Perhaps part was due to the vehement and sometimes condescending presentations made by some organic architects. Louis Sullivan, for example, usually cloaked his thoughts in richly emphatic phrases that were hard to follow. Frank Lloyd Wright still retains an unpleasant reputation for cutting remarks to those who dared question his architectural solutions. Purcell admitted to wearing his principles on his sleeve. The early years of his own practice he referred to as "my Salvation Army period," by which he explained he was "not only practicing the primitive virtues of this art-as-religion, but was quick with real zeal to evangelize the world."[72] While the militant exchanges in this conflict were usually sweetened in print by polite prose, the basic metaphysical incompatibility between the two viewpoints

spawned longlasting gratuitous animosities and petty insistences on each side.

Without doubt, much of the abrasiveness was due to misapprehension. Very likely, the revivalists did not like the criticism that their work was a sham, their hardwon and highly prized architectural credentials derived from Europe being used at home to corrupt society. For their part, organic architects like Purcell and Elmslie believed that they were actively discriminated against by a cabal of Eastern architects centered in New York and Boston. Those damning and the damnation were two sides of the same coin, as Purcell described the situation:

> The whole problem of the architecture of that day was the decorating and enriching of the "finish," as it was called—both exterior and interior. If this was "beautiful" and "correct," no designer bothered to relate to the actualities of doors, windows, and construction, the "architectural material" which he had usually lifted bodily from some book or magazine. Functional inter-relation existing everywhere in nature, as expressed in every animate and inanimate form, was quite ignored and any reference to it classed on as something akin to the "Red" of 1938.[73]

Some revivalist architects who perceived any resemblance in the work of organic designers to their own reproductions accused them of being copyists themselves:

> The practitioners of the French "Beaux Arts" idea, as practiced in America, tried to ease their consciences by calling their copy process "inspiration." Our opponents—perhaps we should call them antagonists from the fury of their dislike—said that we, too, were "copying."[74]

Clearly, reactions on both sides were often rooted in defensiveness. Like many people, most architects depend on peer acceptance to nurture their sense of professional belonging. Purcell and Elmslie felt their strongest convictions were misrepresented by the dominating architectural establishment to the general public, dismissed as a passing trend of little lasting virtue or, worse, ridiculed as the ravings of lunatics. They took the challenge seriously. Conceiving of themselves as insurgents in a war for the American soul the progressive architects staunchly defended their work, though this commitment to their cause varied in strength from one firm to another. Some, like Charles E. White, Jr., George H. Maher, and Robert C. Spencer, wrote commendable articles on the virtues of an indigenous American architecture but of course their own designs were less dedicated than P&E. Of those who had their beginnings with Frank Lloyd Wright, Marion Mahoney, and Walter Burley Griffin were significant contributors to the progressive work, but they were soon to leave for Australia after winning the competition for the Federal Parliament Buildings in Canberra in 1914. Wright himself had departed from the scene under a cloud of scandal in 1909, and the fortunes of Louis Sullivan continued to deteriorate despite the gifted presence of Parker Berry in his office. Purcell, Elmslie, and their associates were more and more

Front entrance, Farmer's and Merchant's Bank. Photograph courtesy of the Northwest Architectural Archives, University of Minnesota Libraries, St. Paul.

on their own as spokesmen for the movement.

Residential work was a mainstay in the business of the firm, but Purcell & Elmslie produced a significant number of designs for commercial and public buildings, churches, factories, landscaping, graphics, and miscellaneous objects. These commissions accounted for about a third of all work done by the firm, but those that were built proved sadly vulnerable to destruction during the following decades. Other than a few bank buildings scattered in small towns across the Midwest, the entire commercial production of Purcell & Elmslie has vanished. Salvage fragments are rare, and color photographs of original appearances almost nonexistent. Surviving bank buildings have often been insensibly mutilated, one example being the defacement of the terra-cotta clock frieze of the Farmers and Merchants State Bank at Hector, minnesota (1916) for an electric time-and-temperature sign. The demolition barely twenty years ago of the exquisite Madison State Bank at Madison, Minnesota (1913), which had remained largely intact, left a single piece of polychrome terra-cotta in place like a gravestone.

By Purcell's count the firm executed designs for jobs in twenty-two states, with the majority in the American midwest. Their message was represented on the East Coast by the work in Massachusetts for Charles R. Crane and,

later, for industrialist Charles O. Alexander in Pennsylvania, Connecticut, New Hampshire, and North Carolina. Two California commissions (a house and a commercial interior for the San Francisco Bay area in the mid-1910s) and a few buildings designed out of the last P&E office in Portland, Oregon, established their presence on the Pacific Coast. Ironically for a practice dedicated to indigenous American architecture, significant designs were developed for two foreign countries. In 1914, they were among the American architects who entered the competition for the new federal capital at Canberra, Australia. The second of their international designs was for a large Young Men's Christian Association building to be built at Siang Tan, Hunan Province, China. Although the work on the YMCA building proceeded through the preparation of enormous

O. L. Branson Company, Bankers. Photograph courtesy of the Northwest Architectural Archives, University of Minnesota Libraries, St. Paul.

Madison State Bank, Madison, Minn. The Western Architect, July 1915.

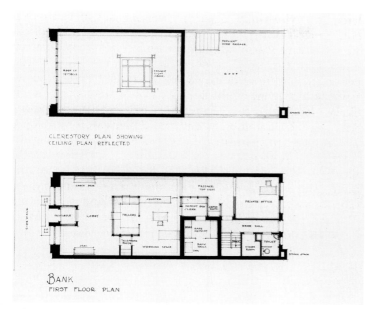

Floor plan. Madison State Bank, Madison, Minn. Photograph courtesy of the Northwest Architectural Archives, University of Minnesota Libraries, St. Paul.

large-scale working drawings, financial difficulties of the client prevented construction.

By the end of the partnership in 1921, P&E had developed schemes for more than twenty banks located in Minnesota, Wisconsin, Iowa, North Dakota, South Dakota, and Nebraska. Eleven of these were constructed. Of the nine remaining extant, seven are still in service as banks. Often, these structures are the sole distinguishing piece of architecture in the small towns where they are situated, still standing on the main street in sharp contrast to the ordinariness of surrounding commercial districts. Despite inevitable alterations over the years to enlarge the buildings, the exteriors of most P&E banks retain a sense of their original presence thanks to the durability of brick, stone, and terra-cotta. Interiors survive only sporadically in their original form, usually through the permanence of architectural features like doors, light fixtures, or terra-cotta detail. Most furnishings, including built-in features such as check desks and teller enclosures, have been removed. Sometimes remodeling actually contributed to the survival of more fragile elements, as with the art glass electroliers at the First National Bank of Adams building at Adams, Minnesota (1920).[75] The best remaining interior of the smaller banks is in the First State Bank of LeRoy, Minnesota (1914), which though slightly altered still shows the kind of integrated working space that P&E believed best for small town banking.

Banks designed by Purcell & Elmslie provided financial and other services to broad areas of dairy and farmland that centered around a small town. Such businesses were often small, run by perhaps one or two individuals who knew each depositor personally. P&E believed that this service relationship reflected a democratic intimacy between

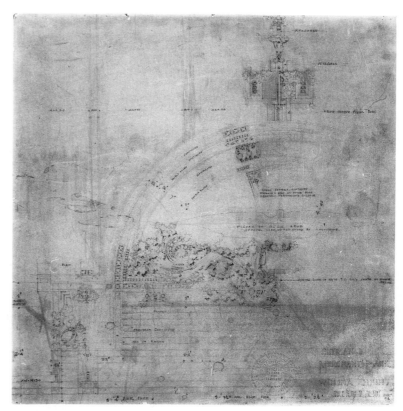

Eagle decoration, front entry, 1912. Merchant's Bank of Winona. Photograph courtesy of David S. Gebhard.

Vault mosaic, 1912. Merchant's Bank of Winona. Photograph courtesy of the Northwest Architectural Archives, University of Minnesota Libraries, St. Paul.

banker and customer that needed to be expressed architecturally. This effect was sought in the Exchange State Bank at Grand Meadow, Minnesota (1910), and suggested for most subsequent banks, by removing the conventional metal wickets that separated teller from customer in order to show a working relationship of trust and egalitarian inter-dependence. The banking rooms were cleared of extraneous walls or other obscuring features so that one person could monitor the interior from a single work position. This spacious flow further reflected openness in the banking transaction. The exterior structures of these buildings enclosed the functional simplicity of the internal arrangements with straightforward geometric planes composed of brick, terra-cotta, and stone.

When designing these banks, P&E knew the sophistication of the form was limited by the skill of contractors at the site. To simplify construction, squared stone spars set flush with the wall allowed the thickness of the masonry to serve as window reveals. Similarly placed terminal coursework eliminated the application of a false cornice. These and other elements combined to make the building a creative expression of modern American life, rather than the illusion of a Greek temple or Roman bath. Because banking hours were confined to the day, the presence of natural light was an integral part of the architectural design. Sunlight introduced through wide, opalescent leaded glass windows prevented glare and obviated the need for unsightly roller shades. Office doors might use the same treatment for privacy. When present, art glass skylights also textured incoming daylight. Electric fixtures, usually at check desks or on light standards above working areas, supplemented natural illumination. Delicate stencils emphasized the plain plaster surfaces of the interior walls, which were unified through an integrated system of wood trim. Although the original stencils in the banks have all long since disappeared, some sense of the intended decorative effect can be seen in a surviving sample screen made for the Grand Meadow bank. Tile floors with white fields were inset with small patterned borders of green and brownish-red. Marble and metal strips were sometimes also used for interior finish.

The largest and most fully developed of the P&E banks was the Merchant's National Bank, built at Winona, Minnesota, in 1912. Using pier-and-lintel framing, massive steel girders set on brick corner piers defined the cubic form of the banking room, relieving the walls of support function to open for great windows in the street-side elevations. The opaque panels that appeared in earlier banks expanded to become vast planes of leaded glass, with a decorative design akin to that Elmslie did for the Farmers National Bank in Owatonna. Both monochrome and polychrome terra-cotta ornaments placed on the facades marked the balance of tension within the structure. The entrance, centered on the axis of the front wall, was mounted by a massive Teco terra-cotta eagle. Inside the banking room two majestic murals painted by Albert Fleury on the upper half of the rear and side walls honored the agricultural character of the river valley. The interior was artificially lit by symmetrically placed groups of light standards that thrust toward a richly colored skylight. Chairs and other furniture were designed to match the architectural elements, and the round doorway to the bank vault was encircled with a halo of glass

Terracotta ornament before glazing, 1912. Merchant's Bank of Winona. Photograph courtesy of the Northwest Architectural Archives, University of Minnesota Libraries, St. Paul.

mosaic. The Merchants National Bank expressed in pier-and-lintel construction the same proud fervor for American life that the arch had borne at the National Farmer's Bank.

The four designs that Purcell & Elmslie executed for firms selling Edison phonograph machines were high points in their commercial work. In 1912 the firm prepared plans for exterior alterations and a completely new interior for the Edison shop owned by Henry B. Babson in Chicago, the most architecturally developed of the series. In these stores, P&E integrated both business functions and advertising functions:

> Each building was designed in a definite attempt to produce sales atmosphere in architecture, interior and exterior, instead of resting content with an architecturalized "store front." Up to this time, the business problems of advertizing, selling, sales psychology, consumer reaction, concern with "package" dramatization of product, employee deportment, had simply not been touched by the architect.[76]

Elmslie & Stavel, architects. First National Bank, Adams, Minn., 1920. Photograph courtesy of the Northwest Architectural Archives, University of Minnesota Libraries, St. Paul.

The Roman brick front of the four-story building extended forward, creating recessed showcase windows and an entrance at ground level, with twin piers rising unimpeded to terra-cotta capitals at the top. A large terra-cotta shield braced the lines of the columns together near the roofline. Terra-cotta urns set in niches and planting boxes that reached across the facade at each floor contained seasonal plantings. Recessed vitrines presented display areas to attract passersby from the sidewalk, and the brightly colored multiple lights of a massive electrolier drew them inside. This light fixture was, in itself, an accomplishment. "At a time when electric light fixtures had practically not advanced at all beyond some modifications of lanterns or torches, it has seemed to me that this superb ceiling fixture for the entrance arcade of this Babson shop represents high tide in Mr. Elmslie's decorative design which he has not

Jardiniere, Atlantic Terracotta and Ceramic, 1905. Farmer's National Bank, Owatonna, Minn. Norwest Bank Owatonna. Photography by Gary Mortensen and Robert Fogt.

Light fixture, *Minnesota Phonograph Company. Photograph courtesy of David S. Gebhard.*

Front elevation, *perspective view. Edison Shop for Henry B. Babson, Chicago, Ill. Photograph courtesy of the Northwest Architectural Archives, University of Minnesota Libraries, St. Paul.*

Minnesota Phonograph Company. Photograph courtesy of the Northwest Architectural Archives, University of Minnesota Libraries, St. Paul.

surpassed and which is not outclassed by anything of the kind produced today."[77] Purcell recalled the reception of the store design by the clients:

> Babsons were tremendously taken up with Mr. Elmslie's solution, which called for a recessed front, the show window being placed some ten feet back of the building line with small, beautifully wrought show cases on either side out on the sidewalk line. This was the very first of the attempts to coax a person away from the sidewalk, the sales psychology being that if you could get a person all on his own initiative to take a step toward entering the building, that he could then be persuaded by proper displays to keep on coming, and finally enter the store.[78]

Every area of the sales floors within created a unified merchandising space. The solid planes of enclosing walls were emphasized by a highly articulated interior trim system. A mezzanine level demonstration space organized in-

dividual listening rooms with a small concert area set beneath a tented ceiling. Specially designed furnishings manufactured by George Niedecken and Company in Milwaukee included chairs, sofas, tables, and rugs. In every respect, the interiors delivered a spirit of modern comfort and pleasure in which to purchase the technological wonders of the new phonograph machines. Within this integrated environment, however, a familiar problem arose. The historicist appearance of the Edison cabinets conflicted with the modern lines of the shop interior. There was only one solution. From time to time, Elmslie designed instrument panels or whole cases to replace the awkwardly styled factory-made woodwork. Although the Chicago store was the most highly developed of the three, other Edison shops were built in Kansas City and San Francisco in 1914. Another phonograph store was designed for the Minnesota Phonograph Company in Minneapolis that same year.

Still faced with an uncomprehending public, however,

Sketch, *showing side elevation, Litchfield Pavilion, Litchfield, Minn. Northwest Architectural Archives, University of Minnesota Libraries, St. Paul. Photography by Gary Mortensen and Robert Fogt.*

many especially experimental forms were fated to remain unbuilt. One of the most architectonically advanced of these projects was a bandstand pavilion designed for the small, largely Scandinavian Minnesota town of Litchfield. In effect, this structure would be the center of the town during summer evenings, when musical performances were the principal entertainment for the community. Recognizing this symbolically, George Elmslie envisioned a structure cast in concrete whose covering roof was mounted on a single supporting stem, very much like the blossom of a flower opening from the pillar. The concept was too radical for a town still questioning the need to hire an architect at all. As a form, however, design would become a commonplace of architecture fifty years later. The faint pencil study done for this small project richly illustrates how far beyond the limitations of traditional architecture Purcell & Elmslie could rise in their efforts to pioneer fresh and vital expressions.

Because of his involvement with Christian Science, Purcell often pursued prospects with these churches. He felt the special service requirements for Christian Science assemblies were an ideal challenge for which he offered an organic solution. Although no results beyond preliminary consultations came of most such contacts, his firm prepared alternate schemes for the Third Christian Science Church in Minneapolis. Accessibility and traffic circulation for those attending services were among the chief difficulties,

The Third Church of Christian Science, project. Photograph courtesy of the Northwest Architectural Archives, University of Minnesota Libraries, St. Paul.

Presentation rendering, 1915. Welcome Inn, Rhinelander, Wisc. *Northwest Architectural Archives, University of Minnesota Libraries, St. Paul. Photography by Gary Mortensen and Robert Fogt.*

as well as the problem of traffic noise from the busy street that fronted the site. The semicircular auditorium proposed by Purcell & Elmslie met these considerations with an intimate and friendly plan made economically attractive by an efficient structural technique, but political divisions within the church membership prevented the project from being realized. The group opted instead to shelter their activities behind the facade of a Greek temple.

Although the firm was never able to realize a commission for a library, school, or hotel, the architects did preliminary work for several such projects. The design of the Welcome Inn in 1915 for George Hermann, the local contractor who built the first National Bank in Rhinelander, Wisconsin, anticipated revolutionary changes in merchandising attitudes later commonplace in hotels. The design for the public spaces was aimed at forming a homelike atmosphere. Restaurant areas for formal and casual dining were segregated, with direct access to the coffee shop from the street. Even the name suggested for the building projected good humor and hospitality. Purcell & Elmslie were confident enough in the approach to provide in their engineering for later multiple story expansion, but the new ideas were too great a departure from the expectations of the client in such a remote Wisconsin town.

A few small public buildings were built by P&E in rural areas. The Jump River Town Hall of 1915 was intended to be a multipurpose meeting place for a Wisconsin lumber town. The low, horizontal appearance of the interlocking board-and-batten siding recalled the logging camps from which the town had come into being. In keeping with the plan, however, even in this economically completed build-

ing simple leaded glass panels were included to enrich the interior. The Municipal Building, built in 1916 at Kasson, Minnesota, represents the most ambitious attempt of the firm to integrate public needs as completely as possible. The design of the two-story plus basement building included a library, post office, rooms for service clubs, police department, and jail. Remarkably, most of these functions continued to serve the town from this structure until the early 1980s, when the library moved and civic functions expanded into that space.

The only major public building to be constructed by any of the progressive architects was designed by Purcell & Elmslie as associated architects in 1916. The commission for the Woodbury County Court House at Sioux City, Iowa, was won by William L. Steele, an architect who had developed a strong friendship with George Elmslie while working in the Sullivan office. His original presentation for the new court house was based on bland neo-classical design. Once the contract was in hand, however, Steele disregarded the approved plans and told his supporters on the county board they could get better than they had bargained for. Steele asked George Elmslie to develop a plan that expressed the wealth of the agricultural region and the populist character of the people who would be served by the building. Despite opposition from several quarters, including a limestone vendors' association, disgruntled politicians, and public incomprehension, the Elmslie concept was accepted, in part because the structure used large quantities of locally manufactured brick, most of the construction money would be spent in the city, and praise for the radical design came from highly respected visitors.

Woodbury County Courthouse. Photograph courtesy of the Northwest Architectural Archives, University of Minnesota Libraries, St. Paul.

George Elmslie moved to Sioux City for the duration of the work and "did about sixty percent of the designing there. The rest was done at our Minneapolis and Chicago offices."[79] The court house was the greatest opportunity that Elmslie ever had to explore architectural treatment on a vast scale. Every drawing for the building, from floor plans to a torrent of ornamental enrichments, poured from his hand. His palette included brick, steel, stone, neutral-glazed and polychrome terra-cotta, bronze, leaded glass, mosaics, and sculpture groups. The central cubic massing of the lower floors contained courtrooms organized around a glass-domed interior atrium, while a tower shaft rose high above to contain office space. A triangular prow on the tower faced west, capped with a massive stone eagle. Inside, the traditional idea of a grand staircase was dismissed and the elevator core moved forward for quick and easy access. Elmslie was so concerned that the work be carried through correctly in every detail that he was twice hospitalized for exhaustion during the course of design and construction.

Although Purcell did not participate directly in the design process, he was responsible for coordinating the work

Side entrance, Woodbury County Courthouse, Sioux City, Iowa. The Western Architect, February 1921.

View in rotunda, Woodbury County Courthouse, Sioux City, Iowa. The Western Architect, *February 1921.*

of contributing artists. Because the fee asked by Gutzon Borglum was more than available for a sculptor, Purcell engaged Alphonso Ianelli, a former student of Borglum who had just opened his own studio in Chicago. For a frugal thirty-five hundred dollars Ianelli executed massive frieze groups symbolizing democratic forms of justice to surmount the principal entrances and whimsically added cow and buffalo heads over the alleyway service dock. On wide, overhanging balconies surrounding the glass-domed lobby, artist John W. Norton painted murals to represent the Elysian richness of the countryside. In the classical tone of these paintings, however, there is clearly a change in the wind for organic design in general. In scale and extent of architectural resolutions, the Woodbury County Court House was the greatest visible monument to the ideals served by Purcell & Elmslie. The building would be among the last of their significant works.

By the time the Woodbury County Court House was completed, America was on the verge of entering World War I. With architectural commissions at a near standstill and wanting to make some contribution to the national defense effort, Purcell made a decision that would temporarily lead away from his primary concerns with architecture and ultimately end in unpleasant litigations. In 1915,

through contacts of his wife's family, Purcell met Charles O. Alexander, the president of the Alexander Brothers Leather Belting Company of Philadelphia. At first blush, the man seemed sympathetic to the progressive movement. Because the production of leather belts that connected pulleys on factory machinery was a war priority industry, Purcell felt encouraged to work for the company in the dual capacities of architect and advertising manager. Purcell sold his properties in Minneapolis and moved his family to Philadelphia in 1916.

The various Alexander Brothers concerns were expanding rapidly to include several other leather manufacturers under the umbrella name of the International Leather Belting Corporation. As corporate architects, Purcell & Elmslie had the task of integrating these diverse businesses, ranging from industrial belting to shoe repair, into a unified identity. The principal architectural opportunity for this was found in a remodeling of the Alexander Brothers offices in Philadelphia in 1916, including executive, reception, and office areas, clerical departments, a library, and a dining room. Purcell & Elmslie considered the requirements of the business operations and designed a functional system of office divisions and furnishings. As clerical stations, chairs were cantilevered from wall mounts

Library, Alexander Brothers Factory. Photograph courtesy of the Northwest Architectural Archives, University of Minnesota Libraries, St. Paul.

to swing back and away from the desk when not in use. The interiors of the management spaces were partly separated by leaded glass screens, and the individual spaces integrated throughout by the familiar interior trim system. Numerous pieces of furniture and lighting fixtures were made to coordinate with the new interior, and decoration of the library included murals by John W. Norton.

One of the most significant and innovative architectural designs for Alexander Brothers was a standardized factory plan to be built in three locations. Only two units, those in Chicago and New Haven, were constructed. Using steel roof framing anchored in pier-buttressed brick endwalls, the architects dismissed intervening side wall supports to leave a continuous 130-foot breadth of window for natural light. The human needs of the worker also were considered in carefully developed machinery layouts. One presentation rendering shows the full development of a factory center with a larger administrative and warehouse building rising between two of the factory units. The powerful streamlined appearance of the image projected a perfect picture of prosperous modern industrialism. The International Leather and Belting Corporation factories were among the first industrial buildings in America to express their utilitarian function with such philosophical conviction.

As advertising manager for Alexander Brothers, Purcell supervised the yearly production of a broad range of promotional materials, including posters, calendars, brochures, labels, mailing cards, and stationery. From 1916 until his resignation in 1919, he applied the principles of organic design in a systematized and coordinated series of campaigns to sell Alexander products. Using artwork and graphic designs commissioned from some of the finest artists of the progressive movement, such as Charles S. Chapman, Charles Livingston Bull, and John W. Norton, the Purcell presentations prophetically anticipated artistic trends in postwar decades. These advertising materials were produced with the finest inks and papers by Norman T. A. Munder & Company, one of the best printers of the time. Although individual brochures and pocket calendars were

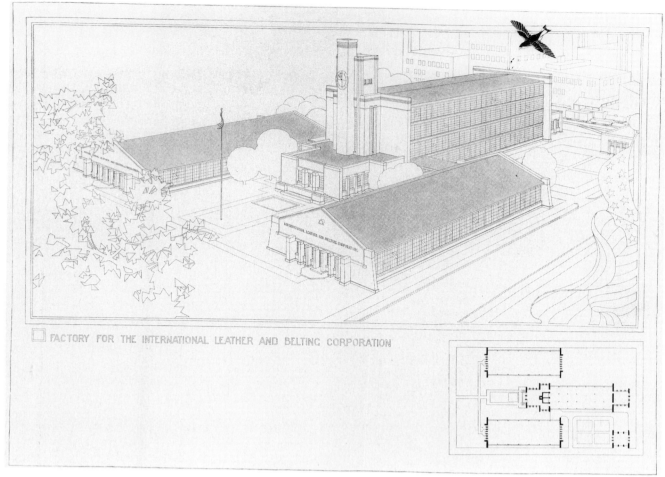

FACTORY FOR THE INTERNATIONAL LEATHER AND BELTING CORPORATION

Presentation rendering, 1916. Factory for the Alexander Brothers
International Leather and Belting Company. Northwest Architectural Archives, University of Minnesota Libraries, St. Paul. Photography by Gary Mortensen and Robert Fogt.

INTERNATIONAL LEATHER AND BELTING CORPORATION

Alexander Brothers Factory. Photograph courtesy of the Northwest
Architectural Archives, University of Minnesota Libraries, St.
Paul.

Charles S. Chapman. Advertisement for Alexander Brothers'
Products. Photograph courtesy of the Northwest Architectural Ar-
chives, University of Minnesota Libraties, St. Paul.

mailed at intervals as their purpose dictated, each series was
also bound together in numbered and signed presentation
annual volumes. P&E also designed a complete suite of
office forms for Alexander Brothers, ranging from bank
drafts to inter-office memoranda.

The firm designed two unbuilt projects for C. O. Alexander personally, but completed some alterations at his
summer residence in Squam Lake, New Hampshire. The
first scheme, a large residence site in Philadelphia, was
begun by Purcell shortly after his meeting with the company president but had to be abandoned at the onset of the
war. Detailed plans were prepared for a large institutional
church building or Y.M.C.A., which C. O. Alexander was
to have contributed to a mission in Siang Tan, China, but
that project ultimately fell through when the Alexander
companies went bankrupt. Sometime before the failure of
Alexander Brothers was evident, however, Purcell realized
his first impressions had failed to recognize the true character of his employer, whom he now understood to be autocratic, ruthless, dishonest, and vain. His involvement with
C. O. Alexander became extremely distasteful, and he resigned after completing his duties for the 1919 advertising

campaign. Despite attempts to leave on cordial terms, Purcell was eventually forced to sue to recover architectural
fees due Purcell & Elmslie as well as his own salary, thus
endowing his three-year stay with a bitterness and personal
disappointment that would remain with him for years.

In the fall of 1919, Purcell relocated to Portland, Oregon, to set up an engineering firm with his cousin, Charles
H. Purcell, who would later go on to design the Oakland
Bay Bridge. The office also was intended to serve the Purcell & Elmslie partnership. Elmslie remained in Chicago,
and the firm maintained a small office in Minneapolis as
well. The distance between the two men was more than
geographical. Purcell saw that the end of the progressive
architecture they had worked so hard to practice was at
hand. Elmslie refused to depart from the forms he knew
and loved. In 1921, Purcell could no longer afford to subsi-
dize the office and sent a letter to Elmslie to explain this.
At first, Elmslie was bitter with defeat, but in time the
two men regained a friendly balance in their relationship.
Purcell eventually established his own practice in Oregon,
while Elmslie attempted to carry on in Chicago with associates from the P&E office. The work of the firm came to
an end.

Of the many fine men and women who came forward
in response to the call for an indigenous American architecture, few consistently achieved the brilliant precision and
comprehensive resolution attained by George Grant Elmslie, William Gray Purcell, and the associates of their office. Most of the people in this community left no
personalized record of their participation, a fact of history
quietly in accord with their democratic humility. More
than Elmslie, Purcell recognized this circumstance when
writing his autobiographical accounts of the firm and honored these contributing citizens "now passed from recorded
life as a summer rain."[80] That same metaphor carried the
description of the progressive movement itself. Aside from
the physical buildings, thinly scattered and vulnerable to
damage from unenlightened owners, the presence of the
Prairie architects moved silently away into history.

Fate had little sympathy for most of the principals, both
architects and clients, in the movement. Louis Sullivan
died, forgotten and destitute in a cheap Chicago hotel. Carl
K. Bennett, one of his greatest clients and a supporter of
Purcell & Elmslie, would go broke and die in an institution
for the mentally insane. George Elmslie, easily the most
brilliant compositionalist of them all, grew ever more bitter
and depressed, rousing himself only from time to time to
remind people of his great master, Sullivan. Purcell was
diagnosed with advanced tuberculosis and spent five years
in a sanitorium before settling down to write about his
experiences and keep the organic message before the reading public in a variety of forms. Unlike Elmslie, Purcell
would live to see the first scholarly recognition of their work
in an exhibition held in 1953. Since then, the reputation of
Purcell & Elmslie has grown steadily among architectural
historians and now has attained a larger public following.
Their message, and the need for it, is all the more with us.

Presentation rendering, 1916. *Institutional Church for Charles O. Alexander, Y.M.C.A., Siang Tan, Hunan, China. Northwest Architectural Archives, University of Minnesota Libraries, St. Paul. Photography by Gary Mortensen and Robert Fogt.*

NOTES

This essay rests on contributions to my work made by many people and institutions over the past fifteen years. I especially want to thank Alan Lathrop and his assistant, Barbara Bezat, at the Northwest Architectural Archives; Michael Conforti, Tran Turner, Jennifer Komar, Brian Kraft, and others at the Minneapolis Institute of Arts; Director Carter J. Manny, Jr. and the Graham Foundation for Advanced Studies in the Fine Arts; Brooks Cavin, FAIA, and the College of Fellows of the American Institute of Architects; Ken Rothchild and the Minnesota Humanities Commission (in honor of the 100th Anniversary of the H. and Val J. Rothchild Company of St. Paul); Roger G. Kennedy, Director Emeritus of the National Museum of American History; Paul and Mary Carson; Arthur Dyson, AIA; Dr. David S. Gebhard; David J. Klaassen; Bruce J. LaBelle; Kenneth Nishimoto, AIA; the late Dorothy O'Brien; Sig Peck; and Helen Purcell. Many the many other individuals whose names do not appear here know that I am grateful for their help and encouragement.

1. The term *midwestern* is a modern usage to describe the eastern interior of the continental United States. This refers generally to a core of states including Illinois, Ohio, Iowa, Wisconsin, Minnesota, and the Dakotas. At the time of Purcell and Elmslie, the same geographical area was usually called the northwest, a term applied from colonial times. In this essay the modern terminology will be observed.

2. Purcell, in "WGP Review of [David S.] Gebhard Thesis, George Grant Elmslie Section part IV" (version of draft dated 7 March 1956. William Gray Purcell Papers, Correspondents record group, David S. Gebhard files [C:124]).

3. The name also recognizes the influence of the surrounding prairie plain in their work, particularly the element of horizonality. A thorough examination of the origins and evolution of the various names that have been used to label the progressive architects appears in the introduction to *The Prairie School: Frank Lloyd Wright and His Midwest Contemporaries,* by architectural historian H. Allen Brooks (Toronto: University of Toronto Press, 1965). This book is the most complete general survey of the entire field of participants, as well as a catalog of many important structures generated by the Prairie architects. Although subsequent research points to some minor errors concerning William Gray Purcell and George Grant Elmslie, this monograph remains the finest and most fulfilling source available on the accomplishments and disappointments of the progressives.

4. For an assessment of the birth of American arts and crafts at Hull House in Chicago and Wright's participation, including the visits by C. R. Ashbee and Walter Crane, see Brooks, *Prairie School,* 17–20. In contrast, Purcell noted that the advanced architectural effects sought by his firm were often limited by clients who installed dark brown craftsman-style furniture. Although this may have been an economic inevitability and perhaps better than other furnishings that also had to be accommodated, the result at least in color value, he considered, was largely old-fashioned. Purcell Papers, Architectural Records, Purcell & Elmslie Archives, *Parabiographies,* entries for commission numbers 23 (1908) and 198 (1913).

5. Gerald Stanley Lee, *The Voice of the Machines* (Northampton, Mass.: Mount Tom Press, 1906).

6. Ibid., 22.

7. At the distance of nearly a century, our own experience of machine-driven life has been too long and too much present to sense easily the stark epiphany that struck men like Lee and Purcell. At the time of the book, for example, animals were not a luxury made possible by surplus wealth but were still very much the means of making ends meet. Drayage or personal transportation over short distances was still often the task of the horse. The removal of the living animal presence from daily human activity was a psychological breakaway whose effects now seem almost trivial. At the time, however, there was a singular sense of change.

8. Purcell, "Sullivan's Personality In Self Expression and Creative Procedures" (version dated 1 October 1952). Purcell Papers, Architectural Records, Louis Sullivan Archives, Manuscripts, Other Writings [AR:A4b3].

9. *The Fourth Dimension Simply Explained: A Collection of Essays Selected from Those Submitted in the Scientific American's Prize Competition,* Henry P. Manning, ed. (New York: Munn & Co., 1910), 91–99.

10. Ibid., 95.

11. Ibid., 280.

12. Although the first American edition of *Tertium Organum* did not appear until 1920, various portions of the draft and related essays by Ouspensky appeared in the press during the 1910s.

13. The scholars of modern day India have written more about the influence of subcontinental philosophies on American literature than their American counterparts. See the bibliography entries for authors Dhawan, Joshi, and Patri.

14. Wright discussed this critical exposure to Hiroshige many times; and when Marian Mahoney, a gifted architect who trained with Wright, was given a compliment on the quality of her presentation renderings, Wright reportedly said, "That's Hiroshige through me, then through Mahoney." Wright also survived financially on occasion by the sale of such valuable Japanese artwork, and avidly collected Orientalia, installing the objects throughout his home at Taliesin. Louis Sullivan highly prized his own collection. Just before Louis Sullivan faced the sale of his possessions in an effort to raise capital, George Grant Elmslie bought two, both by Haronabu. Elmslie later presented these prints to William

Gray Purcell as a wedding gift in 1936, and the pair is now part of the collection of his papers at the Northwest Architectural Archives, University of Minnesota.

15. One reason Japanese prints could so clearly facilitate the organic consciousness lay in the Buddhist philosophy that permeated the art. Although it is outside the scope of this essay, many connections can be made between the organic philosophy and the so-called third basket of esoteric Buddhist teachings called the Abhidharma. A few translations of the Abhidharma texts were available, notably those of the Pali Text Society, yet it is doubtful that these were seen by the progressives until after 1920. This makes their indirect metaphysical perceptions through the artwork all the more remarkable.

16. Because the last names of George Grant Elmslie and William Gray Purcell can refer to both the men and the title of their firm, references to "Purcell and Elmslie" are intended to indicate the individuals. The form "Purcell & Elmslie" (also abbreviated as "P&E" for convenience and because they themselves used this form) is meant o encompass the entire community and activities of the architectural office.

17. This summation of Elmslie's early life is derived from an autobiographical manuscript found in the Purcell Papers, Correspondents [C:99].

18. The essential writing on the Owatonna bank, which also contains an examination of the relationship between Sullivan and Elmslie, is Larry Millett's *The Curve of the Arch* (St. Paul: Minnesota Historical Society Press, 1985).

19. Purcell, in "WGP Review of [David S.] Gebhard Thesis. Part [no number]: George Grant Elmslie, Section III, 2 (version dated 15 February 1956). Purcell Papers, Correspondents [C:124].

20. In 1902, while attending college at Cornell, Purcell won an architectural competition sponsored by Andrew D. White, the American ambassador to Germany. His well-organized but essentially plain and straightforward design took first prize much to the astonishment of his professors and classmates. In a characteristic gesture of community spirit, Purcell donated the prize money to the architecture school for the purchase of art prints.

21. Beyond comments about occasional experiences while at the studio, Purcell left no manuscript in his papers detailing time spent with Wright before leaving for college. One autobiographical record written in 1938 does remark that Wright was genial and friendly, but never too enthusiastic "toward me, because as a bright young kid about town, studying architecture, he had expected that I would enter his office upon leaving college, and when I went, even for a few months in the summer of 1901 [or, possibly, 1902] into the office of Architect E. E. Roberts to please my father, he considered me already a lost soul." Purcell also may have spent less time at the studio because his father disapproved strongly of Wright. Purcell Papers, Architectural Records, purcell & Elmslie Archives, Office Records, *Parabiographies* (volume for 1907), entry for commission no. 5.

22. Purcell met Myron Hunt at the Chicago Architectural club in 1903. After leaving Chicago for his years of apprenticeship on the West Coast, Purcell stopped in Los Angeles to investigate job opportunities. Because Hunt had relocated to southern California, Purcell called on his acquaintance. Hunt was sympathetic but had no work to offer. Instead, he told Purcell to head for San Francisco where architectural work was then more active. In particular, he suggested that Purcell apply to John Galen Howard for work on the University of California campus at Berkeley. Purcell did so and spent the next year as clerk of the works for the construction of California Hall. Although there is no known record of exactly why Purcell agreed to open a practice in Minneapolis with Feick, the city was without a firm devoted to progressive work.

23. Purcell Papers, Architectural Records, Purcell & Elmslie Archives, Office Records, *Parabiographies* (volume for 1907), entry for commission no. 10.

24. Purcell Architectural Records, Purcell & Elmslie Archives, Office Records, *Parabiographies* (volume for 1908), entry for commission no. 24A–B.

25. Ibid. Curiously, further involvement with the Christ Church

commission continued off and on for more than eight years before the building was constructed and long after P&E was well recognized for their organic accomplishments. The firm prepared three sets of modified specifications dated 1910, 1913, and 1915. Financial records show additional work was done in the Purcell & Elmslie office for some kind of substantial plan revision during 1915. This probably accounts for the "A" and "B" designations in the original commission number. The separate memorial window appears under its own assignment and time records (commission no. 287). For understandable reasons, this building has been hitherto omitted from public lists of work done by the firm. Christ Church is a good example, however, of Purcell & Feick's commitment to the needs and desires of people over the colder considerations of an abstract point of view.

26. Purcell Papers, Architectural Records, Purcell & Elmslie Archives, Office Records, *Parabiographies* (volume for 1907), entry for commission no. 8.

27. The Warner design had a unique feature that intended to use living plants as a form of interior decoration. In the living room a four-by-eighteen-foot interior planter was set against the outside wall with windows opening to the outside and separated from the interior by glass panels that could be opened to invite the garden sense inside during winter. A similar treatment was planned later for a residential remodeling in Eau Claire, but the novelty of the concept was too startling and had to be omitted. For the letter to Sullivan, see the Louis Sullivan Archives series, Correspondence, Purcell Papers [AR:A3]. Purcell Papers, Architectural Records, Purcell & Elmslie Archives, Office Records, *Parabiographies* (volume for 1908), entry for commission no. 63.

28. The Sunday school wing was finally built to a design by other architects in the 1920s, after the dissolution of P&E. The wall of sliding door panels was sealed with tar paper and covered with a wooden veneer until this later work was completed.

29. "Expressions in Church Architecture," *The Continent*, 29 June 1911, pp. 937–38.

30. The high-pitched roof experiments for the Gray house were not the first time his enjoyment of this form appeared in a residential design. Purcell submitted a similar, more fancifully dormered house design for Oliver T. Esmond in the Chicago Architectural Club exhibition of 1904.

31. Frank Lloyd Wright, "A Concrete House for $5000," *Ladies Home Journal* (April 1907): 204.

32. Purcell Papers, Architectural Records, Purcell & Elmslie Archives, Office Records, *Parabiographies* (volume for 1907), entry for commission no. 4-1/2.

33. Ibid.

34. Ibid.

35. Ibid. Purcell need not have worried about his failure to recognize the problem with the wall, which he later opened through remodeling to provide a sun porch. In the same *Parabiographies* entry, he also recorded "Ownership changed in 1917 [when Purcell left Minneapolis]. Extensively and very unintelligently redone by new owners in 1918. Still standing in 1938," as is what remains of his original design. Sadly, even the fireplace with raised hearth was removed in a later alteration. The red brick and matching salmon colored plaster finish have long since been submerged beneath a ghostly coat of gray paint meant to bind together additions that are now larger than the original house.

36. Notecard written by Purcell, ca. 1950s. Purcell Papers, Purcell & Elmslie Archives series, commission no. 51.

37. Some sense of the bright color in P&E designs generally can be seen in the exterior orange and blue frieze stencil of the Edna S. Purcell house (Minneapolis, 1913), now restored as part of the permanent collection of The Minneapolis Institute of Arts. Also, a pair of porch door sunscreens were discovered in storage during the restoration process in the 1980s. The stencils on fabric had not been exposed to the sun and retain a bright red color.

38. Later, in 1915, Purcell & Elmslie further added to the house with additional leaded glass panels, sawed wood, and a fireplace mural. After all this work, it must have been a disappointment for Purcell to discover that his father never really liked the house. When it came time to design a second residence in River Forest for his father in 1928,

Charles Purcell insisted on a traditional, Tudor-style design (Helen Purcell in conversation with the author, May 1981).

39. For the Louisiana Purchase Centennial Exposition held at St. Louis, Missouri, in 1904, Jager painted a large mural that formed the main exhibit for Minneapolis and St. Paul. The painting provided a large-scale aerial view of the cities and surrounding communities, which were shown connected together by the existing lines and proposed extensions of the street car system. Using his experiences in city planning, he presented an integrated concept of development for an area totaling two thousand square miles, which he subsequently promoted in publications and public addresses. The mural survives in the history collection of the Minneapolis Public Library, and can be seen on the third floor of the downtown library building.

40. *The Western Architect*, 22, no. 1 (July 1915).

41. John Jager was responsible for the first archival processing of the records of Purcell & Elmslie. When the last foothold of the firm closed in the late 1920s, the records of the practice that remained in Minneapolis passed into his care. Installing them in his basement, Jager worked over the next thirty years to catalog and preserve the body of what is now called the William Gray Purcell Papers. He was instrumental in preparing the P&E materials installed at the Walker Art Center in 1953, an event which was the first scholarly exhibition of the work of the firm.

42. Purcell Papers, Architectural Records, Purcell & Elmslie Archives, Office Records, *Parabiographies* (volume for 1916), fragmentary manuscript, version dated October 1957.

43. The scant biographical information available for Team members reveals some curious personal continuities within this group of people. Marion Parker retired from architectural practice in the 1920s and relocated to Laguna Beach, California. There she joined the active artists colony, opening an arts and crafts shop and exhibiting at the annual summer art fair. In a strange twist of fate, Parker died of a heart attack in 1935 while on her way to visit Purcell at his retirement estate in the Pasadena foothills. At the same time Purcell learned that her residence was so near to him, he also discovered that another Team draftsman, Lawrence Clapp, lived in Santa Barbara and was participating in the same Laguna Beach art fair as Parker.

44. Clapp formed a particular attachment to George Elmslie and returned to work for him during the 1920s after the dissolution of Purcell & Elmslie. He left the midwest in 1929 to follow the boom in Florida real estate, where he suffered financial losses. After a short time in Alaska he returned to Chicago to sell watercolors done on his trip north and by 1935 had moved to southern California.

45. Fournier made significant contributions to later work by Elmslie, particularly the Capital Savings and Loan Association building in Topeka, Kansas. In a situation reminiscent of Sullivan toward Elmslie, Elmslie refused to give substantial credit to Fournier, until the dispirited draftsman finally left in 1922. He then opened his own practice and later in 1935 he became executive architect for a large housing project built during the Depression. Four years later the opportunity arose to become designing engineer for a major bank building if he could meet the license requirements. Fournier overcame the last of his educational hurdles at age sixty by putting himself through three months of intensive technical study in order to qualify for the work. When his health later became impaired, he retired to Minnesota to spend his remaining years writing novels and poetry until his death in 1944 at age sixty-six in an apartment fire.

46. Friend and associate of both Purcell and Elmslie for many years following the end of their partnership, Frederick Strauel continued to work with them for nearly half a century. His presence is implicit in nearly all work done by the architects subsequent to his appearance on the scene. For example, Purcell sent most of his drafting to Strauel during the 1920s and twice brought him out to Portland, Oregon, when the work in his office warranted. Purcell and Strauel collaborated on a number of speculative houses for a developer in Minneapolis, as well as on other projects in Minnesota, from 1928 to 1932. By sharing the rent with Purcell and Elmslie, Strauel was able to maintain a small office in the Architects and Engineers Building in Minneapolis until 1935. He did the working drawings for the last house designed by Purcell for a

client, the K. Paul Carson, Jr., residence in 1940. Except for the periods when he employed Fournier and Clapp, Elmslie, too, used Strauel as draftsman for many of his jobs, including the Yankton College buildings in South Dakota and the Western Springs Congregational Church in Illinois. From 1933 to 1943 Strauel worked in the same WPA office as John Jager, followed by a brief wartime job with a chemical company before taking a staff position with the Minneapolis City Planning Commission from which he retired in 1952. In October of that year he began working with John Jager on preparations for the "Purcell & Elmslie, Architects" exhibition held at the Walker Art Center in Minneapolis in 1953. Thereafter Strauel was periodically involved with the archival preservation of the Purcell & Elmslie records, making detailed catalogs of the drawings and annotating many records with information that he remembered from earlier times. He outlived the rest of those involved in the office and before his own death in 1974, he donated the Purcell & Elmslie materials in his possession to the University of Minnesota.

47. Note by Purcell. Purcell Papers, Architectural Records, Purcell & Elmslies Archives series, Office Records, Biographical materials for the team [AR:B4d4.3]. This text is echoed in greater detail in another manuscript by Purcell in his Review of the [David S.] Gebhard Thesis, Part III: Purcell and Elmslie, Section B: John Jager and Other Personalities (draft updated 2 April 1956) [C:124].

48. Purcell, "Purcell and Elmslie Biographical Notes." Draft dated November 1949. Purcell Papers, Architectural Records, Purcell & Elmslie Archives, Office Records, Manuscripts, Other Writings [AR:B4d2.21(a)].

49. Apparently, Wright was aware when he telephoned that George Elmslie was also in Minneapolis at the same time, making arrangements for his imminent arrival as a full partner. Wright probably knew Elmslie continued to disapprove ever more strongly of Wright's treatment of Sullivan in the years after his departure from the Sullivan office in the mid-1890s. It can be speculated that Wright's desire to sell his practice to Purcell & Elmslie required both the money Purcell was known to have and the self-evident abilities of Elmslie. The younger Purcell would have been easier to influence than the formidably stubborn Elmslie. A full account by Purcell of this incident can be found in his correspondence with Hermann V. von Holst, the architect who finally accepted the Wright proposal. Included in the file is the contract signed by Wright and von Holst, together with letters from the latter describing a nightmarish result. Purcell Papers, Correspondents record group, Frank Lloyd Wright files [C:359].

50. The Griffin request is cited in Brooks, Prairie School, from letters in the possession of David S. Gebhard.

51. The best examples of this ongoing developmental process can be seen in the series of commissions for the Oscar Owre (Minneapolis, Minnesota), E. S. Hoyt (Red Wing, Minnesota), and Louis Heitman (Helena, Montana) residences.

52. This building had many troubles before and during construction. Purcell and Elmslie continued to play a discreet role in an effort to salvage Sullivan's design after the head of the building committee decided he could do better himself. After his botched attempt to economize through haphazard alteration of the Sullivan design, the client turned to P&E to pick up the pieces. Elmslie at first declined out of ethical respect for his former employer, but eventually was convinced to try. He spent substantial time attempting to restore the fundamental concept and restrain the self-impressed fancies of the client, who returned the favor by refusing to pay for the architectural services. When the building was finally finished, Elmslie didn't want acknowledgment for his work. His significant participation in the church design remained hidden until Purcell wrote an account of these remarkable events in his memoirs during the late 1930s. See Purcell Papers, Architectural Records, Purcell & Elmslie Archives, Parabiographies (volume for 1910), entry for commission no. 86.

53. The offended investor could not be mollified, and Purcell thought the commission was lost. Instead bank president D. F. Recker, who had contacted the firm in the first place, refused to be intimidated. The stockholder sold his shares and publicly predicted disaster for any enterprise foolish enough to erect such a structure. See Purcell Papers, Archi-

tectural Records, Purcell & Elmslie Archives, Parabiographies (volume for 1910), entry for commission no. 99.

54. Purcell Papers, Architectural Records, See Parabiographies (volume for 1911), entry for commission no. 124.

55. See "'Why a Greek Colonnade To Lincoln?' Ask American Architects" by Frances Fisher Dyers (Purcell Papers, Architectural Records, Purcell & Elmslie Archives, Office Records, Manuscripts, Publications [AR:B4d4]). This piece was illustrated with photographs of the Catherine Gray house, the Stewart Memorial Church, and a P&E bank. Purcell was extremely careful about how the designs of the firm were presented in the press. In essence, he always asked for creative control. The intent was to prevent progressive work from being shown next to historical forms, so that people would avoid thinking of organic architecture as a style. The result of this was a greatly lessened public exposure, since editors were not always understanding of his purpose. The Dyers piece was an exception. Clippings in the P&E records files show that the article appeared in the New York Herald and the Pioneer Press of St. Paul. For the correspondence with William Channing Whitney, see Purcell Papers, Correspondents [C:348].

56. For examples, see Purcell and Elmslie, "H. P. Berlage, The Creator of a Democratic Architecture in Holland." The Craftsman, 21, no. 5 (February 1912): 547–53; and Purcell, "Walter Burley Griffin, Progressive," The Western Architect 12, no. 12 (September 1912): 93–94.

57. Purcell and Elmslie, "The Statics and Dynamics of Architecture," The Western Architect 19, no. 1 (January 1913): 1–4.

58. Purcell Papers, Architectural Records, Purcell & Elmslie Archives, Parabiographies (volume for 1912), entry for commission no. 132.

59. Purcell, Review of [David S.] Gebhard Thesis (draft dated 7 March 1956) Purcell Papers, Correspondents [C:124].

60. Purcell recounted this learning experience in an article about practical building knowledge titled "Building Superintendence," Northwest Architect, 5, no. 4 (September – October 1940): 4–5.

61. Purcell, untitled fragmentary manuscript dated January 1950, in the possession of the author.

62. Purcell Papers, Architectural Records, Purcell & Elmslie Archives, Parabiographies (volume for 1910), entry for commission no. 98.

63. Annotation by Elmslie on an undated draft by Purcell. In a response that Elmslie probably never say, Purcell noted alongside that "It was the elaboration and cost that bothered me." Purcell Papers, Architectural Records, Purcell & Elmslie Archives, Parabiographies (volume for 1910), entry for commission no. 98.

64. The other was for A. F. Bullen in Red Wing, Minnesota, in 1913 (commission no. 198).

65. Letter from Weber to Purcell dated 17 December 1955. Purcell Papers, Architectural Records, Purcell & Elmslie Archives, Office Records, Biographical Materials [AR:B4d3].

66. Fine organic architecture has not found a friendly environment at Lake Minnetonka. Incredibly, both the Decker house and a large house by Frank Lloyd Wright of the same vintage have been demolished within the last forty years. The Decker house was replaced by a sham red brick Norman chateau, while the original Decker service building was allowed to remain as a gaunt reminder of what had once graced the site. Of all the losses in Purcell & Elmslie residential architecture, the destruction of the Decker house is the most inexcusable and the greatest tragedy. Minute consolation is available in the fact that most of the ornamental treatments were salvaged, though the depth of elegance in their expression has been dimmed by fragmentation.

67. Purcell Papers, Architectural Records, Purcell & Elmslie Archives, Parabiographies (volume for 1914), entry for commission no. 247.

68. Purcell, with following quote from a letter by Josephine Crane Bradley. Purcell Papers, Architectural Records, Purcell & Elmslie Archives, Parabiographies (volume for 1912), entry for commission no. 131 [AR:B4d1.8]..

69. Purcell Papers, Architectural Records, Purcell & Elmslie Archives, Parabiographies (volume for 1915), entry for commission no. 284.

70. Purcell Papers, Architectural Records, Purcell & Elmslie Archives, *Parabiographies* (volume for 1912), entry for commission no. 142B.

71. Purcell went to New York to meet Berlage's ship and escorted him to Chicago and Minneapolis. See Purcell Papers, Architectural Records, Purcell & Elmslie Archives, *Parabiographies* (volume for 1907), entry for commission no. 3; and "'Why a Greek Colonnade To Lincoln?' Ask American Architects," by Frances Fisher Dyers (1912). Office Records, Manuscripts, Publications [B4d4].

72. Purcell, in an untitled fragmentary manuscript dated June 1938. Purcell Papers, Architectural records, Purcell & Elmslie Archives, Office Records, Biographical Materials for the Team [AR:B4d3].

73. Purcell Papers, Architectural Records, Purcell & Elmslie Archives, *Parabiographies* (volume for 1907), entry for commission no. 3. The date of 1938 refers to the time of the original draft of this manuscript.

74. Purcell, Review of [David S.] Gebhard Thesis (WGP Thesis Section III-C4), titled "Relation of Experimental Painting to Progressive Architecture" (version dated 15 December 1956). Purcell Papers, Correspondents [C:124].

75. The interior of this bank featured a high tented ceiling that was later covered by dropped acoustic panels. The electroliers have hung undisturbed above ever since.

76. Purcell Papers, Architectural Records, Purcell & Elmslie Archives, *Parabiographies* (volume for 1912), entry for commission no. 230.

77. Purcell Papers, Architectural Records, Purcell & Elmslie Archives, *Parabiographies* (volume for 1912), entry for commission no. 238.

78. Ibid.

79. Purcell Papers, Architectural Records, Purcell & Elmslie Archives, *Parabiographies* ([fragmentary] volume for 1916), entry for commission no. 276.

80. Purcell, "WGP Review of [David S.] Gebhard Thesis, Purcell and Elmslie III, Section B, John Jager and other personalities" (draft dated 2 April 1956), Correspondents [C:124].

BIBLIOGRAPHY

The principal source of information in this essay derives from manuscripts and other records held in the William Gray Purcell Papers, Northwest Architectural Archives, University of Minnesota Libraries. The endnotes cite specific writings by Purcell and George Elmslie. Most of these are from the series of biographical manuscripts called the *Parabiographies*, written by Purcell beginning in the late 1930s with succeeding revisions during the 1950s. The endnotes also provide references to publications and other materials that can be located within the collection or in general library collections. The voluminous Purcell Papers are an extraordinary rich source of primary materials relating to the Prairie architects. The Purcell and Elmslie Archives series, contained in the Architectural Records record group of the collection, are extensive and have provided much detail to the contents of this manuscript. By using these primary materials, this essay has focused more on an assessment of how the architects viewed themselves, rather than the more encompassing task of seeing Purcell and Elmslie against the larger architectural background against which they worked. To this end, the following sources also contain relevant information.

Bragdon, Claude. *The Beautiful Necessity: Seven Essays on Theosophy and Architecture*. New York: Knopf, 1922.

Bragdon, Claude. *The Frozen Fountain: Being Essays on Architecture and the Art of Design in Space*. New York: Knopf, 1932.

Bragdon, Claude. *Projective Ornament*. Rochester, N.Y.: Manas Press, 1915.

Brooks, H. Allen. *The Prairie School: Frank Lloyd Wright and His Midwestern Contemporaries*. Toronto: University of Toronto Press, 1965.

Dhawan, Rajinder Kumar. *Henry David Thoreau: A Study in Indian Influence*. New Delhi: Classical Publishing Co., 1985.

Ericksen, Richard. *Consciousness, Life, and the Fourth Dimension*. New York: Knopf, 1923.

Francis, E. V. *Emerson and Hindu Scriptures*. Cochin: Academic Publications, 1972.

Gebhard, David S. "William Gray Purcell and George Grant Elmslie and the Early Progressive Movement in American Architecture from 1900–1920." Ph.D. diss., University of Minnesota, 1957.

Joshi, Krishnanand. *The West Looks at India: Studies in the Impact of India Thought on Shelley, Emerson, Thoreau, Whitman, Ruskin, Tennyson, and James Joyce*. Bereilly, India: Prakash Book Depot, 1969.

Lancaster, Clay. *Japanese Influences in America*. New York: Rawls, 1963.

Lathrop, Alan K. "The Prairie School Bank: Patron and Achitect." *Prairie School Architecture in Minnesota Iowa Wisconsin*. Minnesota Museum of Art, 1982: 55–68.

Ouspensky, P. D. *Tertium Organum: The Third Canon of Thought: A Key to the Enigmas of the World*. New York: Knopf, 1920.

Patri, Umesa. *Hindu Scriptures and American Transcendentalists*. New Delhi: Intellectual Publishing House, 1987.

Purcell, William Gray. "Expressions in Church Architecture." *The Continent* (29 June 1911): 937–38.

Purcell, William Gray. "Made in Minnesota." *The Minnesotan* 1, no. 9 (April 1916): 7–13.

Purcell, William Gray. *St. Croix Trail Country*. Minneapolis: University of Minnesota Press, 1967.

Purcell, William Gray. "Walter Burley Griffin, Progressive." *The Western Architect* 18, no. 12 (September 1912): 93–94.

Purcell, William Gray, and George Grant Elmslie. "The American Renaissance?" *The Craftsman* 21, no. 4 (January 1912): 430–35.

Purcell, William Gray, and George Grant Elmslie. "H. P. Berlage, The Creator of a Democratic Architecture in Holland." *The Craftsman* 21, no. 5 (February 1912): 547–553.

Purcell, William Gray, and George Grant Elmslie. "The Statics and Dynamics of Architecture." *The Western Architect* 19, no. 1 (January 1913).

Purcell, William Gray, and George Grant Elmslie. "Work." *The Western Architect* 22, no. 1 (July 1915).

Purcell, William Gray, and George Grant Elmslie. "Work." *The Western Architect* 21, no. 1 (January 1915).

CHECKLIST OF THE EXHIBITION

Dimensions = h × w × d

1. William Purcell and George Feick
   American, 1880–1965 and 1880–1947
   Group of four sketches, 1907

Catherine Gray residence (originally W. G. Purcell residence)
Minneapolis, Minnesota
Wax pencil on paper
8⅞" × 5⅞"
Northwest Architectural Archives, University of Minnesota Libraries, St. Paul

After opening his architectural practice in 1907, Purcell decided to build a house for himself on the shores of Lake of the Isles, then part of the suburban countryside of Minneapolis. The residence was intended to demonstrate the principles of organic design, the work of the Purcell & Feick office. These four sketches reveal the compositional difficulties Purcell encountered as he tried to integrate a functional floor plan with various elements visible in the elevations, including the roof, entrances, fenestration, and pergola.

2. William Purcell and George Feick
   American, 1880–1965 and 1880–1947
   Presentation sketch, "Preconstructional Sketch," 1907
   Minneapolis, Minnesota
   Pencil and colored pencil on tracing paper
   6" × 9½"
   Northwest Architectural Archives, University of Minnesota Libraries, St. Paul

Frustrated in his first attempt to design a house, Purcell abandoned his earlier efforts and consulted with his friend George Elmslie. Elmslie provided an open floor plan that met the project requirements. Purcell then developed the elevations and selected building materials, carefully thinking through the role of each element in organic relationship to the whole. Finally satisfied with his work, he drew this small study to show the new house design to his bride-to-be, Edna Summy. The dwelling was later named in honor of Purcell's maternal grandmother, Catherine Garns Gray, who lived there.

3. William Gray Purcell
   American, 1880–1965
   Transparency from a Lumière Autochrome, showing exterior perspective, 1914
   Charles A. Purcell residence, 1909
   River Forest, Illinois
   William Purcell and George Feick, architects
   Original 8" × 10"; new transparency 16" × 20"
   Northwest Architectural Archives, University of Minnesota Libraries, St. Paul

The Lumière autochrome process for color photography was introduced in 1907 and remained commercially successful until the 1930s. Differing from earlier color methods by exposing a single plate sensitized to red, green, and blue light rather that using multiple plates with separate lens filters, the Lumière autochrome technique produced an image-positive color transparency. These transparencies could be projected or seen in hand-held viewers called Diascopes, small collapsible cases that reflected a light source through the autochrome onto a mirror. An avid photographer, Purcell made autochromes of many Purcell & Elmslie buildings.

4. William Purcell and George Feick
   American, 1880–1965 and 1880–1947
   Presentation rendering, about 1909
   Soldier's Memorial Arch for C. M. Loring
   Colored pencil on tracing paper
   21" × 16"
   Northwest Architectural Archives, University of Minnesota Libraries, St. Paul

C. M. Loring was typical of the influential and well-to-do Minneapolitans who took interest in the progressive ideals represented by the work of Purcell & Feick. Considered the father of the extensive city park system, Loring hired the firm to develop a design for a public memorial dedicated to those citizens of the city who had lost their lives in the Spanish-American war. The unbuilt project turned out to be more of an excuse for Loring to drop into the office for friendly conversation and extend the occasional invitation for dinner to the young architects.

5. William Purcell and George Feick
   American, 1880–1965 and 1880–1947
   Presentation rendering, 1908
   The F. W. Bird Company
   Ink on paper
   20" × 20"
   Northwest Architectural Archives, University of Minnesota Libraries, St. Paul

In 1908, the F. W. Bird Company, manufacturer of building materials, sponsored a contest for the most innovative use for their products. Except for the house's wooden framing, Purcell & Feick's entry was designed to be made entirely of wares sold by the company. The design further developed the open floor plan scheme begun with the Catherine Gray house, showing this type of dwelling in its most fundamental form. Although the design failed to receive recognition in the competition, the simplicity and economy of the basic concept shown here was applied successfully in later houses, notably those for C. T. Backus, Thomas Snelling, and Fred Babson.

6. William Purcell and George Feick
   American, 1880–1965 and 1880–1947
   Advertising card, 1908
   Goosman's "Motor Inn"
   Minneapolis, Minnesota
   Color lithography on card stock
   5½" × 8½"
   Northwest Architectural Archives, University of Minnesota Libraries, St. Paul

Advertising was an implicit element in the commercial architecture of Purcell & Feick and later Purcell & Elmslie. The firm was among the first to include signage as an element of their designs. The polychrome coursework, golden lettering, and pyramidshaped lighting fixtures of the "Motor Inn" facade constituted the earliest example of their colorful approach to making architecture attract the customer. Letting the structure speak for itself, this mailing card uses the image of the building to advertise the service it provides.

7. William Purcell and George Feick
American, 1880–1965 and 1880–1947
Presentation sketch, exterior perspective, 1909
Stewart Memorial Church
Minneapolis, Minnesota
Pencil and colored pencil on paper
14" × 18½"
Northwest Architectural Archives, University of Minnesota Libraries, St. Paul

Stewart Memorial Church was the most ambitious commission realized by the firm prior to the arrival of Elmslie. Planned as a neighborhood or "mission" church, the building required no bell tower or similar traditional elements. Instead, the organizing feature was a cubical massing throughout the entire building. The design eschewed any of the applied revivalist forms typical of ecclesiastical architecture at the time, and instead developed simple cruciform patterns for the ornamental finish of doors, windows, and cornices. This sketch conveys the pleasant character intended for the building. It further reveals Purcell & Feick's increasing willingness to depart from conventional forms.

8. William Purcell and George Feick
American, 1880–1965 and 1880–1947
Presentation rendering, showing interior perspective, 1909
Steward Memorial Church
Minneapolis, Minnesota
Pencil and colored pencil on heavy paper
16" × 21"
Northwest Architectural Archives, University of Minnesota Libraries, St. Paul

A wall-sized window of opaque leaded glass opens in the east side of the Stewart Memorial Church to provide the sanctuary with bright morning light for Sunday services. Massive sliding doors on the opposite side of the space were designed to open into a Sunday school wing to be added at a later date. This drawing shows how the varying heights of the walls and ceiling were to be integrated into a unified whole through a highly articulated system of wooden moldings and trim. The pipe organ indicated behind the pulpit and choir was added after construction was completed and required revisions to the chancel as originally built.

9. William Purcell and George Feick

American, 1880–1965 and 1880–1947
Electrolier, 1909
Stewart Memorial Church
Minneapolis, Minnesota
Oak and iron
About 6" × 20" × 36"
Missionary Redeemer Baptist Church

The design of electric light fixtures was an important element in the efforts of the firm to provide a completely integrated building scheme. This electrolier is the primary artificial light source for the sanctuary balcony. Electric power was unreliable in Minneapolis when the Stewart Church was built, and gas wall sconces also were provided to illuminate the interior for evening services and other community functions.

10. William Purcell and George Feick
American, 1880–1965 and 1880–1947
Presentation rendering, showing grounds and floor plans, 1908
Albert Lea College for Women
Albert Lea, Minnesota
Pencil and watercolor on kraft paper
19" × 24"
Northwest Architectural Archives, University of Minnesota Libraries, St. Paul

The first large commission designed by Purcell & Feick that was accepted by a client, this classroom building was constructed under such severe financial restraints that the firm was unable to supervise construction or select materials. Pioneering time and motion studies were done to maximize traffic efficiency, resulting in carefully placed entrances, exits, and hallways, but the building as a whole remained unavoidably austere in finish. This lush watercolor compensates for plainness of the design. Purcell & Feick hoped to provide comprehensive planning for the entire campus, including landscaping.

11. George Grant Elmslie
American, 1869–1952
Sawed wood screen panel, 1903
Schlesinger & Mayer Store
Chicago, Illinois
William Purcell and George Elmslie, architects
Mahogany
12" × 12"
Arthur Dyson, AIA Collection

A module for a wall divider in a Chicago department store, the design for this screen panel was the work on Elmslie's drafting table when Purcell arrived on his first day of employment in the Sullivan office during 1903. The design represents the most delicate and refined of Elmslie's achievements in ornamental sawed wood, clearly indicating the decorative refinement he would bring to the work of

Purcell & Elmslie seven years later. This panel was probably made as an office sample and likely presented by Elmslie to Purcell as a wedding gift in 1908.

12. William Purcell and George Elmslie
    American, 1880–1965 and 1869–1952
    Dining room chair, 1909
    From Josephine Crane Bradley residence #1
    Madison, Wisconsin
    Oak
    About 52″ × 25″ × 29″
    Sigma Chi Fraternity

The decoration and furnishing of the first Bradley house was being completed at the time Elmslie moved to Minneapolis and was concluded as a Purcell & Elmslie account. This type of chair is typical of the firm at this early period, and the form continued to appear in other dining room suites, notably for E. L. Powers, Bonnie Hunter Elmslie Both (1910), and Amy Hamilton Hunter (1916).

13. Louis Sullivan, architect, and George Elmslie, associate architect
    American, 1856–1924 and 1869–1952
    Transparency from a Lumiere Autochrome, showing exterior perspective, 1908
    Henry B. Babson residence
    Riverside, Illinois
    Original 5″ × 7″; new transparency 16″ × 20″
    Northwest Architectural Archives, University of Minnesota Libraries, St. Paul

When Elmslie left Sullivan's office and joined the partnership with Purcell, he brought with him the wealthy client Henry B. Babson, who would enable the firm to undertake some of its most significant projects. Although Sullivan is credited as author of the house, Elmslie was the one principally responsible for the design. Babson continued to rely on Elmslie to refine his country estate over the years. This extraordinary image is the only known color photograph of this landmark in progressive American residential design and is presented here publically for the first time. The leaded glass executed by P&E as part of an alteration in 1912 can be seen inside the vaulting of the former sleeping porch.

14. William Purcell and George Elmslie
    American, 1880–1965 and 1869–1952
    Andirons. 1912
    From Henry B. Babson residence
    Riverside, Illinois, 1908
    Brass
    10⅞6″ × 7½″ × 7⅞6″
    Art Institute of Chicago 1971.788 a–b

Elmslie designed unique andirons for several fireplaces in the Babson house. Although another form of hearth support was published in *The Western Architect* as belonging to the master bedroom, these playful and bright andirons can be seen in a later photograph being used in that fireplace.

15 William Purcell and George Elmslie
   American, 1880–1965 and 1869–1952
   Presentation rendering, 1915
   Landscaping for Henry B. Babson
   Riverside, Illinois
   Ink and colored pencil on paper, mounted on masonite plate
   About 30″ × 24″ (exclusive of surrounding panel)
   David S. Gebhard Collection

The large grounds of the Babson estate were developed over more than a decade. This drawing illustrates the sense of poetry, and some impracticality, with which George approached landscape design. The Babson main house and a complex of service buildings by Purcell & Elmslie are integrated within a sinuous layout of walks, gardens, and game areas.

16. William Purcell and George Elmslie
    American, 1880–1965 and 1869–1952
    Sketch of front elevation and sketch showing plan, 1915
    Service buildings for Henry B. Babson
    Riverside, Illinois
    Pencil and colored pencil on tracing paper
    8½″ × 14″ and 11″ × 14″
    Northwest Architectural Archives, University of Minnesota Libraries, St. Paul

17. William Purcell and George Elmslie
    American, 1880–1965 and 1869–1952
    Group of four photographs, 1915
    Service buildings for Henry B. Babson
    Riverside, Illinois
    5″ × 7″ mounted on 11″ by 10″ cardboard panel, each
    Northwest Architectural Archives, University of Minnesota Libraries, St. Paul

The service buildings designed by Purcell & Elmslie for Henry Babson accommodate the functional requirements of a large country estate. The structure housed a variety of agricultural and mechanical services and provided living quarters for staff. The highly developed ornamental treatment of the buildings was unusual for this type of structure. Aesthetic elements included a central fountain count, leaded glass, sawed wood, and a wind tower, visible in these early sketches and photographs.

18. William Purcell and George Elmslie
    American, 1880–1965 and 1869–1952
    Transparency from a Lumiere autochrome, exterior perspective, 1911
    E. L. Powers residence, 1910

Minneapolis, Minnesota
Original 4″ × 5″; new transparency 16″ × 20″
Northwest Architectural Archives, University of Minnesota Libraries, St. Paul

Taken from a perspective long obscured by surrounding buildings and landscaping, the image in this Lumiere autochrome reveals the horizontal mounting of the Powers residence along the axis of the lot. Although many houses designed by the firm were finished in a coat of rose-colored plaster, the original light tan color of this house can be seen clearly to match with the dark brown flower boxes and sawed wood ornamentation. This photograph is one of a group of autochromes taken by Purcell of the work of his firm to date during 1914.

19. William Purcell and George Elmslie
    American, 1880–1965 and 1869–1952
    Hall door, 1910
    E. L. Powers residence
    Minneapolis, Minnesota
    84″ × 34″
    Edward and Maureen Labenski Collection

One of the first large commissions designed after Elmslie joined the firm, the Powers house was unique in the addition of specially inlaid doors throughout the interior. Door panels downstairs were made of veneered oak with the same inlay pattern as those upstairs, which were made of darker mahogany. Most doors in the house were inlaid on both faces, even though many were for closet or service areas. The delicate rays of satinwood, kingwood, and ebony draw the eye to the flatness of the doors surface, an effect both honest in function and beautiful in form, echoing the same effect of stencils on the walls.

20. William Purcell and George Elmslie
    American, 1880–1965 and 1869–1952
    Sawed wood panel for sideboard, 1910
    E. L. Powers residence
    Minneapolis, Minnesota
    Oak
    10″ × 6″
    Edward and Maureen Labenski Collection

21. William Purcell and George Elmslie
    American, 1880–1965 and 1869–1952
    Bi-fold doors, 1910
    E. L. Powers residence
    Minneapolis, Minnesota
    Oak and leaded glass
    84″ × 12′
    Edward and Maureen Labenski Collection

The Powers house was the first major residence to be designed by Elmslie after joining the firm. The form of the dwelling recalls elements of the Henry Babson house he had done only a year earlier. The client could afford to ornament the house, and Elmslie took full advantage of the opportunity to unfold the design motive with terracotta, leaded glass, and sawed wood. The pattern seen in the set of living room porch doors matches that found in the sawed wood side panel of the built-in dining room buffet.

22. Gustav Weber
    American, 1870–1960
    Presentation rendering for dining room, showing furniture and decoration, 1910
    E. L. Powers residence
    Minneapolis, Minnesota
    William Purcell and George Elmslie, architects
    Pencil and watercolor
    12½″ × 20½″
    Northwest Architectural Archives, University of Minnesota Libraries, St. Paul

E. L. Powers was on the building committee of the Interlachen Country Club and there met interior designer Gustav Weber. Impressed with the man and his work, Powers requested that Weber consult with Purcell & Elmslie to complete the furnishing of the new house. Weber became an enthusiastic supporter of the organic approach and went on to do many other P&E residential interior designs. This watercolor for the Powers dining room presents the intention of organic interior design to carry through integration of the house and furnishings to the smallest detail.

23. William Purcell, George Feick, and George Elmslie
    American, 1880–1965, 1880–1947, and 1869–1952
    Group of three folio prints: Competition for a Model Village Home, 1914
    Minnesota State Arts Commission
    First prize award, Lawrence A. Fournier
    Second prize award, Marion Alice Parker
    Office entry for Purcell, Feick, and Elmslie
    Ink on paper
    About 17″ × 11″ each
    Northwest Architectural Archives, University of Minnesota Libraries, St. Paul

The Minnesota State Arts Commission sponsored semi-annual design competitions for small house plans that could be built for modest construction costs. Always eager to bring architecture into the reach of the average person, both the Purcell & Elmslie office and individual staff members submitted entries. In 1914, both first and second prizes went to two architects in the office. Two of these drawings were later published in a portfolio that could be obtained by prospective homebuilders through the mail.

24. William Purcell and George Elmslie
    American, 1880–1965 and 1869–1952
    Dining room bay window panel, 1910
    George W. Stricker residence, alterations

Minneapolis, Minnesota
Leaded glass
About 5′ × 2′
Private collection

Like many people, Purcell and Elmslie were very interested in the new field of aviation. Because there were no historical precedents for aircraft design, it would require the designer to work "organically" (i.e., to base all decisions of relevance to function). A vision of the new technology found enthusiastic expression in the remodeling of the dining room for George Stricker, which called for a group of leaded glass panels. In one of the windows, Purcell recorded in a delicately detailed tribute his thrill at the recent initial flight of the Curtis bi-plane.

25. William Purcell and George Elmslie
    American, 1880–1965 and 1869–1952
    Bookcase doors, 1913
    E. S. Hoyt residence
    Red Wing, Minnesota
    Wood and leaded glass
    24″ × 14″ each
    Frank and Jean Chesley Collection

Although William Gray Purcell described the large, two-story residence built in Red Wing, Minnesota, for E. S. Hoyt as an example of the open floor plan design sequence, the size and development of the dwelling go beyond the objective of that form. Specialized areas including a business office on the first floor and domestic areas on the second floor extend the space of the house beyond the compact organization seen in smaller residences by the firm. The large lot, pier-and-lintel elevations, and extended porch spaces reflect design relationships more visible in their larger houses. The budget for the project permitted a rich unfoldment of decorative motifs in leaded glass panels for windows, doors, and bookcases on the same diamond pattern also used in the earlier Edna S. Purcell residence (1913). The most important ornamental treatment in the Hoyt house is an exquisite mosaic panel over the fireplace, executed in Minneapolis by Edward L. Sharretts at his Mosaic Arts Studios. The house was further embellished by massive sawed wood grilles placed in an outdoor breezeway during the later addition of a garage complex.

26. William Purcell and George Elmslie
    American, 1880–1965 and 1869–1952
    Bookcase door panels, 1912
    From Charles I. Buxton residence
    Owatonna, Minnesota
    Leaded glass
    38″ × 14″
    Mark Walbran Collection

Many Purcell & Elmslie houses were embellished with leaded glass panels. When budgets were limited, these enrichments most often occurred on bookcase doors, as in the Buxton house. Although patterns may be similar in type, the firm also intended that each design be unique to a single commission. Something of an exception to the rule, these two panels repeat the pattern motive from the Lyman Wakefield house in Minneapolis (1911), but with a richer palette of color. Curiously, another Wakefield panel was used in the dictionary stand for the Edna S. Purcell residence built in 1913.

27. William Purcell and George Elmslie
    American, 1880–1965 and 1869–1952
    Porch window section, 1912
    Oscar Owre residence
    Minneapolis, Minnesota
    Mahogany
    40″ × 55″ × 2″
    Peter and Nancy Albrecht Collection

Many P&E houses incorporate sitting porches. Storm windows such as this from the Owre house were a standard feature of the firm's more elaborate small dwellings.

28. William Gray Purcell
    American, 1880–1965
    Presentation rendering, 1912
    Josephine Crane Bradley summer residence (aka "Bradley Bungalow")
    Charles R. Crane Estate
    Woods Hole, Massachusetts
    William Purcell and George Elmslie, architects
    Ink on linen
    30″ × 50″
    Northwest Architectural Archives, University of Minnesota Libraries, St. Paul

In the design for the Bradley bungalow, Purcell and Elmslie were given carte blanche by the client with one restriction: the house had to be completed in just over three months. The house was built, completely furnished, and the site landscaped between June and September of 1912. This elaborate rendering was created for an exhibition to show the form and siting of the house on a Cape Cod peninsula in relationship to other structures on the estate, many of which were also designed by P&E.

29. William Purcell and George Elmslie
    American, 1880–1965 and 1869–1952
    Window light panels, 1914
    Edward W. Decker residence
    Holdridge Station
    Lake Minnetonka, Minnesota
    Leaded glass
    42″ × 15″
    Mrs. F. M. Rosekrans Collection

Similar in form to the Bradley bungalow, the vacation house built by P&E for Minneapolis banker Edward Decker was larger and more formal. The structure was richly detailed with sawed wood beam finials and leaded glass windows. In keeping with the client's desire that his house acknowledge and be visually linked with the surrounding woodland, these two panels flanked a large picture window in the dining room. The simplicity of the pattern is consistent with the overall purpose of the vacation house.

30. George Grant Elmslie
    American, 1869–1952
    Side chair, 1914
    Edward W. Decker residence
    Holdridge Station
    Lake Minnetonka, Minnesota
    William Purcell and George Elmslie, architects
    Oak, cloth upholstery
    50" × 19¼" × 20"
    The Minneapolis Institute of Arts
    Gift of Susan Decker Barrows, 93.89.1

Made of rose pine and finished with a rusticated surface, the high back dining room chairs for the Decker vacation house emphasized the relaxed atmosphere of the Lake Minnetonka countryside. Unlike most of the tall chairs designed by the firm, these were not incised with sawed wood or leaded glass ornament. Instead, the double bank of moulding on foot and headboard members provides a gentle emphasis to the straight lines of the chair form. The subtle remark of this detailing visually integrated the suite with the board-and-batten paneling of the dining room.

31. George Grant Elmslie
    American, 1869–1952
    Side table, 1914
    Edward W. Decker residence
    Holdridge Station
    Lake Minnetonka, Minnesota
    William Purcell and George Elmslie, architects
    Oak
    About 24" × 22" × 30"
    Minnesota Historical Society Collections

The Decker house was filled with custom-made furniture. One of a pair, this end table and a matching library table were placed in the central living area of the first floor. The old craftsman who carved the rich curvilinear medallions had trouble at first in pleasing the discriminating eye of the architects. Complaining that years of work on repetitive neo-classicist molding had ruined his artistic hand, he cut the Decker table decorations several times before being satisfied with the result.

32. William Purcell and George Elmslie
    American, 1880–1965 and 1869–1952
    Presentation rendering, 1914

Palmer-Cantini residence, project
Minneapolis, Minnesota
Pencil and colored pencil on tracing paper (mounted on masonite plate)
16¼" × 20½"
David S. Gebhard Collection

This dwelling, which resembles a house less than a jewel box, has the most radical open floor plan ever done by the firm. Of this unbuilt project, Purcell said, "We became so much interested in the mechanical and architectural solution of this small house . . . we fell into the hole which we always tried so hard to avoid and actually produced a paper project which could not have any reality in that world which the client had to face. It deserved not to be built."

33. Miles Sater
    American
    Sketch for living room fireplace mural, 1913
    Edna S. Purcell residence
    Minneapolis, Minnesota
    William Purcell and George Elmslie, architects
    Watercolor on card stock
    9" × 12"
    Northwest Architectural Archives, University of Minnesota Libraries, St. Paul

34. Charles Livingston Bull
    American, 1874–1932
    Two sketches for living room fireplace mural, 1913
    Edna S. Purcell residence
    Minneapolis, Minnesota
    William Purcell and George Elmslie, architects
    9" × 12" each
    Northwest Architectural Archives, University of Minnesota Libraries, St. Paul

The fireplace wall in this residence was meant to have a mural decoration. One of the earliest suggestions for this treatment was made by Miles Sater, a brother-in-law of Walter Burley Griffin, who sometimes worked with George Elmslie in the Chicago P&E office. In 1914, Purcell and his wife sent out letters to various artists whose work they felt expressed the organic ideal, requesting sample mural designs. Charles Livingston Bull, a noted illustrator of children's books, sent this sketch; the final mural design differed in that the ducks were replaced by Louisiana herons.

35. William Purcell and George Elmslie
    American, 1880–1965 and 1869–1952
    Group of five diagrams for leaded glass, 1913
    Edna S. Purcell residence
    Minneapolis, Minnesota
    Ink on paper
    9¼" × 7",   12" × 4½",   8" × 4⅞",   8⅞" × 3½",   and
    7½" × 5⅛"

Northwest Architectural Archives, University of Minnesota Libraries, St. Paul

The Lake Place house was built by Purcell for his wife, Edna. He was determined to fully develop the organic ideal in his new residence, whatever it might cost. These sketches show the decorative pattern of leaded glass panels throughout the house, unfolding from a single decorative pattern according to the size of the window opening.

36. William Purcell and George Elmslie
    American, 1880–1965 and 1869–1952
    Electrolier and wall sconce, 1913
    John H. Adair residence
    Owatonna, Minnesota
    About 24″ × 18″ × 18″
    Private Collection

When budget permitted, P&E included specially designed light fixtures in their houses. In the Adair house, P&E had the opportunity to supply fixtures for ceiling lights and various wall sconces. One of three situated in the living and dining rooms of the Adair house, this electrolier was etched with a stencil pattern on the metal face and glass bowl.

37. William Purcell and George Elmslie, designers
John S. Bradstreet and Co., manufacturer
    American
    Dining room suite, 1915
    For Mrs. Hanna
    William Purcell and George Elmslie, architects
    Table, two chairs, and sideboard
    Cuban mahogany, silver plated brass, and glass inlay
    Buffet: H 35¼″ × W 44″ × D 22⅞″
    Chair: H 40½″ × W 16″ × D 19″
    Table top: W 42″ × L 42″ × 4½″
    Private Collection

Arguably the finest furniture designed by Purcell and Elmslie, this dining room suite was constructed in Minneapolis for a Chicago client. The small scale and refined lines are complemented by delicate inlay and small inset panels of leaded glass. The triangular shape of the chairs is repeated in the drawer pulls on the sideboard, which contains a secret compartment.

38. William Purcell and George Elmslie
    American, 1880–1965 and 1869–1952
    Presentation rendering, 1910
    Saint Paul's Episcopal Church
    Cedar Rapids, Iowa
    Ink on linen
    About 30″ × 32″
    Northwest Architectural Archives, University of Minnesota Libraries, St. Paul

Purcell & Elmslie lost the commission for this large church when the client turned to Louis Sullivan, whom they had honored in their presentation as the fountainhead of the organic architectural movement. When Sullivan and the client later disagreed and parted ways, the firm reluctantly and discreetly tried to salvage as much as possible of the Sullivan design out of respect for their former employer. This large drawing shows the cubical form proposed originally by Purcell & Elmslie.

39. William Gray Purcell
    American, 1880–1965
    Group of 3 presentation renderings, 1912
    Aviation cup trophies for Robert Jarvie
    Pencil and watercolor on colored stock
    30″ × 19″ each
    Northwest Architectural Archives, University of Minnesota Libraries, St. Paul

The first "Flying Machine Meet" was held in Chicago in September 1911. Silversmith Robert Jarvie contacted Purcell & Elmslie for trophy designs. The rush project had to be completed in one weekend. Whether these trophy cups were actually created is not known, but Jarvie later made silver flatware and many other fine objects for the firm.

40. William Purcell and George Elmslie
    American, 1880–1965 and 1869–1952
    Sketch, showing side elevation, 1913
    Litchfield Pavilion
    Litchfield, Minnesota
    Pencil on paper
    13″ × 14″
    Northwest Architectural Archives, University of Minnesota Libraries, St. Paul

When the citizens of the rural village of Litchfield wanted a concrete bandstand for a town square, P&E suggested a single column to support the overhanging canopy. The form shown in this drawing was too radical for the conservative building committee, but the design anticipated ways the proposed building material would be used more than fifty years later.

41. Emil Frank
    American
    Front elevation, perspective view, 1912
    Edison Shop for Henry B. Babson
    Ink and colored ink on linen
    50″ × 24″
    Northwest Architectural Archives, University of Minnesota Libraries, St. Paul

The Edison shops sold photographs and records. Of the three stores designed by the firm for client Henry B. Babson, the most architecturally developed was one on Wabash Avenue in Chicago. This drawing shows the facade of the building, which was designed to draw customers from the sidewalk toward large display windows. Like the other stores in Kansas City and San Francisco, the Chicago Edison shop featured a completely integrated interior finish that included wall moldings, light fixtures, carpets, electric light fixtures, and furniture.

42. William Purcell and George Elmslie
    American, 1880–1965 and 1869–1952
    Light fixture, 1915
    Minnesota Phonograph Company
    Leaded glass
    About 18″ × 6″ × 6″
    David S. Gebhard Collection

The Minnesota Photograph Company was an Edison dealership owned by Lawrence H. Lucker, who wanted a store like the ones Purcell & Elmslie had designed for Henry Babson. Designs for the Lucker shop included upholstered seating, tables, and service counters, which were integrated into an interior design unified by moldings, sawed wood, and leaded glass. This rectangular box light was one of several mounted on top of decorative grille screens.

43. William Purcell and George Elmslie
    American, 1880–1965 and 1869–1952
    Presentation rendering, showing front elevation, 1915
    Hotel
    Rhinelander, Wisconsin
    Pencil and watercolor on paper, mounted on masonite plate
    24″ × 48″
    Northwest Architectural Archives, University of Minnesota Libraries, St. Paul

This hotel project emerged through contacts made when the firm had designed the First National Bank of Rhinelander in 1910. The plan introduced the concept of two entrances for lobby shops, allowing pedestrians direct access to a coffee shop and other services from the street, as well as from inside the hotel. This highly detailed rendering is the most impressive commercial project presentation drawing done by Purcell & Elmslie.

44. William Purcell and George Elmslie
    American, 1880–1965 and 1869–1952
    Photograph of presentation rendering, 1916
    Institutional Church for Charles O. Alexander
    Siang Tan, Hunan, China
    About 12″ × 12″
    Northwest Architectural Archives, University of Minnesota Libraries, St. Paul

Members of the Alexander family were involved with the Young Men's Christian Association mission in China, and this large building was designed to provide an impressive local presence for the institution. The design was approved and working drawings completed, but business reversals of the client prevented construction. This photograph is of an oil on canvas rendering (now lost) by artist Charles S. Chapman.

45. William L. Steele, Architect
    William Purcell and George Elmslie, Associated Architects
    American, 1880–1965 and 1869–1952
    Electroliers, 1916–1917
    Woodbury County Court House
    Sioux City, Iowa
    Metal and art glass
    About 8′ × 2′ × 2′
    Woodbury County Courthouse, Sioux City, Iowa

The Woodbury County Court House was the only major public building erected by Prairie architects. Elmslie, who was responsible for the design, moved to Sioux City while it was under construction. In addition to supervising a large drafting team, Elmslie completed the designs for every decorative element in the structure by hand. Four of these electroliers hang in each of several courtrooms, matching the pattern of window glass and other furnishings.

46. Alphonso Ianelli
    American, b. 1888
    Model for sculpture group, 1916/1917
    Woodbury County Court House
    Sioux City, Iowa
    William L. Steele, architect
    William Purcell and George Elmslie, associated architects
    Plaster
    14½″ × 27½″
    Northwest Architectural Archives

Purcell & Elmslie approached artist Guzton Borglum to do the numerous sculpture groups intended for the courthouse entrances. The fee quoted by Borglum was more than the budget permitted; Borglum recommended one of his students, Alphonso Ianelli. Although Ianelli's nude figures encountered some criticism from local dignitaries, two main groups and some smaller pieces for the court house were eventually completed. This plaster model is one of the later Ianelli studies for the west-facing main entryway.

47. William Purcell and George Elmslie
    American, 1880–1965 and 1869–1952
    Bench, 1905
    Farmers National Bank
    Owatonna, Minnesota
    Oak
    48″ × 56½″ × 22″
    Norwest Bank Owatonna

48. William Purcell and George Elmslie
    American, 1880–1965 and 1869–1952

Table lamp, 1905
Farmers National Bank
Owatonna, Minnesota
Bronze and leaded glass
31″ × 19″ sq.
Norwest Bank Owatonna

49. William Purcell and George Elmslie
    American, 1880–1965 and 1869–1952
    Jardiniere, 1905
    Atlantic Terracotta and Ceramic Company
    Farmers National Bank
    Owatonna, Minnesota
    Terra-cotta
    19″ × 11″ × 6.5″ base dia.
    David Matchan Collection

Although Louis Sullivan is credited with the design of this bank, research has shown that the structure was almost entirely from the hand of George Elmslie. Considered to be the pinnacle of American bank design, the interior was furnished in every detail. The bench shown here is part of a three-piece suite of public seating placed in the main banking room. The table lamp is a very early version of a type that would be developed in later Purcell & Elmslie work.

50. William Purcell and George Feick
    American, 1880–1965 and 1880–1947
    Presentation rendering, perspective, 1909
    First National Bank
    Winona, Minnesota
    Colored pencil on paper, mounted on masonite plate
    ABout 14″ × 22″
    David S. Gebhard Collection

The First National Bank project was one of the most colorful building designs of the Purcell & Feick partnership. This drawing shows the wide wall areas given to windows and decorative features that were intended to convey an enlightened sense of relationship toward the community. The firm invited the banking committee to visit the Farmers National Bank nearby in Owatonna. But the vivacious color treatments in that building were too much for the Winona bankers, who chose instead a granite and marble revivalist design by George H. Maher.

51. William Purcell and George Elmslie
    American, 1880–1965 and 1869–1952
    Presentation drawing, front elevation, 1910
    First National Bank
    Rhinelander, Wisconsin
    Ink on linen
    About 9″ × 12″
    Northwest Architectural Archives, University of Minnesota Libraries, St. Paul

This building was sited on a deep corner lot in the business district of Rhinelander, a small town located in north central Wisconsin. By placing the banking room toward the rear of the lot, P&E was able to provide two useful commercial spaces and still provide access to the bank through an intermediary lobby. Seen in this drawing in front elevation, the resulting design solution so enraged one bank director that he sold his stock and predicted calamity for the institution if the building was constructed.

52. William Purcell and George Elmslie
    American, 1880–1965 and 1869–1952
    Presentation drawing, exterior perspective, 1911
    First National Bank
    Mankato, Minnesota
    Colored pencil and crayon on paper
    About 14″ × 22″
    Northwest Architectural Archives, University of Minnesota Libraries, St. Paul

53. William Purcell and George Elmslie
    American, 1880–1965 and 1869–1952
    Presentation drawing, interior section, 1911
    First National Bank
    Mankato, Minnesota
    Colored pencil and crayon on paper
    About 14″ × 22″
    Northwest Architectural Archives, University of Minnesota Libraries, St. Paul

The First National Bank in Mankato was one of the first bank commissions sought by P&E after Elmslie joined the firm. Convinced that their presentation of the design had been successful and that the client had been won over to the organic design approach, they left these two presentation renderings, among others, with the building committee for further examination. Shortly afterwards a competitor not known for progressive work was given the job, and Purcell felt the result was an "outright transcription" of the P&E proposal.

54. George Grant Elmslie
    American, 1869–1952
    Sketch, terra-cotta ornament, 1912
    Merchants Bank of Winona
    Winona, Minnesota
    William Purcell and George Elmslie, architects
    Pencil on tracing paper
    About 12″ × 9″
    David S. Gebhard Collection

Terra-cotta was a primary form of enrichment for P&E banks, and the elaborate eagle above the front entrance of the Merchants National Bank was one of the most complex pieces ever cast by the Atlantic Terra-cotta Company. This sketch by Elmslie, an outstanding renderer of original ornamental forms, shows the beginning of the design process which brought these decorative features to realization.

55. William Purcell and George Elmslie
    American, 1880–1965 and 1869–1952
    Sketch, diagram for terracotta ornament, 1912
    Merchants Bank of Winona
    Winona, Minnesota
    Pencil on kraft paper
    22¾″ × 14¼
    Northwest Architectural Archives, University of Minnesota Libraries, St. Paul

After roughing out the shape in a preliminary sketch, Elmslie would isolate details of the unique features and indicate the repeating elements of a terra-cotta module. This drawing was prepared for Kristian Schneider, a clay modeler at the Atlantic Terra-Cotta and Ceramic Company in Illinois who had worked with Sullivan and Elmslie since the 1890s. Schneider then rendered the two-dimensional drawing into three-dimensional clay forms.

56. William Purcell and George Elmslie
    American, 1880–1965 and 1869–1952
    Photograph, showing terra-cotta ornament before glazing, 1912
    Merchants Bank of Winona
    Winona, Minnesota
    William Purcell and George Elmslie, architects
    8″ × 5″
    Northwest Architectural Archives, University of Minnesota Libraries, St. Paul

Before molds were made for the production of individual pieces of terra-cotta ornament, the prototype of the clay model was photographed. At this stage, a design could be corrected or altered. This photograph was sent to the P&E office as part of the approval process. At this stage the final glazing colors would be selected and the actual terra-cotta pieces made.

57. Albert Fleury
    American, 1848–1915(?)
    Group of two cartoons for mural, 1912
    Merchants Bank of Winona
    Winona, Minnesota
    William Purcell and George Elmslie, architects
    Oil on canvas
    9″ × 30″
    Nicholas John Steffen Collection

Albert Fleury, a well-known Chicago artist, collaborating with Purcell & Elmslie after Purcell bought a painting from him in 1913. Undertaken by Fleury the year after construction was completed, the decoration of the banking room of the Merchants National Bank in Winona consisted of a pair of paintings stressing the agricultural character of the Mississippi River valley where the bank was suited. The one on the right is now the sole color record of one of the two panels, lost during subsequent remodeling of the bank.

58. George Grant Elmslie
    American, 1869–1952
    Two sketches for vault mosaic, 1912
    Merchants Bank of Winona
    Winona, Minnesota
    William Purcell and George Elmslie, architects
    Sketch for vault mosaic
    Pencil on tracing paper
    14″ × 12½″
    Sketch for vault mosaic colors
    Watercolor on card stock
    9½″ × 8½″
    Northwest Architectural Archives, University of Minnesota Libraries, St. Paul

The vault was at the heart of a bank building. Rather than hide it, Purcell & Elmslie exalted the round vault door with a halo of mosaic tile. This preliminary sketch shows the basic concept of this ornamentation.

The colorful presence of the vault mosaic had to match the rest of the color scheme of the building. The ornamental was to be ordered from a firm in Chicago, which sent this card to the architects to indicate available color choices.

59. William Purcell and George Elmslie
    American, 1880–1965 and 1869–1952
    Mosaic fragments, 1912
    Merchants Bank of Winona
    Winona, Minnesota
    Porcelain tile
    About 6″ × 9″
    David S. Gebhard. Collection

Because of their site specificity, mosaics rarely survive outside the building where they are installed. The beautiful vault mosaic for the Merchants National Bank, however, was removed as early as the 1920s. These remaining fragments provide a glimpse of the final result achieved by P&E in their design.

60. William Purcell and George Elmslie
    American, 1880–1965 and 1869–1952
    Photograph, showing vault mosaic, 1912
    Merchants Bank of Winona
    Winona, Minnesota
    8″ × 10″
    Northwest Architectural Archives, University of Minnesota Libraries, St. Paul

61. William Purcell and George Elmslie
    American, 1880–1965 and 1869–1952
    Chair, 1912
    Merchants Bank of Winona
    Winona, Minnesota
    Oak, leather, metal tacks
    36½″ × 24⅜″ × 26″
    The Minneapolis Institute of Arts
    Driscoll Arts Accession Fund 93.1

As with all fully developed P&E designs, the Winona bank also required specially made furniture. A dozen of these chairs and a small table were built for the director's office. The type of seat for the Winona bank was developed in different formats for residential as well, most notably in two low-back versions for the Edna S. Purcell house (1913) and a high-back style for the Oscar Owre house (1914). The sketch and letter reveal the regard for comfort and practical construction considerations that were characteristic of P&E.

62. William Purcell and George Elmslie
    American, 1880–1965 and 1869–1952
    Letter, 1912
    Concerning the Merchants Bank of Winona bank chair
    Winona, Minnesota
    George Grant Elmslie to William Gray Purcell
    5″ × 7″
    Northwest Architectural Archives, University of Minnesota Libraries, St. Paul

63. George Grant Elmslie
    American, 1869-1952
    Sketch, with annotations, 1912
    Merchants Bank of Winona
    Winona, Minnesota
    William Purcell and George Elmslie, architects
    Pencil on paper
    8.5″ × 11″
    Northwest Architectural Archives, University of Minnesota Libraries, St. Paul

64. William Purcell and George Elmslie
    American, 1880–1965 and 1869–1952
    Transparency from a Lumiere autochrome, showing interior of banking room, 1914
    Merchants Bank of Winona, 1912
    Winona, Minnesota
    Original 4″ × 5″; new transparency 16″ × 20″
    Northwest Architectural Archives, University of Minnesota Libraries, St. Paul

The Merchants National Bank was the largest and most fully developed of the banks designed by Purcell & Elmslie. The interior of the banking room was completed by 1914,

when this color transparency was taken by Purcell. The murals by Albert Fleury are visible on both walls, together with light fixtures, check desks, and the original teller windows.

65. William Purcell and George Elmslie
    American, 1880–1965 and 1869–1952
    Transparency from a Lumière autochrome, showing skylight, 1914
    Merchants Bank of Winona, 1912
    Winona, Minnesota
    Original 4″ × 5″; new transparency 16″ × 20″
    Northwest Architectural Archives, University of Minnesota Libraries, St. Paul

The skylight for the Merchants National Bank is the largest ever designed by the firm. Subsequent insensitive alterations concealed the glasswork, which suffered extensive damage and had to be largely replaced. This unique image shows the original skylight as it appeared in 1914.

66. William Purcell and George Elmslie
    American, 1880–1965 and 1869–1952
    Group of frieze modules, 1916
    Farmers and Merchants Bank
    Hector, Minnesota
    Polychrome terra-cotta
    About 12″ × 24″
    Northwest Architectural Archives, University of Minnesota Libraries, St. Paul, and private collections

Once made, pieces of terra-cotta were packed in hay, crated, and shipped by rail to the construction site. By using factory-produced ornaments in standardized, easily installed modules, P&E was able to enrich small town buildings with sophisticated forms. These segments were removed during a remodeling of the Hector bank during the 1970s.

67. William Purcell and George Elmslie
    American, 1880–1965 and 1869–1952
    Front elevation windows, 1914
    Madison State Bank
    Madison, Minnesota
    Leaded glass
    72″ × 22″
    Private Collection

68. William Purcell and George Elmslie
    American, 1880–1965 and 1869–1952
    Secondary skylight panel, 1914
    Madison State Bank
    Madison, Minnesota
    Leaded glass
    70″ × 32¼″
    Private Collection

69. William Purcell and George Elmslie
American, 1880–1965 and 1869–1952
Office door, 1914
First State Bank
LeRoy, Minnesota
Oak and leaded glass panel
84″ × 30″
First State Bank

Light was always an important factor in designs by Purcell & Elmslie, and many of their bank designs feature large windows. In order to prevent glare, provide solar tempering, and remove the need for unsightly roller shades, windows and door panels were often filled with opaque glass. In this door, the glass panel passes interior light but keeps the office space private from the main banking room.

70. William Purcell and George Elmslie
American, 1880–1965 and 1869–1952
Electrolier, 1920
First National Bank of Adams
Adams, Minnesota
Metal and art glass
About 5′ × 2′ × 2′
City of Adams, Minn.

Even though hours of operation were during the daytime, banking rooms also required supplemental artificial lighting. These fixtures usually dropped from a high tented ceiling in a pendant form that was decorated with art glass. This electrolier is among the last designed by the firm and features the plate-and-hemisphere motive often seen in their residences, commercial, and institutional work.

71. William Purcell and George Elmslie
American, 1880–1965 and 1869–1952
Presentation rendering, perspective, 1916
Factory for Alexander Brothers, International Leather and Belting Company
Reduction print
9″ × 12″
Northwest Architectural Archives, University of Minnesota Libraries, St. Paul

Alexander Brothers was a leather belting manufacturer that assumed the corporate name of International Leather and Belting Company after acquiring several other similar companies. During World War I, Purcell & Elmslie served as company architects to the Alexander concerns. They produced a modular factory design that was built in Philadelphia, Pennsylvania, and New Haven, Connecticut. The Philadelphia site was intended to be the chief manufacturing headquarters of the business, and is shown in this drawing with administrative and warehouse facilities as one integrated building complex.

72. Norman T. A. Munder and Company
Group of eight advertising posters, 1916–1919
Advertising for Alexander Brothers, International Leather and Belting Company
Ink on paper
12″ × 9″ each
Northwest Architectural Archives, University of Minnesota Libraries, St. Paul

73. Norman T. A. Munder and Company
Group of four advertising pocket calendars, 1916–1919
Advertising for Alexander Brothers, International Leather and Belting Company
Ink on paper
5″ × 3″ each
Northwest Architectural Archives, University of Minnesota Libraries, St. Paul

74. Alexander Brothers
Presentation book, 1917
Advertising for Alexander Brothers, International Leather and Belting Company
Leather and ink, with bronze medallion
14″ × 10″
Northwest Architectural Archives, University of Minnesota Libraries, St. Paul

Leather belting was the chief means of industrial power transfer during the 1910s. Before the development of independent electric motors, all machinery was attached to a common steam engine through pulleys, wheels, and stretches of leather belting. Working as a part-time advertising manager for Alexander Brothers, Purcell developed a series of advertising campaigns from 1916 to 1919 that used this arrangement as a basic graphic symbol. Unique and innovative, these materials were developed with artwork by artists John W. Norton, Charles S. Chapman, and Charles Livingston Bull, all of whom had done decorative architectural work for Purcell & Elmslie. The advertising posters, cards, and presentation book seen here were printed with inks and papers by Norman T. A. Munder of Philadelphia.

APPENDIX: PURCELL & ELMSLIE, ARCHITECTS

COMMISSION LIST

Note: The numbers given in this list correspond to the original accounting system of the Purcell & Elmslie office. Commissions with suffix letters are original to that system, unless enclosed in parentheses. Those shown in parentheses represent duplicate account assignments. Date and location are taken from original commission lists. Those shown as "location unknown" are probably for the Minneapolis, Minnesota, area (only one Purcell & Elmslie commission, for John Leuthold [#155], was executed in Saint Paul,

Minnesota). Several Purcell & Elmslie commissions also appear under an accounting system adopted by William Gray Purcell after 1919 in his separate practice in Portland, Oregon, and are given here with those numbers. A series of unnumbered designs is also shown. With the exception of some furniture or decorative designs for family or friends, and a group of unidentified sketches, this list reflects the full record of work by the firm from its founding as Purcell & Feick in 1907 to dissolution of the Purcell & Elmslie partnership in 1921.

1	Duplex residence, project Minneapolis, Minnesota 1907
2	Western Avenue Exchange Block, alterations Minneapolis, Minnesota 1907
2½	A. K. X. Sorority, consultation Wellesley, Massachusetts 1907
3	Garage for Henry Goosman Also known as: "The Motor Inn" Minneapolis, Minnesota 1907/1908
4	Butler Brothers Fireworks Warehouse Minneapolis, Minnesota 1907
4½	Catherine Gray residence, project Also known as: W. G. Purcell residence Minneapolis, Minnesota 1907
5	Catherine Gray residence Also known as: W. G. Purcell residence Minneapolis, Minnesota 1907
5A	Catherine Gray residence, furniture Also known as: W. G. Purcell residence Minneapolis, Minnesota 1909
6A	F. Bullen residence, alterations Red Wing, Minnesota 1907
7	Truman B. Taylor residence Sandusky, Ohio 1907
8	First National Bank, project Winona, Minnesota 1907
9	W. J. Landon duplex residences, projects Winona, Minnesota 1907
10	Cargill Science Hall Albert Lea College for Women Albert Lea, Minnesota 1907
11	Fred A. Larson residence Towner, North Dakota 1908
12	Bookcases and mantel for Dowling Omaha, Nebraska 1908
13	Bank for Mr. Dowling Also known as: Atkinson State Bank Atkinson, Nebraska 1908
15	F. W. Bird Competiton 1908
16	Bank, alterations Bismarck, North Dakota 1908
17	Singer Building, project Bismarck, North Dakota 1908
18	Map for C. H. McHugh, drafting North Dakota 1908

18A	John H. Kahler residence, project Rochester, Minnesota 1908
19	United Brethren Church, project Minneapolis, Minnesota 1908
20	Cover for *The Interior*, graphic design 1908
21	Chicago Architectural Exhibition 1908
22	Handicraft Guild, consultation Minneapolis, Minnesota 1908
23	Arthur Jones residence, alterations Minneapolis, Minnesota 1908
24A–B	Parish House and Chancel for Christ Church Eau Claire, Wisconsin 1908
25	Design for the *Ladies Home Journal* 1908
26	Mrs. W. H. Purcell residence, alterations project Los Angeles, California 1908
27	Elks Club, project Mankato, Minnesota 1908
28	Reel and Rudder Club Lake Minnetonka, Minnesota 1908
29	Nolan R. Best, The Interior consultation 1908
30	J. Trumer, consultation Minneapolis, Minnesota 1908
32	Houses for George Feick, Sr. Sandusky, Ohio 1908
33	H. J. Myers residence Minneapolis, Minnesota 1908
34	Harris, alterations project Minneapolis, Minnesota 1908
35	Soldier's Memorial Arch for C. M. Loring, project Minneapolis, Minnesota 1908
38	Clayton F. Summy, consultation Chicago, Illinois 1908
39	George Stricker residence, alterations Minneapolis, Minnesota 1909
40	Mrs. Terrence W. McCosker residence Minneapolis, Minnesota 1909
41	Office Building for George Feick, Sr. Sandusky, Ohio 1908
42	Warehouse for Sears E. Brace, Jr. & Company Minneapolis, Minnesota 1909
43	Methodist Church, consultation Eau Claire, Wisconsin 1909
44	H. P. Dowling, consultation Harlan, Iowa 1909
45	James Edwin Jensen, consultation Minneapolis, Minnesota 1909
46	Steps for John S. Owen Eau Clair, Wisconsin 1909
47	J. D. R. Steven cottage Eau Claire, Wisconsin 1909

48 J. D. R. Steven residence
Eau Claire, Wisconsin   1909

49 E. M. Thompson residence
Bismarck, North Dakota   1909

50 A. W. Armitage residence, alterations
Minneapolis, Minnesota   1909

51 Charles A. Purcell residence #1
River Forest, Illinois   1909

52 Commercial Building for Carlyle Scott, project
Minneapolis, Minnesota   1909

53 Theodore H. Beaulieu residence
White Earth, Minnesota   1909

54 George W. Wishard residence, alterations
Minneapolis, Minnesota   1909

55 Mrs. P. C. Maxson, alterations
Minneapolis, Minnesota   1909

56 Stewart Memorial Church
Minneapolis, Minnesota   1909

57 Fitting rooms for the Dayton Company, project
Minneapolis, Minnesota   1909

58 Mrs. George H. Simpson, consultation
Oak Park, Illinois   1909

59 Lindsay Brothers Warehouse, alterations project
Minneapolis, Minnesota   1909

60 Henry G. Goosman residence
Minneapolis, Minnesota   1909

61 M. M. Chase, consultation
Lake Minnetonka, Minnesota   1909

62 H. P. Gallagher residence
Lake Minnetonka, Minnesota   1909

63 E. C. Warner residence, project
Minneapolis, Minnesota   1909

64 C. W. Lockwood residence, alterations
Eau Claire, Wisconsin   1909

65 City Hall, project
Eau Claire, Wisconsin   1909

66 Homer M. Stocking, consultation   1909

67 Olaf Noer, consultation   1909

68 Robert G. Morrison, consultation   1909

69 Patrick E. Byrne residence
Bismarck, North Dakota   1909

70 C. L. Browne, consultation   1909

71 Mrs. H. H. Bell residence, alterations
Minneapolis, Minnesota   1910

72 Duplex House for Harry Blair, project
Winona, Minnesota   1910

73 Mrs. T. B. Keith residence, alterations and furniture
Eau Claire, Wisconsin   1910

74 Garage for the Electric Carriage and Battery Company
Minneapolis, Minnesota   1910

75 W. E. Baker residence
Minneapolis, Minnesota   1910

76 Exchange State Bank
Grand Meadow, Minnesota   1910

77 Edward Goetzenberger residence
Minneapolis, Minnesota   1910

78 Westminster Presbyterian Church, alterations
Minneapolis, Minnesota   1910

79 George Stricker residence, project
Minneapolis, Minnesota   1910

80 Leon Warner residence, alterations
Minneapolis, Minnesota   1910

81 T. R. Atkinson residence
Bismarck, North Dakota   1910

82 S. F. Blymer summer residence #1
Lake Minnetonka, Minnesota   1910

83 A. B. C. Dodd residence
Charles City, Iowa   1910

84 C. F. Clark residence, project
Cedar Rapids, Iowa   1910

85 J. H. Waggoner, consultation
Eau Claire, Wisconsin   1910

86 Saint Paul's Episcopal Church, project
Cedar Rapids, Iowa   1910

87 Design for the Perfection Church Company, stationery
(for Carl K. Bennett)
Owatonna, Minnesota   1910

88 Stables for Henry B. Babson
Riverside, Illinois   1910

89 Josephine Crane Bradley residence #1
Madison, Wisconsin   1910

90 H. C. Garvin residence, alterations
Winona, Minnesota 1910/1911

91 Stables and Landscaping for E. B. Ingram
Minneapolis, Minnesota   1910

92 Cabin for James B. Thompson
Northern Minnesota   1910

93 Charles R. Crane residence, alterations
Crane Estate
Woods Hole, Massachusetts   1910

93A Stables for Charles R. Crane, alterations
Crane Estate
Woods Hole, Minnesota   1910

94 Charles W. Sexton summer residence, alterations
Lake Minnetonka, Minnesota   1910

95 W. G. A. Millar residence, alterations
Pittsburgh, Pennsylvania 1910
George Grant Elmslie, architect

96 Frank Horton, consultation
Winona, Minnesota   1910

97 W. B. Hathaway summer residence, alterations
Lake Minnetonka, Minnesota   1910

98 E L. Powers residence
Minneapolis, Minnesota   1910

99 First National Bank
Rhinelander, Wisconsin   1910

100 Elk's Club, project
Winona, Minnesota   1910

101 W. A. Hubbard, consultation
Minneapolis, Minnesota 1910

102 Harold E. Hineline residence
Minneapolis, Minnesota 1910

103 Fireplace for W. A. Benton
Location unknown 1910

104 Studio for Paul Mueller
Minneapolis, Minnesota   1910

105 Citizen's Savings Bank, project
Cedar Falls, Iowa   1911

106 H. W. Baker summer residence, alterations
Minnetonka, Minnesota   1911

107 Christian Church, consultation
Cedar Rapids, Iowa   1911

108 Citizen's National Bank, project
Watertown, South Dakota   1911

109 S. F. Blymer summer residence #2
Lake Minnetonka, Minnesota   1911

110 J. E. Murray residence, alterations
Minneapolis, Minnesota   1911

111 Lyman E. Wakefield, residence
Minneapolis, Minnesota   1911

112 Earl Curtis, consultation   1911

113 Scandinavian American State Bank, alterations project
Minneapolis, Minnesota   1911

114 First National Bank, alterations
Graceville, Minnesota   1911

115 Ruth Rosholt, consultation   1911

116 E. E. Knowlton residence
Rochester, Minnesota   1911

117 Tea Rooms for the Dayton Company, project
Minneapolis, Minnesota   1911

118 Sanitarium for Frank H. Blackmaar, project
Chicago, Illinois   1911

119 Lincoln County Bank, consultation
Merrill, Wisconsin   1911

120 Carlo Jorgenson residence
Bismarck, North Dakota   1911

121 Hattie McIndoe residence, project
Rhinelander, Wisconsin   1911

122 Louis Heitman residence, first scheme, project
Helena, Montana   1911

123 Henry Weber, Jr., consultation
Austin, Minnesota   1911

124 First National Bank, project
Mankato, Minnesota   1911

125 Fowler Methodist Church, consultation
Minneapolis, Minnesota   1911

126 Aviation Cups for Robert Jarvie   1911

127 Gardener's Cottage
Crane Estate
Woods Hole, Massachusetts   1911

128 Chi Psi Fraternity House, alterations
University of Minnesota
Minneapolis, Minnesota   1911

129 J. G. Cross residence, alterations
Minneapolis, Minnesota   1911

130 Oscar Owre residence
Minneapolis, Minnesota   1911

131 Josephine Crane Bradley summer residence
Also known as: the Bradley Bungalow
Crane Estate
Woods Hole, Massachusetts   1911/1912

132 Merchants National Bank
Winona, Minnesota   1912

133 High School, consultation
Rhinelander, Wisconsin   1912

134 Henry W. Benton, consultation
Wayzata, Minnesota   1912

135 Stove for Clayton F. Summy Company
Chicago, Illinois   1912

136 Speculative Houses for Carl K. Bennett, project
Owatonna, Minnesota   1912

137 Third National Bank, project
Sandusky, Ohio   1912

138 High School, project
Sandusky, Ohio   1912

139 H. S. Adams residence, project
Oak Park, Illinois   1912

140 Offices for Eaton, Crane & Pike, consultation
Chicago, Illinois   1912

141 Phi Alpha Theta, alterations
University of Minnesota
Minneapolis, Minnesota   1912

142A Henry B. Babson residence, alterations
Riverside, Illinois   1912

142B Clock for Henry B. Babson   1912

143 Ice House
Crane Estate
Woods Hole, Massachusetts   1912

144 Mrs. Rice, consultation   1912

145 W. F. Braasch residence, project
Rochester, Minnesota   1912

146 Second Cornell Exhibition   1912

147 Cottages
Crane Estate
Woods Hole, Massachusetts   1912

148 George W. Wishard residence, alterations
Minneapolis, Minnesota 1912

149 Buzzard's Bay Cottages
Crane Estate
Woods Hole, Massachusetts 1912

150 A. D. Daniels residence, project
Rhinelander, Wisconsin 1912

151 E. Frank Hussey residence, project
Minneapolis, Minnesota 1912

152 Design for Exchange State Bank, stationery
Grand Meadow, Minnesota 1912

153 T. H. Simmons, consultation
Cedar Rapids, Iowa 1912

154 C. I. Buxton residence
Owatonna, Minnesota 1912

155 John Leuthold residence
Also known as: Ward Beebe residence
Saint Paul, Minnesota 1912

156 Interstate Merchantile Company, consultation
Winona, Minnesota 1912

157 E. C. Tillotson residence
Minneapolis, Minnesota 1912

158 Business Women's Dormitory for Gratia Countryman,
project
Minneapolis, Minnesota 1912

159 Harry D. Page, consultation
Mason City, Iowa 1912

160 Fence
Crane Estate
Woods Hole, Massachusetts 1912

161 Winthrop State Bank, consultation
Winthrop, Minnesota 1912

162 Library, alterations
Crane Estate
Woods Hole, Massachusetts 1912

163 Harry Blair, consultation
Winona, Minnesota 1912

164 J. C. Young, consultation
Paris, France 1912

165 Henry Graefe, alterations
Sandusky, Ohio 1912

166 S. W. Batson, consultation
Wayzata, Minnesota 1912

167 E. W. Decker summer residence, first scheme
Holdridge, Minnesota 1912

168 First National Bank, alterations
Bismarck, North Dakota 1912

169 Westminster Sunday School, alterations
Minneapolis, Minnesota 1912

170 Edison Shop
Chicago, Illinois 1912

171 C. W. Lockwood summer residence
D'Oreille, Wisconsin 1912

172 Design for *The Western Architect* 1912
Volume XIX, #1 (January, 1913).

173 John S. Owen cottage, alterations
Location unknown 1912

174 Maurice I. Wolf residence
Minneapolis, Minnesota 1912

175 Apartment Building for H. H. Newman and G. L.
Marsh, project
Chicago, Illinois 1913

176 William Sufflow, consultation 1913

177 First National Bank, consultation
Janesville, Wisconsin 1913

178 J. E. Meyers residence, project
Minneapolis, Minnesota 1912

179 Charles Parker residence
Minneapolis, Minnesota 1912

180 Chippewa Valley Light & Power Company, consultation
Eau Claire, Wisconsin 1912

181 Charles R. Crane, consultation
Crane Estate
Woods Hole, Massachusetts 1912/1913

182 Western Motor Supply Company, alterations
Minneapolis, Minnesota 1912

183 Swift Cottage, alterations
Crane Estate
Woods Hole, Massachusetts 1913

184 Lamp Posts
Merchants National Bank
Winona, Minnesota 1913

185 Exhibitions
New York, NY
Chicago, Illinois 1913

186 George W. Wishard residence, furniture
Minneapolis, Minnesota 1913

187 J. W. S. Gallagher residence
Winona, Minnesota 1913

188 Greenhouse
Crane Estate
Woods Hole, Massachusetts 1913

189 Pier and Boathouse
Crane Estate
Woods Hold, Massachusetts 1913

190 W. E. Waldron, consultation
Billings, Montana 1913

191 Merton S. Goodnow residence
Hutchinson, Minnesota 1913

192 C. E. Ingersoll residence, project
Sarasota, Florida 1913

193 H. Choate, consultation
Winona, Minnesota 1913

194 Thomas W. Snelling residence
Waukegan, Illinois 1913

195   Mrs. W. B. Harbeson, consultation
       Rapid City, North Dakota   1913

196   P&E Chicago office, accounting   1913

197   Edna S. Purcell residence
       Minneapolis, Minnesota   1913

198   A. F. Bullen residence, alterations
       Red Wing, Minnesota   1913

199   W. E.Baker residence, alterations
       Minneapolis, Minnesota   1913

200   E. S. Hoyt residence
       Red Wing, Minnesota   1913

201   Bolles Rodgers, alterations
       Minneapolis, Minnesota   1913

202   Rectory for the Parish of St. Anthony
       Minneapolis, Minnesota   1913

203   E. W. Decker summer residence, revised scheme
       Holdridge, Minnesota   1913

204   Madison State Bank
       Madison, Minnesota   1913

205   Benjamin A. Paust residence, alterations
       Minneapolis, Minnesota   1913

206   Joseph E. Ware, alterations
       Minneapolis, Minnesota   1913

207   Litchfield Pavilion
       Litchfield, Minnesota   1913

208   Auditorium for the Women's Club, project
       Minneapolis, Minnesota   1913

209   C. A. Wheelock residence, project
       Fargo, North Dakota   1913

210   Garage for E. W. Decker
       Holdridge, Minnesota   1913

211   Clayton F. Summy Company, consultation
       Chicago, Illinois   1913

212   George D. Dayton residence, alterations
       Minneapolis, Minnesota   1913

213   E. W. Decker summer residence, decoration
       Holdrigde, Minnesota   1913

214   Charles A. Purcell residence #1, decoration
       River Forest, Illinois   1913

215   E. W. Decker summer residence, perspective drawing
       Holdridge, Minnesota   1913

216   Cabin for Harold J. McCormick, project
       Island Lake, Wisconsin   1913

217   Landscaping for Carl K. Bennett
       Owatonna, Minnesota   1913

218   John H. Adair residence
       Owatonna, Minnesota   1913

219   E. W. Decker summer residence, entrance gate
       Holdridge, Minnesota   1913

220   Parsonage for the First Congregational Church
       Eau Claire, Wisconsin   1913

221   Community House for the First Congregational Church
       Eau Claire, Wisconsin   1913

222A   Ralph D. Thomas residence, project
       Minneapolis, Minnesota   1913

222B   Ralph D. Thomas residence, alterations
       Lake Minnetonka, Minnesota   1924

223   F. R. Durant summer residence, alterations project
       Crystal Bay, Minnesota   1913

224   Edward L. Somerville summer residence, alterations
       Lake Minnetonka, Minnesota   1913

225   Exhibition
       Chicago, Illinois   1914

226   E. W. Decker summer residence, pump house
       Holdridge, Minnesota   1913

227   Australian Parliament Buildings Competition
       Canberra, Australia   1914

228   Overt Nelson residence, consultation
       Madison, Wisconsin   1913

229   Brick and Tile Competition
       Minnesota State Arts Commission   1914

230   Edison Shop, alterations
       Kansas City, Missouri   1914

231   First State Bank
       LeRoy, Minnesota   1914

232   Walter S. Milnor, consultation   1914

233   First National Bank, alterations
       Graceville, Minnesota   1914

234   Henry B. Babson residence, alterations
       Riverside, Illinois   1914

235   Riverside Country Club, first scheme
       Riverside, Illinois   1914

236   Working People's Cottages for Henry B. Babson, project
       Lyons, Illinois   1914

237   P&E Chicago office, accounting

238   Edison Shop, alterations
       Chicago, Illinois   1914

239   E. H. Foot residence, alterations
       Red Wing, Minnesota   1914

240   R. H. Chute residence, alterations
       Location unknown   1914

241   Charles A. Purcell residence #1, alterations
       River Forest, Illinois   1914

242   Edison Shop
       San Francisco, California   1914
       Walter H. Ratcliff, Jr., associated architect

243   Yale Place Extension, project
       Minneapolis, Minnesota   1914

244   H. B. Sell residence, alterations
       Chicago, Illinois   1914

245   A. W. Sawyer residence, consultation
       Location unknown   1914

246   Open Air Theater for Thaddeus P. Giddings
Anoka, Minnesota   1914

247   Palmer-Cantini residence, project
Saint Paul, Minnesota   1914

248   Fence for Harry F. Baker
Minneapolis, Minnesota   1914

249   E. H. White residence, project
Minneapolis, Minnesota   1914

250   Third Christian Science Church, project
Minneapolis, Minnesota   1914

251   Edison Shop, alterations
San Francisco, California   1914

252   Margaret Little residence
Berkeley, California   1914

253   Edgar Dyar, consultation   1914

254   Durbar Cigarette Company, project
Also known as: Gusto Cigarette Company
Minneapolis, Minnesota   1914

255   Design for *The Western Architect*
Volume XXXI, #1 (January, 1915).

256   Edna S. Purcell residence, alterations, decoration,
furniture
Minneapolis, Minnesota   1914/1915

257   George D. Dayton residence, alterations
Minneapolis, Minnesota   1914

258   Minnesota Phonograph Company
Minneapolis, Minnesota   1914

259   James E. Moore residence, project
Minneapolis, Minnesota   1914

260   Josephine Crane Bradley residence #2
Madison, Wisconsin   1914

261   Carl K. Bennett residence #1, project
Owatonna, Minnesota   1914

262   Catherine Gray residence, alterations project
Also known as: W. G. Purcell residence
Minneapolis, Minnesota   1914

263   Carl K. Bennett, stationery
Owatonna, Minnesota   1914

264   Oscar Owre residence, furniture
Minneapolis, Minnesota   1914

265   Henry Einfeldt residence
River Forest, Illinois   1914

266   Francis Buzzell residence
Lake Bluff, Illinois   1914

267   Landscaping for Henry B. Babson
Riverside, Illinois   1914

268   Rhinelander Inn
Also known as: "The Welcome Inn"
Rhinelander, Wisconsin   1915

269   P&E Chicago office, accounting   1915

270   Garage for Terrence W. McCosker
Minneapolis, Minnesota   1915

271   Design for the Edison Shop, instrument panels
Chicago, Illinois   1915

272   Mrs. Henry L. Simons residence, project
Glencoe, Minnesota   1915

273   Cabin for Francis Buzzell
Lake Bluff, Illinois   1915

274   Cabin for Allen D. Albert, project
Minneapolis, Minnesota   1915

275   Library, consultation
LeRoy, Minnesota   1915

276   Woodbury County Court House
Sioux City, Iowa   1915/1916
William L. Steele, Sr., architect
Purcell & Elmslie, associated architects

277   Open Air Theater for Thaddeus P. Giddings
Anoka, Minnesota   1915

278   A. D. Hirschfelder residence, project
Minneapolis, Minnesota   1915

279   W. G. Purcell, accounting   1915

280   Garage for E. S. Hoyt
Red Wing, Minnesota   1915

281   Design for *The Western Architect*   1915
Volume XXII, #1 (July, 1915)

282   Clayton F. Summy Company, alterations
Chicago, Illinois   1915

283   C. T. Backus residence
Minneapolis, Minnesota   1915

284   Mrs. William H. Hanna, furniture
Chicago, Illinois   1915

285   Jump River Town Hall
Jump River, Wisconsin   1915

286   George D. Dayton residence, alterations
Minneapolis, Minnesota   1915

287   Memorial Window for Christ Church
Eau Claire, Wisconsin   1915

288   Service Buildings for Henry B. Babson
Riverside, Illinois   1915

289   Episcopal Church, consultation
Owen, Wisconsin   1915

290   George S. Blossom residence, consultation
Location unknown   1915

291   Fourteenth Christian Science Church, consultation
Chicago, Illinois   1915

292   Tenth Christian Science Church, consultation
Chicago, Illinois   1915

293   Alexander Brothers, accounting
Philadelphia, Pennsylvania   1915

294   George W. Stricker residence, alterations
Minneapolis, Minnesota   1915

295   J. D. R. Steven residence, alterations
Eau Claire, Wisconsin   1915

296   Commercial Building for F. N. Hegg
      Minneapolis, Minnesota   1915

297   Charles O. Alexander residence, project
      Philadelphia, Pennsylvania   1915

298   Second Christian Science Church, light fixtures
      Minneapolis, Minnesota   1915/1916

299   Louis Heitman residence, first scheme
      Helena, Montana   1916

300   Woodbury County Court House, perspective drawing
      Sioux City, Iowa   1916

301   Farmhouse for Fred Babson
      Hinsdale, Illinois   1916

302   C. J. Hibbard residence, consultation
      Minneapolis, Minnesota   1916

303   Factory for Alexander Brothers, alterations
      Philadelphia, Pennsylvania   1916

304   L. A. Schipfer residence, project
      Bismarck, North Dakota   1916

305   Professor Leavenworth, consultation
      Minneapolis, Minnesota   1916

306   P&E Chicago office, accounting   1916/1917

307   Brick House Competition
      Minnesota State Arts Commission   1917

308   Logan-Branson Bank Building
      Mitchell, South Dakota   1916

309   Farmers and Merchants State Bank
      Hector, Minnesota   1916

310   Institutional Church for Charles O. Alexander, project
      Also known as: Y.M.C.A.
      Siang Tan, Honan, China   1916

311   Alexander Brothers
      Executive and General Offices, alterations
      Philadelphia, Pennsylvania   1916

312   Louis Heitman residence, revised scheme
      Helena, Montana   1916

313   D. F. Recker residence, consultation
      Rhinelander, Wisconsin   1916

314   Louis Heitman residence, accounting
      Helena, Montana   1916

315   Louis Heitman residence, furniture
      Helena, Montana   1916

316   Louis Heitman residence, decoration
      Helena, Montana   1916

317   W. Y. Chute, alterations
      Minneapolis, Minnesota   1916

318   Mrs. Amy Hamilton Hunter residence
      Flossmoor, Illinois   1916

319   Municipal Auditorium Competition
      Minneapolis, Minnesota   1916

320   Land Office Building for the Northwestern Lumber
      Company
      Stanley, Wisconsin   1916

321   Edison Shop, sign
      Chicago, Illinois   1916

322   L. W. Kerugher, consultation
      Mapleton, Minnesota   1916

323   F. W. Sprague residence, alterations
      Sauk Rapids, Minnesota   1916

324   Logan Remodelling Stores, consultation
      Mitchell, South Dakota   1916

325   Australian Parliament Competition
      Canberra, Australia   1916

326   American Institute of Architects, accounting
      Minnesota Chapter   1916

327   Municipal Building
      Kasson, Minnesota   1916

328   Farmers State Bank, alterations
      Also known as: Parkhurst Bank
      Kasson, Minnesota   1916

329   Chute Realty Company, alterations
      Minneapolis, Minnesota   1916

330   Third Church of Christ, Scientist, consultation
      Riverside, Illinois   1916

331   Clark, consultation
      Des Moines, Iowa   1916

332   W. N. Parkhurst residence, project
      Kasson, Minnesota   1916

333   Alexander Brothers, advertising
      Philadelphia, Pennsylvania   1917

334   Commercial Building for James G. Wallace
      Minneapolis, Minnesota   1917

335–335A   Fritz Carlson residence
      Minneapolis, Minnesota   1917/1923

336   P&E Chicago Office, accounting   1917/1918

337   Commercial Building for George E. Logan
      Mitchell, South Dakota   1917

338   Alexander Brothers, accounting
      Philadelphia, Pennsylvania   1917

339   Alexander Brothers, accounting
      Philadelphia, Pennsylvania   1917

340A Alexander Brothers
      Factor for the International Leather & Belting
      Corporation
      Chicago, Illinois   1917

340B Alexander Brothers
      Factory for the International Leather & Belting
      Corporation
      New Haven, Connecticut   1917

340C Alexander Brothers
      Factory for the International Leather & Belting
      Corporation, project
      Cleveland, Ohio   1917

340D Alexander Brothers
      Garage for the International Leather & Belting
      Corporation
      Location unknown 1917

341 Commercial Building and Factory for Mr. Biddle, consultation
Philadelphia, Pennsylvania   1917

342 Alexander Brothers
W. G. Purcell Personal Service, accounting
Philadelphia, Pennsylvania   1917

343 Biddle residence, consultation
Philadelphia, Pennsylvania   1917

344 Landscaping for Mr. Biddle, consultation
Philadelphia, Pennsylvania   1917

345 Charles Weithoff residence
Minneapolis, Minnesota   1917

346 McPhail Studios, consultation
Minneapolis, Minnesota   1917

347 Mrs. Richard Polson residence
Spooner, Wisconsin   1917

348 P&E advertising brochures   1917

349 James Edwin Jensen residence, first scheme
Minneapolis, Minnesota   1918

350 Garage and Fence for Oscar Owre
Minneapolis, Minnesota   1918

351 Speculative Houses for W. Y. Chute
Minneapolis, Minnesota   1918

352 Commercial Building for C. L. Atwood, consultation
St. Cloud, Minnesota   1918

353 Apartments for C. L. Atwood, consultation
St. Cloud, Minnesota   1918

354 Bank Building for C. L. Atwood, consultation
St. Cloud, Minnesota   1918

355 Hotel for C. L. Atwood, consultation
St. Cloud, Minnesota   1918

356 Alexander Brothers
Design for the International Leather & Belting
Corporation, trademark
Philadelphia, Pennsylvania   1918

357 Alexander Brothers
Design for the Shoe Renew Shops, stationery
Philadelphia, Pennsylvania   1918

358 Dental Offices for Drs. Owre and Braasch, alterations
Minneapolis, Minnesota   1918

359 Alexander Brothers
Charlotte Leather Belting Company, consultation
Chicago, Illinois   1918

360 Alexander Brothers, advertising
Philadelphia, Pennsylvania   1918

361 National Farmer's Bank, consultation
Owatonna, Minnesota   1918

362 Helen C. Pierce Public School, consultation
Chicago, Illinois   1918

363 Alexander Brothers
Charlotte Leather Belting Company, alterations
Charlotte, North Carolina   1918

364 Alexander Brothers
International Leather & Belting Corporation, accounting
Philadelphia, Pennsylvania   1918

365 P&E Minneapolis office, accounting   1918

366 Alexander Brothers
Factory for the International Leather & Belting
Corporation, machinery layout
Chicago, Illinois   1918

367 W. G. Purcell residence, accounting (?)
Philadelphia, Pennsylvania   1918

368 Edna S. Purcell summer residence
Rose Valley, Pennsylvania   1918

369 Alexander Brothers
Charlotte Leather & Belting Company, advertising
Charlotte, North Carolina   1918

370A–B Alexander Brothers
International leather & Belting Corporation, advertising
Philadelphia, Pennsylvania   1918

371 Henry B. Babson summer residence, consultation
Riverside, Illinois 1918

372 National Farmer's Bank, consultation
Owatonna, Minnesota   1918

373 National Farmer's Bank, consultation
Owatonna, Minnesota   1918

374 Carl K. Bennett summer residence, project
Owatonna, Minnesota   1918/1920

375 Carl K. Bennett residence #2, project
Owatonna, Minnesota   1918/1920

376 Memorial Design for Carl K. Bennett, consultation
Owatonna, Minnesota   1918

377 Alexander Brothers
Storage Racks
Chicago, Illinois   1918

378 Aloney Rist Owen summer residence, alterations
Drummond, Wisconsin   1918

379 Riverside Country Club, revised scheme
Riverside, Illinois 1918

380 Alexander Brothers
Charlotte Leather Belting Company, consultation
Charlotte, North Carolina   1918

381 Summerhouse for Edna S. Purcell
Rose Valley, Pennsylvania   1918/1919

382 W. G. Purcell, accounting   1918

382(A) Overmantle for Clayton F. Summy, project
Mural Design by John W. Norton
Chicago, Illinois   1918

383 Charles O. Alexander summer residence, alterations
Squam Lake, NH   1919

384 James Edwin Jensen residence, revised scheme
Minneapolis, Minnesota   1919

385 Frank Tustison, consultation
Minneapolis, Minnesota   1919

386   J. S. Ulland, alterations
       Fergus Falls, Minnesota   1919

387   Mrs. Henry L. Simons, consultation
       Glencoe, Minnesota   1919

388   Orlando Simons, consultation
       Glencoe, Minnesota   1919

389   Ralph Owen summer residence, consultation
       Drummond, Wisconsin   1919

390   Bank for the Owen Lumber Company, project
       Drummond, Wisconsin   1919

391   Garage for the Owen Lumber Company, consultation
       Drummond, Wisconsin   1919

392   Church for the Owen Lumber Company, consultation
       Drummond, Wisconsin   1919

393   School for the Owen Lumber Company, consultation
       Drummond, Wisconsin   1919

394   Farmhouse for Aloney Rist Owen, consultation
       Drummond, Wisconsin   1919

395   Business Women's Club, consultation
       Minneapolis, Minnesota   1919

396   Marion Alice Parker, accounting   1919

397   Merchant's National Bank, alterations
       Winona, Minnesota   1919

398   Union Bottling Works, project
       Minneapolis, Minnesota   1920

399   First National Bank of Adams
       Adams, Minnesota   1920

400   Kramer Hotel, consultation
       Mudlava, ID   1920

401   American National Bank
       Aurora, Illinois   1920

402   George Pank (Old Second National Bank)
       Aurora, Illinois   1920

403   Dr. Batrud, consultation
       Minneapolis, Minnesota   1920

404   Not used.

405   K. Paul Carson, Sr., residence, project
       Minneapolis, Minnesota   1920

406   Clayton F. Summy Company, alterations
       Chicago, Illinois   1920

407   E. A. Forbes residence
       Rhinelander, Wisconsin   1920

408   Not used

409   Charles A. Purcell residence #1, alterations
       River Forest, Illinois   1921

410   Albert Lea State Bank, project
       Albert Lea, Minnesota   1921

411   "Purcell & Elmslie, Architects," special accounting
       Exhibition, Walker Art Center
       Minneapolis, Minnesota   1953

412–499   Not used.

500   Cunningham Gray Architectural Service
       Builder's Document Service
       Builder's Plan Service,
       advertising   1920/1921

601   Resort Hotel, project
       Hood River, Oregon   1919
       Purcell & Elmslie, architects

602   Bridge
       Wolf Creek, Oregon   1919
       Purcell & Elmslie, architects

603   Apartment Building, project
       Portland, Oregon   1919
       Purcell & Elmslie, architects

607   William Gray Purcell residence
       Also known as "Georgian Place"
       Portland, Oregon   1920

UNNUMBERED COMMISSIONS

Testimonial Frame for James B. Angell, design   1909

Garage, project
Location unknown   1910

Bank project
Location unknown   1915

J. D. Hussey residence
Philadelphia, Pennsylvania   1919

Cresbard State Bank, project
Cresbard, South Dakota   1920/1921

Memorial Tablet for F. E. Reeve   undated

Apartment Building, project
Location unknown   undated

Apartment building, project
Location unknown   undated

6

Unanswered Questions: Native Americans and Euro-Americans in Minnesota

Louise Lincoln and
Paulette Fairbanks Molin

IN 1893 THE CITY OF CHICAGO OPENED THE WORLD'S Columbian Exposition, a gigantic industrial and cultural fair spread over more than a thousand acres of undeveloped land by the lake on the city's South Side. Marking the four hundredth anniversary of Columbus's arrival in the western hemisphere, the exposition was an unabashedly triumphal celebration of the Euro-American past, present, and future. The dozens of plaster of Paris buildings that made up the fair's main pavilions were extravagantly pseudo-classical in style, invoking Greek and Roman antecedents to assert the legitimacy and permanence of the American government, life, and thought. At night, the buildings, promenades, and fountains were bathed in brilliant artificial light; this unprecedented display of still-novel electrical power was heralded as a culmination of technical progress and an indication of the promise of the future.

Journalists quickly named the pristine buildings, enhanced nightly by arc lights, the White City.[1] Far from finding electrical illumination on antiquarian buildings incongruous, commentators hailed the synthesis as symbolic of the fundamental premise of the fair: the technology of the future could improve even the most revered traditions of the past. That past, like the imagined future, could only be conceived as European.

If there was agreement on the appropriateness of this mixed metaphor, however, there was none on a parallel example of tension between tradition and progress raised by the fair's official displays about American Indians. For all of their educational window-dressing, nineteenth-century world's fairs were primarily an opportunity for nations to promote commercial and industrial development, sweetened by "culture" and exoticism. Pavilions included restaurants with servers in national dress (sometimes invented for the occasion), and troupes of costumed performers, some installed in "authentic" village settings.[2] At fairs preceding Chicago, the representation of Native American life had been confined to material-culture exhibitions or dioramas; now Indian people, too, became part of the spectacle. Under the direction of Frederick Putnam, head of the Peabody Museum at Harvard University, the Columbian Exposition's anthropology department brought Indians from reservations across the country to live in replicas of traditional dwellings on the Midway of the fairgrounds: Navajo hogans sat side by side with long houses and tipis. Richly dressed Indians carried out the tasks of daily life before fairgoers, carefully excluding any hints of the modern world.[3] With its emphasis on "traditional" ways, Putnam's exhibition seemed to freeze Indian peoples in the past, untouched by the notions of progress that the fair celebrated elsewhere.[4]

A second exhibition about Native Americans, sponsored by the Commissioner of Indian Affairs, directly challenged this view. The government's exhibition began with material-culture objects explicitly identified as belonging to the past and culminated with a schoolhouse in which rotating groups of students from reservation schools, neatly dressed in conventional Euro-American clothing, carried out algebra and spelling exercises before large and appreciative audiences. The message here was equally clear: according to Commissioner Thomas Morgan, the exhibition "sets forth the future of the Indian. It shows . . . unmistakably his readiness and ability for the new conditions of civilized life and American citizenship upon which he is entering."[5] The rival interpretations generated considerable controversy in newspaper accounts and among whites involved in Indian issues. Putnam's exhibition was denounced from two sides: by progressives, for failing to acknowledge the reality of contemporary Indian life and condemning Indians to extinction, and by religious conservatives as "an exhibit of savagery in its most repulsive form."[6] Still other commentators argued that Morgan's rose-tinted view held out an unrealistic hope of assimilation. Meanwhile, seemingly oblivious to the controversy, an independent third group of Indians was camped on the lakefront, wearing "traditional" clothing and doing a handsome business in the sale of curios to fair visitors. And on the Midway yet another group, in the employ of Buffalo Bill Cody, performed in the exuberant Wild West shows for huge crowds, while nearby a replica of "Sitting Bull's Cabin" was identified by a sign reading "War Dances Given Daily."[7]

There was, unquestionably, a range of view of Indians, a range of self-presentation by Indians. Nevertheless, the most remarkable aspect of the Indian exhibitions at the fair was what was omitted. By sketching a mythic past in the anthropology section and an almost equally mythic future in the commissioner's schoolhouse, the fair's organizers avoided, perhaps quite consciously, any discussion of the present. The ghastly tragedy of the Wounded Knee Massacre, which had occurred less than two years before, was nowhere mentioned; the disease, hunger, and desperate poverty which were the scourge of the reservations at the time were invisible; the disputes over treaty rights, land allotments, and annuity payments went unnoted.[8]

THE INDIAN PAST IN MINNESOTA

In fact, the decades leading up to the nineties had been a cataclysmic period for Indian people, especially those in the Midwest. With the conclusion of the Civil War, white settlers pressed westward in increasing numbers as returning war veterans on both sides sought homesteads or employment. The railroads, too, penetrated the western regions, cutting strips of land through territories already ceded by treaty to Indian tribes. Lumbering and mining interests pressed for the right to explore and subsequently exploit the natural resources on Indian land. The federal government supported white expansion with increasingly forceful policies. By the 1870s, U.S. Army involvement had moved

from a strategy of sporadic defense of military outposts and wagon trains to one of continuing aggressive action against Indian people. Extermination of the buffalo herds on which many Plains groups depended for sustenance was but one part of a larger plan, carried out with military force, to confine Native Americans to small areas of nonproductive reservation land.

For Northern Plains Indians, the most notable in the long series of military encounters was the stunning defeat of General George Armstrong Custer's troops in 1876 by Lakota and Cheyenne warriors at the Battle of the Little Big Horn. Yet the victory was short-lived; the confinement process continued, with more and more Plains groups yielding their autonomy in exchange for the land and payment of annuity goods promised by the government. The buffalo were gone, the land was insufficient for subsistence, and the annuity payments of food and clothing were always inadequate, their quantity and quality systematically eroded at every stage, from the allocation of funds by Congress to the site of distribution by reservation agents. On the reservations, people struggled to cope with wrenching poverty, illness, and depression. By 1890, many Northern Plains groups turned in their desperation to the messianic vision of a Paiute prophet whose visions promised a return to past times of happiness and plenty. Government agents attempted to suppress the so-called Ghost Dance movement, and their zeal precipitated a series of events that left nearly three hundred Lakota people, mostly women and children, massacred in the snow at Wounded Knee, South Dakota. If the Battle of the Little Big Horn was the zenith of Indian resistance to white expansion, Wounded Knee marked its end.

The situation of Indian people in Minnesota, while driven by many of the same patterns and events, also was conditioned by a unique history. Originally homeland to Dakota and Lakota people, the territory saw an influx of Woodland Anishinabe (often designated Ojibwe or Chippewa) peoples in the eighteenth century, driven westward by the pressure of white expansion. Competition between the two Indian groups over increasingly scarce land led to intertribal conflict, and by 1825 a treaty imposed by federal intervention had separated them, establishing Anishinabe territories to the north and Dakota territories roughly in the southern third of the state. Subsequent treaties ceded control of more and more land to whites and established ever smaller reservations for the various bands.

Relations between Indians and Euro-Americans came to a crisis early in Minnesota. By 1862 people in Dakota reservations were already struggling with hunger and illness brought about by the inadequacy of government provisions—the same problems that would beset reservations further west in subsequent decades. Starving and desperate, Dakota men from the Lower Sioux reservation broke into a government supply warehouse and attacked white homesteads; in the ensuing struggle about 1,400 people died, Indians and whites in roughly equal numbers. The government retaliated quickly, rounding up scores of Dakota and,

Anishinabe men gathering wild rice on the Mille Lacs Reservation, about 1900. Photograph from Roger and Priscilla Buffalohead's Against the Tide of American History: The Story of the Mille Lacs Anishinabe, *p. 15, 1985.*

after a summary trial, executing thirty-eight: the largest public hanging in the history of the nation. It also abrogated all treaties with Minnesota Dakota, voiding their rights of occupancy and selling their lands to whites. The remaining Dakota from Lower Sioux were expelled, first to Nebraska, where many died of hunger and exposure, then to South Dakota. Dakota from other reservations fled the state, fearing continued retaliation, or wandered in small groups. Not until 1886 did Congress reestablish small reservations in southern Minnesota for Dakota people, many of whom had filtered back to Minnesota from their exile.[9]

This catastrophic event shaped relations between Native Americans and Euro-Americans in Minnesota for decades. Subsequent episodes of violence elsewhere, such as the Wounded Knee Massacre, served as an invitation to Minnesota newspaper columnists to rehash the Dakota Conflict.[10] Here, as elsewhere, so-called captivity narratives were a popular literary genre, particularly a handful of putative first-hand accounts of the 1862 episode. The local

narratives, published in the 1860s and 1870s, were reissued around the turn of the century as part of a rather curious national revival of interest in the subject.[11]

As a result of their history, Dakota people in Minnesota were far less numerous, and more impinged upon by whites, than Anishinabe people to the north. The tensions and distrust among Minnesota whites toward Dakota people in fact extended as well to the Anishinabe, who had endured similar privation. Their traditional means of economic subsistence had been curtailed through reduction of tribal lands. Seasonal land-based activities such as hunting, fishing, trapping, and the production of wild rice, once carried out over an extensive region, diminished as the land base became smaller and smaller. The Minnesota reservations were barely established when tribal people began to face additional pressures from Euro-Americans to relinquish still more land, and indeed to give up their way of life. Hereditary leaders such as Bugonaygeshig (Hole in the Day), Flat Mouth, Wabanaquot (White Cloud), Way we ya cumig, and May-dway-gwa-no-nind were hard pressed

Mille Lacs removals with their leader, Wa-way-cumig (Round Earth), at Big Elbow Lake at White Earth, about 1905. Photograph courtesy of the Minnesota Historical Society.

to protect the interests of their bands against the divisive strategies and destructive policies of the government.

Following the treaty-making period, which ended in 1871, relations between Minnesota Indians and the federal government were negotiated through legislative measures and agreements, all of which contributed to the loss of enormous areas of land, destruction of natural resources, displacement of individuals, families, and entire bands, and the abridgment of constitutional rights. The Nelson Act of 1889 (25 Stat. 642) sought to relocate all Anishinabe in the state except the Red Lake band to White Earth Reservation, to allot the land, and to expropriate all other Anishinabe land. Red Lake, which relinquished some acreage but successfully resisted allotting tribal land, has retained its principal territory. The other reservations generally lost land, population, or both through the measure.

A three-member government commission traveled through the reservations in an effort to convince Anishinabe to move to White Earth. At Mille Lacs, leaders told the commissioners about earlier treaty violations, including encroachment of whites on reservation lands, failure to deliver annuity payments, and destruction of wild rice crops as a result of damming. The dismayed commissioners reported, "The principal fault of the Mille Lacs bands seems to lie in possessing lands that the white man wants."[12] Because the Nelson Act permitted Anishinabe to claim their allotments on existing reservation land, Mille Lacs members accepted the agreement, believing it would protect their homeland. During the next decade, however, many

Mille Lacs families lost their land, oftentimes forcibly removed by Euro-American homesteaders. In 1901, the county sheriff reportedly burned the homes of one hundred people to enforce white land claims.[13]

Even White Earth, intended as the ultimate territory of all Minnesota Anishinabe, experienced further loss of land. The *Progress*, the first newspaper published on the reservation, editorialized in its first issue:

> The people of Northern Minnesota may honestly believe that a territory of such portions as the White Earth Reservation, should be thrown open to the public for settlement, they may honestly think that it is a wrong policy which locks up thousands of acres, and allows it to remain unoccupied and uncultivated. But it is a narrow view of the question, it overlooks the numbers, and falsely estimates the character of those who may come here under future agreements with the government.
>
> There will be none too much of arable land should the Chippewas of Minnesota be removed here.[14]

The words were prophetic, for as the land base at White Earth was shrinking, other tribal bands were being pressed to move there by government representatives and "friends of the Indian." Newly arrived Anishinabe began to rebuild communities, construct homes, roads, businesses, and farms, yet whites demanded that still more "surplus land" be opened for their use. Although the Nelson Act ultimately failed to consolidate the Minnesota Anishinabe at White Earth, the measure was incalculably destructive to the peoples' livelihood and social fabric. Way we ya cumig

Last official Red Lake Indian delegation to Washington, D.C. in 1909. Front row (left to right): George Highlanding, Everwind, John English, Chief Nodin, Ponemah. Back row: Joe Mason, P. H. Beaulieu, Kingbird, Basil Lawrence, Attorney John Gibbons of Bemidji, Alex Jourdain, Ba-bee-ge-shig, Eh-mee-we-qua-nobe. Photograph courtesy of the Beltrami County Historical Society.

(Round Earth), the chief of a band that was removed from Mille Lacs to White Earth about 1905, stated: "If all the wrongs that have been done by the white people on this reservation were ascertained there is no scale that is large enough to weigh the losses we have sustained."[15]

Euro-Americans gained further access to land on White Earth reservation with the passage of the Clapp Rider in 1906. While general allotment acts required land to be held in trust for twenty-five years before it could be sold, the new legislation permitted sale of allotted lands by "mixed bloods," while "full bloods" could sell if they were adjudged competent to handle their own affairs.[16] Euro-Americans seeking to buy tribal land "easily procured witnesses who would subscribe to affidavits that the Indian in question had white blood in his veins" and was therefore eligible to sell.[17] Three years after enactment of the Clapp Rider, 90 percent of land allotments that had been in the hands of "full bloods" was sold or mortgaged, and 80 percent of reservation land was privately owned.[18]

Even the land that remained within reservations was vulnerable to exploitation. The Anishinabe historian William W. Warren wrote about the untouched land: "the deep and interminable forests, abounding in beautiful lakes and murmuring streams, whose banks are edged with trees of sweet maple, the useful birch, the tall pine, fir, balsam, cedar, spruce."[19] The forests were a source of maple sugar and other foods as well as materials for homes, canoes, baskets, utensils, snowshoes, and other essentials. At Mille Lacs, the pine trees were said to be so thick in 1868 that "one could walk for miles without seeing direct sunlight."[20] A Euro-American resident, J. W. Nunn, who around 1890 lived near Pine Point, one of the communities on the White Earth reservation, recalled not only the "great pine belts" in every direction, but the subsequent "gigantic slaughter" of the forests by logging operations that turned the land bare. By 1902 the Nichols-Chisholm Lumber Company obtained, through legislation, nearly all of the reservation timber north of Pine Point, comprising, ac-

The dam at Lake Pokegama, 1908. Photograph courtesy of the Minnesota Historical Society.

cording to Nunn, "some of the finest pine forests of northern Minnesota, so much so that it kept this huge outfit in constant operation winter and summer for about fifteen years."[21]

Damming and diversion of water also was destructive, affecting homes, gardens, burial grounds, and resources such as fish and wild rice. Dams and reservoirs constructed at the lakes comprising the headwaters of the Mississippi River as part of a federal project in the 1880s and after the turn of the century flooded thousands of acres of tribal land in the vicinity of Lake Pokegema, Lake Winnibigoshish, and Leech Lake. Not only did people lose sources of subsistence, including ricing areas, but they also received no compensation for the losses.[22] Grievances against the federal government, including anger over the dams and reservoirs, precipitated an uprising at Sugar Point in 1898, the so-called Last Indian War.

THE INDIAN QUESTION

In Minnesota, as in the nation as a whole, the so-called Indian question came in the latter half of the nineteenth century to dominate Euro-American moral discourse in both private and public spheres. In the years after the Civil War, it displaced abolition of slavery as the central and unresolved issue of conscience for whites. Weekly magazines, such as *Harper's* and *Scribner's*, printed serious discussions of the issue, and books by the score advocated solutions;[23] speakers on the Chautauqua circuit debated the merits of various approaches, and religious leaders, especially those of Protestant denominations, cast it in moral terms in sermons and tracts.

Bolstered by a sense of moral right that today seems almost unimaginable, public opinion and government policy veered erratically from a relatively benevolent assimilationist view to fear-driven genocide. Government officials struggled to construct policies that reflected a collective national sentiment at any given time. And while the polarities evident in the World's Columbian Exposition Indian displays correctly suggest a range in public attitudes, they also document a shift in opinion about the Indian question that was taking place around the turn of the century.

In the 1880s, assimilation was the dominant strategy. Its advocates began with a social Darwinist premise that Native Americans were a "savage" race, representing an early stage

*hildren's band at Drexel Indian School, White Earth, Minne-
ta, about 1910. Photograph from the Archives of St. John's Ab-
y courtesy of the Minnesota Historical Society.*

of human evolution. Nonetheless, they reasoned, through education Indians could be advanced quickly through subsequent stages of development ("barbarism") to participate fully in Euro-American civilization. In this view, eradication of game herds such as buffalo was a means of moving Indians from a roaming to a settled existence. Division of the remaining reservation land into allotments owned privately by Indian families would make Indians independent and lessen the need for government annuity payments.[24]

Government and missionary efforts to eradicate culture and language utilized schooling as a tool. Church and state worked hand in glove to "civilize" students in schools such as St. Benedict's at White Earth, St. Mary's at Red Lake,[25] the Morris Indian School, and Pipestone Indian School. Boarding schools in Minnesota or in even more remote locations such as Carlisle, Pennsylvania or Lawrence, Kansas removed Minnesota Indian children from the influence of their families. Besides instruction in English, the schools aimed at training students to adopt Euro-American methods of farming and other occupations in a systematic attempt to change traditional subsistence patterns. The collective effect of these methods, it was assumed, would be to integrate Native Americans quickly into the fabric of Euro-American life.

One of the foremost advocates of this view was Bishop Henry Whipple of the Episcopal diocese of Minnesota. As early as the 1860s Whipple had made Indian rights his cause, serving on government commissions, taking part in treaty negotiations, and traveling widely to speak against injustices, visit Indian reservations, and raise money for support of mission work. Indian people, particularly in Minnesota, largely viewed Whipple as a trustworthy friend,

but it must be noted that self-determination for Indians was not a part of his agenda. Indians in Minnesota, he wrote, "are American Pagans whose degradation and helplessness must appeal to every Christian heart. . . . The only hope for the Indians is in civilization and Christianization."[26] Thus in treaty negotiations he actively intervened on behalf of the government, pressing Lakota people in North and South Dakota as well as Minnesota Anishinabe to accept ever-smaller parcels of reservation land.

Many assimilationists were as sympathetic and well intentioned as Whipple was. Unlike commentators with a harsher view of the problem, their condescension, their notion of Indians as childlike, was tempered by an expectation that education would "advance" Indians. In their naive evolutionism, however, they did not realize how tenaciously many Indian people would retain their cultural traditions, or why. The Native American response to social reformers showed clearly that superficial changes of clothing, hairstyle, even language or profession might leave untouched, perhaps even protectively guarded, a world view and a set of philosophical and ethical principles too fundamental to relinquish, even under considerable duress.

The strategy of assimilation produced some notable successes,[27] but it cannot be said that over time the lives of Indian peoples or the nature of the relation between whites and Indians improved. By the turn of the century, it was becoming apparent that the kind of radical change predicted by some assimilationists was not happening. What is more, the struggles over land were largely in the past, resolved in virtually every instance to the benefit of whites. Euro-American public sentiment and public policy began to redefine the Indian question as intractable and were turning discernibly away from active pursuit of assimilation to avoidance or marginalization of Native Americans and the problems they presented.

Some whites remained engaged in Indian issues, and although they began with the same Darwinist premise of social evolution as the assimilationist view, they parted company on the question of how quickly such change could take place. A small number of Indians might, over generations, be assimilated successfully, but the majority, in this view, were more or less explicitly declared doomed to extinction. The role of interested whites was to document and preserve as much as possible of Indian life and culture. Anthropology, relatively young as an academic discipline, both defined and took on the task, collecting data as avidly as artifacts. The Bureau of American Ethnology, established within the Smithsonian Institution, undertook massive research projects designed to document vanishing ways of life.[28] New natural history museums, such as the American Museum of Natural History, the Peabody Museum at Harvard University, and the Field Museum, included non-European cultures among their specimens. In Minnesota, for example, the ethnologist Frances Densmore began a career devoted not only to recording and annotating Anishinabe music, but also to documenting social and cultural life and collecting objects for display.

Frederick Putnam's seemingly anachronistic display at the World's Columbian Exposition thus in fact represented a more current response to the ethical and practical dilemmas of the Indian question than did Morgan's paean to progress. Although the various mechanisms intended to produce conformity (schools, churches, and government agencies) continued in place, the situation of Indians no longer seemed to weigh so heavily on the national conscience. A Euro-American position that justified both personal and governmental inaction had supplanted one of paternalistic intervention.

THE INDIAN QUESTION IN VISUAL EXPRESSION

Given the presence of the "Indian question" in the late nineteenth century Euro-American discourse, it is no surprise to find those concerns expressed in material and visual forms as well. White objects made with the Indian question in mind can be sorted readily into two groups: those made for white consumption and those made for consumption by Native Americans. While the former can be seen as an insiders' dialogue about the Other, those made for an Indian audience represent an attempt, however partial, to speak to different interests and tastes.

Visual representations of Indian issues by and for whites took a number of forms. The most prominent of these, perhaps, were large-scale public sculpture and mural projects that incorporated romanticized images of Indians in poses of nobility, hostility, or defeat. Smaller works, such as paintings or sculpture on a domestic scale, largely hewed to the same themes. Despite the ascendancy of assimilationism in the 1880s, most of these representations of Indians, which were intended for white consumption, still tended toward the ethnographic, preservationist, or sentimentalizing mode. For the Minnesota building at the World's Columbian exposition, Carl Nykvist created a colossal plaster sculpture based on Henry Wadsworth Longfellow's poem "Hiawatha," showing Hiawatha "bearing Minnehaha in his arms, from the ravages of famine; he is dressed in the most approved Indian style, with the eagle's feather in his hair, and the fringed moccasins indicative of rank."[29] The implicit themes of nobility and tragedy were carried out in a less subtle fashion in images such as the Minnesotan James Earl Fraser's well-known large bronze entitled "End of the Trail," showing an Indian man on horseback, his head bowed and his body slumping, which the artist unsparingly described as representing "a weaker race . . . steadily pushed to the wall."[30]

Another aspect of this nostalgic ethnography among whites, this expectation of extinction, can be found in the interest that the progressive and avant-garde art world showed toward native arts. Reacting against industrialization and machine production of goods, the Arts and Crafts movement of the late nineteenth century placed high value on the work of the individual artisan and on simplicity and refinement of design. Seeking artistic traditions in which these principles of design integrity could be found, its proponents in England turned to Japanese and Islamic models, and their American counterparts, including regional designers such as John Bradstreet of Minneapolis, followed suit. Their craving for exoticism could be satisfied closer to home, however, and it was not long before articles appeared in *The Craftsman*, a leading American Arts and Crafts journal, and other publications on Indian arts and issues. Some reviewed the familiar Indian question from a social perspective. A *Craftsman* article entitled "The North American Indian as a Laborer" contended that the skills used in making traditional goods can simply be transferred to new kinds of objects, such as "a carved bracket or an ornamental door frame," thus allowing Indian people the gratification of profitable labor.[31] Other *Craftsman* articles described the techniques of traditional Native American arts such as basketry, praising the skilled craftsmanship and simple ornamentation in harmony with their form and purpose. Still others, in the classic manner of the appropriation of the exotic, offered hints on adapting Native American design to contemporary purposes, including the decoration of middle-class homes. Of these, an adaptation of Hopi kiva mural designs for infant nurseries is only slightly more surprising and incongruous than the rest: "These designs, which may be executed at little cost, if hung upon our nursery-walls, might show the Indian to our children in a new and better light: no longer as the scalper of men and the murderer of children, but as a being of simple life, possessing crafts, arts, a system of morals and a religious faith not to be despised."[32]

The interest among whites in certain kinds of Native American objects or motifs manifested itself in white-made goods as well. Geometrically patterned woolen blankets, especially those made by the Pendleton Company in Oregon, are perhaps the best example of these Indian-influenced pieces. Inspired by the fashion for Navajo textiles, blankets from Pendleton and other mills began to appear on the market around the turn of the century and were bought not only by whites but also by Indian people, for whom they remain to this day a classic item of ceremonial presentation. Like other goods manufactured for trade across national or ethnic boundaries, they became a kind of specialized commodity directed to a particular audience. In this instance what began as a type of object representing an insiders' dialogue about outsiders came to be consumed by the same outsiders from whom its superficial characteristics were borrowed.[33]

Pendletons are a particularly clear example of the Euro-American goods manufactured with the interest of an Indian audience in mind, and their introduction of the market coincides with a particular moment in white consciousness of Indians. White consciousness of Indian people and Indian issues ebbed and flowed, and its nature changed over time; those changes found expression, as we have suggested above, in a few kinds of objects made by whites. Even taken together, however, the range of goods,

Lace makers at the Redwood Mission, Morton, Minnesota in 1897. Photograph by E. A. Bromley courtesy of the Minnesota Historical Society.

from Pendletons to paintings, that represent awareness of Indian peoples make up only a minuscule portion of the totality of white material culture produced around the turn of the century. Although the Indian question was for many whites a paramount issue of conscience, it was not an issue that confronted them in daily existence. Their interest or sympathy could be represented, even encapsulated, in their ownership and display of certain kinds of objects, but with few exceptions did not extend beyond this.

THE WHITE QUESTION

The situation for Indian people confronting what might be termed the "white question" was considerably different. From the earliest days of contact, Indian people faced the problem of how to accommodate Europeans into an existing world view. In particular, they sought to resolve what their response should be to technology that was perceived

to be superior. In the nineteenth century, as in the seventeenth, the answers were not easy. Over several centuries, a spectrum of Indian views persisted, extending from straightforward resistance through a host of complex intermediate positions to outward assimilation.

In Minnesota in the last decades of the nineteenth century, no Native American was untouched by the rapidly expanding white population. Even in the most remote areas of the northern reservations, missions, schools, and government institutions were an active presence, and some forms of manufactured Euro-American goods were certainly in use in every household. At the same time, however, the persistence of a wide range of attitudes toward Euro-American culture among Minnesota Indian people is clear.

Age and education were not the sole predictors of an assimilationist position, however. On the Lower Sioux Reservation at Birch Coulee, older and younger Dakota women alike earned money by making lace items that were for the most part indistinguishable from the products of

Front page of White Earth Reservation newspaper The Toma-hawk, *9 April 1903. Photograph courtesy of the Minnesota Historical Society.*

European convents. Nor was proximity to white settlements a constant factor; turn-of-the-century missionary accounts often bewail the church's inability to control and thoroughly convert even those Indians employed in missions and schools.[34]

More significant, of course, was an individual's history and present situation in relation to the outside world. Indian people did not arrive at their various positions vis-à-vis whites passively; those who adopted aspects of white life were not simply molded by the will of Euro-Americans. Rather, they made a series of strategic choices, trying to ensure a good outcome for themselves and for their families. Their information was necessarily limited; their views influenced by numerous individual factors. It was easier for families to continue a tribal way of life if their land could still sustain them, if they themselves had been raised in a traditional way, if they had strong reasons to avoid white

presence, if they were remote from centers of white influence.

At a more fundamental level, however, Indian peoples' response to the White Question was often grounded in a philosophical structure and world view that went far deeper than the specifics of the immediate situation. Assumptions about the nature of the universe, of human responsibilities for the natural world, and about appropriate human interactions guided directions and decisions in people's lives. For some assimilated Christians, these principles were those they had learned in churches and schools, and their profound commitment to a new faith was evident. For a far larger number of Indian people, however, the principles were traditional ones, a set of moral codes and precepts that mixed uneasily with Euro-American belief and practices.

Negotiating a course between tradition and "progress" required an endless series of decisions. From the most mundane to the most abstract, every choice was freighted in some measure by the White Question. Some people sought to resolve such issues in a consciously traditional way, through dreams or spirit messages. In her autobiography, Ignatia Broker describes a medicine woman using dreams to find the right path for her people.[35] On White Earth Reservation, Densmore recorded two instances of people who dreamt of flying, seeing telegraph poles, and living in square houses, although at that time they had in their waking lives seen neither.[36]

Resistance, too, took complex forms. While some Indian people simply avoided contact with whites and others used force when they judged it necessary, even up to the end of the century, still others put to use the very tools of white "civilization." In 1886, Augustus H. Beaulieu and a group of other young men at White Earth Reservation founded a newspaper, *The Progress.* Before the first issue could be circulated, however, the federal agent, T. J. Sheehan, ordered the press confiscated and the editor and publisher expelled from the reservation on the grounds that they had failed to obtain authority or license for their actions from government officials.

The Progress became operational again after a federal district court ruled that its suppression was groundless, but the attempt to stifle the paper makes clear how powerful the government feared such "incendiary rot" might be. Later renamed *The Tomahawk,* the paper continued to publish commentary on government policies, land schemes, and other reservation matters. "Believing that 'the pen is mightier than the sword,'" the editors wrote, "we start out on the war-path with a paper tomahawk."[37]

THE WHITE QUESTION IN VISUAL EXPRESSION

It is not surprising that such struggles—personal, political, and economic—should find reflection in the kinds of objects Anishinabe and Dakota people in Minnesota made around the turn of the century. Seen in overview, perhaps

...ishinabe. Makuk, early twentieth century. Science Museum of ...nnesota, St. Paul A83:7:2. Photograph by Gary Mortensen ...d Robert Fogt.

demonstrate virtuosity. In some instances a functional equivalent in manufactured goods existed, and yet the older versions continued to be made and used, perhaps for economic reasons, perhaps by preference.

Anishinabe women also made bark bitings, small pieces of thin inner birch bark folded and incised with the teeth to produce symmetrical patterns. Although the medium does not require elaborate materials or technology, the result is often strikingly complex and beautiful (cat. no. 1). In early times these seem to have been made purely for amusement and pleasure, but by the turn of the century women used them to generate patterns to be worked in beads.[38]

Even past the turn of the century Indians in Minnesota, usually men, continued to make objects for traditional religious practice. Anishinabe men made bark scrolls and other paraphernalia for Midewiwin ceremonies, although these were carried out in increasing secrecy, hidden from outside religious and government authorities. Among Dakota men, the production of catlinite pipes for religious use continued. Because pipestone carving developed into a minor industry, however, as is discussed below, traditional-use pipes could be made more openly.

Clothing, although filling a broad range between traditional and assimilationist expression, also was largely made for internal use. By the reservation period, without access to game animals for hides, Indian people in Minnesota and elsewhere had largely adopted Euro-American dress for daily use, wearing ready-made garments or sewing new ones from cloth included in government annuity payments. Yet a few women still tanned hides, and older styles of shirts or dresses were made from time to time and worn on special occasions. The Dakota dress (cat. no. 5), for example, is said to have been worn to two inaugural balls in Washington, D.C. And many people, both Dakota and Anishinabe, continued to make and wear moccasins (cat. nos. 6, 7), even when the remainder of their dress was conventional Euro-American.[39] The fact that elaborate, laboriously worked moccasins were made for children suggests that they were seen as an important aspect of cultural identity to be passed to succeeding generations.

Although much decorated clothing is often categorized as traditional, in fact the materials, cut, and the medium and style of ornamentation all derive ultimately from European sources. Heavily beaded velvet or stroud "ceremonial" garments and accoutrements, such as the hat belonging to Good Thunder (cat. no. 10) represent a rapid, even dramatic transmuting of ideas and forms culled from a variety of sources and recombined to produce a highly distinctive style of dress.[40] One might classify these pieces, in contradistinction to the traditional works discussed above, as "neo-traditional" objects, made by Native American hands for Native American use, but showing, at least in their initial phase, an interest in innovation and synthesis.

Like the more strictly traditional objects, these, too, were largely made by women, using materials obtained through trade: manufactured cloth, glass beads, sequins, silk rib-

the most striking characteristic of Native American goods at that time was their diversity, their expression of a range of views from traditionalism to assimilation, and the distinctions that were apparent between things made for internal use and those made to sell or give to outsiders.

A number of object types can readily be classified as "traditional," that is, things made for use within Indian society, often having practical or functional purpose, in forms wholly or largely unchanged by Euro-American contact. Many of these were containers of various kinds: bark containers, or makuks (cat. no. 3) for maple sap collection, for storing grains, dried foods, or fats; or trays for winnowing wild rice, for example. Large striped or plaid mats of rushes or cedar strips (cat. no. 4) were still made for use in the home, to sit on, to block drafts, or to decorate interior walls. Many households, both Dakota and Anishinabe, continued to use twined fiber bags (cat. no. 2) for storing clothing and personal effects.

These domestic forms were primarily made by women, and all required considerable skill and experience. Each type allowed for some kind of ornamentation or decoration, and twined bags, in particular, offered an opportunity to

Anishinabe woman weaving bull rush mat, about 1910. Photograph courtesy of the Minnesota Historical Society.

Great Lakes. Bag, about 1900–1920. Cass County Museum, Walker. Photograph courtesy of the Minnesota Historical Society.

Sisseton Dakota. Child's moccasins, *before 1900. The Minneapolis Institute of Arts; The Ethel Morrison Van Derlip Fund 91.95.2 a,b.*

Dakota. Hat, about 1890. Shattuck-St. Mary's School, Faribault on loan to the Science Museum of Minnesota A79.4.119. Photograph by Gary Mortensen and Robert Fogt.

bons, and machine-made trims. Shirts and leggings were more tailored than earlier garments; vests represented a wholly new form. Some garments were sewn by Indian women, others were received as annuity goods or charitable gifts, then decorated. Even non-Euro-American garments such as breechcloths and split skirts (cat. nos. 8, 9) showed the kind of finishing characteristic of the European tradition.

The most distinctive quality of all such garments, however, is the exuberant, brightly colored floral beadwork, often applied to the entire surface. It is generally assumed that the patterns originated in European printed textile design, but in the hands of Woodlands women they quickly evolved in distinctive directions, emphasizing twining vines and fantastic, multicolored flowers. Beaders used bitten bark to inspire geometric patterns and templates of birch bark to trace leaves and flowers.

The most extraordinary of these beaded Woodland forms is certainly the bandolier bag. Evolved over time from a type of European military shoulder bag, bandoliers grew larger and more elaborately beaded until, by the end of the century, they covered large areas of the wearer's torso. Some used panels of loomed beadwork for the body of the bag (cat. no. 16); others featured spot-stitched floral beadwork on wool or velvet (cat. nos. 15, 17). In either case the bags were flamboyant but virtually nonfunctional; some even have a blind "opening" with no pouch inside. Instead, their very purpose lay in their appearance: even more than other items of dress clothing, bandolier bags represented the prestige of the wearer, the ties of blood or friendship between wearer and maker, and a testimony to the maker's skill. It is interesting to note that bandolier bags were often presented to white dignitaries, as were the three in this exhibition; as gifts to government or church officials, they may have been intended not simply to convey the prestige of the wearer, but also to cement a personal relation and to evoke support.

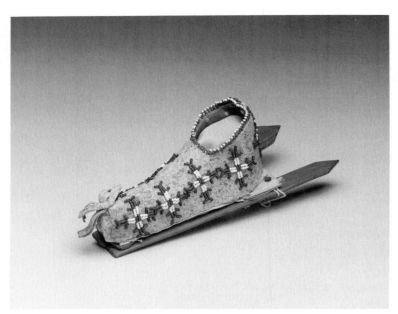

Mrs. Ke-sha-pa-ka-ba-wik, Anishinabe. Cradle board, *about 1900. The Hennepin History Museum, Minneapolis 421/1. Photograph by Gary Mortensen and Robert Fogt.*

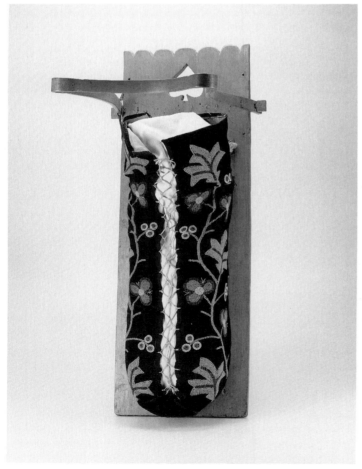

Dakota(?). Model cradleboard. *Rice County Historical Society, Faribault. Photograph by Gary Mortensen and Robert Fogt.*

The development of these new forms of highly decorated clothing was probably stimulated by the growth of new kinds of social and ceremonial events. Although opportunities for wearing dress clothing certainly existed in past times, in the early reservation period powwows and other social dances expanded in scope and size. New events, such as church holidays, the Fourth of July, and school and mission ceremonies were added to the calendar; it is worth noting that these holidays, like the clothing that celebrated them, were transmuted in Native American practice from their source. Reservation Fourth of July festivities emphasized different aspects of American patriotism than might have been found in a small Euro-American town celebration, and the ceremonial activities differed as well.

Finally, as interest in Indians became fashionable among whites, Anishinabe and other peoples elsewhere in the country found that they could dress in their finest clothing and make themselves available for photographers, either professional or amateur, who wished to record "traditional" ways. Thus a large body of photographs exists in which Indian people, elaborately and improbably overdressed, go about cooking, building wigwams, boiling maple sap, or other mundane and inherently messy activities.[41]

These items of clothing may have been made of introduced materials and decorated with European-derived patterns; they may have sometimes been worn on occasions that were new to the Anishinabe calendar. But their symbolic function was entirely traditional. Made by women for members of their families, their real value lay in the amount of skill and labor they demanded. Decorated garments were not only an opportunity to demonstrate virtuosity in needlework, but they were also a vehicle through which that virtuosity could represent sentiment. Beautiful, elaborate clothing was a tangible representation of emotional and familial bonds, just as earlier and more labor-intensive types of garments had represented a woman's domestic skills and devotion to her family.

No such ties of sentiment existed between maker and consumer, however, in the objects Minnesota Indians made to sell to whites. Instead these represent the best guess of the maker (or in some instances the best guess of a white intermediary) about what might appeal to a white consumer. The most familiar of these to outsiders are probably souvenir goods, which often took the form of miniaturized items of Anishinabe or Dakota material culture: tipis, wigwams, canoes (cat. no. 34), cradle boards (cat. no. 36), or dressed dolls. The production of miniatures as souvenirs for a European or Euro-American audience has a long history in the Americas. Through the eighteenth century such models were just that: accurate reproductions in miniature, highly complete and detailed. By the late nineteenth century, however, they had become far more generalized, more simplified, less "authentic." Model canoes, for example, were no longer caulked with pine pitch or equipped with paddles and passengers.[42] What may have begun as images of distinctive aspects of Native American culture evolved into shorthand versions emphasizing the

Anishinabe women making small birch bark canoes, Mille Lacs Reservation, about 1913. Photograph courtesy of the Minnesota Historical Society.

Old Bets, Santee Dakota. Moccasins, *about 1888. Monroe P. Killy Collection. Photograph by Gary Mortensen and Robert Fogt.*

gross characteristics recognizable as "Indian" to whites and eliminating finer points of detail or workmanship by which an Indian audience would judge the quality of a piece. Souvenir miniatures were in fact an Indian reflection of white stereotypes about Native Americans.[43]

From the viewpoint of whites acquiring them, miniature souvenirs may well have implied an objectification or trivialization of Indian people. Not only did such pieces fulfill stereotypes about "primitive" native technology (the more so because of their simplified forms), but they also resonated to the romantic view of Indians frozen in the past, living apart from the modern world. In the hands of their Euro-American buyers, moreover, such pieces could be examined, arranged, and displayed in a privileging power relation echoing that of colonial authority. Ownership and control of small versions of people and objects symbolically represents ownership and control on a larger scale.

From a Native American perspective, such concession to stereotyping surely produced some discomfort. Perhaps as well Indian people were conscious that the objects they made in miniature were increasingly anachronistic. Model wigwams were being made at a time when fewer and fewer full-scale wigwams were produced. Indian people were reduced, almost literally, to making nonfunctional versions of their cultural heritage. Yet it is important to remember, again, that such choices were made strategically—that the production of souvenir items was one means of access to the outside economy, one that did not require outside education or residence. Souvenir makers may also have carried an element of condescension or even contempt for their unknown buyers, who understood as "Indian" a model canoe improbably decorated with strands of wool yarn (cat. no. 34), or who could not distinguish between a correctly dressed doll and one wearing a pastiche of clothing styles.

A few types of Minnesota Indian objects were made full size for sale to whites, most notably moccasins. As with the miniaturized souvenirs, however, such items often were made quickly, their "Indianness" identified with minimal strokes. It is instructive to compare the Dakota moccasins made and sold by "Old Bets" at the St. Paul ice palace (cat. no. 40) to the moccasins made for a Dakota child by her mother (cat. no. 6). Care in workmanship and complexity of design are evident in the child's pair, as is the quality of the tanned hide, while Old Bets, sewing for the undiscriminating eye of an anonymous prospective buyer, could produce moccasins that were more sparsely decorated and less meticulously made.

Other items made for outsiders gained their interest from the transformation of Euroamerican object types through the use of indigenous materials or designs. Such pieces, which ranged from cigar cases to liturgical paraphernalia, were often intended as souvenirs as well, but because many were functional domestic objects, such as napkin rings or

Dakota. Wall pocket, *about 1880. Shattuck-St. Mary's School, Faribault on loan to the Science Museum of Minnesota A79.4.122. Photograph by Gary Mortensen and Robert Fogt.*

Anishinabe(?) Pincushion, *late nineteenth century. Sibley Historic Site, Mendota, 81.36 (1968). Photograph by Gary Mortensen and Robert Fogt.*

William Jones, a Dakota minister, working catlinite at Pipestone, Minnesota on 9 August 1902. Minnesota Historical Society. Photograph by Dr. H. M. Whelpley.

pin cushions, they were more likely to be put to actual use in white households. These items, like other souvenirs, were made for an audience identified broadly as white. A notable example in this exhibition is a beaded Anishinabe wall pocket from the collection of Bishop Whipple which shows considerable wear and may have been used to hold boxes of matches (cat. no. 19).

The materials or decoration of such items, particularly the telltale use of glass beads, signaled their Indian origin just enough, perhaps, to provoke notice or comment. Their presence in a Euro-American domestic interior, one might imagine, would provide the touch of exoticism fashionable at the turn of the century. Some, like the heart-shaped pincushion (cat. no. 21) bear a surprisingly close resemblance to examples in European or American books of patterns for women's fancy-work.[44]

The use of catlinite, or pipestone, in manufacturing items for sale constitutes a special case.[45] A soft, finely grained red sandstone, catlinite is quarried in only a few locations in North America. The largest outcropping is located in southwestern Minnesota near the town of Pipestone. In past centuries Indians from the midwest and further afield had used it to make pipe bowls for ceremonial

purposes, and the stone was associated with sacred stories about the origin of the world. By the late nineteenth century, however, it was being carved into many other forms, often using drills, lathes, and other machinery.[46] From candlesticks and inkwells to crosses, almost all pipestone pieces were intended for souvenirs. In addition to pipe bowls for traditional religious use, souvenir pipes also were made, and because of the simplicity of older forms the two are sometimes difficult to distinguish.

Unlike most other souvenir media, catlinite was worked largely by men, in keeping with the historical Plains and Woodlands tradition of restricting sculpture to males. Students at the Pipestone Indian School made small-scale stone objects to sell for pocket money.[47] To add further complexity to the subject, a number of catlinite carvers around the town of Pipestone at the turn of the century were whites who had found they could earn a living producing such items for sale.[48] A particularly unusual form, which replicates Dutch wooden shoes as paperweights, inkwells, or charms, may derive from these white carvers, perhaps from the nearby town of Holland, the site of Dutch immigrant settlement.

The entry of students and whites into catlinite produc-

Anishinabe or Dakota. Lace making pillow with partial lace,
bobbins and patterns, about 1900. Sibley Historic Site, Mendota
81.232 (1971). Photograph by Gary Mortensen and Robert Fogt.

tion suggests that the profits were large enough to be attractive.[49] By the turn of the century the stone itself was
apparently a source of regional pride for Euro-Americans:
a mantelpiece in the Minnesota building of the Chicago
World's Columbian Exposition was made of catlinite,[50] and
a working model engine in catlinite was displayed there as
well, "a great curiosity."[51] It is hard to know, however,
whether whites were conscious of the ironic or triumphal
overtones in the use of a stone usually associated with Indian ceremonial materials in Euro-American forms, particularly the futuristic image of the engine.

In light of the strong religious associations of catlinite,
use of the stone for trinkets presents an especially sharp
picture of the social and moral dilemmas confronting Indians at the turn of the century. Facing a powerful government backed by military force, heavily proselytized by

Euro-American churches which worked systematically to
undermine traditional religious belief and practice, and
having even fewer available means to enter a cash economy
than women did, Dakota men who worked pipestone chose
a livelihood that seemed least harmful to individual and
collective interests. And while that practice seems painful
from a contemporary perspective, especially that of many
Native American traditionalists, it is clear that attitudes
about catlinite have changed over time, and that a range
of views persists even today.

The most "acculturated" objects made for sale to whites
were, not surprisingly, those which women learned to make
at mission or boarding schools or through other craft training from whites. Lace is perhaps the most dramatic example of these object types. In 1890 Episcopal deaconess Sibyl
Carter, with the encouragement of Bishop Whipple, began

teaching lace making to Anishinabe women at White Earth. Carter's work was inspired by European movements of the time that combined social reform projects with revival of traditional crafts, and her writings, like those of Arts and Crafts reformers, are filled with comments about the dignity of labor and the pride of wage earning, particularly for women.[52] She quickly found that women's considerable skill at needlework transferred readily to lace making, including complex techniques of needlepoint and pillow lace, and that Indian-made lace could compete with European work. Through the Episcopal church lace-making

teachers were sent to other Anishinabe bands, as well as to the Dakota in Minnesota and other tribal groups in the United States.

By 1904 the self-help project had developed into the Sibyl Carter Indian Lace Association, organized by Carter's friends, with headquarters in New York City. The association paid the expenses of teachers on the reservations, who mailed their students' work to be marketed at a Park Avenue shop and at private sales in the homes of wealthy Eastern benefactors, including Mrs. Cornelius Vanderbilt. Indian-made lace, including table linens, other domestic items,

Anishinabe or Dakota. Handkerchief, *about 1900. Sibley Historic Site, Mendota 81.142 (1960). Photograph by Gary Mortensen and Robert Fogt.*

lace clothing, and lace edging by the yard (cat. nos. 28–32), was awarded prizes at various world's fairs and expositions and was widely praised for its high quality, indistinguishable from that of its European antecedents.[53]

In principle, according to the association literature, the lace makers were paid the retail price that would be asked for each piece. In fact, however, there was considerable variance, year to year, between the amount paid out to workers and the total sales of lace, which often considerably exceeded the expenditures. There also was great disparity between the amounts paid to workers and the total expenses of the project. In 1905, for example, sixteen lace makers at Birch Coulee, on the Lower Sioux Reservation, received a total of $442.90, or $27.63 each. Their two resident lace teachers, however, received salaries of $300 plus expenses, while the association's two office workers in New York were each paid $600.[54] Despite such a top-heavy budget, the association made no attempts to transfer the operations to Indian women themselves; probably the condescending tone evident in their writings and pamphlets echoed an assumption of incompetence on the part of their "sisters." Between financial mismanagement, the interruption of the First World War, and changes in fashion, the project began to fade by the mid-teens.

Reservation lace makers produced thousands of items before the organization ceased to function in 1926.[55] Yet because most of it is indistinguishable, it goes unrecognized. Even at the time, however, it was apparently felt that some means of identifying the origin of Indian lace might appeal to consumers, and on some items small "Indian" motifs, including a tipi, men in a canoe, a woman wearing a cradleboard, and men hunting, have been introduced into the pattern (cat. nos. 28, 29). One lace teacher commented that her students sometimes designed their own patterns, borrowing ideas "from carpets, church windows, from leaves and flowers. Many times they take geometrical patterns from their beadwork."[56] It seems likely, however, that the stereotyped native images were designed by the white lace teachers and disseminated as patterns through the association: a white intermediary reintroducing Indian content into a product so acculturated as to conceal its origin.

If the audience wanted to retain some hint of the makers, however, the makers also wanted a glimpse of the audience. Because much of the lace was piecework, made into finished goods by New York seamstresses, its ultimate use puzzled the lacemakers; dress collars seem to have been the only lace item they used themselves. The Sibyl Carter Association annual report for 1913 notes an episode on the Oneida reservation in Wisconsin:

For several years our Oneida teacher, Mrs. [Josephine Hill] Webster, has been telling us of the almost daily questions put to her by one and another of the Oneida workers regarding the ultimate purpose of their work. "What do the New York people do with this and that?" "How do they put these pieces together?" . . . The questions were not only perfectly legitimate ones, showing a pardonable curiosity, but evidenced such a real interest in the work itself that the committee felt it was due the faithful Oneidas to give them the benefit of seeing their excellent work made into useful and salable articles.[57]

The teacher organized a picnic and converted her home into an exhibition of white middle-class domestic life, setting the dining table with lace-trimmed linens and laying out doilies, antimacassars, lace-covered cushions and lampshades in profusion. She reported that the workers brought their family members, and all the guests were awed, gratified, and proud to see their work displayed in its final form.

Lace making was thus perhaps an extreme example of production of goods for consumption by an external audience. Not only were the women making objects for recipients they didn't know, they also were making objects they didn't recognize. Lacking a sense of what the finished goods looked like as well as familiarity with the ornate, largely nonfunctional display in white domestic interiors, the women were thoroughly alienated from the products of their own labor. Although the story of the Oneida workers is presented with a straightforwardly happy ending, it is hard to imagine that the women and their families did not also shake their heads a bit at the display.

What was true for reservation families, however, was not necessarily true for their outside-educated children. The first group of white missionary lace teachers was at times supplanted by Indian women trained in boarding schools, who were not only expert lace makers but also thoroughly schooled in domestic arts.[58] Students who passed through such training had little difficulty recognizing or even aspiring to the trappings of white domestic life.

Elizabeth Cornelius, an Oneida woman who graduated from the Hampton Normal and Agricultural Institute in Virginia and received a teaching diploma from Hampton as well, taught lace making in Canada before marrying James Rock, an Anishinabe man from the White Earth Reservation and settling with him in Minnesota. In 1910 she was appointed pillow lace teacher at the Pine Point School on the White Earth Reservation. Five years later she wrote to a faculty member at Hampton, "I gave up my lace making classes over a year ago. My workers were so irregular and as it was not possible to improve conditions we thought best to drop the work for a time."[59]

By the 1930s Mrs. Rock was living at Cass Lake, where she earned money selling vegetables to tourists during the summer and working to establish a market for handicrafts—"buckskin and beadwork, birch bark work, wood craft, and other things"—during the winter. She wrote: "Some of the work needs adapting to modern requirements." Active in a woman's club at Cass Lake called "The First Daughters of America," she commented, "Among the things which we have made are rush baskets, which are now very rare. We are also learning to weave bags and rugs."[60] Mrs. Rock's career gives a clear picture of the kind of mobility and change introduced into the lives of boarding school students. While many returned to their home reservations and struggled to readjust to a different life, others married into

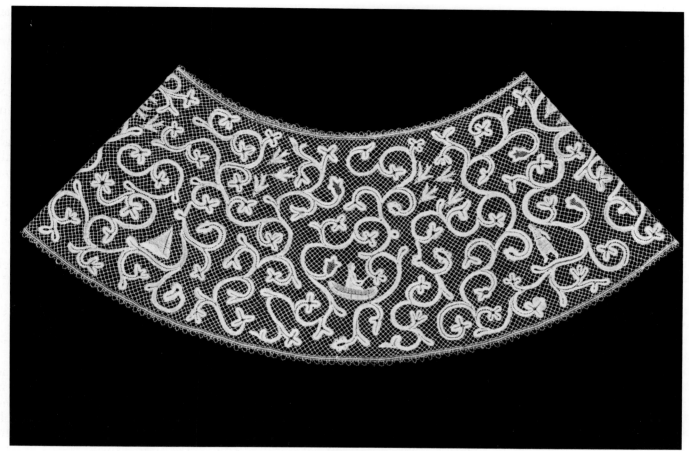

Dakota. Lampshade cover, *early twentieth century. Cooper Hewitt Museum of Design, Smithsonian Institution, New York 1943.44.2.*

other tribes, moved, or continued to live and work in the dominant culture.

* * * *

Taken as a whole, the objects Indian people of Minnesota produced around the turn of the century are striking in several ways. First, what survives in museums and private collections that can be traced to the time is largely the work of women: clothing, domestic items, souvenir goods, and market commodities such as lace. In part, it can be argued that this gender role derives from an earlier period in which women were also the producers of finished goods. In hunting cultures, for example, men and women worked together in complementary ways. It was men who obtained the raw material—game,—and women who dressed that game into usable parts (meat, skins for clothing or shelter, bones for utensils, and so on) and women who created the final products. Around 1900, women remained the primary producers of objects such as clothing intended for internal use and as salable commodities for the outside market. White-sponsored cottage industry projects such as lace making concentrated on women's work, often from a protofeminist perspective that connected women's self-reliance to domestic stability and general social improvement.

Similarly, missions and schools played a supporting role in the development of Anishinabe and Dakota floral beadwork, providing materials and training in needlework and an environment that valued women's domestic arts. In so doing, white teachers and missionaries also were providing models for women's social roles: by encouraging relatively passive work that took place indoors and required a high degree of manual skill and control, they hoped to delegitimate the kinds of active, heavy labor—cutting wood, erecting tipis and wigwams, making canoes—that had formed a part of women' lives in the past.[61]

In the decades of conflict Native American men, specifically warriors, were the target of white attempts to control, to "civilize," to eradicate. They commonly were assumed to be hostile and dangerous. Once forcibly confined to reservations, however, men could not carry out their daily pursuits; the very purpose of their lives was drastically undercut. White reformers in the reservation period transferred their focus of attention to women, often expressing directly the assumption that Indian society could best be reshaped by domesticating women and educating children.

Needlework, and particularly lace making, was understood literally as a means of domestication. Sibyl Carter remarked that she was proud of her students' work, "prouder still of the moral uplift and the material prosperity which the work has brought to my [Indian] sister."[62]

Although beadwork did not bring the same "material prosperity," it continued in production, especially among Anishinabe women. Such persistence argues strongly for a cultural importance that transcends monetary considerations, and in fact this seems to be borne out by patterns of use. Much of what was made was decorated clothing—goods for internal use, goods that were highly distinctive and set apart from the white world outside, worn to mark special occasions. The production of beaded clothing was viewed by whites as an acceptable (although not profitable) domestic activity for women. For Indian people, however, making and wearing such garments took on an entirely different meaning. In the context of Indian-white relations, bandolier bags, moccasins, and dance clothing were a means of subverting the dominant ideology, of discreetly asserting a connection to the past. They were representations of identity, of difference, of the presence of traditional ways in changing times.

Such multiple meanings suggest another characteristic of turn-of-the-century Indian arts in Minnesota: the way in which the objects, by their very range and diversity, represent a complex and evolving response to the issue of dealing with the outside world. Items like the silk rag rug or lace (which was so "white" that Indian motifs had to be introduced into the pattern) were, on the surface at least, the most assimilated, the most accommodating of white aesthetics and values. The resonances between lace patterns and beadwork patterns, or between silk rag rug and rush mat techniques, even if conscious, are covert.

Decorated clothing probably represents the most complex response to the outside world because it held different meanings for Native Americans and Euro-Americans. Deriving, in disparate parts, from Euro-American form and design, Anishinabe (and to a lesser extent Dakota) beaded dress clothing evolved quickly into highly distinctive styles that persist today. In making such garments women signaled both their wish to retain links to traditional culture and a very traditional wish to honor the recipient of the garment through the gift of skill, time, and labor. The wearing of such items, similarly, implied a measure of resistance to total assimilation.

Even objects least touched by white contact, such as traditional styles of housing, birch bark containers, or moccasins, had by the turn of the century taken on associations related to the White Question. Why did some women continue to make bark containers and twined fiber bags when manufactured substitutes were available at the trading post? Perhaps bark was preferable because it didn't require an outlay of cash; perhaps it was more satisfying to exercise a familiar skill. Perhaps, too, these seemed the "proper" containers for certain things, particularly those associated with traditional lifeways. For Anishinabe and Dakota people subsistence activities, even the most mundane, carried a spiritual dimension. Thus gathering maple sap and wild rice, picking berries, or fishing were all seasonal pursuits. Each had an important underlying religious meaning and was successful if relations between the human world and the spiritual were in harmony. To place the harvest that supported life itself and had been obtained with spiritual guidance in containers associated with the outside world would represent a breach in the cycle. To the extent that people were able to continue older subsistence activities, they also may have felt it necessary to continue to make the goods associated with those activities.

Along similar lines, one might wonder what it meant for an older woman to wear moccasins along with her Euro-American calico dress as she sat inside a frame house making European lace. Again, perhaps the reason was an economic one: it was cheaper to make moccasins than to buy manufactured shoes. Perhaps it was an issue of comfort; feet accustomed to soft moccasins would find Euro-American shoes hard and heavy. But soft-soled shoes also may have carried their own meaning. In Native American cosmology the earth is valued as the source and giver of life, often personified as mother to all living beings. As ordinary an activity as walking on the earth thus represents spiritual connectedness between humans and the natural world. Soft shoes impose a minimal barrier between individuals and the earth, and they do not mark or scar its surface. They permit contact and a harmonious interrelationship between the earth and her children.

Like the use of traditional containers, the wearing of moccasins thus may be associated with a core of religious and philosophical principles too deeply held to be eradicated by the proselytizing of missions and schools. Some Indian people may have remained unconscious of the connection between these small outward signs of traditional ways and their fundamental world view. For many, however, the relation between their understanding of the nature of the universe, their recognition of human responsibilities in that universe, and the material representations of their role was clear. White reformers recognized, on an instinctive level at least, the profound effect of this philosophical system and the way it continued to shape people's lives and thought. For this reason they established a boarding school system that removed children from the home as early as possible, to prevent the continuation of that system of belief.

In spite of overwhelming pressure for change, many of these philosophical systems and precepts have survived. Material culture is one means by which aspects of the past have been transmitted over time. Objects people make can be a way of retaining tradition, a vehicle for incorporating certain kinds of change. Particularly in times of great social stress, such as the Minnesota Indian people experienced around the turn of the century, the totality of things produced may reflect the complexity of their existence. Commodities made for the outside market, such as souvenirs or lace, constitute a clear sign of material need. Seemingly anachronistic goods such as moccasins or makuks, on the other hand, suggest the nature and power of ideas and beliefs kept private.

NOTES

1. Considering the demographics of the fair's audience, the term takes on an unpleasantly ironic tone. The few African-American visitors and workers were permitted to eat only in a restaurant in the Haitian pavilion, and when one of the Minnesota building officials hired a "Negro of good character" to help manage the exhibits, the other managers expressed their outrage in overtly racist terms (manuscript report of the Minnesota commissioners, 31 May 1893, World's Columbian Exposition papers, Minnesota Historical Society, St. Paul. Other people of color were represented only as part of the displays.

2. Zeynep Çelik and Leila Kinney, "Ethnography and Exhibitionism at the Exposition Universelles," *Assemblage* 13 (1991): 42.

3. In Minnesota, fair commissioners had difficulty finding Indians who were suitably "authentic" to send to Putnam's display. In a letter dated 29 March 1893, Commissioner George Lamphere reported to the president of the board as follows: "I visited the White Earth Reservation March 27th . . . making as thorough an investigation as possible . . . in relation to the practicability of making an exibit of the Chippewa Indians at Chicago. . . . There is no doubt at all that good specimens of the Chippewa Tribe of both men and women can be induced to go. . . . Most of the Indians on White Earth have had their hair shorn. Whether 'making up' by wearing wigs would be allowed, I am not informed, but if we are compelled to secure as many as ten bucks unshorn it will be necessary to send to Leech Lake ninety miles beyond." Minnesota State Archives, World's Columbian Exposition papers, Minnesota Historical Society, St. Paul.

4. Frederick E. Hoxie, A *Final Promise: The Campaign to Assimilate the Indians, 1880–1920* (Lincoln: University of Nebraska Press, 1984), 87–88.

5. *Annual Report, U.S. Commissioner of Indian Affairs*, 1893, 21.

6. Emma Sickles, *New York Times*, 8 October 1893.

7. Reid Badger, *The Great American Fair: The Columbian Exposition* (Chicago: Nelson Hall, 1979), 108.

8. One of the few references to specific events of Indian history displayed at the World's Fair was a model log cabin shown in the Minnesota pavilion; it was said to be made of the "wood of the log house in which the first blood was shed during the massacre of 1863 [sic]," Report from the various chairmen of the woman's auxiliary of Minnesota, 27 February 1893, Minnesota State Archives, World's Columbian Exposition papers, Minnesota Historical Society, St. Paul.

9. The standard account of the Dakota Conflict is found in William Folwell, *History of Minnesota* (St. Paul: Minnesota Historical Society, 1921–30). See also Kenneth Carley, *The Sioux Uprising of 1862* (St. Paul: Minnesota Historical Society Press, 1976), and Gary Anderson and Alan Woolworth, *Through Dakota Eyes: Narrative Accounts of the Minnesota Indian War of 1862* (St. Paul: Minnesota Historical Society Press, 1988).

10. Anticipating violence a month before the Wounded Knee Massacre, a St. Paul newspaper estimated the number of Lakota willing to fight at about 4,000, further noting that "but a tithe of that number were concerned in the Minnesota massacre, yet they killed more than 500 settlers in a very brief space of time." *St. Paul Pioneer Press*, 3 December 1890. See also Herbert Welsh, "The Meaning of the Dakota Outbreak," *Scribners Magazine* (April): esp. 440.

11. See, for example, Minnie Bruce Carrigan, "Captured by the Indians" (Buffalo Lake, Minn.: The Newsprint, 1912); Urania White, *Captivity among the Sioux* (St. Paul: Minnesota Historical Society, 1901); Oscar G. Wall, *Recollections of the Sioux Massacre* (Lake City, Minn.: The Home Printery, 1909); Mary Schwandt, *The Story of Mary Schwandt: Her Captivity during the Sioux "Outbreak"* (St. Paul: Minnesota Historical Society, 1894); Nancy Huggan, *The Story of Nancy Mc-*

Clure. *Captivity among the Sioux* (St. Paul: Minnesota Historical Society, 1894). For critical studies of the captivity genre, see Richard Van Der Beets, *The Indian Captivity Narrative* (Lanham, Md.: University Press of America, 1984); and June Namias, *White Captives: Gender and Ethnicity on the American Frontier* (Chapel Hill: University of North Carolina Press, 1993).

12. W. Roger Buffalohead and Priscilla Buffalohead, *Against the Tide of American History: The Story of the Mille Lacs Anishinabe* (Cass Lake, Minn.: Minnesota Chippewa Tribe, 1985).

13. Elisabeth Ebbott, for the League of Women Voters of Minnesota. *Indians in Minnesota*, 4th ed. (Minneapolis: University of Minnesota Press, 1985), 34.

14. *The Progress*, 25 March 1886.

15. Buffalohead, *Against the Tide*, 67.

16. Determination of heritage was arbitrary and often erroneous. In 1913 Ales Hrdlicka, a physical anthropologist at the National Museum, registered full-blood and mixed-blood residents of White Earth on the basis of physical characteristics, and although such "evidence" is no longer considered supportable, his register continues to have legal status. See Ebbott, *Indians in Minnesota*, 35.

17. Benno Watrin, *The Ponsfordian 1880–1930* (Park Rapids, Minn.: Press of The Park Rapids Enterprise, 1930), 34.

18. Ebbott, *Indians in Minnesota*, 34.

19. Warren, *History of the Ojibway Nation*, 39.

20. Buffalohead, *Against the Tide*, 61.

21. Nunn in Watrin, *Ponsfordian*, 18.

22. Jane Lamm Carroll, "Dams and Damages: The Ojibway, the United States, and the Mississippi Headwaters Reservoirs," *Minnesota History* 52, no. 1 (Spring 1990): 3–15.

23. See, for example. Lyman Abbott, "Our Indian Problem," *North American Review* 167, no. 505 (1898): 719–28; S. C. Armstrong, *The Indian Question* (Hampton, Va.: Hampton Normal School Steam Press, 1883); Thomas Bland, *The Indian Question* (Boston: F. Wood, 1880); Samuel Gilman, *The Future Indian: A Brief Treatise on the Indian Question* (Indianapolis: Carlon & Hottenbeck, 1891); Francis E. Leupp, *The Indian and His Problem* (New York: Scribner's Sons, 1910); G. W. Owen, *The Indian Question* (Ypsilanti, Mich.: n.p., 1881); James E. Rhoads, *The Indian Question in the Concrete* (Philadelphia: Women's National Indian Association, 1886).

24. Hoxie, *Final Promise*, 17–39.

25. Alban Fruth, A *Century of Missionary Work among the Red Lake Chippewa Indians 1858–1958* (Collegeville, Minn.: Order of St. Benedict, 1958), 27.

26. Henry Benjamin Whipple, *Light and Shadows of a Long Episcopate* (New York: Macmillan Co., 1902), 50–51. Through his advocacy of Indian causes, his mastery of Dakota and Anishinabe languages, and training of Indian men for the Episcopal clergy, Whipple earned of measure of trust exemplified in his Anishinabe name Kichimekadewiconaye, "Straight Tongue."

27. Prominent among these was Charles Eastman (1858–1939) a Minnesota Dakota who was a graduate of Dartmouth College and the first Native American to receive training as a physician. Eastman devoted much of his life to promoting Indian causes, particularly land rights and health issues, to white audiences, but by the 1920s he became despairing of his own assimilationist ideals; see Raymond Wilson, *Ohiyesa: Charles Eastman, Santee Sioux* (Urbana: University of Illinois Press, 1983) and Eastman's own autobiographical works.

28. George W. Stocking, "Philanthropoids and Vanishing Cultures" in *Objects and Others*, ed. George Stocking (Madison, Wis.: University of Wisconsin Press, 1985), 113.

29. James W. Shepp, *Shepp's World's Fair Photographed* (Chicago: Globe Bible Publ. Co., 1893), 398.

30. J. Walker McSpadden, *Famous Sculptors of America* (New York: Dodd, Mead, 1924), 281.

31. C. H. Forbes-Lindsay, "The North American Indian as a Laborer: His Value as a Worker and a Citizen," *The Craftsman* (May 1908): 146–57.

32. "Nursery Wall Coverings in Indian Designs," *The Craftsman* 5,

no. 1 (October 1903): 95–99.

33. George Wharton, *Indian Blankets and Their Makers* (New York: Dover Publications, 1919 [1974]), 162–63. See also Robert W. Kapoun with Charles J. Lohrmann, *Language of the Robe: American Indian Trade Blankets* (Salt Lake City: Gibbs Smith, 1992).

34. Fruth, *Missionary Work*, 27.

35. Ignatia Broker, *Night Flying Woman: An Ojibway Narrative* (St. Paul: Minnesota Historical Society Press, 1983), 69–70.

36. Frances Densmore, *Chippewa Customs* (Minneapolis: Ross & Haines, Inc., 1970 [1929]), 84–86.

37. *The Tomahawk*, 1, no. 1 (9 April 1903). The change in name reflects a move in editorial policy from assimilationism to greater advocacy of Indian rights.

38. Densmore, *Chippewa Customs*, 184.

39. At Hampton Institute in Virginia, Indian students not only preferred to wear moccasins to heavy shoes themselves, but they also converted African American students and the faculty to moccasin wearing, particularly in the summer months. Cora Mae Folsom, unpublished manuscript, 1918, Hampton University Archives.

40. David W. Penney, *Art of the American Indian Frontier: The Chandler-Pohrt Collection* (Seattle and London: University of Washington Press, 1992), 35–38.

41. Patricia Albers and William R. James, "Images and Reality: Post Cards of Minnesota's Ojibway People 1900–80," *Minnesota History* 49, no. 6 (Summer 1985): 230–34.

42. Ruth B. Phillips, "Souvenirs from North America: The Miniature as Image of Woodlands Indian Life," *American Indian Art Magazine* 14, no. 2 (Spring 1989): 59.

43. Ibid., 60–61.

44. Vanda Foster, *Bags and Purses* (New York: Drama Book Publishers, 1932), 47.

45. Although catlinite objects intended for sale to Euro-Americans were made in great quantities at the turn of the century around Pipestone, Minnesota, we have not included any examples in this exhibition or catalogue. The carving and display of any catlinite in a context other than a religious one has become increasingly controversial within the Native American community. Museums are recognizing the authority of native communities around issues of display and interpretation of objects from living cultural traditions.

46. *Pipestone County Star*, 23 February 1900, p. 1.

47. The Anishinabe artist Patrick Des Jarlait describes making such souvenirs as a student at Pipestone Indian School in his autobiography: *Patrick Des Jarlait: The Story of an American Indian Artist*, as told to Neva Williams (Minneapolis: Lerner Publications, 1975), 40.

48. W. H. Holmes, "The Lithic Industries," *Handbook of Aboriginal American Antiquities* (Washington, D.C.: Smithsonian Institution, Bureau of American Ethnology bulletin 60), 263.

49. On the considerable profits from the sale of pipestone items, see *Yankton Sioux vs. U.S.: Red Pipestone Quarry Case*, 1927, testimony of James Austin, pipestone dealer, p. 237.

50. "The laidies [sic] of Pipestone have agreed to construct a mantle (probably in the ladies' reading-room) of pipestone and polished jasper." Minnesota State Archives, World's Columbian Exposition papers, manuscript report from the superintendent of the state exhibit, 23 November 1892, Minnesota Historical Society, St. Paul.

51. Shepp, *Shepp's World's Fair*, 398.

52. Sibyl Carter Indian Lace Association, undated pamphlet, "Indian Mothers and Their Work," n.p.

53. Literature on Native American lace making is sparse. In addition to a few contemporary sources, the Cooper-Hewitt Museum holds the archives of the Lace Association. See also Kate C. Duncan, "American Indian Lace Making," *American Indian Art Magazine* 5, no. 3 (Summer 1980).

54. "Statistical Chart," n.d. (1905, handwritten), Cooper-Hewitt Archives.

55. Production of lace may have continued into the 1930s on the Oneida reservation in Wisconsin and elsewhere. The examples of lace in museum collections recognized as Indian-made probably number fewer than fifty.

56. Lake Mohonk Conference of Friends of the Indians. Proceedings of the Twelfth Annual Meeting, 1894, p. 66.

57. Sibyl Carter Indian Lace Association, annual report, 1913, Cooper-Hewitt Archives, n.p.

58. The Pipestone Indian School, for example, maintained a home economics cottage that included a living room with sewing machines and tables where girls were taught to sew, as well as a dining room and kitchen equipped with a cooking stove, kitchen cabinets, and cooking utensils. A laundry, garden, and poultry house completed the idealized home.

59. Elizabeth Cornelius, student file, Hampton University Archives.

60. *Southern Workman*, March 1932.

61. Patricia Albers, "Sioux Women in Transition: A Study of Their Changing Status in a Domestic and Capitalist Sector of Production," in *The Hidden Half: Studies of Plains Indian Women*, ed. Patricia Albers and Beatrice Medicine (Lanham: University Press of America, 1983), 183–87.

62. Cited in Judith Payne, "The Lace Industry Association and the Native American Women of Minnesota," paper presented at the meeting of the Popular Culture Association, Toronto, 1990.

BIBLIOGRAPHY

Abbott, Lyman. "Our Indian Problem." *North American Review* 167, no. 505 (1898): 719–28.

Albers, Patricia and William R. James. "Images and Reality: Post Cards of Minnesota's Ojibway People 1900–80." *Minnesota History* 49, no. 6 (Summer 1985): 229–40.

Albers, Patricia, and Beatrice Medicine, eds. *The Hidden Half: Studies of Plains Indian Women.* Lanham, Md.: University Press of America, 1983.

Anderson, Marcia G. and Kathy L. Hussey-Arntson. "Anishinabe Bandolier Bags in the Collections of the Minnesota Historical Society." *American Indian Art Magazine* 11, no. 4 (Autumn 1986): 46–56.

———. "Ojibway Beadwork Traditions in the Ayer Collection." *Minnesota History* 48, no. 4 (Winter 1982): 153–57.

Annual Report of the Commissioner of Indian Affairs to the Secretary of the Interior. 1893.

Armstrong, S. C. *The Indian Question.* Hampton, Va.: Hampton Normal School Steam Press, 1883.

Badger, Reid. *The Great American Fair: The Columbian Exposition.* Chicago: Nelson Hall, 1979.

Beaulieu, David. "A Place Among Nations: Experience of Indian People." In *Minnesota in a Century of Change: The State and Its People Since 1900.* St. Paul: Minnesota Historical Society Press, 1989, pp. 391–432.

Bland, Thomas. *The Indian Question.* Boston: F. Wood, 1880.

Broker, Ignatia. *Night Flying Woman: An Ojibway Narrative.* St. Paul: Minnesota Historical Society Press, 1983.

Bromley, Edward A. *Minneapolis Portrait of the Past: A Photographic History of the Early Days in Minneapolis.* Minneapolis: Voyageur Press, Inc., 1973.

Buffalohead, W. Roger and Priscilla Buffalohead. *Against the Tide of American History: The Story of the Mille Lacs Anishinabe.* Cass Lake, Minn.: Minnesota Chippewa Tribe, 1985.

Campisi, Jack and Laurence M. Hauptman, eds. *The Oneida*

Indian Experience: Two Perspectives. Syracuse, N.Y.: Syracuse University Press, 1988.

Carley, Kenneth. *The Sioux Uprising of 1862.* St. Paul: Minnesota Historical Society Press, 1976.

Carrigan, Minnie Bruce. "Captured by the Indians." *The Newsprint.* Buffalo Lake, Minn., 1912.

Carroll, Jane Lamm. "Dams and Damages: The Ojibway, the United States, and the Mississippi Headwaters Reservoirs." *Minnesota History* 52, no. 1 (Spring 1990): 3–15.

Celik, Zeynep and Leila Kinney. "Ethnography and Exhibitionism at the Exposition Universelles." *Assemblage* 13 (1991): 35–59.

Densmore, Frances. *Chippewa Customs.* Minneapolis: Ross & Haines, Inc., [1929] 1970.

Duncan, Kate C. 1980. "American Indian Lace Making." *American Indian Art Magazine* 5, no. 3 (Summer 1980): 28–35, 80.

Ebbott, Elisabeth, for the League of Women Voters of Minnesota. *Indians in Minnesota.* 4th ed. Minneapolis: University of Minnesota Press, 1985.

Ewers, John C. *Plains Indian Sculpture.* Washington, D.C.: Smithsonian Institution Press, 1986.

Flint Institute of Arts. *The American Indian, The American Flag.* Flint, Mich.: Institute of Arts, 1975.

Folwell, William. *A History of Minnesota.* St. Paul: Minnesota Historical Society, 1921–30.

Forbes-Lindsay, C. H. "The North American Indian as a Laborer: His Value as a Worker and a Citizen." *The Craftsman* (May 1908): 146–57.

Foster, Vanda. *Bags and Purses.* The Costume Accessories series. New York: Drama Book Publishers, 1982.

Fruth, Alban. *A Century of Missionary Work Among the Red Lake Chippewa Indians 1858–1958.* Collegeville, Minn.: Order of St. Benedict, Inc., 1958.

Garte, Edna. *Circle of Life: Cultural Continuity in Ojibwe Crafts.* St. Louis County Historical Society, Chisholm Museum, and Duluth Art Institute, 1984.

Gilman, Samuel. *The Future Indian: A Brief Treatise on the Indian Question.* Indianapolis: Carlon & Hottenbeck, 1891.

Gordon, Beverly with Melanie Herzog. *American Indian Art: The Collecting Experience.* Madison: Elvehjem Museum of Art, University of Wisconsin, 1988.

Hagen, Lois D. *A Parish in the Pines.* Cadwell, Ida.: The Caxton Printers, Ltd., 1938.

Holmes, W. H. "The Lithic Industries." In *Handbook of Aboriginal American Antiquities.* Washington D.C.: Smithsonian Institution, Bureau of American Ethnology bulletin 60, 1919.

Hoxie, Frederick E. *A Final Promise: The Campaign to Assimilate the Indians, 1880–1920.* Lincoln: University of Nebraska Press, 1984.

Huggan, Nancy. *The Story of Nancy McClure. Captivity Among the Sioux.* St. Paul: Minnesota Historical Society, 1894.

Kapoun, Robert W. with Charles J. Lohrmann. *Language of the Robe: American Indian Trade Blankets.* Salt Lake City: Gibbs Smith, 1992.

Lee, Art. "Hometown Hysteria: Bemidji at the Start of World War I." *Minnesota History* 49, no. 2 (Summer 1984): 65–66.

Leupp, Francis E. *The Indian and His Problem.* New York: Scribner's Sons, 1910.

Lyford, Carrie. *Ojibwa Crafts.* United States Department of the Interior. Lawrence, Kan.: Publications Service, Haskell Institute, 1943.

McSpadden, J. Walker. *Famous Sculptors of America.* New York: Dodd, Mead, 1924.

Minnesota State Archives, World's Columbian Exposition papers, Minnesota Historical Society, St. Paul.

Namias, June. *White Captives: Gender and Ethnicity on the American Frontier.* Chapel Hill: University of North Carolina Press, 1993.

"Nursery Wall Coverings in Indian Designs." *The Craftsman* 5, no. 1 (October 1903): 95–99.

Owen, G. W. *The Indian Question.* Ypsilanti, Mich.: N.p., 1881.

Payne, Judith. "The Lace Industry Association and the Native American Women of Minnesota." Paper presented at the meeting at the Popular Culture Association, Toronto, 1990.

Penney, David W. *Art of the American Indian Frontier: The Chandler-Pohrt Collection.* Seattle and London: University of Washington Press, 1992.

Phillips, Ruth B. "Souvenirs from North America: The Miniature as Image of Woodlands Indian Life." *American Indian Art Magazine* 14, no. 2 (Spring 1989): 52–63, 78–79.

———. "Great Lakes Textiles: Meaning and Value in Women's Art." In *On the Border: Native American Weaving Traditions of the Great Lakes and Prairie.* Moorhead, Minn.: Plains Art Museum, 1990.

Rhoads, James. E. *The Indian Question in the Concrete.* Philadelphia: Women's National Indian Association, 1886.

Schwandt, Mary. *The Story of Mary Schwandt: Her Captivity during the Sioux "Outbreak."* St. Paul: Minnesota Historical Society, 1894.

Science Museum of Minnesota. *Straight Tongue: Minnesota Indian Art from the Bishop Whipple Collections.* St. Paul: Science Museum of Minnesota, 1980.

Shepp, James W. *Shepp's World's Fair Photographed.* Chicago: Globe Bible Publishing Co., 1893.

Smith, Jane F. and Robert M. Kvasnicka, eds. *Indian-White Relations: A Persistent Paradox.* Washington, D.C.: Howard University Press, 1976.

Stocking, George, ed. *Objects and Others.* Madison, Wis.: University of Wisconsin Press, 1985.

Van Der Beets, Richard. *The Indian Captivity Narrative.* Lanham, Md.: University Press of America, 1984.

Vennum, Jr., Thomas. *The Ojibwa Dance Drum: Its History and Construction.* Smithsonian Folklife Studies 2, 1982.

Vizenor, Gerald. *The Everlasting Sky: New Voices from the People Named the Chippewa.* New York: Crowell-Collier Press, 1972.

———. *The People Named the Chippewa: Narrative Stories.* Minneapolis: University of Minnesota Press, 1984.

Wall, Oscar G. *Recollections of the Sioux Massacre.* Lake City, Minn.: The Home Printery, 1909.

Welsh, Herbert. "The Meaning of the Dakota Outbreak." *Scribners Magazine* (April 1891): 439–52.

Warren, William Whipple. "A History of the Ojibway People." *The Tomahawk* 1, no. 1 (9 April 1903).

————. *History of the Ojibway Nation.* Minneapolis: Ross & Haines, 1957.

Watrin, Benno. *The Ponsfordian 1880–1930.* Park Rapids, Minn.: Press of The Park Rapids Enterprise, 1930.

Wharton, George. *Indian Blankets and Their Makers.* New York: Dover Publications, [1919] 1974.

Whipple, Henry Benjamin. *Light and Shadows of a Long Episcopate.* New York: Macmillan Co., 1902.

White, Urania. *Captivity among the Sioux.* St. Paul: Minnesota Historical Society, 1901.

Williams, Neva. *Patrick Des Jarlait: The Story of An American Indian Artist.* Minneapolis: Lerner Publications Co., 1975.

Wilson, Raymond. *Ohiyesa: Charles Eastman, Santee Sioux.* Urbana: University of Illinois Press, 1983.

CHECKLIST OF THE EXHIBITION

Catalogue entries prepared by Angela Casselton.

1. Anishinabe
   Bitten patterns, early twentieth century
   Birch bark
   3″ × 4⅛″; 3³⁄₁₆″ × 3⅞″
   Science Museum of Minnesota, St. Paul A82:5:82A and A82:5:82G
   Provenance: Collected by Monroe Killy

Folded several times to create symmetrical patterns, birch bark bitings, also called transparencies, were made by older Anishinabe women using their teeth to indent designs on thin pieces of bark. These patterns were then used to create the geometric and floral motifs found on early loom-woven bands and panels for beaded shoulder bags (Densmore 1970, 184–85). This method of creating patterns predates the birch bark cutout forms made after metal scissors were acquired through trade (Densmore 1970, 189).

2. Great Lakes
   Bag, about 1900–20
   Wool yarn, bark fiber, commercial fabric
   16¼″ x 19¾″
   Cass County Museum, Walker
   Provenance: unknown

With the introduction of commercial yarns, woven wool bags gradually replaced the twined bags of cedar, elm, and basswood bark fibers made for carrying and storing personal belongings. Old trade cloth and woolen blankets were painstakingly raveled so the yarn could be respun and dyed again for use as the weft thread in a new bag (Lyford 1943, 81). The twining process, done on a frame of two sticks, permits the creation of many varied horizontal and diago-

Anishinabe. Bitten patterns, early twentieth century. Science Museum of Minnesota, St. Paul A82:5:82A and A82:5:82G. Photograph by Gary Mortensen and Robert Fogt.

nal geometric patterns as well as anthropomorphic and zoomorphic images.

3. Anishinabe
   Makuk, early twentieth century
   Birch bark, split root or spruce twine, wood
   9½″ × 7¼″
   Science Museum of Minnesota, St. Paul A83:7:2
   Provenance: Collected by Mr. & Mrs. Frank Warren, National Park Service, Isle Royale

Makuks are deep birch bark containers with rectangular bases and oval rims made for a variety of household purposes, including the gathering and storing of food. Often pine pitch or spruce gum is used to seal the seams to make the container watertight. The decorative patterns on the exterior of birch bark containers are created by incising and scraping the outer layer.

4. Helen Robinson
   Anishinabe

Mat, early twentieth century
Cedar bark, split spruce root, wood, natural dyes
56½″ × 33¼″
Science Museum of Minnesota, St. Paul A83:7:64
Provenance: Collected by Mr. & Mrs. Frank Warren,
National Park Service, Isle Royale

In Northern Minnesota, where bulrushes do not grow
in abundance, women wove the inner bark of the red cedar
to make woven mats used for floors, beds, walls, and partitions in the summer (Densmore 1970, 146). Striped and
geometric patterns were created by using natural and dyed
strips of cedar plaited on a frame, similar to one used for
rush mats. The making of fiber mats is a labor-intensive
process that was gradually replaced by the introduction of
rag rug weaving at reservation boarding schools and missions. A letter written by the original collector of this mat
identifies Helen Robinson, wife of John Linklater, as the
weaver.

5. Dakota or Lakota
   Dress, late nineteenth century
   Deer skin, glass beads, copper discs and bells
   51″
   The Minneapolis Institute of Arts
   Gift of James David and John David 74.64.5
   Provenance: Collected by Dorothea Record Baumann

This dress is said to have been worn to two inaugural
balls in Washington, D.C. It is typical of the heavily beaded
clothing made and worn on formal occasions by Plains
people at the end of the nineteenth century. The turtle,
a protective female symbol associated with creation and
reproduction, is often represented as a U-shaped design at
the center of the beaded yoke on Dakota and Lakota
dresses.

6. Sisseton Dakota
   Child's moccasins, before 1900
   Hide, glass beads, sinew
   2″ × 6″ × 1½″
   The Minneapolis Institute of Arts
   The Ethel Morrison Van Derlip Fund 91.95.2 a,b
   Provenance: Collected by Burton W. Thayer, Minne-
   apolis, Minn. from Sherman Baird, a Dakota man at
   Pipestone Indian School, Pipestone, Minn., 1933

According to a tag attached by Thayer, these moccasins
were made before 1900 by the mother (1870–1926) of Katherine Rice Hill (Gad-ta-lien), a child who died at age four.
They show clear signs of wear. The tag also notes a Dakota
practice of piercing a small hole in the sole of one of the
child's moccasins in order to allow the release of harmful
spirits.

7. Anishinabe
   Moccasins, 1880s or earlier

Deerskin, black velvet, glass beads, purple ribbon
10¼″ × 4¼″ × 3″
Sibley Historic Site, Mendota 81.91 (1859)
Provenance: From the estate of Evangeline Whipple
in 1938. Bishop Whipple Collection

By the later half of the nineteenth century, most native
people in Minnesota had adopted conventional Euro-
American dress but continued to make and wear moccasins. Although the construction remained largely unchanged, the ornamentation underwent slight
modifications in design and materials including the addition of velvet cuffs and vamps. Often these decorative elements were recycled from one pair to the next (Lyford
1943, 106).

8. Anishinabe
   Pair of breech cloths, about 1900
   Black velvet, cotton fabric, glass beads, metal, pink
   ribbon
   16¾″ × 19¾″; 15¾″ × 19½″
   Minnesota Historical Society Collections 1982.67.4
   and 1982.67.5
   Provenance: Donated by Donald Stewart, Tucson,
   Ariz. in 1978. Collected from Florence Sorenson,
   Minneapolis, Minn. in 1967

According to Mrs. Sorenson, this pair of breechcloths
were once part of a larger dance outfit given to her grandparents by an Anishinabe man as payment for his stay at
their hotel in Detroit Lakes, about 1900. Breechcloths, or
dance aprons, were worn tied about a man's waist, over his
leggings, with one panel in front and the other in back.
Birch bark templates would have been used to create the
identical leaf forms on each of the panels.

9. Anishinabe
   Split skirt, late nineteenth century
   Black velvet, ribbon, cloth, glass beads
   34¾″ × 17¾″
   Sibley Historic Site, Mendota 81.161 (1898)
   Provenance: From the estate of Evangeline Whipple
   in 1938. Bishop Whipple Collection

A split skirt consists of two long rectangular panels worn
around a man's waist like a breechcloth. With the establishment of reservations and the decline in the availability of
natural materials, traditional clothing made of hide was
replaced with commercially manufactured garments and
fabrics. Velvet and dark broadcloth were popular materials
for the elaborately beaded vests, breechcloths, sashes,
gauntlets, leggings, and moccasins worn on special occasions.

10. Dakota
    Hat, about 1890

Black velvet, black (silk?) cloth, glass beads, metal buttons
4⅞" × 6½"
Shattuck-St. Mary's School, Faribault, on loan to the Science Museum of Minnesota A79.4.119
Provenance: Bishop Whipple Collection[1]

This beaded hat was presumably owned by the man whose name it bears, (Andrew) Good Thunder, the first Dakota baptized in Minnesota. Good Thunder (Wa-kin-yan-waste), who aided white settlers during the Dakota Conflict of 1862, was among the Dakota forced out of Minnesota but later returned to assist with the re-establishment of the reservation and became a leader of the Episcopal mission at Morton. Although the use of floral designs is often associated only with the Anishinabe and other Woodland peoples, the Dakota (as well as other Plains groups) also incorporated these designs in their work.

11. Mrs. Ke-sha-pa-ka-ba-wik
    Anishinabe
    Cradleboard, about 1900
    Wood, black velvet, glass beads, green commercial paint, copper wire
    34½" × 11⅜"
    The Hennepin History Museum, Minneapolis 421/1
    Provenance: Donated by Elizabeth Jerome. Collected by Charles W. Jerome in International Falls, Minn. in 1907

Cradleboards were used to carry infants from birth to approximately one year old. The child was supported by a curved wooden lip at the bottom of the fabric pouch and swaddled in blankets. The bentwood frame protected the baby's head and was often adorned with charms or wrapped woven beadwork bands. The cradle would have been made and ornamented by the mother or close female relative while the board was usually constructed by the father of the child. The addition of decorating edging and cutout forms on many late examples may have been the result of training many men received in wood shops and industrial arts classes at mission and government boarding schools. Jerome took a photograph of a woman wearing this carrier in International Falls at the time that it was collected.[2]

12. Dakota (?)
    Visor cap, nineteenth century
    Commercial cap, tanned hide, glass and metal beads
    3" × 7⅜"
    The Hennepin History Museum, Minneapolis 1555/22
    Provenance: Donated by Donald Stein in 1942. Collected by Edwin A. Bowin, donor's grandfather, from the Dakota in the nineteenth century

The practice of overbeading commercially manufactured clothing and accessories was a popular trend at which the Dakota and Lakota excelled. Some acculturated forms, though produced largely for sale, were used internally as special items of prestige. Molin has observed that similar caps were worn by male students at Hampton Institute (and possibly other boarding schools) as part of their military or school uniforms. The beadwork was probably added later by a female relative.

13. Anishinabe
    Breast ornament (?), late nineteenth century
    Glass beads, silk thread, wood
    26½" × 5½" (including fringe and strap)
    Rice County Historical Society, Faribault
    Provenance: Bishop Whipple Collection

Often catalogued as breast ornaments, these long loom-woven (and sometimes chain-woven) beadwork panels may have been suspended from a belt as part of a man's dance outfit at the turn of the century. The simple, flat rectangular ornaments, with short strap and fringe, may also have been adapted and sold as wall hangings.

14. Anishinabe
    Garter, about 1880
    Red and blue yarn, glass beads
    46⅞" × 3" (including fringe)
    Rice County Historical Society, Faribault
    Provenance: Bishop Whipple Collection[3]

Loom-woven beadwork garters, usually made in pairs or matching sets, were used by both men and women to fasten their leggings. The long yarn fringe was used to tie the bands securely in place below the knee.

15. Anishinabe
    Bandolier bag, about 1900
    Red wool tape, glass and metal beads, muslin, black velvet
    15¼" × 21"
    Sibley Historic Site, Mendota 81.30 (1828)
    Provenance: From the estate of Evangeline Whipple in 1938. Bishop Whipple Collection

Beaded bandolier or shoulder bags, which flourished in the nineteenth and early twentieth centuries, were primarily decorative display pieces, valued for their aesthetic rather than functional quality. Thought to have been derived from early European military pouches, many of the later bags were sewn without pockets. Made by women, they were worn by men, and occasionally by women, to indicate wealth or social position.

16. Anishinabe (?)
    Bandolier bag, about 1870–80
    Muslin, red wool fabric, wool tape binding, glass beads, silk ribbon

Dakota(?). Visor cap, nineteenth century. The Hennepin History Museum, Minneapolis 1555/22. Photograph by Gary Mortensen and Robert Fogt.

16½″ × 12⅜″
Minnesota Historical Society Collections 64.155.29
Provenance: Donated by Mr. Thomas G. McGill, St. Paul, Minn. in 1964. Presented to Lucius F. Hubbard (1836–1913), the ninth governor of Minnesota from 1882–87, by six Anishinabe leaders from the Mille Lacs Reservation: Ma-Zu-Nea-Ni, Ba-Gru-na-pu, Cha-ba-ekun, Mar-hi-gar, Wa-wi-eck-ko-nuk, and Ka-gna-dn-sa

By the end of the nineteenth century, loom-woven bandolier bags with geometric designs were eclipsed by the spot-stitched floral motif, possibly as a result of emphasis placed on needlework and embroidery in reservation missions and schools, or in response to an aesthetic preference (Anderson and Hussey-Arntson 1986, 52). The shoulder strap on this bag has been sewn on to the front panel at an angle in order to allow the bag to lie smoothly against the body of the wearer.

17. Anishinabe
Bandolier bag, about 1890–94

Navy blue wool fabric, black velvet, wool yarn, wool tape binding, glass beads
8½″ × 13″
Minnesota Historical Society Collections 70.90
Provenance: Donated by Helen D. Barnes, Cambria, Calif. in 1969. Presented to Rev. William Denley (donor's grandfather), an Episcopal missionary, by a leader of the Cass Lake Anishinabe, about 1890–94[4]

Floral bandolier bags of the late nineteenth century usually feature a single, spot-stitched spray of rather large and elaborated foliate forms. Other bags, like the one seen here, show overall patterns of vinelike stems with smaller, more simplified floral forms reminiscent of the network of stems found in the Renaissance-style laces (see cat. no. 28) taught to Indian women around the same time period (Duncan 1980, 33).

18. Anishinabe
Match holder, about 1891–1919
Glass beads, birch bark
1⅞″ × 1⅜″ (diameter)

Minnesota Historical Society Collections 271.E67
"D.S. Hall" is beaded along the circumference
Provenance: Collected by Darwin Scott Hall (1844–
1919), chairman of the Chippewa Indian Commission
from 1891–98, on the White Earth Reservation

The name woven into the beadwork on this small birch
bark match container is that of the original collector, Darwin Scott Hall. Hall was appointed chairman of the Chippewa Indian Commission in 1891[5] and served for about
five years on the White Earth Reservation. During his last
illness, well-wishers brought him "trinkets and mementos;"
this may have been such a gift, at that time or earlier in
his career.

19. Dakota
    Wall pocket, about 1880
    Black velvet, gold silk ribbon, glass beads
    7 1/16" × 5 1/2"
    Shattuck-St. Mary's School, Faribault, on loan to the
    Science Museum of Minnesota A79.4.122
    Provenance: Bishop Whipple Collection

This wall pocket, probably intended to hold two match
boxes, is an example of the small domestic goods that were
created specifically for an outside market. Unlike many
such pieces, however, this one shows signs of wear and may
have been in use in the Whipple household.

20. Anishinabe
    Loom-woven napkin rings, about 1891–1919
    Glass beads, birch bark
    Various sizes
    Minnesota Historical Society Collections 477.E123
    Provenance: Collected by Darwin Scott Hall (1844–
    1919), chairman of the Chippewa Indian Commis-
    sion, on the White Earth Reservation

    Anishinabe (?)
    Netted napkin rings, early twentieth century
    Glass beads, birch bark
    Various sizes
    Minnesota Historical Society Collections
    1993.153.1–3 (137 IN)
    Provenance: unknown

Bookmarks, pincushions, cigar cases, and napkin rings
were only some of the European forms adapted and modified by Native American beadworkers for sale at local trading posts and curio shops. Similar napkins rings were
collected on the White Earth Reservation in 1893 for display in the Minnesota building at the World's Fair and also
were sold at the H. D. Ayer Trading Post near the Mille
Lacs Reservation well into the first half of the twentieth
century.

21. Anishinabe (?)
    Pincushion, late nineteenth century
    Black velvet, cotton cloth, glass beads, cotton (?)
    stuffing
    5 1/4" × 4" × 1"
    Sibley Historic Site, Mendota 81.36 (1968)
    Provenance: From the estate of Evangeline Whipple
    in 1938. Bishop Whipple Collection

By the turn of the century, black velvet was used as the
supporting material on much of Anishinabe beadwork.
This interest in black backgrounds can be traced to the
early use of smoked and dyed hides for quill decorated
articles. The heart-shaped motif was popular in the late
Victorian period for small decorative items, especially those
intended as gifts.

22. Anishinabe
    Notebook, late nineteenth century
    Birch bark, dyed porcupine quills, sweetgrass, black
    thread
    5 3/4" × 3 1/2"
    Sibley Historic Site, Mendota 81.243 (1874)
    Provenance: From the estate of Evangeline Whipple
    in 1938. Bishop Whipple Collection

This small birch bark notebook with thin bark pages
would have been sold as a souvenir item rather than as a
functional object. The rectangular shape and the use of
sweetgrass and quill decoration may have been derived
from the popular moosehair-embroidered cigar and cigarette cases produced by Woodland peoples further east.

23. Anishinabe or Dakota
    Altar front, about 1890
    Velvet backing, silk binding, glass beads
    4 1/2" (excluding fringe) × 106 1/4"
    "Holy" beaded at the center
    Shattuck-St. Mary's Schools, Faribault, on loan to the
    Science Museum of Minnesota A79.4.188
    Provenance: Bishop Whipple Collection

Despite the prevalence of Christianity on reservations at
the turn of the century, there is surprisingly little documented native-made liturgical material,[6] probably because
use of European-style objects was seen as part of the accul-
turating process. This altar cloth was presumably made by
a Christian Anishinabe or Dakota beadworker. The signifi-
cance of the continuous pattern of crosses and flowers
joined by a chain is unclear. It may be intended to comment on the linking of Christian and Anishinabe spiritual
beliefs.

24. Anishinabe
    Cross, about 1890
    Wood, glass beads, adhesive
    7 1/2" × 4" × 1 1/2"

*Anishinabe or Dakota. Altar front, ca. 1890. Shattuck-St. Mary's
Schools, Faribault on loan to the Science Museum of Minnesota
A79.4.188. Photograph by Gary Mortensen and Robert Fogt.*

Shattuck-St. Mary's Schools, Faribault, on loan to the
Science Museum of Minnesota A79.4.189
Provenance: Bishop Whipple Collection

Given its relatively small size, it is unlikely that this
beaded cross was made for display on a church altar but
may rather have been intended for use as a personal devo-
tional image. As part of the Bishop Whipple Collection, it
may have been given to the bishop for his own use by one
of his many church parishioners or students.

25. Anishinabe
     Pouch with decorated panels, about 1890
     Birch bark, dyed porcupine quills, purple silk
     9⅞" × 9⅞"
     Shattuck-St. Mary's Schools, Faribault, on loan to the
     Science Museum of Minnesota A79.4.135
     Provenance: Bishop Whipple Collection

The form of this silk pouch can be traced to a circular
drawstring reticule fashionable in Europe at the beginning
of the nineteenth century. Easily reproduced, the style became popular with amateur needlewomen who created
their own pricked or embossed card medallions (Foster
1982, 37), or in this case panels of quilled birch bark, to
which wide, pleated strips of silk were sewn.

26. Anishinabe
     Beadwork panel, about 1890
     Glass beads, thread
     7⅛" × 8⅞"
     Sibley Historic Site, Mendota 81.265 (1974)
     Provenance: From the estate of Evangeline Whipple
     in 1938. Bishop Whipple Collection

Loomed panels of this size would have been traditionally
produced for the front panel of a bandolier bag. This particular panel or "picture," derived from an enlarged and
painted photograph provided by Sybil Carter to one of her
lacemakers,[7] may represent an attempt to develop a new
commodity for sale. It is believed to have been on display
at the World's Columbian Exposition in Chicago in 1893.

27. Dakota
     Purse, about 1885
     Commercially manufactured handbag, glass beads,
     cloth, hide
     8⅝" × 5⅛"
     Sibley Historic Site, Mendota A79:15:116
     Provenance: From the estate of Evangeline Whipple
     in 1938. Bishop Whipple Collection[8]

The complete overbeading of commercially manufactured handbags and suitcases was fashionable among the
Lakota and Dakota at the end of the nineteenth century.
Although the floral design on this purse is quite conventional, the bird with a heart line is less common. The bird's
form resembles that of later images derived from conventional patriotic eagle motifs, while the inclusion of a line
connecting the mouth and the heart of the animal is a
standard pictorial representation symbolizing power and
frequently denotes the Thunderbird, an important spiritual
entity embodying the power of the skies in Plains and Great
Lakes mythology.

28. Dakota (?)
     Medallion, late nineteenth century
     Linen thread
     Approx. 6" × 8¼"
     Cooper-Hewitt Museum of Design, Smithsonian Insti-

Anishinabe. Beadwork panel, *about 1890. Sibley Historic Site, Mendota 81.265 (1974). Photograph by Gary Mortensen and Robert Fogt.*

tution, New York 1943.44.4
Provenance: Donated by Mrs. William Bayard Cutting in 1950. Collected through the Sybil Carter Indian Lace Association, Oneida, Wis.

Although Sybil Carter noted that some of the lacemakers began introducing their own designs into their work (Duncan 1980, 32), it is doubtful that they would have chosen the kind of romanticized images found on this lace panel. Identically rendered "Indian" motifs appear on a variety of laces produced both in Minnesota and Wisconsin lace schools, which suggests that patterns were distributed through the Lace Association, perhaps in response to buyers' interest.

29. Anishinabe or Dakota
     Handkerchief, late nineteenth century
     Linen, cotton thread
     11″ × 12″

Sibley Historic Site, Mendota 81.144 (1959)
Provenance: From the estate of Evangeline Whipple in 1938. Bishop Whipple Collection

Cutwork patterns of needlepoint lace, also known as reticella lace, ornament the corners of this otherwise simple linen handkerchief. In this form, the thread is run across the opening in the fabric, then overcast with buttonhole stitches.

30. Anishinabe or Dakota
     Handkerchief, about 1900
     Linen, cotton thread
     13″ × 13″
     Sibley Historic Site, Mendota 81.142 (1960)
     Provenance: From the estate of Evangeline Whipple in 1938. Bishop Whipple Collection

The maple leaf border of tape and needlepoint lace on

this linen handkerchief closely resembles the elaborately detailed foliate forms found on bandolier bags and other beaded items produced during the same period. As in beadwork, an actual leaf or birch bark cutout may have been used as a template for the repeating motif.

31. Anishinabe
    Collar, about 1890–1915
    Linen or cotton thread
    9¼″ × 16″
    Cass County Museum, Walker
    Provenance: unknown

The lace schools active in Minnesota and Wisconsin produced a variety of lace pieces including centerpieces, doilies, handkerchiefs, medallions, edging, veils, boleros, and yokes like this one shown here, probably made by a lacemaker at Onigum on the Leech Lake Reservation. Lace collars may have been the only form of lace used or worn by the Indian lacemakers themselves.[9]

32. Anishinabe
    Purse, late nineteenth century
    Sweetgrass, birch bark, porcupine quills, black thread, wood
    5″ × 9″ × 4″

The Hennepin History Museum, Minneapolis 557/11
Provenance: Donated by Katherine M. Hill, Minneapolis

This distinctly European-style handbag has been skillfully made from traditional basket-weaving materials of coiled sweetgrass and quill-decorated birch bark (see cat. no. 37). It represents the unique productive exchange of forms and aesthetics characteristic of the early reservation period. According to the donor, it was given to her by one of her students at an Indian school.[10]

33. Dakota
    Model canoe, about 1900
    Birch bark, wool yarn
    12⅝″ × 5⅛″ × 2½″
    Sibley Historic Site, Mendota 81.247 (1589)
    Handwritten in ink on side: "Presented to Mrs. Whipple by Mrs. Jane Coupeel(?), Birch Coulee, June 1900, Sioux"
    Provenance: From the estate of Evangeline Whipple in 1938. Bishop Whipple Collection

Once meticulously crafted miniatures of their full-size counterparts, complete with small seated figures and paddles, model canoes were reduced to simple forms produced

Anishinabe. Purse, *late nineteenth century. The Hennepin History Museum, Minneapolis 557/11. Photograph by Gary Mortensen and Robert Fogt.*

in mass throughout the Great Lakes region for tourists. By the second half of the nineteenth century, decorative elements such as moosehair, porcupine quill and, in this case, commercial yarn embroidery began to appear on miniature canoes and on a variety of utilitarian forms. These elaborate embellishments, although enhancing their marketability, only served to create a more convoluted Euro-American understanding of "traditional" Native American arts.

34. Dakota or Anishinabe
    Cane, late nineteenth century
    Wood, commercial paints, catlinite, lead
    34½″ × 3″
    Sibley Historic Site, Mendota 81.255 (1823)
    Provenance: From the estate of Evangeline Whipple in 1938. Bishop Whipple Collection

The carving of effigy canes was a development of the late nineteenth century, stimulated by the interest of collectors as well as internal use (Ewers 1986, 200). The intricate floral carving on the stem of this cane is unusual, possibly influenced by the elaborate floral beadwork patterns of the Anishinabe or the folk-art traditions of European immigrants in surrounding communities. This same incised and painted pattern appears on another cane and on two pipe stems in the Whipple Collection always in conjunction with some element of catlinite, which may suggest the artist worked at or lived near the quarries in southern Minnesota. One such carver, known to have created a cane with a similar dog's head handle,[11] was the Dakota deacon Andrew Good Thunder (1820–1901), a life-long friend of Bishop Whipple.

35. Dakota (?)
    Model cradleboard, about 1900
    Wood, cloth, hide, glass beads
    7¼″ × 2⅜″
    Rice County Historical Society, Faribault
    Provenance: unknown

Cradleboards, canoes, sleds, wigwams, and other unique forms were often miniaturized and sold as souvenir items at trading posts and curio shops. Traditionally, scaled-down versions of everyday objects were made as educational toys. Girls carried dolls in small cradleboards while boys played at hunting with small wooden bows. Although the geometric pattern on this example is not typical, the use of appliqued beadwork and the overall shape and construction of the cradle is distinctly Plains.

36. Anishinabe (?)
    Basket, about 1900–20
    Sweetgrass, birch bark, dyed porcupine quills, black thread
    10″ (diameter)
    Cass County Museum, Walker
    Provenance: unknown

Anishinabe women made baskets of birch bark, split ash, willow, and sweetgrass, the latter consisting of wrapped and sewn coils shaped into small bowls or shallow trays. Birch bark decorated with floral patterns of porcupine quills was often used in conjunction with sweetgrass as a decorative element.

37. Anishinabe
    Pincushion, about 1893
    Black velvet, glass beads, silk ribbon, unbleached muslin, paper stuffing
    8¹⁄₁₆″
    Minnesota Historical Society Collections 519/E144
    Provenance: Donated by the State of Minnesota World's Columbian Exposition Commission. Collected by the Women's Auxiliary Board of the Minnesota Commission from Becker County Indian Industries on the White Earth Reservation in 1893

This beaded pincushion was part of a larger group of objects collected for display in the Minnesota building at the World's Columbian Exposition. The exhibit included a variety of Indian-made objects including traditional forms such as makuks, moccasins, clubs, ladles, and pipes and also a variety of acculturated articles such as wall pockets, table mats, rag rugs, and napkin rings.

38. Anishinabe
    Rag rug, about 1893
    Silk, thread
    124¾″ (excluding fringe) × 38½″
    Minnesota Historical Society Collections 528/E15
    Provenance: Donated by the State of Minnesota World's Columbian Exposition Commission. Collected by the Women's Auxiliary Board of the Minnesota Commission from Becker County Indian Industries[12] on the White Earth Reservation in 1893

With the exception of some lace, rag rug weaving is the only example of an acculturated art form that was not altered to become readily distinguishable from its Euro-American counterpart. Rag rugs gradually replaced fiber mats as more Anishinabe moved into frame houses. Given the fragile nature of silk, it is likely that this particular rug was never meant for use but rather commissioned specifically for display at the World's Fair in Chicago. An unusual amount of wear on the single row of tassels, sewn only to one end of the runner, suggests that it was borrowed or recycled from an older textile.

39. Old Bets
    Santee Dakota
    Moccasins, about 1888
    Tanned hide, glass beads
    9½″ × 3¾″ × 3¾″
    Monroe P. Killy Collection
    Provenance: Acquired from Burton W. Thayer, Min-

neapolis. Collected by L. Ladwig, St. Paul, Minn., in 1888[13]

According to Thayer's tag, these moccasins were originally collected from a Dakota woman known as "Old Bets" at the St. Paul Ice Palace where she was with 150 "Mendota Sioux." It goes on to say that Old Bets was regularly seen at the railroad depot on Washington Avenue where she sold beadwork. Sometimes she was accompanied by her daughter who reportedly continued to sell at the station until the 1910s. Old Bets was said to have helped many whites during the 1862 Dakota conflict and thus was able to remain in the Twin Cities afterwards (Bromley 1973). It also may be why she had to support herself by selling souvenirs, since by aligning herself with whites she would have alienated many other Dakota.

NOTES

1. Reproduced in *Straight Tongue*, p. 21.
2. Per information provided by the donor to the Hennepin History Museum, Minneapolis, 1993.
3. Reproduced as no. 64 in *Straight Tongue*.
4. This bag was thought to be described in a book by Denley's daughter, Lois D. Hagen, titled *A Parish in the Pines*. Of the two beaded items found on pages 70 and 202, neither of the author's descriptions fit this particular bag.
5. The Chippewa Commission was formed to supervise the allotment of land on the White Earth and Red Lake Reservations under the Nelson Act of 1889.
6. A small number of liturgical items exist in the Bishop Whipple Collection, including an early Anishinabe beaded stole made by the wife of Chief Flatmouth. It was given to the bishop for his intervention in the Leech Lake timber controversy of 1873–74 (Science Museum 1980, 69). The stole is presently in the Sibley Historic Site collection in Mendota.
7. This information is noted on the back of a photograph in the collection of the Sibley Historic Site (Science Museum 1980, 76). The panel and photograph are reproduced as no. 72 in *Straight Tongue*.
8. Reproduced as n. 179 in *Straight Tongue*.
9. For contextual reference, see photograph of Mrs. Smith on p. 26 in *Straight Tongue*.
10. Per object label in the "Dark Times, Bright Visions" exhibition at the Hennepin History Museum. Unfortunately, the name of the Indian school is not given.
11. This example can be found in the collections of the Minnesota Historical Society, cat. no. 7401.2. It consists of a simple, undecorated wooden stem and a catlinite handle carved into a dog's head. It was collected as Santee Dakota from Good Thunder at Pipestone, Minn., 1875. Ewers suggests that the cane was probably carved by Good Thunder himself (Ewers 1986, 201).
12. Minnesota Historical Society's records indicate that this rug was "prepared and woven by Indian girls at the Becker County Indian school" with rags collected from all over the state. Although neither of the schools on White Earth in 1893 went by that name, the objects were most likely collected from students at the government industrial boarding school (opened in 1873) which taught young women housework, including "cooking, sewing, knitting, carpetweaving" (Vizenor 1984, 104).
13. There is a ten-year discrepancy between the collection date provided by Thayer and the 1878 death date given for "Old Bets" in Bromley's *Minneapolis Portrait of the Past*.